T0207361

# Lecture Notes in Computer Science 13129

More information about this subseries at https://link.springer.com/bookseries/7410

Maura B. Paterson (Ed.)

# Cryptography and Coding

18th IMA International Conference, IMACC 2021
Virtual Event, December 14–15, 2021
Proceedings

 Springer

*Editor*
Maura B. Paterson ⓘ
Economics, Mathematics and Statistics
University of London Birkbeck
London, UK

ISSN 0302-9743             ISSN 1611-3349  (electronic)
Lecture Notes in Computer Science
ISBN 978-3-030-92640-3     ISBN 978-3-030-92641-0  (eBook)
https://doi.org/10.1007/978-3-030-92641-0

LNCS Sublibrary: SL4 – Security and Cryptology

This Springer imprint is published by the registered company Springer Nature Switzerland AG
The registered company address is: Gewerbestrasse 11, 6330 Cham, Switzerland

# Preface

The 18th edition of the biennial Institute of Mathematics and its Applications (IMA) International Conference on Cryptography and Coding took place during December 14–15, 2021. Due to the continuing global uncertainty arising from the ongoing COVID-19 pandemic it was held as an online event for the first time in its history.

The reviewing process was single-blind, and during the review phase each paper was reviewed independently by at least two reviewers. The reviews and papers were then considered by the Program Committee in a discussion phase. The Program Committee selected 14 papers for presentation at the conference.

I am grateful to the Program Committee members and external reviewers for their efforts in analyzing and discussing the submissions, and to the invited speakers for providing such interesting talks. I would like to thank the Steering Committee for their support and guidance in arranging this event. Finally, particular thanks are due to Maya Everson, Cerys Thompson, and their colleagues for handling all the practical matters of the conference, especially for managing the many challenges inherent in moving to an online event.

November 2021                                                              Maura Paterson

# Organization

## Program Chair

Maura Paterson      Birkbeck, University of London, UK

## Steering Committee

| | |
|---|---|
| Martin Albrecht | Royal Holloway, University of London, UK |
| Liqun Chen | University of Surrey, UK |
| Bahram Honary | University of Lancaster, UK |
| Máire O'Neill | Queen's University Belfast, UK |
| Christopher Mitchell | Royal Holloway, University of London, UK |
| Matthew Parker | University of Bergen, Norway |
| Kenneth Paterson | ETH Zürich, Switzerland |
| Fred Piper | UK |
| Martijn Stam | Simula UiB, Norway |

## Program Committee

| | |
|---|---|
| Martin Albrecht | Royal Holloway, University of London, UK |
| Eimear Byrne | University College Dublin, Ireland |
| Mahdi Cheraghchi | University of Michigan Ann Arbour, USA |
| Tetsu Iwata | Nagoya University, Japan |
| Delaram Kahrobaei | University of York, UK |
| Julien Lavauzelle | Université de Rennes, France |
| Chaoyun Li | KU Leuven, Belgium |
| Chloe Martindale | University of Bristol, UK |
| Atefeh Mashatan | Ryerson University, Canada |
| Siaw-Lynn Ng | Royal Holloway, University of London, UK |
| Frédérique Oggier | Nanyang Technological University, Singapore |
| Léo Perrin | Inria, France |
| Christophe Petit | University of Birmingham, UK |
| Bertram Poettering | IBM Research Research – Zurich, Switzerland |
| Elizabeth Quaglia | Royal Holloway, University of London, UK |
| Ciara Rafferty | Queen's University Belfast, UK |
| Ana Sălăgean | Loughborough University, UK |
| Ben Smith | Inria, France |
| Antonia Wachter-Zeh | TU Munich, Germany |

## Additional Reviewers

Emanuele Bellini
Huck Bennet
Lubjana Beshaj
Alexander Block
Jeremiah Blocki
Ivan Chizhov
Thomas Debris-Alazard
Tako Boris Fouotsa
Erin Hales
Carolin Hannusch
Daniel Kales
Shabnam Khanna
Matluba Khodjaeva
Simon-Philipp Merz

Anderson Nascimento
Jiaxin Pan
Edoardo Persichetti
Albrecht Petzoldt
Nikita Polyanskii
Joe Rowell
Paolo Santini
Boly Seck
Igor Shinkar
Vladimir Shpilrain
Hanh Tang
Yi Tang
Alexandra Veliche
Violetta Weger

# Contents

# Applications of Codes

# Batch Codes from Affine Cartesian Codes and Quotient Spaces

Travis Alan Baumbaugh[1], Haley Colgate[2], Tim Jackman[3], and Felice Manganiello[4(✉)]

[1] ToposWare, Shibuya-ku, Tokyo 150-8010, Japan
[2] University of Wisconsin - Madison, Madison, WI 53706, USA
[3] Boston University, Boston, MA 02215, USA
[4] Clemson University, Clemson, SC 29634, USA
manganm@clemson.edu

**Abstract.** Affine Cartesian codes are defined by evaluating multivariate polynomials at a cartesian product of finite subsets of a finite field. In this work we examine properties of these codes as batch codes. We consider the recovery sets to be defined by points aligned on a specific direction and the buckets to be derived from cosets of a subspace of the ambient space of the evaluation points. We are able to prove that under these conditions, an affine Cartesian code is able to satisfy a query of size up to one more than the dimension of the ambient space.

## 1  Introduction

Batch codes may be used in information retrieval when multiple users want to access potentially overlapping requests from a set of devices while achieving a balance between minimizing the load on each device and minimizing the number of devices used. We can view the buckets as servers and the symbols used from each bucket as the load on each server. In the original scenario, a single user is trying to reconstruct $t$ bits of information. This definition naturally generalizes to the concept of multiset batch codes which have nearly the same definition, but where the indices chosen for reconstruction are not necessarily distinct.

The family of codes known as batch codes was introduced in [9]. They were originally studied as a scheme for distributing data across multiple devices and minimizing the load on each device and total amount of storage consumed. In this paper, we study $[n, k, t, m, \tau]$ batch codes, where $n$ is the code length, $k$ is the dimension of the code, $t$ is the number of entries we wish to retrieve, $m$ is the number of buckets, and $\tau$ is the maximum number of symbols used from each bucket for any reconstruction of $t$ entries. We seek to minimize the load on each device while maximizing the amount of reconstructed data. That is, we want to minimize $\tau$ while maximizing $t$.

This corresponds to $t$ users who each wish to reconstruct a single element, among which there may be duplicates. This is similar to private information retrieval (PIR) codes, which differ in that $t$ duplicates of the same element must

© Springer Nature Switzerland AG 2021
M. B. Paterson (Ed.): IMACC 2021, LNCS 13129, pp. 3–15, 2021.
https://doi.org/10.1007/978-3-030-92641-0_1

be reconstructed. Other schemes dealing with multiple requests are addressed in [15]. For batch and PIR codes where the queries do not all necessarily occur at the same time, see [16]. Restricted recovery set sizes are considered in [19]. Another notable type of batch code defined in [9] is a primitive multiset batch code where the number of buckets is $m = n$.

Much of the related research involves primitive multiset batch codes with a systematic generator matrix. In [9], the authors give results for some multiset batch codes using subcube codes and Reed-Muller codes. They use a systematic generator matrix, which often allows for better parameters. Their goal was to maximize the efficiency of the code for a fixed number of queries $t$. The focus of research on batch codes then shifted to combinatorial batch codes. These were first introduced by [13]. They are replication-based codes using various combinatorial objects that allow for efficient decoding procedures. We do not consider combinatorial batch codes, but some relevant results can be found in [4,5,13], and [17]. There are other constructions that are already known and are based on similar codes. In [1] and [8], the authors suggest to construct primitive multiset batch codes based on multiplicity codes and lifted Reed-Solomon codes. The work [14] proposes finite geometry designs to construct batch codes. There, affine subspaces are used as recovery sets. Finally, in [10] the author state the only known converse bound for linear primitive batch codes.

In order to reduce wait time for multiple users, we may look at locally repairable codes with availability as noted in [6]. A locally repairable code, with locality $r$ and availability $\delta$, provides us the opportunity to reconstruct a particular bit of data using $\delta$ disjoint sets of size at most $r$ [18]. When we only need to reconstruct this one bit multiple times, this gives us properties of the code as a PIR code. However, the research in this paper covers the scenario in which some bits may differ.

The Hamming weights of affine Cartesian codes are studied in [3]. This is a generalization of work in [7], and in a similar fashion, the work in this paper aims to expand the study of batch properties from Reed-Muller codes as studied in [2] to the broader class of affine Cartesian codes. In the same manner, we begin by examining codes with $\tau = 1$. The even broader family of generalized affine Cartesian codes, specifically those with complementary duals, are studied in [11].

This work focuses on studying the properties of affine Cartesian codes as batch codes. In Sect. 2, we formally introduce batch codes and affine Cartesian codes. In Sect. 3, we define the special recovery sets for affine Cartesian codes based on the points in the direction of a coordinate. The main body is Sect. 4; there we define the building blocks of a batch code - the buckets. In this work we suggest the buckets to be cosets of a subset $V$ of $\mathbb{F}_q^\mu$. Under several equivalent conditions, we show in Theorem 2 that a maximal length affine Cartesian code can satisfy queries of size up to $t = n+1$. The specific case with $V = \langle (1, 1, \ldots, 1) \rangle$ is considered in Subsect. 4.1. We conclude by generalizing the result to any affine Cartesian code.

## 2   Background

Batch codes were introduced in [9]. Throughout this work, by batch codes we refer specifically to multiset batch codes, defined by [9]. To build up to this definition, we first introduce several notions. For a given linear code $\mathcal{C} \subseteq \mathbb{F}_q^n$, where $\mathbb{F}_q$ represents the finite field of $q$ elements, and the index set $[n] := \{1, \ldots, n\}$ we give the following definitions.

**Definition 1.** *A* bucket configuration *$B_1, \ldots, B_m$ is a partition on index set $[n]$. For each $k \in [m]$, the $B_k$ is referred to as a* bucket.

**Definition 2.** *For any index $i \in [n]$, a* recovery set *$R_i$ for the index $i$ is a set such that, for any codeword $c \in \mathcal{C}$, the value of $c_i$ may be recovered by reading the symbols $\{c_j \mid j \in R_i\}$.*

At this point, we note two distinct categories of recovery sets. If $R_i = \{i\}$, then we refer to $R_i$ as *direct access*. If instead $i \notin R_i$, then we refer to $R_i$ as an *indirect* recovery set. We also note that while any set containing a recovery set is technically a recovery set, these shall not be considered proper recovery sets in the remainder of the paper. Now we deal with multiple recovery sets at the same time for a query of indices that are not necessarily distinct.

**Definition 3.** *Given a query $Q = (i_1, \ldots, i_t) \in [n]^t$, we say that a set of recovery sets $R^Q = \{R_{i_1}, \ldots, R_{i_t}\}$ is a* query recovery set *with property $\tau$ for $Q$ if*

1. $\left| \left( \bigcup_{s=1}^{t} R_{i_s} \right) \cap B_k \right| \leq \tau \; \forall \; k \in [m]$, *and*
2. $R_{i_r} \cap R_{i_s} = \emptyset \; \forall \; r, s \in [t]$ *where $r \neq s$.*

Having the above mentioned defined property means that not matter which query is selected, we have pairwise disjoint recovery sets that all together use at most $\tau$ elements of each bucket.

**Definition 4.** *We say that a bucket configuration $B_1, \ldots, B_m$ is* $t, \tau$ valid *if, for all queries $Q = (i_1, \ldots, i_t) \in [n]^t$, there exists a query recovery set $R^Q$ with property $\tau$.*

Now, with the building blocks in place, we may more rigorously define batch codes.

**Definition 5.** *A $[n, k, t, m, \tau]$* linear batch code *$\mathcal{C}$ over $\mathbb{F}_q$ is a linear code $\mathcal{C}$ of length $n$ and dimension $k$, together with a $t, \tau$ valid bucket configuration $B_1, \ldots, B_m$.*

Note that we use $k$ for the dimension of the code. Throughout this work, we will focus on the case $\tau = 1$. The following lemma, proven in [9], allows us to do this.

**Lemma 1.** *Any $[n, k, t, m, 1]$ batch code is also an $[n, k, t, \lceil \frac{m}{\tau} \rceil, \tau]$ batch code.*

An affine Cartesian code is defined as follows.

**Definition 6.** *Let $\mathbb{F}_q$ be an arbitrary finite field, and $A_1, \ldots, A_\mu \subseteq \mathbb{F}_q$ be non-empty subsets. Define $X \subseteq \mathbb{F}_q^\mu$ to be the cartesian product $A_1 \times \ldots \times A_\mu \subseteq \mathbb{F}_q^\mu$ where $|A_1 \times \ldots \times A_\mu| = n$. Let $S = \mathbb{F}_q[x_1, \ldots, x_\mu]$ be a multivariate polynomial ring and $S^{\leq \rho}$ be the subspace of $S$ of all polynomials with total degree at most $\rho$. Let $X = \{p_1, \ldots, p_n\}$. The affine Cartesian code $\mathcal{C}_X(\rho)$ of degree $\rho$ is*

$$\mathcal{C}_X(\rho) = \{(f(p_1), \ldots, f(p_n)) \mid f \in S^{\leq \rho}\},$$

*meaning the image of the evaluation map:*

$$ev_\rho : S^{\leq \rho} \to \mathbb{F}_q^n$$
$$f \mapsto (f(p_1), \ldots, f(p_n)).$$

The affine Cartesian code $\mathcal{C}_X(\rho)$ is a linear code of length $n$ which dimension and minimum distance are studied in [12]. Affine Cartesian codes are a generalization of Reed-Muller codes since $\mathcal{C}_{\mathbb{F}_q^\mu}(\rho)$ is a Reed-Muller code. For these codes, the index set of the code corresponds $X$. This is important in the construction of batch codes based on affine Cartesian codes as the entries of the codewords correspond to the evaluations polynomials in the points of $X$.

In the following section, we investigate the recovery sets for an affine Cartesian code that arise from using the structure of the set $X$.

## 3   Recovery Sets

This section focuses on the characterization of some recovery sets for $\mathcal{C}_X(\rho)$. It is well known that a univariate polynomial of degree $\rho - 1$ is uniquely determined by $\rho$ of its evaluations. Furthermore, one can find the polynomial starting from the evaluations by using Lagrange interpolation. The following holds.

**Lemma 2.** *Let $X = A_1 \times \cdots \times A_\mu$. For $p = (a_1, \ldots, a_\mu) \in X$, and $i \in [\mu]$, let*

$$R_{p,i} = \{(b_1, \ldots, b_\mu) \mid b_i \in A_i, \ b_j = a_j \ if \ j \neq i\} \setminus \{p\}.$$

*If $\rho + 1 < |A_i|$, then for any $f \in S^{\leq \rho}$, the value of $f(p)$ can be recovered using the values $f(R_{p,i})$.*

*Proof.* Let $f \in S^{\leq \rho}$, where $\rho + 1 < |A_i|$. By evaluating the multivariate polynomial $f$ in all but the $i$th of the coordinates of $p$, we obtain the univariate polynomial $f_i(x_i) = f(a_1, \ldots, a_{i-1}, x_i, a_{i+1}, \ldots, a_\mu) \in \mathbb{F}_q[x_i]$. By the construction of $R_{p,i}$, we have that $f(R_{p,i}) = f_i(A_i \setminus \{a_i\})$. Since $f$ is a polynomial of total degree at most $\rho$, $f_i(x_i)$ is a polynomial of degree at most $\rho$ in $x_i$. If $\rho + 1 < |A_i|$, then $\rho \leq |A_i| - 2$, so $f_i$ is of degree at most $|A_i| - 2$. By Lagrange interpolation, we may find a unique polynomial $g(x_i) \in \mathbb{F}_q[x_i]$ of degree at most $|A_i \setminus \{a_i\}| - 1 = |A_i| - 2$ such that $g(a) = f_i(a)$ for all $a \in A_i \setminus \{a_i\}$, and so we must have $g = f_i$. We find that $g(a_i) = f_i(a_i) = f(a_1, \ldots, a_\mu) = f(p)$, and so we can recover $f(p)$.

We already recalled that affine Cartesian codes are a generalization of Reed-Muller codes. For simplicity of notation, the remainder of this section and the next section focus on Reed-Muller codes. It is only at the end of the paper that we generalize the results to affine Cartesian codes. We thus initially consider $\mathcal{C}_{\mathbb{F}_q^\mu}(\rho)$ and $\rho < q - 1$.

With $e_i \in \mathbb{F}_q^\mu$ being the vector with 1 in position $i$ and 0 in all other entries, we may take $X = \mathbb{F}_q^\mu$ and obtain the following characterization of some recovery sets for $\mathcal{C}_{\mathbb{F}_q^\mu}(\rho)$.

**Corollary 1.** *For a $p \in \mathbb{F}_q^\mu$, the sets $R_{p,i} = (p + \langle e_i \rangle) \setminus \{p\}$ for $i \in [\mu]$ are recovery sets for $p$ in $\mathcal{C}_{\mathbb{F}_q^\mu}(\rho)$.*

As in Sect. 2, we refer to $R_{p,i}$ for $i \in [\mu]$ as an indirect recovery set of $p$. These sets are in correspondence with one-dimensional affine spaces of $\mathbb{F}_q^\mu$, where $i$ corresponds to the only index that has varying entries. The direct access of $p$ is represented by $R_{p,0} = \{p\}$.

**Corollary 2.** *For any query $Q = (p_1, \ldots, p_{\mu+1}) \in (\mathbb{F}_q^\mu)^{\mu+1}$, using the indices in a set $R^Q = \{R_{p_1,i_1}, \ldots, R_{p_{\mu+1},i_{\mu+1}}\}$, it is possible to recover $f(p_1), \ldots, f(p_{\mu+1})$, where $f \in S^{\leq \rho}$.*

*Proof.* For any $s \in [\mu + 1]$ such that $i_s = 0$, we note that $R_{p_s,i_s} = R_{p_s,0} = \{p_s\}$, and so this is direct access, and we may simply calculate $f(p_s)$. That these are recovery sets for $p_s$ such that $i_s \neq 0$ follows from Corollary 1.

Note that for the previous corollary, we make no claims of non-intersection between the recovery sets. Thus the set $R^Q$ may not be a query recovery set, even for $\tau > 1$, since part 2 of Definition 3 may not be satisfied.

For the rest of the work, we will consider query recovery sets consisting only of sets of the form $R_{p,i}$ for some $p \in \mathbb{F}_q^\mu$ and $i = 0, \ldots, \mu$. We will leave off the $Q$ in $R^Q$ when the context makes the query unambiguous. To be more precise about batch properties, we restate the conditions that every query recovery set must satisfy for a bucket configuration to be valid with $t = \mu + 1$ and $\tau = 1$, the parameters we will be using in the following section:

$$\left| \left( \bigcup_{s=1}^{\mu+1} R_{p_s,i_s} \right) \cap B_k \right| \leq 1 \qquad \forall k \leq m, \tag{1}$$

$$R_{p_r,i_r} \cap R_{p_s,i_s} = \emptyset \qquad \forall r, s \in [\mu + 1], \ r \neq s. \tag{2}$$

The first condition corresponds to using at most $\tau = 1$ indices in any given bucket, while the second corresponds to having non-overlapping recovery sets.

## 4   Quotient-Space Bucket Configuration

With requirements for valid bucket configurations addressed, we now define the bucket configuration used in this paper.

**Definition 7.** *For any subspace $V$ of $\mathbb{F}_q^\mu$, consider the quotient space $\mathbb{F}_q^\mu/V$. The equivalence classes $[p] = p + V$ partition $\mathbb{F}_q^\mu$. We define a quotient-space bucket configuration to be one where the buckets are these equivalence classes.*

Note that the $[\cdot]$ indicates an equivalence in the case that the brackets surround a point $p \in \mathbb{F}_q^\mu$, and a set of indices if they surround a natural number. Its use will be clear from context.

**Definition 8.** *We denote by $\sim$ the equivalence relation on $\mathbb{F}_q^\mu$ induced by $V$, that is, $p_1 \sim p_2$ if and only if $p_1 - p_2 \in V$.*

With this bucket configuration, we have that the number of buckets is $m = q^{\mu - \dim V}$. This configuration provides us with a great deal of symmetry and structure, which allows us to approach determining the validity of a given quotient-space bucket configuration with the following tools.

For any $p \in \mathbb{F}_q^\mu$, the set $[p] = p + V$ is all elements in the same bucket as $p$ by definition. For any subset $U \subseteq \mathbb{F}_q^\mu$, $[U] = \{[p] \mid p \in U\}$ is the set of all buckets corresponding to points in $U$. With this notation, we now note an important result with respect to recovery sets for equivalent points.

**Lemma 3.** *With the subspace construction, if $p_1 \sim p_2$, then $[R_{p_1,i}] = [R_{p_2,i}]$ for all $i \in [\mu]$.*

*Proof.* For all $i \in [\mu]$ and any $\alpha \in \mathbb{F}_q$, $(p_1 + \alpha e_i) - (p_2 + \alpha e_i) = p_1 - p_2 \in V$, so $[p_1 + \alpha e_i] = [p_2 + \alpha e_i]$. Thus we may write

$$[R_{p_1,i}] = \{[p_1 + \alpha e_i] \mid \alpha \in \mathbb{F}_q \setminus \{0\}\} = \{[p_2 + \alpha e_i] \mid \alpha \in \mathbb{F}_q \setminus \{0\}\} = [R_{p_2,i}].$$

This means that under the equivalence relation, the recovery sets for elements in the same bucket are the same. This identical use of buckets for the recovery sets leads to the following:

**Corollary 3.** *Let $Q = (p_1, \ldots, p_{\mu+1}) \in (\mathbb{F}_q^\mu)^{\mu+1}$ be a query such that $p_{i_1} \sim p_{i_2}$ for some $i_1 \neq i_2$. Let $Q' = (p'_1, \ldots, p'_{\mu+1})$ be a query where $p'_{i_2} = p_{i_1}$ and $p'_i = p_i$ for $i \neq i_2$. Then $R$ is a query recovery set for $Q'$ if and only if it is a query recovery set for $Q$.*

In other words, we may effectively treat recovering multiple equivalent points in the same bucket as recovering the same point multiple times. This leads naturally to notation for all recovery sets of a point.

**Definition 9.** *For $p \in \mathbb{F}_q^\mu$, define $R_p = \{R_{p,0}, \ldots, R_{p,\mu}\}$ and $E_p = \bigcup_{i=0}^\mu R_{p,i}$.*

We now reach the central theorem which will be used to verify the validity of quotient-space bucket configurations.

**Theorem 1.** *The following are equivalent:*

*i) $V \cap \langle e_i, e_j \rangle = \{0\}$ $\forall i, j \in [\mu]$.*
*ii) For $p \in \mathbb{F}_q^\mu$, if $a, b \in E_p$ are distinct, then $[a] \neq [b]$.*
*iii) For $p \in \mathbb{F}_q^\mu$, $R_p$ is a query recovery set for $Q = (p, \ldots, p)$.*

*Proof.* We proceed with proving the equivalences.

$i) \Rightarrow ii)$ Let $a, b \in E_p$ be distinct elements for some $p \in \mathbb{F}_q^\mu$. Then, $a = p + \alpha e_i$ and $b = p + \beta e_j$ for some $i, j \in [\mu]$. Since $a \neq b$, it holds that $a - b = \alpha e_i - \beta e_j \neq 0$ which implies that $a - b \notin \mathcal{V}$ as per $i)$, implying that $[a] \neq [b]$.

$ii) \Rightarrow i)$ We prove this implication by contraposition. Assume there are $\alpha, \beta \in \mathbb{F}_q$ such that $\alpha e_i - \beta e_j \in \mathcal{V} \backslash \{0\}$. For arbitrary $p \in \mathbb{F}_q^\mu$, define $a = p + \alpha e_i$ and $b = p + \beta e_j$. Then $a \neq b$, but since $a - b = \alpha e_i - \beta e_j \in \mathcal{V}$, we have $[a] = [b]$.

$ii) \Leftrightarrow iii)$ Since $E_p$ is the union of the sets in $R_p = \{R_{p,i} \mid 0 \leq i \leq \mu\}$, suppose $R_p$ is a query recovery set. Given that $\tau = 1$, by Condition (1) each point in the union of these sets must be in a separate bucket. So for all $a, b \in E_p$, $a \neq b \implies [a] \neq [b]$. Similarly, if each point in $E_p$ is in a different bucket, then Condition (1) is satisfied, and the sets $R_{p,0}, \ldots, R_{p,\mu}$ are all disjoint by construction, so Condition (2) is satisfied. This makes $R_p$ a query recovery set for $Q = (p, \ldots, p)$.

Note that for a non-trivial $\mathcal{V}$, the first condition of this lemma implies $\mu \geq 3$. These equivalent conditions lead to some important necessary conditions.

**Corollary 4.** *When restricted to recovery sets of the form $R_{p,i}$, an affine Cartesian code $\mathcal{C}_{\mathbb{F}_q^\mu}(\rho)$ is a valid batch code with quotient-space bucket configuration induced by $\mathcal{V} \subset \mathbb{F}_q^\mu$ only if $\mathcal{V} \cap \langle e_i, e_j \rangle = \{0\}$ $\forall i, j \in [\mu]$.*

Next, we specify a way that a batch code over $\mathbb{F}_q^{\mu-1}$ may be expanded to a batch code over $\mathbb{F}_q^\mu$. This is then used in constructing a bucket configuration for affine Cartesian codes by induction.

**Theorem 2.** *Consider the puncturing function $\phi : \mathbb{F}_q^\mu \to \mathbb{F}_q^{\mu-1}$ defined by $\phi((a_1, \ldots, a_\mu)) = (u_1, \ldots, a_{\mu-1})$ and let $\mathcal{C} = \mathcal{C}_{\mathbb{F}_q^\mu}(\rho)$ and $\overline{\mathcal{C}} = \mathcal{C}_{\mathbb{F}_q^{\mu-1}}(\rho)$. Let $\mathcal{V} \subseteq \mathbb{F}_q^\mu$ and $\overline{\mathcal{V}} \subseteq \mathbb{F}_q^{\mu-1}$ be subspaces such that $\phi(\mathcal{V}) = \overline{\mathcal{V}}$ and $\mathcal{V} \cap \langle e_i, e_j \rangle = \{0\}$ $\forall i, j \in [\mu]$. If $\overline{\mathcal{C}}$ is a batch code with quotient-space bucket configuration induced by $\overline{\mathcal{V}}$ and $t = \mu$, then $\mathcal{C}$ is a batch code with quotient-space bucket configuration induced by $\mathcal{V}$ and $t = \mu + 1$.*

*Proof.* First, we show that $a \sim b \Rightarrow \phi(a) \sim \phi(b)$. Due to linearity of $\phi$, we have $\phi([a]) = \phi(a + \mathcal{V}) = \phi(a) + \overline{\mathcal{V}} = [\phi(a)]$. From this, we conclude $a \sim b \Rightarrow [a] = [b] \Rightarrow \phi([a]) = \phi([b]) \Rightarrow [\phi(a)] = [\phi(b)] \Rightarrow \phi(a) \sim \phi(b)$.

Now consider any query $Q = (p_1, \ldots, p_\mu, p_{\mu+1})$ of points in $\mathbb{F}_q^\mu$. The multiset $Q' = (\phi(p_1), \ldots, \phi(p_\mu))$ is a query of $\mu$ elements in $\mathbb{F}_q^{\mu-1}$. For any $a \in \mathbb{F}_q^\mu$, let $\overline{a} = \phi(a) \in \mathbb{F}_q^{\mu-1}$. Then we may write $Q' = (\overline{p_1}, \ldots, \overline{p_\mu})$, and since $\overline{\mathcal{C}}$ is a batch code that can satisfy any query of size $t = \mu$, there exists some query recovery set $\overline{R} = \{R_{\overline{p_1}, i_1}, \ldots, R_{\overline{p_\mu}, i_\mu}\}$ such that

1. $\left| \left( \bigcup_{s=1}^\mu R_{\overline{p_s}, i_s} \right) \cap [b] \right| \leq 1$ $\forall [b] \in \mathbb{F}_q^{\mu-1} / \overline{\mathcal{V}}$
2. $R_{\overline{p_r}, i_r} \cap R_{\overline{p_s}, i_s} = \emptyset$ $\forall r, s \in [\mu]$ where $r \neq s$.

Now let $E = \cup_{s=1}^{\mu} R_{p_s,i_s}$. If there exists some $z \in E$ such that $z \sim p_{\mu+1}$, then let $i_{\mu+1} = \mu$, otherwise let $i_{\mu+1} = 0$. We claim that

$$R = \{R_{p_1,i_1}, \ldots, R_{p_\mu,i_\mu}, R_{p_{\mu+1},i_{\mu+1}}\}$$

is a valid recovery set for the query $Q = (p_1, \ldots, p_{\mu+1})$.

First, we check Condition (1) for $R$. Assume for a contradiction that for some $[c] \in \mathbb{F}_q^\mu / \mathcal{V}$, there exist distinct $a, b \in \bigcup_{s=1}^{\mu+1} R_{p_s,i_s} \cap [c]$. Since $a, b \in [c]$, we have $a \sim b$. As seen before, this means that $\phi(a) \sim \phi(b)$. We consider two cases: $\phi(a) = \phi(b)$ or $\phi(a) \neq \phi(b)$.

If $\phi(a) = \phi(b)$, then by the definition of $\phi$, we see that $a - b \in \langle e_\mu \rangle$. This means that $b \in E_a$. Since $\mathcal{V} \cap \langle e_i, e_j \rangle = \{0\} \; \forall i, j \in [\mu]$, part $ii)$ of Theorem 1 implies that $[a] \neq [b]$, a contradiction.

Thus, instead, we must have $\phi(a) \neq \phi(b)$, which we write as $\bar{a} \neq \bar{b}$. This leads to a few possibilities. We distinguish three cases: either $a, b \in E = \bigcup_{s=1}^{\mu} R_{p_s,i_s}$, $a, b \in R_{p_{\mu+1},u_{\mu+1}}$, or without loss of generality $a \in E$ and $b \in R_{p_{\mu+1},i_{\mu+1}}$.

If $a, b \in E = \bigcup_{s=1}^{\mu} R_{p_s,i_s}$, then $\bar{a}, \bar{b} \in \bigcup_{s=1}^{\mu} R_{\overline{p_s},i_s}$. This leads to a contradiction to Condition (1) for $\overline{R}$, as $\bar{a}$ and $\bar{b}$ are in the same bucket. Whether $i_{\mu+1} = 0$ or $i_{\mu_1} = \mu$, our construction means that $\phi(R_{p_{\mu+1},i_{\mu+1}}) = \{\phi(p_{\mu+1})\}$, so $a, b \in R_{p_{\mu+1},i_{\mu+1}}$ implies $\bar{a}, \bar{b} \in \phi(R_{p_{\mu+1},i_{\mu+1}}) = \{\phi(p_{\mu+1})\}$, or $\bar{a} = \bar{b} = \phi(p_{\mu+1})$, and we would have a contradiction to $\bar{a} \neq \bar{b}$.

Thus, we suppose without loss of generality that $a \in E$, and $b \in R_{p_{\mu+1},i_{\mu+1}}$. There are two possibilities. If $i_{\mu+1} = 0$, then by our selection of $i_{\mu+1}$, there is no $z \in E$ such that $p_{\mu+1} \sim z$, but $b \in R_{p_{\mu+1},0} = \{p_{\mu+1}\}$, so $b = p_{\mu+1}$, which means $a \sim b = p_{\mu+1}$, a contradiction. Thus, we may assume $i_{\mu+1} = \mu$, which means $\exists z \in E$ such that $z \sim p_{\mu+1}$. Then there is some $r \in [\mu]$ such that $z \in R_{p_r,i_r}$, and since $a \in E$, we also have some $s \in [\mu]$ such that $a \in R_{p_s,i_s}$. This again leads to two possibilities: either $s = r$ or $s \neq r$.

Suppose $s = r$. Since $b \in R_{p_{\mu+1},\mu}$, we have that $b \neq p_{\mu+1}$ and also $b \in E_{p_{\mu+1}}$. We also have $p_{\mu+1} \in E_{p_{\mu+1}}$, so $b \neq p_{\mu+1} \implies b \not\sim p_{\mu+1}$ by Theorem 1. Since $z \sim p_{\mu+1}$, we must have $b \not\sim z$, or transitivity of $\sim$ would break down. Since $a \sim b$, this also means that $a \not\sim z$, so certainly $z \neq a$. Since $s = r$, we have $a, z \in R_{p_r,i_r} = R_{p_s,i_s}$, so $a - z = \alpha e_{i_r}$ for some $\alpha \in \mathbb{F}_q \setminus \{0\}$. We also have $b = p_{\mu+1} + \beta e_\mu$ for some $\beta \in \mathbb{F}_q \setminus \{0\}$, and we consider that $a \sim b$ and $z \sim p_{\mu+1}$. Since $\sim$ is a congruence relation, we may combine these as $a - z \sim b - p_{\mu+1}$, or $\alpha e_{i_r} \sim \beta e_\mu$. But this means that $\alpha e_{i_r} - \beta e_\mu \in \mathcal{V}$. The only way this would not be a contradiction to $\mathcal{V} \cap \langle e_i, e_j \rangle = \{0\} \; \forall i, j \in [\mu]$ is if $\alpha e_{i_r} = \beta e_\mu$, but that would mean $i_r = \mu$, which is impossible given the construction of $\overline{R}$.

Thus, we consider $s \neq r$. If $\bar{a} = \bar{z}$, then $\bar{a} \in R_{\overline{p_s},i_s}$, and $\bar{a} = \bar{z} \in R_{\overline{p_r},i_r}$, so $\bar{a} \in R_{\overline{p_r},i_r} \cap R_{\overline{p_s},i_s}$. This is a contradiction to (2) for $\overline{R}$. If instead $\bar{a} \neq \bar{z}$, note that $\bar{b} = \overline{p_{\mu+1}} \sim \bar{z}$. This means that $\bar{a} \sim \bar{b} \sim \bar{z}$, so $\bar{a} \sim \bar{z}$, and this is a contradiction to Condition (1) for $\overline{R}$.

This concludes the proof that Condition (1) holds for $R$. Next, we show that Condition (2) holds for $R$.

Again, consider the possibilities for a contradiction. If $R_{p_r,i_r} \cap R_{p_s,i_s} \neq \emptyset$ for some $r, s \in [\mu + 1]$ such that $r \neq s$, then there are two possibilities: either $r, s \in [\mu]$ or without loss of generality $r \in [\mu]$ and $s = \mu + 1$.

If $r, s \in [\mu]$, then this would mean that there exists some $p \in \mathbb{F}_q^\mu$ such that $p \in R_{p_r,i_r} \cap R_{p_s,i_s}$. But then $\overline{p} \in R_{\overline{p_r},i_r}$ and $\overline{p} \in R_{\overline{p_s},i_s}$, a contradiction to Condition (2) for $\overline{R}$.

Thus, without loss of generality, we have $r \in [\mu]$ and $s = \mu + 1$. There are again two possibilities: either $i_{\mu+1} = 0$ or $i_{\mu+1} = \mu$.

If $i_{\mu+1} = 0$, this means $R_{p_s,i_s} = R_{p_{\mu+1},0} = \{p_{\mu+1}\}$, and so the intersection must be $\{p_{\mu+1}\}$. This would mean $p_{\mu+1} \in R_{p_r,i_r}$ and so $p_{\mu+1} \in E$. Since $p_{\mu+1} \sim p_{\mu+1}$ by the reflexive property of $\sim$, it is a $z \in E$ such that $z \sim p_{\mu+1}$, a contradiction to $i_{\mu+1} = 0$.

If instead $i_{\mu+1} = \mu$, we have some $z \in E$ such that $z \sim p_{\mu+1}$, so $z \in R_{p_k,i_k}$ for some $k \in [\mu]$. Since $R_{p_r,i_r} \cap R_{p_{\mu+1},i_{\mu+1}} \neq \emptyset$, we also have some $a \in R_{p_{\mu+1},\mu}$ such that $a \in R_{p_r,i_r}$. If $k = r$, we use the same reasoning as in the case $s = r$ from the proof of Condition (1) above. Since $a \in R_{p_{\mu+1},\mu}$, we have that $a \neq p_{\mu+1}$ and $a \in E_{p_{\mu+1}}$. We also have $p_{\mu+1} \in E_{p_{\mu+1}}$, so $a \neq p_{\mu+1} \implies a \not\sim p_{\mu+1}$ by Theorem 1. Since $z \sim p_{\mu+1}$, we must have $a \not\sim z$, so certainly $z \neq a$. Since $k = r$, we have $a, z \in R_{p_k,i_k} = R_{p_r,i_r}$, so $a - z = \alpha e_{i_r}$ for some $\alpha \in \mathbb{F}_q \setminus \{0\}$. We also have $a = p_{\mu+1} + \beta e_\mu$ for some $\beta \in \mathbb{F}_q \setminus \{0\}$, so $a - p_{\mu+1} = \beta e_\mu$ for some $\beta \in \mathbb{F}_q \setminus \{0\}$. But then $a - z \sim a - p_{\mu+1}$, so $\alpha e_k \sim \beta e_\mu$, which leads to a contradiction as before.

This leaves $k \neq r$. Again, if $\overline{a} = \overline{z}$, this leads to a contradiction to (2) for $\overline{R}$, and if $\overline{a} \neq \overline{z}$, we still have $a \in R_{p_{\mu+1},\mu}$, so $\overline{a} \in \phi(R_{p_{\mu+1},\mu}) = \{\overline{p_{\mu+1}}\}$, which means $\overline{a} = \overline{p_{\mu+1}} \sim \overline{z}$, and so this contradicts Condition (1) for $\overline{R}$.

We have once again contradicted all alternatives, so Condition (2) must be satisfied for $R$. Because $R$ satisfies both conditions, $R$ is a valid query recovery set. Since this holds for any query $Q = (p_1, \ldots, p_{\mu+1})$ of $\mu + 1$ elements in $\mathbb{F}_q^\mu$, $C$ is a batch code that can satisfy $t = \mu + 1$ requests.

## 4.1 The Case of a Diagonal Subspace

Using the subspace $\mathcal{V} = \langle (1, \ldots, 1) \rangle \subset \mathbb{F}_q^\mu$, we are able to generate a valid bucket configuration as long as $q \geq 3$ and $\mu \geq 3$:

**Theorem 3.** *Let $q \geq 3$, $\mu \geq 3$ and $\mathcal{V} = \langle (1, \ldots, 1) \rangle \subset \mathbb{F}_q^\mu$. Then $C_{\mathbb{F}_q^\mu}(\rho)$ is a batch code with quotient-space bucket configuration induced by $\mathcal{V}$ and with properties $m = q^{\mu-1}$, $\tau = 1$, and $t = \mu + 1$.*

*Proof.* With this configuration, since $\dim(\mathcal{V}) = 1$, we have $m = q^{\mu-1}$.

We begin with the base case $\mu = 3$, where $\mathcal{V} = \langle (1, 1, 1) \rangle$, and $t = 4$. Since $\mathcal{V} \cap \langle e_i, e_j \rangle = \{0\} \ \forall i, j \in [\mu]$, recovering four copies of any one point is possible by Theorem 1, and by Corollary 3, so is recovering any four points in the same bucket. Recovering four query points in different buckets is trivial using all direct access. This leaves the cases where the queries belong to either 2 or 3 distinct buckets. Without loss of generality and by Corollary 3, we need to address the queries $Q = (a, a, a, b)$, $Q = (a, a, b, c)$, or $Q = (a, a, b, b)$, where $a, b, c \in \mathbb{F}_q^3$ such that $[a]$, $[b]$, and $[c]$ are all distinct. We handle each of these separately:

1. Consider $Q = (a, a, a, b)$. If $[b] \notin [E_a]$, then any three recovery sets may be used for $a$, and $b$ may be directly accessed. Otherwise, suppose that there are distinct values $i, j \in [\mu]$ such that $[b] \in [R_{a,i}]$ and $[b] \in [R_{a,j}]$. This means that there are some $c \in R_{a,i}$ and $d \in R_{a,j}$ such that $[c] = [b] = [d]$. But since $i \neq j$, $c \neq d$. This makes $c, d \in E_a$ distinct, and so $[c] = [d]$ is a contradiction to part ii of Theorem 1. Thus, there is only one value $i \in [\mu]$ such that $[b] \in [R_{a,i}]$, and we can satisfy the request using $R = \{R_{a,0}, R_{a,j_1}, R_{a,j_2}, R_{b,0}\}$ such that $j_1, j_2 \in [\mu] \setminus i$.

2. Recovering $Q = (a, a, b, c)$ is similar to the first case, using $R_{b,0}$ and $R_{c,0}$. Since these eliminate at most 2 recovery sets of $a$ through intersection with $[E_a]$, there will be at least one remaining recovery set of $a$ besides the direct access.

3. Consider $Q = (a, a, b, b)$. Utilize $R_{a,0}$ and $R_{b,0}$. If $[b] \in [R_{a,i}]$ for some $i \in [\mu]$, let $j \in [\mu] \setminus i$, otherwise let $j$ be any $j \in [\mu]$. This means that $[b] \notin [R_{a,j}]$ by construction. To see that we can use both $R_{a,j}$ and $R_{b,j}$, assume by way of contradiction that there exists some $[p] \in [R_{a,j}] \cap [R_{b,j}]$. Then

$$[p] = [a + \alpha e_j] = [b + \beta e_j],$$

where $\alpha, \beta \in \mathbb{F}_q \setminus \{0\}$. This means $(a + \alpha e_j) - (b + \beta e_j) = a + (\alpha - \beta)e_j - b \in V$, which in turn means $[a + (\alpha - \beta)e_j] = [b]$. Either $\alpha = \beta$, so $[a] = [b]$, a contradiction, or $[b] \in [R_{a,j}]$, also a contradiction. Therefore $[R_{a,j}] \cap [R_{b,j}] = \emptyset$. Thus we may use $R = \{R_{a,0}, R_{a,j}, R_{b,0}, R_{b,j}\}$.

Now, assume that for some $\mu > 3$, $\overline{V} = \langle (1, \ldots, 1) \rangle \subset \mathbb{F}_q^{\mu-1}$ generates a valid batch code with $t = \mu$. Then by Theorem 2, since $V = \langle (1, \ldots, 1) \rangle \in \mathbb{F}_q^{\mu}$ satisfies $V \cap \langle e_i, e_j \rangle = \{0\}$ $\forall i, j \in [\mu]$, we can extend the batch code with quotient-space bucket configuration induced by $\overline{V}$ into a batch code with quotient-space bucket configuration induced by $V$ that can satisfy any query of $t = \mu + 1$ elements. By induction, we then have that for any $\mu \geq 3$, $V = \langle (1, \ldots, 1) \rangle \subset \mathbb{F}_q^{\mu}$ generates buckets for a batch code with $t = \mu + 1$.

## 5   Affine Cartesian Codes

Finally, we want to apply the techniques we have developed so far to all of the affine Cartesian codes.

**Theorem 4.** *Let $C_X(\rho)$ be an affine Cartesian code with $X = A_1 \times \cdots \times A_\mu$ of degree $\rho$ where $\mu \geq 3$. Let $I_\rho = \{i \in [\mu] \mid \rho + 1 < |A_i|\}$ and $\nu(\rho) := |I_\rho|$. If $\nu(\rho) \geq 3$, then $C_X(\rho)$ is a batch code capable of satisfying any $t = \nu(\rho) + 1$ queries.*

*Proof.* For simplicity of notation, let $\nu := \nu(\rho)$. Without loss of generality, under a change of variables, we can consider $I_\rho = \{i \in [\mu] \mid \rho + 1 < |A_i|\} = [\nu]$.

Consider the puncturing function $\phi : \mathbb{F}_q^\mu \to \mathbb{F}_q^\nu$ that is obtained by puncturing the coordinates in the subset $[\mu] \setminus [\nu]$. Let $\mathcal{V} = \langle (1, \ldots, 1) \rangle \subseteq \mathbb{F}_q^\mu$ and define the buckets for $\mathcal{C}_{\phi(X)}(\rho)$ to be the sets $[\tilde{p}]^{\phi(X)} := [\tilde{p}] \cap \phi(X)$ for $\tilde{p} \in \phi(X)$ and where $[\tilde{p}] \in \mathbb{F}_q^\nu/\phi(\mathcal{V})$. Note that since $[\tilde{p}]^{\phi(X)}$ is defined using the equivalence class, it is well-defined. We will show that for a query $Q = (p_1, \ldots, p_{\nu+1}) \in X^{\nu+1} \subseteq (\mathbb{F}_q^\mu)^{\nu+1}$ for which we wish to recover $f(p_1), \ldots, f(p_{\nu+1})$, there exists a valid query recovery set $\{R_{p_1,i_1}, \ldots R_{p_{\nu+1},i_{\nu+1}}\}$ where $R_{p_\ell,i_\ell} \subseteq X$ with $i_\ell \in I_\rho \cup \{0\}$ for all $\ell \in [\nu+1]$.

Consider the affine Cartesian code $\mathcal{C}_{\phi(X)}(\rho)$. We show that this code has the same batch properties as the code $\mathcal{C}_{\mathbb{F}_q^\nu}(\rho)$. Let

$$\phi(Q) = (\phi(p_1), \ldots, \phi(p_{\nu+1})) \subseteq (\phi(X))^{\nu+1} \subseteq (\mathbb{F}_q^\nu)^{\nu+1}.$$

By Theorem 3 there exists a query recovery set $R^{\phi(Q)} = \{R_{\phi(p_1),i_1}, \ldots, R_{\phi(p_{\nu+1}),i_{\nu+1}}\}$ for $\phi(Q)$ in $\mathcal{C}_{\mathbb{F}_q^\nu}(\rho)$ with $R_{\phi(p_s),i_s} \subseteq \mathbb{F}_q^\nu$ as in Corollary 1 and $i_1, \ldots, i_{\nu+1} \in [\nu] \cup \{0\}$.

For all $s \in [\nu+1]$, $R^{\phi(X)}_{\phi(p_s),i_s} = R_{\phi(p_s),i_s} \cap \phi(X)$ matches the definition in Lemma 2. Since $\rho+1 < |A_i|$ for all $i \in [\nu]$, by that lemma the values of $f(R^{\phi(X)}_{\phi(p_\ell),i_\ell})$ are enough to recover $f(\phi(p_\ell))$, for any $\ell \in [\nu+1]$ and $f \in \mathbb{F}_q[x_1, \ldots, x_\nu]^{\leq \rho}$. This means that

$$R^{\phi(Q)} = \{R^{\phi(X)}_{\phi(p_1),i_1}, \ldots, R^{\phi(X)}_{\phi(p_{\nu+1}),i_{\nu+1}}\}$$

is a query recovery set for $\phi(Q)$ in $\mathcal{C}_{\phi(X)}(\rho)$. Furthermore, we have that by Condition (1) for $\mathcal{C}_{\mathbb{F}_q^\nu}(\rho)$, it holds that

$$\left| \left( \bigcup_{s=1}^{\mu+1} R^{\phi(X)}_{\phi(p_s),i_s} \right) \cap [\tilde{p}]^{\phi(X)} \right| = \left| \left( \bigcup_{s=1}^{\mu+1} R_{\phi(p_s),i_s} \right) \cap [\tilde{p}] \cap \phi(X) \right| \leq 1$$

for all $\tilde{p} \in \phi(X)$ and by Condition (2) for $\mathcal{C}_{\mathbb{F}_q^\nu}(\rho)$ it holds that

$$R^{\phi(X)}_{\phi(p_r),i_r} \cap R^{\phi(X)}_{\phi(p_s),i_s} = R_{\phi(p_r),i_r} \cap R_{\phi(p_s),i_s} \cap \phi(X) = \emptyset$$

for all $r, s \in [\nu+1]$ with $r \neq s$.

We have thus shown that the query $\phi(Q) = \{\phi(p_1), \ldots, \phi(p_{\nu+1})\} \subseteq \phi(X)$ can be recovered in $\mathcal{C}_{\phi(X)}(\rho)$ using the recovery sets

$$\{R^{\phi(X)}_{\phi(p_1),i_1}, \ldots, R^{\phi(X)}_{\phi(p_{\nu+1}),i_{\nu+1}}\}. \tag{3}$$

We claim that the set $\{R^X_{p_1,i_1}, \ldots, R^X_{p_{\nu+1},i_{\nu+1}}\}$ is a valid recovery set for $Q$ in $\mathcal{C}_X(\rho)$. Let $R^Q = \{R_{p_1,i_1}, \ldots, R_{p_{\nu+1},i_{\nu+1}}\}$ be the set of recovery sets in $\mathbb{F}_q^\mu$ where the indices correspond to the ones of Eq. (3). Let $\overline{Q}$ be a query obtained by appending $\mu-\nu$ points of $\mathbb{F}_q^\mu$ to $Q$. Using Theorem 2, a query recovery set $R^{\overline{Q}}$ can be constructed recursively by starting from $R^{\phi(Q)}$. That is, we first add one point in $\mathbb{F}_q^{\nu+1}$ to the query, and the query recovery set for such a query will contain

$R^Q$ by construction. This process may be continued until we reach the query $\overline{Q}$ of points in $\mathbb{F}_q^{mu}$, and have $R^Q \subseteq R^{\overline{Q}}$. By taking only the recovery sets for the points in $Q$ and restricting them to $X$, we obtain the set $\{R^X_{p_1,i_1}, \ldots, R^X_{p_{\nu+1},i_{\nu+1}}\}$, which is thus a valid recovery set.

## 6   Conclusions

The work in this paper focuses on the study of batch properties of affine Cartesian codes. For affine Cartesian codes, given a subspace $\mathcal{V} \subseteq \mathbb{F}_q^\mu$, we define a bucket configuration where each bucket is a coset of $\mathcal{V}$ in the quotient space $\mathbb{F}_q^\mu/\mathcal{V}$. We show that when restricted to a certain type of recovery set, for such bucket configuration to define a batch code, one needs to have that the intersection $\mathcal{V} \cap \langle e_i, e_j \rangle$ is trivial for all $i \neq j$. By choosing $\mathcal{V} = \langle (1, \ldots, 1) \rangle$, we demonstrate that the affine Cartesian code $\mathcal{C}_{\mathbb{F}_q^\mu}(\rho)$ can satisfy queries of length $t = \mu + 1$ for any $\mu \geq 3$. We are also able to extend the result for any affine Cartesian code, where the size of the query depends on the total degree and the sizes of the subsets defining the code.

**Acknowledgments.** This research was partially supported by the National Science Foundation under grant DMS-1547399.

## References

1. Asi, H., Yaakobi, E.: Nearly optimal constructions of PIR and batch codes. IEEE Trans. Inf. Theory **65**, 947–964 (2019)
2. Baumbaugh, T., Diaz, Y., Friesenhahn, S., Manganiello, F., Vetter, A.: Batch codes from Hamming and Reed-Muller codes. J. Algebra Comb. Discrete Struct. Appl. **5**, 153–165 (2018)
3. Beelen, P., Datta, M.: Generalized Hamming weights of affine Cartesian codes. Finite Fields Appl. **51**, 130–145 (2018)
4. Bhattacharya, S., Ruj, S., Roy, B.: Combinatorial batch codes: a lower bound and optimal constructions. Adv. Math. Commun. **6**, 165–174 (2012)
5. Bujtás, C., Tuza, Z.: Optimal combinatorial batch codes derived from dual systems, Miskolc. Math. Notes **12**, 11–23 (2011)
6. Dimakis, A.G., Ramchandran, K., Wu, Y., Suh, C.: A survey on network codes for distributed storage. Proc. IEEE **99**, 476–489 (2011)
7. Heijnen, P., Pellikaan, R.: Generalized Hamming weights of $q$-ary Reed-Muller codes. IEEE Trans. Inform. Theory **44**, 181–196 (1998)
8. Holzbaur, L., Polyanskaya, R., Polyanskii, N., Vorobyev, I.: Lifted reed-solomon codes with application to batch codes. In: 2020 IEEE International Symposium on Information Theory (ISIT), pp. 634–639 (2020)
9. Ishai, Y., Kushilevitz, E., Ostrovsky, R., Sahai, A.: Batch codes and their applications. In: Proceedings of the 36th Annual ACM Symposium on Theory of Computing, pp. 262–271. ACM, New York (2004)
10. Li, R., Wootters, M.: Improved batch code lower bounds (2021)
11. López, H.H., Manganiello, F., Matthews, G.L.: Affine Cartesian codes with complementary duals. Finite Fields Appl. **57**, 13–28 (2019)

12. López, H.H., Rentería-Márquez, C., Villarreal, R.H.: Affine Cartesian codes. Des. Codes Cryptogr. **71**, 5–19 (2014)
13. Paterson, M.B., Stinson, D.R., Wei, R.: Combinatorial batch codes. Adv. Math. Commun. **3**, 13–27 (2009)
14. Polyanskaya, R., Polyanskii, N., Vorobyev, I.: Binary batch codes with improved redundancy. IEEE Trans. Inf. Theory **66**, 7360–7370 (2020)
15. Ramakrishnan, P., Wootters, M.: On taking advantage of multiple requests in error correcting codes, CoRR, abs/1802.00875 (2018)
16. Riet, A.-E., Skachek, V., Thomas, E.K.: Asynchronous Batch and PIR Codes from Hypergraphs, arXiv e-prints (2018)
17. Silberstein, N., Gál, A.: Optimal combinatorial batch codes based on block designs. Des. Codes Crypt. **78**(2), 409–424 (2014). https://doi.org/10.1007/s10623-014-0007-9
18. Skachek, V.: Batch and PIR codes and their connections to locally repairable codes. In: Greferath, M., Pavčević, M.O., Silberstein, N., Vázquez-Castro, M.Á. (eds.) Network Coding and Subspace Designs. SCT, pp. 427–442. Springer, Cham (2018). https://doi.org/10.1007/978-3-319-70293-3_16
19. Thomas, E.K., Skachek, V.: Constructions and bounds for batch codes with small parameters. In: Barbero, Á.I., Skachek, V., Ytrehus, Ø. (eds.) ICMCTA 2017. LNCS, vol. 10495, pp. 283–295. Springer, Cham (2017). https://doi.org/10.1007/978-3-319-66278-7_24

# Structural Properties of Self-dual Monomial Codes with Application to Code-Based Cryptography

Vlad-Florin Drăgoi[1,2]([✉]) [iD] and Andreea Szocs[1] [iD]

[1] Aurel Vlaicu University of Arad, Arad, Romania
{vlad.dragoi,andreea.szocs}@uav.com
[2] LITIS, University of Rouen, Normandie, Rouen, France

**Abstract.** This article focuses on the self-dual monomial codes that have an underlying structure of decreasing/weakly decreasing monomial codes. Having such a property permits an in-depth analysis of their structure: The permutation group of a subclass is (significantly) bigger than the affine group. Upon looking at higher powers of the code, we see that its third power is the entire space, but the dual of the square code gives information helpful for decoding. Using operations such as shortening, puncturing and taking the discrete derivative, we extract the subcode generated by the multiples of a certain variable. Recently, self-dual monomial codes have been proposed for a McEliece public key encryption scheme. They seem to possess strong security features - they have a large permutation group, they are self-dual, there are exponentially many of them by counting the possible monomial bases used in their construction. A more detailed analysis allows us to identify subclasses where the square code and shortening methods yield non-trivial results; in these cases, the security is dominated by the complexity of the Information Set Decoding, which is exponential in the square root of the length of the code. This is a solid argument for the security of the McEliece variant based on self-dual monomial codes.

**Keywords:** Monomial code · Self-dual code · Schur product · McEliece cryptosystem · Reed-Muller code

## 1 Introduction

Self-dual codes represent an active field of research in algebraic coding theory. The topic was initiated in the early 70's by Vera Pless, MacWilliams and Sloane [31,42,43]. Results regarding combinatorial aspects such as enumeration of self-dual codes are given in [12,15,43]. In the book of Nebe, Rains, and Sloane [38] one discovers connections between the theory of self-dual codes and invariant theory. In particular, connections with lattices, algebraic combinatorics, and quantum codes are shown. Recently, self-dual codes were applied to the field of cryptography. Secret sharing schemes based on self-dual codes were proposed in

© Springer Nature Switzerland AG 2021
M. B. Paterson (Ed.): IMACC 2021, LNCS 13129, pp. 16–41, 2021.
https://doi.org/10.1007/978-3-030-92641-0_2

[18], highly secure boolean functions from self-dual codes were given in [11], and public-key encryption schemes based on binary self-dual codes were constructed in [24] and more recently analyzed in [33]. In this article, we will focus on the later construction, namely the McEliece variant [24].

The scheme proposed in [24] is based on the construction of self-dual codes proposed by Hannusch and Lakatos [26], where $[2^m, 2^{m-1}, 2^{m/2}]$ binary self-dual codes were defined. These are highly related to binary Reed-Muller codes $(\mathscr{R}(r, m))$. It is well-known that when $m$ is odd the code $\mathscr{R}(\frac{m-1}{2}, m)$ is a self-dual $[2^m, 2^{m-1}, \sqrt{2^{m+1}}]$ code. Currently, there is no self-dual binary Reed-Muller code when $m$ is even. However, in [26] the authors give a method for constructing complement-free sets $I = I_{\leq \frac{m}{2}-1} \cup J$, where $I_{\leq \frac{m}{2}-1}$ denotes the set of all monomials in $m$ variables of degree less than or equal to $m/2 - 1$. The resulting code $\mathscr{C}(I)$, which is the span of the set of $\mathsf{ev}(f)$ for $f \in I$ ($\mathsf{ev}$ is an evaluation function), is a self-dual $[2^m, 2^{m-1}, 2^{m/2}]$ binary code. As the article [26] focuses only on the existence and construction of such codes, several questions regarding the underlying structure of this family of codes are still open. A deeper insight could reveal properties necessary for understanding the security of the McEliece variant [24]. Here, we propose to firstly analyze the structural properties of this family of codes and secondly apply our results on a detailed evaluation of the security of the McEliece variant [24].

## 1.1    Structural Properties of the Binary Self-dual Monomial Codes

As any binary self-dual monomial code $\mathscr{C}$ can be defined as a subcode of the $\mathscr{R}(\frac{m}{2}, m)$, we will use the formalism from [5] to characterize $\mathscr{C}$ in terms of weakly decreasing and decreasing monomial code. More precisely, our first result can be stated as follows:

**Theorem.** Let $\mathscr{C}(I)$ be a self-dual code defined by a max-complement-free monomial set $I = I_{\leq \frac{m}{2}-1} \cup x_i I_{\leq \frac{m}{2}-1}$. Then $\mathscr{C}(I)$ is a weakly decreasing monomial code defined by

$$\mathscr{C}(I) = \mathscr{C}\left(\bigcup_{f \in J} [1, f]_{\preceq_{\mathrm{w}}}\right).$$

Moreover, $\exists \pi^* \in \mathfrak{S}_n$ s.t. $\mathsf{ev}(x_i)^{\pi^*} = \mathsf{ev}(x_0)$ and $\mathscr{C}(I)^{\pi^*}$ is a decreasing monomial code given by

$$\mathscr{C}(I)^{\pi^*} = \mathscr{C}\left([1, x_0 x_{\frac{m}{2}+1} \cdots x_{m-1}]_{\preceq}\right).$$

The fact that $\mathscr{C}$ is a decreasing/weakly decreasing monomial code provides helpful tools for determining

- the structure of the square code $\mathscr{C}^2$ (here, square refers to the Schur product of $\mathscr{C}$ with itself), and higher powers of Schur products $\mathscr{C}^i$;
- the shortened and the punctured codes $\mathcal{S}_{\mathrm{Supp}(\mathsf{ev}(1+x_i))}(\mathscr{C}(I))$ and $\mathcal{P}_{\mathrm{Supp}(\mathsf{ev}(1+x_i))}(\mathscr{C}(I))$;

– the permutation group $\mathsf{Perm}(\mathscr{C}(I))$ of some subclasses of self-dual monomial codes.

The Schur product of two linear codes has recently caught a lot of attention. The possible applications are connected to decoding strategies (error-correcting pairs [16,41], power syndrome decoding [46]), the security of the McElice cryptosystem (square code attacks [14,17,40,52]) and oblivious transfer [39]. More on square and higher powers of linear codes can be found in [45]. Regarding the square of a self-dual monomial code we demonstrate in this article that with high probability $\mathscr{C}(I)^2 = \mathscr{R}(m-1,m)$. The small proportion of $\mathscr{C}(I)$ not satisfying the later condition are those defined by $I = I_{\leq \frac{m}{2}-1} \cup x_i I_{\leq \frac{m}{2}-1}$, in case which we have $\left(\mathscr{C}(I)^2\right)^{\perp} = \mathscr{C}(\{\mathbf{1}, x_i\})$. Our result can also be seen as a constructive way of taking the square root of a Reed-Muller code. Indeed, for odd $m$ we have $\sqrt{\mathscr{R}(m-1,m)} = \mathscr{R}(\frac{m-1}{2}, m)$, and for even $m$ taking the square root of $\mathscr{R}(m-1,m)$ can be reduced to choosing a max-complement-free monomial set $I$ as in [26] (here, the square root is considered with respect to the Schur product operator).

Next, we will analyze the structure of the shortened and punctured codes. Informally, we prove that if we shorten/puncture the code $\mathscr{C}(I)$ on the support of $\mathsf{ev}(1+x_i)$ we obtain a monomial code that is situated in between two consecutive Reed-Muller codes. More precisely, we have:

**Theorem.** Let $I$ be a max-complement-free monomial set, $I = I_{\leq \frac{m}{2}-1} \cup J$, defined as in [24]. Let $L = \mathsf{Supp}(\mathsf{ev}(1 + x_i))$ for some $x_i$. Then we have

$$\mathscr{R}(m/2 - 2, m - 1) \subset \mathcal{S}_L(\mathscr{C}(I)) \subset \mathscr{R}(m/2 - 1, m - 1)$$
$$\mathscr{R}(m/2 - 1, m - 1) \subset \mathcal{P}_L(\mathscr{C}(I)) \subset \mathscr{R}(m/2, m - 1).$$

In particular, $\mathcal{S}_L(\mathscr{C}(I)) = \mathscr{R}\left(\frac{m}{2} - 1, m - 1\right)$ if and only if $I = I_{\leq \frac{m}{2}-1} \cup x_i I_{\leq \frac{m}{2}-1}$.

In order to demonstrate the aforementioned theorem, we will characterize the shortened code $\mathcal{S}_L(\mathscr{C}(I))$ in terms of the monomial code generated by the Hasse derivative of all the monomials $f \in I$ with respect to the variable $x_i$. By doing so, we will be able to recover the subcode of $\mathscr{C}(I)$ which is still a monomial code generated by all the monomials $f \in I$ such that $x_i | f$, or equivalently $x_i \preceq_w f$. A short note on the permutation group of self-dual monomial codes is also provided. We demonstrate that for $I = I_{\frac{m}{2}-1} \cup x_i I_{\frac{m}{2}-1}$ the permutation group can be defined as a triple direct product of $\mathsf{T}(m,2)$ (translation group) and $\mathsf{Aff}(m,2)$ (general affine group).

## 1.2 Evaluating the Security of the McEliece Variant [24]

Code-based cryptography is an active field of research, as pointed out by the finalists in the NIST's post-quantum standardization process. It started with the work of R. McEliece [36] which gained a lot of attention partly due to complexity results regarding the underlying problems, i.e., the decoding problem, which is NP-complete for random codes [7]. McEliece's ideea still stands today, as, after three rounds of reviews in the NIST competition, we are left with one code-based finalist, *Classic McEliece* [2], and two code-based alternatives, BIKE [3] and HQC [1]. The main idea of the generic McEliece scheme is to choose a linear code for which an efficient decoding strategy exists, set a basis for this code as the private key and mask the structure of this code in order to create a trapdoor (change the basis and permute the columns of the private generator matrix in order to obtain a public key), additional to the usual trapdoor based on the difficulty of the Syndrome Decoding Problem. Decoding with the knowledge of the proper basis becomes easy, while decoding with the public basis (which looks similar to the basis of a random code) becomes difficult. That is the idea of the security on which the scheme stands, i.e., decoding a random linear code is NP-complete and hence the cryptosystem should be quantum resistant.

There are several cryptosystems showing several similarities to the McEliece variant based on self-dual monomial codes [24]. The most sticking ones are Sidenlnikov's cryptosystem based on Reed-Muller codes [50] and the McEliece variant based on polar codes proposed by Shrestha and Kim [49]. These were successfully cryptanalysed using efficient techniques [14] or subexponential algorithms [4,37]. However, the self-dual monomial codes come with several advantages, such as:

- the complexity of the attacks on the dual code are identical with that of attacks on the code itself;
- the hull of the code equals the code itself, and hence, generic algorithm for solving the code equivalence problem are unfitted for this scheme;
- as we shall demonstrate, even for a more structured configuration of the monomial set $I$, i.e., $I = I_{\frac{m}{2}-1} \cup x_i I_{\frac{m}{2}-1}$, applying square code and shortening only reduces the code equivalence problem to the most difficult instance of the code equivalence problem on the Reed-Muller codes;
- there is an exponential number of sets $I$ to be considered and hence an exponential number of instances of the code equivalence problem to be solved;
- different choices of $I$ give different permutation groups for $\mathscr{C}(I)$ and, implicitly, different numbers and structures of minimum weight codewords. Again, for more structured choices of $I$ the code spanned by the minimum weight codewords is equivalent to a certain Reed-Muller code for which the attacks such as [14] do not manage to reduce the complexity of [37].

A thorough security analysis of any variant of the McEliece cryptosystem should have at least three components: Message Recovery Attacks - MRA (usually tackled using Information Set Decoding - ISD), Key Recovery Attacks - KRA (more complex and sometimes using ad-hoc techniques, such as attacks based on searching minimum weight codewords, attacks of the square code and filtration type, or generic code equivalence solvers), and distinguishers (weight distribution, square code techniques, hull dimension etc.). Here, we will propose a security level estimation for the McEliece variant [24] based on the analysis of the main cryptanalysis techniques for this type of codes, i.e., square code attacks (like those on the Reed-Muller codes [14]) and structural attacks using shorten and puncture techniques combined with minimum weight codewords search (like the attack on Polar codes [4]). A slightly different distinguisher from the usual one (dimension of the square code) is proposed for self-dual monomial codes.

**Theorem.** Let $\mathscr{C} = [n, \frac{n}{2}]$ be a self-dual code. Then w.h.p. we have

- $\dim(\boldsymbol{c} \star \mathscr{C}) = \frac{n}{2}$, where $\boldsymbol{c} \in \mathscr{C}$ and $\mathscr{C}$ is random;
- $\dim(\mathsf{ev}(f) \star \mathscr{C}) = \dim(\mathscr{C}(fI)) \in \left[\sqrt{n}, \frac{n}{4}\right]$, where $f \in I$ and $\mathscr{C} = \mathscr{C}(I)$ is monomial with $I = I_{\leq \frac{m}{2} - 1} \cup J$ and $J \subset I_{\frac{m}{2}}$.

As message recovery techniques and minimum weight search are exponential in $\sqrt{n}$ in the case of self-dual monomial codes, they are used to set up the first security level. Now, going deeper into the analysis, we will identify a particular subclass of codes for which techniques such as square code reveal some non-trivial information about the private key. More precisely, we will identify, up to a permutation, a variable $x_i$ when the monomial set defining the code is defined by $I = I_{\leq \frac{m}{2} - 1} \cup x_i I_{\leq \frac{m}{2} - 1}$. Moving forward we demonstrate that if we shorten the code on the support of the evaluation of $1 + x_i$ our key recovery problem is equivalent to a key recovery problem on the $\mathscr{R}(\frac{m}{2} - 1, m - 1)$ which is the hardest instance to solve of Sidelnikov's cryptosystem (the Chishov-Borodin attack does not decrease the complexity of the Minder-Shokrollahi attack).

**Theorem.** Let $\pi \in \mathfrak{S}$ and $\mathscr{C}(I)^{\pi}$ be a permuted self-dual code defined by a max-complement-free monomial set $I$. If $I = I_{\leq \frac{m}{2} - 1} \cup x_i I_{\leq \frac{m}{2} - 1}$ then there is an algorithm that outputs a permutation $\pi^{*}$ satisfying $\mathscr{C}^{\pi^{*}} = \mathscr{C}^{\pi}$. Moreover, the overall complexity is $e^{\sqrt{n} c (1 + o(1))}$, where $c$ is a constant.

## 2    Background on Coding Theory

### 2.1    General Considerations

**Groups.** Let $n$ be a positive integer, and denote by $[n] = \{0, \ldots, n - 1\}$. The symmetric group on a set of $n$ elements will be denoted by $\mathfrak{S}_n$. Groups here are considered over finite fields, in particular over $\mathbb{F}_2$. Let us enumerate other groups that are going to be used in this paper. $\mathsf{T}(n, 2)$ denotes the group of translations over $\mathbb{F}_2^n$ and $\mathsf{GL}(n, 2)$ denotes the general linear group over $\mathbb{F}_2$. The semi-direct product of $\mathsf{T}(n, 2)$ and $\mathsf{GL}(n, 2)$ is the general affine group denoted by $\mathsf{Aff}(n, 2)$.

**Error Correcting Codes.** $\mathscr{C}$ is an $[n, k]$ linear code, over a finite field $\mathbb{F}$ if $\mathscr{C}$ is a linear subspace of dimension $k$ of the vector space $\mathbb{F}^n$ ($0 \leq k \leq n$). The subject of this article only refers to binary linear codes, hence we will have $\mathbb{F} = \mathbb{F}_2$. Any vector $\boldsymbol{c} = (c_0, \ldots, c_{n-1}) \in \mathscr{C}$ is called a codeword. We define the support of a codeword $\mathsf{Supp}(\boldsymbol{c}) = \{i \mid c_i \neq 0\}$. Any code $\mathscr{C}$ can be represented either by its generator matrix, $\boldsymbol{G} \in \mathcal{M}_{k,n}(\mathbb{F}_2)$ ($\mathrm{rank}(\boldsymbol{G}) = k$), or by its parity-check matrix, $\boldsymbol{H} \in \mathcal{M}_{n-k,n}(\mathbb{F}_2)$, ($\mathrm{rank}(\boldsymbol{H}) = n - k$), where $\boldsymbol{H} \boldsymbol{G}^T = \boldsymbol{0}$ holds. The dual of a $[n, k]$ linear code $\mathscr{C}$, is a $[n, n - k]$ linear code $\mathscr{C}^{\perp}$ that admits as generator matrix the parity check-matrix of $\mathscr{C}$. The Hamming weight of a vector $\text{wt}(x)$ is the number of non-zero components of $x$. Also, the minimum distance of a code is the minimum over the set of all Hamming weight except from zero.

**Definition 1.** *Given a code* $\mathscr{C} = [n, k]$ *and a subset* $\mathcal{J} \subset [n]$ *define*

- *the* shortened code: $\mathcal{S}_{\mathcal{J}}(\mathscr{C}) = \left\{ (c_i)_{i \notin \mathcal{J}} \mid \exists c \in \mathscr{C} \text{ such that } \forall i \in \mathcal{J}, c_i = 0 \right\}$, *of length* $n - |\mathcal{J}|$;
- *the* punctured code: $\mathcal{P}_{\mathcal{J}}(\mathscr{C}) = \left\{ (c_i)_{i \notin \mathcal{J}} \mid c \in \mathscr{C} \right\}$, *of length* $n - |\mathcal{J}|$;
- *the* extended code: $\mathcal{E}_{\mathcal{J}}(\mathscr{C}) = \left\{ (c_i)_{[n+|\mathcal{J}|]} \mid \mathcal{P}_{\mathcal{J}}(c) \in \mathscr{C} \text{ and } c_i = 0, \forall i \in \mathcal{J} \right\}$, *of length* $n + |\mathcal{J}|$.
  *Denote* $\mathcal{S}_{\mathcal{J}}^{\mathcal{E}}(\mathscr{C}) = \mathcal{E}_{\mathcal{J}}(\mathcal{S}_{\mathcal{J}}(\mathscr{C}))$, *which has length* $n$;
- *the* hull: $\mathcal{H}(\mathscr{C}) = \mathscr{C} \cap \mathscr{C}^{\perp}$, *of length* $n$.

*Example 1.* Consider the code $\mathscr{C} = \{(0\,0\,0\,0), (1\,0\,0\,0), (0\,1\,1\,0), (0\,0\,0\,1), (1\,1\,1\,0), (1\,0\,0\,1), (0\,1\,1\,1), (1\,1\,1\,1)\}$. Then $\mathcal{E}_{\{1,3\}} = \{(0\,0\,0\,0\,0\,0), (1\,0\,0\,0\,0\,0), (0\,0\,1\,0\,1\,0), (0\,0\,0\,0\,0\,1), (1\,0\,1\,0\,1\,0), (1\,0\,0\,0\,0\,1), (0\,0\,1\,0\,1\,1), (1\,0\,1\,0\,1\,1)\}$.

A code $\mathscr{C}$ with dimension $k \leq n/2$ is called *weakly self-dual* if $\mathcal{H}(\mathscr{C}) = \mathscr{C} \subset \mathscr{C}^{\perp}$ and *self-dual* if $\mathcal{H}(\mathscr{C}) = \mathscr{C} = \mathscr{C}^{\perp}$ (in this case $k = n/2$). Next, we define the concept of Schur product of codes, where product refers to component-wise product (see [45] for more details on the topic).

**Definition 2.** *The component-wise product of two codewords* $x$ *and* $y \in \mathbb{F}_2^n$ *is defined as*

$$x \star y = (x_1 y_1, \ldots, x_n y_n) \in \mathbb{F}_2^n. \tag{1}$$

*The Schur product codes of* $\mathscr{C}_1$ *(*$[n, k_1, d_1]$*) and* $\mathscr{C}_2$ *(*$[n, k_1, d_2]$*) is the binary linear code defined as*

$$\mathscr{C}_1 \star \mathscr{C}_2 = \text{Span}_{\mathbb{F}_2} \left\{ c_1 \star c_2 \mid c_1 \in \mathscr{C}_1 \text{ and } c_2 \in \mathscr{C}_2 \right\}. \tag{2}$$

In this article, any power of a code $\mathscr{C}^l$ will refer to the Schur product of a code with itself $l$ times, for a fixed positive integer $l$. Also, the $l^{th}$ root of a code $\mathscr{C}^{1/l}$, if exists, refers to a code $\mathscr{C}_1$ s.t. $\mathscr{C}_1^l = \mathscr{C}$.

**Definition 3 (Permutation group of a code).** *Let* $\mathscr{C} = [n, k]$ *binary linear code and* $\pi \in \mathfrak{S}_n$. *We denote by* $c^{\pi} = (c_{\pi^{-1}(i)})_{i \in [n]}$ *the vector* $c$ *permuted by* $\pi$. $\mathscr{C}^{\pi} = \{c^{\pi} \mid c \in \mathscr{C}\}$ *denotes the permuted code of* $\mathscr{C}$. *The permutation group of a code is*

$$\text{Perm}(\mathscr{C}) = \{\pi \in \mathfrak{S}_n \mid \mathscr{C}^{\pi} = \mathscr{C}\}.$$

## 2.2  Monomial Codes

- We denote the ring of multivariate polynomials

$$\mathbb{R}_{[m]} = \mathbb{F}_2[x_0, x_1, \ldots, x_{m-1}]/(x_0^2 - x_0, \ldots, x_{m-1}^2 - x_{m-1});$$

– Unless it is mentioned the codes that are studied here have length $n = 2^m$;

Let $g \in \mathbb{R}_{[m]}$ and fix an order on the elements in $\mathbb{F}_2^m$. For convenience and to stay in-line with the existing literature, we have chosen the decreasing index order (see [5]). Now, define

$$\begin{array}{rcl} \mathbb{R}_{[m]} & \to & \mathbb{F}_2^n \\ g & \mapsto & \mathsf{ev}(g) = \big(g(\boldsymbol{u})\big)_{\boldsymbol{u} \in \mathbb{F}_2^m} \end{array}.$$

**Notation 1.** *We denote by $\boldsymbol{x}^{\boldsymbol{i}}$ the monomial $x_0^{i_0} \cdots x_{m-1}^{i_{m-1}}$, where $\boldsymbol{i} \in \mathbb{F}_2^m$, and the set of monomials*

$$\mathcal{M}_{[m]} = \big\{ \boldsymbol{x}^{\boldsymbol{i}} \mid \boldsymbol{i} = (i_0, \ldots, i_{m-1}) \in \mathbb{F}_2^m \big\}.$$

For any monomial $g = x_{l_1} \ldots x_{l_s} \in \mathcal{M}_{[m]}$ of degree $1 \le s \le m$ we denote the support of a monomial by $\mathrm{ind}(g) = \{l_1 \ldots, l_s\} \subset [m]$. The subset of all monomials of degree $r$ will be denoted by $I_r = \{f \in \mathcal{M}_{[m]} \mid \deg(f) = r\}$. We extend the definition to $I_{\le r} = \{f \in \mathcal{M}_{[m]} \mid \deg(f) \le r\}$.

For any monomial set $I \subset \mathcal{M}_{[m]}$ and $f \in \mathcal{M}_{[m]}$ we denote $fI = \{fg \mid g \in I\}$. By extension, for $I, J \in \mathcal{M}_{[m]}$, $IJ = \{fg \mid f \in I, g \in J\}$.

For any $i \in [m]$, we denote by $\mathcal{M}_{[m] \setminus \{i\}}$ the image of $\mathcal{M}_{[m-1]}$ under the isomorphism defined by $x_j \to x_j, \forall j < i$ and $x_j \to x_{j+1}, \forall j \ge i$.

**Definition 4.** *Let $I \subseteq \mathbb{R}_{[m]}$ be a finite set of polynomials in $m$ variables. The linear code defined by $I$ is the vector subspace $\mathscr{C}(I) \subseteq \mathbb{F}_2^n$ generated by $\{\mathsf{ev}(f) \mid f \in I\}$.*

These codes are called polynomial codes (see [19]), and when $I \subset \mathcal{M}_{[m]}$ we call $\mathscr{C}(I)$ a monomial code. The Reed-Muller code $\mathscr{R}(r, m)$ is a monomial code with dimension $k = \sum_{i=0}^{r} \binom{m}{i}$, as defined in [32], fact that comes directly from its definition $\mathscr{R}(r, m) = \{\mathsf{ev}(g) \mid g \in \mathbb{R}_{[m]}, \deg g \le r\} = \mathscr{C}(I_{\le r})$.

*Example 2.* Let $m = 3$, and consider $I = \{1, x_0, x_1, x_2, x_0 x_1\}$ a subset of monomials in $\mathcal{M}_{[m]}$.

|  | 111 | 011 | 101 | 001 | 110 | 010 | 100 | 000 |
|---|---|---|---|---|---|---|---|---|
| $\mathsf{ev}(x_0 x_1) =$ | 1 | 0 | 0 | 0 | 1 | 0 | 0 | 0 |
| $\mathsf{ev}(x_2) =$ | 1 | 1 | 1 | 1 | 0 | 0 | 0 | 0 |
| $\mathsf{ev}(x_1) =$ | 1 | 1 | 0 | 0 | 1 | 1 | 0 | 0 |
| $\mathsf{ev}(x_0) =$ | 1 | 0 | 1 | 0 | 1 | 0 | 1 | 0 |
| $\mathsf{ev}(1) =$ | 1 | 1 | 1 | 1 | 1 | 1 | 1 | 1 |

$\mathscr{C}(I)$ is a $[8, 5]$ monomial code, that admits a generator matrix whose rows are the vectors $\mathsf{ev}(f), f \in I$.

## 2.3   Decreasing and Weakly Decreasing Monomial Codes

**Definition 5.** *Let $f$ and $g$ be two monomials in $\mathcal{M}_{[m]}$. Then $f \preceq_w g$ if and only if $f|g$. Also, when $\deg(f) = \deg(g) = s$ say that $f \preceq_{sh} g$ if $\forall\, 1 \le \ell \le s$   $i_\ell \le j_\ell$, where $f = x_{i_1} \ldots x_{i_s}$, $g = x_{j_1} \ldots x_{j_s}$. These two order relations are combined into $f \preceq g$   iff   $\exists g^* \in \mathcal{M}_{[m]}$ s.t. $f \preceq_{sh} g^* \preceq_w g$.*

The notation $f \preceq_{sh} g$ comes the fact that one could obtain $g$ from $f$ by positively shifting all the variables in $f$. For example $x_0 x_3 \preceq_{sh} x_1 x_6$ since $x_1$ is a shift by one positions of $x_0$ and $x_6$ is a shift by 3 positions of $x_3$. This mainly comes from the chain relation on the variables, i.e., $x_0 \preceq x_1 \preceq \cdots \preceq x_{m-1}$. Notice that $\preceq$ is a partial order relation on the set $\mathcal{M}_{[m]}$. However, subsets of $\mathcal{M}_{[m]}$, such as the set of variables are totally ordered by $\preceq$. Such sets are known in the literature as chains in the poset $\{\mathcal{M}_{[m]}, \preceq\}$ (see [8] for more on the properties of this poset). Also notice that in the definition of $\preceq$, $g^*$ might be s.t. $g^* = g$. This implies that if $f \preceq g$ and $\deg(f) = \deg(g)$ we have $\preceq = \preceq_{sh}$ .

**Definition 6.** *Let $f$ and $g$ be two monomials in $\mathcal{M}_{[m]}$ such that $f \preceq_w g$ and $I \subset \mathcal{M}_{[m]}$.*

- *We define the closed interval $[f, g]_{\preceq_w}$ with respect to the partial order $\preceq_w$ as the set of monomials $h \in \mathcal{M}_{[m]}$ such that $f \preceq_w h \preceq_w g$.*
- *The set $I$ is called a weakly decreasing set if and only if $(f \in I$ and $g \preceq_w f)$ implies $g \in I$.*

These definitions can be naturally extended to $\preceq$, and in this case we will simply call a set $I$ decreasing. We will also call $\mathcal{C}(I)$ a weakly decreasing monomial code when $I$ is a weakly decreasing set, respectively $\mathcal{C}(I)$ a decreasing monomial code when $I$ is a decreasing set. Notice that, any decreasing set $I$ is a weakly decreasing set, as $f \preceq_w g \Rightarrow f \preceq g$.

*Example 3.* Let $m = 3$ and $I = \{1, x_0, x_1, x_0 x_1, x_2\}$. As $1 \preceq x_0 \preceq x_1 \preceq x_2$ and $x_1 \preceq x_0 x_1$ we have that $I$ is a decreasing monomial set $I = [1, x_2]_{\preceq} \cup [1, x_0 x_1]_{\preceq}$. Also $I$ is a weakly decreasing monomial set $I = [1, x_0 x_1]_{\preceq_w} \cup [1, x_2]_{\preceq_w}$, since $1 \preceq_w x_0 \preceq_w x_0 x_1, 1 \preceq_w x_1 \preceq_w x_0 x_1$ and $1 \preceq_w x_2$.

**Theorem 2** ([5])**.** *Reed-Muller codes are decreasing monomial codes*

$$\mathcal{R}(r, m) = \mathcal{C}\left([1, x_{m-r} \cdots x_{m-1}]_{\preceq}\right) = \mathcal{C}\left(\cup_{\deg(g)=r}[1, g]_{\preceq_w}\right).$$

Next, basic properties of monomial and weakly monomial codes will be given. To do that, we need to define the *multiplicative complement* of a monomial $g \in \mathcal{M}_{[m]}$ as $\check{g} = \dfrac{x_0 \cdots x_{m-1}}{g}$. By extension, for any $I \subseteq \mathcal{M}_{[m]}$, we define $\check{I} = \{\check{f} \mid f \in I\}$.

**Proposition 1** ([5])**.** *Let $\mathcal{C}(I)$ be a weakly decreasing monomial code. Then its dual is a weakly decreasing monomial code given by*

$$\mathcal{C}(I)^{\perp} = \mathcal{C}(\mathcal{M}_{[m]} \setminus \check{I}). \tag{3}$$

*In particular, we retrieve the result $\mathcal{R}(r, m)^{\perp} = \mathcal{R}(m - r - 1, m)$.*

Another consequence of Proposition 1 is that any weakly decreasing/decreasing monomial code $\mathscr{C}(I)$ is weakly self-dual as long as $\forall f \in I$, $\check{f} \notin I$, or equivalently, $I \subseteq \mathcal{M}_{[m]} \setminus \check{I}$ (see Corollary 3.4.14 in [19]). Hence, in order to construct self-dual monomial codes one needs to define the concept of *complement-free* monomial sets, as in the following section.

## 2.4   Construction of Self-dual Monomial and Weakly Monomial Codes

**Definition 7.** *A set $I \subseteq \mathcal{M}_{[m]}$ is called* complement-free *if $I \cap \check{I} = \emptyset$ and* max-complement-free *if $I$ is complement-free and $I \cup \check{I} = \mathcal{M}_{[m]}$.*

From now on the parameter $m \in \mathbb{N}$ will always be even.

*Remark 1.* If the maximum degree of the monomials in $I$ is $\frac{m}{2}$, then one only needs to look at the monomials of degree $\frac{m}{2}$ to determine whether $I$ is complement-free.

**Lemma 1.** *Let $I \in \mathcal{M}_{[m]}$ be a complement-free set, s.t., $I_{\leq \frac{m}{2}-1} \subset I$ and $|I| = 2^{m-1}$. Then $I$ is max-complement-free.*

The proof of this lemma is trivial.

*Example 4.* Let $m = 4$ and $I = \{1, x_0, x_1, x_2, x_3, x_0x_1, x_0x_2, x_1x_2\}$. Then $I$ is a complement-free set satisfying the conditions from Lemma 1. We can easily verify that $I$ is max-complement-free since $\check{I} \cap I = \emptyset$ and $\check{I} \cup I = \mathcal{M}_{[m]}$. Take another example $J = \{1, x_0, x_1, x_2, x_3, x_0x_1, x_2x_3, x_0x_2\}$. Notice that $I_{\leq \frac{m}{2}-1} \subset J$ and $|J| = 2^{m-1}$. However, $J$ is not a complement-free set, as $x_0x_1, x_2x_3 \in J$ and $x_2x_3$ is the multiplicative complement of $x_0x_1$.

*Remark 2.* Any max-complement-free set can be obtained from another max-complement-free set $I$ by taking each element of $I$ and placing either the element or its complement into the new set. There are $2^{2^{m-1}}$ such sets.

The authors in [26] provided a method for constructing a max-complement-free set containing the set $I_{\leq \frac{m}{2}-1}$. Algorithm 1 describes this procedure.

**Proposition 2.** *Algorithm 1 generates a valid max-complement-free set $I = I_{\leq \frac{m}{2}-1} \cup J$. The corresponding code $\mathscr{C}(I)$ is a $[2^m, 2^{m-1}, 2^{\frac{m}{2}}]$ binary self-dual linear code. Moreover, there are $2^{\binom{m-1}{\frac{m}{2}}}$ such codes.*

*Proof.* Directly from Lemma 1 and $|J| = \binom{m-1}{\frac{m}{2}}$, which yields $|I| = 2^{m-1}$.

Notice that Algorithm 1 can be generalized in a certain manner.

**Proposition 3.** *Algorithm 2 generates a valid max-complement-free set. It is a generalisation of Algorithm 1, as it can generate all the sets generated by Algorithm 1 by picking $r = 0, \forall j \leq 2^{\frac{m}{2}-1}$ and $r = 1, \forall j \geq 2^{\frac{m}{2}}+1$.*

---

**Algorithm 1.** Generate max-complement-free set $I$ as per [26]

---

**Require:** $m$ even integer, $i \in [m]$
**Ensure:** $I$ max-complement-free monomial set

$\quad I \leftarrow I_{\leq \frac{m}{2}-1}$
$\quad S = \text{GenerateSubsets}([m] \setminus \{i\}, \frac{m}{2})$ $\qquad$ {all subsets of $[m] \setminus \{i\}$ of cardinality $\frac{m}{2}$}
$\quad \textbf{for } j \leftarrow 1, \binom{m-1}{\frac{m}{2}} \textbf{ do}$
$\quad\quad r = \text{Random}\{0, 1\}$
$\quad\quad \textbf{if } r == 0 \textbf{ then}$
$\quad\quad\quad \text{Append}(I, S[j])$
$\quad\quad \textbf{else}$
$\quad\quad\quad \text{Append}(I, \check{S}[j])$
$\quad\quad \textbf{end if}$
$\quad \textbf{end for}$

---

---

**Algorithm 2.** Generate max-complement-free set $I$

---

**Require:** $m$ even integer, $i \in [m]$
**Ensure:** $I$ max-complement-free monomial set

$\quad I = \emptyset$
$\quad S = \text{GenerateAllSubsets}([m] \setminus \{i\})$ $\qquad$ {all subsets of $[m] \setminus \{i\}$}
$\quad \textbf{for } j \leftarrow 1, 2^{m-1} \textbf{ do}$
$\quad\quad r = \text{Random}\{0, 1\}$
$\quad\quad \textbf{if } r == 0 \textbf{ then}$
$\quad\quad\quad \text{Append}(I, S[j])$
$\quad\quad \textbf{else}$
$\quad\quad\quad \text{Append}(I, \check{S}[j])$
$\quad\quad \textbf{end if}$
$\quad \textbf{end for}$

---

*Proof.* Just check that any set $I$ generated by Algorithm 2 is complement-free and $|I| = 2^{m-1}$.

**Theorem 3.** *Algorithm 2 can generate any of the $2^{2^{m-1}}$ max-complement-free sets.*

*Proof.* We have that Algorithm 2 can generate $2^{2^{m-1}}$ distinct codes; this, by Remark 2, is the same number as that of all the max-complement-free codes.

### 2.5 Schur Product and Square Code of Weakly Decreasing Monomial Codes

**Proposition 4** ([20]). *Let $I$ and $J$ be two monomial sets. Then we have*

$$\mathscr{C}(I) \star \mathscr{C}(J) = \mathscr{C}(IJ).$$

**Proposition 5** ([20]). *Let $l$ and $s$ be two positive integers and $(f_i)_{1 \leq i \leq l}$ and $(g_j)_{1 \leq j \leq s}$ be two sequences of noncomparable monomials. Let $I = \bigcup\limits_{1 \leq i \leq l} [1, f_i]_{\preceq_{\text{w}}}$ and $J = \bigcup\limits_{1 \leq j \leq s} [1, g_j]_{\preceq_{\text{w}}}$, be two weakly decreasing sets. Then*

$$\mathscr{C}(I) \star \mathscr{C}(J) = \mathscr{C}\left(\cup_{\substack{1 \le i \le l \\ 1 \le j \le s}} [1, f_i g_j]_{\preceq_w}\right).$$

*In particular,* $\mathscr{R}(r_1, m) \star \mathscr{R}(r_2, m) = \mathscr{R}(r_1 + r_2, m)$.

# 3    Structural Properties of Self-dual Monomial Codes

In what follows, we will only deal with codes generated by Algorithm 1. We will simply call such codes $\mathscr{C}(I)$ self-dual monomial codes defined by a max-complement-free monomial set $I$.

## 3.1    Self-dual Monomial Codes are Decreasing/Weakly Decreasing Monomial Codes

**Theorem 4.** *Let* $\mathscr{C}(I)$ *be a self-dual code defined by a max-complement-free monomial set* $I = I_{\le \frac{m}{2} - 1} \cup J$. *Then* $\mathscr{C}(I)$ *is a weakly decreasing monomial code given by*

$$\mathscr{C}(I) = \mathscr{C}\left(\bigcup_{\substack{f \in I \\ \deg(f) \ge \frac{m}{2} - 1}} [1, f]_{\preceq_w}\right). \tag{4}$$

*Moreover, if* $\exists i \in [m]$ *s.t.* $\forall f \in J$ *we have* $x_i | f$, *then the following holds*

– $\mathscr{C}(I)$ *is a weakly decreasing monomial code defined by*

$$\mathscr{C}(I) = \mathscr{C}\left(\bigcup_{f \in J} [1, f]_{\preceq_w}\right). \tag{5}$$

– *Let* $\pi \in \mathfrak{S}_n$ *be s.t.* $\pi(\mathsf{ev}(x_i)) = \mathsf{ev}(x_0)$. *Then* $\mathscr{C}(I)^\pi$ *is a decreasing monomial code given by*

$$\mathscr{C}(I)^\pi = \mathscr{C}\left([1, x_0 x_{\frac{m}{2} + 1} \ldots x_{m-1}]_{\preceq}\right). \tag{6}$$

*Proof.* We will demonstrate the two qualities by proving the double inclusion of the monomial bases, instead of taking all linear combinations of monomials from each basis.

– $\mathscr{C}(I)$ **is a weakly decreasing monomial code**
  - The first inclusion: take $g \in I$. Then, either $g \in J$ and then $g \in \bigcup_{f \in J} [1, f]_{\preceq_w}$, or $g \in I_{\le \frac{m}{2} - 1}$ and then $g \preceq_w x_i g \in J \subset \bigcup_{f \in J} [1, f]_{\preceq_w}$.
  - The second inclusion: take $g \preceq_w f$ for an $f \in J$. Then, by definition $g | f$, and either $g = f \in J \subset I$, or $g \ne f$ and then $\deg(g) \le \frac{m}{2} - 1$, which implies that $g \in I_{\frac{m}{2} - 1} \subset I$.

– $\mathscr{C}(I)^\pi$ **is a decreasing monomial code**
  As $\exists i \in [m]$ s.t. $\forall f \in J \ x_i | f$, when $i = 0$ we simply denote such a set by $J_0$.
  Notice that $\mathscr{C}(I_{\leq \frac{m}{2}-1})^\pi = \mathscr{C}(I_{\leq \frac{m}{2}-1})$ and $\mathscr{C}(J)^\pi = \mathscr{C}(J_0)$. Hence, we have

$$\mathscr{C}(I)^\pi = \mathscr{C}(I_{\frac{m}{2}-1} \cup J_0) \tag{7}$$

$$= \mathscr{C}([1, x_{\frac{m}{2}+1} \ldots x_{m-1}]_{\preceq} \cup [x_0 x_1 \ldots x_{\frac{m}{2}-1}, x_0 x_{\frac{m}{2}+1 \ldots x_{m-1}}]_{\preceq}) \tag{8}$$

$$= \mathscr{C}\left([1, x_0 x_{\frac{m}{2}+1} \ldots x_{m-1}]_{\preceq}\right). \tag{9}$$

*Remark 3.* Notice that any self-dual code defined by a max-complement-free monomial set $I = I_{\leq \frac{m}{2}-1} \cup J$ satisfies

$$\mathscr{R}\left(\frac{m}{2} - 1, m\right) \subset \mathscr{C}(I) \subset \mathscr{R}\left(\frac{m}{2}, m\right). \tag{10}$$

## 3.2 Some Notes on the Permutation Group of Self-dual Monomial Codes

As self-dual monomial codes are weakly decreasing (see Theorem 4), their permutation group contains the subgroup induced by the group of translations $\mathsf{T}(m, 2)$ on the set of variables. This implies that any variable change $x_i \to x_i + 1$ leaves the code $\mathscr{C}(I)$ globally invariant. In the particular case of $I = I_{\leq \frac{m}{2}-1} \cup x_i I_{\leq \frac{m}{2}-1}$ ($\mathscr{C}(I)$ is decreasing by Theorem 4), the permutation group contains a bigger subgroup, i.e., the lower triangular affine group ($\mathsf{LTA}(m, 2)$, see [5] for details). Simulations show that, in general ($I$ is generated by Algorithm 1 without any particular condition), the cardinal of $\mathsf{Perm}\,(\mathscr{C}(I))$ is small compared to the cardinal of $\mathsf{Perm}\,(\mathscr{R}(r, m))$, for any $1 \leq r \leq m - 2$. Also, when $I = I_{\leq \frac{m}{2}-1} \cup x_i I_{\leq \frac{m}{2}-1}$, the size of $\mathsf{Perm}\,(\mathscr{C}(I))$ is significantly greater than in the general case, being greater than the size of $\mathsf{Aff}(m, 2)$. This is mainly due to the particular structure of $I$. Our next result characterizes this large subgroup of $\mathsf{Perm}\,(\mathscr{C}(I))$.

**Theorem 5.** *Let $\mathscr{C}(I)$ be a self-dual monomial code with $I = I_{\leq \frac{m}{2}-1} \cup x_i I_{\leq \frac{m}{2}-1}$. Then $\mathsf{Perm}\,(\mathscr{C}(I))$ is defined by $\{(\sigma_1, \sigma_2, \sigma_3) \mid \sigma_1 \in \mathsf{T}(1, 2), \sigma_2, \sigma_3 \in \mathsf{Aff}(m - 1, 2)\}$.*

*Moreover, we have $|\mathsf{Perm}\,(\mathscr{C}(I))| = 2^{2m-1} \prod\limits_{i=0}^{m-2} (2^{m-1} - 2^i)^2$.*

*Proof.* Let us start by splitting the support of our code ($[n]$) into two disjoint sets $[n] = \mathsf{Supp}(\mathsf{ev}(x_i)) \cup \mathsf{Supp}(\mathsf{ev}(1 + x_i))$. Any translation on the variable $x_i$ induce a permutation between the two sets $\mathsf{Supp}(\mathsf{ev}(x_i))$ and $\mathsf{Supp}(\mathsf{ev}(1 + x_i))$. Let us denote this permutation by $\sigma_1$, and notice that it leaves the code $\mathscr{C}(I)$ globally invariant as it belongs to $\mathsf{T}(m, 2)$ (see Proposition 3.6.4 in [19]). Let us prove that on each of the two disjoint sets $\mathsf{Supp}(\mathsf{ev}(x_i))$ and $\mathsf{Supp}(\mathsf{ev}(1 + x_i))$ the action of the group $\mathsf{Aff}(m - 1, 2)$ leaves the code globally invariant. This is equivalent to showing that $\forall f \in \mathcal{M}_{[m]\setminus\{i\}}, \deg(f) \leq \frac{m}{2} - 1$ the set of all $\mathsf{ev}(x_i \mathsf{Aff}(m - 1, 2) \cdot f) \subset \mathscr{C}(I)$ and $\mathsf{ev}((1 + x_i)\mathsf{Aff}(m - 1, 2) \cdot f) \subset \mathscr{C}(I)$. As $\mathscr{C}(I)$ is weakly decreasing we are only left to prove one of the inclusions, for example

$\mathsf{ev}(x_i \mathsf{Aff}(m-1,2) \cdot f) \subset \mathscr{C}(I)$. Any element in $x_i \mathsf{Aff}(m-1,2) \cdot f$ can be written as a sum of monomial $x_i g$ where $g \in \mathcal{M}_{[m] \setminus \{i\}}$ and $\deg(g) \le \frac{m}{2} - 1$. Hence, as linear combination of monomials from $x_i I_{\le \frac{m}{2}-1}$ the evaluation of the polynomial belongs to the linear code $\mathscr{C}(I)$, fact that ends the proof.

The order of this group is the product of the order of its group components, i.e., $2^1$ for $\mathsf{T}(1,2)$ and $2^{m-1} \prod_{i=0}^{m-2}(2^{m-1} - 2^i)$ for $\mathsf{Aff}(m-1,2)$. Let us now prove that this is the entire permutation group. As the properties we have demonstrated do not depend on the variable $x_i$ we might fix it to $x_{m-1}$. We can now write $\mathscr{C}(I)$ as a juxtaposition of two Reed-Muller codes, i.e., $\mathscr{C}(I) = \left(\mathscr{R}(\frac{m}{2} - 1, m-1) | \mathscr{R}(\frac{m}{2} - 1, m-1)\right)$. Here, the juxtaposition of two linear codes $\mathscr{C}_1, \mathscr{C}_2$ is the code $\mathscr{C} = \{(\boldsymbol{c}_1 | \boldsymbol{c}_2), \boldsymbol{c}_1 \in \mathscr{C}_1, \boldsymbol{c}_2 \in \mathscr{C}_2\}$. From this, one can easily deduce the permutations that leave $\mathscr{C}(I)$ globally invariant, i.e. we have $\mathsf{Perm}\left(\mathscr{R}(\frac{m}{2} - 1, m-1)\right) = \mathsf{Aff}(m-1,2)$ which acts independently on the two blocks and $\mathfrak{S}_2$ which permutes the two blocks.

An example related to Theorem 5 is given in Appendix A. Notice that the order of $\mathsf{Perm}(\mathscr{C}(I))$ is much bigger than the order of $\mathsf{Aff}(m,2)$, the permutation group of Reed-Muller codes. Indeed, the following holds

$$\frac{|\mathsf{Perm}(\mathscr{C}(I))|}{|\mathsf{Aff}(m,2)|} = \frac{(2^m - 2^1) \dots (2^m - 2^{m-2})}{2^m - 1}.$$

It would be interesting, but at the same time much more complex, to determine a characterization of the permutation group of any self-dual monomial code.

## 3.3    Square and Higher Powers of Self-dual Monomial Codes

The square of a self-dual monomial code can be characterized in general by means of Proposition 4.

**Lemma 2.** *Let $I$ be a max-complement-free monomial set. Then we have*

$$\mathscr{C}(I)^2 = \mathscr{C}(I_{\le m-2} \cup JI_{\le \frac{m}{2}-1} \cup J^2). \tag{11}$$

*Moreover,*

$$\mathscr{R}(m-2, m) \subset \mathscr{C}(I)^2 \subset \mathscr{R}(m, m). \tag{12}$$

**Theorem 6.** *Let $I \subset \mathcal{M}_{[m]}$ be a max-complement-free monomial set, $I = I_{\le \frac{m}{2}-1} \cup J$. Then $\mathscr{C}(I)^2$ is a weakly decreasing monomial code defined by*

$$\mathscr{C}(I)^2 = \begin{cases} \mathscr{C}(\mathcal{M}_{[m]} \setminus \{\check{\mathbf{1}}, \check{x}_i\}) & \text{if } \exists i, \forall f \in J, x_i | f \\ \mathscr{C}(\mathcal{M}_{[m]} \setminus \{\check{\mathbf{1}}\}) & \text{if not} \end{cases} \tag{13}$$

*Proof.* Recall from Lemma 2 that $\mathscr{C}(I)^2 = \mathscr{C}(I_{\le m-2} \cup JI_{\le \frac{m}{2}-1} \cup J^2)$. Since $\exists i \in [m]$ such that $\forall f \in J$, $x_i | f$, we deduce that for all $f \in JI_{\le \frac{m}{2}-1} \cup J^2$, $x_i | f$. As $x_i \nmid \check{x}_i$, it follows that $\check{x}_i \notin JI_{\le \frac{m}{2}-1} \cup J^2$. So, because $\deg(\check{x}_i) = m-1 > m-2$, we have $\check{x}_i \notin I^2$. As $J$ is complement-free with elements of degree $\frac{m}{2}$, $\check{\mathbf{1}} \notin J^2$; and $\forall f \in JI_{\le \frac{m}{2}-1}, \deg(f) \le m-1$, so $\check{\mathbf{1}} \notin I^2$ either. Then $\mathscr{C}(I)^2 \subseteq \mathscr{C}(\mathcal{M}_{[m]} \setminus \{\check{\mathbf{1}}, \check{x}_i\})$.

For the reverse inclusion, assume that $\exists f \in \mathcal{M}_{[m]} \setminus \{\check{1}, \check{x}_i\}$ such that $f \notin I^2$. Then $\deg(f) = m - 1$, equivalent to $f = \check{x}_j$ for some $j \in [m] \setminus \{i\}$. As $J = \{x_i g \mid g \in I_{\frac{m}{2}-1}, x_i \not\wedge g\}$, one can pick an $f_1 \in J$ such that $x_j \wedge f_1$. Then $f = f_1 f_2$, where $f_2 \in I_{\leq \frac{m}{2}-1}$. So $f \in J I_{\leq \frac{m}{2}-1} \subset I^2$, contradiction. Thus, $\mathcal{C}(I)^2 = \mathcal{C}(\mathcal{M}_{[m]} \setminus \{\check{1}, \check{x}_i\})$.

Moving on to the second case, assume $\forall i \in [m], \exists g \in J$ such that $x_i \not\wedge g$. Same as above, as $J$ is complement-free with elements of degree $\frac{m}{2}$, $\check{1} \notin J I_{\leq \frac{m}{2}-1} \cup J^2$, so $\check{1} \notin I^2$. Let $f \in \mathcal{M}_{[m]}$ of degree $m - 1$. Then $\exists j \in [m]$ such that $f = \check{x}_j$. Suppose $\forall f_1 \in \mathcal{M}_{[m]}$ with $\deg(f_1) = \frac{m}{2}$ and $f_1 | f$, have $f_1 \notin J$. This implies that $x_j | g, \forall g \in J$, contradiction. So $\exists f_1 \in J$ such that $f_1 | f$. Write $f = f_1 f_2$. By comparing degrees, $f_2 \in I_{\frac{m}{2}-1} \subset I_{\leq \frac{m}{2}-1}$. Therefore, $f \in J I_{\leq \frac{m}{2}-1} \subset I^2$. This gives that $I^2 = \mathcal{M}_{[m]} \setminus \{\check{1}\}$.

**Corollary 1.** *Let $I \subset \mathcal{M}_{[m]}$ be a max-complement-free monomial set. Then*

$$(\mathcal{C}(I)^2)^{\perp} = \begin{cases} \mathcal{C}(\{1, x_i\}) & \text{if } \exists i, \forall f \in J, x_i | f \\ \mathcal{C}(\{1\}) & \text{if not} \end{cases} \tag{14}$$

A direct consequence of Theorem 6 is

**Corollary 2.** *Let $I \subset \mathcal{M}_{[m]}$ be a max-complement-free monomial set and $n = 2^m$. Then with probability $1 - O\left(\dfrac{\log(n)}{2^{\frac{n}{\sqrt{\log(n)}}}}\right)$ we have that $\mathcal{C}(I)^2 = \mathcal{R}(m-1, m)$.*

*Moreover, for $m$ even, one constructive way of taking square roots of $\mathcal{R}(m - 1, m)$ is using Algorithm 1.*

The proof of Corollary 2 follows directly from Theorem 6, combined with the combinatorial argument regarding the proportion of max-complement-free monomial sets $I$ satisfying the condition $\exists i, \forall f \in J, x_i | f$. More exactly, there are $m$ out of $2^{\binom{m-1}{\frac{m}{2}}}$ such sets. Using the Stirling approximation for the binomial coefficient one gets the desired result.

Under the hypothesis that self-dual codes are uniformly distributed within the set of $[n, \frac{n}{2}]$ random linear codes, Corollary 2 holds true if we loosen the condition and simply consider a self-dual code that is not necessarily also a decreasing monomial code.

**Proposition 6.** *Let $\mathcal{C}$ be a self-dual code. Then, if self-dual codes are uniformly distributed within the set of $[n, \frac{n}{2}]$ random linear codes, w.h.p. $\mathcal{C}^2$ is the space of even-weight vectors of length $n$.*

*In particular, for $n = 2^m$ we have that $\mathcal{C}^2 = \mathcal{R}(m - 1, m)$.*

*Proof.* Since $\mathcal{C}$ is a self-dual code, $\forall c_1, c_2 \in \mathcal{C}$, have $0 = c_1 \cdot c_2 = \text{wt}(c_1 \star c_2)$ mod 2. So all the codewords in $\mathcal{C}^2$ have even weight. As self-dual codes are uniformly distributed within the set of $[n, \frac{n}{2}]$ linear codes, the probability for the former to satisfy a property is the same as for the latter. Thus, by [13], w.h.p. $\dim(\mathcal{C}^2) = \min\left\{n, \binom{\frac{n}{2}+1}{2}\right\} = n$. Therefore, w.h.p. $\mathcal{C}^2$ is the space of even-weight vectors of length $n$.

*Remark 4.* In the case that $\exists i, \forall f \in J, x_i | f$, the set $I$ can be written as $I = I_{\leq \frac{m}{2}-1} \cup x_i I_{\leq \frac{m}{2}-1}$.

Moving forward, we compute higher powers of monomial max-complement-free sets in the special case where $I = I_{\leq \frac{m}{2}-1} \cup x_i I_{\leq \frac{m}{2}-1}$.

**Lemma 3.** *For a max-complemet-free monomial set $I = I_{\leq \frac{m}{2}-1} \cup x_i I_{\leq \frac{m}{2}-1}$, we have the following:*

- $x_i I = x_i I_{\leq \frac{m}{2}-1}$;
- $I^2 = I_{\leq m-2} \cup x_i I_{\leq m-2}$;
- $x_i I^2 = x_i I_{\leq m-2} = x_i \mathcal{M}_{[m]} \setminus \{\check{1}\}$;
- $I^3 = \mathcal{M}_{[m]}$.

**Proposition 7.** *The monomial set $x_i I^2$ generates a $[2^m, 2^{m-1} - 1, 2]$-code $\mathscr{C}(x_i I^2)$.*

*Proof.* The dimension is given by that multiplication by $x_i$ halves the number of monomials and $\check{1}$ is excluded. The minimal distance of the code is given by any element of the set $\bigcup_{j \neq i} \mathsf{T}(m, 2) \cdot \check{x}_j$, for example by $\check{x}_j$ for some $j \neq i$.

**Proposition 8.** *Let $\mathcal{D} = \mathscr{C}(x_i I^3)$. Then $\mathcal{D}$ is a $[2^m, 2^{m-1}, 1]$-code with dual $\mathcal{D}^\perp = \mathscr{C}\left((1 + x_i)\mathcal{M}_{[m]}\right)$ and basis $W_{\min}(\mathcal{D}) = \{\mathsf{ev}(f) \mid f \in x_i\left(\mathsf{T}(m, 2) \cdot \check{x}_i\right)\}$.*

*Proof.* Since $I^3 = \mathcal{M}_{[m]}$, $\mathcal{D} = \mathscr{C}\left(x_i \mathcal{M}_{[m]}\right)$ and then it is clear that $\mathcal{D}^\perp = \mathscr{C}\left((1 + x_i)\mathcal{M}_{[m]}\right)$. The code has dimension $2^{m-1}$ as it consists of the evaluation of half of the monomials and it has minimum weight 1, as it contains $\check{1}$. The minimum weight is 1, so

$$W_{\min}(\mathcal{D}) = \mathrm{Span}\left(\{\mathsf{ev}(f) \mid f \in x_i\mathcal{M}_{[m]} \text{ with } \deg(f) = m\}\right) \tag{15}$$

$$= \{\mathsf{ev}(f) \mid f = x_i \prod_{j \neq i}(x_j + e_j), \text{ for } e_j \in \{0, 1\}, \forall j \neq i\} \tag{16}$$

$$= \{\mathsf{ev}(f) \mid f \in x_i\left(\mathsf{T}(m, 2) \cdot \check{x}_i\right)\} \tag{17}$$

As $x_i\mathsf{T}(m, 2) \cdot \check{x}_i$ is a linearly independent set of size $2^{m-1}$, so is $W_{\min}(\mathcal{D})$. This makes $W_{\min}(\mathcal{D})$ a basis for $\mathcal{D}$.

### 3.4  Shortened Self-dual Monomial Codes

**Definition 8.** *The discrete derivative of a monomial $f \in \mathcal{M}_{[m]}$ with respect to a variable $x_i$ is a monomial $\frac{\partial f}{\partial x_i} \in \mathcal{M}_{[m] \setminus \{i\}}$ given by*

$$\frac{\partial f}{\partial x_i} = \begin{cases} \dfrac{f}{x_i} & \text{if } x_i | f \\ 0 & \text{if not} \end{cases} \tag{18}$$

*Let $I \subset \mathcal{M}_{[m]}$. The discrete derivative of a monomial set is a monomial set* $\frac{\partial I}{\partial x_i} \subset \mathcal{M}_{[m] \setminus \{i\}}$ *given by*

$$\frac{\partial I}{\partial x_i} = \left\{ \frac{\partial f}{\partial x_i} \mid f \in I \right\}.$$

**Lemma 4.** *Let $I$ be a monomial set. We have*

$$\{ f \in I \mid x_i | f \} = x_i \cdot \frac{\partial I}{\partial x_i} \setminus \{0\}. \tag{19}$$

*Moreover, $\mathscr{C}\left( x_i \cdot \frac{\partial I}{\partial x_i} \right)$ is a monomial subcode of $\mathscr{C}(I)$.*

**Theorem 7.** *Let $I \subset \mathcal{M}_{[m]}$ and $L = \mathrm{Supp}(\mathrm{ev}(1 + x_i))$. The code $\mathcal{S}_L(\mathscr{C}(I))$ is a monomial code defined over $\mathcal{M}_{[m] \setminus \{i\}}$ and given by*

$$\mathcal{S}_L(\mathscr{C}(I)) = \mathscr{C}\left( \frac{\partial I}{\partial x_i} \right). \tag{20}$$

*Proof.* Consider a generator matrix $\boldsymbol{G}$ for the code $\mathscr{C}(I)$ given by the evaluation of the monomials in $I$. By the definition of the shortened code (see Definition 1), one can construct a basis for the shortened code starting from $\boldsymbol{G}$ by taking only those vectors that equal 0 on $L$. Any monomial $f$ in $I$ such that $\mathrm{ev}(f)_j = 0$ for all $j \in L$ has to admit $x_i$ as factor, i.e., $f = x_i f^*$ with $f^* \in \mathcal{M}_{[m] \setminus \{i\}}$. Hence, any $f$ satisfying the aforementioned condition is sent (by the shortening operator) onto $f^* = \frac{\partial f}{\partial x_i}$, which proves the $\subseteq$ inclusion. For the converse, take any element of the monomial set $\frac{\partial I}{\partial x_i}$. It either equals 0, which implies that $x_i \nmid f$ (and the zero vector belongs to $\mathcal{S}(\mathscr{C}(I))$), or it equals $f^* \in \mathcal{M}_{[m] \setminus \{i\}}$, which implies that $\exists f \in I$ such that $f = x_i f^*$. This gives that $\mathrm{ev}(f)_j = 0, \forall j \in L$, and ends the proof.

**Corollary 3.** *Let $I \in \mathcal{M}_{[m]}$ and $L = \mathrm{Supp}(\mathrm{ev}(1 + x_i))$. The monomial subcode of $\mathscr{C}(I)$ generated by $f \in I$ with the property $x_i | f$ is*

$$\mathcal{S}_L^{\mathcal{E}}(\mathscr{C}(I)) = \mathscr{C}\left( x_i \cdot \frac{\partial I}{\partial x_i} \right). \tag{21}$$

*Proof.* Use Lemma 4 and Theorem 7.

*Remark 5.* As $I = I_{\leq \frac{m}{2} - 1} \cup x_i I_{\leq \frac{m}{2} - 1}$, we have $\mathscr{C}\left( x_i \cdot \frac{\partial I}{\partial x_i} \right) = \mathscr{C}(x_i I)$. Notice that the equality

$\mathscr{C}\left( x_i \cdot \frac{\partial I}{\partial x_i} \right) = \mathscr{C}(x_i I)$ does not hold for the general monomial set.

**Corollary 4.** *Let $I = I_{\leq \frac{m}{2} - 1} \cup J \subset \mathcal{M}_{[m]}$ be a max-complement-free monomial set, and $L = \mathrm{Supp}(\mathrm{ev}(1 + x_i))$. Then*

$$\mathcal{P}_L(\mathscr{C}(I)) = \mathscr{C}\left( \frac{\partial I}{\partial x_i} \right)^{\perp}. \tag{22}$$

**Theorem 8.** *Let $I = I_{\leq \frac{m}{2}-1} \cup J \subset \mathcal{M}_{[m]}$ be a max-complement-free monomial set, and $L = \mathrm{Supp}(\mathrm{ev}(1 + x_i))$. Then*

$$\mathscr{R}(m/2 - 2, m - 1) \subset \mathcal{S}_L(\mathscr{C}(I)) \subset \mathscr{R}(m/2 - 1, m - 1) \tag{23}$$

$$\mathscr{R}(m/2 - 1, m - 1) \subset \mathcal{P}_L(\mathscr{C}(I)) \subset \mathscr{R}(m/2, m - 1). \tag{24}$$

*In particular, $\mathcal{S}_L(\mathscr{C}(I)) = \mathcal{P}_L(\mathscr{C}(I)) = \mathscr{R}\left(\frac{m}{2} - 1, m - 1\right)$ if and only if $I = I_{\leq \frac{m}{2}-1} \cup x_i I_{\leq \frac{m}{2}-1}$.*

*Proof.* Differentiate the inclusions $I_{\leq \frac{m}{2}-1} \subset I \subset I_{\leq \frac{m}{2}}$ by $x_i$ to get

$$I_{\leq \frac{m}{2}-2} \simeq \frac{\partial I_{\leq \frac{m}{2}-1}}{\partial x_i} \subset \frac{\partial I}{\partial x_i} \subset \frac{\partial I_{\leq \frac{m}{2}}}{\partial x_i} \simeq I_{\leq \frac{m}{2}-1}, \tag{25}$$

where $I_{\leq \frac{m}{2}-2}, I_{\leq \frac{m}{2}-1} \subset \mathcal{M}_{[m-1]}$ and the isomorphisms are given by restricting the isomorphism $\mathcal{M}_{[m-1]} \to \mathcal{M}_{[m]\setminus\{i\}}$ from Definition 4 to the respective sets.

Then, by Theorem 7 and considering the codes generated by these monomial sets, we get

$$\mathscr{R}(m/2 - 2, m - 1) \subset \mathcal{S}_L(\mathscr{C}(I)) \subset \mathscr{R}(m/2 - 1, m - 1). \tag{26}$$

Taking the dual of the above gives

$$\mathscr{R}(m/2 - 1, m - 1) \subset \mathcal{P}_L(\mathscr{C}(I)) \subset \mathscr{R}(m/2, m - 1). \tag{27}$$

For the equality, if $I = I_{\leq \frac{m}{2}-1} \cup x_i I_{\leq \frac{m}{2}-1}$, then

$$\mathcal{S}_L(\mathscr{C}(I)) = \mathscr{C}\left(\frac{\partial I_{\leq \frac{m}{2}-1} \cup x_i I_{\leq \frac{m}{2}-1}}{\partial x_i}\right) \tag{28}$$

$$= \mathscr{C}\left(I_{\leq \frac{m}{2}-1}\right), \text{ where } I_{\leq \frac{m}{2}-1} \subset \mathcal{M}_{[m]\setminus\{i\}} \tag{29}$$

$$= \mathscr{R}\left(\frac{m}{2} - 1, m - 1\right) \tag{30}$$

Where as, if $I \neq I_{\leq \frac{m}{2}-1} \cup x_i I_{\leq \frac{m}{2}-1}$, then $\frac{\partial I}{\partial x_i} \subsetneq I_{\leq \frac{m}{2}-1}$, where $I_{\leq \frac{m}{2}-1} \subset \mathcal{M}_{[m]\setminus\{i\}}$. It follows that $\mathcal{S}_L(\mathscr{C}(I)) \subsetneq \mathscr{R}\left(\frac{m}{2} - 1, m - 1\right)$.

## 4    Security of the McEliece Public Key Encryption Scheme Based on Self-dual Monomial Codes

### 4.1    The McEliece Encryption Scheme

The McEliece public key encryption scheme [36] is composed of three algorithms: *key generation* (KeyGen), *encryption* (Encrypt) and *decryption* (Decrypt) (see Table 1).

Instantiating the McEliece scheme with a different family of codes than the original proposal (using binary Goppa codes) gives a plethora of alternatives that were analyzed and some successfully cryptanalyzed [9,48]. The [24] variant could overcome many of the security problems encountered in the past. The idea of using self-dual codes comes with several advantages.

**Table 1.** McEliece PKE scheme

| KeyGen$(n, k, t) = (\mathsf{pk}, \mathsf{sk})$ | $G$-generator matrix of $\mathscr{C}$ \\ $\mathscr{C}$ an $[n, k]$ that corrects $t$ errors |
|---|---|
| | An $n \times n$ permutation matrix $P$ |
| | A $k \times k$ invertible matrix $S$ |
| | Compute $G_{\mathrm{pub}} = SGP$ |
| | Return $\mathsf{pk} = (G_{\mathrm{pub}}, t)$ $\mathsf{sk} = (S, G, P)$ |
| Encrypt$(m, \mathsf{pk}) = z$ | Encode $m \to c = mG_{\mathrm{pub}}$ |
| | Choose $e$ \\ $e$ a vector of weight $t$ |
| | Return $z = c + e$ |
| Decrypt$(z, \mathsf{sk}) = m$ | Compute $z^* = zP^{-1}$ |
| | $z^* = mSG + eP^{-1}$ |
| | $m^* = \mathcal{D}ecode(z^*, G)$ |
| | Return $m$ from $m^* S^{-1}$ |

- As the dual equals the code itself, no extra information about the structure of the code could be revealed via the dual code. Moreover, the complexity of the attacks on the dual code are identical with that of attacks on the code itself.
- Generic algorithms for solving the code equivalence problem, such as the Support Splitting Algorithm [47], are unfitted for such codes. There are two reasons for that: i) the hull of the code equals the code itself (large dimension) ii) the permutation group is non-trivial, making the SSA unfeasible.
- The efficient techniques used for distinguishers and structural attacks such as the square code technique are not able to retreive any non-trivial information about the code in general (see Theorem 6). Even for more symmetric configurations, e.g., $I = I_{\frac{m}{2}-1} \cup x_i I_{\frac{m}{2}-1}$, applying square code and shortening only reduces the code equivalence problem to the most difficult instance of the code equivalence problem on a certain Reed-Muller code.
- There is an exponential number of monomial sets $I$ to be considered and, hence, an exponential number of instances of the code equivalence problem to be solved. On top of that, different choices of $I$ give different permutation groups for $\mathscr{C}(I)$.

In their article [24], the authors do not give a feasible solution to the decoding problem. Here, we are dealing with a unique decoding problem (up to half the minimum distance) or a list decoding problem up to the minimum distance, for subcodes of a certain Reed-Muller code. Known solutions for such scenarios are the Dummer's list decoding algorithms [22,23] or a modified version of the recent recursive projection-aggregation decoding [53]. Notice that we are in a more particular case, i.e. a code that is situated between two consecutive Reed-Muller codes. Hence, in this case the work of Jamali et al. is more suitable

(Section III in [27]). However, there is no clear evidence that such decoders perform well enough for parameters as in [24].

## 4.2  Security Analysis

In [24] the authors propose a basic security analysis based only on the ISD technique. Hence, we propose to explore other techniques of cryptanalysis and show how these affect the security of the scheme.

**Distinguisher.** It is known from [13] that with high probability the dimension of the square code of a random linear code $\mathscr{C} = [n, k]$ is

$$\dim (\mathscr{C}^2) = \min \left\{ n, \ \binom{k+1}{2} \right\}. \tag{31}$$

Straightforwardly, one can deduce that with high probability a random linear self-dual code $\mathscr{C} = [n, n/2]$ with $n > 2$ has a square code that covers the whole space, i.e., $\dim(\mathscr{C}^2) = n$. Now, by Theorem 6 the dimension of a self-dual monomial code $\mathscr{C}(I)$ generated by Algorithm 1 has dimension either $n - 1$ or $n - 2$. Even though there is a slight difference between the random case and the structured monomial case, this difference is too small to be convincing. Hence, we will propose another distinguisher, as efficient as the former in terms of complexity, but more relevant to our context.

**Theorem 9** ([13]). *With high probability, the dimension of the product code of two random linear codes $\mathscr{C}_1 = [n, k_1]$ and $\mathscr{C}_2 = [n, k_2]$ is*

$$\dim (\mathscr{C}_1 \star \mathscr{C}_2) = \min \left\{ n, \ k_1 k_2 - \binom{\dim (\mathscr{C}_1 \cap \mathscr{C}_2)}{2} \right\}.$$

**Corollary 5.** *The dimension of the product code between a random code $\mathscr{C} = [n, k]$ and a randomly chosen codeword of $\mathscr{C}$ is, with high probability,*

$$\dim(c \star \mathscr{C}) = k.$$

The equivalent of Corollary 5 for self-dual monomial codes is more cumbersome, as the dimension of the product code depends on the degree and makeup of the polynomial by which the initial code is multiplied. We do however have results for the extreme cases in which the multiplying codeword is the evaluation of a monomial; the dimension of the product code in the case of a polynomial will be a linear combination of the dimensions resulting from multiplying by monomials. These show a significant difference between the case in which a code $\mathscr{C} = [n, \frac{n}{2}]$ is random, where w.h.p. $\dim(c \star \mathscr{C}) = \frac{n}{2}$, and a self-dual monomial code generated by $I = I_{\leq \frac{m}{2}-1} \cup J$ with $J \subset I_{\frac{m}{2}}$, where w.h.p. $\dim(\mathsf{ev}(f) \star \mathscr{C}) = \dim(\mathscr{C}(fI)) \in \left[ \sqrt{n}, \frac{n}{4} \right]$.

**Theorem 10.** *Let $f \in \mathcal{M}_{[m]}, I \subset \mathcal{M}_{[m]}$ s.t. $I = I_{\leq \frac{m}{2}-1} \cup J$ is a max-complement-free monomial set. Then for any $f$ with $\deg(f) \leq \frac{m}{2}$ we have*

$$\sum_{i=0}^{\frac{m}{2}-1} \binom{m-\deg(f)}{i} \leq \dim(\mathrm{ev}(f) \star \mathscr{C}) \leq \sum_{i=0}^{\frac{m}{2}} \binom{m-\deg(f)}{i}. \tag{32}$$

*In particular, the following holds for the extreme cases.*

$$\dim(\mathrm{ev}(f) \star \mathscr{C}) = \begin{cases} \frac{n}{2} & \text{if } \deg(f) = 0 \\ \sqrt{n}-1 \text{ or } \sqrt{n} & \text{if } \deg(f) = \frac{m}{2} \end{cases},$$

$$\dim(\mathrm{ev}(f) \star \mathscr{C}) \simeq \begin{cases} \frac{n}{4} & \text{if } \deg(f) = 1 \\ 2\sqrt{n} & \text{if } \deg(f) = \frac{m}{2} - 1 \end{cases}.$$

*Proof.* Let $f$ and $I$ be as in stated in the theorem and denote $J_{\mathrm{ind}(f)} = \{g \in J \mid \mathrm{ind}(g) \cap \mathrm{ind}(f) \neq \emptyset\}$, and $J^c_{\mathrm{ind}(f)} = J \setminus J_{\mathrm{ind}(f)}$. Then we have

$$fI = fI_{\leq \frac{m}{2}-1} \cup fJ$$
$$= \{g \in I_{\leq \deg(f)+\frac{m}{2}-1} \mid f|g\} \cup f\{h \in J \mid \mathrm{ind}(h) \cap \mathrm{ind}(f) = \emptyset\}$$
$$= \{g \in I_{\leq \deg(f)+\frac{m}{2}-1} \mid f|g\} \cup fJ^c_{\mathrm{ind}(f)}.$$

Notice that we have a disjoint decomposition of $fI$, as $\deg(g) = \deg(f) + \frac{m}{2}$ for any $g \in fJ^c_{\mathrm{ind}(f)}$. So when computing the dimension we obtain $\dim(\mathrm{ev}(f) \star \mathscr{C}) = \dim(\mathscr{C}(fI)) = \sum_{i=0}^{\frac{m}{2}-1} \binom{m-\deg(f)}{i} + |J^c_{\mathrm{ind}(f)}|$. Now, by definition of $J^c_{\mathrm{ind}(f)}$ we have that any $g \in J^c_{\mathrm{ind}(f)}$ satisfies $\deg(g) = \frac{m}{2}$ and $\mathrm{ind}(g) \in \mathrm{ind}(\check{f})$. This implies a maximum number of choices for $g$ as $\binom{\deg(\check{f})}{\frac{m}{2}} = \binom{m-\deg(f)}{\frac{m}{2}}$, which leads to (32).

If we plug into (32) the four particular cases we obtain:

1. $\dim(\mathrm{ev}(1) \star \mathscr{C}) = \dim(\mathscr{C}(1 \cdot I)) = \dim(\mathscr{C}(I)) = \dim(\mathscr{C}) = \frac{n}{2}$.
2. $\dim(\mathrm{ev}(x_i) \star \mathscr{C}) = \sum_{j=0}^{\frac{m}{2}-1} \binom{m-1}{j} + |J^c_{\{i\}}| = 2^{m-2} + |J^c_{\{i\}}|$, which yields $\lim_{m\to\infty} \dim(\mathrm{ev}(x_i) \star \mathscr{C}) = \frac{n}{4}$.
3. If $\deg(f) = \frac{m}{2} - 1$ we have $\dim(\mathrm{ev}(f) \star \mathscr{C}) = \sum_{i=0}^{\frac{m}{2}-1} \binom{\frac{m}{2}+1}{i} + |J^c_{\mathrm{ind}(f)}| = 2^{\frac{m}{2}+1} - (\frac{m}{2} + 2) + |J^c_{\mathrm{ind}(f)}|$. This yields $\lim_{m\to\infty} \dim(\mathrm{ev}(f) \star \mathscr{C}) = 2\sqrt{n}$.
4. If $\deg(f) = \frac{m}{2}$ then $2^{\frac{m}{2}} - 1 \leq \dim(\mathrm{ev}(f) \star \mathscr{C}) \leq 2^{\frac{m}{2}}$.

**Message Recovery Attacks.** Given a chipertext, an adversary is confronted in this scenario with the well-known decoding problem. More precisely, given pk and $z$ an adversary is challenged to retrieve $m$. In most of the cases one would tackle this problem using ISD [10,21,25,29,30,35,44,51]. In Table 2 the complexity of some of the variants is computed for three different sets of parameters. If the weight of the error is set for unique decoding, i.e., $t = \lfloor \frac{d-1}{2} \rfloor$ then the only parameters with a reasonable security level are for $m = 14$, which give $2^{245.74}$ complexity of the ISD variant [6] for $t = 128$. This would yield a quantum security

**Table 2.** Security level given by the complexity of the ISD variants for the McEliece variant based on self-dual monomial codes for $m = 10, 12, 14$, as well as the key size of the cryptosystem.

| Parameters $[n, k, d]$ | Information Set Decoding variant | | | | | Key size (Kbytes) |
|---|---|---|---|---|---|---|
| | [44] | [29] | [21] | [34] | [6] | |
| Unique decoding up to $t = \lfloor \frac{d-1}{2} \rfloor$ | | | | | | |
| $[1024, 512, 32]$ | 35.17 | 28.51 | 17.07 | 12.75 | 6.38 | 32 |
| $[4096, 2048, 128]$ | 87.72 | 76.98 | 64.69 | 59.43 | 53.53 | 512 |
| $[16384, 8192, 512]$ | 285.92 | 271.16 | 256.26 | 250.34 | 245.74 | 8192 |
| Search for minimum weight codewords | | | | | | |
| $[1024, 512, 32]$ | 51.72 | 42.91 | 32.97 | 28.87 | 22.65 | 32 |
| $[4096, 2048, 128]$ | 153.96 | 141.11 | 129.13 | 123.70 | 119.44 | 512 |
| $[16384, 8192, 512]$ | 550.89 | 534.03 | 514.35 | 512.15 | 510.57 | 8192 |

of about $2^{122.87}$ [28]. Now, if list decoding is used, which could increase the weight of the error vector up to the minimum distance $t = d$, the security levels would be of about $2^{119.44}$ and $2^{510.57}$ for $m = 12$, respectively $m = 14$. In the quantum scenario the security levels would decrease down to $2^{59.72}$ and $2^{255.28}$. The latter scenario is probably the most suitable for cryptographic purposes, even though list decoding comes with an extra computation requirement.

**Key Recovery Attacks.** Since the generator matrix $G$ for the code $\mathscr{C}(I)$ is generated via Algorithm 1, by Proposition 2 we have an exponential number of distinct codes $\mathscr{C}(I)$ and thus matrices $G$. More exactly we have $2^{\binom{m-1}{\frac{m}{2}}}$ distinct codes, which gives $2^{126}, 2^{462}, 2^{1716}$ for $m \in \{10, 12, 14\}$. Some of them are equivalent, as pointed out in Theorem 4, fact that reduces the factor in the exponent. However, the quantity remains out-of-reach on any classic computer. Hence, reducing the key recovery problem to the code equivalence problem seems unlikely. The best we can hope for is to identify sub-classes of self-dual codes, which are distinguishable by means of signatures such as dimension of the dual of the shortened code, the number of minimum weight codewords in the dual of the shortened code etc. In the case of monomial codes the code equivalece problem can be defined as follows.

**Definition 9 (Code Equivalence Problem for Monomial Codes).** *Let $I \subset \mathcal{M}_{[m]}$ and $G = \langle \text{ev}(f) \mid f \in I \rangle$ such that the matrix $G$ generates an $[n, k]$-code. Let $G^*$ also be the generating matrix for an $[n, k]$ binary linear code. Find matrices $S \in \mathsf{GL}(k, 2)$ and $P \in \mathfrak{S}_n$ such that $G^* = SGP$.*

Notice that for the Sidelnikov's scheme and the McEliece based on polar codes the key recovery problem reduced to the code equivalence problem for monomial codes. We will demonstrate here that for $I = I_{\leq \frac{m}{2} - 1} \cup x_i I_{\leq \frac{m}{2} - 1}$ the code equivalence problem can be solved using the following algorithm.

---

**Algorithm 3.** Key Recovery on self-dual monomial McEliece

---

**Require:** $\mathscr{C}(I)^\pi$ a public self-dual monomial code
**Ensure:** $\pi^*$ a permutation s.t. $\mathscr{C}^{\pi^*} = \mathscr{C}^\pi$ if $I = I_{\leq \frac{m}{2}-1} \cup x_i I_{\leq \frac{m}{2}-1}$ or ERROR if not

   Compute $\mathcal{D} = \left((\mathscr{C}(I)^\pi)^2\right)^\perp$
   **if** $\dim(\mathcal{D}) = 2$ **then**
      Retrieve $c \in \mathcal{D}$ s.t. $c \neq \text{ev}(0), c \neq \text{ev}(1)$.
      Compute $\mathcal{S}_{\text{Supp}(c)}(\mathscr{C}(I)^\pi)$
      Solve $\pi^* \leftarrow \text{CEP}(\mathscr{R}(\frac{m}{2} - 1, m - 1), \mathcal{S}_{\text{Supp}(c)}(\mathscr{C}(I)^\pi))$
      Return $\pi^*$
   **else**
      Return ERROR
   **end if**

---

**Theorem 11.** *Let $\pi \in \mathfrak{S}_n$ and $\mathscr{C}(I)^\pi$ be a permuted self-dual code defined by a max-complement-free monomial set $I$. If $I = I_{\leq \frac{m}{2}-1} \cup x_i I_{\leq \frac{m}{2}-1}$ then Algorithm 3 outputs a permutation $\pi^*$ satisfying $\mathscr{C}^{\pi^*} = \mathscr{C}^\pi$. Moreover, the overall complexity is dominated by the algorithm that solves $\text{CEP}(\mathscr{R}(\frac{m}{2}-1, m-1), \mathcal{S}_{\text{Supp}(c)}(\mathscr{C}(I)^\pi))$, having time complexity $e^{\sqrt{n}c(1+o(1))}$, where $c$ is a constant.*

*Proof.* By Theorem 6 if $I = I_{\leq \frac{m}{2}-1} \cup x_i I_{\leq \frac{m}{2}-1}$ then $\dim(\mathcal{D}) = 2$ and if not $\dim(\mathcal{D}) = 1$. Hence, Algorithm 3 outputs ERROR each time the set $I$ does not satisfy the condition $I = I_{\leq \frac{m}{2}-1} \cup x_i I_{\leq \frac{m}{2}-1}$. Going further, when $\dim(\mathcal{D}) = 2$ by Corollary 1 the code $\mathcal{D} = \mathscr{C}(\{1, x_i\})^\pi$. Hence, one can easily choose a random element $c \in \mathcal{D}$ and verify that $c \neq \text{ev}(0)$ or $c \neq \text{ev}(1)$. This implies that either $c = \text{ev}(x_i)^\pi$ or $c = \text{ev}(1+x_i)^\pi$. As $\text{T}(m, 2) \subset \text{Perm}(\mathcal{D})$ we can set $c = \text{ev}(1+x_i)^\pi$. Next, using Theorem 7 we deduce that the two codes $\mathscr{R}(\frac{m}{2} - 1, m - 1)$ and $\mathcal{S}_{\text{Supp}(c)}(\mathscr{C}(I)^\pi))$ are equivalent. Hence, we are left to solve the code equivalence problem for these two codes. According to [14] there is an efficient algorithm that transforms a permuted $\mathscr{R}(r, m)^\pi$ into $\mathscr{R}(\gcd(r, m - 1), m)^\pi$. This resumes in our case to transforming $\mathscr{R}(\frac{m}{2} - 1, m - 1)^\pi$ into itself as $\gcd(\frac{m}{2} - 1, m - 2) = \frac{m}{2} - 1$. Hence, the best strategy up-to-date for solving the $\text{CEP}(\mathscr{R}(\frac{m}{2} - 1, m - 1), \mathcal{S}_{\text{Supp}(c)}(\mathscr{C}(I)^\pi))$ is given by the algorithm proposed in [37], and having time complexity $e^{\sqrt{n}c(1+o(1))}$, $c$ being constant. The permutation obtained in solving the $\text{CEP}(\mathscr{R}(\frac{m}{2} - 1, m - 1), \mathcal{S}_{\text{Supp}(c)}(\mathscr{C}(I)^\pi))$ is a valid permutation for the initial problem. Indeed, by Theorem 5 any $\sigma \in \text{Perm}(\mathscr{R}(\frac{m}{2} - 1, m - 1))$ gives a valid permutation for $\text{Perm}(\mathscr{C}(I))$, by setting $(\sigma_1, \sigma, \sigma) \in \text{Perm}(\mathscr{C}(I))$, with $\sigma_1 \in \text{T}(1, 2)$. $\square$

**Acknowledgments.** We would like to thank the anonymous reviewers for their suggestions and comments that helped us improve the quality of our article.

   V-F. Drăgoi was supported by a grant of the Ministry of Research, Innovation and Digitization, CNCS/CCCDI – UEFISCDI, project number PN-III-P1-1.1-PD-2019-0285, within PNCDI III.

# A    Example on the Permutation Group of Self-dual Monomial Codes

*Example 5.* Let $m = 4$. The code defined by

$$I = I_{\leq \frac{m}{2} - 1} \cup x_0 I_{\leq \frac{m}{2} - 1} = \{1, x_0, x_1, x_2, x_3, x_0 x_1, x_0 x_2, x_0 x_3\}$$

is the code generated by

$$G = \begin{pmatrix} 1\,0\,1\,0\,1\,0\,1\,0\,0\,0\,0\,0\,0\,0\,0\,0 \\ 1\,0\,1\,0\,0\,0\,0\,0\,1\,0\,1\,0\,0\,0\,0\,0 \\ 1\,0\,0\,0\,1\,0\,0\,0\,1\,0\,0\,0\,1\,0\,0\,0 \\ 1\,1\,1\,1\,1\,1\,1\,1\,0\,0\,0\,0\,0\,0\,0\,0 \\ 1\,1\,1\,1\,0\,0\,0\,0\,1\,1\,1\,1\,0\,0\,0\,0 \\ 1\,1\,0\,0\,1\,1\,0\,0\,1\,1\,0\,0\,1\,1\,0\,0 \\ 1\,0\,1\,0\,1\,0\,1\,0\,1\,0\,1\,0\,1\,0\,1\,0 \\ 1\,1\,1\,1\,1\,1\,1\,1\,1\,1\,1\,1\,1\,1\,1\,1 \end{pmatrix}$$

Let us first split the set $[n]$ into two disjoint sets, i.e., the sets $\mathrm{Supp}(x_0) = \{1, 3, 5, 7, 9, 11, 13, 15\}$ and $\mathrm{Supp}(1 + x_0) = \{2, 4, 6, 8, 10, 12, 14, 16\}$. We have that $\mathscr{C}(I) = \mathscr{C}(I)^{\sigma_1}$, where

$$\sigma_1([n]) = \{2, 4, 6, 8, 10, 12, 14, 16, 1, 3, 5, 7, 9, 11, 13, 15\},$$

here the sets are indexed, i.e., the order of the elements matters. One can apply the same splitting idea to the matrix $G$ and obtain two matrices $G_1$ and $G_2$, column subtarices of $G$ indexed by $\mathrm{Supp}(x_0)$, respectively $\mathrm{Supp}(1 + x_0)$

$$G_1 = \begin{pmatrix} 1\,1\,1\,1\,0\,0\,0\,0 \\ 1\,1\,0\,0\,1\,1\,0\,0 \\ 1\,0\,1\,0\,1\,0\,1\,0 \\ 1\,1\,1\,1\,0\,0\,0\,0 \\ 1\,1\,0\,0\,1\,1\,0\,0 \\ 1\,0\,1\,0\,1\,0\,1\,0 \\ 1\,1\,1\,1\,1\,1\,1\,1 \\ 1\,1\,1\,1\,1\,1\,1\,1 \end{pmatrix}, \quad G_2 = \begin{pmatrix} 0\,0\,0\,0\,0\,0\,0\,0 \\ 0\,0\,0\,0\,0\,0\,0\,0 \\ 0\,0\,0\,0\,0\,0\,0\,0 \\ 1\,1\,1\,1\,0\,0\,0\,0 \\ 1\,1\,0\,0\,1\,1\,0\,0 \\ 1\,0\,1\,0\,1\,0\,1\,0 \\ 0\,0\,0\,0\,0\,0\,0\,0 \\ 1\,1\,1\,1\,1\,1\,1\,1 \end{pmatrix}$$

Notice that $G_1$ and $G_2$ generate the same code, namely the code with generator matrix

$$G^* = \begin{pmatrix} 1\,1\,1\,1\,0\,0\,0\,0 \\ 1\,1\,0\,0\,1\,1\,0\,0 \\ 1\,0\,1\,0\,1\,0\,1\,0 \\ 1\,1\,1\,1\,1\,1\,1\,1 \end{pmatrix}$$

Finally, the code generated by $G^*$ is the Reed-Muller code $\mathscr{R}(1, 3)$ which has permutation group $\mathrm{Aff}(3, 2)$.

# References

1. Aguilar-Melchor, C., et al.: Hamming quasi-cyclic (HQC) (2017). Submission to the NIST post quantum standardization process. https://pqc-hqc.org/doc/hqc-specification_2020-10-01.pdf
2. Albrecht, M.R., et al.: Classic McEliece, November 2017. Submission to the NIST post quantum standardization process. https://classic.mceliece.org/nist/mceliece-20201010.pdf
3. Aragon, N., et al.: BIKE: Bit Flipping Key Encapsulation, December 2017. Submission to the NIST post quantum standardization process. https://bikesuite.org/files/v4.1/BIKE_Spec.2020.10.22.1.pdf
4. Bardet, M., Chaulet, J., Dragoi, V., Otmani, A., Tillich, J.-P.: Cryptanalysis of the McEliece public key cryptosystem based on polar codes. In: Takagi, T. (ed.) PQCrypto 2016. LNCS, vol. 9606, pp. 118–143. Springer, Cham (2016). https://doi.org/10.1007/978-3-319-29360-8_9
5. Bardet, M., Dragoi, V., Otmani, A., Tillich, J.: Algebraic properties of polar codes from a new polynomial formalism. In: IEEE International Symposium on Information Theory, ISIT 2016, Barcelona, Spain, 10–15 July 2016, pp. 230–234 (2016)
6. Becker, A., Joux, A., May, A., Meurer, A.: Decoding random binary linear codes in 2n/20: how 1+1=0 improves information set decoding. In: Pointcheval, D., Johansson, T. (eds.) EUROCRYPT 2012. LNCS, vol. 7237, pp. 520–536. Springer, Heidelberg (2012). https://doi.org/10.1007/978-3-642-29011-4_31
7. Berlekamp, E., McEliece, R., van Tilborg, H.: On the inherent intractability of certain coding problems. IEEE Trans. Inform. Theory **24**(3), 384–386 (1978)
8. Beiu, V., Dragoi, V.-F.: Fast reliability ranking of matchstick minimal networks. Networks 1–22 (2021, in press)
9. Bucerzan, D., Dragoi, V., Kalachi, H.T.: Evolution of the McEliece public key encryption scheme. In: Farshim, P., Simion, E. (eds.) SecITC 2017. LNCS, vol. 10543, pp. 129–149. Springer, Cham (2017). https://doi.org/10.1007/978-3-319-69284-5_10
10. Canteaut, A., Chabaud, F.: A new algorithm for finding minimum-weight words in a linear code: application to McEliece's cryptosystem and to narrow-sense BCH codes of length 511. IEEE Trans. Inform. Theory **44**(1), 367–378 (1998)
11. Carlet, C., Gaborit, P., Kim, J.L., Sole, P.: A new class of codes for boolean masking of cryptographic computations. IEEE Trans. Inf. Theor. **58**(9), 6000–6011 (2012)
12. Cary Huffman, W.: On the classification and enumeration of self-dual codes. Finite Fields Their Appl. **11**(3), 451–490 (2005)
13. Cascudo, I., Cramer, R., Mirandola, D., Zémor, G.: Squares of random linear codes. IEEE Trans. Inform. Theory **61**(3), 1159–1173 (2015)
14. Chizhov, I.V., Borodin, M.A.: Effective attack on the McEliece cryptosystem based on Reed-Muller codes. Discrete Math. Appl. **24**(5), 273–280 (2014)
15. Conway, J., Pless, V.: On the enumeration of self-dual codes. J. Comb. Theory Ser. A **28**(1), 26–53 (1980)
16. Corbella, I., Pellikaan, R.: Error-correcting pairs: a new approach to code-based cryptography. ACM Commun. Comput. Algebra **49**, 21 (2015)
17. Couvreur, A., Gaborit, P., Gauthier-Umaña, V., Otmani, A., Tillich, J.P.: Distinguisher-based attacks on public-key cryptosystems using Reed-Solomon codes. Des. Codes Cryptogr. **73**(2), 641–666 (2014)
18. Dougherty, S.T., Mesnager, S., Sole, P.: Secret-sharing schemes based on self-dual codes. In: 2008 IEEE Information Theory Workshop, pp. 338–342 (2008)

19. Dragoi, V.: Algebraic approach for the study of algorithmic problems coming from cryptography and the theory of error correcting codes. Theses, Université de Rouen, France, July 2017. https://hal.archives-ouvertes.fr/tel-01627324

20. Drăgoi, V., Beiu, V., Bucerzan, D.: Vulnerabilities of the McEliece variants based on polar codes. In: Lanet, J.-L., Toma, C. (eds.) SECITC 2018. LNCS, vol. 11359, pp. 376–390. Springer, Cham (2019). https://doi.org/10.1007/978-3-030-12942-2_29

21. Dumer, I.: Two decoding algorithms for linear codes. Probl. Inf. Transm. **25**(1), 17–23 (1989)

22. Dumer, I., Shabunov, K.: Recursive list decoding for reed-muller codes and their subcodes. In: Blaum, M., Farrell, P.G., van Tilborg, H.C.A. (eds.) Information, Coding and Mathematics. The Springer International Series in Engineering and Computer Science (Communications and Information Theory), vol. 687. Springer, Boston (2002). https://doi.org/10.1007/978-1-4757-3585-7_17

23. Dumer, I., Shabunov, K.: Soft-decision decoding of Reed-Muller codes: recursive lists. IEEE Trans. Inf. Theory **52**(3), 1260–1266 (2006)

24. Dömösi, P., Hannusch, C., Horváth, G.: A cryptographic system based on a new class of binary error-correcting codes. Tatra Mountains Math. Publ. **73**(1), 83–96 (2019)

25. Finiasz, M., Sendrier, N.: Security bounds for the design of code-based cryptosystems. In: Matsui, M. (ed.) ASIACRYPT 2009. LNCS, vol. 5912, pp. 88–105. Springer, Heidelberg (2009). https://doi.org/10.1007/978-3-642-10366-7_6

26. Hannusch, C., Lakatos, P.: Construction of self-dual binary $[2^{2k}, 2^{2k-1}, 2^k]$-codes. Algebra Discrete Math. **21**(1), 59–68 (2016)

27. Jamali, M.V., Liu, X., Makkuva, A., Mahdavifar, H., Oh, S., Viswanath, P.: Reed-Muller Subcodes: machine learning-aided design of efficient soft recursive decoding. In: 2021 IEEE International Symposium on Information Theory (ISIT), pp. 1088–1093 (2021)

28. Kachigar, G., Tillich, J.-P.: Quantum information set decoding algorithms. In: Lange, T., Takagi, T. (eds.) PQCrypto 2017. LNCS, vol. 10346, pp. 69–89. Springer, Cham (2017). https://doi.org/10.1007/978-3-319-59879-6_5

29. Lee, P.J., Brickell, E.F.: An observation on the security of McEliece's public-key cryptosystem. In: Barstow, D., et al. (eds.) EUROCRYPT 1988. LNCS, vol. 330, pp. 275–280. Springer, Heidelberg (1988). https://doi.org/10.1007/3-540-45961-8_25

30. Leon, J.: A probabilistic algorithm for computing minimum weights of large error-correcting codes. IEEE Trans. Inform. Theory **34**(5), 1354–1359 (1988)

31. MacWilliams, F., Sloane, N., Thompson, J.: Good self dual codes exist. Discrete Math. **3**(1), 153–162 (1972)

32. MacWilliams, F.J., Sloane, N.J.A.: The Theory of Error-Correcting Codes, 5th edn. North-Holland, Amsterdam (1986)

33. Mariot, L., Picek, S., Yorgova, R.: On McEliece type cryptosystems using self-dual codes with large minimum weight. Cryptology ePrint Archive, Report 2021/837 (2021)

34. May, A., Meurer, A., Thomae, E.: Decoding random linear codes in $\tilde{\mathcal{O}}(2^{0.054n})$. In: Lee, D.H., Wang, X. (eds.) ASIACRYPT 2011. LNCS, vol. 7073, pp. 107–124. Springer, Heidelberg (2011). https://doi.org/10.1007/978-3-642-25385-0_6

35. May, A., Ozerov, I.: On computing nearest neighbors with applications to decoding of binary linear codes. In: Oswald, E., Fischlin, M. (eds.) EUROCRYPT 2015. LNCS, vol. 9056, pp. 203–228. Springer, Heidelberg (2015). https://doi.org/10.1007/978-3-662-46800-5_9

36. McEliece, R.J.: A Public-Key System Based on Algebraic Coding Theory, pp. 114–116. Jet Propulsion Lab (1978). dSN Progress Report 44
37. Minder, L., Shokrollahi, A.: Cryptanalysis of the Sidelnikov cryptosystem. In: Naor, M. (ed.) EUROCRYPT 2007. LNCS, vol. 4515, pp. 347–360. Springer, Heidelberg (2007). https://doi.org/10.1007/978-3-540-72540-4_20
38. Nebe, G., Rains, E.M., Sloane, N.J.A.: Self-Dual Codes and Invariant Theory. Algorithms and Computation in Mathematics, Springer, Heidelberg (2006). https://doi.org/10.1007/3-540-30731-1
39. Oggier, F., Z'emor, G.: Coding constructions for efficient oblivious transfer from noisy channels (2020)
40. Otmani, A., Kalachi, H.T.: Square code attack on a modified sidelnikov cryptosystem. In: El Hajji, S., Nitaj, A., Carlet, C., Souidi, E.M. (eds.) C2SI 2015. LNCS, vol. 9084, pp. 173–183. Springer, Cham (2015). https://doi.org/10.1007/978-3-319-18681-8_14
41. Pellikaan, R.: On decoding by error location and dependent sets of error positions. Discrete Math. **106–107**, 368–381 (1992)
42. Pless, V.: A classification of self-orthogonal codes over GF(2). Discrete Math. **3**(1), 209–246 (1972)
43. Pless, V., Sloane, N.: On the classification and enumeration of self-dual codes. J. Comb. Theory Ser. A **18**(3), 313–335 (1975)
44. Prange, E.: The use of information sets in decoding cyclic codes. IRE Trans. Inf. Theory **8**(5), 5–9 (1962)
45. Randriambololona, H.: On products and powers of linear codes under component-wise multiplication. Contemporary Mathematics (2015). https://hal.telecom-paris.fr/hal-02287120
46. Schmidt, G., Sidorenko, V.R., Bossert, M.: Syndrome decoding of Reed-Solomon codes beyond half the minimum distance based on shift-register synthesis. IEEE Trans. Inf. Theory **56**(10), 5245–5252 (2010)
47. Sendrier, N.: Finding the permutation between equivalent linear codes: the support splitting algorithm. IEEE Trans. Inform. Theory **46**(4), 1193–1203 (2000)
48. Sendrier, N.: Code-based cryptography: state of the art and perspectives. IEEE Secur. Privacy **15**(4), 44–50 (2017)
49. Shrestha, S.R., Kim, Y.S.: New McEliece cryptosystem based on polar codes as a candidate for post-quantum cryptography. In: 2014 14th International Symposium on Communications and Information Technologies (ISCIT), pp. 368–372. IEEE (2014)
50. Sidelnikov, V.M.: A public-key cryptosytem based on Reed-Muller codes. Discrete Math. Appl. **4**(3), 191–207 (1994)
51. Stern, J.: A method for finding codewords of small weight. In: Cohen, G., Wolfmann, J. (eds.) Coding Theory 1988. LNCS, vol. 388, pp. 106–113. Springer, Heidelberg (1989). https://doi.org/10.1007/BFb0019850
52. Wieschebrink, C.: Cryptanalysis of the niederreiter public key scheme based on GRS subcodes. In: Sendrier, N. (ed.) PQCrypto 2010. LNCS, vol. 6061, pp. 61–72. Springer, Heidelberg (2010). https://doi.org/10.1007/978-3-642-12929-2_5
53. Ye, M., Abbe, E.: Recursive projection-aggregation decoding of Reed-Muller codes. IEEE Trans. Inf. Theory **66**(8), 4948–4965 (2020)

# Cryptanalysis

# Cryptanalysis of the Rank Preserving Signature

Nicolas Aragon[1]([✉]), Maxime Bros[2], and Philippe Gaborit[2]

[1] Univ. Rennes, CNRS, Inria, IRISA, Rennes, France
nicolas.aragon@irisa.fr
[2] University of Limoges, CNRS, XLIM, UMR 7252, Limoges, France
{maxime.bros,philippe.gaborit}@unilim.fr

**Abstract.** In code-based cryptography, the rank metric usually allows one to have smaller keys and signatures than the traditional Hamming metric. Recently, a new rank-based signature was proposed: Durandal [4]. It relies on the use of proofs of knowledge, namely the Schnorr-Lyubashevsky approach. The authors of the Rank Preserving Signature (RPS) [9] built upon this approach and proposed even smaller keys and signatures than Durandal.

In this paper, we describe attacks against the RPS scheme which break all sets of parameters proposed in [9].

More precisely, our attacks enable us to forge valid signatures in $2^{68}$ and $2^{47}$ operations for sets of parameters whose claimed securities are, respectively, 128 and 192 bits. In addition to this, we give a quantum adaptation of our attack which yields an attack on the last two sets of parameters given in [9].

Overall, our attacks highlight weaknesses of the RPS scheme and give new constraints when designing new parameter sets.

In order to describe the complexities of our attacks, this paper contains theoretical arguments together with experimental results for which we give the source code of our programs.

**Keywords:** Rank-metric based cryptography · Post-quantum cryptography · Signature

## 1 Introduction

*Context.* The interest for rank-metric based cryptography has grown rapidly since the beginning of the NIST post-quantum standardization process in 2017.

While two rank-metric encryption schemes (ROLLO [3] and RQC [1]) were selected for the second round of the standardization process, designing rank-metric signature schemes is a more challenging task. Code based signature schemes, and rank metric schemes in particular, can essentially be split in two categories: the hash-and-sign schemes and the proof of knowledge ones.

For building a hash-and-sign signature scheme, one needs to be able to find a low rank error vector associated to a syndrome. Ranksign [8] was built using this technique together with LRPC (Low Rank Parity Check) codes. However, it has been shown in [6] that it is possible to recover the secret LRPC matrix from the public key.

© Springer Nature Switzerland AG 2021
M. B. Paterson (Ed.): IMACC 2021, LNCS 13129, pp. 45–58, 2021.
https://doi.org/10.1007/978-3-030-92641-0_3

Designing proof of knowledge signature schemes can be done in two ways. The first one consists in turning a zero-knowledge authentication scheme into a signature scheme using the Fiat-Shamir transformation. This approach usually leads to schemes with large signature sizes, since the protocol needs to be repeated multiple times (depending on the soundness of the underlying authentication scheme) in order to reach an arbitrary security level. Instead of using zero-knowledge authentication schemes, one can build upon the work of Lyubashevsky [10], which adapts the Schnorr signature scheme [11] to the Euclidian metric. In this scheme, the public key consists of a random matrix $H$ and a matrix $T = HS$ where $S$ is a secret matrix of low weight syndromes. To prove the knowledge of $S$, the signer outputs a signature consisting of a challenge $c$ and a vector $z = y + cS$. The idea is that $y$ acts as a mask that hides the secret value $cS$.

In the rank metric, this idea gave rise to the Durandal [4] and RPS [9] schemes. While the Durandal scheme reuses the same secret matrix $S$ across all signatures and checks that the techniques used in the decoding algorithm of the LRPC codes do not leak information, the RPS scheme uses ephemeral keys in order to randomize this matrix for each signature.

*Our Contributions.* In this paper, we describe a cryptanalysis of the RPS signature scheme. It is divided in two attacks: one that uses information leakage in the signatures, and one that uses the fact that random vectors have a non-negligible chance to behave like valid signatures for particular parameter values.

The first attack breaks the second set of parameters proposed in [9], i.e. RPS-C2, using $2^{47}$ operations whereas the claimed security is 192 bits, and the second attack breaks RPS-C1 with $2^{68}$ operations for a claimed security of 128 bits.

We give a complexity formula for both of our attacks, as well as experimental results to support them, which give new constraints that can be used to design parameter sets for the RPS scheme.

Then, we show that using a quantum computer yields a quadratic speedup for both of our attacks, this allows us to break the RPS-P1 and RPS-P2 parameter sets.

## 2  Preliminaries

In this section, we recall some definitions on rank metric codes and then present the RPS signature scheme.

### 2.1  Rank Metric

**Definition 1 (Rank metric over $\mathbb{F}_{q^m}^n$).** *Let $x = (x_1, \ldots, x_n) \in \mathbb{F}_{q^m}^n$ and $(\beta_1, \ldots, \beta_m) \in \mathbb{F}_{q^m}^m$ a basis of $\mathbb{F}_{q^m}$ viewed as an $m$-dimensional vector space over $\mathbb{F}_q$. Each coordinate $x_j$ is associated to a vector of $\mathbb{F}_q^m$ in this basis: $x_j = \sum_{i=1}^{m} x_{ij}\beta_i$. The $m \times n$ matrix associated to $x$ is given by $M(v) = (x_{ij})_{\substack{1 \leqslant i \leqslant m \\ 1 \leqslant j \leqslant n}}$.*

*The rank weight $\|x\|$ of $x$ is defined as*

$$\|x\| \overset{def}{=} \operatorname{Rank} M(x).$$

*The associated distance $d(x, y)$ between elements $x$ and $y$ in $\mathbb{F}_{q^m}^n$ is defined by $d(x, y) = \|x - y\|$.*

**Definition 2 ($\mathbb{F}_{q^m}$-linear code).** *An $\mathbb{F}_{q^m}$-linear code $\mathcal{C}$ of dimension $k$ and length $n$ is a subspace of dimension $k$ of $\mathbb{F}_{q^m}^n$ embedded with the rank metric. It is denoted $[n, k]_{q^m}$. Such a code $\mathcal{C}$ can be represented in two equivalent ways:*

- *with a generator matrix $G \in \mathbb{F}_{q^m}^{k \times n}$; each row of $G$ is an element of a basis of $\mathcal{C}$:*

$$\mathcal{C} = \{xG, x \in \mathbb{F}_{q^m}^k\}.$$

- *with a parity-check matrix $H \in \mathbb{F}_{q^m}^{(n-k) \times n}$; each row of $H$ determines a parity-check equation verified by the elements of $\mathcal{C}$:*

$$\mathcal{C} = \{x \in \mathbb{F}_{q^m}^n : Hx^\mathsf{T} = 0\}.$$

*$Hv^\mathsf{T}$ is called the syndrome of $v$ (with respect to $H$).*

*We say that $G$ (respectively $H$) is under systematic form if and only if it is of the form $(I_k | A)$ (respectively $(I_{n-k} | B)$).*

**Definition 3 (Support of a word).** *Let $x = (x_1, \ldots, x_n) \in \mathbb{F}_{q^m}^n$, the support $E$ of $x$, denoted $\operatorname{Supp}(x)$, is the $\mathbb{F}_q$-subspace of $\mathbb{F}_{q^m}$ generated by the coordinates of $x$:*

$$E = \langle x_1, \ldots, x_n \rangle_{\mathbb{F}_q},$$

*note that $\dim E = \|x\|$.*

The RPS scheme uses a particular family of rank metric codes, namely ideal codes, in order to obtain smaller parameters.

Let $P \in \mathbb{F}_q[X]$ a polynomial of degree $n$. We can identify the vector space $\mathbb{F}_{q^m}^n$ with the ring $\mathbb{F}_{q^m}[X]/\langle P \rangle$, where $\langle P \rangle$ denotes the ideal of $\mathbb{F}_{q^m}[X]$ generated by $P$.

$$\Psi : \mathbb{F}_{q^m}^n \simeq \mathbb{F}_{q^m}[X]/\langle P \rangle$$

$$(v_0, \ldots, v_{n-1}) \mapsto \sum_{i=0}^{n-1} v_i X^i$$

For $u, v \in \mathbb{F}_{q^m}^n$, we define their product similarly as in $\mathbb{F}_{q^m}[X]/\langle P \rangle$: $w = uv \in \mathbb{F}_{q^m}^n$ is the only vector such that $\Psi(w) = \Psi(u)\Psi(v)$. From now on, in order to lighten the formulas, we will omit the symbol $\Psi$.

To a vector $\boldsymbol{v} \in \mathbb{F}_{q^m}^n$, one can associate an $n \times n$ square matrix with entries in $\mathbb{F}_{q^m}^n$ corresponding to the product by $\boldsymbol{v}$. Indeed,

$$
\begin{aligned}
\boldsymbol{u} \cdot \boldsymbol{v} &= & & \boldsymbol{u}(X)\boldsymbol{v}(X) \pmod{P} \\
&= & & \sum_{i=0}^{n-1} u_i X^i \boldsymbol{v}(X) \pmod{P} \\
&= & & \sum_{i=0}^{n-1} u_i (X^i \boldsymbol{v}(X) \mod P) \\
&= & (u_0, \ldots, u_{n-1}) & \begin{pmatrix} \boldsymbol{v}(X) \mod P \\ X\boldsymbol{v}(X) \mod P \\ \vdots \\ X^{n-1}\boldsymbol{v}(X) \mod P \end{pmatrix}
\end{aligned}
$$

Such a matrix is called the ideal matrix generated by $\boldsymbol{v}$ and $P$, or simply by $\boldsymbol{v}$ when there is no ambiguity in the choice of $P$.

**Definition 4 (Ideal Matrix).** *Let $P \in \mathbb{F}_q[X]$ be a polynomial of degree $n$ and $\boldsymbol{v} \in \mathbb{F}_{q^m}^n$. The ideal matrix generated by $\boldsymbol{v}$ is the $n \times n$ square matrix denoted $\mathcal{IM}(\boldsymbol{v})$ of the form:*

$$
\mathcal{IM}(\boldsymbol{v}) = \begin{pmatrix} \boldsymbol{v} \\ X\boldsymbol{v} \mod P \\ \vdots \\ X^{n-1}\boldsymbol{v} \mod P \end{pmatrix}
$$

As a consequence, the product of two elements of $\mathbb{F}_{q^m}[X]/\langle P \rangle$ is equivalent to the usual vector-matrix product:

$$
\boldsymbol{u} \cdot \boldsymbol{v} = \boldsymbol{u}\mathcal{IM}(\boldsymbol{v}) = \mathcal{IM}(\boldsymbol{u})^{\mathsf{T}}\boldsymbol{v} = \boldsymbol{v} \cdot \boldsymbol{u}.
$$

**Definition 5 (Ideal codes).** *Let $P(X) \in \mathbb{F}_q[X]$ be a polynomial of degree $n$. An $[ns, nt]_{q^m}$ code $\mathcal{C}$ is an $(s,t)$-ideal code if its generator matrix under systematic form is of the form*

$$
G = \begin{pmatrix} & \mathcal{IM}(\boldsymbol{g}_{1,1}) \ldots \mathcal{IM}(\boldsymbol{g}_{1,s-t}) \\ I_{tn} & \vdots \quad \ddots \quad \vdots \\ & \mathcal{IM}(\boldsymbol{g}_{t,1}) \ldots \mathcal{IM}(\boldsymbol{g}_{t,s-t}) \end{pmatrix}
$$

*where $(\boldsymbol{g}_{i,j})_{\substack{i\in[1..s-t] \\ j\in[1..t]}}$ are vectors of $\mathbb{F}_{q^m}^n$. In this case, we say that $\mathcal{C}$ is generated by the $(\boldsymbol{g}_{i,j})$.*

In the following, we are going to consider only $[2n, n]$ ideal codes, that is to say codes that can be represented by two vectors $\boldsymbol{x}, \boldsymbol{y} \in \mathbb{F}_{q^m}^n$ and admit a generator matrix of the form:

$$G = \left( \mathcal{IM}(x) \; \mathcal{IM}(y) \right).$$

## 2.2  Some Useful Propositions

In this paper, we will need several propositions about vector spaces of $\mathbb{F}_{q^m}$ or vector spaces in general, there are given in this section.

**Proposition 1 (Dimension of random vectors).** *Let $X$ be a vector space of $\mathbb{F}_{q^m}$ of dimension $w_r$ and let $x$ be a random vector in $X^n$.*
*The probability that $\|x\| = w_r - i$ can be approximated by:*

$$q^{-i(max(n,w_r) - min(n,w_r) + i)}$$

This proposition comes from [5], for a proof of it, reader may refer to [5].

**Lemma 1 (Intersection of 2 vector spaces).** *Let $A$ and $B$ be two vector spaces of $\mathbb{F}_{q^m}$, their dimensions fulfill the following inequality:*

$$\dim(A \cap B) \geq \dim(A) + \dim(B) - m.$$

*Proof.* Straightforward using the classic equality $\dim(A \cap B) = \dim(A) + \dim(B) - \dim(A + B)$ and the fact that $A + B$ has a dimension bounded from above by $m$, i.e. the dimension of the whole space $\mathbb{F}_{q^m}$. $\qquad\square$

Lemma 1 can easily be generalized to the intersection of 3 subspaces of $\mathbb{F}_{q^m}$. The proof is straightforward and only requires to use lemma 1.

**Lemma 2 (Intersection of 3 vector spaces).** *Let $A$, $B$, and $C$, be 3 vector spaces of $\mathbb{F}_{q^m}$, their dimensions fulfill the following inequality:*

$$\dim(A \cap B \cap C) \geq \dim(A) + \dim(B) + \dim(C) - 2m.$$

**Lemma 3 (Random vector in vector space).** *Let $X \subset Y$ be two vector spaces of $\mathbb{F}_{q^m}$ of dimensions $x$ and $y$, respectively. If one picks at random a vector $v \in Y$, it will belongs to $X$ with probability $q^{x-y}$.*

*Proof.* Straightforward by computing the ratio of favorable vectors over all possible vectors. $\qquad\square$

**Proposition 2.** *Let $X \subset Y$ be two vector spaces of $\mathbb{F}_{q^m}$ of dimensions $x$ and $y$, respectively. If one picks at random $x$ vectors $v_1, \ldots, v_x$ in $Y$, $\{v_1, \ldots, v_x\}$ will be a basis of $X$ with probability*

$$\prod_{j=0}^{x-1} q^{-y}(q^x - q^j).$$

*Proof.* When one picks $x$ vectors in the vector space $Y$, the probability that these vectors form a basis of a subvector space of dimension $x$, i.e. that they are linearly independent, is

$$\prod_{j=0}^{x-1} (1 - q^{j-y}) = \prod_{j=0}^{x-1} q^{-y}(q^y - q^j). \tag{1}$$

There are

$$\begin{bmatrix} y \\ x \end{bmatrix}_q := \prod_{j=0}^{x-1} \frac{q^y - q^j}{q^x - q^j}$$

distinct vector spaces of dimension $x$ in the vector space $Y$. Thus, each time one picks a random vector space in $Y$, it will be $X$ with probability

$$\prod_{j=0}^{x-1} \frac{q^x - q^j}{q^y - q^j}. \tag{2}$$

One ends the proof by multiplying the two probabilities given by (1) and (2). □

## 2.3   The RPS Scheme

We now present the RPS scheme from [9]. Let us denote the set of vectors of length $n$ and weight $w$ over $\mathbb{F}_{q^m}$ by $\mathcal{S}_n^w$.

*Keygen:*

- Sample $\boldsymbol{x} \xleftarrow{\$} \mathcal{S}_k^{r_x}$ and $\boldsymbol{y} \xleftarrow{\$} \mathcal{S}_k^{r_y}$.
- Let $\boldsymbol{h} = \boldsymbol{x}^{-1}\boldsymbol{y}$.
- Output $(pk = \boldsymbol{h}, sk = (\boldsymbol{x}, \boldsymbol{y}))$.

Sign($\mu$, pk, sk): for $1 \leqslant i \leqslant l$, sample:

- $\boldsymbol{e}_i \xleftarrow{\$} \mathcal{S}_k^{r_e}$
- $\boldsymbol{f}_i \xleftarrow{\$} \mathcal{S}_k^{r_f}$
- $\boldsymbol{u}_i \xleftarrow{\$} \mathcal{S}_k^{r_u}$
- $\boldsymbol{v}_i \xleftarrow{\$} \mathcal{S}_k^{r_v}$

Let $\mathcal{H}$ be a hash function which outputs values in $\mathcal{S}_k^1$ and $H$ be the parity-check matrix generated by $(\boldsymbol{h}, \boldsymbol{h}^{-1})$. Compute:

- $\boldsymbol{s}_i = (\boldsymbol{e}_i\boldsymbol{x}, \boldsymbol{f}_i\boldsymbol{y})H^\mathsf{T}$
- $\boldsymbol{w}_i = (\boldsymbol{u}_i\boldsymbol{x}, \boldsymbol{v}_i\boldsymbol{y})H^\mathsf{T}$
- $\boldsymbol{c}_i = \mathcal{H}(\{\boldsymbol{w}_i, \boldsymbol{s}_i\}, \mu, pk)$
- $\boldsymbol{a}_i = (\boldsymbol{u}_i + \boldsymbol{c}_i\boldsymbol{e}_i)\boldsymbol{x}$
- $\boldsymbol{b}_i = (\boldsymbol{v}_i + \boldsymbol{c}_i\boldsymbol{f}_i)\boldsymbol{y}$

Then output $\sigma = (\{\boldsymbol{c}_i, \boldsymbol{a}_i, \boldsymbol{b}_i, \boldsymbol{s}_i\}_{1 \leqslant i \leqslant l})$.

Verify($\sigma$, $\mu$, pk): for $1 \leqslant i \leqslant l$, we check the rank of the following values:

- $\|a_i\| = (r_u + r_e)r_x$
- $\|a_i h\| = (r_u + r_e)r_y$
- $\|b_i\| = (r_v + r_f)r_y$
- $\|b_i h\| = (r_v + r_f)r_x$
- $\|s_i\| = r_e r_y + r_f r_x$
- $\|s_i h\| \geqslant min(m - 1, k)$
- $\|s_i h^{-1}\| \geqslant min(m - 1, k)$

If one of them is not valid, reject the signature. Otherwise, compute $w_i$ as $(a_i, b_i)H^\top - c_i s_i$. Accept the signature if $c_i = \mathcal{H}(\{w_i, s_i\}, \mu, pk)$ for $1 \leqslant i \leqslant l$.

In [9], the authors proposed the following parameter sets, where $r_x = r_y$, $r_e = r_v$ and $r_u = r_f$:

| Parameter set | $(l, q, m, k, r_x, r_e, r_u)$ | Security |
|---|---|---|
| RPS-C1 | (3, 2, 61, 59, 5, 6, 5) | 128 (classical) |
| RPS-C2 | (4, 2, 67, 59, 5, 6, 5) | 192 (classical) |
| RPS-P1 | (3, 2, 89, 83, 7, 6, 5) | 128 (post-quantum) |
| RPS-P2 | (3, 2, 89, 107, 11, 4, 3) | 192 (post-quantum) |

## 3  Our Attacks

### 3.1  Information Leakage Attack

In this section, we present our first attack, which shows that one can exploit information leakage from the signatures when $m$ is high enough in order to recover the ephemeral keys $e_i x, u_i x, v_i y$ and $f_i y$.

In what follows, let us assume that $q = 2$. With a signature $\sigma = (\{c_i, a_i, b_i, s_i\}_{1 \leqslant i \leqslant l})$ and using the public key $h$, one can easily compute the following vectors:

$$a_i h = u_i y + c_i e_i y,$$

$$w_i = u_i y + v_i x,$$

$$w_i + b_i h^{-1} = u_i y + c_i f_i x.$$

The weights of those vectors are respectively bounded from above by the following values: $(r_u + r_e)r_y$, $r_u r_y + r_v r_x$, $r_u r_y + r_f r_x$; however, in practice, with high probability, those inequalities are equalities. Moreover, those 3 vectors have length $k$ and their weight are bounded from above by values that are always strictly smaller than $k$ for the given sets of parameters. Thus, using Proposition 1, we can consider that, with high probability:

$$\|a_i h\| = (r_u + r_e)r_y, \quad \|w_i\| = r_u r_y + r_v r_x, \quad \|w_i + b_i h^{-1}\| = r_u r_y + r_f r_x.$$

Thus, one can easily compute the intersection of the supports of those vectors and using Lemma 2, one gets the following bound:

$$\dim\left(\mathrm{Supp}(a_i h) \cap \mathrm{Supp}(w_i) \cap \mathrm{Supp}(w_i + b_i h^{-1})\right) \geq 2(r_x(r_e + 2r_u) - m). \tag{3}$$

Note that, for the sake of clarity, we considered, like the authors of [9] that $r_x = r_y$, $r_v = r_e$, and $r_f = r_u$. One can get an equality from (3) by replacing $m$ by

$$\dim(\mathrm{Supp}(a_i h) + \mathrm{Supp}(w_i) + \mathrm{Supp}(w_i + b_i h^{-1}))$$

which is exactly $m$ with high probability.

So far, one has computed an intersection of 3 vector spaces, denoted $Z$ in the following, whose dimension is $2(r_x(r_e + 2r_u) - m)$ and which contains $\mathrm{Supp}(u_i y)$ of dimension $r_u r_y = r_u r_x$.

*Finding $u_i y_i$.* We then use the knowledge of $Z$ to recover the ephemeral key $u_i y_i$. We use the following procedure:

– Sample a random subspace $T$ of $Z$ of dimension $r_u r_x$.
– Let $A = Supp(a_i h)$. Find a vector space $T'$ such that $A = T + T'$ where $T$ and $T'$ are in direct sum.
– Write $a_i h$ as $t + t'$ where $t \in T^k$ and $t' \in T'^k$. $t$ is a candidate for $u_i y_i$.
– If $\|t h^{-1}\| = \|t\|$, then with overwhelming probability $t = u_i y_i$. Otherwise, start over by sampling an other vector space $T$.

*Finishing the Attack.* Once we recover $u_i y_i$ for $1 \leqslant i \leqslant l$, we can recover the other ephemeral keys:

– $u_i x = h^{-1} u_i y_i$
– $v_i y = h(w_i - u_i y)$
– $e_i x = c_i^{-1}(a_i - u_i x)$
– $f_i y = c_i^{-1}(b_i - v_i y)$

Using these keys and a valid signature $\sigma = (\{c_i, a_i, b_i, s_i\}_{1 \leqslant i \leqslant l})$ on a message $\mu$, one can forge a valid signature $\sigma' = (\{c_i', a_i', b_i', s_i'\}_{1 \leqslant i \leqslant l})$ for a message $\mu'$ using the following procedure for $1 \leqslant i \leqslant l$:

– Compute $w_i = (a_i, b_i)H^{\mathsf{T}} - c_i s_i$
– Set $s_i' = s_i$ and $w_i' = w_i$
– Compute $c_i' = \mathcal{H}(\{w_i, s_i\}, \mu, pk)$

- Set $a'_i = u_i x + c'_i e_i x$
- Set $b'_i = v_i y + c'_i f_i y$

Finally, we derive the complexity of this attack:

**Theorem 1.** *The information leakage attack forges a valid signature using:*

$$l \times m \times k \times min(m, k) \times \prod_{j=0}^{r_u r_x - 1} q^z (q^{r_u r_x} - q^j)$$

*operations over $\mathbb{F}_q$, where $z$ is dimension of the recovered vector space $Z$.*

*Proof.* Using proposition 2, we know that the probability of finding the correct support of $u_i y$ is $\prod_{j=0}^{r_u r_x - 1} q^{-z} (q^{r_u r_x} - q^j)$.

The most costly step in verifying that the sampled support $T$ is the correct one is checking the rank of $th^{-1}$, which can be done using a Gaussian elimination in $m \times k \times min(m, k)$ operations over $\mathbb{F}_q$.

This process needs to be repeated $l$ times to forge a complete signature, hence the result.  □

For sets of parameters given in [9], we obtain the following complexities:

| Parameter set | Claimed security | Success probability | Complexity |
|---|---|---|---|
| RPS-C1 | 128 | $2^{-327}$ | $2^{347}$ |
| RPS-C2 | 192 | $2^{-27}$ | $2^{47}$ |

## 3.2   Random Low Rank Vectors Attack

We now describe a procedure that can be used to forge valid signatures for the RPS scheme when the parameters $m$ and $k$ are too close to the weight of the vectors $a_i$ and $b_i$.

On input $(pk, \mu)$, our goal is to find a signature $\sigma$ such that Verify($\sigma$, $\mu$, pk) accepts it. For each $1 \leqslant i \leqslant l$, we start by computing $s_i$, $w_i$ and $c_i$ as follows:

- Sample $s_i$ as a random vector of weight $r_e r_y + r_f r_x$
- Sample $w_i$ as a random vector of weight $r_u r_y + r_v r_x$
- Let $c_i = \mathcal{H}(\{w_i, s_i\}, \mu, pk)$

Since $s_i$ is chosen randomly, the following conditions are fulfilled:

- $\|s_i h\| \geqslant min(m - 1, k)$
- $\|s_i h^{-1}\| \geqslant min(m - 1, k)$

Now we need to find $a_i$ and $b_i$ such that:

$$(a_i, b_i)H^\intercal - c_i s_i = w_i$$
$$(a_i, b_i)H^\intercal = w_i + c_i s_i$$
$$a_i h + b_i h^{-1} = w_i + c_i s_i$$

Let $z = w_i + c_i s_i$. We start by splitting $z$ into a sum of two vectors $z_1$ and $z_2$ such that $\|z_1\| = (r_u + r_e)r_y$ and $\|z_2\| = (r_v + r_f)r_x$. In order to do so, one needs to write the vector $z$ as matrix $Z$ in $\mathbb{F}_{q^m}^{m \times k}$ using a basis of $\mathbb{F}_{q^m}$ seen as an $\mathbb{F}_q$-vector space. Then, one picks 2 matrices $Z_1$ and $Z_2$ at random in $\mathbb{F}_{q^m}^{m \times k}$ and solves the following linear system:

$$V \times (Z_1 | Z_2)^\intercal = Z$$

where $V$ is a $m \times m^2$ matrix containing unknowns.

Since $\|z_1\|$ and $\|z_2\|$ have the same order of magnitude as $k$, this system has far more unknowns than equations, thus, it has a lot of solutions. Those solution are of the form $V_0 + K$ where $K$ is a matrix containing random linear combinations of vectors belonging to the left kernel of $(Z_1 | Z_2)^\intercal$. Each one of these solutions yields different matrices $Z_1'$ and $Z_2'$ which can easily be turned into vectors $z_1$ and $z_2$ in $\mathbb{F}_{q^m}^k$. The two vectors $z_1$ and $z_2$ will have correct weights (respectively $(r_u + r_e)r_y$ and $(r_v + r_f)r_x$) with a probability bounded from above by $0.28^2 \approx 8\%$. This is due to the fact that one is looking for a solution matrix $V_0 + K$ whose two first blocks of size $m \times m$ are non-singular. This happens with probability asymptotically close to 1 when $q$ grows but bounded from above by $0.28$ when $q = 2$.

In order to verify this heuristic, we computed 10.000 solutions for a system with parameters $q = 2, m = 100, k = 90, r_1 = r_2 = 80$, and it appeared that $8.1\%$ of the associated $z_1$ and $z_2$ had the expected weights.

The cost of computing this decomposition is basically the one of performing linear algebra (solving a system, computing rank, multiplying two matrices, ...) on matrices of size $m^2 \times k$, $m \times m$ and $m \times k$.

Most importantly, the number of different decompositions of the form $z = z_1 + z_2$ (with correct weights) that can be found is huge, roughly

$$\left[ \begin{matrix} m \\ (r_u + r_e)r_y \end{matrix} \right]_q \times \left[ \begin{matrix} m \\ (r_v + r_f)r_x \end{matrix} \right]_q \times 0.28^2 \times 2^{m(2m-k)}. \tag{4}$$

The two first terms concern the choice of the two supports of $z_1$ and $z_2$, the third one the aforementioned probability and the last one the number of possible choices for the matrix $K$. This is only a very rough estimation since it does not consider the probability that the 2 vector spaces have a non trivial intersection nor the probability that the rank of $(Z_1 | Z_2)^\intercal$ is maximal; however, it gives an heuristic to grasp the order of magnitude of the number of distinct solutions.

Then we compute $a_i = z_1 h^{-1}$ and $b_i = z_2 h$. By construction, the following conditions are verified:

- $(\boldsymbol{a}_i, \boldsymbol{b}_i) H^\intercal - c_i \boldsymbol{s}_i = \boldsymbol{w}_i$
- $\|\boldsymbol{a}_i \boldsymbol{h}\| = (r_u + r_e) r_y$
- $\|\boldsymbol{b}_i \boldsymbol{h}\| = (r_v + r_f) r_x$

Applying Proposition 1 with $X = \mathbb{F}_{q^m}$ and $\boldsymbol{a}_i \in \mathbb{F}_{q^m}^k$ gives the following result:

**Proposition 3.** *The probability that this procedure outputs $\boldsymbol{a}_i$ and $\boldsymbol{b}_i$ such that $\|\boldsymbol{a}_i\| = (r_u + r_e) r_y$ and $\|\boldsymbol{b}_i\| = (r_v + r_f) r_x$ is:*

$$q^{-i_1(max(m,k) - min(m,k) + i_1)} \times q^{-i_2(max(m,k) - min(m,k) + i_2)}$$

*where $i_1 = min(m,k) - (r_u + r_e) r_x$ and $i_2 = min(m,k) - (r_v + r_f) r_y$.*

Finally, we derive the complexity of this attack:

**Theorem 2.** *The random low rank vectors attack forges a valid signature using:*

$$l \times 2(m \times k \times min(m,k)) \times \frac{1}{p}$$

*operations over $\mathbb{F}_q$, where $p$ is the probability of success given in Proposition 3.*

*Proof.* Checking the rank of $\boldsymbol{a}_i$ and $\boldsymbol{b}_i$ is done by performing two Gaussian eliminations on $m \times k$ matrices over $\mathbb{F}_q$, and each Gaussian elimination costs $m \times k \times min(m,k)$ operations over $\mathbb{F}_q$.

This process needs to be repeated $\frac{1}{p}$ times on average in order to find a valid pair of vectors.

Finally, this process needs to be repeated for $l$ times, hence the result.  □

For sets of parameters given in [9], we obtain the following complexities:

| Parameter set | Claimed security | Sucess probability | Attack complexity |
|---|---|---|---|
| RPS-C1 | 128 | $2^{-48}$ | $2^{68}$ |
| RPS-C2 | 192 | $2^{-96}$ | $2^{117}$ |

## 4  Implementation Results

We performed simulations for both of our attacks in order to support our theoretical claims. Our code is available at github.com/nicolas-aragon/cryptanalysis-RPS, it is based on the RBC (Rank Based Cryptography) library [2].

*Information Leakage Attack.* We realized an implementation of the RPS scheme, as well as an implementation of the recovery of the vector space $Z$. Our experiments show that $Z$ has the expected dimension most of the time, and when it does not, one can simply start the procedure over with another signature.

**Table 1.** Implementation results for the random low rank vectors attack.

| $m$ | $k$ | $\|z_1\|$ | $P(\|z_1\| = \|z_1 h^{-1}\|)$ from Proposition 1 | Observed $P(\|z_1\| = \|z_1 h^{-1}\|)$ |
|---|---|---|---|---|
| 61 | 59 | 57 | $2^{-8}$ | $2^{-6.6}$ |
| 61 | 59 | 55 | $2^{-24}$ | $2^{-22.3}$ |

**Table 2.** Timings (in seconds) for the low rank vectors attack.

| $m$ | $k$ | $\|z_1\|$ | Time to find a correct $z_1$ | Time to perform the attack |
|---|---|---|---|---|
| 61 | 59 | 57 | 0.2 | 4 |
| 61 | 59 | 55 | 474 | Not performed |

*Random Low Rank Vectors Attack.* We implemented a code that samples vectors $z_1$ and $z_2$ randomly, and checks the rank of $z_1 h^{-1}$ and $z_2 h$ in order to verify the probabilities from Propositions 1 and 3. We used $m = 61, k = 59$ and $\|z_i\| = 55$ or 57, results are reported in Table 1.

We measured the time needed to find $z_1$ such that $\|z_1\| = \|z_1 h^{-1}\|$ as well as the time needed to perform the attack (i.e. finding $z_1$ and $z_2$ both with the right property). These results are reported in Table 2. We did not finish the actual attack with $m = 61, k = 59, \|z_i\| = 55$.

These results show that for $q = 2$, the probability that $\|z_1 h^{-1}\|$ is higher than stated in Proposition 1, which is favorable for the attacker. Reported timings were performed using a single core, but the nature of both our attacks make them easily parallelizable.

## 5   Quantum Speedup

In [7], the authors described how solving the rank syndrome decoding problem using a quantum computer gives a quadratic speed-up when considering combinatorial algorithms. We will use similar techniques to show that we obtain a quadratic speedup for both attacks described in Sect. 3.

**Theorem 3.** *[7], Theorem 1.*

*Let $f$ be a Boolean function $f : \{0,1\}^b \to \{0,1\}$ that is computable by a NAND circuit of size $S$. Let $p$ be the proportion of roots of the Boolean function*

$$p \overset{def}{=} \frac{\#\{x \in \{0,1\}^b : f(x) = 0\}}{2^b}$$

*Then there is a quantum algorithm based on iterating a quantum circuit $\mathcal{O}\left(\frac{1}{\sqrt{p}}\right)$ many times that outputs with probability at least $\frac{1}{2}$ one of the roots of the Boolean function. The size of this circuit is $\mathcal{O}(S)$.*

*Information Leakage Attack.* For this attack, we want to speed up the process of finding the correct vector space $Supp(\boldsymbol{u}_i\boldsymbol{y})$ from the vector space leaked from the signatures. From Proposition 2 we have:

$$p = \prod_{j=0}^{x-1} q^{-y}(q^x - q^j)$$

As explained in Sect. 3.1, checking whether the vector space is the right one can be done by solving a linear system with $r_u r_y$ unknowns, performing a multiplication in $\mathbb{F}_{q^m}[X]/P$, and checking the rank of the resulting vector, which is the most costly operation. Hence, there exists a NAND classical circuit that performs this verification using $\mathcal{O}\left(max(m,k)^3\right)$ gates.

*Random Low Rank Vectors Attack.* For this attack, we want to speed up the search of vectors $\boldsymbol{a}_i = \boldsymbol{z}_1\boldsymbol{h}^{-1}$ and $\boldsymbol{b}_i = \boldsymbol{z}_2\boldsymbol{h}$ with correct weights. Proposition 3 gives the value for $p$:

$$p = q^{-i_1(max(m,k)-min(m,k)+i_1)} \times q^{-i_2(max(m,k)-min(m,k)+i_2)}$$

where $i_1 = min(m,k) - (r_u + r_e)r_x$ and $i_2 = min(m,k) - (r_v + r_f)r_y$.

As for the previous attack, checking whether the two resulting vectors have the desired weight can be performed by a NAND classical circuit using $\mathcal{O}\left(max(m,k)^3\right)$ gates.

*Resulting Complexities.* These results show that, for both of our attacks, the search for, respectively, the correct vector space and vectors with right weight, can be performed in $\mathcal{O}\left(\frac{1}{\sqrt{p}}\right)$ iterations of the circuit when using a quantum computer. The cost of evaluating this circuit remains unchanged. This yields the following complexities for the RPS parameters targetting quantum security, using the random low rank vectors attack against RPS-P1 and the information leakage attack against RPS-P2:

| Parameter set | Claimed security | Quantum attack complexity |
| --- | --- | --- |
| RPS-P1 | 128 | $2^{94}$ |
| RPS-P2 | 192 | $2^{170}$ |

# 6    Conclusion

In this paper, we presented two attacks against the RPS signature scheme: the information leakage attack, effective when $m$ is high enough, and the random low rank vectors attack, effective when both $m$ and $k$ are low enough. Using these two attacks, we broke the RPS-C1 and RPS-C2 parameter sets. We demonstrated the effectiveness of both attacks with a complexity analysis and implementation results. Finally, we showed that our attacks benefit from a quantum speedup, which allows us to break the RPS-P1 and RPS-P2 parameter sets, targetting quantum security.

Theses results indicate that, when designing parameters for the RPS scheme, $m$ must be small enough to avoid information leakage, and $k$ must be significantly larger in order to avoid forgery using random vectors of low rank.

# References

1. Melchor, C.A., et al.: Rank quasi cyclic (RQC). Second Round submission to the NIST post-quantum cryptography call, April 2020
2. Aragon, N., et al.: The rank based cryptography library. In: International Workshop on Code-Based Cryptography (2021)
3. Aragon, N., et al.: ROLLO (merger of Rank-Ouroboros, LAKE and LOCKER). Second round submission to the NIST post-quantum cryptography call, March 2019
4. Aragon, N., Blazy, O., Gaborit, P., Hauteville, A., Zémor, G.: Durandal: a rank metric based signature scheme. In: Ishai, Y., Rijmen, V. (eds.) EUROCRYPT 2019. LNCS, vol. 11478, pp. 728–758. Springer, Cham (2019). https://doi.org/10.1007/978-3-030-17659-4_25
5. Aragon, N., Gaborit, P., Hauteville, A., Ruatta, O., Zémor, G.: Low rank parity check codes: New decoding algorithms and applications to cryptography. CoRR, abs/1904.00357 (2019)
6. Debris-Alazard, T., Tillich, J.-P.: Two attacks on rank metric code-based schemes: RankSign and an IBE Scheme. In: Peyrin, T., Galbraith, S. (eds.) ASIACRYPT 2018. LNCS, vol. 11272, pp. 62–92. Springer, Cham (2018). https://doi.org/10.1007/978-3-030-03326-2_3
7. Gaborit, P., Hauteville, A., Tillich, J.P.: Ranksynd a PRNG based on rank metric. In: Post-Quantum Cryptography 2016, pp. 18–28. Fukuoka, Japan, February 2016
8. Gaborit, P., Ruatta, O., Schrek, J., Zémor, G.: RankSign: an efficient signature algorithm based on the Rank Metric. In: Mosca, M. (ed.) PQCrypto 2014. LNCS, vol. 8772, pp. 88–107. Springer, Cham (2014). https://doi.org/10.1007/978-3-319-11659-4_6
9. Lau, T.S.C., Tan, C.H.: Rank preserving code-based signature. In: 2020 IEEE International Symposium on Information Theory (ISIT), pp. 846–851. IEEE (2020)
10. Lyubashevsky, V.: Fiat-Shamir with aborts: applications to lattice and factoring-based signatures. In: Matsui, M. (ed.) ASIACRYPT 2009. LNCS, vol. 5912, pp. 598–616. Springer, Heidelberg (2009). https://doi.org/10.1007/978-3-642-10366-7_35
11. Schnorr, C.P.: Efficient signature generation by smart cards. J. Cryptol. 4(3), 161–174 (1991). https://doi.org/10.1007/BF00196725

# Attacks on a Privacy-Preserving Publish-Subscribe System and a Ride-Hailing Service

Srinivas Vivek$^{(\boxtimes)}$

IIIT Bangalore, Bangalore, India
`srinivas.vivek@iiitb.ac.in`

**Abstract.** A privacy-preserving Context-Aware Publish-Subscribe System (CA-PSS) enables an intermediary (broker) to match the content from a publisher and the subscription by a subscriber based on the current context while preserving confidentiality of the subscriptions and notifications. While a privacy-preserving Ride-Hailing Service (RHS) enables an intermediary (service provider) to match a ride request with a taxi driver in a privacy-friendly manner. In this work, we attack a privacy-preserving CA-PSS proposed by Nabeel et al. (2013), where we show that any entity in the system including the broker can learn the confidential subscriptions of the subscribers. We also attack a privacy-preserving RHS called lpRide proposed by Yu et al. (2019), where we show that any rider/driver can efficiently recover the secret keys of all other riders and drivers. Also, we show that any rider/driver will be able to learn the location of any rider. The attacks are based on our cryptanalysis of the modified Paillier cryptosystem proposed by Nabeel et al. that forms a building block for both the above protocols.

**Keywords:** Privacy · Publish-subscribe system · Ride-hailing service · Homomorphic encryption · Modified Paillier cryptosystem · lpRide

## 1 Introduction

Publish-Subscribe systems (also written as pub/sub systems) are a well-known paradigm to disseminate information among multiple parties in a distributed and asynchronous manner. Subscribers subscribe for content from publishers, who create content and push notifications to the intermediaries' network (aka. brokers). Brokers route the content to subscribers based on their subscription. A Context-Aware Publish-Subscribe System (CA-PSS) extends a pub/sub system by taking into account the subscriber context. For instance, the context could be the location of a subscriber in a traffic information service, and the content from a publisher could correspond to the traffic situation in the neighbourhood of the subscriber. Hence, the context of a subscriber could change frequently over time. It is important to protect the confidentially of the context, subscription and notification. The goal of a Privacy-Preserving CA-PSS (PP-CA-PSS) is

© Springer Nature Switzerland AG 2021
M. B. Paterson (Ed.): IMACC 2021, LNCS 13129, pp. 59–71, 2021.
https://doi.org/10.1007/978-3-030-92641-0_4

to protect the above confidential information. The scheme from Nabeel et al. [NABB13a] is one of the early proposals of a privacy-preserving CA-PSS. There have many works on this topic and we refer to [Mun18, CBDA+] and references therein for more details.

On the other hand, a Ride-Hailing Service (RHS) too provides location-based services. RHSs have become increasingly popular in recent years. Uber, Ola, Lyft, Didi, Grab, etc. are some popular RHSs. With these services also comes the risk of misuse of personal data. The Ride matching Service Providers (RSPs) collect personal information regarding the riders and drivers along with their ride statistics. There have been many instances of violation of individual privacy of the users using these RHSs [Nor20]. A Privacy-Preserving RHS (PP-RHS) aims to provide privacy guarantees to the users of the RHS, namely, riders and drivers. Recent years have witnessed many proposals of PP-RHS [PDJ+17, PDE+17, KFZC18, BLM+19, HNW+18, LJFX19, YSJ+19, WZL+18, YJZ+19]. Recently, the ORide RHS's [PDE+17] security was revisited in [KMV21].

The focus of this work is on the PP-CA-PSS from [NABB13a] and the lpRride PP-RHS proposed by Yu et al. [YSJ+19]. These two seemingly disparate protocols share the following common features: a) both offer or potentially can offer location-based services, and b) both the protocols are based on the modified Paillier cryptosystem that was proposed in [NABB13a]. The modified Paillier cryptosystem (yet another variant of the Paillier cryptosystem [Pai99]) is an additively homomorphic (digital signature-like) cryptosystem and both the protocols use this cryptosystem to blind the subscriptions and notifications (resp. locations of riders and taxis) but still can perform subscription-notification matching (resp. ride-matching) on the blinded data using the additive homomorphism property.

## 1.1    Our Contribution

In this work, we analyse the security of the PP-CA-PSS from [NABB13a] and the lpRide protocol. For the PP-CA-PSS we demonstrate an attack where any entity in the system including the broker can fully learn the confidential subscriptions of the subscribers. This invalidates the claim in [NABB13a] that subscriptions remain confidential. We would like to note that we do not target notifications from publishers or the content. Yet, subscriptions can leak confidential information such as locations of subscribers.

On the lpRide protocol we exhibit a key recovery attack by any rider or driver that can efficiently recover the secret keys of all other riders and drivers. Also, we show that any rider or driver will be able to learn the location of any rider. We were unable to recover drivers' locations as they are blinded by random values.

All our adversaries are honest-but-curious. The basis of our attack is our cryptanalysis of the modified Paillier cryptosystem mentioned above. In particular, we show that anyone will be able to forge the "signatures" and that these signatures are deterministic. Hence, this result is of independent interest to the security of protocols that are based on the modified Paillier cryptosystem. It is somewhat surprising that a simple attack on this cryptosystem went unnoticed despite many follow-up works of [NABB13a].

In Sect. 2, we recall and then cryptanalyse the modified Paillier cryptosystem. In Sect. 3, we briefly recall the PP-CA-PSS, and then describe our attack. In Sect. 4, we briefly recall the lpRide protocol, and then describe our attack. Section 5 concludes the paper.

## 2   Cryptanalysis of Modified Paillier Cryptosystem

### 2.1   Recall of the Modified Paillier Cryptosystem

As mentioned earlier, the modified Paillier cryptosystem was proposed in the article [NABB13a]. A preliminary use of this cryptosystem was already made in [NSB12]. As the name suggests, this cryptosystem is a variant of the Paillier encryption scheme [Pai99]. It consists of the following three algorithms:

- **Key generation**: choose two distinct large primes $p$ and $q$. Compute $N = p \cdot q$ and $\lambda = \text{lcm}(p - 1, q - 1)$, the Carmichael function of $N$. Randomly sample a base $g_p \xleftarrow{\$} \mathbb{Z}^*_{N^2}$, such that the order of $g_p$ is a multiple of $N$. The latter condition can be ensured by checking the condition

$$\gcd(L(g_p^\lambda \pmod{N^2})), \ N) = 1,$$

where

$$L(x) = \frac{x - 1}{N}, \tag{1}$$

for

$$x \in \{y \mid y \in \mathbb{Z}_{\geq 0}, \ y < N^2, \ y \equiv 1 \pmod{N}\}.$$

Compute

$$\mu = \left(L(g_p^\lambda \pmod{N^2}))\right)^{-1} \pmod{N}. \tag{2}$$

The public "decryption" key is

$$PK' = (N, g_p, \mu),$$

and the secret "encryption" key is

$$SK' = \lambda.$$

- **Encryption.** $E'(m, r, SK')$: let the plaintext $m \in \mathbb{Z}_N$. Sample a random value $r \xleftarrow{\$} \mathbb{Z}^*_N$. Compute the "ciphertext"

$$c = g_p^{m\lambda} r^{N\lambda} \pmod{N^2}. \tag{3}$$

When the randomness and the secret key is implicit from the context, we simply denote the encryption of a message $m$ as $E'(m)$.

– **Decryption.** $D'(c, PK')$: compute the plaintext

$$m = L(c \pmod{N^2}) \cdot \mu \pmod{N}. \tag{4}$$

The scheme described above resembles a digital signature scheme more than an encryption scheme, but we will follow the terminology from the previous works. Note that in the original Paillier scheme [Pai99], the public key is $(N, g_p)$ and the secret key is $(\lambda, \mu)$. Hence, in the modified scheme described above $\mu$ is made a public parameter in order to make the decryption algorithm a) to be publicly computable (that is, make it like the verification algorithm of a digital signature scheme), and b) more efficient. The rationale to make $\mu$ public is the claim in [NABB13a] that it is hard to compute the discrete logarithm of $\mu$ w.r.t. base $g_p$ to obtain $\lambda$. Also, note that the modified scheme is also additively homomorphic, i.e.,

$$E'(m_1 + m_2, r_1 r_2) = E'(m_1, r_1) \cdot E'(m_2, r_2),$$

and

$$E'^{m_2}(m_1, r_1) = E'(m_1 m_2, r_1^{m_2}).$$

## 2.2 Cryptanalysis

We now show that the modified Paillier scheme is insecure. Namely, an adversary having access only to the public key can produce encryptions of messages, contrary to the claims in [YSJ+19, NABB13a] that only those who possess the secret key would be able to encrypt. Moreover, we also show that the ciphertexts are deterministic.

**Lemma 1.** *The ciphertexts of the modified Paillier cryptosystem (see (3)) are deterministic.*

*Proof.* Since $c = g_p^{m\lambda} r^{N\lambda} \pmod{N^2}$, by the properties of the Carmichael function $\lambda$, we have $r^{N\lambda} \equiv 1 \pmod{N^2}$ (see for e.g., [Pai99, pp. 2]). Hence $c = \left(g_p^{\lambda}\right)^m \pmod{N^2}$ and is independent of $r$.    □

Next, we show how to efficiently compute $g_p^{\lambda} \pmod{N^2}$ from the public key.

**Lemma 2.** $g_p^{\lambda} \pmod{N^2} = N \cdot (\mu^{-1} \pmod{N}) + 1$.

*Proof.* From (2),

$$L(g_p^{\lambda} \pmod{N^2}) \equiv \mu^{-1} \pmod{N}.$$

Since $1 \leq L(g_p^{\lambda} \pmod{N^2}) < N$ , the lemma follows from the definition of the $L$ function in (1).    □

From Lemmas 1 and 2 and their proofs, we have

**Corollary 1.** $E'(m) = (N \cdot (\mu^{-1} \pmod N)) + 1)^m \pmod{N^2}$.

Hence, anyone with access to the public key can easily produce the (unique) ciphertext corresponding to a given message without knowing the secret key (or equivalently, will be able to forge the signature). Note that we were able to compute $g_p^\lambda \pmod{N^2}$ without explicitly computing $\lambda$. This constitutes a complete break of the modified Paillier cryptosystem.

# 3 Attack on the PP-CA-PSS from [NABB13a]

## 3.1 Recall of the Scheme

For completeness, we briefly recall the relevant steps of the privacy-preserving context-aware publish-subscribe system from [NABB13a] that are necessary to understand our attack. For other details, we refer the reader to [NABB13a] and its full version [NABB13b]. This protocol consists of the following types of entities:

- **Context manager**: it is a trusted third party (TTP) responsible for initialising the system and registering other entities. There is a context manager for each context (e.g. location) and the context could change frequently. It provides secret keys to publishers (resp. subscribers) to encrypt (resp. decrypt) the content payload during the initialisation phase and there will be no further interaction with publishers/subscribers unless the system must be reinitialised.
- **Publisher**: owner of the messages/content that they like to publish and notify the subscribers.
- **Subscriber**: entity interested to subscribe for the content from the publishers.
- **Broker**: intermediary that matches the blinded/encrypted notifications and subscriptions, and if there is a match, then forward the encrypted message to the corresponding subscriber.

The threat model assumed in [NABB13a] is that the context manager is fully trusted. The brokers are assumed to be honest-but-curious, i.e., they honestly follow the protocol but are curious to learn the confidential notifications and subscriptions. Publishers are expected to not collude with any other entity and to follow the protocol honestly. Subscribers are not trusted. Brokers may collude with one another and also collude with malicious subscribers.

The steps of the protocol are as follows:

- **System initialisation**: The context manager generates the parameters of the modified Paillier cryptosystem. It maintains a set of contexts $\mathcal{C}$. Each context $C_i \in \mathcal{C}$ is a tuple $C_i = (\lambda_i, \mu_i, t_i, r_i)$, where $\lambda_i$ and $\mu_i$ are modified Paillier parameters described in Sect. 2. Implicit in the description is the modulus $N_i$ that is different for each context, and $t_i, r_i \xleftarrow{\$} \mathbb{Z}_{N_i}$ are random values. Brokers only match notifications with subscriptions within the same context.

The parameters $\lambda_i$ and $t_i$ are private to the context manager but $\mu_i$ (also $N_i$) are public.

The context manager also deploys an Attribute-based Group Key Management (AB-GKM) scheme [NB14] to manage the secret keys issued to the subscribers that is used to decrypt the payload message of the notification. An AB-GKM scheme enables group key management while also enabling fine-grained access control among a group of users each of whom is identified by a set of attributes. Subscribers need to provide their identity attributes (in an oblivious manner) to the context manager and obtain the secrets that is also shared with the subscribed publishers by the context manager. These secrets are later used to derive the secret encryption key for the publisher to encrypt the payload content, and also derive decryption keys for the subscribers. Since in this work we do not target the encrypted payload content, we omit the details corresponding to the AB-GKM scheme.

- **Subscriber registration**: every subscriber registers with the context manager. A subscriber with context $C_i$ receives the following parameters during the registration:

$$(E'(-r_i),\ E'(-1),\ g^{-t_i}E'(-r_i)),$$

where $g \xleftarrow{\$} \mathbb{Z}_{N^2}^*$. The subscriber uses these parameters to "blind" its subscriptions. Since $\mu_i$ is public, the subscriber may decrypt $E'(-r_i)$ using the decryption procedure $D'$ to obtain $r_i$. Note that the parameter $r_i$ is common to all the subscribers within a given context. It is claimed in [NABB13a] that the subscriber can neither recover $g^{-t_i}$ nor $t_i$ from $g^{-t_i}E'(-r_i)$. Needless to say, it was believed until now that the ciphertexts $E'(-r_i)$ are randomised.

As briefly mentioned above, the subscribers also receive their secret of the AB-GKM scheme depending on the identity attributes they possess but without revealing them to the context manager.

- **Publisher registration**: every publisher too registers with the context manager. A publisher with context $C_i$ receives the following parameters during the registration:

$$(E'(r_i),\ E'(1),\ g^{t_i}E'(r_i)).$$

As in the case of subscribers, the publisher uses these parameters to blind its notifications. In addition to the modified Paillier parameters, the publishers also receive the set of secrets for the AB-GKM scheme issued to the subscribers, from the context manager. The publisher uses these secrets to derive a secret encryption key to selectively encrypt the payload of the notification of a subscriber depending on the latter's subscription.

- **Notifications**: in this system, every notification and subscription is represented as a Boolean expression over a set of attribute/value pairs. The publisher blinds a value $v$ ($0 \le v < 2^\ell \ll N_i$) for an attribute $a$ as follows:

$$
\begin{aligned}
v' &= g^{t_i} \cdot E'(r_i) \cdot E'(r_i(v-1)) \cdot E'(r_v) \\
&= g^{t_i} \cdot E'(r_i v + r_v),
\end{aligned}
\tag{5}
$$

where $r_v$ is a suitably sampled random value in $\mathbb{Z}_{N_i}$. For reasons that will be more clear when describing the matching phase, the value $r_v$ is chosen such that $0 \leq r_i(v-x)+r_v \leq N_i/2$ for $x \in \{0,1,\ldots,v\}$, else $N_i/2 < r_i(v-x)+r_v < N_i$ for $x \in \{v+1, v+2, \ldots, 2^\ell - 1\}$.

The publisher also generates the encryption key $k$ of the AB-GKM scheme using the secret it received from the context manager for the corresponding subscriber. The publisher then encrypts the payload (denoted as *payload*) of the notification $\langle a_i = v_i \rangle_{i \in I}$ as $\mathcal{E}_k(payload)$.

- **Subscriptions**: suppose a subscriber wants to subscribe for the attribute $a$ with the value $x$. It blinds $x$ as follows:

$$x' = g^{-t_i} \cdot E'(-r_i) \cdot E'(r_i(1-x))$$
$$= g^{-t_i} \cdot E'(-r_i x). \tag{6}$$

For each such attribute/value pairs $(a, x)$, a tuple $(a, x', \alpha)$, where $\alpha \in \{<, \geq\}$ is sent to the broker. Each such atomic subscription thus allows a homomorphic greater/less than comparison between the value and the notification. These atomic subscriptions are combined using a Boolean formula to create the complete subscription.

- **Broker matching**: the brokers are assumed to know the public parameters for all the contexts $C_i$. Suppose a broker receives the blinded subscription $x'$ and the blinded notification $v'$ for the attribute $a$. It first computes $x' \cdot v'$ and, since the blinding values $g^{t_i}$ and $g^{-t_i}$ get cancelled, the product is now a typical modified Paillier ciphertext that can be decrypted using the public parameters. It then decrypts the ciphertext to obtain the randomised difference between the original values $x$ and $v$ as follows:

$$d' = D'(x' \cdot v') = r_i(v - x) + r_v. \tag{7}$$

The broker decides $v \geq x$ if $d' \leq N_i/2$, otherwise $v < x$. For a full/composite subscription, the broker evaluates the Boolean formula. After successful matching, it forwards the encrypted payload $\mathcal{E}_k(payload)$ to the subscriber. The subscriber having valid credentials will be able to derive the secret key $k$ and decrypt the payload ciphertext.

## 3.2 Attack on the Scheme

The basis of our attack on the PP-CA-PSS scheme from [NABB13a] is our attack on the modified Paillier cryptosystem that we presented in Sect. 2. First, we show that any registered publisher or subscriber will be able to compute the blinding value $g^{t_i}$ used to hide notifications and subscriptions, respectively.

**Lemma 3.** *Within a context $C_i$, any publisher or subscriber will be able to efficiently compute $g^{t_i}$.*

*Proof.* Consider the case of a subscriber who receives the tuple $(E'(-r_i)$, $E'(-1)$, $g^{-t_i}E'(-r_i))$ from the context manager during its registration. From Lemma 1, the value of $E'(-r_i)$ is unique and so is the value $g^{-t_i} \cdot E'(-r_i)$. Hence by dividing the latter by the former, the subscriber can easily recover the value $g^{-t_i}$. Analogously, the publisher too can recover the blinding value.                    □

Hence, the claim in [NABB13a] that publishers/subscriber cannot efficiently recover $g^{t_i}$ is incorrect.

**Corollary 2.** *Within a context $C_i$, any broker, by colluding with a subscriber, will be able to efficiently recover the subscription $x$ from its blinded subscription $x'$.*

The above corollary follows immediately from the above lemma since a broker can collude with any subscriber and learn the blinding value $g^{t_i}$ (and hence $g^{-t_i}$) and the parameter $r_i$, and then remove the blinds from the blinded subscription $x'$ (see (6)) and eventually decrypt the ciphertext $E'(-r_i x)$ to recover $x$.

The broker can also attempt to recover the notifications from publishers but since these values $v$ are blinded by the random values $r_v$ (see (5)), we do not know how to recover the notifications. As already observed in [NABB13a], there will be a small leakage on the value of $v - x$ leaked by the randomised difference $d'$ (see (7)) since $r_v$ is not sampled from the uniform distribution. Since we now know $x$, this directly translates to a small leakage on the value of the notification $v$ itself. Also, note that we do not get learn anything about the payload of the notification.

## 4    Attack on the LpRide RHS Protocol

### 4.1    Recall of LpRide

For completeness, we briefly recall the relevant steps of the lpRide RHS protocol that are necessary to understand our attack. For other details, we refer to [YSJ+19]. The lpRide protocol consists of the following entities:

- **Authority**: responsible for the registration of riders and taxis/drivers.
- **RSP**: the ride matching service provider that provides the online service of matching riders' encrypted locations with the "nearest" taxis whose locations too are encrypted.
- **Rider**: a rider $u$ provides the encryption of its location $l_u$ to the RSP to request a nearby taxi.
- **Taxi** (*aka.* driver): a taxi $t_k$ provides the encryption of its location $l_{t_k}$ to the RSP and waits for a match with its potential client.

The threat model assumed in [YSJ+19] is that the authority is fully trusted and that its communications with other entities happen over authenticated channels. The riders and taxis are honest-but-curious so is the RSP. Further, it is assumed that the RSP will not collude with any rider or taxi.

The steps of the lpRide protocol are as follows:

- **System initialisation**: the RSP prepares the road network embedding [SKS03] and partitions it into zones. The authority initialises the system parameters $(PK, SK) \leftarrow \text{Init}_{\text{auth}}(\ell, \kappa)$, and by using the modified Paillier cryptosystem generates and broadcasts its public key

$$PK = (N, g_p, g, \boldsymbol{\mu}, \ell, \kappa), \tag{8}$$

where $\ell$ is the bit length of the location coordinates in the road network embedding, $\kappa - 1 \leq \log_2 N - 2$ is the size of the random values used to blind the location coordinates of drivers, and $g \xleftarrow{\$} \mathbb{Z}_{N^2}^*$ is a random base, and $\boldsymbol{\mu} = \langle \mu_i \rangle_{0 \leq i \leq \omega}$ is a $\omega$-tuple of modified Paillier cryptosystem public parameter $\mu$. The secret key is

$$SK = (\boldsymbol{\lambda}, \boldsymbol{\epsilon}, \boldsymbol{\xi}),$$

where $\boldsymbol{\lambda} = \langle \lambda_i \rangle_{0 \leq i \leq \omega}$ is a $\omega$-tuple of modified Paillier cryptosystem secret parameter $\lambda$. The parameters $\boldsymbol{\epsilon} = \langle \epsilon_i \rangle_{1 \leq i \leq \omega}$ and $\boldsymbol{\xi} = \langle \xi_i \rangle_{1 \leq i \leq \omega}$ are $\omega$-tuples of random values from $\mathbb{Z}_N$.

*Remark 1.* In the lpRide protocol, the same modulus $N$, and the same bases $g_p$ and $g$ are suggested to be used for all the coordinates $1 \leq i \leq \omega$. In this case, $\lambda_i$ are all identical, so are all $\mu_i$. But the protocol can be easily generalised to use different moduli and bases (and our attack applies for this variant too).

- **Rider and Taxi registration**:
  - **Rider registration**: the authority assigns a rider $u$ its secret key $sk_u \leftarrow$ RiderKeyGen$(u, PK, SK)$. It chooses a set of random integers $\langle r_i \rangle_{0 \leq i \leq \omega}$ from $\mathbb{Z}_N^*$, and computes

$$E'(-1) = g_p^{-\lambda_0} r_0^{\lambda_0 N} \pmod{N^2},$$
$$g^{-\epsilon_i} E'(-1) = g^{-\epsilon_i} g_p^{-\lambda_i} r_i^{\lambda_i N} \pmod{N^2},$$
$$g^{-\xi_i} E'(-1) = g^{-\xi_i} g_p^{-\lambda_i} r_i^{\lambda_i N} \pmod{N^2}.$$

Then, the secret key of the rider is

$$sk_u = (E'(-1), \langle g^{-\epsilon_i} E'(-1) \rangle_{1 \leq i \leq \omega}, \langle g^{-\xi_i} E'(-1) \rangle_{1 \leq i \leq \omega}). \tag{9}$$

Note that $g^{-\epsilon_i}$ and $g^{-\xi_i}$ serve as blinding values. It is claimed in [YSJ+19], as was done in [NABB13a], that the rider can neither recover $g^{-\epsilon_i}$ (resp. $g^{-\xi_i}$) nor $\epsilon_i$ (resp. $\xi_i$) from $g^{-\epsilon_i} E'(-1)$ (resp. $g^{-\xi_i} E'(-1)$).

  - **Taxi registration**: the authority assigns a taxi $t_k$ its secret key $sk_{t_k} \leftarrow$ TaxiKeyGen$(t_k, PK, SK)$. It chooses a set of random integers $\langle r'_i \rangle_{0 \leq i \leq \omega}$

from $\mathbb{Z}_N^*$, and computes

$$E'(1) = g_p^{\lambda_0} r'_0{}^{\lambda_0 N} \pmod{N^2},$$

$$g^{\epsilon_i} E'(1) = g^{\epsilon_i} g_p^{\lambda_i} r'_i{}^{\lambda_i N} \pmod{N^2},$$

$$g^{\xi_i} E'(1) = g^{\xi_i} g_p^{\lambda_i} r'_i{}^{\lambda_i N} \pmod{N^2}.$$

Then, the secret key of the taxi is

$$sk_{t_k} = (E'(1), \langle g^{\epsilon_i} E'(1) \rangle_{1 \leq i \leq \omega}, \langle g^{\xi_i} E'(1) \rangle_{1 \leq i \leq \omega}). \tag{10}$$

- **Ride request**: a rider $u$ generates an encrypted ride request $\widehat{R}_u \leftarrow$ ReqGen $(c_u, sk_u)$ by computing its location $c_u = \langle c_u[i] \rangle_{1 \leq i \leq \omega}$ in the embedded road network encoding, where $0 \leq c_u[i] < 2^\ell$ is an integer. Then, two vectors of *blinded* ciphertexts $\widehat{c}_u^+$ and $\widehat{c}_u^-$ are computed from $c_u$ and $sk_u$ by element-wise multiplication.
  - $\widehat{c}_u^+ = \langle \widehat{c}_u^+[i] \rangle_{1 \leq i \leq \omega}$, where

$$\widehat{c}_u^+[i] = sk_u[2] \cdot sk_u[1]^{-c_u[i]-1} = g^{-\epsilon_i} E'(c_u[i]). \tag{11}$$

  - $\widehat{c}_u^- = \langle \widehat{c}_u^-[i] \rangle_{1 \leq i \leq \omega}$, where

$$\widehat{c}_u^-[i] = sk_u[3] \cdot sk_u[1]^{c_u[i]-1} = g^{-\xi_i} E'(-c_u[i]). \tag{12}$$

The rider sends $\widehat{R}_u = (\widehat{c}_u^+, \widehat{c}_u^-, z_u)$ to the RSP, where $z_u$ is the identity of the zone of the rider.

- **Taxi location update**: a taxi $t_k$ computes its encrypted updated location $\widehat{L}_{t_k} \leftarrow$ TaxiUpdate$(c_{t_k}, sk_{t_k})$ by computing its location $c_{t_k} = \langle c_{t_k}[i] \rangle_{1 \leq i \leq \omega}$ in the embedded road network encoding, where $0 \leq c_{t_k}[i] < 2^\ell$ is an integer. Two vectors $r_1 = \langle r_1[i] \rangle_{1 \leq i \leq \omega}$ and $r_2 = \langle r_2[i] \rangle_{1 \leq i \leq \omega}$ of $\kappa - 1$-bit random integers are sampled. These random values are used to blind the driver locations and, eventually, the differences of the distances between rider and drivers. Then, two vectors of *blinded* ciphertexts $\widehat{c}_{t_k}^+$ and $\widehat{c}_{t_k}^-$ are computed from $c_{t_k}$ and $sk_{t_k}$ by element-wise multiplication.
  - $\widehat{c}_{t_k}^+ = \langle \widehat{c}_{t_k}^+[i] \rangle_{1 \leq i \leq \omega}$, where

$$\widehat{c}_{t_k}^+[i] = sk_{t_k}[3] \cdot sk_{t_k}[1]^{c_{t_k}[i]-1+r_1[i]}$$
$$= g^{\xi_i} E'(c_{t_k}[i] + r_1[i]). \tag{13}$$

  - $\widehat{c}_{t_k}^- = \langle \widehat{c}_{t_k}^-[i] \rangle_{1 \leq i \leq \omega}$, where

$$\widehat{c}_{t_k}^-[i] = sk_{t_k}[2] \cdot sk_{t_k}[1]^{-c_{t_k}[i]-1+r_2[i]}$$
$$= g^{\epsilon_i} E'(-c_{t_k}[i] + r_2[i]). \tag{14}$$

The taxi $t_k$ sends $\widehat{L}_{t_k} = (\widehat{c}_{t_k}^+, \widehat{c}_{t_k}^-, z_{t_k})$ to the RSP, where $z_{t_k}$ is the identity of the zone of the taxi.

– **Ride matching**: the RSP receives the ride request $\widehat{R}_u$ and the set of taxi locations $\{\widehat{L}_{t_k}\}_{t_k \in \mathcal{T}}$ and filters the list of taxis based on the zone information of the rider. Then, it computes the products $\widehat{c}_{t_k}^+[i]\widehat{c}_u^-[i]$ and $\widehat{c}_{t_k}^-[i]\widehat{c}_u^+[i]$ for all $1 \leq i \leq \omega$. Note that the blinding values $g^{\xi_i}$ or $g^{\epsilon_i}$ or their inverses that are present in the individual ciphertexts gets cancelled upon multiplication of the ciphertexts, and hence the products are typical modified Paillier ciphertexts that can be decrypted with the public key $PK$. Note that the resulting difference of plaintexts is still blinded by the random values $r_1$ and $r_2$. A detailed procedure to recover the sign of the differences from these decrypted blinded sums is given [YSJ+19] and we do not recall it here as it is not needed for the present purpose.

## 4.2   Attack on LpRide

The basis of our attack on lpRide is again our attack on the modified Paillier cryptosystem that we presented in Sect. 2. In particular, Corollary 1 shows that any one with the knowledge of the public key $PK$ of lpRide will be able to compute the modified Paillier ciphertexts. First, we show that any registered rider or a taxi will be able to compute the secret keys of all the other riders and drivers.

**Lemma 4.** *The secret keys of riders (resp. taxis) are identical. Moreover, knowing any one secret key will suffice to compute all the remaining secret keys of riders and drivers.*

*Proof.* The first part of the lemma follows directly from Lemma 1. For the second part, suppose a rider $u$ has its secret key

$$sk_u = (E'(-1), \langle g^{-\epsilon_i}E'(-1)\rangle_{1 \leq i \leq \omega}, \langle g^{-\xi_i}E'(-1)\rangle_{1 \leq i \leq \omega}).$$

From Corollary 1, it can efficiently compute the (unique value of) $E'(-1)$ and $E'(1)$. Hence, any rider (analogously, any taxi) can easily determine all the values $g^{\epsilon_i}$, $g^{\xi_i}$. Once these values are obtained, it can compute the (identical) secret keys of all the taxis. Similarly, any taxi can easily compute the secret keys of all the riders and other taxis.                                                      □

The above attack effectively makes the role of the trusted authority redundant as any registered rider or taxi will be able to add others into the system without the consent of the authority.

**Lemma 5.** *Any rider or taxi will be able to infer the locations of all the riders.*

*Proof.* From the proof of Lemma 4, any rider or taxi can easily determine all the values $g^{\epsilon_i}$ and $g^{\xi_i}$. Using these computed values, it can unmask the ciphertexts (see (11) and (12)) that correspond to the locations of the riders, and eventually decrypt them using the public key $PK$. Note that these location values are not blinded by the random values $r_1$ and $r_2$ unlike the case of taxi location data. □

*Remark 2.* Note that the RSP will not be able to learn the blinding values $g^{\epsilon_i}$ or $g^{\xi_i}$ or the exact locations of the riders since it assumed that it cannot collaborate with any rider or driver. However, if the RSP is allowed to disguise itself as a rider or a driver, then it will be able to learn all the secret keys and locations of the rider.

## 5 Conclusion

We demonstrated an attack on the PP-CA-PSS from [NABB13a] where any honest-but-curious entity (publisher/broker/subscriber) can learn the subscriptions of any subscriber. We also exhibited a key recovery attack on the lpRide RHS protocol of [YSJ+19] by any honest-but-curious rider or driver who can efficiently recover the secret keys of all other riders and drivers, and also learn the location of any rider. The basis of our attack is our cryptanalysis of the modified Paillier cryptosystem. This attack was possible since the reasoning about the security of this primitive in [NABB13a] is flawed. The weaknesses in the PP-CA-PSS and the lpRide protocols were direct consequences of the insecurity of the modified Paillier primitive. We did not exploit any weakness, if at all there are any, in other parts of the above protocols or their security analysis.

Since the notifications in the case of PP-CA-PSS protocol and the driver locations in the case of lpRide are blinded by random values, we do not know how to recover these values, if at all it is possible. It will be interesting to explore this attack scenario. Also, it will be interesting to explore candidate constructions that are equivalent to the functionality of the modified Paillier cryptosystem but offer better security. This way it may possible to prevent our attacks against these two protocols.

**Acknowledgements.** This work was funded by the INSPIRE Faculty Award (by DST, Govt. of India) for the author.

## References

[BLM+19] Baza, M., Lasla, N., Mahmoud, M., Srivastava, G., Abdallah, M.: B-Ride: Ride sharing with privacy-preservation, trust and fair payment atop public blockchain. IEEE Transactions on Network Science and Engineering, pp. 1–1 (2019)

[CBDA+] Cui, S., Belguith, S., De Alwis, P., Asghar, M.R., Russello, G.: Collusion defender: preserving subscribers' privacy in publish and subscribe systems. IEEE Transactions on Dependable and Secure Computing (2019)

[HNW+18] He, Y., Ni, J., Wang, X., Niu, B., Li, F., Shen, X.: Privacy-preserving partner selection for ride-sharing services. IEEE Trans. Veh. Technol. **67**(7), 5994–6005 (2018)

[KFZC18] Khazbak, Y., Fan, J., Zhu, S., Cao, G.: Preserving location privacy in ride-hailing service. In: 2018 IEEE Conference on Communications and Network Security, CNS 2018, Beijing, China, May 30 - June 1, 2018, pp. 1–9. IEEE (2018)

[KMV21] Dunkelman, O., Jacobson, Jr., M.J., O'Flynn, C. (eds.): SAC 2020. LNCS, vol. 12804. Springer, Cham (2021). https://doi.org/10.1007/978-3-030-81652-0

[LJFX19] Luo, Y., Jia, X., Shaojing, F., Ming, X.: pRide: privacy-preserving ride matching over road networks for online ride-hailing service. IEEE Trans. Inform. Forensics Secur. **14**(7), 1791–1802 (2019)

[Mun18] Munster, J.: Securing publish/subscribe. Master's thesis, University of Toronto (2018). http://msrg.org/publications/pdf. Publish-Subcribe.pdf

[NABB13a] Nabeel, M., Appel, S., Bertino, E., Buchmann, A.: Privacy preserving context aware publish subscribe systems. In: Lopez, J., Huang, X., Sandhu, R. (eds.) NSS 2013. LNCS, vol. 7873, pp. 465–478. Springer, Heidelberg (2013). https://doi.org/10.1007/978-3-642-38631-2_34

[NABB13b] Nabeel, M., Appel, S., Bertino, E., Buchmann, A.P.: Privacy preserving context aware publish subscribe systems 2013-1. Technical Report CCTECH-6, Cyber Center Technical Reports, Purdue University (2013)

[NB14] Nabeel, M., Bertino, E.: Attribute based group key management. Trans. Data Priv. **7**(3), 309–336 (2014)

[Nor20] NortonLifeLock. Uber Announces New Data Breach Affecting 57 million Riders and Drivers (2020). https://us.norton.com/internetsecurity-emerging-threats-uber-breach-57-million.html. Retrieved: April 10 2020

[NSB12] Nabeel, M., Shang, N., Bertino, E.: Efficient privacy preserving content based publish subscribe systems. In: Atluri, V., Vaidya, J., Kern, A., Kantarcioglu, M. (eds.) 17th ACM Symposium on Access Control Models and Technologies, SACMAT '12, Newark, NJ, USA - June 20–22, 2012, pp. 133–144. ACM (2012)

[Pai99] Paillier, P.: Public-key cryptosystems based on composite degree residuosity classes. In: Stern, J. (ed.) EUROCRYPT 1999. LNCS, vol. 1592, pp. 223–238. Springer, Heidelberg (1999). https://doi.org/10.1007/3-540-48910-X_16

[PDE+17] Pham, A., Dacosta, I., Endignoux, G., Ramón Troncoso-Pastoriza, J., Huguenin, K., Hubaux, J.P.: ORide: a privacy-preserving yet accountable ride-hailing service. In: Kirda, E., Ristenpart, T. (eds.) 26th USENIX Security Symposium, USENIX Security 2017, Vancouver, BC, Canada, August 16–18, 2017, pp. 1235–1252. USENIX Association (2017)

[PDJ+17] Pham, A., et al.: PrivateRide: a privacy-enhanced ride-hailing service. PoPETs **2017**(2), 38–56 (2017)

[SKS03] Shahabi, C., Kolahdouzan, M.R., Sharifzadeh, M.: A road network embedding technique for k-nearest neighbor search in moving object databases. GeoInformatica **7**(3), 255–273 (2003)

[WZL+18] Wang, F., et al.: Efficient and privacy-preserving dynamic spatial query scheme for ride-hailing services. IEEE Trans. Veh. Technol. **67**(11), 11084–11097 (2018)

[YJZ+19] Yu, H., Jia, X., Zhang, H., Yu, X., Shu, J.: PSRide: Privacy-preserving shared ride matching for online ride hailing systems. IEEE Transactions on Dependable and Secure Computing, pp. 1–1 (2019)

[YSJ+19] Haining, Y., Shu, J., Jia, X., Zhang, H., Xiangzhan, Y.: lpRide: lightweight and privacy-preserving ride matching over road networks in online ride hailing systems. IEEE Trans. Veh. Technol. **68**(11), 10418–10428 (2019)

# Encryption Schemes

# Tightness Subtleties for Multi-user PKE Notions

Hans Heum[ID] and Martijn Stam[(✉)][ID]

Simula UiB, Bergen, Norway
{hansh,martijn}@simula.no

**Abstract.** Public key encryption schemes are increasingly being studied concretely, with an emphasis on tight bounds even in a multi-user setting. Here, two types of formalization have emerged, one with a single challenge bit and one with multiple challenge bits. Another modelling choice is whether to allow key corruptions or not. How tightly the various notions relate to each other has hitherto not been studied in detail. We show that in the absence of corruptions, single-bit left-or-right indistinguishability is the preferred notion, as it tightly implies the other (corruption-less) notions. However, in the presence of corruptions, this implication no longer holds; we suggest the use of a more general notion that tightly implies both existing options. Furthermore, for completeness we study how the relationship between left-or-right versus real-or-random evolves in the multi-user PKE setting.

**Keywords:** Indistinguishability · Public key encryption · Multi-user security · Adaptive corruptions

## 1 Introduction

Historically, a primitive like public key encryption (PKE) is often studied in a setting where a single key-pair is generated for an adversary to attack, often based on a single challenge ciphertext only [27]. Yet, in reality there will be many users, each generating their own key pairs, to be used repeatedly. To study the concrete security risk of having very many keys in play simultaneously, Bellare et al. [5] introduced the multi-user setting. They considered an adversary with access to $n$ different public keys and the ability to challenge (in an indistinguishability fashion) each of them, and concluded that the security loss is at worst linear in the total number challenge queries. Loosely speaking, such a linear security loss implies that a scheme that is believed to offer, say, 128-bit security in the single user setting, may only guarantee 80-bit security if there are $2^{20}$ users each receiving $2^{28}$ messages (based on the same hardness assumption).

Unfortunately, there have been ample examples of schemes where practical attacks can indeed exploit the increased attack surface, demonstrating that these theoretical security losses can be realized. Consequently, the generic tightness losses to move from a single-user, single-challenge setting to a more realistic

© Springer Nature Switzerland AG 2021
M. B. Paterson (Ed.): IMACC 2021, LNCS 13129, pp. 75–104, 2021.
https://doi.org/10.1007/978-3-030-92641-0_5

multi-user, multi-challenge setting are problematic as, conservatively, one would have to increase key sizes to compensate. Alternatively, a growing number of works have looked at schemes with tighter security guarantees, either if the number of users goes up, the number of challenge encryptions per key goes up, or both [2,5,12,16,21,22,28].

Moreover, in a system with many users, it is not inconceivable that some private keys eventually become available to an adversary, which can be modelled using key corruptions. An adversary learning a private key can obviously decrypt all ciphertexts that were encrypted under the corresponding public key, thus some care has to be taken to avoid trivial wins when allowing key corruptions. The two simplest mechanisms are either using independent challenge bits for each key or disallowing an adversary to both challenge and corrupt a single key. As we detail in Appendix A, both these mechanisms have been used, also in related contexts such as key encapsulation mechanisms (KEMs), authenticated encryption (AE), and authenticated key exchange (AKE), raising the inevitable question which notion should be the preferred one.

In the context of lower bounding tightness losses for multi-user AE, Jager et al. [25] employed a novel multi-key, multi-challenge-bit notion that generalizes both mechanisms; however, the main motivation of this generalized mechanism was universality of their impossibility result, allowing them to side-step the question which mechanism to focus on. Recently, in the context of AKE, Jager et al. [24] argued in favour of the single-bit notion, primarily as it composes more easily. For KEMs a similar argument holds, yet for PKE composition is arguably less relevant. Instead, a more direct interpretation of what the various notions entail might well be preferable.

**Our Contribution.** Both the single-bit and multi-bit approaches are implied by the single user notion at the cost of a tightness loss linear in the number of users. Consequently, the two multi-user notions are also within that linear factor in the number of user. As our goal is to avoid such tightness losses, we are interested in identifying the most suitable, general notion as possible, guaranteeing that there are no "hidden" linear losses in the choice of notion—an issue already pointed to by Jager et al. [24]

To this end, we adapt the multi-key, multi-bit notion of Jager et al. [25] to the PKE setting, slightly generalizing it in the process. We show how it tightly implies, and therefore unifies, the previous multi-user notions, and give novel interpretations of each (see Sect. 3).

We then shift our focus to how tightly the different notions relate to each other, with the goal of identifying the strongest, and therefore preferred, multi-user notions. We find that the answer depends on whether or not corruptions are present: in the absence of corruptions, we find that the single-challenge-bit notion is *as strong or stronger* than any of the other (see Sect. 4.2). Given that this notion is significantly simpler than the fully general game, this makes the single-bit notion the preferred one in the absence of corruptions. With corruptions, this relation breaks down, and the general "free-bit" game indeed seems the stronger, and therefore preferred, notion (see Sect. 4.3).

Finally, we fill some holes largely left as folklore until now regarding how the well-known factor-2 reduction from real-or-random to left-or-right indistinguishability, as shown by Bellare et al. [7] for the single-user, single-challenge setting, generalizes to the multi-user setting. We find that, as expected, the relation remains intact in the single-bit setting, regardless of whether corruptions are present (see Sect. 4.4). In contrast, with multiple challenge bits the best-known reductions turn lossy. Whether these losses are inevitable remains open; however, it reinforces the by now established notion that left-or-right indistinguishability is to be preferred over its real-or-random counterpart whenever possible.

The appendices contain much additional material: highlights include Appendix A giving context to the present work by presenting a more complete history of multi-user indistinguishability than that presented here, and Appendix F, illustrating the difficulty of achieving tight composition in multi-bit settings, as alluded to by Jager et al. [24], by giving an overview of how additional losses can appear in PKE schemes built using the widely used KEM/DEM paradigm.

## 2   Preliminaries

### 2.1   Notation

For an integer $n$, we will write $[n]$ for the set $\{1, \ldots, n\}$. We will also use the abbreviation $X \xleftarrow{\cup} x$ for the operation $X \leftarrow X \cup \{x\}$. The event of an adversary $\mathbb{A}$ outputting 0 is denoted $0 \leftarrow \mathbb{A}$. We use $\Pr[Code : Event \mid Condition]$ to denote the conditional probability of $Event$ occurring when $Code$ is executed, conditioned on $Condition$. We omit $Code$ when it is clear from the context and $Condition$ when it is not needed.

### 2.2   PKE Syntax

A public key encryption scheme PKE consists of three algorithms: the probabilistic *key generation* algorithm Pk.Kg, which takes as input some system parameter pm and outputs a public/private key pair $(\mathsf{pk}, \mathsf{sk}) \in (\mathcal{PK}, \mathcal{SK})$; the probabilistic *encryption* algorithm Pk.Enc, which on input a public key $\mathsf{pk} \in \mathcal{PK}$ and a message $m \in \mathcal{M}$, outputs a ciphertext $c$; and the deterministic *decryption* algorithm Pk.Dec, which on input of a secret key $\mathsf{sk} \in \mathcal{SK}$ and a ciphertext $c$, outputs either the message $m$, or a special symbol $\perp$ denoting failure.

We allow the message space $\mathcal{M}$ to depend on the parameters pm, but insist it is independent of the public key pk. We furthermore assume that there exists an equivalence relation $\sim$ on the message space that partitions $\mathcal{M}$ into finite equivalence classes. For $m \in \mathcal{M}$, we let $[\![m]\!]$ denote its equivalence class, so $[\![m]\!] = \{\tilde{m} \in \mathcal{M} : m \sim \tilde{m}\}$. Often $\mathcal{M}$ consists of arbitrary length bitstrings, or at least all bitstrings up to some large length (e.g. $2^{64}$), and two messages are equivalent iff they have the same length, so $[\![m]\!] = \{0, 1\}^{|m|}$; for other cryptosystems, such as ElGamal, messages are group elements that are essentially all equivalent, so $[\![m]\!] = \mathcal{M}$. (Note that the case where $[\![m]\!] = \{m\}$ for all $m$ is degenerate and 'security' is often trivially satisfied.)

The scheme must satisfy $\epsilon$-correctness [20], namely that for any pm:

$$\mathbb{E}_{(\mathsf{pk},\mathsf{sk}) \leftarrow\$ \, \mathsf{Pk}.\mathsf{Kg}(\mathsf{pm})} \left[ \max_{m \in \mathcal{M}} \Pr[c \leftarrow\$ \, \mathsf{Pk}.\mathsf{Enc}_{\mathsf{pk}}(m)) \; : \; \mathsf{Pk}.\mathsf{Dec}_{\mathsf{sk}}(c) \neq m] \right] \leq \epsilon.$$

If $\epsilon = 0$ we speak of perfect correctness; the case $\epsilon > 0$ is especially useful to model decryption errors typical to lattice-based schemes.

*Remark 1.* The system parameters pm are implicitly input to Pk.Enc and Pk.Dec as well; for concreteness, they can for instance be the description of an elliptic curve group with generator for an ECDLP-based system or the dimensions and noise sampling algorithm for an LWE-based system. When one is interested in re-phrasing our results in an asymptotic setting, the parameters pm will be generated by a probabilistic, polynomial-time algorithm that only takes the security parameter as input.

## 2.3    Concrete Security

**Indistinguishability.** The standard notion of security for encryption systems has become that of indistinguishability. Here the adversary is given access to a challenge encryption oracle implementing one of two "worlds"; the adversary needs to find out which. Several choices appear regarding the exact nature of these worlds, leading to different notions of indistinguishability such as real-or-random and left-or-right. Henceforth we refer to those two notions ROR and LOR, respectively, and we will refer to them collectively as IND. We will flesh out the details in Sect. 3.

Security definitions furthermore take into account the POWER given to the adversary, for example that of chosen plaintext attacks (CPA), or chosen ciphertext attacks (CCA). The distinguishing advantage of an adversary $\mathbb{A}$ against a scheme relative to some notion will then be IND-POWER$_{\mathrm{PKE}}(\mathbb{A})$, see Definition 1. As randomly guessing a world is correct half of the time, the distinguishing advantage is of course suitably offset.

**Definition 1.** *The* distinguishing advantage *of an adversary* $\mathbb{A}$ *against an encryption scheme* PKE *is*

$$\mathrm{IND\text{-}POWER}_{\mathrm{PKE}}(\mathbb{A}) := 2 \cdot \Pr\left[\mathsf{Exp}_{\mathrm{PKE}}^{\mathrm{ind\text{-}power}}(\mathbb{A}) = 1\right] - 1.$$

**Implications and Separations.** Our main focus will be comparing different notions of security, especially showing that if security is met under one notion, then it is also met under another one. We will prove these implication using fully black box reductions [4,31] that are furthermore simple [29]. A fully black box reduction works for all schemes and adversaries, and only accesses them in a black box manner. Moreover, if the reduction only runs its adversary once and without rewinding, then the reduction is simple.

To allow for black-box access to the scheme, we will add an auxiliary oracle for the PKE to operate on the message space and the key space. A simple fully-black box (SFBB) reduction has access to this auxiliary oracle, as well as to the oracles corresponding to the PKE's algorithms, the oracles provided to the reduction by the game it is playing, and finally its single straight copy of the adversary. We will insist that the overhead of such a reduction, namely the number of oracle calls it makes more than the adversary it is running, is not undue: it can be upper bounded in terms of the parameters that define the security game(s) at hand, such as the number of keys in the system.

**Definition 2 (Tightness).** *Let* $\mathrm{IND}_1$ *and* $\mathrm{IND}_2$ *be two indistinguishability notions for PKE schemes, let* $c$ *be a positive real number, then* $\mathrm{IND}_1 \overset{\leq c}{\Longrightarrow} \mathrm{IND}_2$ *iff there exists a simple fully-black box reduction* $\mathbb{B}_1$ *such that for all PKE schemes PKE and adversaries* $\mathbb{A}_2$,

$$\mathrm{IND}_2(\mathbb{A}_2) \leq c \cdot \mathrm{IND}_1(\mathbb{B}_1^{\mathbb{A}_2,\mathrm{PKE}})$$

*and the overhead of* $\mathbb{A}_2$ *is not undue.*

Refer also to Jager et al. [25] for a discussion on how to express tightness for more general reductions. They also formalize the folklore that simple reductions compose neatly; in our case if $\mathrm{IND}_1 \overset{\leq c}{\Longrightarrow} \mathrm{IND}_2$ and $\mathrm{IND}_2 \overset{\leq d}{\Longrightarrow} \mathrm{IND}_3$ then also $\mathrm{IND}_1 \overset{\leq c \cdot d}{\Longrightarrow} \mathrm{IND}_3$.

If $c = 1$, the reduction is called tight; if $c > 1$ we call the reduction lossy. Note that our notion of tightness is stricter than in some other works where a constant factor of say 2 will still be considered tight [18]; our convention has the benefit of not depending on any (security) parameter. A natural question for lossy reductions is whether the loss is inevitable or not—if it is, the bound is called sharp. Questions of sharpness are not the focus of our work, although we do remark upon it in more detail in Appendix B.

# 3    A General Definition of PKE Multi-user Security

## 3.1    A General Game

In order to compare various flavours of multi-user notions for PKE, we take Jager et al.'s framework for multi-user AE notions [25] and port it to the PKE setting, using some slightly different game-mechanics in the process. A multi-user security game is parametrized by the number of keys $\kappa$ and the number of bits $\beta$. Usually one can imagine $\beta \leq \kappa$ and in fact Jager et al. only considered $\beta = \kappa$. However, keeping $\kappa$ and $\beta$ distinct helps when expressing and interpreting security losses.

$$\mathsf{Exp}_{\mathrm{PKE}}^{\mathrm{ind\text{-}cca},\not\kappa,\beta}(\mathbb{A})$$

---

$(\mathsf{pk}_1,\mathsf{sk}_1),\ldots,(\mathsf{pk}_\kappa,\mathsf{sk}_\kappa)\leftarrow\!\!\$\,\mathsf{Pk}.\mathsf{Kg}$

$b_1,\ldots,b_\beta,\delta\leftarrow\!\!\$\,\{0,1\}$

$\mathsf{C}_1,\ldots,\mathsf{C}_\kappa,\mathtt{I}_1^{\mathcal{E}},\ldots,\mathtt{I}_\beta^{\mathcal{E}},\mathtt{I}^{\mathcal{K}}\leftarrow\emptyset$

$(j,\hat{b}_j)\leftarrow\!\!\$\,\mathbb{A}^{\mathcal{E},\mathcal{D},\mathcal{K}}(\mathsf{pk}_1,\ldots,\mathsf{pk}_\kappa)$

if $\mathtt{I}_j^{\mathcal{E}}\cap\mathtt{I}^{\mathcal{K}}\neq\emptyset$ then return $\delta$

else return $b_j=\hat{b}_j$

$\mathcal{E}_{\mathrm{LOR}}(i,j,m_0,m_1)$

---

if $m_0\not\sim m_1$ then return $\mathcal{t}$

$\mathtt{I}_j^{\mathcal{E}}\xleftarrow{\cup}i$

$c^*\leftarrow\!\!\$\,\mathsf{Pk}.\mathsf{Enc}_{\mathsf{pk}_i}(m_{b_j})$

$\mathsf{C}_i\xleftarrow{\cup}c^*$

return $c^*$

$\mathcal{E}_{\mathrm{ROR}}(i,j,m)$

---

$m'\leftarrow\!\!\$\,[\![m]\!]$

return $\mathcal{E}_{\mathrm{LOR}}(i,j,m,m')$

$\mathcal{D}(i,c)$

---

if $c\in\mathsf{C}_i$ then return $\mathcal{t}$

$m\leftarrow\mathsf{Pk}.\mathsf{Dec}_{\mathsf{sk}_i}(c)$

return $m$

$\mathcal{K}(i)$

---

$\mathtt{I}^{\mathcal{K}}\xleftarrow{\cup}i$

return $\mathsf{sk}_i$

**Fig. 1.** The generalised multi-user distinguishing experiment $\mathsf{Exp}_{\mathrm{PKE}}^{\mathrm{ind\text{-}cca},\not\kappa,\beta}(\mathbb{A})$; the adversary has access to either the left-or-right $\mathcal{E}_{\mathrm{LOR}}$ or the real-or-random $\mathcal{E}_{\mathrm{ROR}}$ challenge oracle.

Given a public key encryption scheme PKE, let $\mathsf{Exp}_{\mathrm{PKE}}^{\mathrm{ind\text{-}cca},\not\kappa,\beta}(\mathbb{A})$ be the experiment given in Fig. 1, where $\mathbb{A}$ is the adversary. The corresponding distinguishing advantage (see Definition 1) is denoted by $\mathrm{IND\text{-}CCA}_{\mathrm{PKE}}^{\not\kappa,\beta}(\mathbb{A})$. The $\kappa$ is slashed to denote the presence of a key corruption oracle; the corresponding notion without corruptions is $\mathrm{IND\text{-}CCA}_{\mathrm{PKE}}^{\kappa,\beta}$. Without the decryption oracle the notion becomes a chosen-plaintext attack (CPA) instead. Often our results are oblivious of whether the power is CPA or CCA; we will then use CXA to refer to them collectively.

In the game, an adversary is given $\kappa$ public keys, and a choice of $\beta$ bits to try and attack through one of the two challenge oracles depending on the flavour of indistinguishability: for left-or-right indistinguishability, it gains access to $\mathcal{E}_{\mathrm{LOR}}$, whereas for real-or-random, it instead gains access to $\mathcal{E}_{\mathrm{ROR}}$. Both oracles have the usual interface, augmented by a key handle $i$ and a bit handle $j$. For instance, for $\mathcal{E}_{\mathrm{LOR}}$ an adversary picks handles $i$ and $j$ as well as two equivalent messages $m_0$ and $m_1$ to receive the encryption of $m_{b_j}$ under public key $\mathsf{pk}_i$. For $\mathcal{E}_{\mathrm{ROR}}$ only a single message $m$ is provided in addition to the two handles and, depending on the value of $b_j$, $\mathbb{A}$ receives the encryption of either the message or of a uniformly chosen equivalent message.

The adversary has possible access to two additional powers: a decryption oracle $\mathcal{D}$ and a corruption oracle $\mathcal{K}$. The former takes as input a ciphertext $c$ together with a key handle $i$, and returns the decryption of $c$ under private key $\mathsf{sk}_i$. The latter takes as input a key handle $i$ and directly returns said $\mathsf{sk}_i$.

The adversary has in principle unlimited adaptive access to the available oracles, necessitating some admin in the game to deal with trivial wins. Firstly, if $m_0\not\sim m_1$ for $\mathcal{E}_{\mathrm{LOR}}$, or if a challenge ciphertext is submitted to the decryption oracle under its handle of creation, then the adversary receives the special symbol $\mathcal{t}$ instead. Secondly, once the adversary outputs a bit handle $j$ and a guess $\hat{b}_j$, the game checks through $I_j^{\mathcal{E}} \cap I^{\mathcal{K}} = \emptyset$ whether the challenge bit has become compromised by virtue of being challenged together with a corrupted key. If so, the game outputs the uniformly random bit $\delta$, yielding the adversary no advantage; otherwise, the game outputs whether $\hat{b}_j = b_j$.

Unlike Jager et al., we do not consider valid or invalid adversaries, but rather deal with bad behaviour in-game. Specifically, we want the adversary to be able to challenge on a key both before and after it becomes corrupted, but trying to win by attacking any of the corrupted challenge bits must of course be disallowed, regardless of the order of the queries. Thus, for problematic combinations of challenge/corrupt/target we necessarily had to wait until the adversary announced its target $j$ before, if need be, penalizing. For bad decryption queries, penalizing at the end is discouraged [8], moreover it is easy to check on-the-fly.

Finally, we use $q_i^{\mathcal{E}}$ to refer to the number of challenge queries on public key $\mathsf{pk}_i$; $q_{\Sigma}^{\mathcal{E}}$ for the total number of challenge oracle calls; and $q_{\max}^{\mathcal{E}}$ for the maximum number of challenge queries per key. Similarly, $q_i^{\mathcal{D}}$ is the number of decryption calls on private key $\mathsf{sk}_i$ and $q^{\mathcal{K}}$ the number of corruption calls.

## 3.2 Notational Conventions

Jager et al. [25] introduced their unified game in order to show that, for authenticated encryption, tightness losses are inevitable in a multi-key with corruption setting, irrespective of certain definitional choices. Thus they can avoid having to choose one notion over the other. We are interested in finding out, for public key encryption, whether some notion is preferred over the other. To that end, we will introduce some notation to more easily identify known notions and express relationships between them.

One can visualize the IND-CXA$^{\kappa,\beta}$ experiment using a binary matrix of dimension $\kappa \times \beta$, where an entry be set wherever a key and a bit may be called together. For the general game, the matrix has every entry filled (see the leftmost matrix of Fig. 2). We will refer to this as the free-bit notion. By restricting the matrix, we can easily express existing notions.

Bellare et al.'s original single-challenge-bit notion [5] corresponds to a $\kappa \times \beta$-matrix (for arbitrary $\beta$) with only a single set row to force all challenge queries to the same bit handle (see the middle matrix of Fig. 2). If $\beta = 1$, the notion matches the free-bit notion, so we may write IND-CXA$^{\kappa,1}$, or IND-CXA$^{\hat{\kappa},1}$ if corruptions are present, for the single-bit notion.

On the other hand, for the one-challenge-bit-per-key notion we have that $\beta = \kappa$ and the restriction $i = j$ for all challenge queries. These restrictions correspond to a square matrix in which only the diagonal is set (see the rightmost matrix of Fig. 2), inspiring us to refer to this notion as *diagonal-bit*, or just diagonal, and denote it by IND-CXA$^{\kappa,\boxdot}$, or IND-CXA$^{\hat{\kappa},\boxdot}$ with corruptions.

The single-bit and diagonal-bit notions we will collectively refer to as the simple notions. Our notation and terminology differs from prior art, which is to some extent inevitable. The distinction between the various notions has only recently received explicit attention [24, 25] and no clear terminology has yet been set. For instance, we drop the prefix MU (for multi-user, to contrast with the

$$
\begin{array}{c}
\begin{array}{ccccc} b_1 & b_2 & b_3 & \cdots & b_\beta \end{array} \\
\begin{array}{c} \mathrm{pk}_1 \\ \mathrm{pk}_2 \\ \mathrm{pk}_3 \\ \vdots \\ \mathrm{pk}_\kappa \end{array}
\left(\begin{array}{ccccc}
\circ & \circ & \circ & \cdots & \circ \\
\circ & \circ & \circ & \cdots & \circ \\
\circ & \circ & \circ & \cdots & \circ \\
\vdots & \vdots & \vdots & \ddots & \vdots \\
\circ & \circ & \circ & \cdots & \circ
\end{array}\right) \\
\mathrm{IND}^{\kappa,\beta}
\end{array}
\qquad
\begin{array}{c}
\begin{array}{ccccc} b_1 & b_2 & b_3 & \cdots & b_\beta \end{array} \\
\left(\begin{array}{ccccc}
\circ & \times & \times & \cdots & \times \\
\circ & \times & \times & \cdots & \times \\
\circ & \times & \times & \cdots & \times \\
\vdots & \vdots & \vdots & \ddots & \vdots \\
\circ & \times & \times & \cdots & \times
\end{array}\right) \\
\mathrm{IND}^{\kappa,1}
\end{array}
\qquad
\begin{array}{c}
\begin{array}{ccccc} b_1 & b_2 & b_3 & \cdots & b_\kappa \end{array} \\
\left(\begin{array}{ccccc}
\circ & \times & \times & \cdots & \times \\
\times & \circ & \times & \cdots & \times \\
\times & \times & \circ & \cdots & \times \\
\vdots & \vdots & \vdots & \ddots & \vdots \\
\times & \times & \times & \cdots & \circ
\end{array}\right) \\
\mathrm{IND}^{\kappa,\boxtimes}
\end{array}
$$

**Fig. 2.** Matrices of allowed key/bit combinations in challenge oracle calls for the free-bit, single-bit, and diagonal-bit multi-user notion, respectively; circles mark allowed queries, while crosses mark disallowed ones. The visualization highlights that the free-bit notion is a strict generalization of the two other, simple notions.

older single user notions) as on the one hand we believe that these days multi-user security should be the default from which single user notions can be derived if needed, and on the other hand we wish to maintain a clean GOAL–POWER nomenclature: having multiple users to target primarily modifies an adversary's power, not its goal.

### 3.3 Interpretation

Both simple notions with corruptions have appeared in the literature, both in a PKE setting but also in related KEM, AKE, and to a lesser extent AE settings. One key question is which notion to opt for when. Establishing relationships between the notions, as in the next section, helps answer this question. Here, we want to address the meaning and usefulness of the notions as they are.

In the context of AKE, Jager et al. [24] discuss the difference between the single-bit notion ("single-bit guess") and the diagonal notion ("multi-bit guess"). Earlier works on tight security for AKE focused on the diagonal setting [2], yet as Cohn-Gorden et al. [13, Section 3] point out, that notion does not lend itself very well for tight composition: when the keys produced by an AKE are subsequently used, in a proof it is convenient to swap out all keys from real to random in one fell swoop. The single-bit notion allows such a massive substitution, but the diagonal notion does not. Moreover, Jager et al. wonder whether the diagonal notion is meaningful, which would "provide a good intuition of what [it] tries to model".

Whereas AKE and KEMs are primarily tools to set up symmetric keys for subsequent use, the situation for PKE is different as it is much closer to the end user. The difference is reflected in the kind of indistinguishability as well: for AKE and KEMs, a ROR-style notion is used where the adversary cannot even control the real world's "message", yet for PKE's LOR-notion, an adversary has full control over the left-versus-right challenge messages. Thus, for PKE the diagonal-LOR notion does seem meaningful, as we explain below.

Suppose we interpret each key to correspond to a *user* and each challenge bit to correspond to a *conversation*. Then the different notions model different scenarios. For instance, the diagonal notion models a scenario where the users take part in independent conversations, and an adversary can decide which honest conversation to target after corrupting a number of other ones. In contrast, the single-bit notion models a scenario where all users are engaged in the *same* conversation. The latter scenario allows an adversary to accumulate information on the conversation across users, although none of the active parties may be corrupted.

Finally, the free-bit notion models a situation where there are a number of independent conversations, each with their own potentially overlapping set of users. The adversary can adaptively corrupt a number of users, and finally targets a conversation conducted by honest users only.

Of course, there are already existing notions that study PKE security in the presence of corruptions, under the term "selective opening attacks" (SOA, [9, 15]). There are various formalizations of SOA, the most relevant ones to our work are receiver SOA [19] where an adversary can corrupt private keys (as opposed to sender SOA, where an adversary learns how a ciphertext was created). Most of these SOA notions are considerably stronger than the notions we consider: our strongest notion is still implied by the customary single-user single-challenge LOR–CCA (just rather lossy), yet for SOA strong separations, and in some cases impossibility results, are known [23]. The link between multi-user security with corruptions on the one hand and SOA on the other has largely been ignored and appears worth expanding further.

We remark that the multi-bit notion also occurs naturally when studying multi-instance security [10], which has been studied in the context of PKE [1]. We leave the adaptation of our work, and specifically the general free-bit game to that setting as an enticing open problem.

# 4  Relations Between Indistinguishability Notions

In this section we investigate how tightly the various multi-user notions relate to each other, and how each relates to single-user notions. Some implications are known or folklore and others follow quite naturally from the literature, but not all. As expected, most of the notions are equivalent within a factor linear in the number of users. Yet, some notions turn out to be more, or less, tightly related.

There is for instance the surprising and completely tight reduction from $\text{LOR-CXA}_{\text{PKE}}^{\kappa,1}$ to $\text{LOR-CXA}_{\text{PKE}}^{\kappa,\boxtimes}$ (Theorem 1). However, the proof technique breaks down for real-or-random indistinguishability and in notions with corruptions. Furthermore, for the latter, there doesn't seem to be a way of relating the notions more tightly than by a linear loss. We conjecture this linear loss to be sharp, yet proving so we leave open.

*Shorthand for Unified Implications.* Given the large number of notions resulting from the various orthogonal definitional choices, we use shorthand, as presented in Table 1, to state various theorems. The shorthand serves as an implicit quantifier, so a theorem statement in shorthand essentially holds for all notions included in the shorthand. To avoid clutter, we will sometimes abbreviate $\text{IND-CXA}^{u,c}$ to

**Table 1.** A modular framework for multi-user security notions.

| Shorthand | Stand-in for | Relates to |
|---|---|---|
| IND | $\{\text{LOR}, \text{ROR}\}$ | Type of challenge oracle |
| CXA | $\{\text{CPA}, \text{CCA}\}$ | Presence of decryption oracle |
| $u$ | $\{\kappa, \not{\kappa}\}$ | Number of keys; presence of corruption oracle |
| $c$ | $\{1, \boxminus, \beta\}$ | Number of challenge bits; relation with keys |

just $\text{IND}^{u,c}$, and let it be implied that the result holds for both CPA and CCA. We will refer to single-user, multi-challenge notions by dropping the superscripts, e.g. IND.

As a concrete example, consider the trivial statement

$$\text{IND}^{u,c} \implies \text{IND}.$$

This is then to be read as, "Both in the cpa and the cca setting, and regardless of the nature of the challenge oracle, the presence or absense of corruptions, or the number and structure of the challenge bits, security under a multi-user notion implies security under the corresponding single-user notion." Written out in full, the statement becomes:

**Lemma 1.** *For all* $\text{IND} \in \{\text{LOR}, \text{ROR}\}$, $\text{CXA} \in \{\text{CPA}, \text{CCA}\}$, $u \in \{\kappa, \not{\kappa}\}$, *and* $c \in \{1, \boxminus, \beta\}$, *there is a reduction* $\mathbb{B}$ *such that, for every adversary* $\mathbb{A}$,

$$\text{IND-CXA}_{\text{PKE}}(\mathbb{A}) \leq \text{IND-CXA}_{\text{PKE}}^{u,c}(\mathbb{B}),$$

*where* $\mathbb{B}$ *calls* $\mathbb{A}$ *once, with no undue overhead.*

*Tight Implications From Strict Generalizations.* Security under a multi-user notion tightly implies single-user security under the corresponding notion, and adding helper oracles (like decryption for CCA, or a corruption oracle) yields strictly more general notions; as does increasing the parameters (number of users/number of challenge bits), and for all notions, left-or-right security implies real-or-random security, as can be seen from Fig. 1. For completeness, we summarize these trivial implications in the full version.

### 4.1   Simple Multi-user Notions Versus Classical Single-Key Notions

Bellare et al. [5] used a hybrid argument to show that single-user single-challenge security implies $\text{LOR}^{\kappa,1}$ with a security loss linear in the total number of challenge encryption queries. They phrased this total as the product of the number of users and the number of challenges per user. As all our notions are explicitly multi-challenge, we will ignore the number of challenge queries, meaning the loss simply becomes linear in the number of users (in line with the original claim).

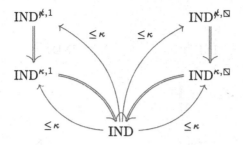

**Fig. 3.** Known relations between single-user (but multi-challenge) indistinguishability and the two different generalizations to multi-user indistinguishability, with and without corruptions; refer to Table 1 for an overview of the shorthand. Recall that IND without any superscripts means single-user notions. (Double arrows: trivially tight.)

Bellare et al. did not consider the diagonal notion or corruption, however later, when Jager et al. [25] introduced the free-bit notion to the setting of AE, they also showed that the simple notions are implied by the single-user notion, again with a linear loss, even when corruptions are considered. For completeness, we reprove the relevant linear losses in our new PKE context in Appendix C. The resulting relations are summarized in Fig. 3.

As explained in Sect. 3.1, Jager et al. used slightly different game mechanics by prohibiting certain adversarial behaviour. In contrast, we allow such bad behaviour and just ignore the adversary's output instead. We introduce a useful lemma (Lemma 3) that formalizes that, in the single-key setting, our mechanism is sound and corrupting that single-key yields no adversarial advantage. This single-key-with-corruptions game is often easier to use in reductions.

Existing sharpness results can be used to show that linear losses are inevitable, see Appendix B.2 for details.

### 4.2 Relationship Between Simple Multi-user Notions

Now that we have affirmed that the single-user notion implies any of the four simple multi-user notions with a loss linear in the number of users, a natural question is how the simple multi-user notions relate to each other. As the multi-user notions all tightly imply the single-user notion, one can always just go via the single-user notion. As already noted by Jager et al. [25], this strategy will again lead to a loss linear in the number of users. Lemma 2 formalizes this trivial loss and Fig. 4 provides an overview of the relations. One notable exception from the linear losses is the implication from the single-bit notion to the diagonal notion if there are no corruptions, which is tight for the case of left-or-right indistinguishability and almost tight for real-or-random indistinguishability. We will explain why this is in the next paragraph.

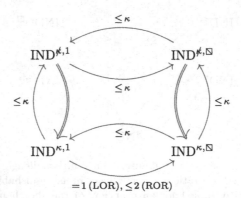

$$=1\,(\mathrm{LOR}),\ \leq 2\,(\mathrm{ROR})$$

**Fig. 4.** Relations between the simple multi-user notions, including the non-trivially tight relation between $\mathrm{LOR}^{\kappa,\beta}$ and $\mathrm{LOR}^{\kappa,\boxtimes}$ as captured by Corollaries 1 and 2 for LOR and ROR, respectively. (Double arrows: trivially tight.)

**Lemma 2** ($\mathrm{IND}^{u,c} \overset{\leq\kappa}{\Longrightarrow} \mathrm{IND}^{u,c'}$). *Let $c' \in \{1, \boxtimes\}$. Then, there is an SFBB reduction $\mathbb{B}$ such that, for every adversary $\mathbb{A}$,*

$$\mathrm{IND\text{-}CXA}_{\mathrm{PKE}}^{u',c'}(\mathbb{A}) \leq \kappa \cdot \mathrm{IND\text{-}CXA}_{\mathrm{PKE}}^{u,c}(\mathbb{B})\,.$$

*Proof (sketch).* Trivially, $\mathrm{IND}^{\kappa,c} \implies \mathrm{IND}$. Meanwhile, Theorems 3 and 4 together say that $\mathrm{IND} \overset{\leq\kappa}{\Longrightarrow} \mathrm{IND}^{\kappa,c}$. Combining (in the manner discussed in Sect. 2) gives $\mathrm{IND}^{\kappa,c} \implies \mathrm{IND} \overset{\leq\kappa}{\Longrightarrow} \mathrm{IND}^{\kappa,c'}$.

**A Tight Relation: From Single-Bit to Multi-bit Without Corruptions.** Surprisingly, left-or-right indistinguishability allows for a 'bit-hiding' argument that lets an adversary playing a single-bit multi-user game simulate the full free-bit game (and therefore also the diagonal-bit game), by simply exchanging the order in which it forwards its two messages. We formalize this argument in Theorem 1 and its proof. Consequently, $\mathrm{LOR}^{\kappa,1}$ tightly implies of $\mathrm{LOR}^{\kappa,\boxtimes}$ (Corollary 1), whereas the implication in the other direction appears lossy, this clearly renders $\mathrm{LOR}^{\kappa,1}$ the preferred notion.

**Theorem 1** ($\mathrm{LOR}^{\kappa,1} \implies \mathrm{LOR}^{\kappa,\beta}$). *There is an SFBB reduction $\mathbb{B}$ such that, for every adversary $\mathbb{A}$,*

$$\mathrm{LOR\text{-}CXA}_{\mathrm{PKE}}^{\kappa,\beta}(\mathbb{A}) \leq \mathrm{LOR\text{-}CXA}_{\mathrm{PKE}}^{\kappa,1}(\mathbb{B})\,,$$

*where $\mathbb{B}$'s overhead is limited to drawing $\beta$ uniformly random bits.*

*Proof.* The reduction $\mathbb{B}$, playing $\mathsf{Exp}_{\mathrm{PKE}}^{\mathrm{lor\text{-}cxa},\kappa,1}$, simulates $\mathsf{Exp}_{\mathrm{PKE}}^{\mathrm{lor\text{-}cxa},\kappa,\beta}$ for $\mathbb{A}$ by drawing $\beta$ fresh challenge bits, and simply exchanging the order of $m_0$ and $m_1$

| $\mathbb{B}(\mathsf{pk}_1, \ldots, \mathsf{pk}_\kappa)$ | if $\mathbb{A}$ calls $\mathcal{E}(i, j, m_0, m_1)$ | if $\mathbb{A}$ calls $\mathcal{D}(i, c)$ |
| --- | --- | --- |
| $b_1, \ldots, b_\beta \leftarrow\!\!\$ \, \{0, 1\}$ | $c^* \leftarrow \mathcal{E}(i, m_{b_j}, m_{\bar{b}_j})$ | $m \leftarrow \mathcal{D}(i, c)$ |
| $(j, \hat{b}_j) \leftarrow\!\!\$ \, \mathbb{A}^{\mathcal{E}, \mathcal{D}}(\mathsf{pk}_1, \ldots, \mathsf{pk}_\kappa)$ | return $c^*$ | return $m$ |
| return $\hat{b}_j \oplus b_j$ | | |

**Fig. 5.** The adversary $\mathbb{B}$, playing $\mathsf{Exp}_{\mathrm{PKE}}^{\mathrm{lor\text{-}cxa}, \kappa, 1}$ while simulating $\mathsf{Exp}_{\mathrm{PKE}}^{\mathrm{lor\text{-}cxa}, \kappa, \beta}$ for $\mathbb{A}$.

in accordance to the value of the simulated challenge bit when forwarding to its own left-or-right oracle (see Fig. 5). Denoting the challenge bit of $\mathsf{Exp}_{\mathrm{PKE}}^{\mathrm{lor\text{-}cxa}, \kappa, 1}(\mathbb{B})$ by $b$, the ciphertext that $\mathbb{A}$ receives upon the query $\mathcal{E}(i, j, m_0, m_1)$ will be an encryption of the message $m_{b \oplus b_j}$ under $\mathsf{pk}_i$; $\mathbb{B}$ then simply makes sure to undo this xor again before returning its final guess. $\qquad\square$

**Corollary 1 ($\mathrm{LOR}^{\kappa, 1} \implies \mathrm{LOR}^{\kappa, \boxtimes}$).** *There is an SFBB reduction $\mathbb{B}$ such that, for every adversary $\mathbb{A}$,*

$$\mathrm{LOR\text{-}CXA}_{\mathrm{PKE}}^{\kappa, \boxtimes}(\mathbb{A}) \leq \mathrm{LOR\text{-}CXA}_{\mathrm{PKE}}^{\kappa, 1}(\mathbb{B}).$$

In the presence of a corruption oracle, the reduction breaks down as it is no longer able to simulate properly: it cannot both challenge on and corrupt the same key (a behaviour that is allowed in the diagonal and free-bit games). We will return to the free-bit game in the presence of corruptions below, but first we turn our attention to that other indistinguishability notion, real-or-random.

*Extending the Argument to Real-or-Random.* The proof of Theorem 1 makes use of the fact that the LOR challenge oracle allows both a left and a right message to be input, enabling us to hide the bit in the ordering of the two messages. For ROR, the challenge oracle only accepts a single message, so hiding the bit as above is no longer possible.

However, when Bellare et al. [6] introduced the distinction between LOR versus ROR indistinguishability in the context of single-user probabilistic symmetric encryption, they also showed a factor-2 loss from ROR to LOR. As we will show in Theorem 5 (to be presented shortly), their proof technique is readily adapted to a relation between single-bit multi-user PKE notions. Theorems 1 and 5 can then be combined into the corollary below (which itself implies the equivalent of Corollary 1 for ROR, again with a factor 2 loss).

**Corollary 2 ($\mathrm{ROR}^{\kappa, 1} \overset{\leq 2}{\implies} \mathrm{ROR}^{\kappa, \beta}$).** *There is an SFBB reduction $\mathbb{B}$ such that, for every adversary $\mathbb{A}$,*

$$\mathrm{ROR\text{-}CXA}_{\mathrm{PKE}}^{\kappa, \beta}(\mathbb{A}) \leq 2 \cdot \mathrm{ROR\text{-}CXA}_{\mathrm{PKE}}^{\kappa, 1}(\mathbb{B}).$$

*Proof (Sketch).* Theorem 5 states that $\text{ROR}^{\kappa,1} \overset{\leq 2}{\Longrightarrow} \text{LOR}^{\kappa,1}$, while trivially $\text{LOR}^{\kappa,\beta} \Longrightarrow \text{ROR}^{\kappa,\beta}$. Then, using Theorem 1, we get $\text{ROR}^{\kappa,1} \overset{\leq 2}{\Longrightarrow} \text{LOR}^{\kappa,1} \Longrightarrow \text{LOR}^{\kappa,\beta} \Longrightarrow \text{ROR}^{\kappa,\beta}$.

### 4.3   The Free-Bit Game with Corruptions

In the free-bit game, the adversary can both challenge on and corrupt keys, provided the final targeted bit remains uncorrupted. In the single-bit game, however, challenging on and corrupting a key are mutually exclusive, causing the bit-hiding argument, that tightly related $\text{LOR}^{\kappa,1}$ to $\text{LOR}^{\kappa,\beta}$, to break down in the presence of corruptions. Seemingly, the best we can do is a standard bit-guessing argument, suffering a $\beta$ loss, as formalized in Theorem 2 below (see Appendix E for a full proof).

**Theorem 2** ($\text{IND}^{\cancel{\kappa},1} \overset{\leq \beta}{\Longrightarrow} \text{IND}^{\cancel{\kappa},\beta}$). *There is an SFBB reduction* $\mathbb{B}$ *such that, for any adversary* $\mathbb{A}$,

$$\text{IND-CXA}_{\text{PKE}}^{\cancel{\kappa},\beta}(\mathbb{A}) \leq \beta \cdot \text{IND-CXA}_{\text{PKE}}^{\cancel{\kappa},1}(\mathbb{B}),$$

*where* $\mathbb{B}$*'s overhead consists of drawing* $\beta$ *uniformly random bits.*

Combining with $\text{IND} \overset{\leq \kappa}{\Longrightarrow} \text{IND}^{\cancel{\kappa},1}$ (Theorem 3) yields an upper bound on the free-bit advantage as it relates to single-user advantage, see Corollary 3. Notably, when Jager et al. [25] introduced the free-bit notion (for AE), they observed that proving a linear loss was beyond them, yet they did not provide an alternative, looser bound instead. We therefore plug this gap in the literature. Figure 6 provides an overview of how the single-user and simple multi-user notions relate to the free-bit notions.

**Corollary 3** ($\text{IND} \overset{\leq \kappa\beta}{\Longrightarrow} \text{IND}^{\cancel{\kappa},\beta}$). *There is a reduction* $\mathbb{B}$ *such that, for any adversary* $\mathbb{A}$,

$$\text{IND-CXA}_{\text{PKE}}^{\cancel{\kappa},\beta}(\mathbb{A}) \leq \kappa \cdot \beta \cdot \text{IND-CXA}_{\text{PKE}}(\mathbb{B}).$$

$\mathbb{B}$ *calls* $\mathbb{A}$ *once, and additionally uses the resources needed to draw* $\kappa$ *fresh keypairs and* $\beta$ *uniformly random bits.*

Interestingly, Corollary 3 tightly implies Theorem 3, but not Theorem 4: setting $\kappa = \beta$ in Corollary 3 yields a $\kappa^2$ loss. This gives some hope that a tighter relation than that of Corollary 3 might still be possible, one that would imply both Theorems 3 and 4. We leave this an open problem, although present some initial thoughts in Appendix B.

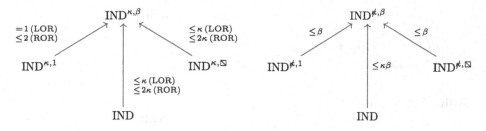

**Fig. 6.** Relations between different multi-user notions, without corruptions (left), and with corruptions (right).

## 4.4 LOR Versus ROR, or When the Challenge Oracle Matters

Until now, we have for the most part treated the two flavours of indistinguishability as one. However, as we saw for Theorem 1, the choice of challenge oracle can sometimes make a difference. Of course, left-or-right indistinguishability always implies real-or-random indistinguishability. Furthermore, for single-user notions, it has been long been known that ROR implies LOR with only a factor 2 tightness loss [5]. However, for multi-instance security [10], the loss is known to blow up exponentially. Thus, it is a priori unclear what losses one should expect for the multi-user setting, both between corresponding LOR and ROR notions, but also between the ROR notions themselves.

Jager et al. [26, Theorem 21] showed a general result that a loss $L$ in the single user setting can be turned into a loss $L\kappa$ for the simple notions (for AE); the free-bit case is not addressed. We complement their results for the PKE setting, as summarized in Fig. 7 and formalized in Appendix D.

Some relations are worth highlighting. First, note that the same factor 2 reduction still lends itself to the single-bit multi-key setting (with or without corruptions). The argument is very similar to that of the single-user case: either the bit is "real", in which case the simulated game is equivalent to the left-or-right one, or the bit is "random", in which case the simulated challenge bit is information-theoretically hidden from the adversary; the main complication in going to a multi-key setting with corruptions being dealing with disallowed guesses. See Theorem 5. This contrasts to the diagonal-bit setting, in which the tightest known reduction loses a factor $2\kappa$, as achieved via the single-user relation: $\text{ROR}^{u,\boxdot} \implies \text{ROR} \overset{\leq 2}{\implies} \text{LOR} \overset{\leq \kappa}{\implies} \text{LOR}^{u,\boxdot}$.

Second, note that the fact that $\text{LOR}^{\kappa,1} \implies \text{LOR}^{\kappa,\beta}$ (Theorem 1) allows us to conclude that the factor 2 reduction still holds for the free-bit notion absent corruptions: $\text{ROR}^{\kappa,\beta} \implies \text{ROR}^{\kappa,1} \overset{\leq 2}{\implies} \text{LOR}^{\kappa,1} \implies \text{LOR}^{\kappa,\beta}$. Compare with the situation in the presence of corruptions, where the corresponding implications yield $\text{ROR}^{\sharp,\beta} \overset{\leq 2\beta}{\implies} \text{LOR}^{\sharp,\beta}$.

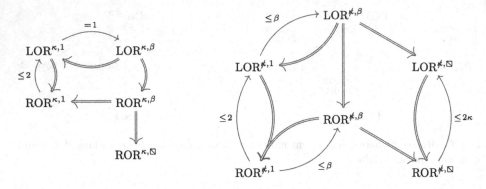

**Fig. 7.** Relations between lor and ror for the different multi-user notions, without corruptions (left) and with corruptions (right). The placement of notions roughly translate to their relative strength, with stronger notions placed higher, (see Fig. 6 for the implications missing from the figure.) As before, double arrows indicate trivially tight.

As before, we leave the question of whether there exist tighter reductions, or these losses really are inevitable, as open questions. Nevertheless, these additional losses serve to reinforce the folklore that left-or-right notions should be preferred over real-or-random whenever possible.

## 5   Conclusion

In this article, we surveyed several possible notions of multi-user security, showing how they relate to each other, and identifying a unified and general free-bit notion. We also conclusively answered the question of which canonical multi-user notion is the preferred one in the absence of corruptions, namely the single-bit left-or-right notion, as it is as strong or stronger than any of the others. In the presence of corruptions, the situation is less clear, particularly as it is not currently known whether the ability to both challenge and corrupt a key yields the adversary any additional power. What *is* known, however, is that the ability to challenge the same bit on several keys *does* give the adversary extra power. Until these questions have been definitively settled, we therefore suggest aiming for security under a free-bit notion whenever multi-user security with adaptive corruptions is to be considered.

## A    A Brief History of Indistinguishability

The traditional 'IND-CPA' security notion for public key encryption (PKE) is an indistinguishability notion (IND) under adaptively chosen plaintext attacks

(CPA). Here an adversary receives a challenge ciphertext either for a plaintext of its choosing or an alternative challenge ciphertext, and needs to decide which one was received. The alternate challenge ciphertext can be generated in different ways, leading to subtly different notions [6]. The two common choices are: left-or-right (LOR), in which the adversary supplies two messages and receives the encryption of one of them; and real-or-random (ROR), in which the adversary supplies a message and either receives its encryption or the encryption of a random bit string. When Bellare et al. [7] considered various PKE security notions they showed that LOR-security tightly implies ROR-security, whereas the other direction incurs a modest security loss of a factor 2.

Stronger, more realistic notions are indistinguishability under adaptively chosen ciphertext attacks (CCA), or IND-CCA (historically also called IND-CCA2 to distinguish it from its non-adaptive counterpart IND-CCA1 [7]). Here, in addition to choosing the plaintexts to be challenged on, the adversary is given access to a decryption oracle, which it can query on any valid ciphertext receiving the corresponding plaintext, or the ciphertext-reject symbol $\perp$. To avoid trivial wins, some care needs to be taken when the challenge ciphertext is submitted to the encryption oracle; there are several mechanisms to deal with this subtlety [8]. Ignoring the decryption oracle gives back IND-CPA, making IND-CCA the stronger notion. Moreover, several real-world attacks not covered by IND-CPA (such as Bleichenbacher's attack [11]) are captured by IND-CCA, making the latter the preferred notion to aim for.

We are concerned with the multi-user setting, leading to further definitional choices. Although it might appear that these choices are largely irrelevant in an asymptotic context, as they are all polynomially equivalent, a concrete security treatment can surface non-trivial differences. These differences are often amplified with the introduction of multiple users, particularly when considering adaptive corruptions (see below).

First of all, while the notions above initially only allowed for a single challenge query, when Bellare et al. [5] investigated multi-user security, they simultaneously generalized the single-user notions by giving each user multiple challenges. Moreover, they showed that security under single-challenge implies security under multi-challenge with an (inevitable) loss linear in the number of challenges (cf. [6]).

In the present work, we consider all notions, including the single-user notions, to be multi-challenge. To adapt our results to a single-challenge setting, simply note that our single-user notions imply the corresponding single-challenge notion with a tightness loss $q^{\mathcal{E}}$, and insert the factor as needed. For instance, writing SC-IND for single-challenge indistinguishability, the analogue to Corollary 3 becomes SC-IND $\xrightarrow{\leq q^{\mathcal{E}} \kappa\beta}$ IND$^{\kappa,\beta}$.

Another choice is how to 'multiplex' the challenge oracles: should each user be independent of the others, or should they depend on each other? When multi-user security was introduced [5], the game only had a single challenge bit shared across all users for an adversary to guess. This choice intuitively leads to a stronger notion than if each user was given its own challenge bit as, with a single shared bit, an adversary can 'gather evidence' for the true value of this challenge bit across the users (we provide evidence to this intuition in Corollary 1). Yet, the notion feels awkward when introducing corruptions, given that both corrupting and challenging on the same key would immediately yield a trivial win. One option is to disallow corrupting 'challenge' keys, and vice versa, leading to the single-bit notion $\text{IND}^{\kappa,1}$ [3,24,28]. Another option is to introduce user-specific bits. This was the approach employed by Bader et al. [2] in their study of authenticated key exchange: they considered a multi-user KEM notion with corruptions where each user was associated with its own challenge bit and the adversary had to declare at the end which uncorrupted bit it was guessing. Thus, even if a user was both challenged on and corrupted, a non-trivial win would still be possible. In the present work, we refer to this notion as *diagonal-bit* ($\text{IND}^{\not\kappa,\boxtimes}$), as explained in Sect. 3.

Recently, Jager et al. [24] pointed out that this notion is problematic in the AKE setting, as unlike in the single-bit setting, a KEM secure under the diagonal-bit notion is not known to tightly compose to an AKE. They went on to construct a KEM tightly secure under the single-bit notion instead, which was therefore guaranteed to compose tightly.

Apart from the multi-user setting, the diagonal notion has seen use in the multi-*instance* setting [1,10], in which the adversary is asked to make a guess on *every* bit; in such settings, single-bit notions make little sense.

When Jager et al. [25] investigated the inevitability of multi-user tightness losses in the setting of authenticated encryption, they wanted their result to capture both of the the single-bit and the diagonal-bit notions, without having to provide separate proofs for the distinct cases. They therefore introduced a generalized notion, in which an adversary was free to choose the exact relations between the keys and challenge bits. This notion, which avoids the awkwardness of not being able to both challenge and corrupt the same key without sacrificing the ability to "gather evidence" on a bit over several keys, sits at the centre of much of the present work, and we refer to it as the *free-bit* notion ($\text{IND}^{\not\kappa,\beta}$).

# B    Sharpness or When Tightness Losses are Inevitable

## B.1    Sharpness and Inevitably Lossy Reductions

A natural question for lossy reductions is whether the loss is inevitable or not. To determine inevitability, we only need to 'invert' Definition 2, as below in Definition 3.

**Definition 3 (Lossy).** *Let* $\text{IND}_1$ *and* $\text{IND}_2$ *be two indistinguishability notions for PKE schemes, and let* $c$ *be a positive real number, then* $\text{IND}_1 \stackrel{\geq c}{\Longrightarrow} \text{IND}_2$ *iff for all simple fully-black box reductions* $\mathbb{B}_1$ *there exist PKE schemes* PKE *and adversary* $\mathbb{A}_2$,

$$\text{IND}_2(\mathbb{A}_2) \geq c \cdot \text{IND}_1(\mathbb{B}_1^{\mathbb{A}_2,\text{PKE}}).$$

If both $\mathrm{IND}_1 \overset{\leq c}{\Longrightarrow} \mathrm{IND}_2$ and $\mathrm{IND}_1 \overset{\geq c}{\Longrightarrow} \mathrm{IND}_2$, then the reduction (for the first term) is sharp and we may write $\mathrm{IND}_1 \overset{=c}{\Longrightarrow} \mathrm{IND}_2$.

## B.2    Sharpness of Single-to-Simple Reductions

Below we discuss some relevant methods and results regarding the inevitability of lossy reductions in the context of multi-user PKE, showing that linear losses (in the number of users) is often sharp. Such results are often called impossibility results, yet to contrast with impossibility results that show that no constructions can achieve a notion (irrespective of the lossiness of the reduction), we prefer the term sharpness result when the impossibility is restricted to tightness only. The two main techniques are counterexamples and meta-reductions.

**Counterexamples.** As already pointed out by Bellare et al. [5], a simple counterexample shows that the bounds are generally sharp. They modified a PKE scheme that was identical to a 'secure' one except that with a small probability its encryption would be trivial and essentially just output the plaintext as the ciphertext (with some additional modifications to ensure correctness and that this event is easily recognizable publicly). Thus, when the challenge encryption oracle hits the trivial encryption, an adversary can trivially win its game; moreover the probability of this event happening at some point during the game is roughly linear with the number of challenge encryption queries.

However, given that we consider all our notions to be multi-challenge, we prefer a counterexample whose security degrades linearly in the number of available *keys*, not challenges. One might therefore instead consider a scheme for which a small-but-nonempty subset of the public keyspace returns messages in the clear. This "weak key" counterexample already works without corruptions for both of the simple multi-user notions, which implies sharpness for the more general notions.

Note that a similar critique of Bellare et al.'s original counterexample and (more refined) link with weak keys was made by Luykx et al. [30].

**Meta-reductions.** Another line of work has aimed to show sharpness through meta-reduction, thus ruling out tight reductions for a larger class of PKE schemes. The gain in generality is however traded for restrictions on the type of reductions that are ruled out, typically referred to as "simple" reductions (e.g., blackbox, no rewinding, etc.).

Bader et al. [3] showed that, for a large class of PKE systems, any simple reduction from a multi-user notion with corruptions to an underlying non-interactive hardness assumption must be lossy, with the loss linear in the number of keys. Meanwhile, Jager et al. [25] showed a similar result in the setting of authenticated encryption when reducing to single-user notions. In both cases, though, the proof technique crucially relied on the ability to corrupt keys, meaning that sharpness for the corruptionless notions aren't covered by their results.

Meta-reductions also don't rule out tight reductions for schemes outside the class considered; in fact, part of the usefulness of these results is the ability to look for tightly secure constructions outside these classes. This is exactly what Bader et al. [2] did when they constructed a tightly secure authenticated key exchange by deliberately breaking the requirement of public–private key uniqueness.

### B.3    Tightening the Single-to-Free Implication?

Corollary 3, $\text{IND} \xrightarrow{\leq \kappa \beta} \text{IND}^{\not\kappa,\beta}$, tightly implies Theorem 3, but not Theorem 4: setting $\kappa = \beta$ in Corollary 3 yields a $\kappa^2$ loss. This gives some hope that we might be able to show a tighter relation than that of Corollary 3, as in order to imply both Theorem 3 and 4, the statement would have to look something like the following.

*Conjecture 1* ($\text{IND} \xrightarrow{\leq \mathrm{I}^{\mathcal{E}}_{\max}\beta} \text{IND}^{\not\kappa,\beta}$). Let $\mathrm{I}^{\mathcal{E}}_{\max}$ be the maximum number of keys called together with any one challenge bit, (i.e., for any run of the game, we now require that $\forall j, |\mathrm{I}_j| \leq \mathrm{I}^{\mathcal{E}}_{\max}$; see Fig. 1). Then, there is a reduction $\mathbb{B}$ such that, for every adversary $\mathbb{A}$,

$$\text{IND-CXA}^{\not\kappa,\beta}_{\text{PKE}}(\mathbb{A}) \leq \mathrm{I}^{\mathcal{E}}_{\max} \cdot \beta \cdot \text{IND-CXA}_{\text{PKE}}(\mathbb{B}),$$

where $\mathbb{B}$ calls $\mathbb{A}$ once, and the overhead of $\mathbb{B}$ is small.

Then, for $\text{IND}^{\not\kappa,1}$, we would set $\mathrm{I}^{\mathcal{E}}_{\max} = \kappa$ and $\beta = 1$, while for $\text{IND}^{\not\kappa,\boxtimes}$, $\mathrm{I}^{\mathcal{E}}_{\max} = 1$ and $\beta = \kappa$. Thus, both theorems are recovered.

To prove the statement, a natural strategy would be to combine the proof techniques of each of the theorems it is generalising, i.e. by first guessing a challenge bit, and then doing a hybrid argument over the keys relating to that bit. However, given that the free-bit game allows the adversary to choose the relations between keys and bits adaptively, this hybrid argument does not work without incurring losses larger than that of Corollary 3. We nevertheless present Conjecture 1 as an interesting open problem.

## C    Formalization of Single to Simple Implications

*A Single-User Notion with Corruptions.* First, let us establish the trivial yet useful Lemma 3. Let $\text{Exp}^{\text{lor-cxa},1,1}_{\text{PKE}}(\mathbb{A})$ be exactly as the single-key game, except that the player now has the option to corrupt the key. In other words, the game will be equivalent to that of Fig. 1, with $\kappa = \beta = 1$ (and with or without decryption oracle). Given that in this game, an adversary that both challenges and corrupts will trigger the game to output the uniformly random value $\delta$, the presence of a corruption oracle should yield it no extra power. We formalize this intuition next.

**Lemma 3** (IND $\implies$ IND$^{1,1}$). *There is an SFBB reduction $\mathbb{B}$ with no additional overhead such that, for every adversary $\mathbb{A}$,*

$$\text{IND-CXA}^{1,1}_{\text{PKE}}(\mathbb{A}) \leq \text{IND-CXA}_{\text{PKE}}(\mathbb{B}).$$

*Proof.* The following argument works the same whether IND = LOR or ROR, and whether CXA = CCA or CPA. The reduction $\mathbb{B}$, playing the regular single-key game, simulates the game with corruptions to $\mathbb{A}$ by forwarding every oracle call and mimicking $\mathbb{A}$'s output, unless at some point $\mathbb{A}$ asks to corrupt: in that case $\mathbb{B}$ aborts $\mathbb{A}$ and simply returns 0. This works because if $\mathbb{A}$ corrupts, either $\mathbb{A}$ also challenges, in which case the advantage will be forced to 0, or it corrupts the key and outputs a guess without challenging, in which case the challenge bit will be information-theoretically hidden from it, so that its advantage is 0 by necessity. Thus, in the event that $\mathbb{A}$ corrupts at all, its win advantage will be exactly 0; the same that $\mathbb{B}$ gets from simply aborting $\mathbb{A}$ and outputting 0. We provide a formal derivation below.

$$\Pr\left[\text{Exp}^{\text{ind-cxa}}_{\text{PKE}}(\mathbb{B}) = 1\right] = \Pr[\mathbb{A}\text{ did not corrupt} \wedge \mathbb{A}\text{ wins}]$$
$$+ \Pr[\mathbb{A}\text{ did corrupt} \wedge b = 0]$$
$$= \Pr[\mathbb{A}\text{ did not corrupt} \wedge \mathbb{A}\text{ wins}]$$
$$+ \Pr[\mathbb{A}\text{ did corrupt}] \cdot \Pr[b = 0 \mid \mathbb{A}\text{ did corrupt}]$$
$$= \Pr[\mathbb{A}\text{ did not corrupt} \wedge \mathbb{A}\text{ wins}]$$
$$+ \Pr[\mathbb{A}\text{ did corrupt}] \cdot 1/2$$
$$= \Pr[\mathbb{A}\text{ did not corrupt} \wedge \mathbb{A}\text{ wins}]$$
$$+ \Pr[\mathbb{A}\text{ did corrupt}] \cdot \Pr[\mathbb{A}\text{ wins} \mid \mathbb{A}\text{ did corrupt}]$$
$$= \Pr[\mathbb{A}\text{ did not corrupt} \wedge \mathbb{A}\text{ wins}]$$
$$+ \Pr[\mathbb{A}\text{ did corrupt} \wedge \mathbb{A}\text{ wins}]$$
$$= \Pr[\mathbb{A}\text{ wins}],$$
$$\Rightarrow \text{IND-CXA}_{\text{PKE}}(\mathbb{B}) \geq \text{IND-CXA}^{1,1}_{\text{PKE}}(\mathbb{A}).$$

$\square$

*Single-Bit Security with Corruptions.* We can then show a reduction from IND-CXA$^{\kappa,1}_{\text{PKE}}$ to IND-CXA$^{1,1}_{\text{PKE}}$, using exactly same hybrid argument that was used by Bellare et al. [5] in the absence of corruptions, and let Lemma 3 imply the result.

**Theorem 3** (IND $\overset{\leq \kappa}{\implies}$ IND$^{\kappa,1}$). *There is a SFBB reduction $\mathbb{B}$ such that, for every adversary $\mathbb{A}$,*

$$\text{IND-CXA}^{\kappa,1}_{\text{PKE}}(\mathbb{A}) \leq \kappa \cdot \text{IND-CXA}_{\text{PKE}}(\mathbb{B}),$$

*where $\mathbb{B}$'s overhead consists of $\kappa - 1$ fresh keypair generations.*

*Proof (sketch).* Through a standard hybrid argument completely analogous to that used to prove the corruptionless version, we can show that there is an adversary $\mathbb{B}$ such that for every adversary $\mathbb{A}$,

$$\text{IND-CXA}_{\text{PKE}}^{\kappa,1}(\mathbb{A}) \leq \kappa \cdot \text{IND-CXA}_{\text{PKE}}^{1,1}(\mathbb{B}).$$

Then, Lemma 3 implies the result.

See the full version for the complete proof.

*Diagonal-Bit Security with Corruptions.* For the diagonal notion, showing the relation to the single-user notion is done using a different—and arguably simpler—proof technique: the reduction $\mathbb{B}$ simply guesses which user $\mathbb{A}$ is going to attack, forwarding the oracles called to that user to its own oracles and simulating the rest; it will guess correctly with probability $1/\kappa$, leading to the $\kappa$ security loss.

**Theorem 4** (IND $\overset{\leq \kappa}{\Longrightarrow}$ IND$^{\kappa,\boxtimes}$). *There is an SFBB reduction $\mathbb{B}$ such that, for every adversary $\mathbb{A}$,*

$$\text{IND-CXA}_{\text{PKE}}^{\kappa,\boxtimes}(\mathbb{A}) \leq \kappa \cdot \text{IND-CXA}_{\text{PKE}}(\mathbb{B}),$$

*where $\mathbb{B}$'s overhead consists of $\kappa - 1$ fresh keypair generations.*

*Proof (sketch).* $\mathbb{B}$ draws a key handle $i^* \in [\kappa]$ uniformly at random. Whenever $\mathbb{A}$ calls an oracle using this handle, $\mathbb{B}$ will forward the call to its own oracle. To simulate the rest of the users, $\mathbb{B}$ draws fresh keypairs and challenge bits, simulating the oracles as needed. If $\mathbb{A}$ returns a guess on challenge bit $i^*$, $\mathbb{B}$ forwards the guess, gaining the winning advantage of $\mathbb{A}$. Given that the value of $i^*$ is information-theoretically hidden from $\mathbb{A}$, this happens with probability exactly $1/\kappa$. Otherwise, $\mathbb{B}$ returns 0, achieving advantage 0.

The full proof can be found in the full version.

# D    Formalization of ROR to LOR Implications

**Theorem 5** (ROR$^{u,1} \overset{\leq 2}{\Longrightarrow}$ LOR$^{u,1}$). *There is a simple, fully black box reduction $\mathbb{B}$ such that, for any adversary $\mathbb{A}$,*

$$\text{LOR-CXA}_{\text{PKE}}^{u,1}(\mathbb{A}) \leq 2 \cdot \text{ROR-CXA}_{\text{PKE}}^{u,1}(\mathbb{B}),$$

*where $\mathbb{B}$'s overhead consists of drawing one uniformly random bit.*

*Proof (Sketch).* Essentially, there are only two, equally likely cases: either the bit is "real", in which case $\mathbb{B}$ is able to simulate the left-or-right game perfectly; or the bit is "random", in which case the advantage of $\mathbb{A}$ against the simulated game will be exactly 0—and the addition of corruptions does nothing to change this fact.

| $\mathbb{B}(\mathsf{pk}_1, \ldots, \mathsf{pk}_\kappa)$ | if A calls $\mathcal{E}(i, m_0, m_1)$ | if A calls $\mathcal{D}(i, c)$ |
|---|---|---|
| $d \leftarrow\!\!\$ \{0, 1\}$ | $c^* \leftarrow \mathcal{E}(i, m_d)$ | $m \leftarrow \mathcal{D}(i, c)$ |
| $\hat{d} \leftarrow\!\!\$ \mathbb{A}^{\mathcal{E}, \mathcal{D}, \mathcal{K}}(\mathsf{pk}_1, \ldots, \mathsf{pk}_\kappa)$ | **return** $c^*$ | **return** $m$ |
| $\hat{b} \leftarrow d \neq \hat{d}$ | | |
| **return** $\hat{b}$ | | if A calls $\mathcal{K}(i)$ |
| | | $\mathsf{sk}_i \leftarrow \mathcal{K}(i)$ |
| | | **return** $\mathsf{sk}_i$ |

**Fig. 8.** The adversary $\mathbb{B}$, playing $\mathsf{Exp}_{\mathrm{PKE}}^{\mathrm{ror\text{-}cca}, \kappa, 1}$ while simulating $\mathsf{Exp}_{\mathrm{PKE}}^{\mathrm{lor\text{-}cca}, \kappa, 1}$ for $\mathbb{A}$.

*Proof.* We will show the theorem for the case $u = \kappa$ and CXA = CCA; by inspection, the proof also holds for the cases $u = \kappa$ (by setting $\Pr[1 \in \mathsf{J}^{\mathcal{K}}] = 0$), and CXA = CPA.

In the following, let $b$ be the challenge bit of $\mathbb{B}$'s game $\mathsf{Exp}_{\mathrm{PKE}}^{\mathrm{ror\text{-}cca}, \kappa, 1}$ (see Fig. 1, with $\beta = 1$). Let $\mathsf{J}^{\mathcal{K}}$ denote the set of compromised bits; note however that there is now only one challenge bit per game, meaning its bit handle is 1, and the event that it was compromised is denoted by $1 \in \mathsf{J}^{\mathcal{K}}$. Using the strategy of Fig. 8, we then get $\Pr\left[\mathsf{Exp}_{\mathrm{PKE}}^{\mathrm{ror\text{-}cca}, \kappa, 1}(\mathbb{B}) = 1\right]$

$$= \Pr\left[1 \notin \mathsf{J}^{\mathcal{K}} \wedge d = \hat{d} \wedge b = 0\right]$$
$$+ \Pr\left[1 \notin \mathsf{J}^{\mathcal{K}} \wedge d \neq \hat{d} \wedge b = 1\right]$$
$$+ \Pr\left[1 \in \mathsf{J}^{\mathcal{K}} \wedge \delta = 1\right]$$
$$= \Pr[b = 0]\left(\Pr\left[1 \notin \mathsf{J}^{\mathcal{K}} \wedge d = \hat{d} \,\middle|\, b = 0\right] + \Pr\left[1 \in \mathsf{J}^{\mathcal{K}} \wedge \delta = 1 \,\middle|\, b = 0\right]\right)$$
$$+ \Pr[b = 1]\left(\Pr\left[1 \notin \mathsf{J}^{\mathcal{K}} \wedge d \neq \hat{d} \,\middle|\, b = 1\right] + \Pr\left[1 \in \mathsf{J}^{\mathcal{K}} \wedge \delta = 1 \,\middle|\, b = 1\right]\right) .$$

Note that if $b = 1$, then the value of $d$ is information-theoretically hidden from $\mathbb{A}$, so we have that $\Pr\left[d \neq \hat{d} \,\middle|\, b = 1\right] = \Pr[\delta = 1 \,|\, b = 1] = 1/2$, allowing us to write

$$= \Pr[b = 0]\left(\Pr\left[1 \notin \mathsf{J}^{\mathcal{K}} \wedge d = \hat{d} \,\middle|\, b = 0\right] + \Pr\left[1 \in \mathsf{J}^{\mathcal{K}} \wedge \delta = 1 \,\middle|\, b = 0\right]\right)$$
$$+ \Pr[b = 1]\left(\Pr\left[1 \notin \mathsf{J}^{\mathcal{K}} \wedge \delta = 1 \,\middle|\, b = 1\right] + \Pr\left[1 \in \mathsf{J}^{\mathcal{K}} \wedge \delta = 1 \,\middle|\, b = 1\right]\right)$$
$$= \Pr[b = 0]\left(\Pr\left[1 \notin \mathsf{J}^{\mathcal{K}} \wedge d = \hat{d} \,\middle|\, b = 0\right] + \Pr\left[1 \in \mathsf{J}^{\mathcal{K}} \wedge \delta = 1 \,\middle|\, b = 0\right]\right)$$
$$+ \Pr[b = 1] \cdot \Pr[\delta = 1 \,|\, b = 1]$$
$$= \frac{1}{2}\left(\Pr\left[1 \notin \mathsf{J}^{\mathcal{K}} \wedge d = \hat{d} \,\middle|\, b = 0\right] + \Pr\left[1 \in \mathsf{J}^{\mathcal{K}} \wedge \delta = 1 \,|\, b = 0\right] + \frac{1}{2}\right)$$
$$= \frac{1}{2}\left(\Pr\left[\mathsf{Exp}_{\mathrm{PKE}}^{\mathrm{lor\text{-}cca}, \kappa, 1}(\mathbb{A}) = 1\right] + \frac{1}{2}\right) .$$

Which implies that $\text{ROR-CCA}_{\text{PKE}}^{\not k,1}(\mathbb{B})$

$$
\begin{aligned}
&= 2 \cdot \Pr\left[\text{Exp}_{\text{PKE}}^{\text{ror-cca},\not k,1}(\mathbb{B}) = 1\right] - 1 \\
&= 2 \cdot \frac{1}{2}\left(\Pr\left[\text{Exp}_{\text{PKE}}^{\text{lor-cca},\not k,1}(\mathbb{A}) = 1\right] + \frac{1}{2}\right) - 1 \\
&= \frac{1}{2}\left(2 \cdot \Pr\left[\text{Exp}_{\text{PKE}}^{\text{lor-cca},\not k,1}(\mathbb{A}) = 1\right] - 1\right) \\
&= \frac{1}{2} \cdot \text{LOR-CCA}_{\text{PKE}}^{\not k,1}(\mathbb{A}),
\end{aligned}
$$

which is what we aimed to show.                                            □

Taken together with Theorem 1, this implies that the left-or-right free-bit notion without corruptions is separated from the single-bit real-or-random notion by at most a factor 2.

**Corollary 4** ($\text{ROR}^{\kappa,1} \overset{\leq 2}{\Longrightarrow} \text{LOR}^{\kappa,\beta}$)**.** *There is a reduction $\mathbb{B}$ such that, for any adversary $\mathbb{A}$,*

$$
\text{LOR-CXA}_{\text{PKE}}^{\kappa,\beta}(\mathbb{A}) \leq 2 \cdot \text{ROR-CXA}_{\text{PKE}}^{\kappa,1}(\mathbb{B}).
$$

$\mathbb{B}$ *calls $\mathbb{A}$ once, and additionally uses the resources needed to draw $\beta$ uniformly random bits.*

*Proof (Sketch).* Theorem 5 states that $\text{ROR}^{\kappa,1} \overset{\leq 2}{\Longrightarrow} \text{LOR}^{\kappa,1}$, while Theorem 1 states that $\text{LOR}^{\kappa,1} \implies \text{LOR}^{\kappa,\beta}$, allowing us to conclude that $\text{ROR}^{\kappa,1} \overset{\leq 2}{\Longrightarrow} \text{LOR}^{\kappa,\beta}$.

Given that the free-bit notion generalises the single-bit notion, this in turn implies that LOR and ROR are separated by at most a factor 2 between the corruptionless free-bit notions, even if the number of challenge bits varies between them.

With corruptions, however, any direct simulation would become trivially recognisable—meaning that in order to do a faithful simulation, the reduction would have to guess which bit the adversary is going to attack, leading to a loss linear in $\beta$. Instead of reformulating this argument, we let it follow as a corollary to previous results, yielding a slightly tighter statement by letting $\mathbb{B}$ play a single-bit game.

**Corollary 5** ($\text{ROR}^{\not k,1} \overset{\leq 2\beta}{\Longrightarrow} \text{LOR}^{\not k,\beta}$)**.** *For every adversary $\mathbb{A}$, there is an adversary $\mathbb{B}$, such that*

$$
\text{LOR-CXA}_{\text{PKE}}^{\not k,\beta}(\mathbb{A}) \leq 2 \cdot \beta \cdot \text{ROR-CXA}_{\text{PKE}}^{\not k,1}(\mathbb{B}).
$$

$\mathbb{B}$ *calls $\mathbb{A}$ once, and additionally uses the resources needed to draw $\beta$ uniformly random bits.*

*Proof (Sketch).* Theorem 5 states that $\mathrm{ROR}^{\not{k},1} \overset{\leq 2}{\Longrightarrow} \mathrm{LOR}^{\not{k},1}$, while Theorem 2 states that $\mathrm{LOR}^{\not{k},1} \overset{\leq \beta}{\Longrightarrow} \mathrm{LOR}^{\not{k},\beta}$, allowing us to conclude that $\mathrm{ROR}^{\not{k},1} \overset{\leq 2\beta}{\Longrightarrow} \mathrm{LOR}^{\not{k},\beta}$.

Interestingly, the tightest known relation from the diagonal-bit $\mathrm{ROR}^{\kappa,\boxtimes}$ to $\mathrm{LOR}^{\kappa,\boxtimes}$ is one that loses a factor $2\kappa$, even in the absense of corruptions. This is once again achieved going through the single-user notion.

**Corollary 6** ($\mathrm{ROR} \overset{\leq 2\kappa}{\Longrightarrow} \mathrm{LOR}^{u,\boxtimes}$). *There is a reduction $\mathbb{B}$ such that, for every adversary $\mathbb{A}$,*

$$\mathrm{LOR\text{-}CXA}_{\mathrm{PKE}}^{u,\boxtimes}(\mathbb{A}) \leq 2 \cdot \kappa \cdot \mathrm{ROR\text{-}CXA}_{\mathrm{PKE}}(\mathbb{B}).$$

*$\mathbb{B}$ calls $\mathbb{A}$ once, and additionally uses the resources needed to draw $\kappa$ fresh key-pairs and $\kappa$ uniformly random bits.*

*Proof (Sketch).* It is well established [6] that $\mathrm{ROR} \overset{\leq 2}{\Longrightarrow} \mathrm{LOR}$, and we know from Theorem 4 that $\mathrm{LOR} \overset{\leq \kappa}{\Longrightarrow} \mathrm{LOR}^{\not{k},\boxtimes}$, allowing us to conclude that $\mathrm{ROR} \overset{\leq 2\kappa}{\Longrightarrow} \mathrm{LOR}^{\not{k},\boxtimes}$.

# E     Deferred Proof of Theorem 2

**Theorem 2** ($\mathrm{IND}^{\not{k},1} \overset{\leq \beta}{\Longrightarrow} \mathrm{IND}^{\not{k},\beta}$). *There is an SFBB reduction $\mathbb{B}$ such that, for any adversary $\mathbb{A}$,*

$$\mathrm{IND\text{-}CXA}_{\mathrm{PKE}}^{\not{k},\beta}(\mathbb{A}) \leq \beta \cdot \mathrm{IND\text{-}CXA}_{\mathrm{PKE}}^{\not{k},1}(\mathbb{B}),$$

*where $\mathbb{B}$'s overhead consists of drawing $\beta$ uniformly random bits.*

We will show the result for $\mathrm{IND} = \mathrm{LOR}$ and $\mathrm{CXA} = \mathrm{CCA}$; the proof transfers directly to the ROR and CPA cases.

*Proof.* We will prove the statement by constructing an adversary $\mathbb{B}$ that achieves the claimed advantage by leveraging any advantage an adversary $\mathbb{A}$ has against the free-bit game, and making a guess on the bit that $\mathbb{A}$ is going to attack. $\mathbb{B}$ will guess correctly with probability $1/\beta$, leading to the $\beta$ security loss. The proof is very similar to that of Theorem 4, the main complication being that we now need to keep track of compromised challenge bits, instead of just which keys are corrupted.

$\mathbb{B}$ is given in Fig. 9. In the following, let $b$ be the challenge bit of $\mathbb{B}$'s game $\mathsf{Exp}_{\mathrm{PKE}}^{\mathrm{lor\text{-}cca},\not{k},1}$ (see Fig. 1, with $\beta = 1$), let the set of compromised bits (i.e., bits used by $\mathbb{A}$ to challenge a corrupted key) be denoted by $\mathsf{J}^{\mathcal{K}}$, and assume that $\mathbb{A}$ returns the guess $(j, \hat{b}_j)$. Finally, note that the value of $j^*$ is

| $\mathbb{B}(\mathsf{pk}_1,\dots,\mathsf{pk}_\kappa)$ | if $\mathbb{A}$ calls $\mathcal{E}(i,j,m_0,m_1)$ | if $\mathbb{A}$ calls $\mathcal{D}(i,c)$ |
|---|---|---|
| $j^* \leftarrow\!\!\$ \, [\beta]$ | if $m_0 \not\sim m_1$ then return $\ell$ | if $c \in \mathsf{C}_i$ then return $\ell$ |
| for $j \in [\beta], j \neq j^*$ do : | if $j = j^*$ | $m \leftarrow \mathcal{D}(i,c)$ |
| $\quad b_j \leftarrow\!\!\$ \, \{0,1\}$ | $\quad c^* \leftarrow \mathcal{E}(i,m_0,m_1)$ | return $m$ |
| $\mathsf{C}_1,\dots,\mathsf{C}_\kappa \leftarrow \emptyset$ | else $c^* \leftarrow\!\!\$ \, \mathsf{Pk.Enc}_{pk_i}(m_{b_j})$ | |
| $(j,\hat{b}_j) \leftarrow\!\!\$ \, \mathbb{A}^{\mathcal{E},\mathcal{D},\mathcal{K}}(\mathsf{pk}_1,\dots,\mathsf{pk}_\kappa)$ | $\mathsf{C}_i \leftarrow c^*$ | if $\mathbb{A}$ calls $\mathcal{K}(i)$ |
| if $j \neq j^*$ then return 0 | return $c^*$ | $\mathsf{sk}_i \leftarrow \mathcal{K}(i)$ |
| return $\hat{b}_j$ | | return $\mathsf{sk}_i$ |

**Fig. 9.** The adversary $\mathbb{B}$, playing $\mathrm{Exp}_{\mathrm{PKE}}^{\mathrm{lor\text{-}cca},\kappa,1}$ while simulating $\mathrm{Exp}_{\mathrm{PKE}}^{\mathrm{lor\text{-}cca},\kappa,\beta}$ for $\mathbb{A}$.

information-theoretically hidden from $\mathbb{A}$. Then, $\mathbb{B}$ achieves the following advantage, $\Pr\left[\mathrm{Exp}_{\mathrm{PKE}}^{\mathrm{lor\text{-}cca},\kappa,1}(\mathbb{B}) = 1\right]$

$$= \Pr\left[j = j^* \wedge j^* \notin \mathsf{J}^\mathcal{K} \wedge b_{j^*} = \hat{b}_{j^*}\right] + \Pr\left[j = j^* \wedge j^* \in \mathsf{J}^\mathcal{K} \wedge \delta = 1\right]$$
$$\quad + \Pr\left[j \neq j^* \wedge j^* \notin \mathsf{J}^\mathcal{K} \wedge b = 0\right] + \Pr\left[j \neq j^* \wedge j^* \in \mathsf{J}^\mathcal{K} \wedge \delta = 1\right]$$
$$= \Pr[j = j^*]\left(\Pr\left[j^* \notin \mathsf{J}^\mathcal{K} \wedge b_{j^*} = \hat{b}_{j^*} \mid j = j^*\right] + \Pr\left[j^* \in \mathsf{J}^\mathcal{K} \wedge \delta = 1 \mid j = j^*\right]\right)$$
$$\quad + \Pr[j \neq j^*]\left(\Pr[b = 0] \cdot \Pr\left[j^* \notin \mathsf{J}^\mathcal{K} \mid j \neq j^*\right] + \Pr[\delta = 1] \cdot \Pr\left[j^* \in \mathsf{J}^\mathcal{K} \mid j \neq j^*\right]\right)$$
$$= \frac{1}{\beta}\left(\Pr\left[j \notin \mathsf{J}^\mathcal{K} \wedge b_j = \hat{b}_j\right] + \Pr\left[j \in \mathsf{I}^\mathcal{K} \wedge \delta = 1\right]\right)$$
$$\quad + \frac{1}{2}\left(1 - \frac{1}{\kappa}\right)\left(\Pr\left[j^* \notin \mathsf{J}^\mathcal{K} \mid j \neq j^*\right] + \Pr\left[j^* \in \mathsf{J}^\mathcal{K} \mid j \neq j^*\right]\right)$$
$$= \frac{1}{\beta}\Pr\left[\mathrm{Exp}_{\mathrm{PKE}}^{\mathrm{lor\text{-}cca},\kappa,\beta}(\mathbb{A}) = 1\right] + \frac{1}{2}\left(1 - \frac{1}{\kappa}\right)$$
$$= \frac{1}{2\beta}\left(2 \cdot \Pr\left[\mathrm{Exp}_{\mathrm{PKE}}^{\mathrm{lor\text{-}cca},\kappa,\beta}(\mathbb{A}) = 1\right] - 1\right) + \frac{1}{2}$$

which implies that $\mathrm{LOR\text{-}CCA}_{\mathrm{PKE}}^{\kappa,1}(\mathbb{B})$

$$= 2 \cdot \Pr\left[\mathrm{Exp}_{\mathrm{PKE}}^{\mathrm{lor\text{-}cca},\kappa,1}(\mathbb{B}) = 1\right] - 1$$
$$= 2 \cdot \left(\frac{1}{2\beta}\mathrm{LOR\text{-}CCA}_{\mathrm{PKE}}^{\kappa,\beta}(\mathbb{A}) + \frac{1}{2}\right) - 1$$
$$= \frac{1}{\beta} \cdot \mathrm{LOR\text{-}CCA}_{\mathrm{PKE}}^{\kappa,\beta}(\mathbb{A}),$$

which is what we set out to show.    □

# F     Multi-bit Composability of Hybrid Encryption

As shown by Cramer and Shoup [14], one can combine the practicality of asymmetric encryption with the efficiency of symmetric encryption into a highly efficient public key encryption system. The idea is to encrypt the message under an ephemeral symmetric key, which is itself encapsulated under a public key. This paradigm, which already saw widespread use at the time, has become known as the KEM/DEM paradigm, after its constituent Key Encapsulation Mechanism and Data Encapsulation Mechanism; it is also known as *hybrid* encryption.

Recently, Lee et al. [28] built on earlier work by Giacon et al. [17] and showed that a KEM and a DEM tightly compose to a PKE in a single-bit multi-user setting with corruptions. We paraphrase their result in Theorem 3.

**Theorem 3 (Lee, Lee, Park, DCC'20).** *There are SFBB reductions* $\mathbb{B}$ *and* $\mathbb{C}$ *such that, for every adversary* $\mathbb{A}$,

$$\text{LOR-CXA}_{\text{PKE}}^{\mathit{k},1}(\mathbb{A}) \leq 2 \cdot \text{ROR-CCA}_{\text{KEM}}^{\mathit{k},1}(\mathbb{B}) + 1\text{LOR-CCA}_{\text{DEM}}(\mathbb{C})\,.$$

Here, 1LOR means "one-time left-or-right"; see their paper for definitions and proof. Combining their result with Theorem 2 yields the following, more general, corollary.

**Corollary 7 (Free-bit composability).** *There are SFBB reductions* $\mathbb{B}$ *and* $\mathbb{C}$ *such that, for every adversary* $\mathbb{A}$,

$$\text{LOR-CXA}_{\text{PKE}}^{\mathit{k},\beta}(\mathbb{A}) \leq 2 \cdot \beta \cdot \text{ROR-CCA}_{\text{KEM}}^{\mathit{k},1}(\mathbb{B}) + \beta \cdot 1\text{LOR-CCA}_{\text{DEM}}(\mathbb{C})\,.$$

*Proof.* Immediately follows from Theorems 2 and 3.

While lossy in the number of challenge bits, it matches Lee et al.'s Theorem for $\beta = 1$. However, the implication to the diagonal-bit notion, with $\beta = \kappa$, results in a rather lossy composition, as made explicit below.

**Corollary 8 (Diagonal-bit composability).** *There are SFBB reductions* $\mathbb{B}$ *and* $\mathbb{C}$ *such that, for every adversary* $\mathbb{A}$,

$$\text{LOR-CXA}_{\text{PKE}}^{\mathit{k},\boxtimes}(\mathbb{A}) \leq 2 \cdot \kappa \cdot \text{ROR-CCA}_{\text{KEM}}(\mathbb{B}) + \kappa \cdot 1\text{LOR-CCA}_{\text{DEM}}(\mathbb{C})\,.$$

*Proof.* Follows from Theorems 4 and 3.

No tighter composition is known for multi-bit security notions, for much the same reason that no tight composition is known for AKE: as pointed out by Jager et al. [24], the multi-bit KEM notion does not easily allow for a game hop in which real keys are exchanged for fake ones, making the resulting game something in between the 'real' and 'random' worlds. Any attempt to circumvent this issue (without specialising to specific constructions) seems to lead to hybrid or guessing arguments, yielding similar linear losses.

# References

1. Auerbach, B., Giacon, F., Kiltz, E.: Everybody's a target: scalability in public-key encryption. In: Canteaut, A., Ishai, Y. (eds.) EUROCRYPT 2020. LNCS, vol. 12107, pp. 475–506. Springer, Cham (2020). https://doi.org/10.1007/978-3-030-45727-3_16

2. Bader, C., Hofheinz, D., Jager, T., Kiltz, E., Li, Y.: Tightly-secure authenticated key exchange. In: Dodis, Y., Nielsen, J.B. (eds.) TCC 2015. LNCS, vol. 9014, pp. 629–658. Springer, Heidelberg (2015). https://doi.org/10.1007/978-3-662-46494-6_26

3. Bader, C., Jager, T., Li, Y., Schäge, S.: On the impossibility of tight cryptographic reductions. In: Fischlin, M., Coron, J.-S. (eds.) EUROCRYPT 2016. LNCS, vol. 9666, pp. 273–304. Springer, Heidelberg (2016). https://doi.org/10.1007/978-3-662-49896-5_10

4. Baecher, P., Brzuska, C., Fischlin, M.: Notions of black-box reductions, revisited. In: Sako, K., Sarkar, P. (eds.) ASIACRYPT 2013. LNCS, vol. 8269, pp. 296–315. Springer, Heidelberg (2013). https://doi.org/10.1007/978-3-642-42033-7_16

5. Bellare, M., Boldyreva, A., Micali, S.: Public-key encryption in a multi-user setting: security proofs and improvements. In: Preneel, B. (ed.) EUROCRYPT 2000. LNCS, vol. 1807, pp. 259–274. Springer, Heidelberg (2000). https://doi.org/10.1007/3-540-45539-6_18

6. Bellare, M., Desai, A., Jokipii, E., Rogaway, P.: A concrete security treatment of symmetric encryption. In: 38th FOCS, pp. 394–403. IEEE Computer Society Press, October 1997. https://doi.org/10.1109/SFCS.1997.646128

7. Bellare, M., Desai, A., Pointcheval, D., Rogaway, P.: Relations among notions of security for public-key encryption schemes. In: Krawczyk, H. (ed.) CRYPTO 1998. LNCS, vol. 1462, pp. 26–45. Springer, Heidelberg (1998). https://doi.org/10.1007/BFb0055718

8. Bellare, M., Hofheinz, D., Kiltz, E.: Subtleties in the definition of IND-CCA: when and how should challenge decryption be disallowed? J. Cryptol. 28(1), 29–48 (2015). https://doi.org/10.1007/s00145-013-9167-4

9. Bellare, M., Hofheinz, D., Yilek, S.: Possibility and impossibility results for encryption and commitment secure under selective opening. In: Joux, A. (ed.) EUROCRYPT 2009. LNCS, vol. 5479, pp. 1–35. Springer, Heidelberg (2009). https://doi.org/10.1007/978-3-642-01001-9_1

10. Bellare, M., Ristenpart, T., Tessaro, S.: Multi-instance security and its application to password-based cryptography. In: Safavi-Naini, R., Canetti, R. (eds.) CRYPTO 2012. LNCS, vol. 7417, pp. 312–329. Springer, Heidelberg (2012). https://doi.org/10.1007/978-3-642-32009-5_19

11. Bleichenbacher, D.: Chosen ciphertext attacks against protocols based on the RSA encryption standard PKCS #1. In: Krawczyk, H. (ed.) CRYPTO 1998. LNCS, vol. 1462, pp. 1–12. Springer, Heidelberg (1998). https://doi.org/10.1007/BFb0055716

12. Canetti, R., Halevi, S., Katz, J.: Adaptively-secure, non-interactive public-key encryption. In: Kilian, J. (ed.) TCC 2005. LNCS, vol. 3378, pp. 150–168. Springer, Heidelberg (2005). https://doi.org/10.1007/978-3-540-30576-7_9

13. Cohn-Gordon, K., Cremers, C., Gjøsteen, K., Jacobsen, H., Jager, T.: Highly efficient key exchange protocols with optimal tightness. In: Boldyreva, A., Micciancio, D. (eds.) CRYPTO 2019. LNCS, vol. 11694, pp. 767–797. Springer, Cham (2019). https://doi.org/10.1007/978-3-030-26954-8_25

14. Cramer, R., Shoup, V.: A practical public key cryptosystem provably secure against adaptive chosen ciphertext attack. In: Krawczyk, H. (ed.) CRYPTO 1998. LNCS, vol. 1462, pp. 13–25. Springer, Heidelberg (1998). https://doi.org/10.1007/BFb0055717

15. Dwork, C., Naor, M., Reingold, O., Stockmeyer, L.J.: Magic functions. In: 40th FOCS, pp. 523–534. IEEE Computer Society Press, October 1999. https://doi.org/10.1109/SFFCS.1999.814626

16. Gay, R., Hofheinz, D., Kiltz, E., Wee, H.: Tightly CCA-secure encryption without pairings. In: Fischlin, M., Coron, J.-S. (eds.) EUROCRYPT 2016. LNCS, vol. 9665, pp. 1–27. Springer, Heidelberg (2016). https://doi.org/10.1007/978-3-662-49890-3_1

17. Giacon, F., Kiltz, E., Poettering, B.: Hybrid encryption in a multi-user setting, revisited. In: Abdalla, M., Dahab, R. (eds.) PKC 2018. LNCS, vol. 10769, pp. 159–189. Springer, Cham (2018). https://doi.org/10.1007/978-3-319-76578-5_6

18. Han, S., Liu, S., Gu, D.: Key encapsulation mechanism with tight enhanced security in the multi-user setting: impossibility result and optimal tightness. In: ASIACRYPT 2021. LNCS. Springer, Heidelberg (2021, to appear)

19. Hazay, C., Patra, A., Warinschi, B.: Selective opening security for receivers. In: Iwata, T., Cheon, J.H. (eds.) ASIACRYPT 2015. LNCS, vol. 9452, pp. 443–469. Springer, Heidelberg (2015). https://doi.org/10.1007/978-3-662-48797-6_19

20. Hofheinz, D., Hövelmanns, K., Kiltz, E.: A modular analysis of the Fujisaki-Okamoto transformation. In: Kalai, Y., Reyzin, L. (eds.) TCC 2017. LNCS, vol. 10677, pp. 341–371. Springer, Cham (2017). https://doi.org/10.1007/978-3-319-70500-2_12

21. Hofheinz, D., Jager, T.: Tightly secure signatures and public-key encryption. Des. Codes Cryptogr. 80(1), 29–61 (2016)

22. Hofheinz, D., Nguyen, N.K.: On tightly secure primitives in the multi-instance setting. In: Lin, D., Sako, K. (eds.) PKC 2019. LNCS, vol. 11442, pp. 581–611. Springer, Cham (2019). https://doi.org/10.1007/978-3-030-17253-4_20

23. Hofheinz, D., Rao, V., Wichs, D.: Standard security does not imply indistinguishability under selective opening. In: Hirt, M., Smith, A. (eds.) TCC 2016. LNCS, vol. 9986, pp. 121–145. Springer, Heidelberg (2016). https://doi.org/10.1007/978-3-662-53644-5_5

24. Jager, T., Kiltz, E., Riepel, D., Schäge, S.: Tightly-secure authenticated key exchange, revisited. In: Canteaut, A., Standaert, F.-X. (eds.) EUROCRYPT 2021. LNCS, vol. 12696, pp. 117–146. Springer, Cham (2021). https://doi.org/10.1007/978-3-030-77870-5_5

25. Jager, T., Stam, M., Stanley-Oakes, R., Warinschi, B.: Multi-key authenticated encryption with corruptions: reductions are lossy. In: Kalai, Y., Reyzin, L. (eds.) TCC 2017. LNCS, vol. 10677, pp. 409–441. Springer, Cham (2017). https://doi.org/10.1007/978-3-319-70500-2_14

26. Jager, T., Stam, M., Stanley-Oakes, R., Warinschi, B.: Multi-key authenticated encryption with corruptions: reductions are lossy. Cryptology ePrint Archive, Report 2017/495 (2017). https://eprint.iacr.org/2017/495

27. Katz, J., Lindell, Y.: Introduction to Modern Cryptography, 2nd edn. Chapman & Hall/CRC, London (2015)

28. Lee, Y., Lee, D.H., Park, J.H.: Tightly CCA-secure encryption scheme in a multi-user setting with corruptions. Des. Codes Cryptogr. 88(11), 2433–2452 (2020)

29. Lewko, A., Waters, B.: Why proving HIBE systems secure is difficult. In: Nguyen, P.Q., Oswald, E. (eds.) EUROCRYPT 2014. LNCS, vol. 8441, pp. 58–76. Springer, Heidelberg (2014). https://doi.org/10.1007/978-3-642-55220-5_4

30. Luykx, A., Mennink, B., Paterson, K.G.: Analyzing multi-key security degradation. In: Takagi, T., Peyrin, T. (eds.) ASIACRYPT 2017. LNCS, vol. 10625, pp. 575–605. Springer, Cham (2017). https://doi.org/10.1007/978-3-319-70697-9_20
31. Reingold, O., Trevisan, L., Vadhan, S.: Notions of reducibility between cryptographic primitives. In: Naor, M. (ed.) TCC 2004. LNCS, vol. 2951, pp. 1–20. Springer, Heidelberg (2004). https://doi.org/10.1007/978-3-540-24638-1_1

# Asymptotically Tight Lower Bounds in Anonymous Broadcast Encryption and Authentication

Hirokazu Kobayashi[1(✉)], Yohei Watanabe[2], and Junji Shikata[1]

[1] Yokohama National University, 79-7 Tokiwadai,
Hodogaya-ku, Yokohama, Kanagawa 240-8501, Japan
kobayashi-hirokazu-dr@ynu.jp, shikata-junji-rb@ynu.ac.jp
[2] The University of Electro-Communications, 1-5-1 Chofugaoka,
Chofu, Tokyo 182-8585, Japan
watanabe@uec.ac.jp

**Abstract.** Broadcast Encryption (BE) is a cryptosystem that allows a sender to specify recipients so that only the specified recipients can perform decryption. Anonymity, which is one of additional but important security requirements of BE, guarantees that no information of the designated recipients is leaked from ciphertexts, and several BE schemes with anonymity (ANO-BE) have been proposed so far.

Kiayias and Samari (IH 2013) analyzed a lower bound on the ciphertext size required for ANO-BE. In their analysis, they derived the lower bound under the assumption that ANO-BE schemes meets a special property. However, it is unclear whether the special property holds for existing ANO-BE schemes. In other words, their analysis is insufficient to show that the existing ANO-BE schemes achieve the optimal ciphertext size.

In this paper, we derive a lower bound on the ciphertext size in ANO-BE, assuming only properties that most existing ANO-BE schemes satisfy. In our analysis, we newly define several properties abstracted from existing (even non-anonymous) BE schemes and carefully analyze them to replace the Kiayias–Samari assumption with ours. As a result, we show that the existing ANO-BE schemes achieve the optimal ciphertext size. We further show that our analysis can be extended to the authentication setting. Specifically, we first derive a lower bound on the authenticator size required for anonymous broadcast authentication.

**Keywords:** Broadcast encryption · Anonymity · Lower bound

© Springer Nature Switzerland AG 2021
M. B. Paterson (Ed.): IMACC 2021, LNCS 13129, pp. 105–128, 2021.
https://doi.org/10.1007/978-3-030-92641-0_6

# 1   Introduction

**(Anonymous) Broadcast Encryption.** *Broadcast Encryption* (BE) is public-key encryption in which a sender can choose a set of recipients so that only designated recipients can decrypt the ciphertext encrypted by the sender. In BE, the sender specifies a subset $\mathcal{S}$, called a *privileged set*, from $N$ recipients when encrypting a message m. Only designated recipients in $\mathcal{S}$ can decrypt the corresponding ciphertexts $ct_{\mathcal{S}}$, and non-designated recipients cannot decrypt them. Thanks to the functionality, BE has many applications such as pay-TV. BE is said to satisfy *collusion resistance*, which is a de-facto standard security notion of BE, if BE is secure against any number of colluders. To date, many collusion-resistant BE schemes have been proposed (e.g., [1,2,4,5,7,8,14,15]).

In addition, there are several work [3,9–11] on BEs meeting anonymity,[1] which guarantees that no information on the designated set of recipients $\mathcal{S}$ is leaked from ciphertexts $ct_{\mathcal{S}}$. Indeed, anonymity is an important security notion from a practical perspective. For example, the pay-TV service sometimes requires users' privacy as well as the confidentiality of contents. Specifically, there are two main notions for anonymity, called *anonymity* and *full anonymity*, or *Anonymous BE*, introduced by Barth et al. [3] and Kiayias and Samari [9], respectively.[2] The differences between them are as follows: anonymity guarantees that no information on a set of designated recipients is leaked from ciphertexts except for its size; full anonymity guarantees that ciphertexts do not leak even the information on the size of the set. In this paper, we refer to BE meeting anonymity and full anonymity as ANO-BE and full-ANO-BE, respectively.

**Ciphertext Size of Anonymous BE.** The existing anonymous BE schemes [3, 10,11] achieve the ciphertext-size being linear in the number of designated recipients or all recipients. Specifically, the ciphertext sizes in the existing schemes are shown as $O(|\mathcal{S}| \cdot \kappa)$ for ANO-BE and $O(N \cdot \kappa)$ for full-ANO-BE, where $|\mathcal{S}|$ and $N$ are the numbers of designated recipients and all recipients, respectively, and $\kappa$ is a security parameter. Therefore, we see that they are the upper bounds on ciphertext-sizes of Anonymous BEs.

On the other hand, lower bounds on ciphertext-sizes of Anonymous BEs (i.e., ANO-BE and full-ANO-BE) are derived by Kiayias and Samari [9]. More precisely, they deived lower bounds on the ciphertext-size, $\Omega(|\mathcal{S}| \cdot \kappa)$ for ANO-BE and $\Omega(N \cdot \kappa)$ for full-ANO-BE, for *a limited class* of (anonymous) BE and listed several BE schemes in [3,11,12] in the class[3]. We emphasize that in their analysis on lower bounds, they implicitly assume a special property for BE schemes in their main theorem [9, Theorem 1]. Namely, they indeed proved "if a BE scheme

---

[1] The term *privacy* is often used instead of anonymity (e.g., [3,9]).

[2] There is another notion of "outsider anonymity" [6], weaker than both anonymity and full anonymity. We do not deal with the notion in this paper.

[3] Kiayias and Samari also derived lower bounds on the ciphertext sizes $\Omega(N + \kappa)$ required for *any* full-ANO-BE [9, Lemma 2]. However, it is unclear whether the lower bound is asymptotically tight, because no full-ANO-BE construction attains it.

is anonymous and satisfies the special property, then the lower bound holds."
However, it is hard to check whether the existing anonymous BE schemes in
the limited class (e.g., [3,9,11]) satisfy the property (see Sect. 1.2 for details). In
other words, it is not cleary stated that those anonymous BE schemes achieve
asymptotically the optimal ciphertext-size.

## 1.1  Our Contributions

In this paper, assuming only properties found in most existing (anonymous)
BE schemes, we show that lower bounds on ciphertext size for ANO-BE and
full-ANO-BE are $\Omega\left(|\mathcal{S}| \cdot \kappa\right)$ and $\Omega\left(N \cdot \kappa\right)$, respectively. As a result, we first
show that existing ANO-BE schemes indeed achieve the optimal ciphertext sizes.
Since the properties we assume are applicable for existing (even non-anonymous)
BE schemes, our results also show that extending existing non-anonymous BE
schemes to meet anonymity is impossible unless its ciphertext size attains our
lower bound.

   In order to facilitate our analysis, we take a similar approach to Kiayias and
Samari's one: we consider Atomic BE (AtBE), which covers a broad range of
(both anonymous and non-anonymous) BE schemes. AtBE allows each ciphertext and decryption key to be divided into multiple sub-elements, called *atomic
ciphertexts and decryption keys*, respectively. We then derive lower bounds on the
ciphertext sizes by showing lower bounds in the number of atomic ciphertexts
required for any anonymous BE scheme with the properties that most of the
existing anonymous BE schemes have. We summarize the differences between
our and Kiayias and Samari's analysis as follows.

- As described above, we assume several properties that most of the existing BE
  schemes have. To formally describe them, we give a formal syntax of AtBE,
  whereas Kiayias and Samari considered an informal syntax of AtBE.
- Our lower bounds hold for most of the existing anonymous BE schemes (i.e.,
  BE schemes in [3,10,11]), since we only assume the properties common to
  them. Almost all non-anonymous BE schemes in [1,2,4,5,7,8,12,14] also meet
  the properties, our results are applicable for their variants. On the other hand,
  it is unclear that the special property implicitly assumed in [9] holds for the
  existing anonymous BE schemes.

We emphasize that the syntax and properties of AtBE we consider cannot trivially obtained from Kiayias and Samari's results.

   We further extend our results to authentication systems. More specifically,
we derive lower bounds on authenticator-size required for Anonymous Broadcast Authentication (ABA) in [13] via the same approach above, and show
that the authenticator-size should be $\Omega\left(|\mathcal{S}| \cdot \kappa\right)$ and $\Omega\left(N \cdot \kappa\right)$ for BA with
anonymity (ANO-BA) or full anonymity (full-ANO-BA), respectively. Interest-
ingly, concrete ABA schemes proposed in [13] asymptotically meet our lower
bounds on authenticator-size tightly, and it is shown that our lower bounds on
authenticator-size in ABA are asymptotically tight.

## 1.2   Technical Overview

**Kiayias and Samari's Analysis** [9]. To facilitate an analysis, Kiayias and Samari introduced AtBE in which ciphertexts and decryption keys can be broken down to atomic ciphertexts and decryption keys. In their AtBE, ciphertext $\mathsf{ct}_\mathcal{S}$ consists of $\rho$ atomic ciphertexts $\mathsf{ct}_\mathcal{S}^{(\theta)}$ ($\theta \in [\rho]$), and decryption key of a recipient id consists of $\tau$ atomic decryption keys $\mathsf{sk}_{\mathsf{id}}^{(\gamma)}$ ($\gamma \in [\tau]$). If the recipient id is in $\mathcal{S}$, there exists at least one pair of an atomic ciphertext $\mathsf{ct}_\mathcal{S}^{(\theta)}$ and decryption key $\mathsf{sk}_{\mathsf{id}}^{(\gamma)}$ that produces a message m (i.e., $\mathsf{ct}_\mathcal{S}^{(\theta)}$ can be decrypted with $\mathsf{sk}_{\mathsf{id}}^{(\gamma)}$).

They showed lower bounds on ciphertext sizes in any anonymous AtBE scheme by deriving lower bounds on the number of atomic ciphertexts in each ciphertext. Specifically, they showed in [9, Theorem 2] that "for any AtBE scheme, if there exists a set $\mathcal{S}$ such that the number of atomic ciphertexts in $\mathsf{ct}_\mathcal{S}$ is smaller than $|\mathcal{S}|$, then the AtBE scheme does not satisfy anonymity." However, they implicitly assumed the following property for AtBE in their proof:

**Assumption 1:** For all message m, all privileged set $\mathcal{S} \subseteq \mathcal{ID}$, let $\{\mathsf{ct}_\mathcal{S}^{(\theta)}\}_{\theta \in [\rho]} = \mathsf{ct}_\mathcal{S} \leftarrow \mathsf{Enc}(\mathsf{pk}, \mathsf{m}, \mathcal{S})$, where $\mathcal{ID}$ is a set of all recipients. For all $\mathsf{id}, \mathsf{id}' \in \mathcal{S}$, if they can decrypt the same atomic ciphertext $\mathsf{ct}_\mathcal{S}^{(\theta)}$ contained in $\mathsf{ct}_\mathcal{S}$ to obtain m, atomic decryption keys $\mathsf{sk}_{\mathsf{id}}^{(\gamma)}$ and $\mathsf{sk}_{\mathsf{id}'}^{(\gamma')}$ used for the decryption are identical.

Namely, they indeed proved "for any AtBE scheme, if Assumption 1 holds (i.e., the AtBE scheme meets the above property) and there exists a set $\mathcal{S}$ such that the number of atomic ciphertexts in $\mathsf{ct}_\mathcal{S}$ is less than $|\mathcal{S}|$, then the AtBE scheme does not satisfy anonymity." However, it is difficult to check whether the anonymous BE schemes meet the above property; in any existing anonymous BE schemes [3, 9–11], a situation where "any two recipients $\mathsf{id}, \mathsf{id}' \in \mathcal{S}$ decrypt the same atomic ciphertext $\mathsf{ct}_\mathcal{S}^{(\theta)}$ contained in $\mathsf{ct}_\mathcal{S}$" never occurs, whereas Kiayias and Samari considered such a situation and then assumed the above property in their proof. Since the contraposition of their theorem is "for any AtBE scheme, if it satisfies anonymity, then Assumption 1 does not hold, or the number of atomic ciphertext in $\mathsf{ct}_\mathcal{S}$ is greater than or equal to $|\mathcal{S}|$ for all privileged set $\mathcal{S}$," their lower bounds hold only if an AtBE scheme satisfies anonymity and Assumption 1 holds. Hence, their lower bounds are insufficient to show that existing anonymous BE schemes achieve optimal ciphertext sizes, since it is unclear whether Assumption 1 holds for existing (anonymous) AtBE schemes.

**Our Approach.** In this paper, we only assume that AtBE scheme satisfies properties existing BE schemes have, not a special property mentioned above, and derive lower bounds on ciphertext sizes required for anonymous AtBE with the properties.

First of all, we give a formal definition of AtBE to describe these properties. Specifically, we consider AtBE in which a public key pk can be divided into several sub-elements, called atomic public key $\mathsf{pk}^{(\delta)}$, in addition to ciphertexts and decryption keys. We also define Enc-at and Dec-at algorithms as an encryption and decryption algorithms of AtBE, and they capture encryption and decryption procedures for each atomic ciphertext in the Enc and Dec algorithms, respectively. In Enc-at, multiple atomic public keys $\{pk^{(\delta)}\}_{\delta \in \Delta'}$ are used to generate the atomic ciphertext $ct_{S,id}$ corresponding to the recipient id in $S$. In Dec-at, an atomic ciphertext $ct_{S,id}$ is decrypted using multiple atomic decryption keys $\{sk_{id}^{(\gamma)}\}_{\gamma \in \Gamma_{id}'}$. Note that almost all (even non-anonymous) BE schemes [1–5,7–12,14] indeed have the above algorithms inside.

With the formal syntax of AtBE, we formalize the following four properties of AtBE that we consider in our analysis:

1. When a ciphertext has intended recipient set $S$, then any recipient in $S$ can obtain the underlying plaintext by decrypting at least one of the corresponding atomic ciphertexts.
2. A triplet of recipient, recipient set, and message $(id, S, m)$ uniquely determine the minimum subset of atomic public keys required to generate an atomic ciphertext $ct_{S,id}$.
3. A pair of recipient and recipient set $(id, S)$ uniquely determine the minimum subset of atomic decryption keys required to decrypt a (correctly-generated) atomic ciphertext $ct_{S,id}$.
4. If two atomic ciphertexts $ct_{S,id}, ct_{S,id'}$ are identical, then the two corresponding minimum subsets of atomic public keys generating $ct_{S,id}$ and $ct_{S,id'}$ are also identical.

In Sect. 3.2, we show that most existing BE schemes satisfy the above four properties.

**Overview for Derivation of Lower Bounds.** First, we analyze conditions under which BE scheme with the above properties satisfies anonymity. Specifically, we show that "if an AtBE scheme satisfies the four properties and anonymity, then atomic decryption keys used for decryption is not shared among different recipients" (see Lemma 2 in Sect. 4). We then additionally assume the following property that most existing anonymous BE schemes have [3,10,11], to derive lower bounds for any anonymous AtBE scheme with the above four properties:

**Assumption 2:** For any $S \subset \mathcal{ID}$, any $id \in S$, and any m, let $pk'$ be a subset of atomic public keys that produces $ct_{S,id} \leftarrow$ Enc-at$(pk', S, m, id)$. Then, $pk'$ uniquely determines a minimum subset of atomic decryption keys to be used to decrypt $ct_{S,id}$.

We emphasize that, unlike Assumption 1, one can easily check Assumption 2 holds for all existing anonymous BE schemes [3,10,11].

Finally, we show that for any AtBE scheme with the four properties and Assumption 2, if there exists a set $S$ such that the number of atomic ciphertexts in the corresponding ciphertext $ct_S$ is smaller than $|S|$, then it contradicts to Lemma 2 in Sect. 4.

**Notation.** For all natural number $n \in \mathbb{N}$, $\{1, \ldots, n\}$ is denoted by $[n]$. For a finite set $\mathcal{X}$, we denote by $|\mathcal{X}|$ the cardinality of $\mathcal{X}$. For finite sets $\mathcal{X}, \mathcal{Y}$, let $\mathcal{X} \triangle \mathcal{Y}$ be the symmetric difference $\mathcal{X} \triangle \mathcal{Y} := (\mathcal{X} \setminus \mathcal{Y}) \cup (\mathcal{Y} \setminus \mathcal{X})$. For any finite set $\mathcal{X}$ and any natural number $\ell \in \mathbb{N}$, let $2_{\leq \ell}^{\mathcal{X}} := \{ \mathcal{Y} \subset \mathcal{X} \mid |\mathcal{Y}| \leq \ell \}$ be a family of subsets of $\mathcal{X}$ such that its cardinality is at most $\ell$ (i.e., a part of a power set of $\mathcal{X}$). For any algorithm A, out $\leftarrow$ A(in) means that A takes in as input and outputs out. For any set $\mathcal{X}$, if we write $x \xleftarrow{\mathsf{U}} \mathcal{X}$, $x$ is chosen uniformly at random from $\mathcal{X}$. Throughout the paper, we denote a security parameter by $\kappa$ and consider probabilistic polynomial-time algorithms (PPTAs). For any element $x \in \{0,1\}^*$, let $|x|$ be the number of bits of $x$. We say a function $\mathsf{negl}(\cdot)$ is negligible if for any polynomial $\mathsf{poly}(\cdot)$, there exists some constant $\kappa_0$, such that $\mathsf{negl}(\kappa) < 1/\mathsf{poly}(\kappa)$ for all $\kappa \geq \kappa_0$.

## 2   Broadcast Encryption

We begin by defining Broadcast Encryption (BE) and its security notions based on [11,13]. In this paper, we assume that the maximum number of recipients $N$ in BE is determined at the time of setup and an arbitrary set of recipients can be specified at the time of encryption.

**Syntax.** A BE scheme $\Pi^{\mathsf{BE}}$ consists of four algorithms (Setup, Join, Enc, Dec).

1. $(\mathsf{mk}, \mathsf{pk}) \leftarrow \mathsf{Setup}(1^\kappa, N, \ell)$: a probabilistic algorithm for setup. It takes a security parameter $1^\kappa$, the maximum number of recipients $N \in \mathbb{N}$, the maximum number of recipients $\ell$ designated at once as input, and outputs a master secret key $\mathsf{mk}$ and a public key $\mathsf{pk}$.
2. $\mathsf{sk_{id}} \leftarrow \mathsf{Join}(\mathsf{mk}, \mathsf{id})$: a decryption key generation algorithm. It takes $\mathsf{mk}$ and an identifier $\mathsf{id} \in \mathcal{ID}$, as input, and outputs a decryption key $\mathsf{sk_{id}}$ for id. Here, $\mathcal{ID}$ is a set of all possible identifiers, and $|\mathcal{ID}| := \mathsf{poly}(\kappa)$ for some polynomial $\mathsf{poly}(\cdot)$.
3. $\mathsf{ct}_{\mathcal{S}} \leftarrow \mathsf{Enc}(\mathsf{pk}, \mathsf{m}, \mathcal{S}; r)$: an encryption algorithm. It takes $\mathsf{pk}$, a message $\mathsf{m} \in \mathcal{M}$, randomness $r \in \mathcal{R}$, and a privileged set $\mathcal{S} \subseteq \mathcal{ID}$ as input, and outputs a ciphertext $\mathsf{ct}_{\mathcal{S}}$, where $\mathcal{M}$ is a message-space and $\mathcal{R}$ is a randomness-space. It is also possible to omit r from the input.
4. $\mathsf{m} \leftarrow \mathsf{Dec}(\mathsf{sk_{id}}, \mathsf{ct}_{\mathcal{S}})$: a decryption algorithm. It takes $\mathsf{sk_{id}}$ and $\mathsf{ct}_{\mathcal{S}}$ as inputs, and outputs $\mathsf{m} \in \mathcal{M} \cup \{\bot\}$.

To describe properties of the existing anonymous BE schemes, we regard Join as a deterministic algorithm in this paper[4].

**Correctness.** For all $\kappa, N \in \mathbb{N}$, all $\ell$ such that $1 \leq \ell \leq N$, all $\mathsf{mk} \leftarrow \mathsf{Setup}(1^\kappa, N, \ell)$, all $\mathsf{m} \in \mathcal{M}$, all $r \in \mathcal{R}$, all $\mathcal{S} \subseteq \mathcal{ID}$ such that $|\mathcal{S}| \leq \ell$, and all $\mathsf{id} \in \mathcal{S}$, we have $\mathsf{m} \leftarrow \mathsf{Dec}(\mathsf{Join}(\mathsf{mk}, \mathsf{id}), \mathsf{Enc}(\mathsf{pk}, \mathsf{m}, \mathcal{S}; r))$ with overwhelming probability.

**Collusion Resistance.** We define indistinguishability against chosen plaintext attack (IND-CPA) for BE. Let A be any PPT adversary against IND-CPA security. We consider an experiment $\mathsf{Exp}_{\Pi^{\mathsf{BE}},\mathsf{A}}^{\mathsf{IND\text{-}CPA}}(\kappa, N, \ell)$ between a challenger C and A as follows.

---

[4] Although Join behaves probabilistically, we can realize Join as a deterministic algorithm by pseudo-random function.

$\mathsf{Exp}_{\Pi,\mathsf{A}}^{\mathsf{IND\text{-}CPA}}(\kappa, N, \ell)$ C randomly chooses $b \in \{0, 1\}$. C runs $\mathsf{Setup}(1^\kappa, N, \ell)$ to get mk and randomly chooses $b \in \{0, 1\}$. Let $\mathcal{D}, \mathcal{CD}$ be a empty sets. We denote $\mathcal{D}$ as a set of recipients currently participating in the protocol, and $\mathcal{CD}$ as a set of identifiers of recipient from which A obtained its decryption key, respectively. A may adaptively issue the following queries to C.

- Key-generation Query: Upon a query id $\in \mathcal{ID}$ from A, C adds id to $\mathcal{D}$ and generates $\mathsf{sk}_{\mathsf{id}} \leftarrow \mathsf{Join}(\mathsf{mk}, \mathsf{id})$. Note that A obtains nothing, and that A is allowed to make this query at most $N$ times.
- Corruption Query: Upon a query id $\in \mathcal{D}$ from A, C adds id to $\mathcal{CD}$, and returns $\mathsf{sk}_{\mathsf{id}}$ to A.
- Challenge Query: Upon a query $(\mathsf{m}_0, \mathsf{m}_1, \mathcal{S}) \in \mathcal{M}^2 \times \left(2_{\leq \ell}^{\mathcal{D}}\right)$ from A, C runs $\mathsf{ct}_{\mathcal{S}} \leftarrow \mathsf{Enc}(\mathsf{pk}, \mathsf{m}_b, \mathcal{S})$ and returns $\mathsf{ct}_{\mathcal{S}}$ to A. A is allowed to make this query only once under the restriction that $\mathcal{S} \cap \mathcal{CD} = \emptyset$.

At some point, A outputs $b'$. If $b' = b$, C then sets 1 as the output of $\mathsf{Exp}_{\Pi^{\mathsf{BE}},\mathsf{A}}^{\mathsf{IND\text{-}CPA}}(\kappa, N, \ell)$. Otherwise, C then sets 0. C terminates the experiment.

**Definition 1 (IND-CPA).** We say $\Pi^{\mathsf{BE}}$ is IND-CPA secure if for any PPTA A, for all sufficiently-large $\kappa \in \mathbb{N}$, all $N \in \mathbb{N}$ and all $\ell (\leq N)$, it holds that $\mathsf{Adv}_{\Pi^{\mathsf{BE}},\mathsf{A}}^{\mathsf{IND\text{-}CPA}}(\kappa, N, \ell) < \mathsf{negl}(\kappa)$, where $\mathsf{Adv}_{\Pi^{\mathsf{BE}},\mathsf{A}}^{\mathsf{IND\text{-}CPA}}(\kappa, N, \ell) := |\Pr[\mathsf{Exp}_{\Pi^{\mathsf{BE}},\mathsf{A}}^{\mathsf{IND\text{-}CPA}}(\kappa, N, \ell) \to 1] - \frac{1}{2}|$.

**Anonymity.** We define two kinds of anonymity for BE, full anonymity (full-ANO-CPA) and anonymity (ANO-CPA). Let A be any PPT adversary against Full-ANO-CPA security. We define Full-ANO-CPA by $\mathsf{Exp}_{\Pi^{\mathsf{BE}},\mathsf{A}}^{\mathsf{full\text{-}ANO\text{-}CPA}}(\kappa, N, \ell)$ which is the same as $\mathsf{Exp}_{\Pi^{\mathsf{BE}},\mathsf{A}}^{\mathsf{IND\text{-}CPA}}$ except for the following changes to challenge query:

- Challenge Query: Upon a query $(\mathsf{m}, \mathcal{S}_0, \mathcal{S}_1) \in \mathcal{M} \times \left(2_{\leq \ell}^{\mathcal{D}}\right)^2$ from A, C runs $\mathsf{ct}_{\mathcal{S}_b} \leftarrow \mathsf{Enc}(\mathsf{pk}, \mathsf{m}, \mathcal{S}_b)$ and returns $\mathsf{ct}_{\mathcal{S}_b}$ to A. A is allowed to make this query only once under the restriction that $(\mathcal{S}_0 \triangle \mathcal{S}_1) \cap \mathcal{CD} = \emptyset$.

We can also define ANO-CPA with an experiment $\mathsf{Exp}_{\Pi^{\mathsf{BE}},\mathsf{A}}^{\mathsf{ANO\text{-}CPA}}(\kappa, N, \ell)$ which is the same as $\mathsf{Exp}_{\Pi^{\mathsf{BE}},\mathsf{A}}^{\mathsf{full\text{-}ANO\text{-}CPA}}(\kappa, N, \ell)$ except for the following additional condition of the restriction for challenge query: $|\mathcal{S}_0| = |\mathcal{S}_1|$.

**Definition 2 (Anonymity).** We say $\Pi^{\mathsf{BE}}$ is X-CPA secure (X $\in \{$full-ANO, ANO$\}$) if for any PPTA A, for all sufficiently-large $\kappa \in \mathbb{N}$, all $N \in \mathbb{N}$ and all $\ell (\leq N)$, it holds that $\mathsf{Adv}_{\Pi^{\mathsf{BE}},\mathsf{A}}^{X}(\kappa, N, \ell) < \mathsf{negl}(\kappa)$, where $\mathsf{Adv}_{\Pi^{\mathsf{BE}},\mathsf{A}}^{X}(\kappa, N, \ell) := |\Pr[\mathsf{Exp}_{\Pi^{\mathsf{BE}},\mathsf{A}}^{X}(\kappa, N, \ell) \to 1] - \frac{1}{2}|$.

## 3    Atomic Broadcast Encryption

In this section, we give a formal syntax of Atomic Broadcast Encryption (AtBE) to formally describe properties satisfied by existing BE schemes. These properties are used to formalize properties of existing anonymous BE and derive lower bounds. We further provide security definitions for BE covered with AtBE.

## 3.1   Syntax of AtBE

Our AtBE aims to describe encryption and decryption for each recipient in a designated set performed inside Enc and Dec algorithms of BE. Towards that aim, ciphertexts, decryption keys, and public keys are divided into multiple sub-elements. An AtBE scheme $\Pi^{\mathsf{At\text{-}BE}}$ consists of four algorithms (Setup-at, Join-at, Enc-at, Dec-at).

1. $(\mathsf{mk}, \{\mathsf{pk}^{(\delta)}\}_{\delta \in \Delta}) \leftarrow \mathsf{Setup\text{-}at}(1^\kappa, N, \ell)$: a probabilistic algorithm for setup. It takes a security parameter $1^\kappa$, the maximum number of receivers $N \in \mathbb{N}$, the maximum number of receivers $\ell$ designated at once as input, and outputs a master secret key $\mathsf{mk}$ and a public key $\mathsf{pk}$ consisting of $|\Delta|$ atomic public keys $\{\mathsf{pk}^{(\delta)}\}_{\delta \in \Delta}$.
2. $\{\mathsf{sk}_{\mathsf{id}}^{(\gamma)}\}_{\gamma \in \Gamma_{\mathsf{id}}} \leftarrow \mathsf{Join\text{-}at}(\mathsf{mk}, \mathsf{id})$: a decryption key generation algorithm. It takes $\mathsf{mk}$ and an identifier $\mathsf{id} \in \mathcal{ID}$, as input, and outputs a decryption key $\mathsf{sk}_{\mathsf{id}}$ for $\mathsf{id}$ consisting of $|\Gamma_{\mathsf{id}}|$ atomic decryption keys $\{\mathsf{sk}_{\mathsf{id}}^{(\gamma)}\}_{\gamma \in \Gamma_{\mathsf{id}}}$.
3. $\mathsf{ct}_{\mathcal{S},\mathsf{id}} \leftarrow \mathsf{Enc\text{-}at}(\{\mathsf{pk}^{(\delta)}\}_{\delta \in \Delta'}, \mathcal{S}, \mathsf{m}, \mathsf{id}; \mathsf{r})$: an atomic encryption algorithm. It takes a subset of the atomic public key $\{\mathsf{pk}^{(\delta)}\}_{\delta \in \Delta'}$, a privileged set $\mathcal{S} \subseteq \mathcal{ID}$, a message $\mathsf{m} \in \mathcal{M}$, an identifier $\mathsf{id} \in \mathcal{ID}$, and randomness $\mathsf{r}$ as input, and outputs an atomic ciphertext $\mathsf{ct}_{\mathcal{S},\mathsf{id}}$, where $\Delta' \subseteq \Delta$.
4. $\mathsf{m} \leftarrow \mathsf{Dec\text{-}at}(\{\mathsf{sk}_{\mathsf{id}}^{(\gamma)}\}_{\gamma \in \Gamma_{\mathsf{id}}'}, \mathsf{ct}_{\mathcal{S},\mathsf{id}})$: an atomic decryption algorithm. It takes a subset of atomic decryption keys $\{\mathsf{sk}_{\mathsf{id}}^{(\gamma)}\}_{\gamma \in \Gamma_{\mathsf{id}}'}$, and $\mathsf{ct}_{\mathcal{S},\mathsf{id}}$ as input, and outputs a message $\mathsf{m} \in \mathcal{M} \cup \{\bot\}$, where $\Gamma_{\mathsf{id}}' \subseteq \Gamma_{\mathsf{id}}$.

Setup-at and Join-at are essentially equivalent to Setup and Join in BE respectively, except for difference that public and decryption keys are explicitly divided into multiple sub-elements. As in the case of Join in BE, we regard Join-at as being a deterministic algorithm. We require a natural property for AtBE that an atomic ciphertext $\mathsf{ct}_{\mathcal{S},\mathsf{id}}$ contained in ciphertext $\mathsf{ct}_{\mathcal{S}}$ will be correctly decrypted by a decryption key $\{\mathsf{sk}_{\mathsf{id}}^{(\gamma)}\}_{\gamma \in \Gamma_{\mathsf{id}}}$ of a recipient $\mathsf{id} \in \mathcal{S}$ as follows:

**Atomic Correctness.** For all $\kappa, N \in \mathbb{N}$, all $\ell$ such that $1 \leq \ell \leq N$, all $(\mathsf{mk}, \{\mathsf{pk}^{(\delta)}\}_{\delta \in \Delta}) \leftarrow \mathsf{Setup\text{-}at}(1^\kappa, N, \ell)$, all $\mathcal{S} \subseteq \mathcal{ID}$ such that $|\mathcal{S}| \leq \ell$, all $\mathsf{id} \in \mathcal{S}$, all $\mathsf{m} \in \mathcal{M}$, all $\{\mathsf{sk}_{\mathsf{id}}^{(\gamma)}\}_{\gamma \in \Gamma_{\mathsf{id}}} \leftarrow \mathsf{Join\text{-}at}(\mathsf{mk}, \mathsf{id})$, all $\mathsf{r} \xleftarrow{\mathsf{U}} \mathcal{R}$, for some $\Delta' \subseteq \Delta, \Gamma_{\mathsf{id}}' \subseteq \Gamma_{\mathsf{id}}$, for all $\mathsf{ct}_{\mathcal{S},\mathsf{id}} \leftarrow \mathsf{Enc\text{-}at}(\{\mathsf{pk}^{(\delta)}\}_{\delta \in \Delta'}, \mathsf{id}, \mathsf{m}, \mathcal{S}; \mathsf{r})$, we have $\mathsf{m} \leftarrow \mathsf{Dec\text{-}at}(\{\mathsf{sk}_{\mathsf{id}}^{(\gamma)}\}_{\gamma \in \Gamma_{\mathsf{id}}'}, \mathsf{ct}_{\mathcal{S},\mathsf{id}})$ with overwhelming probability.

## 3.2   Properties in Existing BE Schemes

As described in Sect. 1.2, Kiayias and Samari assumed a special property for anonymous BE in their analysis, and it is difficult to check whether the property holds for existing anonymous BE schemes. Therefore, our goal is to replace that property with a natural one that could be checked if it holds for existing anonymous BE schemes. In order to achieve this, we describe four properties that holds in most of existing (i.e., both non-anonymous and anonymous) BE schemes in this section. In particular, we show that they hold for the pairing-based BE scheme of Boneh et al. [4]. The four properties are described as follows.

**Property 1.** Ciphertext $ct_{\mathcal{S}}$ output from $\Pi^{BE}$.Enc algorithm consists of atomic ciphertext $ct_{\mathcal{S},id}$ obtained by $\Pi^{At\text{-}BE}$.Enc-at algorithm, and other elements. [5] In other words, let a set of atomic ciphertext contained in $ct_{\mathcal{S}}$ be $\{ct_{\mathcal{S},id}\}_{id \in \mathcal{S}}$, and let union of $\{ct_{\mathcal{S},id}\}_{id \in \mathcal{S}}$ and other elements contained in $ct_{\mathcal{S}}$ be $\{ct_{\mathcal{S}}^{(\theta)}\}_{\theta \in [\beta_{\mathcal{S}}]}$, it holds that $\{ct_{\mathcal{S},id}\}_{id \in \mathcal{S}} \subseteq \{ct_{\mathcal{S}}^{(\theta)}\}_{\theta \in [\beta_{\mathcal{S}}]} \subseteq ct_{\mathcal{S}}$. Here, a randomness r input to $\Pi^{At\text{-}BE}$.Enc-at is the same when generating each atomic ciphertext in $\{ct_{\mathcal{S},id}\}_{id \in \mathcal{S}}$. Also, inside $\Pi^{BE}$.Dec algorithm, $\Pi^{At\text{-}BE}$.Dec-at algorithm takes atomic ciphertext and a set of atomic decryption key as input, and outputs a message. If $ct_{\mathcal{S}}$ is valid ciphertext, then there is an atomic ciphertext $ct_{\mathcal{S}}^{(\theta)}$ in $ct_{\mathcal{S}}$ that can be decrypted using a subset of atomic decryption keys of a recipient id in $\mathcal{S}$. Formally, we require the following property for BE $\Pi^{BE}$:

For all $\kappa, N \in \mathbb{N}$, all $\ell$ such that $1 \leq \ell \leq N$, all $(mk, pk) \leftarrow \Pi^{BE}$.Setup($1^{\kappa}$, $N, \ell$), all $m \in \mathcal{M}$, all $\mathcal{S} \subseteq \mathcal{ID}$ such that $|\mathcal{S}| \leq \ell$, all $id \in \mathcal{ID}$, all $\{sk_{id}^{(\gamma)}\}_{\gamma \in \Gamma_{id}} \leftarrow \Pi^{At\text{-}BE}$.Join-at(mk, id), all $r \xleftarrow{U} \mathcal{R}$, all $\{ct_{\mathcal{S}}^{(\theta)}\}_{\theta \in [\beta_{\mathcal{S}}]} \subseteq ct_{\mathcal{S}} \leftarrow \Pi^{BE}$.Enc(pk, m, $\mathcal{S}$; r), if $id \in \mathcal{S}$, then for some $\Gamma'_{id} \subseteq \Gamma_{id}$, there exists $\theta \in [\beta_{\mathcal{S}}]$ such that $m \leftarrow$ Dec-at($\{sk_{id}^{(\gamma)}\}_{\gamma \in \Gamma'_{id}}, ct_{\mathcal{S}}^{(\theta)}$) with overwhelming probability. If $id \notin \mathcal{S}$, then for all $\Gamma'_{id} \subseteq \Gamma_{id}$, there is no $\theta \in [\beta_{\mathcal{S}}]$ such that $m \leftarrow$ Dec-at($\{sk_{id}^{(\gamma)}\}_{\gamma \in \Gamma'_{id}}, ct_{\mathcal{S}}^{(\theta)}$) with overwhelming probability.

**Property 2.** When generating $ct_{\mathcal{S},id}$ such that $m \leftarrow$ Dec-at($\{sk_{id}^{(\gamma)}\}_{\gamma \in \Gamma'_{id}}, ct_{\mathcal{S},id}$) for some $\gamma \in \Gamma'_{id}$, let $\Delta^*_{id,\mathcal{S},m}$ be the minimum subset of atomic public keys required for input to Enc-at. In this case, for any $\mathcal{S} \subset \mathcal{ID}$, any $id \in \mathcal{S}$, and any $m, \in \mathcal{M}$, $\Delta^*_{id,\mathcal{S},m}$ is uniquely determined by pairs of $(id, m, \mathcal{S})$ to input to Enc-at.

**Property 3.** When $m \leftarrow$ Dec-at($\{sk_{id}^{(\gamma)}\}_{\gamma \in \Gamma'_{id}}, ct_{\mathcal{S},id}$) holds, let $\Gamma^*_{id,\mathcal{S}}$ be the minimum subset of atomic decryption keys required for input to Dec-at. In this case, for any $\mathcal{S} \subset \mathcal{ID}$ and any $id \in \mathcal{S}$, $\Gamma^*_{id,\mathcal{S}}$ is uniquely determined by pairs of $(id, \mathcal{S})$ to input to Enc-at when generating $ct_{\mathcal{S},id}$.

**Property 4.** For all $(mk, \{pk^{(\delta)}\}_{\delta \in \Delta}) \leftarrow$ Setup($1^{\kappa}, N, \ell$), id, id' $\in \mathcal{ID}$, all $\mathcal{S} \subset \mathcal{ID}$ such that $\{id, id'\} \subseteq \mathcal{S}$, all $m \in \mathcal{M}, r \in \mathcal{R}$, all $ct_{\mathcal{S},id} \leftarrow$ Enc-at($\{pk^{(\delta)}\}_{\delta \in \Delta^*_{id,\mathcal{S},m}}$, id, m, $\mathcal{S}$; r), $ct_{\mathcal{S},id'} \leftarrow$ Enc-at($\{pk^{(\delta')}\}_{\delta' \in \Delta^*_{id',\mathcal{S},m}}$, id', m, $\mathcal{S}$; r), if $ct_{\mathcal{S},id} = ct_{\mathcal{S},id'}$ holds, then we have $\{pk^{(\delta)}\}_{\delta \in \Delta^*_{id,\mathcal{S},m}} = \{pk^{(\delta')}\}_{\delta' \in \Delta^*_{id',\mathcal{S},m}}$ with overwhelming probability.

Here, we can see that most of the existing BE schemes satisfy the above properties. In particular, we show that the BE scheme in [4] meets the properties described above. The outline of the BE scheme is as follows: Let $p$ be a prime, $g$ be a random generator chosen randomly from a bilinear group $\mathbb{G}$ whose order is $p$, $\mathbb{Z}_p := \{1, \ldots, p-1\}, \alpha, s \xleftarrow{U} \mathbb{Z}_p$. Its public key, private key

---

[5] The "other elements" indicate, e.g., signatures for atomic ciphertexts (found in [11]).

of a recipient $\text{id} \in [N]$, and ciphertext with $\mathcal{S}$ is as follows: $\{\mathsf{pk}^{(\delta)}\}_{\delta \in \Delta} := \{g, g_1, \ldots, g_N, g_{N+2}, \ldots, g_{2N}, v\}, \{\mathsf{sk}_{\mathsf{id}}^{(\gamma)}\}_{\gamma \in \Gamma_{\mathsf{id}}} := \{g_{\mathsf{id}}^s\} \cup \{\mathsf{pk}^{(\delta)}\}_{\delta \in \Delta}, \{\mathsf{ct}_{\mathcal{S}}^{(\theta)}\}_{\theta \in [\beta_s]}$
$= \mathsf{ct}_{\mathcal{S}} := \{(g^r, (v \cdot \prod_{j \in \mathcal{S}} g_{N+1-j})^r)\}$, where $g_i := g^{\alpha^i} (i \in [2N]), v := g^s, r \xleftarrow{\mathsf{U}} \mathbb{Z}_p$.

According to an atomic ciphertext,

$$\mathsf{ct}_{\mathcal{S}, \mathsf{id}} := \{(g^r, (v \cdot \prod_{j \in \mathcal{S}} g_{N+1-j})^r)\},$$

$$\{\mathsf{sk}_{\mathsf{id}}^{(\gamma)}\}_{\gamma \in \Gamma'_{\mathsf{id}}} := \{g_{\mathsf{id}}^s, g, \{g_{N+1-j+\mathsf{id}}\}_{\substack{j \in \mathcal{S} \\ j \neq \mathsf{id}}}, v\},$$

$$\mathsf{m} \leftarrow \mathsf{Dec\text{-}at}(\{\mathsf{sk}_{\mathsf{id}}^{(\gamma)}\}_{\gamma \in \Gamma'_{\mathsf{id}}}, \mathsf{ct}_{\mathcal{S}, \mathsf{id}}).$$

Hence, Property 1 is satisfied.

According to a public key, a minimum subset of atomic public keys used to generate $\mathsf{ct}_{\mathcal{S}, \mathsf{id}}$ is uniquely determined as $\{\mathsf{pk}^{(\delta)}\}_{\delta \in \Delta^*_{\mathsf{id}, \mathcal{S}, \mathsf{m}}} := \{g, \{g_{N+1-j}\}_{j \in \mathcal{S}}, v\}$. Therefore, Property 2 is met.

According to a decryption key, a minimum subset of atomic decryption keys used to decrypt $\mathsf{ct}_{\mathcal{S}, \mathsf{id}}$, is uniquely determined as $\{\mathsf{sk}_{\mathsf{id}}^{(\gamma)}\}_{\gamma \in \Gamma^*_{\mathsf{id}, \mathcal{S}}} := \{g_{\mathsf{id}}^s, g, \{g_{N+1-j+\mathsf{id}}\}_{\substack{j \in \mathcal{S} \\ j \neq \mathsf{id}}}, v\}$. Therefore, Property 3 is satisfied.

An atomic ciphertext with $\mathsf{id}'$ is given as $\mathsf{ct}_{\mathcal{S}, \mathsf{id}'} := \{(g^r, (v \cdot \prod_{j \in \mathcal{S}} g_{N+1-j})^r)\}$, and if $\mathsf{ct}_{\mathcal{S}, \mathsf{id}} = \mathsf{ct}_{\mathcal{S}, \mathsf{id}'}$ holds, then we have $\{\mathsf{pk}^{(\delta)}\}_{\delta \in \Delta^*_{\mathsf{id}, \mathcal{S}, \mathsf{m}}} = \{\mathsf{pk}^{(\delta')}\}_{\delta' \in \Delta^*_{\mathsf{id}', \mathcal{S}, \mathsf{m}}}$ with overwhelming probability. Therefore, Property 4 is also satisfied.

From the above, we can see that the BE scheme in [4] meets Properties 1, 2, 3 and 4. In addition, we can similarly show that the existing (both non-anonymous and anonymous) BE schemes [1–3, 5, 7, 8, 10–12, 14] satisfy Properties 1, 2, 3 and 4 as well, thus it is reasonable to assume Properties 1, 2, 3 and 4 in this paper.

### 3.3   Security Definitions for BE Covered with AtBE

We define collusion resistance and anonymity for BE covered with AtBE in the same way as in BE. In the following, we give definitions of IND-CPA (**INDat-CPA**), full anonymity (**full-ANOat-CPA**) and anonymity (**ANOat-CPA**).

Security games for BE covered with AtBE are the same as those for BE except that an attacker obtains decryption keys and a challenge ciphertext is explicitly devided into multiple sub-elements. Essentially, there is no difference between IND-CPA and INDat-CPA, also between anonymity for BE and AtBE in that information attackers obtain. Therefore, we consider INDat-CPA, full-ANOat-CPA and ANOat-CPA defined below to be the same security as IND-CPA, full-ANO-CPA and ANO-CPA, respectively.

**Indistinguishability for AtBE.** Let A be any PPT adversary against INDat-CPA security. We define INDat-CPA with an experiment $\mathsf{Exp}_{\Pi^{\mathsf{BE}}, \mathsf{A}}^{\mathsf{INDat\text{-}CPA}}$ which is the same as $\mathsf{Exp}_{\Pi^{\mathsf{BE}}, \mathsf{A}}^{\mathsf{IND\text{-}CPA}}$ except for the following changes to Key-generation Query and Corruption Query:

- Key-generation Query: Upon a query id $\in \mathcal{ID}$ from A, C adds id to $\mathcal{D}$ and generates $\{sk_{id}^{(\gamma)}\}_{\gamma \in \Gamma_{id}} \leftarrow$ Join-at(mk, id), not $sk_{id} \leftarrow$ Join(mk, id).
- Corruption Query: Upon a query id $\in \mathcal{D}$ from A, C adds id to $\mathcal{CD}$, and returns $\{sk_{id}^{(\gamma)}\}_{\gamma \in \Gamma_{id}}$ to A, not $sk_{id}$.

**Definition 3 (Indistinguishability for AtBE).** We say $\Pi^{BE}$ is INDat-CPA secure if for any PPTA A, for all sufficiently-large $\kappa \in \mathbb{N}$, all $N \in \mathbb{N}$ and all $\ell\ (\leq N)$, it holds that $|Adv_{\Pi^{BE},A}^{INDat-CPA}(\kappa, N, \ell)| < negl(\kappa)$, where $Adv_{\Pi^{BE},A}^{INDat-CPA}(\kappa, N, \ell) :=$ $|\Pr[Exp_{\Pi^{BE},A}^{INDat-CPA}(\kappa, N, \ell) \to 1] - \frac{1}{2}|$.

**Anonymity for AtBE.** Let A be any PPT adversary against full-ANOat-CPA security. We define full-ANOat-CPA with an experiment $Exp_{\Pi^{BE},A}^{full-ANOat-CPA}(\kappa, N, \ell)$ which is the same as $Exp_{\Pi^{BE},A}^{INDat-CPA}$ except for the following changes on challenge query:

- Challenge Query: Upon a query $(m, \mathcal{S}_0, \mathcal{S}_1) \in \mathcal{M} \times \left(2_{\leq \ell}^{\mathcal{D}}\right)^2$ from A, C runs $ct_{\mathcal{S}_b} \leftarrow$ Enc(pk, m, $\mathcal{S}_b$) and returns $ct_{\mathcal{S}_b}$ to A. A is allowed to make this query only once under the restriction that $(\mathcal{S}_0 \triangle \mathcal{S}_1) \cap \mathcal{CD} = \emptyset$.

We also define ANOat-CPA with an experiment $Exp_{\Pi^{BE},A}^{ANOat-CPA}(\kappa, N, \ell)$ which is the same as $Exp_{\Pi^{BE},A}^{full-ANOat-CPA}(\kappa, N, \ell)$ except for the following additional condition of the restriction for challenge query: $|\mathcal{S}_0| = |\mathcal{S}_1|$.

**Definition 4 (Anonymity for AtBE).** We say $\Pi^{BE}$ is X-CPA secure (X $\in$ {full-ANOat, ANOat}) if for any PPTA A, for all sufficiently-large $\kappa \in \mathbb{N}$, all $N \in \mathbb{N}$ and all $\ell\ (\leq N)$, it holds that $|Adv_{\Pi^{BE},A}^{X}(\kappa, N, \ell)| < negl(\kappa)$, where $Adv_{\Pi^{BE},A}^{X}(\kappa, N, \ell) := |\Pr[Exp_{\Pi^{BE},A}^{X}(\kappa, N, \ell) \to 1] - \frac{1}{2}|$.

# 4 Lower Bounds on Ciphertext Sizes in BE

We derive lower bounds for BE schemes with ANOat-CPA security and full-ANOat-CPA security. First, we define a property assumed for BE schemes and show that it holds for ANO-BE scheme of Libert et al. [11]. Then, we derive lower bounds for ANO-BE and full-ANO-BE with the property described in Sect. 4.1. In the following analysis, we assume that BE scheme satisfies INDat-CPA security, although not explicitly stated.

## 4.1 A Property of ANO-BE and Full-ANO-BE

In order to derive lower bounds for ANO-BE and full-ANO-BE, we assume a property that "a minimum subset of atomic decryption keys used to decrypt ciphertexts is uniquely determined by a subset of public keys used to generate the ciphertext." Specifically, we consider the following property for both ANO-BE and full-ANO-BE:

**Assumption 2:** When $(\mathsf{mk}, \{\mathsf{pk}^{(\delta)}\}_{\delta \in \Delta}) \leftarrow \mathsf{Setup}(1^\kappa, N, \ell)$ is generated, we denote $\mathcal{PK}^*$ as a set of all atomic public keys, namely $\mathcal{PK}^* := \{\mathsf{pk}^{(\delta)}\}_{\delta \in \Delta}$. And, when $\{\mathsf{sk}_{\mathsf{id}}^{(\gamma)}\}_{\gamma \in \Gamma_{\mathsf{id}}} \leftarrow \mathsf{Join\text{-}at}(\mathsf{mk}, \mathsf{id})$ is generated, $\mathcal{SK}^*$ denotes a set of a minimum subset of atomic decryption keys to be input to $\mathsf{Dec\text{-}at}$, namely $\mathcal{SK}^* := \{\{\mathsf{sk}_{\mathsf{id}}^{(\gamma)}\}_{\gamma \in \Gamma_{\mathsf{id}, S}^*}\}_{\mathsf{id} \in \mathcal{ID}, S \subseteq \mathcal{ID}}$. Here, we note that $\mathcal{SK}^*$ is uniquely determined, since $\mathsf{Join\text{-}at}$ is a deterministic algorithm. At this time, for all $\mathsf{id} \in \mathcal{ID}$, all $S \subseteq \mathcal{ID}$, all $\mathsf{m} \in \mathcal{M}$, all $\mathsf{r} \in \mathcal{R}$, all $\mathsf{pk}' \in 2^{\mathcal{PK}^*}$, all $\mathsf{ct}_{S, \mathsf{id}} \leftarrow \mathsf{Enc\text{-}at}(\mathsf{pk}', \mathsf{id}, \mathsf{m}, S; \mathsf{r})$, a set of atomic decryption keys $\mathsf{sk}' \in \mathcal{SK}^* \cup \{\bot\}$ such that $\mathsf{m} \leftarrow \mathsf{Dec\text{-}at}(\mathsf{sk}', \mathsf{ct}_{S, \mathsf{id}})$ is uniquely determined by the set of atomic public keys $\mathsf{pk}'$.

ANO-BE schemes satisfying the above property include Libert et al.'s scheme [11], which is a generic construction using public key encryption PKE and one-time signature OTS. Its outline is as follows.

$\varPi^{\mathsf{BE}}.\mathsf{Setup}(1^\kappa, N, \ell)$ : For all $\mathsf{id} \in [N]$, run $(\mathsf{pke.pk}_{\mathsf{id}}, \mathsf{pke.sk}_{\mathsf{id}}) \leftarrow \mathsf{PKE.KGen}(1^\kappa)$, and output $\mathsf{pk} := \{\mathsf{pke.pk}_{\mathsf{id}}\}_{\mathsf{id} \in [N]}, \mathsf{mk} := \{\mathsf{pke.sk}_{\mathsf{id}}\}_{\mathsf{id} \in [N]}$.

$\varPi^{\mathsf{BE}}.\mathsf{Join}(\mathsf{mk}, \mathsf{id})$ : Output $\mathsf{pke.sk}_{\mathsf{id}}$.

$\varPi^{\mathsf{BE}}.\mathsf{Enc}(\mathsf{pk}, \mathsf{m}, S)$ : Compute $(\mathsf{ots.sk}, \mathsf{ots.vk}) \leftarrow \mathsf{OTS.KGen}(1^\kappa)$. Then for all $\mathsf{id} \in S$, run $\mathsf{ct}_{S, \mathsf{id}} \leftarrow \mathsf{PKE.Enc}(\mathsf{pke.pk}_{\mathsf{id}}, \mathsf{m} \| \mathsf{ots.vk})$ and $\sigma \leftarrow \mathsf{OTS.Sign}(\mathsf{ots.sk}, \{\mathsf{ct}_{S, \mathsf{id}}\}_{\mathsf{id} \in S})$. Then output $\mathsf{ct}_S := (\sigma, \{\mathsf{ct}_{S, \mathsf{id}}\}_{\mathsf{id} \in S})$.

$\varPi^{\mathsf{BE}}.\mathsf{Dec}(\mathsf{sk}_{\mathsf{id}}, \mathsf{ct}_S)$ : Parse $\mathsf{ct}_S$ as $(\sigma, \{\mathsf{ct}_{S, \mathsf{id}}\}_{\mathsf{id} \in S})$. For all $\mathsf{ct}_{S, \mathsf{id}} \in \{\mathsf{ct}_{S, \mathsf{id}}\}_{\mathsf{id} \in S}$, compute $\mathsf{m}' \leftarrow \mathsf{PKE.Dec}(\mathsf{pke.sk}_{\mathsf{id}}, \mathsf{ct}_{S, \mathsf{id}})$, and parse $\mathsf{m}$ as $\mathsf{m}' \| \mathsf{ots.vk}$. Then, if $1 \leftarrow \mathsf{OTS.Vrfy}(\mathsf{ots.vk}, \sigma, \{\mathsf{ct}_{S, \mathsf{id}}\}_{\mathsf{id} \in S})$, output $\mathsf{m}$.

In the above scheme, PKE.Enc executed inside Enc corresponds to Enc-at, and PKE.Dec executed inside Dec corresponds to Dec-at. Then, $\mathcal{PK}^*$ and $\mathcal{SK}^*$ indicates $\{\mathsf{pke.pk}_{\mathsf{id}}\}_{\mathsf{id} \in [N]}$ and $\{\{\mathsf{pke.sk}_1\}, \ldots, \{\mathsf{pke.sk}_N\}\}$ respectively, and $\mathsf{pke.sk}_{\mathsf{id}} = \mathsf{sk}'$ such that $\mathsf{m}' \leftarrow \mathsf{PKE.Dec}(\mathsf{pke.sk}_{\mathsf{id}}, \mathsf{ct}_{S, \mathsf{id}})$ is uniquely determined by $\mathsf{pke.pk}_{\mathsf{id}} \in 2^{\mathcal{PK}^*}$. Therefore, Libert et al.'s scheme satisfies the above property.

In addition, we can similarly show that all of the existing ANO-BE and full-ANO-BE schemes in [3, 9–11] satisfy Assumption 2.

## 4.2   Lower Bounds in ANOat-CPA Secure BE

First, we show two lemmas, Lemma 1 and 2, for ANOat-CPA secure BE with Properties 1, 2, 3 and 4 described in Sect. 3.2. In Lemma 1, we show that "if BE is ANOat-CPA secure, then for ciphertexts with a set $S_0, S_1$ whose size is equal, sets of atomic decryption keys used by a receipient id for each decryption is equal." Then, in Lemma 2, we show that "if BE is ANOat-CPA secure, then for any set $S$ with more than two elements, recipients $\mathsf{id}, \mathsf{id}' \in S$ must not share a set of atomic decryption keys used to decrypt $\mathsf{ct}_S$."

Then, for ANOat-CPA secure BE with the property described in Assumption 2, we will derive a lower bound on ciphertext-size by Theorem 1.

**Lemma 1.** If BE $\varPi^{\mathsf{BE}}$ is ANOat-CPA secure, for all $\mathsf{id} \in \mathcal{ID}$, all $S_0, S_1$ such that $\mathsf{id} \in S_0 \cap S_1$ and $|S_0| = |S_1|$, we have $\{\mathsf{sk}_{\mathsf{id}}^{(\gamma)}\}_{\gamma \in \Gamma_{\mathsf{id}, S_0}^*} = \{\mathsf{sk}_{\mathsf{id}}^{(\gamma)}\}_{\gamma \in \Gamma_{\mathsf{id}, S_1}^*}$.

*Proof.* We show this lemma by contraposition. Suppose $\{\mathsf{sk}_{\mathsf{id}}^{(\gamma)}\}_{\gamma \in \Gamma_{\mathsf{id},\mathcal{S}_0}^*} \neq \{\mathsf{sk}_{\mathsf{id}}^{(\gamma)}\}_{\gamma \in \Gamma_{\mathsf{id},\mathcal{S}_1}^*}$ for some $\mathsf{id} \in \mathcal{ID}$ and some $\mathcal{S}_0, \mathcal{S}_1$ such that $\mathsf{id} \in \mathcal{S}_0 \cap \mathcal{S}_1, |\mathcal{S}_0| = |\mathcal{S}_1|$. We will construct PPT adversary against ANOat-CPA security as follows. Let $\mathsf{id}^*$ be $\mathsf{id}$ as above. Initially, the adversary guesses sizes of $\mathcal{S}_0, \mathcal{S}_1$ as $\ell^* \xleftarrow{\mathsf{U}} [\ell]$. Next, the adversary guesses $\mathsf{id}^*, \mathcal{S}_0$, and $\mathcal{S}_1$. A probability that the adversary succeeds in guessing is $\frac{1}{|\mathcal{ID}|} \cdot \frac{1}{\ell} \cdot \binom{|\mathcal{ID}|}{\ell^*-1}^{-1} \cdot \left(\binom{|\mathcal{ID}|}{\ell^*-1}-1\right)^{-1}$. The adversary also issues Key-Generation queries for all $\mathsf{id}$ in $\mathcal{S}_0 \cup \mathcal{S}_1$ and Corruption queries for $\mathsf{id}^*$ to obtain decryption key $\{\mathsf{sk}_{\mathsf{id}^*}^{(\gamma)}\}_{\gamma \in \Gamma_{\mathsf{id}^*}}$. Then, the adversary issues a challenge query $(\mathsf{m}, \mathcal{S}_0, \mathcal{S}_1)$ to obtain $\{\mathsf{ct}_{\mathcal{S}_b}^{(\theta)}\}_{\theta \in [\beta_{\mathcal{S}_b}]} \subseteq \mathsf{ct}_{\mathcal{S}_b}$. Finally, the adversary outputs $b' = 0$ if there exists $\theta \in [\beta_{\mathcal{S}_b}]$ such that $\mathsf{m} \leftarrow \mathsf{Dec\text{-}at}(\{\mathsf{sk}_{\mathsf{id}^*}^{(\gamma)}\}_{\gamma \in \Gamma_{\mathsf{id}^*,\mathcal{S}_0}^*}, \mathsf{ct}_{\mathcal{S}_b}^{(\theta)})$, and $b' = 1$ otherwise. In this case, the adversary can output $b'$ such that $b = b'$ with probability $\frac{1}{2}\left(\frac{1}{|\mathcal{ID}|} \cdot \frac{1}{\ell} \cdot \binom{|\mathcal{ID}|}{\ell^*-1}^{-1} \cdot \left(\binom{|\mathcal{ID}|}{\ell^*-1}-1\right)^{-1}+1\right)$. Note that $|\mathcal{ID}|$ is polynomial in $\kappa$.                                                                $\square$

**Lemma 2.** *If BE $\Pi^{\mathsf{BE}}$ is ANOat-CPA secure, for all $\mathsf{id}, \mathsf{id}' \in \mathcal{ID}$, all $\mathcal{S} \subseteq \mathcal{ID}$ such that $\{\mathsf{id}, \mathsf{id}'\} \subseteq \mathcal{S}, |\mathcal{S}| \geq 2$, we have $\{\mathsf{sk}_{\mathsf{id}}^{(\gamma)}\}_{\gamma \in \Gamma_{\mathsf{id},\mathcal{S}}^*} \neq \{\mathsf{sk}_{\mathsf{id}'}^{(\gamma')}\}_{\gamma' \in \Gamma_{\mathsf{id}',\mathcal{S}}^*}$.*

*Proof.* Assume on the contrary that we have $\{\mathsf{sk}_{\mathsf{id}}^{(\gamma)}\}_{\gamma \in \Gamma_{\mathsf{id},\mathcal{S}}^*} = \{\mathsf{sk}_{\mathsf{id}'}^{(\gamma')}\}_{\gamma' \in \Gamma_{\mathsf{id}',\mathcal{S}}^*}$ for some $\mathsf{id}, \mathsf{id}' \in \mathcal{ID}$ and some $\mathcal{S} \subseteq \mathcal{ID}$ such that $\{\mathsf{id}, \mathsf{id}'\} \subseteq \mathcal{S}, |\mathcal{S}| \geq 2$. Then, we will show that it contradicts correctness of BE with AtBE structure (see Sect. 3.2, Property 1). First, we choose $\mathcal{S}'$ such that $\mathsf{id} \in \mathcal{S}', \mathsf{id}' \notin \mathcal{S}', |\mathcal{S}| = |\mathcal{S}'|$. In this case, since $\mathsf{id} \in \mathcal{S}'$, we have $\mathsf{m} \leftarrow \mathsf{Dec\text{-}at}(\{\mathsf{sk}_{\mathsf{id}}^{(\gamma)}\}_{\gamma \in \Gamma_{\mathsf{id},\mathcal{S}'}^*}, \mathsf{ct}_{\mathcal{S}',\mathsf{id}})$. And, since $\{\mathsf{sk}_{\mathsf{id}}^{(\gamma)}\}_{\gamma \in \Gamma_{\mathsf{id},\mathcal{S}'}^*} = \{\mathsf{sk}_{\mathsf{id}}^{(\gamma)}\}_{\gamma \in \Gamma_{\mathsf{id},\mathcal{S}}^*}$ from Lemma 1, we have $\mathsf{m} \leftarrow \mathsf{Dec\text{-}at}(\{\mathsf{sk}_{\mathsf{id}}^{(\gamma)}\}_{\gamma \in \Gamma_{\mathsf{id},\mathcal{S}}^*}, \mathsf{ct}_{\mathcal{S}',\mathsf{id}})$. Here, since $\{\mathsf{sk}_{\mathsf{id}}^{(\gamma)}\}_{\gamma \in \Gamma_{\mathsf{id},\mathcal{S}}^*} = \{\mathsf{sk}_{\mathsf{id}'}^{(\gamma')}\}_{\gamma' \in \Gamma_{\mathsf{id}',\mathcal{S}}^*}$ from the assumption, we have $\mathsf{m} \leftarrow \mathsf{Dec\text{-}at}(\{\mathsf{sk}_{\mathsf{id}'}^{(\gamma')}\}_{\gamma' \in \Gamma_{\mathsf{id}',\mathcal{S}}^*}, \mathsf{ct}_{\mathcal{S}',\mathsf{id}})$. However, by $\mathsf{id}' \notin \mathcal{S}'$, the above contradicts Property 1.                                                                $\square$

In the following, we derive a lower bound on ciphertext-size in ANOat-CPA secure BE with the property described in Assumption 2. Specifically, we show the statement: When there exists a set $\mathcal{S}$ such that the number of atomic ciphertexts $\mathsf{ct}_{\mathcal{S}}$ contained in $\mathsf{ct}_{\mathcal{S}}$ is less than $|\mathcal{S}|$, a contradiction occurs for Lemma 2.

**Theorem 1.** *If BE with the property shown in Assumption 2 is ANOat-CPA secure, the size of ciphertext with any recipient set $\mathcal{S} \subseteq \mathcal{ID}$ is $\Omega(|\mathcal{S}| \cdot k)$, where $k = \min_{\mathcal{S} \subseteq \mathcal{ID}, \theta \in [\beta_{\mathcal{S}}]} |\mathsf{ct}_{\mathcal{S}}^{(\theta)}|$.*

*Proof.* For some set of recipients $\mathcal{S}^*$, we assume $\beta_{\mathcal{S}^*} < |\mathcal{S}^*|$, and then show that this contradicts Lemma 2. Now, from $\beta_{\mathcal{S}^*} \geq 1$, we consider that $|\mathcal{S}^*| \geq 2$ holds. From $\beta_{\mathcal{S}^*} < |\mathcal{S}^*|$, for a set of atomic ciphertexts $\{\mathsf{ct}_{\mathcal{S}^*}^{(\theta)}\}_{\theta \in \beta_{\mathcal{S}^*}}$, there exists at least one atomic ciphertext $\mathsf{ct}_{\mathcal{S}^*}^{(\theta^*)}$ that can be decrypted by two recipients

$id, id' \in S^*$. That is, for $id, id' \in S^*$ and for any $m \in \mathcal{M}, r \in \mathcal{R}$, it holds that $ct_{S^*}^{(\theta^*)} = ct_{S,id} = ct_{S,id'}$, when $ct_{S,id}, ct_{S,id'}$ is generated by

$$ct_{S,id} \leftarrow \text{Enc-at}(\{pk^{(\delta)}\}_{\delta \in \Delta_{id,S^*,m}^*}, id, m, S^*; r),$$

$$ct_{S,id'} \leftarrow \text{Enc-at}(\{pk^{(\delta)}\}_{\delta \in \Delta_{id',S^*,m}^*}, id', m, S^*; r).$$

Therefore, by Property 4 , we have $\{pk^{(\delta)}\}_{\delta \in \Delta_{id,S^*,m}^*} = \{pk^{(\delta)}\}_{\delta \in \Delta_{id',S^*,m}^*}$.
In addition, we have the following by Atomic Correctness:

$$m \leftarrow \text{Dec-at}(\{sk_{id}^{(\gamma)}\}_{\gamma \in \Gamma_{id,S^*}^*}, ct_{S^*}^{(\theta^*)}), \tag{1}$$

$$m \leftarrow \text{Dec-at}(\{sk_{id'}^{(\gamma')}\}_{\gamma' \in \Gamma_{id',S^*}^*}, ct_{S^*}^{(\theta^*)}). \tag{2}$$

In this case, a set of atomic encryption keys used to encrypt $ct_{S^*}^{(\theta^*)}$ is $\{pk^{(\delta)}\}_{\delta \in \Delta_{id,S^*,m}^*} = \{pk^{(\delta)}\}_{\delta \in \Delta_{id',S^*,m}^*}$. Then, by Assumption 2, a set of a minimum subset of atomic decryption keys used to decrypt $ct_{S^*}^{(\theta^*)}$ is uniquely determined by $\{pk^{(\delta)}\}_{\delta \in \Delta_{id,S^*,m}^*}$. Therefore, in order that (1) and (2) holds, the following must hold true: $\{sk_{id}^{(\gamma)}\}_{\gamma \in \Gamma_{id,S^*}^*} = \{sk_{id'}^{(\gamma')}\}_{\gamma' \in \Gamma_{id',S^*}^*}$. However, the above equality contradicts Lemma 2. □

### 4.3   Lower Bounds in Full-ANOat-CPA Secure BE

First, we show Lemma 3 that states "if BE is full-ANOat-CPA secure, then for all privileged set $S, S'$, $\beta_S = \beta_{S'}$ holds , where $\beta_S, \beta_{S'}$ are the number of atomic ciphertexts in $ct_S, ct_{S'}$, respectively." Then, we derive a lower bound on ciphertext size in Theorem 2 for full-ANOat-CPA secure BE with the property described in Assumption 2, using Lemma 3 and Theorem 1.

**Lemma 3.** If BE $\Pi^{BE}$ is full-ANOat-CPA secure, we have $\beta_S = \beta_{S'}$ for all $S, S'$.

*Proof.* We show the statement: If $\beta_S \neq \beta_{S'}$ for some set $S, S'$, then we can construct a PPT adversary that breaks the full-ANOat-CPA security.

The adversary guesses the size of $S, S'$ as $\ell_0 \xleftarrow{U} [\ell], \ell_1 \xleftarrow{U} [\ell]$, respectively. We then randomly select a set whose size is $\ell_0, \ell_1$. Here, the probability that the adversary can obtain the set $S, S'$ such that $\beta_S \neq \beta_{S'}$ is $\ell^{-1} \cdot \binom{|\mathcal{ID}|}{\ell_0}^{-1} \cdot \ell^{-1} \cdot \binom{|\mathcal{ID}|}{\ell_1}^{-1}$. Then, the adversary issues $(m, S, S')$ as a challenge query, and obtains $\{ct_{S_b}^{(\theta)}\}_{\theta \in [\beta_{S_b}]}$. If $\beta_{S_b} = \ell_0$, the adversary outputs $b' = 0$, otherwise $b' = 1$. □

**Theorem 2.** If BE with the property shown in Assumption 2 is full-ANOat-CPA secure, the size of ciphertext with an arbitrary recipient set $S \subseteq \mathcal{ID}$ is $\Omega(N \cdot k)$, where $k = \min_{S \subseteq \mathcal{ID}, \theta \in [\beta_S]} |ct_S^{(\theta)}|$.

*Proof.* We assume $\beta_S < N$ for some $S$, and show a contradiction. First, if $S^* := [N]$, then $\beta_{S^*} = \beta_S < N$ holds from Lemma 3. On the other hand, since a full-ANOat-CPA secure BE meets ANOat-CPA security, we have $\beta_{S^*} \geq N$ by Theorem 1, but it contradicts $\beta_{S^*} < N$. □

## 5   Lower Bounds in Anonymous Broadcast Authentication

In recent years, with the spread of IoT devices, a system for safely control-ling a large number of IoT devices at once is desired. For doing it, Anonymous Broadcast Authentication (ABA) was proposed in [13]. ABA is an authentica-tion scheme that allows a sender to specify recipients so that only the specified recipients can perform verification-process correctly. A sender uses an authen-tication key ak to generate an authenticated command $cmd_S$ from a command m with a privileged set $S$. A recipient id can check validity of $cmd_S$ using its verification key $vk_{id}$. If a designated recipient $id \in S$ receives $cmd_S$ and it is not forged, the recipient accepts m. If $cmd_S$ is forged or a recipient is not designated, the recipient rejects it. ABA is also required to satisfy anonymity in addition to the functionality of broadcast authentication mentioned above, which guarantees that information of designated recipients $S$ is never leaked from the authenti-cated command $cmd_S$. Watanabe et al. [13] introduced two anonymity notions, anonymity and full-anonymity, like anonymity and full-anonymity in anonymous BA. Syntax and security definitions of ABA is provided in Appendix A. How-ever, a tight lower bound on authenticator-size of authenticated commands in ABA is not given in the previous work.

We can derive lower bounds on authenticator-size of authenticated commands in ABA by extending our analysis in anonymous BE to ABA, and the result-ing bounds are shown to be asymptotically tight. In fact, lower bounds in ABA can be obtained in a similar way as in anonymous BE in the previous sections: First, for simplicity, we define Atomic Broadcast Authentication (AtBA) allow-ing authenticators, authentication keys and verification keys to be split into multiple elements (see the syntax provided in Appendix B.1). Also, we define anonymity notions corresponding to anonymity and full-anonymity for ABA cov-ered with AtBA and call them as ANOat and full-ANOat, respectively (see also Appendix B.2). Next, we describe properties that the existing ABA scheme in [13] has, by which we derive lower bounds in ABA. (see Appendix C). By taking it into account, we define the property assumed for ABA schemes (see Appendix D.1). Then, we derive lower bounds on authenticator-size for ABA that sat-isfy the property (see Appendix D.2). Specifically, we can obtain the following results:

**Theorem 3.** If an ABA scheme with the property shown in Appendix D.1 is ANOat secure, then the size of authenticator with an arbitrary recipient set $S \subseteq \mathcal{ID}$ is $\Omega(|S| \cdot k)$, where $k = \min_{S \subseteq \mathcal{ID}, \theta \in [\beta_S]} |cmd_S^{(\theta)}|$.

**Theorem 4.** If an ABA scheme with the property shown in Appendix D.1 is full-ANOat secure, then the size of the authenticator with an arbitrary recipient set $S \subseteq \mathcal{ID}$ is $\Omega(N \cdot k)$, where $k = \min_{S \subseteq \mathcal{ID}, \theta \in [\beta_S]} |cmd_S^{(\theta)}|$.

We note that ABA schemes provided in [13] asymptotically meet the above bounds tightly. Therefore, we can conclude that our lower bounds on authenticator-size for ANO-BA and full-ANO-BA are asymptotically tight.

**Acknowledgements.** This research was conducted under a contract of "Research and development on IoT malware removal/make it non-functional technologies for effective use of the radio spectrum" among "Research and Development for Expansion of Radio Wave Resources (JPJ000254)," which was supported by the Ministry of Internal Affairs and Communications, Japan.

# A  Anonymous Broadcast Authentication

We define Anonymous Broadcast Authentication (ABA) and its security notions. In this paper, we assume that the maximum number of recipients $N$ is determined at the time of setup and an arbitrary set of recipients can be specified at the time of authentication.

**Syntax.** An Anonymous Broadcast Authentication scheme $\Pi^{\mathsf{ABA}}$ consists of four algorithms (Setup, Join, Auth, Vrfy).

1. $\mathsf{ak} \leftarrow \mathsf{Setup}(1^\kappa, N, \ell)$: a probabilistic algorithm for setup. It takes a security parameter $1^\kappa$, the maximum number of recipients $N \in \mathbb{N}$, the maximum number of recipients $\ell$ designated at once as input, and outputs authentication key $\mathsf{ak}$.
2. $\mathsf{vk}_{\mathsf{id}} \leftarrow \mathsf{Join}(\mathsf{ak}, \mathsf{id})$: a verification key generation algorithm. It takes $\mathsf{ak}$ and an identifier $\mathsf{id} \in \mathcal{ID}$, as input, and outputs verification key $\mathsf{vk}_{\mathsf{id}}$ for $\mathsf{id}$. Here, $\mathcal{ID}$ is a set of all possible identifiers, and $|\mathcal{ID}| := \mathsf{poly}(\kappa)$ for some polynomial $\mathsf{poly}(\cdot)$.
3. $\mathsf{cmd}_{\mathcal{S}} \leftarrow \mathsf{Auth}(\mathsf{ak}, \mathsf{m}, \mathcal{S}; \mathsf{r})$: an authentication algorithm. It takes $\mathsf{ak}$, a message $\mathsf{m} \in \mathcal{M}$, a randomness $\mathsf{r} \in \mathcal{R}$, and a privileged set $\mathcal{S} \subseteq \mathcal{ID}$ as input, and outputs ciphertext $\mathsf{cmd}_{\mathcal{S}}$, where $\mathcal{M}$ is a message space and $\mathcal{R}$ is a randomness space. It is also possible to omit $\mathsf{r}$ from the input.
4. $\mathsf{m} \leftarrow \mathsf{Vrfy}(\mathsf{vk}_{\mathsf{id}}, \mathsf{cmd}_{\mathcal{S}})$: a verification algorithm. It takes $\mathsf{vk}_{\mathsf{id}}$ and $\mathsf{cmd}_{\mathcal{S}}$ as inputs, and outputs $\mathsf{m} \in \mathcal{M}$ (accept) or $\perp$ (reject).

To describe properties of the existing ABA scheme, we regard Join as a deterministic algorithm in this paper.

**Correctness.** For all $\kappa, N \in \mathbb{N}$, all $\ell$ such that $1 \leq \ell \leq N$, all $\mathsf{ak} \leftarrow \mathsf{Setup}(1^\kappa, N, \ell)$, all $\mathsf{m} \in \mathcal{M}$, all $\mathsf{r} \in \mathcal{R}$, and all $\mathcal{S} \subseteq \mathcal{ID}$ such that $|\mathcal{S}| \leq \ell$, if $\mathsf{id} \in \mathcal{S}$, then $\mathsf{m} \leftarrow \mathsf{Vrfy}(\mathsf{Join}(\mathsf{ak}, \mathsf{id}), \mathsf{Auth}(\mathsf{ak}, \mathsf{m}, \mathcal{S}))$ holds with overwhelming probability. Otherwise, $\perp \leftarrow \mathsf{Vrfy}(\mathsf{Join}(\mathsf{ak}, \mathsf{id}), \mathsf{Auth}(\mathsf{ak}, \mathsf{m}, \mathcal{S}))$ holds with overwhelming probability

**Anonymity.** We define two kinds of anonymity for ABA, full anonymity (full-ANO) and anonymity (ANO).

Let A be any PPT adversary against full-ANO security. We consider an experiment $\mathsf{Exp}_{\Pi^{\mathsf{ABA}}, \mathsf{A}}^{\mathsf{full\text{-}ANO}}(\kappa, N, \ell)$ between a challenger C and A.

$\mathsf{Exp}_{\varPi^{\mathsf{ABA}},\mathsf{A}}^{\mathsf{full\text{-}ANO}}(\kappa, N, \ell).$

C randomly chooses $b \in \{0,1\}$. C runs $\mathsf{Setup}(1^\kappa, N, \ell)$ to get $\mathsf{ak}$ and randomly chooses $b \in \{0,1\}$. Let $\mathcal{D}, \mathcal{CD}$ be a empty sets. We denote $\mathcal{D}$ as a set of recipients currently participating in the protocol, and $\mathcal{CD}$ as a set of identifiers of recipient from which A obtained its verification key, respectively. A may adaptively issue the following queries to C.

- Key-generation Query: Upon a query $\mathsf{id} \in \mathcal{ID}$ from A, C adds $\mathsf{id}$ to $\mathcal{D}$ and generates $\mathsf{vk}_{\mathsf{id}} \leftarrow \mathsf{Join}(\mathsf{ak}, \mathsf{id})$. Note that A obtains nothing, and that A is allowed to make this query at most $N$ times.
- Corruption Query: Upon a query $\mathsf{id} \in \mathcal{D}$ from A, C adds $\mathsf{id}$ to $\mathcal{CD}$, and returns $\mathsf{vk}_{\mathsf{id}}$ to A.
- Challenge Query: Upon a query $(\mathsf{m}, \mathcal{S}_0, \mathcal{S}_1) \in \mathcal{M} \times \left(2_{\leq \ell}^{\mathcal{D}}\right)^2$ from A, C runs $\mathsf{cmd}_{\mathcal{S}_b} \leftarrow \mathsf{Auth}(\mathsf{ak}, \mathsf{m}, \mathcal{S}_b)$ and returns $\mathsf{cmd}_{\mathcal{S}_b}$ to A. A is allowed to make this query only once under the restriction that $(\mathcal{S}_0 \triangle \mathcal{S}_1) \cap \mathcal{CD} = \emptyset$.

At some point, A outputs $b'$. If $b' = b$, C then sets 1 as the output of $\mathsf{Exp}_{\varPi^{\mathsf{ABA}},\mathsf{A}}^{\mathsf{full\text{-}ANO}}(\kappa, N, \ell)$. Otherwise, C then sets 0. C terminates the experiment.

We can also define ANO with an experiment $\mathsf{Exp}_{\varPi^{\mathsf{ABA}},\mathsf{A}}^{\mathsf{ANO}}(\kappa, N, \ell)$ which is the same as $\mathsf{Exp}_{\varPi^{\mathsf{ABA}},\mathsf{A}}^{\mathsf{full\text{-}ANO}}(\kappa, N, \ell)$ except for the following additional condition of the restriction for challenge query: $|\mathcal{S}_0| = |\mathcal{S}_1|$.

**Definition 5 (Anonymity).** We say $\varPi^{\mathsf{ABA}}$ is X secure (X $\in \{\mathsf{full\text{-}ANO}, \mathsf{ANO}\}$) if for any PPTA A, for all sufficiently-large $\kappa \in \mathbb{N}$, all $N \in \mathbb{N}$ and all $\ell (\leq N)$, it holds that $\mathsf{Adv}_{\varPi^{\mathsf{ABA}},\mathsf{A}}^{X}(\kappa, N, \ell) < \mathsf{negl}(\kappa)$, where $\mathsf{Adv}_{\varPi^{\mathsf{ABA}},\mathsf{A}}^{X}(\kappa, N, \ell) := \left| \Pr[\mathsf{Exp}_{\varPi^{\mathsf{ABA}},\mathsf{A}}^{X}(\kappa, N, \ell) \to 1] - \frac{1}{2} \right|.$

# B    Atomic Broadcast Authentication

In this section, we give a formal syntax of Atomic Broadcast Authentication (AtBA) to formally describe properties satisfied by the existing ABA scheme. These properties are used to formalize existing properties of ABA and derive lower bounds. We further provide security definitions for ABA covered with AtBA.

## B.1    Syntax of AtBA

Our AtBA describes authentication and verification for each recipient in a designated set performed inside $\mathsf{Auth}$ and $\mathsf{Vrfy}$ algorithms of ABA. We define a model for Atomic BA $\varPi^{\mathsf{At\text{-}BA}} = (\mathsf{Setup\text{-}at}, \mathsf{Join\text{-}at}, \mathsf{Auth\text{-}at}, \mathsf{Vrfy\text{-}at})$ as follows.

1. $\{\mathsf{ak}^{(\delta)}\}_{\delta \in \Delta} \leftarrow \mathsf{Setup\text{-}at}(1^\kappa, N, \ell)$: a probabilistic algorithm for setup. It takes a security parameter $1^\kappa$, the maximum number of receivers $N \in \mathbb{N}$, the maximum number of receivers $\ell$ designated at once as input, and outputs authentication key $\mathsf{ak}$ consisting of $|\Delta|$ atomic authentication keys $\{\mathsf{ak}^{(\delta)}\}_{\delta \in \Delta}$.

2. $\{vk_{id}^{(\gamma)}\}_{\gamma \in \Gamma_{id}} \leftarrow$ Join-at($\{ak^{(\delta)}\}_{\delta \in \Delta}$, id): a verification key generation algorithm. It takes $\{ak^{(\delta)}\}_{\delta \in \Delta}$ and an identifier id $\in \mathcal{ID}$, as input, and outputs verification key $vk_{id}$ for id consisting of $|\Gamma_{id}|$ atomic verification keys $\{vk_{id}^{(\gamma)}\}_{\gamma \in \Gamma_{id}}$.

3. $cmd_{\mathcal{S},id} \leftarrow$ Auth-at($\{ak^{(\delta)}\}_{\delta \in \Delta'}$, $\mathcal{S}$, m, id; r): an atomic authenticate algorithm. It takes $\{ak^{(\delta)}\}_{\delta \in \Delta'}$, a message m $\in \mathcal{M}$, a privileged set $\mathcal{S} \subseteq \mathcal{ID}$, an identifier id $\in \mathcal{ID}$ and randomness r $\in \mathcal{R}$ as input, and outputs an atomic authenticator $cmd_{\mathcal{S},id}$, where $\Delta' \subseteq \Delta$.

4. m/$\perp \leftarrow$ Vrfy-at($\{vk_{id}^{(\gamma)}\}_{\gamma \in \Gamma_{id}'}$, $cmd_{\mathcal{S},id}$): an atomic verification algorithm. It takes a subset of atomic verification keys $\{sk_{id}^{(\gamma)}\}_{\gamma \in \Gamma_{id}'}$, and $cmd_{\mathcal{S},id}$ as input, and outputs a message m(accept) or $\perp$(reject), where $\Gamma_{id}' \subseteq \Gamma_{id}$.

Setup-at and Join-at are essentially equivalent to Setup and Join in ABA respectively, except for difference that authentication and verification keys are explicitly divided into multiple sub-elements. As in the case of Join in BE, we regard Join-at as being a deterministic algorithm. We require a natural property for AtBA that an atomic authenticator $cmd_{\mathcal{S},id}$ contained in authenticator $cmd_{\mathcal{S}}$ will be correctly verified by a verification key $\{vk_{id}^{(\gamma)}\}_{\gamma \in \Gamma_{id}}$ of a recipient id $\in \mathcal{S}$ as follows:

**Atomic Correctness.** For all $\kappa, N \in \mathbb{N}$, all $\ell$ such that $1 \leq \ell \leq N$, all $\{ak^{(\delta)}\}_{\delta \in \Delta} \leftarrow$ Setup-at($1^\kappa, N, \ell$), all id $\in \mathcal{ID}$, all m $\in \mathcal{M}$, all r $\overset{U}{\leftarrow} \mathcal{R}$, all $\mathcal{S} \subseteq \mathcal{ID}$ such that $|\mathcal{S}| \leq \ell$, all $\{vk_{id}^{(\gamma)}\}_{\gamma \in \Gamma_{id}} \leftarrow$ Join-at($\{ak^{(\delta)}\}_{\delta \in \Delta}$, id), for some $\Delta' \subseteq \Delta$ and $\Gamma_{id}' \subseteq \Gamma_{id}$, for all $cmd_{\mathcal{S},id} \leftarrow$ Auth-at($\{ak^{(\delta)}\}_{\delta \in \Delta}$, id, m, $\mathcal{S}$), if id $\in \mathcal{S}$, then m $\leftarrow$ Vrfy-at($\{vk_{id}^{(\gamma)}\}_{\gamma \in \Gamma_{id}}$, $cmd_{\mathcal{S},id}$) with overwhelming probability. Otherwise, $\perp \leftarrow$ Vrfy-at($\{vk_{id}^{(\gamma)}\}_{\gamma \in \Gamma_{id}}$, $cmd_{\mathcal{S},id}$) with overwhelming probability.

## B.2   Security Definitions for ABA Covered with AtBA

We define anonymity for ABA covered with AtBA in the same way as in BE. In the following, we give definitions of full anonymity (**full-ANOat**) and anonymity (**ANOat**).

Security games for ABA covered with AtBA are the same as those for ABA except that an attacker obtains verification keys and a challenge authenticator is explicitly devided into multiple sub-elements. Essentially, there is no difference between anonymity for ABA and AtBA in that information attackers obtain. Therefore, we consider AnonymityAt defined below to be the same security as Anonymity.

Let A be any PPT adversary against full-ANOat security. We consider an experiment $\text{Exp}_{\Pi^{ABA},A}^{full\text{-}ANOat}(\kappa, N, \ell)$ between a challenger C and A. Let $\text{Exp}_{\Pi^{ABA},A}^{full\text{-}ANOat}$ be the experiment with the following changes to Key-generation Query and Corruption Query in experiment $\text{Exp}_{\Pi^{ABA},A}^{full\text{-}ANO}$.

- Key-generation Query: Upon a query id $\in \mathcal{ID}$ from A, C adds id to $\mathcal{D}$ and generates $\{vk_{id}^{(\gamma)}\}_{\gamma \in \Gamma_{id}} \leftarrow$ Join-at(ak, id), not $vk_{id} \leftarrow$ Join(ak, id).

– Corruption Query: Upon a query $id \in \mathcal{D}$ from A, C adds $id$ to $\mathcal{CD}$, and returns $\{vk_{id}^{(\gamma)}\}_{\gamma \in \Gamma_{id}}$ to A, not $vk_{id}$.

We also define ANOat with an experiment $Exp_{\Pi^{ABA},A}^{ANOat}(\kappa, N, \ell)$ which is the same as $Exp_{\Pi^{ABA},A}^{full\text{-}ANOat}(\kappa, N, \ell)$ except for the following additional condition of the restriction for challenge query: $|\mathcal{S}_0| = |\mathcal{S}_1|$.

**Definition 6 (Anonymity for AtBA).** We say $\Pi^{ABA}$ is X secure (X $\in$ full-ANOat, ANOat) if for any PPTA A, for all sufficiently-large $\kappa \in \mathbb{N}$, all $N \in \mathbb{N}$ and all $\ell \, (\leq N)$, it holds that $|Adv_{\Pi^{ABA},A}^{X}(\kappa, N, \ell)| < negl(\kappa)$, where $Adv_{\Pi^{ABA},A}^{X}(\kappa, N, \ell) := |\Pr[Exp_{\Pi^{ABA},A}^{X}(\kappa, N, \ell) \to 1] - \frac{1}{2}|$.

# C   Properties in An Existing ABA Scheme

In this section, we describe four properties that holds for an existing ABA scheme. The four properties is as follows.

**Property 5.** Authenticator $cmd_{\mathcal{S}}$ output from $\Pi^{ABA}$.Auth algorithm consists of atomic authenticator $cmd_{\mathcal{S},id}$ obtained by $\Pi^{At\text{-}BA}$.Auth-at algorithm, and other elements. In other words, let a set of atomic authenticators contained in $cmd_{\mathcal{S}}$ be $\{cmd_{\mathcal{S},id}\}_{id \in \mathcal{S}}$, and let union of $\{cmd_{\mathcal{S},id}\}_{id \in \mathcal{S}}$ and some elements contained in $cmd_{\mathcal{S}}$ be $\{cmd_{\mathcal{S}}^{(\theta)}\}_{\theta \in [\beta_{\mathcal{S}}]}$, it holds that $\{cmd_{\mathcal{S},id}\}_{id \in \mathcal{S}} \subseteq \{cmd_{\mathcal{S}}^{(\theta)}\}_{\theta \in [\beta_{\mathcal{S}}]} \subseteq cmd_{\mathcal{S}}$. Here, a randomness r input to $\Pi^{At\text{-}BA}$.Auth-at is the same when generating $\{cmd_{\mathcal{S},id}\}_{id \in \mathcal{S}}$ respectively. Also, inside ABA's $\Pi^{ABA}$.Vrfy algorithm, $\Pi^{At\text{-}BA}$.Vrfy-at algorithm takes atomic authenticator and a set of atomic verification key as input, and outputs a message. If $cmd_{\mathcal{S}}$ is valid authenticator, then there is an atomic authenticator $cmd_{\mathcal{S}}^{(\theta)}$ in $cmd_{\mathcal{S}}$ that can be verified using a subset of atomic verification keys of a recipient $id$ in $\mathcal{S}$. Formally, we require the following property for ABA $\Pi^{ABA}$:

For all $\kappa, N \in \mathbb{N}$, all $\ell$ such that $1 \leq \ell \leq N$, all $ak \leftarrow \Pi^{ABA}$.Setup($1^{\kappa}, N, \ell$), all $m \in \mathcal{M}$, all $\mathcal{S} \subseteq \mathcal{ID}$ such that $|\mathcal{S}| \leq \ell$, all $id \in \mathcal{ID}$, all $\{vk_{id}^{(\gamma)}\}_{\gamma \in \Gamma_{id}} \leftarrow \Pi^{At\text{-}BA}$.Join-at($ak, id$), all $r \xleftarrow{U} \mathcal{R}$, all $\{cmd_{\mathcal{S}}^{(\theta)}\}_{\theta \in [\beta_{\mathcal{S}}]} \subseteq cmd_{\mathcal{S}} \leftarrow \Pi^{ABA}$.Auth($ak, m, \mathcal{S}; r$), if $id \in \mathcal{S}$, then for some $\Gamma_{id}' \subseteq \Gamma_{id}$, there exists $\theta \in [\beta_{\mathcal{S}}]$ such that $m \leftarrow$ Vrfy-at($\{vk_{id}^{(\gamma)}\}_{\gamma \in \Gamma_{id}'}, cmd_{\mathcal{S}}^{(\theta)}$). If $id \notin \mathcal{S}$, then for all $\Gamma_{id}' \subseteq \Gamma_{id}$, there is no $\theta \in [\beta_{\mathcal{S}}]$ such that $m \leftarrow$ Vrfy-at($\{vk_{id}^{(\gamma)}\}_{\gamma \in \Gamma_{id}'}, cmd_{\mathcal{S}}^{(\theta)}$).

**Property 6.** When generating $cmd_{\mathcal{S},id}$ such that $m \leftarrow$ Vrfy-at($\{vk_{id}^{(\gamma)}\}_{\gamma \in \Gamma_{id}'}, cmd_{\mathcal{S},id}$) for some $\gamma \in \Gamma_{id}'$, let $\Delta_{id,\mathcal{S},m}^{*}$ be a minimum subset of atomic authentication keys required for the input to Auth-at. In this case, $\Delta_{id,\mathcal{S},m}^{*}$ is uniquely determined by pairs of the recipient's identifier, the message, and the set $(id, m, \mathcal{S})$ to input to Auth-at.

**Property 7.** When $m \leftarrow$ Vrfy-at($\{vk_{id}^{(\gamma)}\}_{\gamma \in \Gamma_{id}'}, cmd_{\mathcal{S},id}$) holds, let $\Gamma_{id,\mathcal{S}}^{*}$ be a minimum subset of atomic verification keys required for the input to Vrfy-at. In this case, $\Gamma_{id,\mathcal{S}}^{*}$ is uniquely determined by pairs of the recipient's identifier, and the set $(id, \mathcal{S})$ to input to Auth-at when generating $cmd_{\mathcal{S},id}$.

**Property 8.** For all $(\mathsf{ak}, \{\mathsf{ak}^{(\delta)}\}_{\delta \in \Delta}) \leftarrow \mathsf{Setup}(1^\kappa, N, \ell), \mathsf{id}, \mathsf{id}' \in \mathcal{ID}$, all $\mathcal{S}$ such that $\{\mathsf{id}, \mathsf{id}'\} \subseteq \mathcal{S}$, all $\mathsf{m} \in \mathcal{M}, \mathsf{r} \in \mathcal{R}$, all $\mathsf{cmd}_{\mathcal{S}, \mathsf{id}} \leftarrow \mathsf{Auth\text{-}at}(\{\mathsf{ak}^{(\delta)}\}_{\delta \in \Delta^*_{\mathsf{id}, \mathcal{S}, \mathsf{m}}},$ $\mathsf{id}, \mathsf{m}, \mathcal{S}; \mathsf{r}), \mathsf{cmd}_{\mathcal{S}, \mathsf{id}'} \leftarrow \mathsf{Auth\text{-}at}(\{\mathsf{ak}^{(\delta')}\}_{\delta' \in \Delta^*_{\mathsf{id}', \mathcal{S}, \mathsf{m}}}, \mathsf{id}', \mathsf{m}, \mathcal{S}; \mathsf{r})$, if $\mathsf{cmd}_{\mathcal{S}, \mathsf{id}} = \mathsf{cmd}_{\mathcal{S}, \mathsf{id}'}$ holds, then we have $\{\mathsf{ak}^{(\delta)}\}_{\delta \in \Delta^*_{\mathsf{id}, \mathcal{S}, \mathsf{m}}} = \{\mathsf{ak}^{(\delta')}\}_{\delta' \in \Delta^*_{\mathsf{id}', \mathcal{S}, \mathsf{m}}}$ with overwhelming probability.

Here, we can see that the existing ABA scheme [13] satisfy the above properties in a similar way in Sect. 3.2.

# D    Lower Bounds of authenticator Size in ABA

## D.1    A Property of ANO-BA and Full-ANO-BA

In order to derive lower bounds for ANO-BA and full-ANO-BA, we assume a property that "a minimum subset of atomic verification keys used to verify authenticators is uniquely determined by a subset of authentication keys used to generate the authenticator." Specifically, we consider the following property for ANO-BA and full-ANO-BA:

**Assumption 3.** When $\{\mathsf{ak}^{(\delta)}\}_{\delta \in \Delta} \leftarrow \mathsf{Setup}(1^\kappa, N, \ell)$ is generated, we denote $\mathcal{AK}^*$ as a set of all authentication keys, namely $\mathcal{AK}^* := \{\mathsf{ak}^{(\delta)}\}_{\delta \in \Delta}$. And, when $\{\mathsf{vk}^{(\gamma)}_{\mathsf{id}}\}_{\gamma \in \Gamma_{\mathsf{id}}} \leftarrow \mathsf{Join}(\mathsf{ak}, \mathsf{id})$ is generated, $\mathcal{VK}^*$ denotes a set of a minimum subset of atomic verification keys to be input to $\mathsf{Vrfy\text{-}at}$, namely $\mathcal{VK}^* := \{\{\mathsf{vk}^{(\gamma)}_{\mathsf{id}}\}_{\gamma \in \Gamma^*_{\mathsf{id}, \mathcal{S}}}\}_{\mathsf{id} \in \mathcal{ID}, \mathcal{S} \subseteq \mathcal{ID}}$. Here, we note that $\mathcal{VK}^*$ is uniquely determined, since $\mathsf{Join} - at$ is a deterministic algorithm. At this time, for all $\mathsf{id} \in \mathcal{ID}$, all $\mathcal{S} \subseteq \mathcal{ID}$, all $\mathsf{m} \in \mathcal{M}$, all $\mathsf{r} \in \mathcal{R}$, all $\mathsf{ak}' \in 2^{\mathcal{AK}^*}$, all $\mathsf{cmd}_{\mathcal{S}, \mathsf{id}} \leftarrow \mathsf{Auth\text{-}at}(\mathsf{ak}', \mathsf{id}, \mathsf{m}, \mathcal{S}; \mathsf{r})$, a set of atomic verification keys $\mathsf{vk}' \in \mathcal{VK}^* \cup \{\bot\}$ such that $\mathsf{m} \leftarrow \mathsf{Vrfy\text{-}at}(\mathsf{vk}', \mathsf{cmd}_{\mathcal{S}, \mathsf{id}})$ is uniquely determined by the set of atomic authentication keys $\mathsf{ak}'$.

The above property holds for Watanabe et al.'s ANO-BA and full-ANO-BA schemes [13], which is a generic construction using message authentication code and pseudo-random function. Since it can be shown that they satisfies the above property in the same way as ANO-BE scheme of Libert et al. [11], we omit a detailed discussion here.

## D.2    Lower Bounds in ANOat Secure ABA

First, we show two lemmas, Lemmas 4 and 5, for ANOat secure ABA with Properties 5, 6, 7 and 8 described in Section C. In Lemma 4, we show that "if ABA is ANOat secure, then for authenticators with a set $\mathcal{S}_0, \mathcal{S}_1$ whose size is equal, sets of atomic verification keys used by a receipient id for each verification is equal." Then, in Lemma 5, we show that "if ABA is ANOat secure, then for any set $\mathcal{S}$ with more than two elements, recipients $\mathsf{id}, \mathsf{id}' \in \mathcal{S}$ must not share a set of atomic verification keys used to verify $\mathsf{cmd}_{\mathcal{S}}$."

Then, for ANOat secure ABA with the property described in Assumption 3, we will derive a lower bound on authenticator-size by Theorem 5.

**Lemma 4.** If ABA $\Pi^{\mathsf{ABA}}$ is ANOat secure, for all id $\in \mathcal{ID}$, all $\mathcal{S}_0, \mathcal{S}_1$ such that id $\in \mathcal{S}_0 \cap \mathcal{S}_1$ and $|\mathcal{S}_0| = |\mathcal{S}_1|$, we have $\{\mathsf{vk}_{\mathsf{id}}^{(\gamma)}\}_{\gamma \in \Gamma_{\mathsf{id}, \mathcal{S}_0}^*} = \{\mathsf{vk}_{\mathsf{id}}^{(\gamma)}\}_{\gamma \in \Gamma_{\mathsf{id}, \mathcal{S}_1}^*}$.

*Proof.* We show this lemma by contraposition. Suppose $\{\mathsf{vk}_{\mathsf{id}}^{(\gamma)}\}_{\gamma \in \Gamma_{\mathsf{id}, \mathcal{S}_0}^*} \neq \{\mathsf{vk}_{\mathsf{id}}^{(\gamma)}\}_{\gamma \in \Gamma_{\mathsf{id}, \mathcal{S}_1}^*}$ for some id $\in \mathcal{ID}$ and some $\mathcal{S}_0, \mathcal{S}_1$ such that id $\in \mathcal{S}_0 \cap \mathcal{S}_1, |\mathcal{S}_0| = |\mathcal{S}_1|$. We will construct PPT adversary against ANOat security as follows. Let id* be id as above. Initially, the adversary guesses sizes of $\mathcal{S}_0, \mathcal{S}_1$ as $\ell^* \overset{\mathsf{U}}{\leftarrow} [\ell]$. Next, the adversary guesses id*, $\mathcal{S}_0$, and $\mathcal{S}_1$. A probability that the adversary succeeds in guessing is $\frac{1}{|\mathcal{ID}|} \cdot \frac{1}{\ell} \cdot \binom{|\mathcal{ID}|}{\ell^*-1}^{-1} \cdot \left( \binom{|\mathcal{ID}|}{\ell^*-1} - 1 \right)^{-1}$. The adversary also issues Key-Generation queries for all id in $\mathcal{S}_0 \cup \mathcal{S}_1$ and Corruption queries for id* to obtain verification key $\{\mathsf{vk}_{\mathsf{id}*}^{(\gamma)}\}_{\gamma \in \Gamma_{\mathsf{id}*}}$. Then, the adversary issues a challenge query $(\mathsf{m}, \mathcal{S}_0, \mathcal{S}_1)$ to obtain $\{\mathsf{cmd}_{\mathcal{S}_b}^{(\theta)}\}_{\theta \in [\beta_{\mathcal{S}_b}]} \subseteq \mathsf{cmd}_{\mathcal{S}_b}$. Finally, the adversary outputs $b' = 0$ if there exists $\theta \in [\beta_{\mathcal{S}_b}]$ such that $\mathsf{m} \leftarrow \mathsf{Dec\text{-}at}(\{\mathsf{vk}_{\mathsf{id}*}^{(\gamma)}\}_{\gamma \in \Gamma_{\mathsf{id}*, \mathcal{S}_0}^*}, \mathsf{cmd}_{\mathcal{S}_b}^{(\theta)})$, and $b' = 1$ otherwise. In this case, the adversary can output $b'$ such that $b = b'$ with probability $\frac{1}{2} \left( \frac{1}{|\mathcal{ID}|} \cdot \frac{1}{\ell} \cdot \binom{|\mathcal{ID}|}{\ell^*-1}^{-1} \cdot \left( \binom{|\mathcal{ID}|}{\ell^*-1} - 1 \right)^{-1} + 1 \right)$. □

**Lemma 5.** If ABA $\Pi^{\mathsf{ABA}}$ is ANOat secure, for all id, id' $\in \mathcal{ID}$, all $\mathcal{S} \subseteq \mathcal{ID}$ such that $\{\mathsf{id}, \mathsf{id}'\} \subseteq \mathcal{S}, |\mathcal{S}| \geq 2$, we have $\{\mathsf{vk}_{\mathsf{id}}^{(\gamma)}\}_{\gamma \in \Gamma_{\mathsf{id}, \mathcal{S}}^*} \neq \{\mathsf{vk}_{\mathsf{id}'}^{(\gamma')}\}_{\gamma' \in \Gamma_{\mathsf{id}', \mathcal{S}}^*}$.

*Proof.* Assume on the contrary that we have $\{\mathsf{vk}_{\mathsf{id}}^{(\gamma)}\}_{\gamma \in \Gamma_{\mathsf{id}, \mathcal{S}}^*} = \{\mathsf{vk}_{\mathsf{id}'}^{(\gamma')}\}_{\gamma' \in \Gamma_{\mathsf{id}', \mathcal{S}}^*}$ for some id, id' $\in \mathcal{ID}$ and some $\mathcal{S} \subseteq \mathcal{ID}$ such that $\{\mathsf{id}, \mathsf{id}'\} \subseteq \mathcal{S}, |\mathcal{S}| \geq 2$. Then, we will show that it contradicts correctness of ABA with AtABA structure (see Section C, Property 5). First, we choose $\mathcal{S}'$ such that id $\in \mathcal{S}', \mathsf{id}' \notin \mathcal{S}', |\mathcal{S}| = |\mathcal{S}'|$. In this case, since id $\in \mathcal{S}'$, we have $\mathsf{m} \leftarrow \mathsf{Dec\text{-}at}(\{\mathsf{vk}_{\mathsf{id}}^{(\gamma)}\}_{\gamma \in \Gamma_{\mathsf{id}, \mathcal{S}'}^*}, \mathsf{cmd}_{\mathcal{S}', \mathsf{id}})$. And, since $\{\mathsf{vk}_{\mathsf{id}}^{(\gamma)}\}_{\gamma \in \Gamma_{\mathsf{id}, \mathcal{S}'}^*} = \{\mathsf{vk}_{\mathsf{id}}^{(\gamma)}\}_{\gamma \in \Gamma_{\mathsf{id}, \mathcal{S}}^*}$ from Lemma 4, we have $\mathsf{m} \leftarrow \mathsf{Dec\text{-}at}(\{\mathsf{vk}_{\mathsf{id}}^{(\gamma)}\}_{\gamma \in \Gamma_{\mathsf{id}, \mathcal{S}}^*}, \mathsf{cmd}_{\mathcal{S}', \mathsf{id}})$. Here, since $\{\mathsf{vk}_{\mathsf{id}}^{(\gamma)}\}_{\gamma \in \Gamma_{\mathsf{id}, \mathcal{S}}^*} = \{\mathsf{vk}_{\mathsf{id}'}^{(\gamma')}\}_{\gamma' \in \Gamma_{\mathsf{id}', \mathcal{S}}^*}$ from the assumption, we have $\mathsf{m} \leftarrow \mathsf{Dec\text{-}at}(\{\mathsf{vk}_{\mathsf{id}'}^{(\gamma')}\}_{\gamma' \in \Gamma_{\mathsf{id}', \mathcal{S}}^*}, \mathsf{cmd}_{\mathcal{S}', \mathsf{id}})$. However, by id' $\notin \mathcal{S}'$, the above contradicts Property 5. □

In the following, we derive a lower bound on authenticator-size in ANOat secure ABA with the property described in Assumption 3. Specifically, we show the statement: When there exists a set $\mathcal{S}$ such that the number of atomic authenticators $\mathsf{cmd}_{\mathcal{S}}$ contained in $\mathsf{cmd}_{\mathcal{S}}$ is less than $|\mathcal{S}|$, a contradiction occurs for Lemma 5.

**Theorem 5.** If ABA with the property shown in Assumption 3 is ANOat secure, the size of authenticator with any recipient set $\mathcal{S} \subseteq \mathcal{ID}$ is $\Omega(|\mathcal{S}| \cdot k)$, where $k = \min_{\mathcal{S} \subseteq \mathcal{ID}, \theta \in [\beta_{\mathcal{S}}]} |\mathsf{cmd}_{\mathcal{S}}^{(\theta)}|$.

*Proof.* For some set of recipients $\mathcal{S}^*$, we assume $\beta_{\mathcal{S}^*} < |\mathcal{S}^*|$, and then show that this contradicts Lemma 5. Now, from $\beta_{\mathcal{S}^*} \geq 1$, we consider that $|\mathcal{S}^*| \geq 2$ holds. From $\beta_{\mathcal{S}^*} < |\mathcal{S}^*|$, for a set of atomic authenticators $\{\mathsf{cmd}_{\mathcal{S}^*}^{(\theta)}\}_{\theta \in \beta_{\mathcal{S}^*}}$, there exists at least one atomic authenticator $\mathsf{cmd}_{\mathcal{S}^*}^{(\theta^*)}$ that can be verified by two recipients $\mathsf{id}, \mathsf{id}' \in \mathcal{S}^*$. That is, for $\mathsf{id}, \mathsf{id}' \in \mathcal{S}^*$ and for any $\mathsf{m} \in \mathcal{M}, \mathsf{r} \in \mathcal{R}$, it holds that $\mathsf{cmd}_{\mathcal{S}^*}^{(\theta^*)} = \mathsf{cmd}_{\mathcal{S},\mathsf{id}} = \mathsf{cmd}_{\mathcal{S},\mathsf{id}'}$, when $\mathsf{cmd}_{\mathcal{S},\mathsf{id}}, \mathsf{cmd}_{\mathcal{S},\mathsf{id}'}$ is generated by

$$\mathsf{cmd}_{\mathcal{S},\mathsf{id}} \leftarrow \mathsf{Enc\text{-}at}(\{\mathsf{ak}^{(\delta)}\}_{\delta \in \Delta^*_{\mathsf{id},\mathcal{S}^*,\mathsf{m}}}, \mathsf{id}, \mathsf{m}, \mathcal{S}^*; \mathsf{r}),$$

$$\mathsf{cmd}_{\mathcal{S},\mathsf{id}'} \leftarrow \mathsf{Enc\text{-}at}(\{\mathsf{ak}^{(\delta)}\}_{\delta \in \Delta^*_{\mathsf{id}',\mathcal{S}^*,\mathsf{m}}}, \mathsf{id}', \mathsf{m}, \mathcal{S}^*; \mathsf{r}).$$

Therefore, by Property 8, we have $\{\mathsf{ak}^{(\delta)}\}_{\delta \in \Delta^*_{\mathsf{id},\mathcal{S}^*,\mathsf{m}}} = \{\mathsf{ak}^{(\delta)}\}_{\delta \in \Delta^*_{\mathsf{id}',\mathcal{S}^*,\mathsf{m}}}$.

In addition, we have the following by Atomic Correctness:

$$\mathsf{m} \leftarrow \mathsf{Dec\text{-}at}(\{\mathsf{vk}_{\mathsf{id}}^{(\gamma)}\}_{\gamma \in \Gamma^*_{\mathsf{id},\mathcal{S}^*}}, \mathsf{cmd}_{\mathcal{S}^*}^{(\theta^*)}), \tag{3}$$

$$\mathsf{m} \leftarrow \mathsf{Dec\text{-}at}(\{\mathsf{vk}_{\mathsf{id}'}^{(\gamma')}\}_{\gamma' \in \Gamma^*_{\mathsf{id}',\mathcal{S}^*}}, \mathsf{cmd}_{\mathcal{S}^*}^{(\theta^*)}). \tag{4}$$

In this case, a set of atomic authentication keys used to authenticate $\mathsf{cmd}_{\mathcal{S}^*}^{(\theta^*)}$ is $\{\mathsf{ak}^{(\delta)}\}_{\delta \in \Delta^*_{\mathsf{id},\mathcal{S}^*,\mathsf{m}}} = \{\mathsf{ak}^{(\delta)}\}_{\delta \in \Delta^*_{\mathsf{id}',\mathcal{S}^*,\mathsf{m}}}$. Then, by Assumption 3, a set of a minimum subset of atomic verification keys used to verify $\mathsf{cmd}_{\mathcal{S}^*}^{(\theta^*)}$ is uniquely determined by $\{\mathsf{ak}^{(\delta)}\}_{\delta \in \Delta^*_{\mathsf{id},\mathcal{S}^*,\mathsf{m}}}$. Therefore, in order that (3) and (4) holds, the following must hold true: $\{\mathsf{vk}_{\mathsf{id}}^{(\gamma)}\}_{\gamma \in \Gamma^*_{\mathsf{id},\mathcal{S}^*}} = \{\mathsf{vk}_{\mathsf{id}'}^{(\gamma')}\}_{\gamma' \in \Gamma^*_{\mathsf{id}',\mathcal{S}^*}}$. However, the above equality contradicts Lemma 5. □

### D.3  Lower Bounds in full-ANOat secure ABA

First, we show Lemma 6 that states "if ABA is full-ANOat secure, then for all privileged set $\mathcal{S}, \mathcal{S}'$, $\beta_{\mathcal{S}} = \beta_{\mathcal{S}'}$ holds , where $\beta_{\mathcal{S}}, \beta_{\mathcal{S}'}$ are the number of atomic authenticators in $\mathsf{cmd}_{\mathcal{S}}, \mathsf{cmd}_{\mathcal{S}'}$, respectively." Then, we derive a lower bound on authenticator size in Theorem 6 for full-ANOat secure ABA with the property described in Assumption 3, using Lemma 6 and Theorem 5.

**Lemma 6.** *If ABA $\Pi^{\mathsf{ABA}}$ is full-ANOat secure, we have $\beta_{\mathcal{S}} = \beta_{\mathcal{S}'}$ for all $\mathcal{S}, \mathcal{S}'$.*

*Proof.* We show the statement: If $\beta_{\mathcal{S}} \neq \beta_{\mathcal{S}'}$ for some set $\mathcal{S}, \mathcal{S}'$, then we can construct a PPT adversary that breaks the full-ANOat security.

the adversary guesses the size of $\mathcal{S}, \mathcal{S}'$ as $\ell_0 \xleftarrow{\mathsf{U}} [\ell], \ell_1 \xleftarrow{\mathsf{U}} [\ell]$, respectively. We then randomly select a set whose size is $\ell_0, \ell_1$. Here, the probability that the adversary can obtain the set $\mathcal{S}, \mathcal{S}'$ such that $\beta_{\mathcal{S}} \neq \beta_{\mathcal{S}'}$ is $\ell^{-1} \cdot \binom{|\mathcal{ID}|}{\ell_0}^{-1} \cdot \ell^{-1} \cdot \binom{|\mathcal{ID}|}{\ell_1}^{-1}$. Then, the adversary issues $(\mathsf{m}, \mathcal{S}, \mathcal{S}')$ as a challenge query, and obtains $\{\mathsf{cmd}_{\mathcal{S}_b}^{(\theta)}\}_{\theta \in [\beta_{\mathcal{S}_b}]}$. If $\beta_{\mathcal{S}_b} = \ell_0$, the adversary outputs $b' = 0$, otherwise $b' = 1$. □

**Theorem 6.** If ABA with the property shown in Assumption 3 is full-ANOat secure, the size of authenticator with an arbitrary recipient set $\mathcal{S} \subseteq \mathcal{ID}$ is $\Omega(N \cdot k)$, where $k = \min_{\mathcal{S} \subseteq \mathcal{ID}, \theta \in [\beta_\mathcal{S}]} |\mathsf{cmd}_\mathcal{S}^{(\theta)}|$.

*Proof.* We assume $\beta_\mathcal{S} < N$ for some $\mathcal{S}$, and show a contradiction. First, if $\mathcal{S}^* := [N]$, then $\beta_{\mathcal{S}^*} = \beta_\mathcal{S} < N$ holds from Lemma 6. On the other hand, since a full-ANOat secure ABA meets ANOat security, we have $\beta_{\mathcal{S}^*} \geq N$ by Theorem 5, but it contradicts $\beta_{\mathcal{S}^*} < N$. $\qquad\square$

# References

1. Agrawal, S., Wichs, D., Yamada, S.: Optimal broadcast encryption from LWE and pairings in the standard model. In: Pass, R., Pietrzak, K. (eds.) TCC 2020. LNCS, vol. 12550, pp. 149–178. Springer, Cham (2020). https://doi.org/10.1007/978-3-030-64375-1_6

2. Agrawal, S., Yamada, S.: Optimal broadcast encryption from pairings and LWE. In: Canteaut, A., Ishai, Y. (eds.) EUROCRYPT 2020. LNCS, vol. 12105, pp. 13–43. Springer, Cham (2020). https://doi.org/10.1007/978-3-030-45721-1_2

3. Barth, A., Boneh, D., Waters, B.: Privacy in encrypted content distribution using private broadcast encryption. In: Di Crescenzo, G., Rubin, A. (eds.) FC 2006. LNCS, vol. 4107, pp. 52–64. Springer, Heidelberg (2006). https://doi.org/10.1007/11889663_4

4. Boneh, D., Gentry, C., Waters, B.: Collusion resistant broadcast encryption with short ciphertexts and private keys. In: Shoup, V. (ed.) CRYPTO 2005. LNCS, vol. 3621, pp. 258–275. Springer, Heidelberg (2005). https://doi.org/10.1007/11535218_16

5. Boneh, D., Waters, B., Zhandry, M.: Low overhead broadcast encryption from multilinear maps. In: Garay, J.A., Gennaro, R. (eds.) CRYPTO 2014. LNCS, vol. 8616, pp. 206–223. Springer, Heidelberg (2014). https://doi.org/10.1007/978-3-662-44371-2_12

6. Fazio, N., Perera, I.M.: Outsider-anonymous broadcast encryption with sublinear ciphertexts. In: Fischlin, M., Buchmann, J., Manulis, M. (eds.) PKC 2012. LNCS, vol. 7293, pp. 225–242. Springer, Heidelberg (2012). https://doi.org/10.1007/978-3-642-30057-8_14

7. Gay, R., Kowalczyk, L., Wee, H.: Tight adaptively secure broadcast encryption with short ciphertexts and keys. In: Catalano, D., De Prisco, R. (eds.) SCN 2018. LNCS, vol. 11035, pp. 123–139. Springer, Cham (2018). https://doi.org/10.1007/978-3-319-98113-0_7

8. Gentry, C., Waters, B.: Adaptive security in broadcast encryption systems (with short ciphertexts). In: Joux, A. (ed.) EUROCRYPT 2009. LNCS, vol. 5479, pp. 171–188. Springer, Heidelberg (2009). https://doi.org/10.1007/978-3-642-01001-9_10

9. Kiayias, A., Samari, K.: Lower bounds for private broadcast encryption. In: Kirchner, M., Ghosal, D. (eds.) IH 2012. LNCS, vol. 7692, pp. 176–190. Springer, Heidelberg (2013). https://doi.org/10.1007/978-3-642-36373-3_12

10. Li, J., Gong, J.: Improved anonymous broadcast encryptions. In: Preneel, B., Vercauteren, F. (eds.) ACNS 2018. LNCS, vol. 10892, pp. 497–515. Springer, Cham (2018). https://doi.org/10.1007/978-3-319-93387-0_26

11. Libert, B., Paterson, K.G., Quaglia, E.A.: Anonymous broadcast encryption: adaptive security and efficient constructions in the standard model. In: Fischlin, M., Buchmann, J., Manulis, M. (eds.) PKC 2012. LNCS, vol. 7293, pp. 206–224. Springer, Heidelberg (2012). https://doi.org/10.1007/978-3-642-30057-8_13
12. Naor, D., Naor, M., Lotspiech, J.: Revocation and tracing schemes for stateless receivers. In: Kilian, J. (ed.) CRYPTO 2001. LNCS, vol. 2139, pp. 41–62. Springer, Heidelberg (2001). https://doi.org/10.1007/3-540-44647-8_3
13. Watanabe, Y., Yanai, N., Shikata, J.: Anonymous broadcast authentication for securely remote-controlling IoT devices. In: Barolli, L., Woungang, I., Enokido, T. (eds.) AINA 2021. LNNS, vol. 226, pp. 679–690. Springer, Cham (2021). https://doi.org/10.1007/978-3-030-75075-6_56
14. Waters, B.: Dual system encryption: realizing fully secure IBE and HIBE under simple assumptions. In: Halevi, S. (ed.) CRYPTO 2009. LNCS, vol. 5677, pp. 619–636. Springer, Heidelberg (2009). https://doi.org/10.1007/978-3-642-03356-8_36
15. Zhang, L., Wu, Q., Mu, Y.: Anonymous identity-based broadcast encryption with adaptive security. In: Wang, G., Ray, I., Feng, D., Rajarajan, M. (eds.) CSS 2013. LNCS, vol. 8300, pp. 258–271. Springer, Cham (2013). https://doi.org/10.1007/978-3-319-03584-0_19

# Optimizing Registration Based Encryption

Kelong Cong[1], Karim Eldefrawy[2], and Nigel P. Smart[1,3(✉)]

[1] imec-COSIC, KU Leuven, Leuven, Belgium
kelong.cong@esat.kuleuven.be, nigel.smart@kuleuven.be
[2] SRI International, Menlo Park, CA, USA
karim.eldefrawy@sri.com
[3] Department of Computer Science, University of Bristol, Bristol, UK

**Abstract.** The recent work of Garg et al. from TCC'18 introduced the notion of registration based encryption (RBE). The principal motivation behind RBE is to address the key escrow issue of identity based encryption (IBE), where an IBE authority is trusted to generate private keys for all users in the system. Although RBE has excellent asymptotic properties, it is currently impractical; in our estimate, ciphertext size would be about 11 TB in an RBE deployment supporting 2 billion users.

Motivated by this observation, our work attempts to reduce the concrete communication and computation cost of the current state-of-the-art construction. Our contribution is two-fold. First, we replace the usage of Merkle trees in RBE with crit-bit trees, a form of PATRICIA trie, without relaxing any of the original efficiency requirements introduced by Garg et al. This change reduces the ciphertext size by 15% and the computation cost of decryption by 30%. Second, we observe that increasing RBE's public parameters by a few hundred kilobytes could reduce the ciphertext size by an additional 50%. Overall, our work decreases the ciphertext size by 57.5%.

## 1 Introduction

Identity based encryption (IBE), introduced by Shamir [33], allows Alice to encrypt a message to Bob as long as she knows Bob's identity, such as his email address or pseudonym. This notion significantly simplifies the key-management issue of public key encryption [10,19,31] (PKE) since it removes the need of a public key infrastructure (PKI). Starting with the first concrete instantiation by Boneh and Franklin [5], a long line of research has developed many IBE instantiations from a variety of assumptions. Generalizations of IBE such as attribute based encryption (ABE) [32] and functional encryption (FE) [6] have also been recently studied.

Despite the success of the research community in developing practical IBE, IBE has not replaced public key encryption due to the key escrow problem. In an IBE scheme, there exists a key-generation authority that generates decryption keys for every user enrolled in the system. Users must fully trust such an authority to behave honestly, since it has the ability to decrypt every (private) message

© Springer Nature Switzerland AG 2021
M. B. Paterson (Ed.): IMACC 2021, LNCS 13129, pp. 129–157, 2021.
https://doi.org/10.1007/978-3-030-92641-0_7

that it captures. In an age where end-to-end encryption is widely deployed[1], requiring a central authority that can eavesdrop on private communication is considered a major downgrade in security.

An obvious mitigation to this key escrow problem is to homogeneously distribute the power of the key generation authority, which was already suggested by Boneh and Franklin [5]. The work of Kate and Goldberg [23], for example, presented a solution based on distributed key generation. Another approach is to distribute the authority heterogeneously. In the work of Chow [9], authentication and key-issuance are performed by two different authorities, identity certifying authority and key generation authority. This approach ensures that the key generation authority, which has the master private key, does not know the identities of users. Without the identities, the key generation authority cannot decrypt the messages as long as the two authorities do not collude. While these ideas mitigate the escrow problem, they do not solve it completely since the authority (or a collective authority) still has the ability to eavesdrop on users.

In another direction, Al-Riyami and Paterson [1] put forward the notion of Certificateless Public Key Cryptography; there is no escrow problem and there is no need for certificates in such schemes. Thus, this notion can be seen as a hybrid between PKE+PKI and IBE. Unfortunately, it does not have the convenient features of IBE since users cannot encrypt messages using only the identities of the receivers (assuming some known system-wide public parameter).

## 1.1  Registration Based Encryption: Prior Work

Motivated by the shortcomings discussed above, Garg et al. [16] initiated the study of Registration-Based Encryption (RBE) where the authority does not hold any secret and is fully transparent.

There are three roles in RBE. The key curator (KC), the encryptor and the decryptor. Of course, a single entity may have multiple roles. Every decryptor registers their public key and identity with a KC. In contrast to a typical IBE scheme, the KC does not generate decryption keys nor does it hold any secret information; it simply acts as an accumulator. Although the KC may sound like a PKI, it does not answer queries for public keys. Instead, it publishes a relatively short public parameter that *every* encryptor can use to perform encryption. Similar to IBE, the encryptor only needs to know the identity of the receiver/decryptor and the short public parameter to generate a ciphertext. The decryptor needs some "supporting information", that does not need to be kept secret from the KC, and its *own* private key to decrypt. The public parameters in some sense "encode" identities and public keys of all users, in a highly compact form.

To make RBE more attractive, the formal definition of RBE [16] formulates the following efficiency requirements:

1. The public parameters must be short, i.e., $\mathsf{poly}(\lambda, \log n)$, where $n$ is the number of registered users and $\lambda$ is the security parameter.

---

[1] WhatsApp implements end-to-end encryption and has 2 billion users [13].

2. The registration process and the generation of supporting information must be efficient, i.e., they must run in time $\mathsf{poly}(\lambda, \log n)$ per user registration.
3. The number of times that a decryptor must request supporting information must be low, i.e., $\mathsf{poly}(\lambda, \log n)$ over the lifetime of the system.

Below we give an overview of the RBE literature. The detailed explanation is deferred to when we describe our contribution, since all constructions share a similar blueprint. See Sect. 2 for a gentle introduction to the blueprint which all constructions follow.

The authors of [16] described a construction based on indistinguishability obfuscation (iO) [2,15] and somewhere statistically-binding hash functions (SSBH) [21] which satisfies all the efficiency requirements. They also proposed a weakly efficient construction based on standard assumptions but the registration process must run in time $\mathsf{poly}(\lambda, n)$.

Followup work [17] solved the issue above and introduced the first RBE scheme that satisfies all the efficiency requirements from standard assumptions. Their "efficient" RBE construction is achieved via a two-step approach, where they used the construction of [16] to bootstrap the fully efficient construction. Further, the authors introduce anonymous RBE which requires that the ciphertext generated on a uniformly random message looks uniformly random (irrespective of the recipient).

An outstanding security issue is that the KC could maliciously register duplicate identities with different public keys where it knows the corresponding secret key. A malicious user could do the same if the KC does not check for uniqueness. This behavior essentially gives the attacker a trapdoor, allowing him to read messages that are encrypted for an honestly registered user. The same attack also applies to PKI systems. Motivated by the above, the third work on RBE [20] studied the verifiability aspect and described an efficient construction where the user who has identity id can ask the KC to prove that id is unique. Further, the authors introduced the "snapshot trick" that removed the bootstrapping step of previous constructions [17].

## 1.2   Our Contributions

As mentioned above, existing RBE constructions already achieve very appealing asymptotic complexity, i.e., short public parameters, and efficient generation and requesting of (updated) supporting information, that scale with $\mathsf{poly}(\lambda, \log n)$, where $n$ is the number of registered users and $\lambda$ is the security parameter. Unfortunately, the requirement to garble public key operations, which is a key building block in all existing RBE schemes, makes such schemes impractical.

Concretely, suppose this operation is implemented using elliptic curve cryptography, for example based on secp192k1 [8]. One (garbled) curve multiplication in this case requires 19.2 billion non-XOR gates[2] and 366 GB of communication [22]. Worse, this operation is performed $O(\log n)$ times, where $n$ is the

---

[2] Free-XOR [26] is an optimization for garbled circuits which allows the garbler to create the garbled truth table "for free", without symmetric key operations.

number of users. For example, using the most efficient construction [20], Alice would need to send approximately 11 TB to Bob if there are 2 billion users and $\lambda$ is 256 bits. Undoubtedly, for RBE to be of practical use, we need to focus on reducing the concrete computation and communication cost. To this end, we make the following contributions that aim to improve the concrete efficiency.

1. We introduce an authenticated version of crit-bit trees [4] (which might be of independent interest), a form of authenticated PATRICIA trie [29]. It is used in our RBE construction instead of Merkle trees. This modification reduces the number of input bits of the circuits that we need to garble, which directly decreases the number of public key encryption circuits. We estimate a 15% reduction in computation and communication (ciphertext size) by the encryptor and a 30% reduction in computation by the decryptor. Our construction preserves the verifiability property introduced in [20].
2. Furthermore, we suggest a modification to the RBE public parameter which reduces computation and communication of the encryptor by a half, in addition to the improvement above. However, this modification requires us to relax the compactness requirement in typical RBE schemes from $\mathsf{poly}(\lambda, \log n)$ to $O(\lambda, \sqrt{n})$, where $n$ is the number of users registered in the system and $\lambda$ is the security parameter. For many applications, we argue that this is a reasonable assumption since the total number of users would reach a saturation point, eventually. For example, WhatsApp uses end-to-end encryption and has 2 billion users [13]; with an $n$ of 2 billion our construction would only add 187 kilobytes to the public parameters.

The two optimizations can be combined. Overall, the ciphertext size (communication cost) can be reduced by 57.5% on average.

Our work follows the original RBE security definition [16] which does not include a decryption oracle. In other words, we do not handle active attacks, this limitation is not unique to our scheme, existing RBE constructions in the literature exhibit the same limitation. Defining and designing an RBE scheme that is secure under chosen ciphertext attacks is still currently an open question and left for future work.

## 2 Registration Based Encryption: a Tutorial

Before giving the formal definitions, we describe the key idea behind all RBE constructions using a series of strawman constructions so that readers unfamiliar with RBE can build an intuition of how it works and why the key building block, hash garbling, is needed. We begin our discussion by considering a fixed set of (n) users, and only focus on the encryption and decryption functionalities. We then describe a dynamic setting where new users are allowed to register.

### 2.1 Encryption and Decryption

Consider three parties, the encryptor Alice, the decryptor Bob and the key curator (KC). Alice wants to send an encrypted message to Bob using only Bob's identity, e.g., his email address, and a short public parameter pp provided by the KC. Bob should be able to decrypt the message using his secret key (which he generated by himself) and some short, non-secret "supporting information" $u$, provided by the KC. What follows is a series of strawman constructions that we will refine one at a time. Eventually, we will arrive at a construction that is very close to what is described in the literature.

**Strawman 1 (RBE from iO):** Let the KC store a Merkle tree where intermediate nodes have the form $(\text{id}^*\|\alpha\|\beta)$, where $\text{id}^*$ is the largest identity[3] of the left sub-tree, $\alpha$ is the digest of the left node and $\beta$ is the digest of the right node. The digests are computed using some hash function $\mathsf{H}: \{0,1\}^* \to \{0,1\}^\lambda$, where $\lambda$ is the security parameter. For example, $\alpha_1 = \mathsf{H}(\text{id}_2^*\|\alpha_2\|\beta_2)$ in Fig. 1. The leaf nodes store the user identities and their corresponding public keys, i.e., they have the form $(0^\lambda\|\text{id}\|\text{pk})$. For brevity, we assume the tree is perfectly balanced, i.e., the number of leaves is a power of two. We denote the depth of the tree with $d$ and the Merkle root by rt. The public parameter is $\text{pp} \leftarrow (\text{rt}, d)$ and we let the $u$ data of Bob be the authenticating path from the root to the leaf that contains Bob's identity.

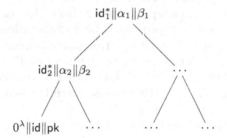

**Fig. 1.** The Merkle tree structure used for RBE. The leaves are sorted by id. Consider a node, $\text{id}^*$ is the identity of the largest identity in its left sub-tree.

The reason for storing the identity of the left sub-tree is so that the KC can search for an identity in $O(\log n)$ time, using the binary search algorithm, when a decryptor asks for his path $u$. Consequently, the identities stored in the leaves must be sorted.

Another ingredient we need for encryption and decryption is a circuit $P$. This circuit takes Bob's $u$ as input, checks whether $u$ is a valid path that begins with rt and ends with a leaf node containing Bob's identity, and finally outputs $\text{ct} \leftarrow \mathsf{Enc}(\text{pk}, m)$ where pk is Bob's public key taken from the leaf node. For a path to be valid we require that, for every node $(\text{id}^*\|\alpha\|\beta)$, the hash of the child node is $\beta$ if

---

[3] We assume the identities can be ordered.

Bob's identity is greater than $\mathsf{id}^*$ otherwise $\alpha$. We write $P(u; m, \mathsf{pp})$ for the circuit, where $m$ and $\mathsf{pp}$ is hardwired into the circuit and $u$ is the undetermined input.

If Alice wants to send an encrypted message $m$ to Bob using only $\mathsf{pp}$ and Bob's identity, she creates an obfuscated version of the circuit $\tilde{P} \leftarrow \mathsf{Obf}(P(?; m, \mathsf{pp}))$ and then sends it to Bob. Upon receiving $\tilde{P}$, Bob simply evaluates it to obtain $\mathsf{ct}$ and attempts to decrypt it using his secret key $\mathsf{sk}$. Note that anyone who has the path $u$, e.g., the KC, can evaluate $\tilde{P}$, but it is not possible to recover the underlying message $m$ since they do not have Bob's secret key.

To achieve ciphertext indistinguishability, we need to argue that two obfuscated programs with different hardwired $m$ are indistinguishable. However, indistinguishability obfuscation (iO) only guarantees that the two obfuscated programs are indistinguishable if they have the same functionality which is not the case here. Fortunately, [16, Theorem 4.3] states that one can achieve indistinguishability for this particular type of program $P$. The proof relies on the semantic security of the PKE scheme used in the program.

**Strawman 2 (Replacing iO by Using GC):** Strawman 1 already has most of ingredients of a typical RBE scheme and it is essentially the idea of the very first RBE construction from [16]. While it works, it needs to assume that iO exists, which is not a standard assumption.

In the second strawman, we replace the iO idea with a garbling scheme [3,18]. The garbling scheme has two algorithms. The first algorithm, $\mathsf{Garble}$, takes a circuit (e.g., $P$) as input, and then outputs the garbled circuit (GC) $\tilde{P}$ and all the input labels $\mathbf{k}$, two labels for every bit in the input of $P$. The evaluation algorithm, $\mathsf{Eval}$, evaluates the GC using the labels that correspond to the evaluator's input $x$ (denoted using $\mathbf{k}_x$). Everything goes correctly when $\mathsf{Eval}(\tilde{P}, \mathbf{k}_x) = P(x)$. A detailed definition is given in Sect. 3.2.

For this construction to be secure, we need to make a modification to the circuit $P$. Before the values $m$ and $\mathsf{pp}$ are hardwired. But this is not secure since two garbled circuits with different topologies (different message $m$) are not indistinguishable. Thus we need to modify $P(u; m, \mathsf{pp})$ to become $P(u, m; \mathsf{pp})$, where $m$ is also undetermined.

Using a garbling scheme, Alice creates a GC and input labels $(\tilde{P}, \mathbf{k}) \leftarrow \mathsf{Garble}(P)$ and then sends $\tilde{P}$ to Bob. But we run into a problem when Bob attempts to evaluate $\tilde{P}$ on the undetermined input $(u, m)$, since he does not have the input labels. The wire labels corresponding to $m$ can be sent along with the ciphertext, but for Bob to obtain the wire labels corresponding to his input $u$ it seems that we require interaction. In the next two strawman constructions we show how to resolve this issue.

**Strawman 2.5 (Breaking up the Large Circuit):** Removing interaction is not trivial. Thus, we need to take an intermediate step where we break up one large circuit $P$ into many smaller ones, one for every level of the tree. Below we give a description of a circuit that does *not* work, but it illustrates the idea of what we want to achieve.

For every level $j \in [d]$ in the Merkle tree, the corresponding circuit $P_j$ will have the following logic.

1. Take a Merkle tree node $u_j = (\mathsf{id}_j^* \| \alpha_j \| \beta_j)$ as input.
2. Check whether $\mathsf{H}(u_j) = \mathsf{y}$ where $\mathsf{y}$ is some hardwired value, if the check fails then abort.
3. If $\mathsf{id}^* = \alpha_j$, return $\mathsf{Enc}(\beta_j, m)$. Recall that $\alpha_j$ stores the identity and $\beta_j$ stores the corresponding public key in the leaf node.
4. Else, return the labels that correspond to the preimage of $\alpha_j$ if $\mathsf{id} > \mathsf{id}_j^*$, otherwise return the labels that correspond to $\beta_j$.

If Alice sends these circuits to Bob, and if Bob also has the input labels $\mathbf{k}_{u_1}$ then he can evaluate every circuit. That is because the output of every circuit is the input label for the next circuit. The final output is $\mathsf{Enc}(\beta_j, m)$, which Bob can decrypt using his secret key.

The reader may have already notice that in Item 2 above, Alice does not have the digest $\mathsf{y}$ to create these circuits. Further, in Item 4, Alice also does not have the preimage of $\alpha_j$ or $\beta_j$ to generate the labels. Nevertheless, this impossible strawman construction illustrates the idea of "chaining" GCs such that the output of one is used as the input of the next. This idea is crucial for understanding the final strawman construction.

**Strawman 3 (Putting Everything Together Using Hash Garbling):** In the final strawman, we realise the idea of chaining GCs and remove the need for interaction using an important primitive called hash garbling, first introduced in [16].

One can think of hash garbling as an extension to a garbling scheme with an HG.Input algorithm and a modified evaluation algorithm HG.Eval. HG.Input outputs *encrypted* labels, denoted by $\tilde{\mathbf{k}}$, given some input $\mathsf{y}$. These encrypted labels are crafted in a way that the actual labels that represent $\mathsf{y}$ are only revealed if the preimage, under $\mathsf{H}$, of $\mathsf{y}$ is known. Next, HG.Eval is a modified Eval, it still takes the garbled circuit $\tilde{P}$, but also takes the encrypted labels $\tilde{\mathbf{k}}$ and the preimage $x$. As we noted earlier, it is only possible to evaluate $\tilde{P}$ on input $\mathsf{y}$ if $\mathsf{H}(x) = \mathsf{y}$. We formally define hash garbling in Sect. 3.3.

Now we are ready to put everything together in the final strawman. We modify the circuit $P_j$ as follows.

1. Take a Merkle tree node $u_j = (\mathsf{id}_j^* \| \alpha_j \| \beta_j)$ as input.
2. If $\mathsf{id} = \alpha_j$, return $\mathsf{Enc}(\beta_j, m)$.
3. Else, return HG.Input$(\alpha_j)$ if $\mathsf{id} > \mathsf{id}_j^*$ otherwise return HG.Input$(\beta_j)$.

Alice creates a garbled circuits $\tilde{P}_j$ as before, but she also runs $\tilde{\mathbf{k}}_1 \leftarrow$ HG.Input(rt), and then sends $(\{\tilde{P}_j\}_{j \in [d]}, \tilde{\mathbf{k}}_1)$ to Bob. Upon receiving the message, Bob begins to evaluate the first circuit with HG.Eval$(\tilde{P}_1, \tilde{\mathbf{k}}_1, u_1)$. Suppose Bob's identity is in the left sub-tree, the output of HG.Eval becomes $\tilde{\mathbf{k}}_2 \leftarrow$ HG.Input$(\alpha_1)$. Bob continues the evaluation by running HG.Eval$(\tilde{P}_2, \tilde{\mathbf{k}}_2, u_2)$, and so on. Eventually,

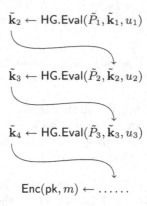

**Fig. 2.** Illustration of RBE decryption.

Bob obtains $\mathsf{Enc}(\mathsf{pk}, m)$ which he can decrypt using his secret key. An illustration of this process is in Fig. 2.

The construction is complete. To understand why it removes interaction and correctly checks the Merkle path, we make the following two observations.

1. Interaction is no longer needed in this construction. Alice does not need to stay online after sending a series of garbled circuits and an encrypted input label.
2. Due to the properties of hash garbling, the evaluator must input the correct preimage and encrypted labels to $\mathsf{HG.Eval}$ at every step, otherwise the circuits cannot output the ciphertext at the end. In other words, the evaluator cannot generate the encrypted labels by himself which forces him to use the correct preimage $x$ in $\mathsf{HG.Eval}$, i.e. the path provided to the evaluator by the KC.

## 2.2   Adding Registration

We now turn to registration. Performing registration the naive way, i.e., adding a new leaf node to the Merkle tree whenever a new user registers, leads to $O(n)$ updates for the supporting information $u$, the path that contains his leaf.

A simple idea, first introduced in [16], is to keep multiple Merkle trees. Whenever a new user registers, a new Merkle tree with a single leaf is created. Then, trees that have the same number of leaves are merged to form a new tree. Observe that the sizes of the trees are unique powers of two. The KC needs to publish $O(\log n)$ Merkle roots, so the public parameters are kept small. The encryptor Alice needs to run the encryption procedure for every tree since she does not know where Bob's leaf is. The number of updates that Bob needs to do for $u$ is reduced to $O(\log n)$ due to the following reason. Bob's identity must be in a tree with $2^i$ leaves, for some integer $i$. Bob needs to update $u$ whenever $2^i$ users are registered in the system after him. When that happens, his identity will be in a tree with $2^{i+1}$ leaves and the process repeats.

Unfortunately, the registration idea above does not guarantee $\mathsf{poly}(\lambda, \log n)$ computational complexity. Concretely, whenever two Merkle trees are merged, their leaves need to be re-sorted. As such, it is not possible to merge to trees in time $\mathsf{poly}(\lambda, \log n)$ while keeping the leaves sorted. Subsequent works [17,20] resolved this issue. We use the same idea in our construction thus we defer the details to Sect. 4.2.

## 3    Preliminaries

We first present definitions used throughout this paper.

### 3.1    Public Key Encryption

A public key encryption (PKE) scheme consists of the following PPT algorithms.

- $\mathsf{KGen}(1^\lambda) \to (\mathsf{pk}, \mathsf{sk})$. The key generation algorithm takes the security parameter as input, and then outputs a public key and a private key.
- $\mathsf{Enc}(\mathsf{pk}, m) \to \mathsf{ct}$. The encryption algorithm takes a public key $\mathsf{pk}$ and a message $m$ as input, and then outputs a ciphertext $\mathsf{ct}$. Sometimes we write $\mathsf{Enc}(\mathsf{pk}, m; r)$ to explicitly specify the randomness $r \subset \{0,1\}^\lambda$.
- $\mathsf{Dec}(\mathsf{sk}, \mathsf{ct}) \to m$. The decryption algorithm takes a secret key $\mathsf{sk}$ and a ciphertext $\mathsf{ct}$ as input, and then outputs a message $m$.

**Definition 1** *(Correctness of PKE).*    *A PKE scheme is correct if for all $\lambda$, $m \in \mathcal{M}$ and $(\mathsf{pk}, \mathsf{sk}) \leftarrow \mathsf{KGen}(1^\lambda)$, it holds that*

$$\Pr[\mathsf{Dec}(\mathsf{sk}, \mathsf{Enc}(\mathsf{pk}, m)) = m].$$

**Definition 2** *(IND-CPA security of PKE).*    *The PKE scheme is IND-CPA secure if there exists a negligible function $\mathsf{negl}(\lambda)$ such that any PPT adversary $\mathcal{A}$ wins the following game with probability $\frac{1}{2} + \mathsf{negl}(\lambda)$.*

- *The challenger $\mathcal{C}$ generates $(\mathsf{pk}, \mathsf{sk}) \leftarrow \mathsf{KGen}(\lambda)$ and sends $\mathsf{pk}$ to $\mathcal{A}$.*
- *$\mathcal{A}$ picks two messages $m_0, m_1$ and sends them to $\mathcal{C}$.*
- *$\mathcal{C}$ samples $b \leftarrow_\$ \{0,1\}$ and sends $\mathsf{ct} \leftarrow \mathsf{Enc}(\mathsf{pk}, m_b)$ to $\mathcal{A}$.*
- *$\mathcal{A}$ outputs $b'$ and wins if $b = b'$.*

### 3.2    Garbled Circuits

To build a hash garbling scheme, we also need garbled circuits (GC). We review Yao's GC next using the notation adapted from [7]. A garbling scheme consist of the following two algorithm.

- $\mathsf{Garble}(1^\lambda, 1^n, 1^m, C, \mathsf{state}) \to (\tilde{C}, \{k_{i,b}\}_{i \in [n], b \in \{0,1\}})$ is a deterministic algorithm that generates the input labels $\{k_{i,b}\}_{i \in [n], b \in \{0,1\}}$ as well as all the intermediate labels using $\mathsf{state}$ as the seed, and then creates the garbled circuit $\tilde{C}$, which has an input length of $n$ bits and an output length of $m$ bits.

- Eval($1^\lambda, \tilde{C}, \{k_{i,x_i}\}_{i\in[n]}$) evaluates the garbled circuit using the given input labels $k_{i,x_i}$. Each label corresponds to a bit of the desired input $x$.

**Definition 3** *(Correctness of garbling). For all circuits $C$, inputs $x$ and secret state* state $\in \{0,1\}^\lambda$, *correctness holds when* Eval($1^\lambda, \tilde{C}, \mathbf{k}$) = $C(x)$, *where* $(\tilde{C}, \{k_{i,b}\}_{i\in[n],b\in\{0,1\}}) \leftarrow$ Garble($1^\lambda, 1^n, 1^m, C$, state) *and* $\mathbf{k} \leftarrow \{k_{i,x_i}\}_{i\in[n]}$.

**Definition 4** *(Security of garbling). For any circuit $C : \{0,1\}^n \rightarrow \{0,1\}^m$, input $x \in \{0,1\}^n$ and secret state* state $\in \{0,1\}^\lambda$, *there exists a simulator* Sim *such that the following distributions are computationally indistinguishable:*

$$\{(\tilde{C}, \tilde{\mathbf{k}}) : (\tilde{C}, \{\tilde{k}_{i,b}\}_{i\in[n],b\in\{0,1\}}) \leftarrow \text{Garble}(1^\lambda, 1^n, 1^m, C, \text{state}), \tilde{\mathbf{k}} \leftarrow \{\tilde{k}_{i,x_i}\}_{i\in[n]}\}$$
$$\stackrel{c}{\approx} \{(\tilde{C}, \tilde{\mathbf{k}}) : (\tilde{C}, \tilde{\mathbf{k}}) \leftarrow \text{Sim}(1^\lambda, 1^{|C|}, 1^n, C(x))\}.$$

### 3.3    Hash Garbling

The main ingredient in RBE is hash garbling; it is first introduced in [16] and then used in a similar manner in subsequent works on RBE [17,20]. In this section, we review its definition from the literature. A hash garbling scheme is defined by the following five algorithms HG.Gen, HG.Hash, HG.Garble, HG.Input, HG.Eval:

- HG.Gen($1^\lambda, 1^n$) $\rightarrow$ hk. This algorithm takes a security parameter $\lambda$ and an input length parameter $n$, and outputs a hash key hk.
- HG.Hash(hk, $x$) $\rightarrow$ y. This is a deterministic algorithm that takes a hash key hk and a preimage $x \in \{0,1\}^n$ as input, and outputs a digest y $\in \{0,1\}^\lambda$.
- HG.Garble(hk, $C$, state) $\rightarrow \tilde{C}$. This algorithm takes a hash key hk, a circuit $C$ and a secret state state $\in \{0,1\}^\lambda$ as input, and outputs a garbled circuit $\tilde{C}$ (without labels).
- HG.Input(hk, y, state) $\rightarrow \tilde{\mathbf{k}}$. This algorithm takes a hash key hk, a value y $\in \{0,1\}^\lambda$ and a secret state state $\in \{0,1\}^\lambda$ as input, and outputs encrypted labels $\tilde{\mathbf{k}}$.
- HG.Eval($\tilde{C}, \tilde{\mathbf{k}}, x$) $\rightarrow$ z. This algorithm takes a garbled circuit $\tilde{C}$, encrypted labels $\tilde{\mathbf{k}}$ and a value $x \in \{0,1\}^n$, and outputs a value $z$.

**Definition 5** *(Correctness of Hash Garbling). For all $\lambda$, $n$, hash key* hk $\leftarrow$ HG.Gen($1^\lambda, 1^n$), *circuit $C$, input $x \in \{0,1\}^n$,* state $\in \{0,1\}^\lambda$, *garbled circuit* $\tilde{C} \leftarrow$ HG.Garble(hk, $C$, state) *and* $\tilde{\mathbf{k}} \leftarrow$ HG.Input(hk, HG.Hash(hk, $x$), state), *we require that*

$$\text{HG.Eval}(\tilde{C}, \tilde{\mathbf{k}}, x) = C(x).$$

**Definition 6** *(Security of Hash Garbling). There exists a PPT simulator* Sim *such that for all $\lambda, n$ and PPT adversary $\mathcal{A}$ we have*

$$(\text{hk}, x, \tilde{\mathbf{k}}, \tilde{C}) \stackrel{c}{\approx} (\text{hk}, x, \text{Sim}(\text{hk}, x, C(x), 1^{|C|})),$$

*where hash key* hk $\leftarrow$ HG.Gen($1^\lambda, 1^n$), $(C, x) \leftarrow \mathcal{A}(\text{hk})$, state $\leftarrow \{0,1\}^\lambda$, *garbled circuit* $\tilde{C} \leftarrow$ HG.Garble(hk, $C$, state) *and* $\tilde{\mathbf{k}} \leftarrow$ HG.Input(hk, HE.Hash(hk, $x$), state).

In the full version we give a construction based on the Decision Diffie–Hellman (DDH) problem in a finite Abelian group, which may help the reader understand the specific details.

## 3.4  Hash Encryption

Hash Encryption is the key building block needed to construct Hash Garbling schemes. We use the definition from [11, Definition 9].

- $\mathsf{HE.Gen}(1^\lambda, 1^n) \to \mathsf{hk}$. This is the key generation algorithm that takes a security parameter and a output length parameter, and then outputs a hash key $\mathsf{hk}$.
- $\mathsf{HE.Hash}(\mathsf{hk}, x) \to \mathsf{y}$. This algorithm takes a hash key $\mathsf{hk}$ and some input $x \in \{0,1\}^n$ and outputs a digest $\mathsf{y}$.
- $\mathsf{HE.Enc}(\mathsf{hk}, (\mathsf{y}, i, b), m) \to \mathsf{ct}$. This is the encryption algorithm that takes a hash key $\mathsf{hk}$, a value $\mathsf{y}$, an integer $i \in [n]$, a bit $b$ and a message $m$, and then outputs a ciphertext $\mathsf{ct}$.
- $\mathsf{HE.Dec}(\mathsf{hk}, x, \mathsf{ct}) \to \{m, \bot\}$. This is the decryption algorithm that takes a hash key $\mathsf{hk}$, a value $x$ and a ciphertext $\mathsf{ct}$, and then outputs a message $m$ if the decryption is successful, otherwise it outputs $\bot$.

**Definition 7** *(Correctness of Hash Encryption).*  *For all $x \in \{0,1\}^n$ and $i \in [n]$, correctness holds when*

$$\Pr[\mathsf{HE.Dec}(\mathsf{hk}, x, \mathsf{HE.Enc}(\mathsf{hk}, (\mathsf{HE.Hash}(\mathsf{hk}, x), i, x_i), m)) = m] \geq 1 - \mathsf{negl}(\lambda),$$

*where $\mathsf{hk} \leftarrow \mathsf{HE.Gen}(1^\lambda, 1^n)$ and $x_i$ denotes the $i$th bit of $x$.*

**Definition 8** *(Security of Hash Encryption).*  *The security is defined using the game $\mathsf{IND}^{\mathsf{HE}}$ shown below. The hash encryption scheme is secure when, for any PPT adversary $\mathcal{A} = (\mathcal{A}_1, \mathcal{A}_2, \mathcal{A}_3)$,*

$$\left| \frac{1}{2} - \Pr[\mathsf{IND}^{\mathsf{HE}}(1^\lambda, \mathcal{A}) = 1] \right| \leq \mathsf{negl}(\lambda).$$

$\mathsf{IND}^{\mathsf{HE}}(\mathcal{A})$

---

$1:$  $(x, \mathsf{state}_1) \leftarrow \mathcal{A}_1(1^\lambda)$

$2:$  $\mathsf{hk} \leftarrow \mathsf{HE.Gen}(1^\lambda, 1^n)$

$3:$  $(i \in [n], m_0, m_1, \mathsf{state}_2) \leftarrow \mathcal{A}_2(\mathsf{state}_1, \mathsf{hk})$

$4:$  $b \leftarrow_\$ \{0,1\}$

$5:$  $\mathsf{ct} \leftarrow \mathsf{HE.Enc}(\mathsf{hk}, (\mathsf{HE.Hash}(\mathsf{hk}, x), i, 1 - x_i), m_b)$

$6:$  $b' \leftarrow \mathcal{A}_3(\mathsf{state}_2, \mathsf{ct})$

$7:$  **return if** $b = b'$ **then** $1$ **else** $0$

In contrast to witness encryption, where the ciphertext can only be decrypted if the preimage is known, hash encryption has the extra property that the $i$th bit of $x$ must be $b$. Batch encryption schemes, described in [7], can be used to construct hash garbling schemes as well. This fact is shown in [17].

## 3.5  Registration Based Encryption

We recall the original definition of registration based encryption (RBE) [16]. An RBE scheme involves two types of parties. The first is the key curator (KC) that maintains a public parameter pp and some auxillary information aux. The second is the user which can register with the KC and then communicate privately with other users using only the identity of the recipient and pp.

RBE consists of six PPT algorithms: RBE.Setup, KGen, RBE.Reg[aux], RBE.Enc, RBE.Upd[aux] and RBE.Dec. The aux superscript means that the algorithm associated with it has read access to the auxiliary information aux. Having a bracket around aux means that it is mutable by the associated algorithm.

- RBE.Setup($1^\lambda$) → crs. This is the common reference string (CRS) generation algorithm which outputs a CRS crs based on the security parameter $\lambda$.
- KGen($1^\lambda$) → (pk, sk). This is the key generation algorithm of the PKE scheme.
- RBE.Reg[aux](crs, pp, id, pk) → pp′. The registration algorithm takes a CRS crs, a public parameter pp, an identity id and a its corresponding public key pk as input. It outputs a new public parameter pp′. This algorithm has read and write oracle access to the auxillary information aux.
- RBE.Enc(crs, pp, id, $m$) → ct. The encryption algorithm takes as input the CRS crs, public parameters pp, an identity id of the recipient, and a message $m$, and then outputs a ciphertext ct that encrypts $m$.
- RBE.Upd[aux](pp, id) → $u$. The update algorithm takes as input the current public parameter pp stored at the KC and an identity id, and then outputs some information $u \in \{0, 1\}^*$ that would help the user who has the identity id with decryption. This algorithm has read-only oracle access to aux.
- RBE.Dec(sk, $u$, ct) → $\{m, \bot, \texttt{GetUpd}\}$. The decryption algorithm takes as input a secret key sk, decryption information $u$ and a ciphertext ct, and then it outputs either a message $m$, an error $\bot$ or $\texttt{GetUpd}$ which indicates that $u$ is out of date.

RBE.Reg[aux] and RBE.Upd[aux] are *deterministic* algorithm executed by the KC. This property implies that the KC is fully auditable. The other algorithms are randomized.

We recall the definition of completeness, compactness, and efficiency from the literature. We use $\mathsf{Comp}_{\mathcal{A}}^{\mathsf{RBE}}$ to define the definitions. It is a game where the adversary $\mathcal{A}$ can register non-target identities and a target identity, and then make encryption and decryption requests.

**Definition 9** (*Completeness, compactness, and efficiency of RBE*). *For any stateful, interactive computationally bounded adversary $\mathcal{A}$ that has a* poly($\lambda$) *round complexity, consider the following game* $\mathsf{Comp}_{\mathcal{A}}^{\mathsf{RBE}}$ *between $\mathcal{A}$ and a challenger $\mathcal{C}$.*

1. *Initialization. The challenger $\mathcal{C}$ initializes parameters as*

$$(\mathsf{pp}, \mathsf{aux}, S_{\mathsf{id}}, \mathsf{id}^*, t) = (\epsilon, \epsilon, \epsilon, \emptyset, \bot, 0),$$

*samples* crs $\leftarrow$ RBE.Setup($1^\lambda$) *and sends* crs *to* $\mathcal{A}$. $S_{id}$ *is the set of registered identities,* id* *is the target identity and* $t$ *acts as a counter for the number of decryption attempts.*

2. **Query phase.** $\mathcal{A}$ *makes polynomially many queries of the following form, where each query is considered as a single round of interaction between* $\mathcal{C}$ *and* $\mathcal{A}$.

   (a) **Registering a non-target identity.** *On a query of the form* (regnew, id, pk), $\mathcal{C}$ *checks that* id $\notin S_{id}$. *It aborts if the check fails. Otherwise,* $\mathcal{C}$ *registers* (id, pk) *by running the registration algorithm*

   $$\text{pp} \leftarrow \text{RBE.Reg}^{[\text{aux}]}(\text{crs}, \text{pp}, \text{id}, \text{pk}).$$

   *It adds* id *to the set as* $S_{id}$. *After every query,* $\mathcal{C}$ *updates the parameters* pp, aux *and* $S_{id}$.

   (b) **Registering target identity.** *On a query of the form* (regtgt, id), $\mathcal{C}$ *first checks if* id* $=\perp$. *Again, it aborts if the check fails. Otherwise,* $\mathcal{C}$ *sets* id* $\leftarrow$ id, *samples a challenge key pair* (pk*, sk*) $\leftarrow$ KGen($1^\lambda$), *updates the public parameter (and* aux) *using* pp $\leftarrow$ RBE.Reg$^{[\text{aux}]}$(crs, pp, id*, pk*) *and inserts* id* *into* $S_{id}$. *We remark that the challenger stores the secret key* sk* *in addition to updating all other parameters. Also, note that the adversary here is restricted to make such a query at most once, since the challenger would abort otherwise.*

   (c) **Target identity encryption.** *On a query of the form* (enctgt, m), $\mathcal{C}$ *checks if* id* $\neq\perp$. *If the check fails, abort. Otherwise, it sets* $t \leftarrow t+1$, $\tilde{m}_t \leftarrow m$, *and computes ciphertext* $\text{ct}_t \leftarrow$ RBE.Enc(crs, pp, id*, $\tilde{m}_t$). *It stores*[4] *the tuple* $(t, \tilde{m}_t, \text{ct}_t)$ *and then sends the* $\text{ct}_t$ *to* $\mathcal{A}$.

   (d) **Target identity decryptions.** *On a query of the form* (dectgt, j), $\mathcal{C}$ *checks if* id* $\neq\perp$ *and* $j \in [t]$. *If the check fails, abort. Otherwise,* $\mathcal{C}$ *computes* $y_j \leftarrow$ RBE.Dec(sk*, $u$, $\text{ct}_j$). *If* $y_j =$ GetUpd, *then it computes* $u \leftarrow$ RBE.Upd$^{\text{aux}}$(p, id*) *and then recomputes* $y_j \leftarrow$ Dec(sk*, $u$, $\text{ct}_j$). *Finally,* $\mathcal{C}$ *stores the tuple* $(j, y_j)$.

3. **Output Phase.** *We say that* $\mathcal{A}$ *wins the game if there is some* $j \in [t]$ *for which* $\tilde{m}_j \neq y_j$.

*Let* $n \leftarrow |S_{id}|$ *denote the number of identities registered until a specific round in the game above. We require the following properties to hold for any* $\mathcal{A}$ *at any moment during the game* $\text{Comp}_{\mathcal{A}}^{\text{RBE}}$.

- **Completeness.** $\Pr[\mathcal{A}$ *wins* $\text{Comp}_{\mathcal{A}}^{\text{RBE}}(\lambda)] \leq \text{negl}(\lambda)$.
- **Compactness.** $|\text{pp}|, |u|$ *are both* $\leq \text{poly}(\lambda, \log n)$.
- **Efficiency of registration and update.** *The time complexity of each invocation of* RBE.Reg$^{[\text{aux}]}$ *and* RBE.Upd$^{\text{aux}}$ *is at most* $\text{poly}(\lambda, \log n)$.
- **Efficiency of the number of updates.** *The total number of invocations of* RBE.Upd$^{\text{aux}}$ *for identity* id* *during the decryption phase is at most* $\text{poly}(\lambda, \log n)$ *for every* $n$.

---

[4] If $\mathcal{C}$ stores a tuple, it means appending the tuple to $\mathcal{C}$'s local state so that it can be accessed later.

**Definition 10** *(Security of RBE). For any interactive PPT adversary $\mathcal{A}$, consider the game $\mathsf{Sec}_{\mathcal{A}}^{\mathsf{RBE}}(\lambda)$ below. The definition is similar to the IND-CPA public key encryption definition except that $\mathcal{A}$ can register one target and polynomially many non-target identities.*

1. **Initialization.** *The challenger $\mathcal{C}$ initializes parameters as*

$$(\mathsf{pp}, \mathsf{aux}, u, S_{\mathsf{id}}, \mathsf{id}^*) = (\epsilon, \epsilon, \epsilon, \emptyset, \perp),$$

   *samples $\mathsf{crs} \leftarrow \mathsf{RBE.Setup}(1^\lambda)$ and sends $\mathsf{crs}$ to $\mathcal{A}$.*
2. **Query Phase.** *$\mathcal{A}$ makes polynomially many queries of the following form.*
   (a) **Registering non-target identity.** *On a query of the form $(\mathsf{regnew}, \mathsf{id}, \mathsf{pk})$, $\mathcal{C}$ checks that $\mathsf{id} \notin S_{\mathsf{id}}$. It aborts if the check fails. Otherwise, $\mathcal{C}$ registers $(\mathsf{id}, \mathsf{pk})$ by running the registration algorithm $\mathsf{RBE.Reg}^{[\mathsf{aux}]}(\mathsf{crs}, \mathsf{pp}, \mathsf{id}, \mathsf{pk})$. It adds $\mathsf{id}$ to the set as $S_{\mathsf{id}}$. Note that $\mathsf{pp}, \mathsf{aux}$ and $S_{\mathsf{id}}$ is updated after every query.*
   (b) **Registering target identity.** *On a query of the form $(\mathsf{regtgt}, \mathsf{id})$, $\mathcal{C}$ first checks if $\mathsf{id}^* = \perp$. Again, it aborts if the check fails. Otherwise, $\mathcal{C}$ sets $\mathsf{id}^* \leftarrow \mathsf{id}$, samples a challenge key pair $(\mathsf{pk}^*, \mathsf{sk}^*) \leftarrow \mathsf{KGen}(1^\lambda)$, updates the $\mathsf{pp}$ and $\mathsf{aux}$ using $\mathsf{pp} \leftarrow \mathsf{RBE.Reg}^{[\mathsf{aux}]}(\mathsf{crs}, \mathsf{pp}, \mathsf{id}^*, \mathsf{pk}^*)$ and inserts $\mathsf{id}^*$ into $S_{\mathsf{id}}$. Finally, $\mathcal{C}$ sends $\mathsf{pk}^*$ to $\mathcal{A}$.*
3. **Challenge Phase.** *On a query of the form $(\mathsf{chal}, \mathsf{id}, m_0, m_1)$, the challenger checks whether $\mathsf{id} \notin S_{\mathsf{id}} \setminus \{\mathsf{id}^*\}$. If the check fails, abort. Otherwise, $\mathcal{C}$ samples $b \in \{0, 1\}$ and computes the challenge ciphertext $\mathsf{ct} \leftarrow \mathsf{RBE.Enc}(\mathsf{crs}, \mathsf{pp}, \mathsf{id}, m_b)$.*
4. **Output Phase.** *$\mathcal{A}$ outputs a bit $b'$ and wins the game if $b' = b$.*

*We say that an RBE scheme is message-hiding secure if for every PPT $\mathcal{A}$ and every $\lambda \in \mathbb{N}$, there exists a negligible function $\mathsf{negl}(\lambda)$ such that*

$$\Pr[\mathcal{A} \text{ wins } \mathsf{Sec}_{\mathcal{A}}^{\mathsf{RBE}}(\lambda)] \leq \frac{1}{2} + \mathsf{negl}(\lambda).$$

## 3.6    Crit-Bit Tree

One of the key building blocks in our optimized RBE construction is crit-bit trees. We describe a crit-bit tree by comparing it to the trie structure. Tries look like binary trees but the path for searching and inserting an item depends on the binary encoding of the item. For example to find the value $3_{10} = 011_2$, the algorithm would take the path "right, right, left", assuming 0 represents "left" and 1 represents "right". This idea implies that there are at least two types of nodes, (1) intermediate nodes only hold pointers to their children and (2) leaf nodes hold the actual values. An example is given in Fig. 3.

PATRICIA Trie [29], also known as radix tree, is a type of trie where some of the intermediate nodes are "compressed". The idea is simple: nodes on a path that do not branch are compressed into one internal node. There are many varieties of PATRICIA tries. In this work, we use crit-bit trees [4]. The name comes from "critical bit", which is an integer stored in all the internal nodes that indicates the next bit location where two items differ. Typically, this integer increases with depth. The main reason behind this choice is that crit-bit trees have very small node size, using only two pointers and an integer of size at most the log of bit-length of the leaf size.

An example is given in Fig. 4. Note that the two internal nodes in the standard trie on Fig. 3 are compressed into one internal node in the crit-bit example. Suppose we want to find the value $100_2$, the search algorithm first visits the root node and sees a critical bit of 0, and then decides to go left since the 0th bit (the LSB) of $100_2$ is 0. Then the algorithm reaches an intermediate node with a critical bit of 2, it would decide to go right since the 2nd bit of $100_2$ (the MSB) is 1.

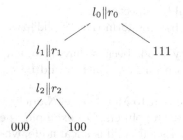

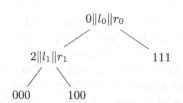

**Fig. 3.** An example of a trie. Each node has two pointers $l_d, r_d$ which refer to the left or the right child, where $d$ is the depth.

**Fig. 4.** An example of a crit-bit tree. In addition to the two pointers which it inherited from the trie structure, every node contains a positive integer which represents the "critical bit".

Key properties of PATRICIA tries, which also apply to crit-bit trees, include the following. For random items, the average depth is approximately $\log n + 0.33279$ [25, p. 507]. Szpankowski computed the variance of the depth [34, Eq. 2.9] which turned out to be a constant for a fixed branching factor. In the binary case, the variance is 1. We are also interested in the worst-case performance. In the literature, the maximum depth is called the height. The expected value of the height is $\log n + \sqrt{2 \log n} + O(1)$ [12,24]. The final $O(1)$ term is small, typically ranging between 1 and $-1$ [24]. Many of the results above are confirmed experimentally in the literature [30].

In Sect. 4.1, we will describe how a crit-bit tree is augmented to be an authenticated crit-bit tree and give algorithms for searching and inserting in such an authenticated crit-bit tree.

## 4 Optimizing RBE Using Crit-Bit Trees

In this section we describe our optimized RBE construction based on crit-bit trees. Before describing the construction, we define the authenticated crit-bit tree by drawing inspiration from CONIKS [28] which uses a similar construction but based on tries.

## 4.1 Authenticated Crit-Bit Tree

Assume $\lambda$ is a power of 2, every node in the tree has $1 + \log \lambda + 2\lambda$ bits and has the format

$$(\tau \in \{0,1\} \parallel \sigma \in \{0,1\}^{\log \lambda} \parallel \alpha \in \{0,1\}^{\lambda} \parallel \beta \in \{0,1\}^{\lambda}),$$

where $\tau$ represents the node type and $\sigma$ represents the critical bit index. For clarity, we let $\mathsf{I} \leftarrow 0$ and $\mathsf{L} \leftarrow 1$. The tree consists of two types of nodes:

1. the intermediate node has the form $(\mathsf{I} \parallel \sigma \parallel \alpha \parallel \beta)$, where $\alpha$ and $\beta$ correspond to the digest of the left child and the right child, respectively;
2. the leaf node holds the registered user and has the form $(\mathsf{L} \parallel 0^{\log \lambda} \parallel \mathsf{id} \parallel \mathsf{pk})$.

Unlike CONIKS [28], we do not need an "empty" node because having an empty node implies that there is a path that has no branches, which would be compressed in crit-bit trees.

   Authentication is performed in a manner similar to Merkle-tree. Namely, the pointers described in Sect. 3.6 are replaced by hash pointers. For example, the $\alpha$ value of an internal node is $\mathsf{H}(\mathsf{L} \parallel 0^{\log \lambda} \parallel \mathsf{id} \parallel \mathsf{pk})$ if its left child is a leaf node, where $\mathsf{H}$ is a hash function. In our RBE construction (Sect. 4.2), we use $\mathsf{HG.Hash}$ as the hash function.

**Search:** The search algorithm follows directly from the crit-bit tree definition. We give a high level description based on [27]. Before giving the search algorithm, we define an algorithm that walks down the tree to find the node that is "closest" to the target identity id. If id exists, then the leaf node containing id is returned. We call this algorithm the "walk algorithm".

1. Let id be the input and we use the $\mathsf{id}[i]$ notation to access the $i$th bit, $\mathsf{id}[0]$ represents the LSB of id.
2. Let currNode be the root node, recursively perform the following steps until currNode is a leaf node.
   (a) Determine the traversal direction, i.e., $\mathsf{dir} \leftarrow \mathsf{id}[\mathsf{currNode}.\sigma]$.
   (b) Set currNode to the left child if $\mathsf{dir} = 0$, otherwise set it to the right child.
3. Output currNode.

The search algorithm is simply an equality test added to the algorithm above.

1. Run the "walk algorithm" above and obtain a leaf node.
2. Output the leaf node if the leaf node contains id, otherwise output $\perp$.

**Insertion:** The insertion algorithm is a bit more involved because we need make sure the critical bits are always increasing with depth. We give a high level description based on [27] for inserting (id, pk).

1. Create a leaf node newLeaf $\leftarrow$ (L$\|0^{\log \lambda}\|$id$\|$pk).
2. Find the closest leaf node to id using the "walk algorithm" from above and call it closestLeaf.
3. Starting at the LSB, let $\sigma^*$ be the critical bit between id and closestLeaf.$\alpha$.
4. From the root, walk the tree in the same way (using id as the target) and stopping at a node, which we call pNode, if
   (a) it is a leaf node, or
   (b) the critical bit is greater than $\sigma^*$.
5. Compute the direction dir $\leftarrow$ id[$\sigma^*$].
6. Create a new internal node (I$\|\sigma^*\|\alpha\|\beta$), where $\alpha = $ H(newLeaf) if dir $= 0$, otherwise $\alpha = $ H(pNode). The other digest $\beta$ is set the same way except it's the mirror image of $\alpha$. In essence, the new internal node took the position of pNode, and pNode and newLeaf are its two children.
7. Traverse back up the tree to the root and recompute the digests.

## 4.2 Optimized RBE Construction with Compact Public Parameters

**Tree Structure:** Similar to the work of [20], our construction uses two data structures, IDTree and CBTree. The first is IDTree, which is a self-balancing binary tree (e.g., Red–black trees) used for internal book-keeping by the KC. Concretely, the nodes have the form (id, $t$) where id is a user identity and $t$ is a timestamp which always increments by 1. The re-balancing operation is based on the order of id, thus we assume the identities have an ordering.

The second is CBTree, which are crit-bit trees. These trees have the structure describe in Sect. 4.1. We use $\ell$ to denote the total number of such trees at any moment in time.

**Optimized RBE Construction:** We detail our RBE construction below. Most of the algorithms follow a similar idea as [20] but are adapted to use crit-bit trees. In particular, the registration algorithm is functionally the same as the one in [20] but the description is simplified using the critical bit idea.

The KC holds public parameters pp $= $ (crs, $\{$rt$_i, d_i\}_{i \in [\ell]}$) and auxillary information aux $= \{$IDTree, $\{($CBTree$_i, n_i)\}_i\}$, where rt$_i$ is the digest of the root node of CBTree$_i$ and $d_i$ is the maximum depth of CBTree$_i$.

- RBE.Setup($1^\lambda$) $\rightarrow$ crs. Let hk $\leftarrow$ HG.Gen($1^\lambda, 1^{1+\log \lambda + 2\lambda}$). Output hk as crs. Note that the reason for using $1^{1+\log \lambda + 2\lambda}$ is because the preimage of the hash function, which is the size of a node, has $1 + \log \lambda + 2\lambda$ bits.
- KGen($1^\lambda$) $\rightarrow$ (pk, sk). Generate a public and a secret key pair (pk, sk) using the public key generation algorithm.
- RBE.Reg$^{[\text{aux}]}$(crs, pp, id, pk) $\rightarrow$ pp$'$. The registration is described in the steps below. An example can be found in Fig. 5.

1. Let $(\mathsf{IDTree}, \{(\mathsf{CBTree}_i, n_i)\}_{i \in [\ell]}) \leftarrow \mathsf{aux}$, and let $n = \sum_{i \in [\ell]} n_i$.
2. Insert $(\mathsf{id}, n + 1)$ to $\mathsf{IDTree}$ and call it $\mathsf{IDTree}'$.
3. Copy the latest tree $\mathsf{CBTree}_\ell$ and call it $\mathsf{NewTree}$, and then insert the leaf $(\mathsf{L}\|0^{\log \lambda}\|\mathsf{id}\|\mathsf{pk})$ into $\mathsf{NewTree}$.
4. Find the critical bit index $\sigma$ between $n$ and $n + 1$ counting from the MSB.
5. Set $T \leftarrow \{(\mathsf{CBTree}_i, n_i) : i \in [\ell], n_i > 2^\sigma\} \cup \{(\mathsf{NewTree}, 2^\sigma)\}$.
6. Let the new auxillary information be $\mathsf{aux}' \leftarrow \{\mathsf{IDTree}', T\}$.
7. Finally, the KC sets the new public parameter $\mathsf{pp}' \leftarrow (\mathsf{crs}, \{(\mathsf{rt}'_i, d'_i)\}_{i \in [\|T\|]})$, where $\mathsf{rt}'_i$ and $d'_i$ are the new Merkle root and the maximum depth of the trees in $T$, respectively.

- $\mathsf{RBE.Enc}(\mathsf{crs}, \mathsf{pp}, \mathsf{id}, m) \to \mathsf{ct}$. The encryption algorithm uses a program $P_{i,j}$ which we describe first. For clarity, we use Greek alphabet symbols to denote values that are unknown to the encryptor. The others are constants.

$P_{i,j}(\tau\|\sigma\|\alpha\|\beta)$ [Constants: $\mathsf{crs}, \mathsf{state}_{i,j+1}, \mathsf{id}, m, r$]

```
 1:  if τ = I then
 2:      if id[σ] = 0
 3:          return HG.Input(crs, α, state_{i,j+1})
 4:      else
 5:          return HG.Input(crs, β, state_{i,j+1})
 6:      endif
 7:  elseif τ = L ∧ id = α then
 8:      return Enc(β, m; r)
 9:  else
10:      return ⊥
11:  endif
```

Using the program above, the encryption algorithm works as follows.
1. Sample a random value $r \in \{0,1\}^\lambda$.
2. Parse $\mathsf{pp}$ as $(\mathsf{hk}, \{(\mathsf{rt}_1, d_1), \ldots, (\mathsf{rt}_\ell, d_\ell)\})$.
3. For each tree index $i \in [\ell]$ and each depth $j \in \{1, \ldots, d_i\}$ of the $i$th tree, sample $\mathsf{state}_{i,j} \leftarrow_\$ \{0,1\}^\lambda$, and then execute

$$\tilde{P}_{i,j} \leftarrow \mathsf{HG.Garble}(\mathsf{hk}, P_{i,j}, \mathsf{state}_{i,j}).$$

4. For every root $\mathsf{rt}_i$, compute $\tilde{\mathbf{k}}_{i,1} \leftarrow \mathsf{HG.Input}(\mathsf{hk}, \mathsf{rt}_i, \mathsf{state}_{1,j})$.
5. Output the ciphertext $\mathsf{ct} = (\mathsf{pp}, \{\tilde{P}_{i,j}\}_{i,j}, \{\tilde{\mathbf{k}}_{i,1}\}_i)$.

- $\mathsf{RBE.Upd}^{\mathsf{aux}}(\mathsf{pp}, \mathsf{id}) \to u$. Let $\mathsf{aux} = (\mathsf{IDTree}, \{(\mathsf{CBTree}_i, n_i)\}_{i \in [\ell]})$ and $\mathsf{pp} = \{(\mathsf{rt}_i, d_i)\}_{i \in [\ell]}$, the update algorithm works as follows.
  1. The algorithm performs a binary search in $\mathsf{IDTree}$ to find the timestamp $t$ associated with $\mathsf{id}$. If the timestamp does not exist, the algorithm aborts.

2. Otherwise, the algorithm computes an index $i \in [\ell]$ such that

$$\sum_{j \in [i-1]} n_j < t \leq \sum_{j \in [i]} n_j.$$

The index $i$ represents the smallest tree index that contains id.

3. Finally, traverse $\mathsf{CBTree}_i$ to find the identity and output the traversed path as $u \leftarrow (u_1, \ldots, u_{d_{\mathsf{id}}})$. We use $d_{\mathsf{id}}$ to indicate the depth of the path containing id which may be less than the maximum depth of $\mathsf{CBTree}_i$.

- $\mathsf{RBE.Dec(sk}, u, \mathsf{ct}) \rightarrow \{m, \perp, \mathsf{GetUpd}\}$.
  1. Let $(u_1, \ldots, u_{d_{\mathsf{id}}}) \leftarrow u$, where $u_1$ is a root node and $u_{d_{\mathsf{id}}}$ should be $(\mathsf{L} \| 0^{\log_2 \lambda} \| \mathsf{id} \| \mathsf{pk})$ and $d_{\mathsf{id}}$ is the depth of the leaf node $u_{d_{\mathsf{id}}}$. If $u$ does not exist, output $\mathsf{GetUpd}$.
  2. Let $(\mathsf{pp}, \{\tilde{P}_{i,j}\}_{i,j}, \{\tilde{\mathbf{k}}_{i,1}\}_i) \leftarrow \mathsf{ct}$.
  3. Let $i$ be the tree index such that $\mathsf{rt}_i = \mathsf{HG.Hash(hk}, u_1)$. If no such $i$ exists then output $\mathsf{GetUpd}$.
  4. For $j \in [d_{\mathsf{id}}]$:
     - Compute $\tilde{\mathbf{k}}_{i,j+1} \leftarrow \mathsf{HG.Eval}(\tilde{P}_{i,j}, \tilde{\mathbf{k}}_{i,j}, u_j)$.
     - If $\tilde{\mathbf{k}}_{i,j+1} = \perp$ then output $\perp$.
  5. The final $\tilde{\mathbf{k}}_{i,d_{\mathsf{id}}+1}$ is the ciphertext, so the algorithm decrypts it using the secret key $\mathsf{sk}$, i.e., $\mathsf{Dec(sk}, \tilde{\mathbf{k}}_{i,d_{\mathsf{id}}+1}) \rightarrow m$, and finally output $m$.

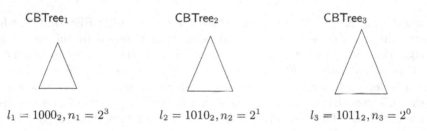

CBTree₁                          CBTree₂                          CBTree₃

$l_1 = 1000_2, n_1 = 2^3$      $l_2 = 1010_2, n_2 = 2^1$      $l_3 = 1011_2, n_3 = 2^0$

**Fig. 5.** There are three crit-bit trees in this example, each tree contains $l_i$ identities. Further, every tree has $n_i$ users that must use the path in the corresponding $\mathsf{CBTree}_i$ to decrypt. The trees can be considered as snapshots where the last one is the latest snapshot that contains all the users, i.e., $n = l_3$. If a new user registers, there will be $1100_2$ users. The critical bit between $1011_2$ and $1100_2$ is 1st bit from the MSB, which suggests that $\mathsf{CBTree}_1$ will be kept but the two others will be replaced by $\mathsf{CBTree}_{\mathsf{new}}$ that has $l_{\mathsf{new}} = 1100_2$ and $n_{\mathsf{new}} = 2^2$, according to the registration algorithm.

## 4.3   Completeness, Efficiency and Compactness

Using the correctness property of PKE (Definition 1) and hash garbling (Definition 5), the completeness of the RBE scheme, from Definition 9, follows by simply following the construction. We can also prove our scheme is efficient and compact according to Definition 9.

- **Compactness.** There are at most $\log n$ roots since there are at most $\log n$ trees in aux, thus the public parameter is compact. The number of nodes from a root to any leaf is $O(\log n)$, thus the path $u$ is also compact.
- **Efficiency of registration and update.** Our registration algorithm first inserts an item into the self-balancing IDTree, which takes $O(\log n)$ time. Then we make a copy of CBTree$_\ell$ to produce NewTree and then insert a new leaf node. Insertion takes time $O(\log n)$ for a crit-bit tree, but implementing the copy operation natively will take $O(n)$ time. Fortunately, we can use techniques such as copy-on-write and only allocate storage for the $O(\log n)$ nodes in NewTree that are different from CBTree$_\ell$ since the insertion algorithm (Sect. 4.1) only modifies nodes on a single path. Finally, finding the critical bit and then selecting which trees to delete takes $O(\log n)$ time. Thus, the overall time complexity for registration is $O(\log n)$.
  The update algorithm finds the timestamp $t$ of id which takes time $O(\log n)$ since IDTree is balanced. Then, the algorithm computes the tree index that contains id which also takes $O(\log n)$ since there are only $\log n$ indices. Finally, finding the correct leaf and outputting the path to the leaf is $O(\log n)$ as well due to the tree structure. Thus, the overall time complexity for the update algorithm is $O(\log n)$.
- **Efficiency of the number of updates.** An identity registered at time $t$ is associated with CBTree$_i$ if

$$\sum_{j \in [i-1]} n_j < t \leq \sum_{j \in [i]} n_j,$$

where $n_i \geq 2n_{i+1}$. A user needs to fetch a new $u$, using RBE.Upd$^{\mathsf{aux}}$, whenever the tree CBTree$_i$ containing his identity is removed by the registration algorithm. Suppose CBTree$_i$ exists at a moment in time, the registration algorithm only deletes it after $n_i$ new identities are registered after it. In other words, for a particular identity, the $n_i$ value associated to the earliest snapshot CBTree$_i$ that contains the identity will grow in powers of 2 as new users are registered. Thus we conclude that the number of updates needed by any user is $\log n$.

## 4.4   Security Proof

In this section, we follow the template of [16] and present the security proof. To build intuition, we begin by presenting a proof for when only one user has registered. Then we move on to the general case.

**Proof for One User:** Single-user security is defined below, which is essentially ciphertext indistinguishability.

**Theorem 1** *(RBE security for one user). For any identity* id *we have*

$$\mathsf{ct}_0 = (\mathsf{HG.Garble}(\mathsf{hk}, P[\mathsf{id}, 0, r], \mathsf{state}), \mathsf{HG.Input}(\mathsf{hk}, \mathsf{rt}, \mathsf{state})) \stackrel{c}{\approx}$$
$$(\mathsf{HG.Garble}(\mathsf{hk}, P[\mathsf{id}, 1, r], \mathsf{state}), \mathsf{HG.Input}(\mathsf{hk}, \mathsf{rt}, \mathsf{state})) = \mathsf{ct}_1,$$

*where* hk $\leftarrow$ RBE.Setup$(1^\lambda)$, state $\leftarrow \{0,1\}^\lambda$, rt $\leftarrow$ HG.Hash(hk, $(\mathsf{L}\|0^\lambda\|\mathsf{id}\|\mathsf{pk}))$, $r \in \{0,1\}^\lambda$, $(\mathsf{pk}, \mathsf{sk}) \leftarrow$ KGen$(1^\lambda)$ $m \in \{0,1\}$ *and the circuit P is defined below. This circuit is an equivalent but simplified version of $P_{i,j}$ in Sect. 4.2 that works for only one user. We abuse the notation and use $P[\mathsf{id}, m, r]$ to indicate the constants used in the circuit.*

$$P(\tau\|\sigma\|\alpha\|\beta) \text{ [Constants: id}, m, r]$$

---

1 : **if** $\tau \neq \mathsf{L} \wedge \alpha \neq \mathsf{id}$

2 : **else return** $\mathsf{Enc}(\beta, m; r)$

3 : **endif**

*Proof.* For $m \in \{0,1\}$, let $\mathsf{ct}_m$ denote the challenge ciphertext, i.e.,

$$\mathsf{ct}_m \leftarrow (\mathsf{HG.Garble}(\mathsf{hk}, P[\mathsf{id}, m, r], \mathsf{state}), \mathsf{HG.Input}(\mathsf{hk}, \mathsf{rt}, \mathsf{state})).$$

We show that $\mathsf{ct}_0 \overset{c}{\approx} \mathsf{ct}_1$. By simulation security of the hash garbling scheme (Definition 6), for $m \in \{0,1\}$, we have

$$\mathsf{ct}_m \overset{c}{\approx} \mathsf{Sim}(\mathsf{hk}, (\mathsf{L}\|0^\lambda\|\mathsf{id}\|\mathsf{pk}), \mathsf{Enc}(\mathsf{pk}, m; r), 1^{|P|}).$$

By semantic security of the public key encryption scheme, we can write

$$\mathsf{Sim}(\mathsf{hk}, (\mathsf{L}\|0^\lambda\|\mathsf{id}\|\mathsf{pk}), \mathsf{Enc}(\mathsf{pk}, 0; r), 1^{|P|})$$
$$\overset{c}{\approx} \mathsf{Sim}(\mathsf{hk}, (\mathsf{L}\|0^\lambda\|\mathsf{id}\|\mathsf{pk}), \mathsf{Enc}(\mathsf{pk}, 1; r), 1^{|P|}),$$

which concludes the proof. $\qquad\square$

**General Proof:** Now we are ready to prove RBE security for the general case. Without loss of generality, we will only consider one crit-bit tree. Recall that for encryption, if we have $\ell$ roots, we create circuits individually for each root. Suppose at the time of encryption, we have $\ell$ trees with roots $\mathsf{rt}_1, \ldots, \mathsf{rt}_\ell$. Then, between the two hybrids which correspond to an encryption of zero and an encryption of one, we may consider $\ell$ intermediate hybrids, where under the $i$th hybrid we encrypt 0 under the roots $\mathsf{rt}_1, \ldots \mathsf{rt}_i$ and we encrypt 1 under the roots $\mathsf{rt}_{i+1}, \ldots \mathsf{rt}_\ell$. Thus, using the hybrid argument above, it is enough to only consider one crit-bit tree.

When only considering one tree, the proof is a straightforward hybrid argument. Recall that the ciphertext contains $d$ garbled programs, one for every level of the tree. Starting with the correctly computed ciphertext. We define a series of hybrids where the garbled program and the garbled input are replaced by the *simulated* version one by one. From the security of the hash garbling scheme, these hybrids are computationally indistinguishable. In the final hybrid, we can switch the underlying plaintext using Theorem 1.

**Theorem 2.** *Our crit-bit tree based RBE construction is secure with respect to the standard RBE security definition given in Definition 10.*

*Proof.* Since we are only considering one tree, we will ignore the tree index. That is, $P_{i,j}$ becomes $P_j$, $\mathsf{state}_{i,j}$ becomes $\mathsf{state}_j$ and so on.

Consider an identity id, the path leading to it is $(u_1, u_2, \ldots, u_d)$, where $u_1$ is the root node and $u_d = (\mathsf{L}\|0^\lambda\|\mathsf{id}\|\mathsf{pk})$. For $j > 1$, let $\tilde{\mathbf{k}}_j \leftarrow$ HG.Input$(\mathsf{hk}, u_j, \mathsf{state}_j)$. Now we are ready to give the hybrids.

- **Hybrid 0 (encryption in real game).** Let the ciphertext be $\mathsf{ct}_0 \leftarrow$ $(\tilde{P}_1, \ldots, \tilde{P}_d, \tilde{\mathbf{k}}_1)$, where every value is sampled from the construction.
- **Hybrid 1.** Let $\mathsf{ct}_1 \leftarrow (\hat{P}_1, \ldots, \tilde{P}_d, \hat{\mathbf{k}}_1)$, where we use a circumflex to denote simulated values, i.e.,

$$(\hat{P}_1, \hat{\mathbf{k}}_1) \leftarrow \mathsf{Sim}(\mathsf{hk}, u_1, \tilde{\mathbf{k}}_2, 1^{|P_1|}).$$

The other values are sampled as the construction. Recall that $\tilde{P}_j$ is generated using $P_j$ and $\mathsf{state}_j$ in the construction. But in this hybrid, and the ones below, we simulate $\tilde{P}_j$ without $P_j$ or $\mathsf{state}_j$.

- **Hybrid $i \in [d-1]$.** Let $\mathsf{ct}_i \leftarrow (\hat{P}_1, \ldots, \hat{P}_i, \tilde{P}_{i+1}, \ldots, \tilde{P}_d, \hat{\mathbf{k}}_1)$, where for $j \in [i]$ $(\hat{P}_j, \hat{\mathbf{k}}_j) \leftarrow \mathsf{Sim}(\mathsf{hk}, u_{j+1}, \tilde{\mathbf{k}}_{j+1}, 1^{|P_j|})$.
- **Hybrid $d$.** Let $\mathsf{ct}_d \leftarrow (\hat{P}_1, \ldots, \hat{P}_d, \hat{\mathbf{k}}_1)$, where all the values are simulated like the hybrid above for $j \in [d-1]$ and

$$(\hat{P}_d, \hat{\mathbf{k}}_d) \leftarrow \mathsf{Sim}(\mathsf{hk}, u_d, \mathsf{Enc}(\mathsf{pk}, m; r), 1^{|P_d|}).$$

From the security of hash garbling (Definition 6), any two adjacent hybrids are indistinguishable. In the final hybrid, we use the same argument as Theorem 1, i.e.,

$$\mathsf{Sim}(\mathsf{hk}, (\mathsf{L}\|0^\lambda\|\mathsf{id}\|\mathsf{pk}), \mathsf{Enc}(\mathsf{pk}, 0; r), 1^{|P|})$$
$$\overset{c}{\approx} \mathsf{Sim}(\mathsf{hk}, (\mathsf{L}\|0^\lambda\|\mathsf{id}\|\mathsf{pk}), \mathsf{Enc}(\mathsf{pk}, 1; r), 1^{|P|}),$$

to claim that the ciphertexts are indistinguishable. Hence, the security of our RBE construction is proved.  □

### 4.5   Performance Improvement over Prior Work

Our main performance improvement comes from reducing the number of bits stored in the tree node from $1 + 3\lambda$ to $1 + \log\lambda + 2\lambda$. The reason this is important is because HG.Input needs to perform 2 public key operations in the garbled circuit per bit, which is exceptionally costly.

The tradeoff is that the depth is higher than a balanced Merkle tree which has $\lceil\log n\rceil$ depth. The decryption algorithm RBE.Dec is only affected by the average depth $\log n + 0.33279$ (discussed in Sect. 3.6) so it is a small price to pay to benefit from crit-bit trees. Suppose $n = 2^{31}$, which is a reasonable number for popular applications considering WhatsApp has 2 billion users [13], and $\lambda = 256$. Our construction makes 30% fewer public key operations in the garbled circuit (GC) compared to the best prior work [20] on average.

The encryption algorithm RBE.Enc, however, is affected by the maximum depth which is $\log n + \sqrt{2 \log n} + O(1)$. It tends to $\log n$ as $n$ tends to infinity. This property implies that our encryption performance becomes better as the number of registered user grows. In practice, $n$ is not infinite. Suppose $n = 2^{31}$ and $\lambda = 256$ again, the encryption algorithm in our construction makes 15% fewer public key operations in the GC on average.

The calculations above is purely based on the number of public key operations that must be performed in the GC. For every circuit, we assume the PKE uses one pubic key operation and HG.Input uses $2 \cdot \lambda$ public key operations. The circuit that the encryptor needs to garble also contains other operations such as branching and string comparison. But the cost of these operations are negligible as they only require a few logic gates, relatively speaking. Naively, a branching operation can be implemented with a 2-to-1 multiplexer where the input is $\lambda$ bits using $3\lambda + 1$ gates compared to billions of gates in the case of one public key operation.

In Sect. 5 we slightly weaken the compactness requirement of RBE and further reduce the number of public key operations in the encryption algorithm.

### 4.6 Verifiability

The work of [20] introduced verifiable RBE. This property allows users to request a pre-registration proof and a post-registration proof. The former is a proof of non-membership. The latter is a proof of unique-membership. While we do not give the full verification algorithm and prove its soundness and completeness, we argue that it is possible to add pre/post-registration proofs, which essentially only depend on the authenticity of aux (crit-bit trees in our case), without changing the underlying construction.

Before presenting our argument, we introduce the notion of adjacent paths. A pair of adjacent paths in a crit-bit tree is two valid paths[5] with leaf nodes containing $\mathsf{id}^{(0)}$ and $\mathsf{id}^{(1)}$ such that there does not exist another leaf node with id such that $\mathsf{id}^{(0)} < \mathsf{id} < \mathsf{id}^{(1)}$. Concretely, the two paths have the following form,

$$- \ u^{(0)} = \{(\mathsf{I}\|\sigma_1^{(0)}\|\alpha_1^{(0)}\|\beta_1^{(0)}), \ldots, (\mathsf{I}\|\sigma_k^{(0)}\|\alpha_k^{(0)}\|\beta_k^{(0)}), \ldots, (\mathsf{L}\|0^{\log \lambda}\|\mathsf{id}^{(0)}\|\mathsf{pk}^{(0)})\},$$

$$- \ u^{(1)} = \{(\mathsf{I}\|\sigma_1^{(1)}\|\alpha_1^{(1)}\|\beta_1^{(1)}), \ldots, (\mathsf{I}\|\sigma_k^{(1)}\|\alpha_k^{(1)}\|\beta_k^{(1)}), \ldots, (\mathsf{L}\|0^{\log \lambda}\|\mathsf{id}^{(1)}\|\mathsf{pk}^{(1)})\}.$$

For every $i \in [k]$, $u_i^{(0)} = u_i^{(1)}$. That is, the two paths share the same prefix of length $k$ and $\sigma_k$ is the critical bit that distinguishes $\mathsf{id}^{(0)}$ and $\mathsf{id}^{(1)}$, e.g., $\mathsf{id}^{(0)}[\sigma_k] = 0$ and $\mathsf{id}^{(1)}[\sigma_k] = 1$. Further, for $b \in \{0,1\}$ and $i \in [k+1, d^{(b)}]$, we require that $\mathsf{id}^{(b)}[\sigma^{(b)}] = 1 - b$, where $d^{(b)}$ is the length of the two paths. Intuitively, the two paths diverge after the $k$th node. But after this point, the left path ($u^{(0)}$) must always follow the *right* branch and the right path $u^{(1)}$ must always follow the *left* branch.

For the non-membership proof in the pre-registration phase, the KC simply constructs the pair of adjacent paths described above to prove id does not exist.

---

[5] A path is valid when the adjacent nodes obey the hash-pointer constraint.

That is, constructing a pair of adjacent paths with $\text{id}^{(0)}$ and $\text{id}^{(1)}$ in the leaves such that $\text{id}^{(0)} < \text{id} < \text{id}^{(1)}$. The KC can perform this step efficiently and the prove size is compact, i.e., $O(\log n)$. Clearly, verification is also efficient and runs in time $O(\log n)$. This idea generalizes to multiple trees by making one such proof for every tree.

For the unique-membership proof in the post-registration phase, the KC constructs two pairs of adjacent paths. Suppose we want to prove the uniqueness of id, then the KC constructs one pair of adjacent paths with leaves $\text{id}^{(0)}$ and id, and another with the leaves id and $\text{id}^{(1)}$. As a result, for every identity that is unique registered, the KC is able to create the two pairs of adjacent paths. Extending this idea to multiple trees is a bit different than the pre-registration phase above. Similar to [20], we can view the trees as snapshots. Which means the KC needs to produce non-membership proofs for identities that are not yet in the snapshots and unique-membership proof for identities that are in the snapshot.

## 5    Further Optimization Using Larger Public Parameter

Using even fewer public key operations is possible if we relax the compactness requirement of RBE. Concretely, the original definition requires pp to have size $\text{poly}(\lambda, \log n)$. However, if we relax the requirement to $\text{poly}(\lambda, \sqrt{n})$, it is possible to reduce the number of public key operations needed in the GC by a half for the encryptor. In practice, if there are $2^{31}$ registered users and the identities of $\sqrt{2^{31}}$ users are published using a cuckoo filter [14] with a false positive rate of $2^{-40}$, then the size of the public parameter is only increased by 187 kilobytes. We argue that this is a reasonable tradeoff to make to alleviate the bottleneck.

Below we describe the intuition before detailing the modification of the registration and the encryption algorithm. Starting from the scheme in Sect. 4.2, recall that aux stores $(\{\text{CBTree}_i, n_i\}_{i \in [\ell]})$, where $n_i$ is a power of 2 representing the number of identities that needs to use a path in $\text{CBTree}_i$ to decrypt. For brevity, assume $n_i = 2 \cdot n_{i+1}$ for all $i \in [\ell]$. Then majority of the users only need the first half of the trees $\{\text{CBTree}_i\}_{i \in [\ell/2]}$ to decrypt and only a minority need the second half. If the encryptor knows whether a user belongs to the first half or the second half, then he only needs to iterate over half of the trees in the encryption algorithm. Thus, if we allow the KC to publish the identities that belong the second half of the trees (there will be $O(\sqrt{n})$ of them), then the number public key operations in the GC would be halved. The same argument applies in the general case where $n_i \geq 2 \cdot n_{i+1}$ since the bit-pattern of $n$ is uniformly distributed at any moment in time.

### 5.1    Optimized RBE Construction with Larger Public Parameters

First we describe the new format of the public parameter and then highlight the changes in the two algorithms. The public parameter now has the form

$$\{\text{IDTree}, \{(\text{rt}_i, d_i, n_i)\}_{i \in [\ell]}, \mathcal{I} = \{I_i : i \in [\ell], n_i < \sqrt{2^{\lfloor \log_2 n \rfloor}}\}\},$$

where $I_i$ represent the set of identities that need a path in $\mathsf{CBTree}_i$ to decrypt. Note that $|I_i| = n_i$ and $\lfloor \log_2 n \rfloor$ gives the number of bits of $n$. We view $\mathcal{I}$ as a flattened set to simplify notation but it can be implemented using a cuckoo filter as mentioned above.

The modified registration and encryption algorithms are shown below. We copy the algorithms verbatim from Sect. 4.2 and highlight the differences (modified steps) with the "*" symbol. The other algorithms remain unchanged.

- $\mathsf{RBE.Reg}^{[\mathsf{aux}]}(\mathsf{crs}, \mathsf{pp}, \mathsf{id}, \mathsf{pk}) \to \mathsf{pp}'$.

  1. Let $(\mathsf{IDTree}, \{(\mathsf{CBTree}_i, n_i)\}_{i \in [\ell]}) \leftarrow \mathsf{aux}$, and let $n = \sum_{i \in [\ell]} n_i$.
  2. Insert $(\mathsf{id}, n+1)$ to $\mathsf{IDTree}$ and call it $\mathsf{IDTree}'$.
  3. Copy the latest tree $\mathsf{CBTree}_\ell$ and call it $\mathsf{NewTree}$, and then insert the leaf $(\mathsf{L} \| 0^{\log \lambda} \| \mathsf{id} \| \mathsf{pk})$ into $\mathsf{NewTree}$.
  4. Find the critical bit index $\sigma$ between $n$ and $n+1$ counting from the MSB.
  5. Set $T \leftarrow \{(\mathsf{CBTree}_i, n_i) : i \in [\ell], n_i > 2^\sigma\} \cup \{(\mathsf{NewTree}, 2^\sigma)\}$.
  6. Let the new auxillary information be $\mathsf{aux}' \leftarrow \{\mathsf{IDTree}', T\}$.
  *7. Update the set $\mathcal{I}$ according to its definition and call it $\mathcal{I}'$.
  *8. Finally, the KC sets the new public parameter

$$\mathsf{pp}' \leftarrow (\mathsf{crs}, \{(\mathsf{rt}'_i, d'_i, n'_i)\}_{i \in [\|T\|]}, \mathcal{I}'),$$

  where $\mathsf{rt}'_i$, $d'_i$ and $n'_i$ are the new Merkle root, the maximum depth and the number of users of the trees in $T$, respectively.

- $\mathsf{RBE.Enc}(\mathsf{crs}, \mathsf{pp}, \mathsf{id}, m) \to \mathsf{ct}$. The encryption algorithm uses a program $P_{i,j}$ which we describe first. For clarity, we use Greek alphabet sybmols to denote values that are unknown to the encryptor. The others are constants.

$P_{i,j}(\tau \| \sigma \| \alpha \| \beta)$ [Constants: $\mathsf{crs}, \mathsf{state}_{i,j+1}, \mathsf{id}, m, r$]

```
 1 :  if τ = I then
 2 :      if id[σ] = 0
 3 :          return HG.Input(crs, α, state_{i,j+1})
 4 :      else
 5 :          return HG.Input(crs, β, state_{i,j+1})
 6 :      endif
 7 :  elseif τ = L ∧ id = α then
 8 :      return Enc(β, m; r)
 9 :  else
10 :      return ⊥
11 :  endif
```

Using the program above, the encryption algorithm works as follows.
  1. Sample a random value $r \in \{0,1\}^\lambda$.
  *2. Parse $\mathsf{pp}$ as $(\mathsf{hk}, \{(\mathsf{rt}_1, d_1, n_1), \ldots, (\mathsf{rt}_\ell, d_\ell, n_\ell)\}, \mathcal{I})$.

*3. Let $L \leftarrow \{1, \ldots, v\}$ if id $\notin \mathcal{I}$, otherwise let $L \leftarrow \{v+1, \ldots, \ell\}$, where $v$ is an index to a crit-bit tree such that $n_v < \sqrt{2^{\lfloor \log_2 n \rfloor}}$.

*4. For each crit-bit tree $i \in L$ and each depth $j \in \{1, \ldots, d_i\}$ of the $i$th tree, sample $\mathsf{state}_{i,j} \leftarrow_\$ \{0,1\}^\lambda$, and then execute

$$\tilde{P}_{i,j} \leftarrow \mathsf{HG.Garble}(\mathsf{hk}, P_{i,j}, \mathsf{state}_{i,j}).$$

5. For every root $\mathsf{rt}_i$, compute $\tilde{\mathbf{k}}_{i,1} \leftarrow \mathsf{HG.Input}(\mathsf{hk}, \mathsf{rt}_i, \mathsf{state}_{1,j})$.

6. Output the ciphertext $\mathsf{ct} = (\mathsf{pp}, \{\tilde{P}_{i,j}\}_{i,j}, \{\tilde{\mathbf{k}}_{i,1}\}_i)$.

### 5.2  Correctness, Security and Efficiency

Correctness and security hold since this construction is similar to the one given in Sect. 4.2 except that the public parameter has some additional information to help the encryptor select which trees to use. If id $\in \mathcal{I}$, then the encryption algorithm uses the "smaller" trees, i.e., $\{\mathsf{CBTree}_i : i \in [\ell], n_i < \sqrt{2^{\lfloor \log_2 n \rfloor}}\}$. Otherwise id must be in the "bigger" trees. The construction guarantees that the encryptor will always use roots of the trees that contain id.

The time complexity of the new registration algorithm does not change since updating the set $\mathcal{I}$ can be performed at the same time as selecting which trees to include in the new auxillary information (Item 5). The update algorithm stays the same so the time complexity does not change as well.

However, our public parameters are not compact anymore since $O(\sqrt{n})$ identities are included in them. But we argue that this is a good tradeoff, since the additional data can be stored in a compressed format cuckoo filter as mentioned in Sect. 5.1.

## 6  Conclusion

Our work gives two optimizations that reduce the concrete cost of RBE. The first optimization maintains the excellent asymptotic complexity of existing RBE schemes while reducing the ciphertext size by 15% and the computation cost, incurred by the decryptor, by 30%. The second optimization relaxes the public parameter size from $\mathsf{poly}(\lambda, \log n)$ to $\mathsf{poly}(\lambda, \sqrt{n})$. Combining the two optimizations, the ciphertext size is reduced by 57.5% on average (e.g., from 11 to 4.5 TB when an RBE deployment supports 2 billion users).

Although our contribution does not make RBE practical, we believe it is a significant step in the right direction. A promising future work could study public key operations that are garbled-circuit friendly. The communication cost could be significantly reduced if such a primitives exist.

**Acknowledgments.** This work was supported in part by CyberSecurity Research Flanders with reference number VR20192203, by ERC Advanced Grant ERC-2015-AdG-IMPaCT, by the Defense Advanced Research Projects Agency (DARPA) and Space and Naval Warfare Systems Center, Pacific (SSC Pacific) under contract No. FA8750-19-C-0502 (Approved for Public Release, Distribution Unlimited), and by the FWO under an Odysseus project GOH9718N. Any opinions, findings and conclusions or recommendations expressed in this material are those of the author(s) and do not necessarily reflect the views of the ERC, DARPA, the US Government or the FWO. The U.S. Government is authorized to reproduce and distribute reprints for governmental purposes notwithstanding any copyright annotation therein.

# References

1. Al-Riyami, S.S., Paterson, K.G.: Certificateless public key cryptography. In: Laih, C.-S. (ed.) ASIACRYPT 2003. LNCS, vol. 2894, pp. 452–473. Springer, Heidelberg (2003). https://doi.org/10.1007/978-3-540-40061-5_29

2. Barak, B., et al.: On the (Im)possibility of obfuscating programs. In: Kilian, J. (ed.) CRYPTO 2001. LNCS, vol. 2139, pp. 1–18. Springer, Heidelberg (2001). https://doi.org/10.1007/3-540-44647-8_1

3. Bellare, M., Hoang, V.T., Rogaway, P.: Foundations of garbled circuits. In: Yu, T., Danezis, G., Gligor, V.D. (eds.) ACM CCS 2012, pp. 784–796. ACM Press, October 2012

4. Bernstein, D.J.: Crit-bit trees. https://cr.yp.to/critbit.html. Accessed 10 Feb 2021

5. Boneh, D., Franklin, M.: Identity-based encryption from the Weil pairing. In: Kilian, J. (ed.) CRYPTO 2001. LNCS, vol. 2139, pp. 213–229. Springer, Heidelberg (2001). https://doi.org/10.1007/3-540-44647-8_13

6. Boneh, D., Sahai, A., Waters, B.: Functional encryption: definitions and challenges. In: Ishai, Y. (ed.) TCC 2011. LNCS, vol. 6597, pp. 253–273. Springer, Heidelberg (2011). https://doi.org/10.1007/978-3-642-19571-6_16

7. Brakerski, Z., Lombardi, A., Segev, G., Vaikuntanathan, V.: Anonymous IBE, leakage resilience and circular security from new assumptions. In: Nielsen, J.B., Rijmen, V. (eds.) EUROCRYPT 2018. LNCS, vol. 10820, pp. 535–564. Springer, Cham (2018). https://doi.org/10.1007/978-3-319-78381-9_20

8. Certicom Research: SEC 2: Recommended elliptic curve domain parameters, January 2010. https://www.secg.org/sec2-v2.pdf. Accessed 26 Feb 2021

9. Chow, S.S.M.: Removing Escrow from identity-based encryption. In: Jarecki, S., Tsudik, G. (eds.) PKC 2009. LNCS, vol. 5443, pp. 256–276. Springer, Heidelberg (2009). https://doi.org/10.1007/978-3-642-00468-1_15

10. Diffie, W., Hellman, M.E.: New directions in cryptography. IEEE Trans. Inf. Theory **22**(6), 644–654 (1976)

11. Döttling, N., Garg, S., Hajiabadi, M., Masny, D.: New constructions of identity-based and key-dependent message secure encryption schemes. In: Abdalla, M., Dahab, R. (eds.) PKC 2018. LNCS, vol. 10769, pp. 3–31. Springer, Cham (2018). https://doi.org/10.1007/978-3-319-76578-5_1

12. Drmota, M., Fuchs, M., Hwang, H.K., Neininger, R.: External profile of symmetric digital search trees (extended abstract). In: 2017 Proceedings of the Meeting on Analytic Algorithmics and Combinatorics (ANALCO), pp. 124–130 (2017). https://epubs.siam.org/doi/abs/10.1137/1.9781611974775.12

13. Facebook: Two billion users-connecting the world privately, February 2020. https://about.fb.com/news/2020/02/two-billion-users/. Accessed 12 Feb 2021

14. Fan, B., Andersen, D.G., Kaminsky, M., Mitzenmacher, M.D.: Cuckoo filter: practically better than bloom. In: Proceedings of the 10th ACM International on Conference on Emerging Networking Experiments and Technologies, pp. 75–88, CoNEXT 2014. Association for Computing Machinery, New York, NY, USA (2014). https://doi.org/10.1145/2674005.2674994

15. Garg, S., Gentry, C., Halevi, S., Raykova, M., Sahai, A., Waters, B.: Candidate indistinguishability obfuscation and functional encryption for all circuits. In: 54th FOCS, pp. 40–49. IEEE Computer Society Press, October 2013

16. Garg, S., Hajiabadi, M., Mahmoody, M., Rahimi, A.: Registration-based encryption: removing private-key generator from IBE. In: Beimel, A., Dziembowski, S. (eds.) TCC 2018. LNCS, vol. 11239, pp. 689–718. Springer, Cham (2018). https://doi.org/10.1007/978-3-030-03807-6_25

17. Garg, S., Hajiabadi, M., Mahmoody, M., Rahimi, A., Sekar, S.: Registration-based encryption from standard assumptions. In: Lin, D., Sako, K. (eds.) PKC 2019. LNCS, vol. 11443, pp. 63–93. Springer, Cham (2019). https://doi.org/10.1007/978-3-030-17259-6_3

18. Goldreich, O., Micali, S., Wigderson, A.: How to play any mental game. In: Proceedings of the Nineteenth Annual ACM Symposium on Theory of Computing, pp. 218–229, STOC 1987. Association for Computing Machinery, New York, NY, USA (1987). https://doi.org/10.1145/28395.28420

19. Goldwasser, S., Micali, S.: Probabilistic encryption and how to play mental poker keeping secret all partial information. In: 14th ACM STOC, pp. 365–377. ACM Press, May 1982

20. Goyal, R., Vusirikala, S.: Verifiable registration-based encryption. In: Micciancio, D., Ristenpart, T. (eds.) CRYPTO 2020. LNCS, vol. 12170, pp. 621–651. Springer, Cham (2020). https://doi.org/10.1007/978-3-030-56784-2_21

21. Hubacek, P., Wichs, D.: On the communication complexity of secure function evaluation with long output. In: Roughgarden, T. (ed.) ITCS 2015, pp. 163–172. ACM, January 2015

22. Jayaraman, B., Li, H., Evans, D.: Decentralized certificate authorities (2017). https://arxiv.org/pdf/1706.03370.pdf

23. Kate, A., Goldberg, I.: Distributed private-key generators for identity-based cryptography. In: Garay, J.A., De Prisco, R. (eds.) SCN 2010. LNCS, vol. 6280, pp. 436–453. Springer, Heidelberg (2010). https://doi.org/10.1007/978-3-642-15317-4_27

24. Knessl, C., Szpankowski, W.: Limit laws for the height in Patricia tries. J. Algorithms 44(1), 63–97 (2002). https://doi.org/10.1016/S0196-6774(02)00212-2

25. Knuth, D.E.: The Art of Computer Programming, vol. 3, 2nd edn. Addison Wesley Longman, Redwood City (1998)

26. Kolesnikov, V., Schneider, T.: Improved garbled circuit: free XOR gates and applications. In: Aceto, L., Damgård, I., Goldberg, L.A., Halldórsson, M.M., Ingólfsdóttir, A., Walukiewicz, I. (eds.) ICALP 2008. LNCS, vol. 5126, pp. 486–498. Springer, Heidelberg (2008). https://doi.org/10.1007/978-3-540-70583-3_40

27. Langley, A.: Crit-bit trees, September 2008. https://www.imperialviolet.org/binary/critbit.pdf. Accessed 10 Feb 2021

28. Melara, M.S., Blankstein, A., Bonneau, J., Felten, E.W., Freedman, M.J.: CONIKS: bringing key transparency to end users. In: Jung, J., Holz, T. (eds.) USENIX Security 2015, pp. 383–398. USENIX Association, August 2015

29. Morrison, D.R.: Patricia-practical algorithm to retrieve information coded in alphanumeric. J. ACM 15(4), 514–534 (1968). https://doi.org/10.1145/321479.321481

30. Nilsson, S., Tikkanen, M.: An experimental study of compression methods for dynamic tries. Algorithmica **33**(1), 19–33 (2002). https://doi.org/10.1007/s00453-001-0102-y

31. Rivest, R.L., Shamir, A., Adleman, L.M.: A method for obtaining digital signatures and public-key cryptosystems. Commun. Assoc. Comput. Mach. **21**(2), 120–126 (1978)

32. Sahai, A., Waters, B.: Fuzzy identity-based encryption. In: Cramer, R. (ed.) EURO-CRYPT 2005. LNCS, vol. 3494, pp. 457–473. Springer, Heidelberg (2005). https://doi.org/10.1007/11426639_27

33. Shamir, A.: Identity-based cryptosystems and signature schemes. In: Blakley, G.R., Chaum, D. (eds.) CRYPTO 1984. LNCS, vol. 196, pp. 47–53. Springer, Heidelberg (1984). https://doi.org/10.1007/3-540-39568-7_5

34. Szpankowski, W.: Patricia tries again revisited. J. ACM **37**(4), 691–711 (1990). https://doi.org/10.1145/96559.214080

# Hash Functions

# A Note on Quantum Collision Resistance of Double-Block-Length Compression Functions

Shoichi Hirose[1]([⊠])[iD] and Hidenori Kuwakado[2]

[1] University of Fukui, Fukui, Japan
hrs_shch@u-fukui.ac.jp
[2] Kansai University, Osaka, Japan
kuwakado@kansai-u.ac.jp

**Abstract.** In 2005, Nandi presented a class of double-block-length compression functions specified as $h^{\pi}(x) := (h(x), h(\pi(x)))$, where $h$ is assumed to be a random oracle producing an $n$-bit output and $\pi$ is a non-cryptographic permutation. He showed that the collision resistance of $h^{\pi}$ is optimal if $\pi$ has no fixed point. This manuscript discusses the quantum collision resistance of $h^{\pi}(x)$. First, it shows that the quantum collision resistance of $h^{\pi}$ is not always optimal even if $\pi$ has no fixed point: One can find a colliding pair of inputs for $h^{\pi}$ with only $O(2^{n/2})$ queries to $h$ by using the Grover search if $\pi$ is an involution. Second, this manuscript shows that there really exist cases that the quantum collision resistance of $h^{\pi}$ is optimal. More precisely, a sufficient condition on $\pi$ is presented for the optimal quantum collision resistance of $h^{\pi}$, that is, any collision attack needs $\Omega(2^{2n/3})$ queries to find a colliding pair of inputs. The proof uses the recent technique of Zhandry's compressed oracle. Finally, this manuscript makes some remarks on double-block-length compression functions using a block cipher.

**Keywords:** Hash function · Compression function · Double-block-length · Grover's search · Zhandry's compressed oracle

## 1 Introduction

*Background.* Cryptographic hash functions are important primitives in cryptography and are used in almost all cryptographic schemes. SHS [7] is a standardized family of cryptographic hash functions, which are called iterated hash functions from their structure of sequential chaining of a compression function due to Merkle [18] and Damgård [5]. The hash functions in SHS have their dedicated compression functions. The other more classical method to construct a compression function is to use a block cipher. The examples are MDC-2 and MDC-4 [19]. MDC-2 is standardized in ISO/IEC 10118-2 [12]. Both MDC-2 and MDC-4 adopt double-block-length (DBL) construction to achieve sufficient level

This work was supported by JSPS KAKENHI Grant Number JP20K21798.

M. B. Paterson (Ed.): IMACC 2021, LNCS 13129, pp. 161–175, 2021.
https://doi.org/10.1007/978-3-030-92641-0_8

of collision resistance. Namely, the output length of a DBL compression function is double the output length of its component such as a block cipher.

Nandi [20] defined a class of DBL compression functions $h^\pi : \{0,1\}^m \to \{0,1\}^{2n}$ such that

$$h^\pi(x) := (h(x), h(\pi(x))),$$

where $h : \{0,1\}^m \to \{0,1\}^n$ and $\pi$ is a non-cryptographic permutation over $\{0,1\}^m$. It was shown by Nandi [20] that the collision resistance of $h^\pi$ is optimal if $h$ is a random oracle and $\pi$ has no fixed point. More precisely, it was shown that any collision attack on $h^\pi$ needs $\Omega(2^n)$ queries to $h$.

Recently, post quantum cryptography has been attracting much interest. In accordance with this trend, security analyses of cryptographic schemes against quantum attacks have become important research topics.

*Our Contribution.* We analyze the quantum collision resistance of the class of DBL compression functions $h^\pi$ assuming that $h$ is a random oracle. We show that it is not always optimal even if $\pi$ has no fixed point. First, we show a quantum collision attack which is able to find a colliding pair of inputs for $h^\pi$ with only $O(2^{n/2})$ queries to $h$ if $\pi$ is an involution, that is, $\pi \circ \pi$ is the identity permutation. The attack simply uses the Grover search [9]. Second, we present a sufficient condition on $\pi$ for the optimal quantum collision resistance of $h^\pi$, that is, $\Omega(2^{2n/3})$ query complexity. The proof uses the technique of Zhandry's compressed oracle [23] and it is similar to the proof for the lower bound of quantum collision resistance by Liu and Zhandry [16]. We also give a few examples of $\pi$ satisfying the sufficient conditions. They are quite simple and suitable for instantiation of $h^\pi$. Finally, we make some remarks on two DBL compression functions using a block cipher. Due to the non-optimality result above, the DBL compression function proposed by Hirose [10] is not optimally collision resistant against quantum adversaries. A Grover oracle of the collision attack is also presented, which is similar to that of the quantum exhaustive key search of a block cipher [8,14]. On the other hand, the DBL compression function proposed by Jonsson and Robshaw [15] uses a permutation satisfying the sufficient condition for optimal collision resistance of $h^\pi$, though it is still an open question if the DBL compression function by Jonsson and Robshaw is optimally collision resistant against quantum adversaries.

*Other Related Work.* Brassard et al. [3] presented an algorithm to find a colliding pair of inputs for any $r$-to-one hash function with $O((N_d/r)^{1/3})$ quantum queries, where $N_d$ is the cardinality of the domain of the given hash function. Zhandry [22] showed the $\Theta(N_r^{1/3})$ quantum query complexity to find a colliding pair of inputs for any hash function with the cardinality of its range $N_r$.

Chauhan et al. [4] presented a quantum collision attack on the DBL compression function [10] instantiated with AES-256. Their attack uses a quantum version [6,11] of the rebound attack [17].

DBL compression functions using a tweakable block cipher are adopted by a leakage-resilient AEAD mode TEDT [1] and a family of lightweight cryptographic schemes Romulus [13].

*Organization.* Section 2 introduces some notations and definitions necessary for the discussions. Section 3 describes the construction of DBL compression functions proposed by Nandi and its classical collision resistance. Section 4 discusses the quantum collision resistance of Nandi's DBL compression functions. Section 5 makes some remarks on the DBL compression functions using a block cipher related to the results in the previous section. Section 6 gives a brief concluding remark.

## 2    Preliminaries

For integers $n_1$ and $n_2$ such that $n_1 \leq n_2$, let $[n_1, n_2]$ be the set of integers between $n_1$ and $n_2$ inclusive.

### 2.1   Collision Resistance

For a hash function, collision resistance means the intractability of finding a colliding pair of inputs. A pair of inputs to a hash function are called colliding if they are distinct and mapped to the same output by the hash function.

Let $\mathsf{H}^P$ be a hash function using $P$ as its component. The collision resistance of $\mathsf{H}^P$ is often discussed under the assumption that $P$ is an ideal primitive such as a random oracle or an ideal block cipher [2]. Let $\mathbf{A}$ be an adversary trying to find a colliding pair of inputs for $\mathsf{H}^P$. $\mathbf{A}$ is allowed to make queries to $P$. Then, the advantage of $\mathbf{A}$ is defined as

$$\mathrm{Adv}^{\mathrm{col}}_{\mathsf{H}^P}(\mathbf{A}) := \Pr[(x, x') \leftarrow \mathbf{A}^P : \mathsf{H}^P(x) = \mathsf{H}^P(x') \wedge x \neq x'].$$

The maximum advantage with at most $q$ queries is defined as

$$\mathrm{Adv}^{\mathrm{col}}_{\mathsf{H}^P}(q) := \max_{\mathbf{A}} \mathrm{Adv}^{\mathrm{col}}_{\mathsf{H}^P}(\mathbf{A}),$$

where $\mathbf{A}^P$ makes at most $q$ queries. If quantum adversaries are concerned, then $\mathrm{Adv}^{\mathrm{col}}_{\mathsf{H}^P}$ is denoted by $\mathrm{Adv}^{\mathrm{qcol}}_{\mathsf{H}^P}$.

### 2.2   Quantum Computation

For quantum computation [21], we assume the quantum circuit model. We further assume that any unitary transformation can be implemented by a quantum circuit. For a unitary transformation $U$, $U^\dagger$ is its Hermitian conjugate.

Some quantum gates are explicit in the remaining parts. $I$, $X$, and $H$ are quantum gates for a single qubit defined as follows:

$$I := |0\rangle \langle 0| + |1\rangle \langle 1|, \qquad\qquad X := |1\rangle \langle 0| + |0\rangle \langle 1|,$$

$$H := \frac{|0\rangle + |1\rangle}{\sqrt{2}} \langle 0| + \frac{|0\rangle - |1\rangle}{\sqrt{2}} \langle 1|.$$

The controlled NOT is a quantum gate for two qubits defined as

$$|0\rangle\langle 0| \otimes I + |1\rangle\langle 1| \otimes X.$$

The Toffoli gate is a quantum gate for three qubits defined as

$$(I \otimes I - |11\rangle\langle 11|) \otimes I + |11\rangle\langle 11| \otimes X.$$

**Grover Search.** The quantum search algorithm of Grover [9] is usually described as an algorithm to find a solution $x^*$ of a given Boolean function $f : \{0,1\}^m \to \{0,1\}$ such that $f(x^*) = 1$. The Grover search uses a unitary operator $O_f$ called the Grover oracle such that $O_f(|x\rangle \otimes |z\rangle) := |x\rangle \otimes |z \oplus f(x)\rangle$, where $x \in \{0,1\}^m$ and $z \in \{0,1\}$. Let $|-\rangle := (|0\rangle - |1\rangle)/\sqrt{2}$. Then, $O_f(|x\rangle \otimes |-\rangle) = (-1)^{f(x)}|x\rangle \otimes |-\rangle$.

The Grover search first prepares the state

$$H^{\otimes(m+1)}(I^{\otimes m} \otimes X)(|0^m\rangle \otimes |0\rangle) = \frac{1}{\sqrt{2^m}} \sum_{x \in \{0,1\}^m} |x\rangle \otimes |-\rangle.$$

Then, it repeatedly applies the Grover operator

$$G := ((H^{\otimes m}(2|0^m\rangle\langle 0^m| - I^{\otimes m})H^{\otimes m}) \otimes I)O_f$$

to the state. Finally, it measures the first $m$ qubits.

Let $M$ be the number of solutions of $f$, that is, $M := |\{x \mid f(x) = 1\}|$. Then, by applying the Grover operator $q$ times, one can find a solution of $f$ with probability $O(q^2 M/2^m)$.

**Zhandry's Compressed Oracle [23].** Let $F : \{0,1\}^m \to \{0,1\}^\ell$ be a random oracle. Let $\mathbf{A}$ be a quantum adversary with oracle access to $F$. We assume that a basis state of $\mathbf{A}$ is represented as $|x, z, w\rangle$, where $x \in \{0,1\}^m$ is a query register, $z \in \{0,1\}^\ell$ is a response register, and $w \in \{0,1\}^l$ is a private working register. We also assume that a basis state of the random oracle $F$ is represented as $|T_F\rangle$, where $T_F \in \{0,1\}^{\ell 2^m}$ is the table of $F$. Namely, $|T_F\rangle := |F(0)\rangle \otimes |F(1)\rangle \otimes \cdots \otimes |F(2^m - 1)\rangle$. Then, a query of $\mathbf{A}$ to $F$ and the corresponding response can be represented by a unitary operator StO such that

$$\mathsf{StO}(|x, z, w\rangle \otimes |T_F\rangle) := |x, z \oplus F(x), w\rangle \otimes |T_F\rangle.$$

Zhandry called it a standard oracle. He also introduced a phase oracle such that

$$\mathsf{PhO}(|x, z, w\rangle \otimes |T_F\rangle) := |x, z, w\rangle \otimes ((-1)^{F(x) \cdot z}|T_F\rangle).$$

The unitary operator PhO is equivalent to StO in that

$$\mathsf{PhO} = (I^{\otimes m} \otimes H^{\otimes \ell} \otimes I^{\otimes l} \otimes I^{\otimes \ell 2^m}) \circ \mathsf{StO} \circ (I^{\otimes m} \otimes H^{\otimes \ell} \otimes I^{\otimes l} \otimes I^{\otimes \ell 2^m}).$$

For these oracles, the random oracle $F$ is initialized to the uniform superposition of all the basis states:

$$\frac{1}{\sqrt{2^{\ell 2^m}}} \sum_{T_F \in \{0,1\}^{\ell 2^m}} |T_F\rangle.$$

Zhandry further presented the compressed standard oracle and the compressed phase oracle which implement the lazy evaluation of a quantum random oracle. He also confirmed the equivalence of these oracles to the standard oracle and the phase oracle. Here, we only refer to the compressed phase oracle.

For the compressed phase oracle, the random oracle is simulated by a superposition of databases. Suppose that $\mathbf{A}$ makes at most $q$ quantum queries to the random oracle. Then, a database $D$ is an element in $((\{0,1\}^m \cup \{\bot\}) \times \{0,1\}^{\ell})^q$. Specifically, $D$ is represented as

$$\underbrace{((x_1, y_1), (x_2, y_2), \ldots, (x_k, y_k), (\bot, 0^{\ell}), \ldots, (\bot, 0^{\ell})),}_{q \text{ elements in } (\{0,1\}^m \cup \{\bot\}) \times \{0,1\}^{\ell}}$$

where $x_i \neq \bot$ for $i \in [1,k]$ and $x_1 < x_2 < \cdots < x_k$. For $(x_i, y_i) \in \{0,1\}^m \times \{0,1\}^{\ell}$, let $(x_i, y_i) \in D$ and $D(x_i) = y_i$ represent that $(x_i, y_i)$ appears in $D$. For $x_i \in \{0,1\}^m$, let $D(x_i) = \bot$ represent that $(x_i, y_i) \notin D$ for any $y_i \in \{0,1\}^{\ell}$. $D(x_i) = y_i$ means that the random oracle $F$ is specified to output $y_i$ for the input $x_i$. $D(x_i) = \bot$ means that the output of the random oracle $F$ is not yet specified for the input $x_i$. Let $|D|$ represent the number of elements $(x,y)$ in $D$ such that $x \neq \bot$.

For a database $D$ such that $D(x) = \bot$ and $|D| < q$, let $D \cup (x,y)$ represent that $(\bot, 0^{\ell})$ is removed from $D$ and $(x,y)$ is added to $D$ in its appropriate position. To describe how the compressed phase oracle processes a query, a unitary operator $\mathsf{StdDecomp}_x$ over a database is introduced. It works as follows:

– For $D$ such that $D(x) = \bot$ and $|D| < q$,

$$\mathsf{StdDecomp}_x |D\rangle = \frac{1}{\sqrt{2^{\ell}}} \sum_{y \in \{0,1\}^{\ell}} |D \cup (x,y)\rangle.$$

– For $D$ such that $D(x) = \bot$ and $|D| < q$,

$$\mathsf{StdDecomp}_x \left( \frac{1}{\sqrt{2^{\ell}}} \sum_{y \in \{0,1\}^{\ell}} (-1)^{z \cdot y} |D \cup (x,y)\rangle \right)$$

$$= \begin{cases} \frac{1}{\sqrt{2^{\ell}}} \sum\limits_{y \in \{0,1\}^{\ell}} (-1)^{z \cdot y} |D \cup (x,y)\rangle & \text{if } z \neq 0^{\ell}, \\ |D\rangle & \text{if } z = 0^{\ell}. \end{cases}$$

Let $\mathsf{StdDecomp}$ be a unitary operator over $|x, z, w\rangle \otimes |D\rangle$ defined as follows:

$$\mathsf{StdDecomp}(|x, z, w\rangle \otimes |D\rangle) := |x, z, w\rangle \otimes (\mathsf{StdDecomp}_x |D\rangle).$$

Let CPhO' be a unitary operator such that

$$\text{CPhO}'(|x, z, w\rangle \otimes |D\rangle) := (-1)^{z \cdot D(x)} |x, z, w\rangle \otimes |D\rangle,$$

where $D(x) \neq \perp$. The compressed phase oracle CPhO is defined as follows:

$$\text{CPhO} := \text{StdDecomp} \circ \text{CPhO}' \circ \text{StdDecomp}.$$

Initially, only $(\perp, 0^\ell)$'s appear in the database.

Zhandry showed the relationship between the output of an adversary on the random oracle and the entries of compressed standard/phase oracle database:

**Lemma 1 ([23]).** *Let $F$ be a random oracle producing an $\ell$-bit output for each input. Let $\mathbf{A}$ be a quantum algorithm making queries to $F$ and outputting a tuple $(x_1, \ldots, x_k; y_1, \ldots, y_k)$. Let $\mathcal{R}$ be a collection of such tuples. Suppose that, with probability $p$, $\mathbf{A}$ outputs a tuple such that (1) the tuple is in $\mathcal{R}$ and (2) $F(x_i) = y_i$ for every $i \in [1, k]$. Consider running $\mathbf{A}$ with the compressed standard/phase oracle and suppose that the database $D$ is measured after $\mathbf{A}$ produces its output. Let $p'$ be the probability that (1) the tuple is in $\mathcal{R}$ and (2) $D(x_i) = y_i$ for every $i \in [1, k]$. Then,*

$$\sqrt{p} \leq \sqrt{p'} + \sqrt{k/2^\ell}.$$

## 3    Nandi's Class of DBL Compression Functions

Let $m$ and $n$ be positive integers such that $m > 2n$. Let $h : \{0, 1\}^m \to \{0, 1\}^n$. Let $\pi$ be a permutation over $\{0, 1\}^m$. $a \in \{0, 1\}^m$ is called a fixed point of $\pi$ if $\pi(a) = a$. $\pi$ is called an involution if $\pi^2 := \pi \circ \pi$ is the identity permutation, that is, $\pi(\pi(x)) = x$ for every $x \in \{0, 1\}^m$.

Nandi [20] defined a class of DBL compression functions $h^\pi : \{0, 1\}^m \to \{0, 1\}^{2n}$ such that

$$h^\pi(x) := (h(x), h(\pi(x))).$$

He discussed the classical collision resistance of $h^\pi$ on the assumption that $h$ is a random oracle. He showed that the classical collision resistance of $h^\pi$ is optimal if $\pi$ has no fixed points. Namely, any classical adversary needs $\Omega(2^n)$ queries to find a colliding pair of inputs for $h^\pi$ with some constant probability:

**Theorem 1 (Theorem 1 [20]).** *Suppose that $h$ is a random oracle and that $\pi$ has no fixed points. Then,*

$$\text{Adv}_{h^\pi}^{\text{col}}(q) = \begin{cases} O(q^2/2^{2n}) & \text{if } \pi^2 \text{ has no fixed points,} \\ O(q/2^n) & \text{otherwise.} \end{cases}$$

# 4   Quantum Collision Resistance of Nandi's DBL Compression Functions

## 4.1   Result on Non-optimality

It is shown that the quantum collision resistance of $h^\pi$ is not optimal if $\pi$ is an involution:

**Theorem 2.** *Suppose that $h$ is a random oracle and that $\pi$ is an involution. Then,*

$$\mathrm{Adv}_{h^\pi}^{\mathrm{qcol}}(q) = \Omega(q^2/2^n).$$

*Proof.* Since $\pi$ is an involution,

$$h^\pi(\pi(x)) = (h(\pi(x)), h(\pi^2(x))) = (h(\pi(x)), h(x)).$$

Thus, $x$ and $\pi(x)$ are a colliding pair of inputs for $h^\pi$ if $h(x) = h(\pi(x))$. Let $f : \{0,1\}^m \to \{0,1\}$ be a Boolean function such that $f(x) = 1$ if and only if $h(x) = h(\pi(x))$. Then, since $h$ is a random oracle, the expected value of $|\{x \mid f(x) = 1\}|$ is $2^{m-n}$. Thus, by applying the Grover search to $f$, the probability that a colliding pair of inputs for $h^\pi$ are found with $q$ iterations is $\Omega(q^2/2^n)$.     □

## 4.2   Result on Optimality

It has been shown that the quantum collision resistance of $h^\pi$ is not optimal if $\pi$ is an involution. If $\pi$ is an involution with no fixed points, then its domain $\{0,1\}^m$ is divided into pairs of elements $\{x, \pi(x)\}$. In the remaining part, permutations satisfying the following property are considered:

**Lemma 2.** *For $\pi$, suppose that $\pi^4$ is the identity permutation and that, for any $x \in \{0,1\}^m$, $x$, $\pi(x)$, $\pi^2(x)$, and $\pi^3(x)$ are distinct from each other. For $x \in \{0,1\}^m$, let $\mathcal{C}^\pi(x) := \{x, \pi(x), \pi^2(x), \pi^3(x)\}$. Then,*

- $\mathcal{C}^\pi(x) \cap \mathcal{C}^\pi(x') = \emptyset$ *if* $\mathcal{C}^\pi(x) \neq \mathcal{C}^\pi(x')$, *and*
- $\bigcup_{x \in \{0,1\}^m} \mathcal{C}^\pi(x) = \{0,1\}^m.$

The proof of Lemma 2 is easy and omitted.

*Example 1.* Let $c \in \{0,1\}^{m/2} \setminus \{0\}$ be a constant. Then, the following permutations over $\{0,1\}^m$ satisfy the condition specified in Lemma 2:

- $(x_0, x_1) \mapsto (x_0 \oplus x_1, x_1 \oplus c)$;
- $(x_0, x_1) \mapsto (x_1, x_0 \oplus c)$,

where $x_0, x_1 \in \{0,1\}^{m/2}$. Both of them are quite simple and seem suitable for instantiation of $h^\pi$.

The following theorem implies that the quantum collision resistance of $h^\pi$ is optimal if $\pi$ satisfies the condition given in Lemma 2. Namely, to find a colliding pair of inputs for $h^\pi$ with some constant probability, any quantum adversary needs $\Omega(2^{2n/3})$ queries.

**Theorem 3.** *For $\pi$, suppose that $\pi^4$ is the identity permutation and that, for every $x \in \{0,1\}^m$, $x$, $\pi(x)$, $\pi^2(x)$, and $\pi^3(x)$ are distinct from each other. Then,*

$$\mathrm{Adv}_{h^\pi}^{\mathrm{qcol}}(q) = O(q^3/2^{2n}).$$

A pair of colliding inputs $x$ and $x'$ for $h^\pi$ are divided into two classes based on whether $x' \in C^\pi(x)$ or $x' \notin C^\pi(x)$. Lemmas 3 and 4, which are given below, show the intractability of finding a pair of colliding inputs $x$ and $x'$ for $h^\pi$ which satisfy $x' \in C^\pi(x)$ and $x' \notin C^\pi(x)$, respectively. Thus, Theorem 3 directly follows from them. The proofs of Lemmas 3 and 4 are similar to that of Theorem 4 by Liu and Zhandry [16].

Let $\mathcal{X}^\pi := \{x \,|\, x \in \{0,1\}^m$ is the lexicographically first element in $C^\pi(x)\}$. Then, $|\mathcal{X}^\pi| = 2^{m-2}$. Let $g : \mathcal{X}^\pi \to \{0,1\}^{4n}$ be defined as follows:

$$g(x) := (h(x), h(\pi(x)), h(\pi^2(x)), h(\pi^3(x))).$$

Then, $g$ is a random oracle since $h$ is a random oracle.

**Lemma 3.** *For $\pi$, suppose that $\pi^4$ is the identity permutation and that, for any $x \in \{0,1\}^m$, $x$, $\pi(x)$, $\pi^2(x)$ and $\pi^3(x)$ are distinct from each other. Then, for any adversary making at most $q$ quantum queries, the probability that it succeeds in finding a colliding pair of inputs $x$ and $x'$ for $h^\pi$ satisfying $x' \in C^\pi(x)$ is $O(q^2/2^{2n})$.*

*Proof.* The problem to find a colliding pair of inputs $x$ and $x'$ for $h^\pi$ satisfying $x' \in C^\pi(x)$ is equivalent to the problem to find an input $x \in \mathcal{X}^\pi$ for $g$ satisfying (1) $g_0(x) = g_1(x) = g_2(x)$, (2) $g_0(x) = g_2(x)$ and $g_1(x) = g_3(x)$, or (3) $g_3(x) = g_0(x) = g_1(x)$, where $g(x) = (g_0(x), g_1(x), g_2(x), g_3(x)) \in (\{0,1\}^n)^4$.

Let $\mathcal{Y}_{c1}$ be the sets of $y = (y_0, y_1, y_2, y_3) \in (\{0,1\}^n)^4$ satisfying (1) $y_0 = y_1 = y_2$, (2) $y_0 = y_2$ and $y_1 = y_3$, or (3) $y_3 = y_0 = y_1$. Then, $|\mathcal{Y}_{c1}| \leq 3 \cdot 2^{2n}$.

Let $P_{c1}$ be the projection spanned by all the states containing a database $D$ for $g$ including at least a tuple $(x^*, y^*) \in \mathcal{X}^\pi \times \mathcal{Y}_{c1}$. Let

$$\mathcal{D}_{c1} = \{D \,|\, D \text{ has at least an entry } (x^*, y^*) \in \mathcal{X}^\pi \times \mathcal{Y}_{c1}\}.$$

Then,

$$P_{c1} = \sum_{x,z,w} \sum_{D \in \mathcal{D}_{c1}} |x, z, w, D\rangle\langle x, z, w, D|.$$

For $k \in [1, q]$, let $|\psi_{k-1}\rangle$ be the state right before the $k$-th oracle query is made and $|\psi_k'\rangle$ be the state right after the $k$-th oracle query is made. Let $|\psi_0'\rangle$ be the initial state and $|\psi_q\rangle$ be the state right before the measurement. Let $O_g$ be the operator making an oracle query to $g$. Then, $|\psi_k'\rangle = O_g|\psi_{k-1}\rangle$. For $k \in [0, q]$, let $U_k$ be the operator such that $|\psi_k\rangle = U_k|\psi_k'\rangle$. Thus, $U_k$ represents the local computation on $|x, z, w\rangle$ by the adversary and it does not affect the database.

A colliding pair of inputs $x$ and $x'$ for $h^\pi$ satisfying $x' \in C^\pi(x)$ is found with probability at most $\|P_{c1}|\psi_q\rangle\|^2 := \langle\psi_q|P_{c1}^\dagger P_{c1}|\psi_q\rangle = \langle\psi_q|P_{c1}|\psi_q\rangle$. In the remaining parts, an upper bound of $\|P_{c1}|\psi_k\rangle\|$ is evaluated.

Since $U_k$ does not affect the database,

$$\|P_{c1}|\psi_k\rangle\| = \|P_{c1}U_k|\psi_k'\rangle\| = \|P_{c1}|\psi_k'\rangle\|.$$

In addition,

$$
\begin{aligned}
\|P_{c1}|\psi_k'\rangle\| &= \|P_{c1}O_g|\psi_{k-1}\rangle\| \\
&= \|P_{c1}O_g(P_{c1} + (I^{\otimes L} - P_{c1}))|\psi_{k-1}\rangle\| \\
&\leq \|P_{c1}O_gP_{c1}|\psi_{k-1}\rangle\| + \|P_{c1}O_g(I^{\otimes L} - P_{c1})|\psi_{k-1}\rangle\| \\
&\leq \|P_{c1}|\psi_{k-1}\rangle\| + \|P_{c1}O_g(I^{\otimes L} - P_{c1})|\psi_{k-1}\rangle\|,
\end{aligned}
$$

where $L$ is the number of qubits in $|\psi_{k-1}\rangle$. For the last term, let

$$|\psi_{k-1}\rangle = \sum_{x,z,w}\sum_D \alpha_{x,z,w,D}|x,z,w\rangle \otimes |D\rangle.$$

Then,

$$\|P_{c1}O_g(I - P_{c1})|\psi_{k-1}\rangle\| = \left\|P_{c1}O_g \sum_{x,z,w}\sum_{D\notin\mathcal{D}_{c1}} \alpha_{x,z,w,D}|x,z,w\rangle \otimes |D\rangle\right\|.$$

If $D(x) \neq \bot$, then $D(x) \notin \mathcal{Y}_{c1}$ since $D \notin \mathcal{D}_{c1}$. Thus,

$$
\begin{aligned}
&\left\|P_{c1}O_g \sum_{x,z,w}\sum_{D\notin\mathcal{D}_{c1}} \alpha_{x,z,w,D}|x,z,w\rangle \otimes |D\rangle\right\| \\
&= \left\|P_{c1} \sum_{x,z,w}\sum_{D\notin\mathcal{D}_{c1},D(x)=\bot} \frac{1}{\sqrt{2^{4n}}}\sum_{y'}(-1)^{z\cdot y'}\alpha_{x,z,w,D}|x,z,w\rangle \otimes |D\cup(x,y')\rangle\right\| \\
&= \left\|\frac{1}{\sqrt{2^{4n}}} \sum_{x,z,w}\sum_{D\notin\mathcal{D}_{c1},D(x)=\bot}\sum_{y'\in\mathcal{Y}_{c1}}(-1)^{z\cdot y'}\alpha_{x,z,w,D}|x,z,w\rangle \otimes |D\cup(x,y')\rangle\right\| \\
&= \left(\frac{1}{2^{4n}} \sum_{x,z,w}\sum_{D\notin\mathcal{D}_{c1},D(x)=\bot}\sum_{y'\in\mathcal{Y}_{c1}}|\alpha_{x,z,w,D}|^2\right)^{1/2} \\
&\leq \left(\frac{3\cdot 2^{2n}}{2^{4n}} \sum_{x,z,w}\sum_{D\notin\mathcal{D}_{c1},D(x)=\bot}|\alpha_{x,z,w,D}|^2\right)^{1/2} \\
&\leq \frac{\sqrt{3}}{2^n}.
\end{aligned}
$$

Thus,

$$\|P_{c1}|\psi_k\rangle\| \leq \|P_{c1}|\psi_{k-1}\rangle\| + \sqrt{3}/2^n,$$

which implies $\|P_{c1}|\psi_q\rangle\| = O(q/2^n)$. This completes the proof together with Lemma 1. $\qquad\square$

**Lemma 4.** *For $\pi$, suppose that $\pi^4$ is the identity permutation and that, for any $x \in \{0,1\}^m$, $x$, $\pi(x)$, $\pi^2(x)$ and $\pi^3(x)$ are distinct from each other. Then, for any adversary making at most $q$ quantum queries, the probability that it succeeds in finding a colliding pair of inputs $x$ and $x'$ for $h^\pi$ satisfying $x' \notin C^\pi(x)$ is $O(q^3/2^{2n})$.*

*Proof.* The problem to find a colliding pair of inputs $x$ and $x'$ for $h^\pi$ satisfying $x' \notin C^\pi(x)$ is equivalent to the problem to find a pair of distinct inputs $x, x' \in \mathcal{X}^\pi$ for $g$ satisfying $(g_i(x), g_{i+1 \bmod 4}(x)) = (g_j(x'), g_{j+1 \bmod 4}(x'))$ for some $i, j \in [0,3]$, where $g(x) = (g_0(x), g_1(x), g_2(x), g_3(x)) \in (\{0,1\}^n)^4$.

Let $P_{c2}$ be the projection spanned by all the states containing a database $D$ for $g$ including at least a pair of tuples $(x^*, y^*)$ and $(x^{**}, y^{**})$ in $\mathcal{X}^\pi \times (\{0,1\}^n)^4$ such that $(y_i^*, y_{i+1 \bmod 4}^*) = (y_j^{**}, y_{j+1 \bmod 4}^{**})$ for some $i, j \in [0,3]$, where $y^* = (y_0^*, y_1^*, y_2^*, y_3^*)$ and $y^{**} = (y_0^{**}, y_1^{**}, y_2^{**}, y_3^{**})$. Then,

$$P_{c2} = \sum_{x,z,w} \sum_{D \in \mathcal{D}_{c2}} |x,z,w,D\rangle\langle x,z,w,D|,$$

where $\mathcal{D}_{c2}$ is the set of the databases including at least a pair of tuples described above.

For $k \in [1,q]$, let $|\psi_{k-1}\rangle$ be the state right before the $k$-th oracle query is made and $|\psi_k'\rangle$ be the state right after the $k$-th oracle query is made. Let $|\psi_0'\rangle$ be the initial state and $|\psi_q\rangle$ be the state just before the measurement. Let $O_g$ be the operator making an oracle query. Then, $|\psi_k'\rangle = O_g|\psi_{k-1}\rangle$. For $k \in [0,q]$, let $U_k$ be the operator such that $|\psi_k\rangle = U_k|\psi_k'\rangle$. Thus, $U_k$ represents the local computation on $|x,z,w\rangle$ by the adversary and it does not affect the database.

A colliding pair of inputs $x$ and $x'$ for $h^\pi$ satisfying $x' \notin C^\pi(x)$ is found with probability at most $\|P_{c2}|\psi_q\rangle\|^2$. In the remaining parts, an upper bound of $\|P_{c2}|\psi_k\rangle\|$ is evaluated.

Since $U_k$ does not affect the database,

$$\|P_{c2}|\psi_k\rangle\| = \|P_{c2}U_k|\psi_k'\rangle\| = \|P_{c2}|\psi_k'\rangle\|.$$

In addition,

$$\begin{aligned}\|P_{c2}|\psi_k'\rangle\| &= \|P_{c2}O_g|\psi_{k-1}\rangle\| \\ &= \|P_{c2}O_g(P_{c2} + (I^{\otimes L} - P_{c2}))|\psi_{k-1}\rangle\| \\ &\leq \|P_{c2}O_gP_{c2}|\psi_{k-1}\rangle\| + \|P_{c2}O_g(I^{\otimes L} - P_{c2})|\psi_{k-1}\rangle\| \\ &\leq \|P_{c2}|\psi_{k-1}\rangle\| + \|P_{c2}O_g(I^{\otimes L} - P_{c2})|\psi_{k-1}\rangle\|,\end{aligned}$$

where $L$ is the number of qubits in $|\psi_{k-1}\rangle$. For the last term, let

$$|\psi_{k-1}\rangle = \sum_{x,z,w} \sum_D \alpha_{x,z,w,D}|x,z,w\rangle \otimes |D\rangle.$$

Then,

$$\|P_{c2}O_g(I - P_{c2})|\psi_{k-1}\rangle\| = \left\| P_{c2}O_g \sum_{x,z,w} \sum_{D \notin \mathcal{D}_{c2}} \alpha_{x,z,w,D}|x,z,w\rangle \otimes |D\rangle \right\|.$$

If $D(x) \neq \perp$, then $D \notin \mathcal{D}_{c2}$ and the database after the application of $O_g$ has no pair of tuples containing a collision for $h^\pi$. For $D \notin \mathcal{D}_{c2}$, let $\mathcal{Y}_D$ be the set of $y' = (y'_0, y'_1, y'_2, y'_3) \in (\{0,1\}^n)^4$ such that there exists $(x^*, y^*) \in D$ satisfying $(y_i^*, y_{i+1 \bmod 4}^*) = (y'_j, y'_{j+1 \bmod 4})$ for some $i, j \in [0,3]$. Then,

$$
\left\| P_{c2} O_g \sum_{x,z,w} \sum_{D \notin \mathcal{D}_{c2}} \alpha_{x,z,w,D} |x, z, w\rangle \otimes |D\rangle \right\|
$$

$$
= \left\| P_{c2} \sum_{x,z,w} \sum_{D \notin \mathcal{D}_{c2}, D(x)=\perp} \frac{1}{\sqrt{2^{4n}}} \sum_{y'} (-1)^{z \cdot y'} \alpha_{x,z,w,D} |x, z, w\rangle \otimes |D \cup (x, y')\rangle \right\|
$$

$$
= \left\| \frac{1}{\sqrt{2^{4n}}} \sum_{x,z,w} \sum_{D \notin \mathcal{D}_{c2}, D(x)=\perp} \sum_{y' \in \mathcal{Y}_D} (-1)^{z \cdot y'} \alpha_{x,z,w,D} |x, z, w\rangle \otimes |D \cup (x, y')\rangle \right\|
$$

$$
= \left( \frac{1}{2^{4n}} \sum_{x,z,w} \sum_{D \notin \mathcal{D}_{c2}, D(x)=\perp} \sum_{y' \in \mathcal{Y}_D} |\alpha_{x,z,w,D}|^2 \right)^{1/2}
$$

$$
\leq \left( \frac{16 \cdot 2^{2n}(k-1)}{2^{4n}} \sum_{x,z,w} \sum_{D \notin \mathcal{D}_{c2}, D(x)=\perp} |\alpha_{x,z,w,D}|^2 \right)^{1/2}
$$

$$
\leq \frac{4\sqrt{k-1}}{2^n}.
$$

Altogether,

$$
\|P_{c2}|\psi_k\rangle\| \leq \|P_{c2}|\psi_{k-1}\rangle\| + 4\sqrt{k-1}/2^n.
$$

Thus,

$$
\|P_{c2}|\psi_q\rangle\| \leq \frac{1}{2^{n-2}} \sum_{k=1}^{q-1} \sqrt{k} \leq \frac{(q-1)\sqrt{q-1}}{2^{n-2}},
$$

which implies $\|P_{c2}|\psi_q\rangle\| = O(q^{3/2}/2^n)$. This completes the proof together with Lemma 1. □

## 5    Observation on DBL Compression Functions Using a Block Cipher

### 5.1    Related to Non-optimality Result

Let $E : \{0,1\}^\ell \times \{0,1\}^n \to \{0,1\}^n$ be a block cipher with its key space $\{0,1\}^\ell$ and $\ell > n$. Let $h_E : \{0,1\}^\ell \times \{0,1\}^n \to \{0,1\}^n$ be the function such that $h_E(x_0, x_1) := E(x_0, x_1) \oplus x_1$. Let $\varpi$ be a permutation over $\{0,1\}^\ell \times \{0,1\}^n$ such that $\varpi(x_0, x_1) := (x_0, x_1 \oplus c)$, where $c \in \{0,1\}^n \setminus \{0\}$ is a constant. Then, $h_E^\varpi$ represents the DBL compression function using the block cipher $E$ proposed by Hirose [10]. It is depicted in Fig. 1a.

Since $\varpi$ is an involution, the collision attack presented in the proof of Theorem 2 can be applied to the DBL compression function $h_E^\varpi$. The Grover oracle of the collision attack is depicted in Fig. 2, which is very similar to that of the exhaustive key search for a block cipher by Jaques et al. [14]. The components of the oracle is specified in Fig. 3. $U_E$ is the unitary operator of $E$. For the component to check equality in Fig. 3b, eq is a predicate such that eq$(u, c) = 1$ if and only if $u = c$. The component in Fig. 3b can be constructed, for example, with a controlled NOT gate, $O(n)$ Toffoli gates, $O(n)$ $X$ gates, and $O(n)$ additional qubits [21]. Notice that $E(x_0, x_1) = E(x_0, x_1 \oplus c) \oplus c$ if $h_E(x_0, x_1) = h_E(\varpi(x_0, x_1))$. For the Grover oracle in Fig. 2, the plaintext inputs to $U_E$ are fixed constants $0^n$ and $c$.

*Remark 1.* It was shown [10] that the collision resistance of the Merkle-Damgård iterated hash function using $h_E^\varpi$ can be reduced only to the intractability of finding a colliding pair of inputs $(x_0, x_1)$ and $(x_0', x_1')$ for $h_E^\varpi$ such that $(x_0', x_1') \neq \varpi(x_0, x_1)$.

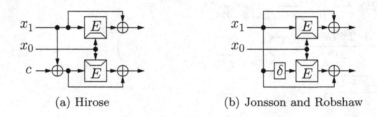

(a) Hirose                    (b) Jonsson and Robshaw

**Fig. 1.** DBL compression functions using a block cipher

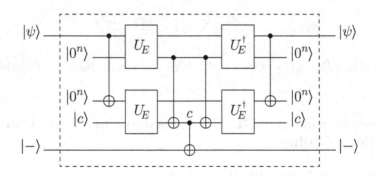

**Fig. 2.** Grover oracle for the collision attack

## 5.2   Related to Optimality Result

Let $\delta$ be a permutation over $\{0, 1\}^n$ applying addition of 1 modulo 4 to the two most significant bits of an input, which is equivalent to addition of $2^{n-2}$ modulo $2^n$. Then, $\hat{h}_E^\delta(x_0, x_1) := (E(x_0, x_1) \oplus x_1, E(x_0, \delta(x_1)) \oplus x_1)$ represents the DBL compression function using the block cipher $E$ proposed by Jonsson and Robshaw [15], which is depicted in Fig. 1b.

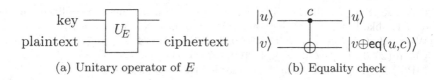

(a) Unitary operator of $E$          (b) Equality check

**Fig. 3.** Components of the Grover oracle in Fig. 2

Addition of 1 modulo 4 to $(b_1, b_0) \in \{0,1\}^2$ can be represented by a permutation shown in Example 1: $(b_1, b_0) \mapsto (b_1 \oplus b_0, b_0 \oplus 1)$. Thus, $\delta$ satisfies the sufficient condition for optimal quantum collision resistance. However, it is still an open question if $\hat{h}_E^\delta$ is optimally collision resistant against quantum adversaries.

## 6   Conclusion

We have analyzed the quantum collision resistance of the compression function $h^\pi$ assuming that $h$ is a random oracle. Though our analysis has covered some permutations $\pi$ of practical interest, it leaves the quantum collision resistance for the other permutations as an open question. It is also an open question if there exists an optimally collision resistant DBL compression function using a block cipher against quantum adversaries.

**Acknowledgements.** We would like to thank the reviewers for their valuable comments to improve the presentation of this manuscript. One of the reviewers pointed out our misunderstanding about Theorem 1 by Nandi [20].

## References

1. Berti, F., Guo, C., Pereira, O., Peters, T., Standaert, F.: TEDT, a leakage-resist AEAD mode for high physical security applications. IACR Trans. Cryptographic Hardware Embedded Syst. **2020**(1), 256–320 (2020). https://doi.org/10.13154/tches.v2020.i1.256-320

2. Black, J., Rogaway, P., Shrimpton, T.: Black-box analysis of the block-cipher-based hash-function constructions from PGV. In: Yung, M. (ed.) CRYPTO 2002. LNCS, vol. 2442, pp. 320–335. Springer, Heidelberg (2002). https://doi.org/10.1007/3-540-45708-9_21

3. Brassard, G., Høyer, P., Tapp, A.: Quantum cryptanalysis of hash and claw-free functions. SIGACT News **28**(2), 14–19 (1997). https://doi.org/10.1145/261342.261346

4. Chauhan, A.K., Kumar, A., Sanadhya, S.K.: Quantum free-start collision attacks on double block length hashing with round-reduced AES-256. IACR Trans. Symmetric Cryptol. **2021**(1), 316–336 (2021). https://doi.org/10.46586/tosc.v2021.i1.316-336

5. Damgård, I.B.: A design principle for hash functions. In: Brassard, G. (ed.) CRYPTO 1989. LNCS, vol. 435, pp. 416–427. Springer, New York (1990). https://doi.org/10.1007/0-387-34805-0_39

6. Dong, X., Sun, S., Shi, D., Gao, F., Wang, X., Hu, L.: Quantum collision attacks on AES-like hashing with low quantum random access memories. In: Moriai, S., Wang, H. (eds.) ASIACRYPT 2020. LNCS, vol. 12492, pp. 727–757. Springer, Cham (2020). https://doi.org/10.1007/978-3-030-64834-3_25

7. FIPS PUB 180–4: Secure hash standard (SHS), August 2015

8. Grassl, M., Langenberg, B., Roetteler, M., Steinwandt, R.: Applying Grover's algorithm to AES: quantum resource estimates. In: Takagi, T. (ed.) PQCrypto 2016. LNCS, vol. 9606, pp. 29–43. Springer, Cham (2016). https://doi.org/10.1007/978-3-319-29360-8_3

9. Grover, L.K.: A fast quantum mechanical algorithm for database search. In: Miller, G.L. (ed.) Proceedings of the Twenty-Eighth Annual ACM Symposium on the Theory of Computing, pp. 212–219. ACM (1996). https://doi.org/10.1145/237814.237866

10. Hirose, S.: Some plausible constructions of double-block-length hash functions. In: Robshaw, M. (ed.) FSE 2006. LNCS, vol. 4047, pp. 210–225. Springer, Heidelberg (2006). https://doi.org/10.1007/11799313_14

11. Hosoyamada, A., Sasaki, Y.: Finding hash collisions with quantum computers by using differential trails with smaller probability than birthday bound. In: Canteaut, A., Ishai, Y. (eds.) EUROCRYPT 2020. LNCS, vol. 12106, pp. 249–279. Springer, Cham (2020). https://doi.org/10.1007/978-3-030-45724-2_9

12. ISO/IEC 10118–2: Information technology - security techniques - hash-functions - part 2: Hash-functions using an $n$-bit block cipher (2000)

13. Iwata, T., Khairallah, M., Minematsu, K., Peyrin, T.: New results on Romulus. NIST Lightweight Cryptography Workshop 2020 (2020). https://csrc.nist.gov/events/2020/lightweight-cryptography-workshop-2020

14. Jaques, S., Naehrig, M., Roetteler, M., Virdia, F.: Implementing Grover Oracles for quantum key search on AES and LowMC. In: Canteaut, A., Ishai, Y. (eds.) EUROCRYPT 2020. LNCS, vol. 12106, pp. 280–310. Springer, Cham (2020). https://doi.org/10.1007/978-3-030-45724-2_10

15. Jonsson, J., Robshaw, M.J.B.: Securing RSA-KEM via the AES. In: Vaudenay, S. (ed.) PKC 2005. LNCS, vol. 3386, pp. 29–46. Springer, Heidelberg (2005). https://doi.org/10.1007/978-3-540-30580-4_4

16. Liu, Q., Zhandry, M.: On finding quantum multi-collisions. In: Ishai, Y., Rijmen, V. (eds.) EUROCRYPT 2019. LNCS, vol. 11478, pp. 189–218. Springer, Cham (2019). https://doi.org/10.1007/978-3-030-17659-4_7

17. Mendel, F., Rechberger, C., Schläffer, M., Thomsen, S.S.: The rebound attack: cryptanalysis of reduced Whirlpool and Grøstl. In: Dunkelman, O. (ed.) FSE 2009. LNCS, vol. 5665, pp. 260–276. Springer, Heidelberg (2009). https://doi.org/10.1007/978-3-642-03317-9_16

18. Merkle, R.C.: One way hash functions and DES. In: Brassard, G. (ed.) CRYPTO 1989. LNCS, vol. 435, pp. 428–446. Springer, New York (1990). https://doi.org/10.1007/0-387-34805-0_40

19. Meyer, C.H., Schilling, M.: Secure program load with manipulation detection code. In: Proceedings of the 6th Worldwide Congress on Computer and Communications Security and Protection (SECURICOM 1988), pp. 111–130 (1988)

20. Nandi, M.: Towards optimal double-length hash functions. In: Maitra, S., Veni Madhavan, C.E., Venkatesan, R. (eds.) INDOCRYPT 2005. LNCS, vol. 3797, pp. 77–89. Springer, Heidelberg (2005). https://doi.org/10.1007/11596219_7

21. Nielsen, M.A., Chuang, I.L.: Quantum Computation and Quantum Information. Cambridge University Press, Cambridge (2000)

22. Zhandry, M.: A note on the quantum collision and set equality problems. Quantum Inf. Comput. **15**(7&8), 557–567 (2015). https://doi.org/10.26421/QIC15.7-8-2
23. Zhandry, M.: How to record quantum queries, and applications to quantum indifferentiability. In: Boldyreva, A., Micciancio, D. (eds.) CRYPTO 2019. LNCS, vol. 11693, pp. 239–268. Springer, Cham (2019). https://doi.org/10.1007/978-3-030-26951-7_9

# Isogeny-Based Cryptography

# An Isogeny-Based ID Protocol Using Structured Public Keys

Karim Baghery$^{(\boxtimes)}$, Daniele Cozzo, and Robi Pedersen

imec-COSIC, KU Leuven, Leuven, Belgium
{karim.baghery,daniele.cozzo,robi.pedersen}@kuleuven.be

**Abstract.** Isogeny-based cryptography is known as one of the promising approaches to the emerging post-quantum public key cryptography. In cryptography, an IDentification (ID) protocol is a primitive that allows someone's identity to be confirmed. We present an efficient variation of the isogeny-based interactive ID scheme used in the base form of the CSI-FiSh signature [BKV19], which was initially proposed by Couveignes-Rostovtsev-Stolbunov [Cou06, RS06], to support a larger challenge space, and consequently achieve a better soundness error rate in each execution. To this end, we prolong the public key of the basic ID protocol with some *well-formed* elements that are generated by particular factors of the secret key. Due to the need for a well-formed (or structured) public key, the (secret and public) keys are generated by a trusted authority. Our analysis shows that, for a particular security parameter, by extending a public key of size 64B to 2.1 MB, the prover and verifier of our ID protocol can be more than $14\times$ faster than the basic ID protocol which has a binary challenge space, and moreover, the proof in our case will be about $13.5\times$ shorter. Using standard techniques, we also turn the presented ID protocol into a signature scheme that is as efficient as the state-of-the-art CSI-FiSh signature, and is existentially unforgeable under chosen message attacks in the (quantum) random oracle model. However, in our signature scheme, a verifier should get the public key of a signer from a trusted authority, which is standard in a wide range of current uses of signatures. Finally, we show how to eliminate the need for a trusted authority in our proposed ID protocol.

**Keywords:** Isogeny-based cryptography · Identification protocols · Digital signatures · Quantum random oracle model

## 1 Introduction

An IDentification (ID) protocol is an interactive cryptographic protocol between two parties called Prover and Verifier, that allows to prove the identity of the former to the latter [Sch89]. At the end of a successful execution of an ID protocol, the Verifier is convinced that it is interacting with the Prover that knows the secret key sk corresponding to a particular public key pk. ID protocols are deployed in a wide range of cryptographic protocols and practical applications,

© Springer Nature Switzerland AG 2021
M. B. Paterson (Ed.): IMACC 2021, LNCS 13129, pp. 179–197, 2021.
https://doi.org/10.1007/978-3-030-92641-0_9

and above all, they can be used to build digital signatures. Constructions like Schnorr's ID protocol and its corresponding signature [Sch89] are known for their simplicity and efficiency, but rely on the intractability of the discrete logarithm problem, which is known to be insecure against sufficiently powerful quantum computers [Sho94].

There are various research areas that are exploring post-quantum cryptographic techniques to design primitives and protocols that can remain secure in the presence of quantum computers. One of these is isogeny-based cryptography, which was independently proposed by Couveignes [Cou06] and by Rostovtsev and Stolbunov [RS06,Sto10]. The security of these isogeny-based constructions mainly relies on the difficulty of finding an explicit isogeny connecting two isogenous ordinary elliptic curves over a finite field, while the construction of such isogenies can be efficiently computed as the action of elements of the ideal-class group of the endomorphism ring of these elliptic curves. In these original works, the authors also independently proposed an isogeny-based interactive ID protocol. In his Ph.D. thesis, Stolbunov [Sto12] further mentioned how to convert the ID protocol to the first isogeny-based signature scheme using the Fiat–Shamir transform. However, these constructions have many drawbacks. First, they work with a binary challenge space, and therefore need to be repeated many times to achieve a reasonable soundness rate. Second, in order to allow the uniform sampling and efficiently computable canonical representations of elements in the class group needed in these protocols, the class group structure has to be known, which is a difficult problem for quadratic imaginary fields [HM89]. Finally, a quantum attack by Childs, Jao, and Soukharev [CJS14] pushed the security parameter sizes of these schemes to an impractical scale. Even with current optimizations [DFKS18], these schemes are inefficient in practice.

Later works have tried to mitigate these shortcomings. In 2018, Castryck et al. [CLM+18] proposed CSIDH (Commutative Supersingular Isogeny Diffie-Hellman) and showed that using supersingular curves over $\mathbb{F}_p$ instead of ordinary ones, combined with the action by $\mathbb{F}_p$-rational ideals, greatly increases the efficiency of isogeny computations and thus makes these schemes again usable in practice. De Feo and Galbraith [DFG19] used the tools of CSIDH to construct a signature scheme that does not need the knowledge of the class group, but rather uses rejection sampling. With later improvements by Decru, Panny, and Vercauteren [DPV19], Seasign signatures could be performed in a few minutes. Later that same year Beullens, Kleinjung and Vercauteren [BKV19] performed a record class-group computation for the CSIDH-512 parameter set (a class group of size $\approx 2^{257}$) that finally allowed class group elements to be uniformly sampled and efficiently represented, leading to a practical signature scheme, called CSI-FiSh. In its simplest version, using a binary challenge space, a CSI-FiSh signature takes slightly less than 3 s. Then, with further improvements, the authors managed to decrease it to a few hundred milliseconds by increasing the public-key size and using a different $\Sigma$-protocol which is an ID protocol for a different language, but supports a larger challenge space.

A very different approach to isogeny-based ID protocols and signatures was taken based on the SIDH scheme proposed by Jao and De Feo [JDF11], which uses supersingular elliptic curves over $\mathbb{F}_{p^2}$, where the endomorphism ring is isomorphic to an order in a quaternion algebra, rather than a quadratic imaginary field. The original paper also proposes an ID protocol, based on which later signature schemes have been proposed [YAJ+17, GPS17], although not very practical. The work of Galbraith et al. [GPS17] however also introduced a signature scheme based on the KLPT algorithm [KLPT14], which uses the knowledge of the endomorphism ring of two supersingular elliptic curves over $\mathbb{F}_{p^2}$ to compute an isogeny connecting them. In 2020, De Feo et al. [DFKL+20] showed that with further assumptions, this scheme can be made practical and proposed the signature scheme SQI-Sign. At the NIST security level 1, SQI-Sign runs in a few seconds and has public-key sizes a magnitude smaller than any other post-quantum secure signature scheme.

***Our Contributions.*** Our main contribution is to extend the ID protocol used in the base form of CSI-FiSh signature [BKV19], which was initially proposed by Couveignes-Rostovtsev-Stolbunov [Cou06, RS06], to work with a larger challenge space rather than a binary space. By extending the challenge space, the proposed ID protocol achieves an arbitrarily small soundness error rate in each execution. To this end, we modify the ID protocol with binary challenge space [Cou06, RS06, BKV19] and prolong its public key with some new *structured* elements. Particularly, each new element in the public key is built from a distinct specific multiple of the secret key, where the coefficients are taken from a public *exceptional set* [BCPS18, DLSV20]. The latter is a crucial requirement in the security proof for knowledge soundness. Then, we show that using the *structured public key*, we can build an ID protocol that works with a larger challenge space, and consequently achieves a bigger soundness error rate in each run. Due to the need for a *well-formed* or structured public key, in the basic and more efficient version of our ID protocol, we assume that the (secret and public) keys are generated by a trusted authority and shared with parties. Our performance analysis shows that, in practice, for a particular security parameter, with an honestly generated public key of size 2.1 MB, the prover and verifier of our ID protocol can be more than 14× faster than using repetitions of the basic ID protocol with a binary challenge space and also the proof will be about 13.5× shorter. In order to apply further optimizations to the soundness security, we define *superexceptional sets* (in Definition 3.2) as a particular form of exceptional sets, which can be of independent interest.

As our second contribution, we use standard techniques to turn the proposed ID protocol into a signature scheme that has the same efficiency as the state-of-the-art isogeny-based signature scheme CSI-FiSh [BKV19], constructed to work in the CSIDH setting. In our signature scheme, the verifier needs to get the public key of the signer from a trusted authority rather than from the signer itself, which is standard in applications like public key certificates. Similar to CSI-FiSh, our signature scheme would allow to generate and verify a signature of size less than 400 bytes in less than 0.5 s.

In our basic ID protocol, to guarantee the well-formedness of the public keys, we assume that these are generated by a trusted authority. As the next contribution of the paper, we show how this trust can be eliminated by letting the prover generate the key pair themselves, while appending a proof of well-formedness to the public key. We also show that in order to increase the efficiency, this proof can be incrementally generated, i.e. that the correctness of the $i$-th public key element can be proven more efficiently by using the fact that elements $1, \ldots, i - 1$ have already been proven.

***Organization.*** Section 2 presents some preliminaries used in the paper. In Sect. 3, we present our ID protocol in the setting where a trusted authority has generated the keys. In Sect. 4, we detail the corresponding signature scheme. In Sect. 5, we propose two protocols to eliminate the trust on the key generation and also discuss some applications. We present some benchmarks in Sect. 6. Finally, we conclude the paper in Sect. 7.

## 2    Preliminaries

We denote by $\mathbb{Z}_N = \mathbb{Z}/N\mathbb{Z}$ the integers modulo $N$, where we assume that $N$ is a composite number of known prime factorisation $N = \prod_{i=1}^{m} q_i^{r_i}$ with $q_1 < \cdots < q_m$ primes and all $r_i \in \mathbb{N}$. We further say that a function $\mu(x)$ is a negligible function of $x$, if for any constant $c$, there exists $x_0$, such that for all $x > x_0$, we have $\mu(x) < \frac{1}{x^c}$.

### 2.1    ID Protocols

**Sigma-Protocols.** Let $\lambda$ be a security parameter and let $X = X(\lambda)$ and $W = W(\lambda)$ be sets. Let $\mathcal{R}$ be a relation on $X \times W$ that defines a language $\mathbf{L} = \{x \in X : \exists w \in W, \mathcal{R}(x, w) = 1\}$. Given $x \in \mathbf{L}$, an element $w \in W$ such that $\mathcal{R}(x, w) = 1$ is called a witness. Let R be a PPT algorithm such that $R(1^\lambda)$ outputs pairs $(x, w)$ such that $\mathcal{R}(x, w) = 1$.

A sigma-protocol ($\Sigma$-protocol) for the relation $\mathcal{R}$ is a 3-round interactive protocol between two PPT algorithms: a prover P and a verifier V. P holds a witness w for $x \in \mathbf{L}$ and V is given x. P first sends a value $a$ to V, and then V answers with a challenge $c$ , and finally P answers with $z$. V accepts or rejects the proof. The triple trans $= (a, c, z)$ is called a transcript of the $\Sigma$-protocol. A $\Sigma$-protocol is supposed to satisfy *Completeness, Honest Verifier Zero-Knowledge* (HVZK), and *Special Soundness* defined below.

**Definition 2.1 (Completeness).** *A $\Sigma$-protocol $\Pi$ with parties* $(P, V)$ *is complete for* R, *if for all* $(x, w) \in \mathcal{R}$, *the honest* V *will always accept the honest* P.

**Definition 2.2 (HVZK).** *A $\Sigma$-protocol satisfies HVZK for* R, *if there exists a PPT algorithm* Sim *that given* $x \in X$, *can simulate the* trans *of the scheme, s.t. for all* $x \in \mathbf{L}$, $(x, w) \in \mathcal{R}$,

$$\mathsf{trans}(\mathsf{P}(\mathcal{R}, x, w) \leftrightarrow \mathsf{V}(\mathcal{R}, x)) \approx \mathsf{trans}(\mathsf{Sim}(\mathcal{R}, x) \leftrightarrow \mathsf{V}(\mathcal{R}, x))$$

*where* $\mathsf{trans}(\mathsf{P}(\cdot) \leftrightarrow \mathsf{V}(\cdot))$ *indicates the transcript of $\Pi$ with* $(P, V)$, *and $\approx$ denotes the indistinguishability of transcripts.*

**Definition 2.3 (Special Soundness).** *The $\Sigma$-protocol $\Pi$ with parties* $(P, V)$ *is special sound for* R, *if there exists a PPT extractor* Ext, *such that for any* $x \in \mathbf{L}$, *given two valid transcripts* $(a, c, z)$ *and* $(a, c', z')$ *for the same message* $a$ *but* $c \neq c'$, *then* $\mathsf{Ext}(a, c, z, c', z')$ *outputs a witness* w *for the relation $\mathcal{R}$.*

**Identification Protocols.** An ID protocol is a special case of a $\Sigma$-protocol between two parties $(P, V)$, with respect to a hard relation defined by a key generator KGen, as $(\mathsf{pk}, \mathsf{sk}) \leftarrow \mathsf{KGen}(1^\lambda)$, where one thinks of sk as a witness for the public key pk.

## 2.2 Building NIZK ID Protocols and Signatures

An HVZK $\Sigma$-protocol $\Pi$ can be transformed to a Non-Interactive Zero-Knowledge (NIZK) argument $\Pi_{\mathsf{NIZK}}$ in the Random Oracle Model (ROM) via the Fiat–Shamir (FS) transformation [FS87]. The transformation also allows to build signatures from an ID protocol [AABN02]; we describe this procedure in Appendix A. Next we define strong existential unforgeability under chosen message attacks, the primary security notion for signatures.

**Definition 2.4 (Strong Existential Unforgeability under Chosen Message Attacks).** *A signature scheme* $\Pi_{\mathsf{Sign}} = (\mathsf{KGen}, \mathsf{Sign}, \mathsf{Vf})$ *is said to be strong Existentially Unforgeable under adaptive Chosen-Message Attacks (sEU-CMA) if for all PPT adversaries $\mathcal{A}$,*

$$\left| \Pr \left[ \begin{array}{l} (\mathsf{pk}, \mathsf{sk}) \leftarrow \mathsf{KGen}(1^\lambda), \ \sigma_i \leftarrow \mathsf{Sign}(\mathsf{sk}, m_i) \ for \ 1 \leq i \leq k; \\ (m, \sigma) \leftarrow \mathcal{A}^{\mathsf{Sign}(\cdot)}(\mathsf{pk}, (m_i, \sigma_i)_{i=1}^k) : \mathsf{Vf}(m, \sigma, \mathsf{pk}) = 1 \wedge (m, \sigma) \notin Q \end{array} \right] \right|$$

*is negligible in the security parameter $\lambda$, where* $Q := \{(m_1, \sigma_1) \cdots , (m_k, \sigma_k)\}$ *is the set of the messages requested by $\mathcal{A}$ and the signatures returned from the signing oracle.*

## 2.3    CSI-FiSh

The digital signature scheme CSI-FiSh [BKV19] is based on the ID protocol with *binary challenge space* initially proposed by Couveignes-Rostovtsev-
Stolbunov [Cou06, RS06], that closely follows the lines of the Schnorr identification protocol as introduced in [Sch89]. We will introduce it in the notation
of hard homogeneous spaces, a notion introduced by Couveignes [Cou06], which
generalizes group actions that contain hard computational problems.

**Definition 2.5 (Hard homogeneous space [Cou06]).** *A Hard Homogeneous
Space (HHS) is a pair of a finite Abelian group $\mathcal{G}$ acting on a finite set $\mathcal{E}$ with
a free and transitive map $\star : \mathcal{G} \times \mathcal{E} \to \mathcal{E}$, that is efficiently computable.*
*Furthermore, operations, sampling and membership checks in $\mathcal{G}$, as well as mem-
bership and equality checks in $\mathcal{E}$ are efficiently computable. Given an element of
$\mathcal{G}$, one can also efficiently compute a unique representation. The following are
hard algorithmic problems:*

- *Vectorization: Given $E_1, E_2 \in \mathcal{E}$, find $\mathfrak{a} \in \mathcal{G}$, such that $\mathfrak{a} \star E_1 = E_2$.*
- *Parallelization: Given $E_1, E_2, F_1 \in \mathcal{E}$ with $E_2 = \mathfrak{a} \star E_1$, compute $F_2 = \mathfrak{a} \star F_1$.*

When $\mathcal{G}$ is cyclic of order $N$ and $\mathfrak{g}$ is a given generator of $\mathcal{G}$, we can also define
the group action $[\ ] : \mathbb{Z}_N \times \mathcal{E} \to \mathcal{E}$ as $[a]E = \mathfrak{g}^a \star E$ for $a \in \mathbb{Z}_N, E \in \mathcal{E}$. It holds
$[a][b]E = [a + b]E$.

The ID protocol underlying CSI-FiSh allows to prove knowledge of a secret
group action $[a]$ connecting two given set elements $(E_0, E_1 = [a]E_0)$, where
$E_0 \in \mathcal{E}$ is a public starting element. Similar to the Schnorr protocol, the prover
first commits to a random $b \in \mathbb{Z}_N$ via $E_b = [b]E_0$, then after receiving a random
bit $c$ from the verifier, sends the response $r = b - ca \mod N$. The verifier
checks whether $[r]E_c = E_b$. While in Schnorr protocols, the soundness error
can be increased by choosing challenges as bit-strings of length $k$, computing
$[r]E_c = [r][ca]E_0$ for non-binary $c$ is not directly possible in the more restrictive
HHS setting, since there is no way for the verifier to compute the action of $ca$
without knowing $a$.

In order to decrease the soundness error of their ID protocol, the authors
rather increase the challenge space by using larger keys: the secret key is a set
$a_1, \ldots, a_{S-1}$ which defines the corresponding public key $E_1, \ldots, E_{S-1}$. Then the
prover proves knowledge of any isogeny connecting two elements of its public
key, which results in a $\Sigma$-protocol with soundness error rate $\frac{1}{S}$. We note at this
point, that this protocol cannot be used as an identification protocol for the
knowledge of the secret key, in that an extractor can only extract a difference
$a_i - a_j$ of secret keys. The purpose of the next sections is to construct such an
identification protocol.

The authors of [BKV19] instantiate the HHS by identifying $\mathcal{E}$ with the set
of supersingular elliptic curves defined over a prime field $\mathbb{F}_p$ with $\log_2 p \approx 512$.
The class group $\mathsf{Cl}(\mathcal{O})$ of the $\mathbb{F}_p$-rational endomorphism ring $\mathcal{O}$ acts freely and
transitively on these elements by isogenies, which allows the identification $\mathcal{G}$ with

$\mathsf{Cl}(\mathcal{O})$. The full class group structure has also been determined in [BKV19]. It has size

$$\#\mathsf{Cl}(\mathcal{O}) = 3 \cdot 37 \cdot 1407181 \cdot 51593604295295867744293584889$$
$$\cdot 31599414504681995853008278745587832204909$$

and is cyclic with generator $\mathfrak{g} = (3, \pi - 1)$. The starting element $E_0 : y^2 = x^3 + x$ enjoys the special symmetry, that the twist of $[a]E_0$ is $[-a]E_0$. Since twisting can be performed efficiently, the authors implicitly include twists in the public key and thus double the challenge space, reducing the soundness error rate to $\frac{1}{2S-1}$. For the sake of generality, we also describe this concept for HHS by introducing the following notion of a *symmetric* HHS. In this setting, we generally use the index notation to identify the "twists", i.e. we write $E_a = [a]E_0$ and $E_{-a} = [-a]E_0$ for the twists.

**Definition 2.6 (Symmetric hard homogeneous space).** *We call a hard homogeneous space* symmetric around $E_0 \in \mathcal{E}$, *if, given an element* $\mathfrak{a} \star E_0$, *one can efficiently compute* $\mathfrak{a}^{-1} \star E_0$ *without any extra information.*

# 3  An Efficient ID Protocol

Next, we generalize the ID scheme with binary challenge space used in the basic version of CSI-FiSh [BKV19] to support a larger challenge space. Their protocol allows to prove the knowledge of secret key $x$ for the public key $E_1 = [x]E_0$, but works with a binary challenge space. As a consequence, this construction requires a large number of parallel executions and large communication to achieve a reasonable soundness error rate. In order to extend the ID protocol to support a larger challenge space, we assume that there exists a trusted authority in the protocol that generates the pair of secret and (structured) public keys. The trusted authority sends both keys to the prover, while only the public key to the verifier. We later discuss how to eliminate the need for a trusted authority.

## 3.1  Construction and Security Proofs

To efficiently prove the knowledge of $x$ in $E_1 = [x]E_0$, our key idea is to ask a trusted authority to generate $k - 2$ new curves $E_2, E_3, \cdots, E_{k-1}$ using other multiples of $x$, say $E_i = [c_i x]E_0$ for $i = 2, \cdots, k-1$, where $c_i$ are public integers.

**The Issue with Composite $N$.** In order to achieve special soundness and build an efficient extraction algorithm that can extract the witness from two acceptable transcripts of our construction, we need to assume that the difference of any two challenge values is always invertible. Since $N$ can be composite, we need to define the challenge set to only contain elements, whose pairwise difference is invertible. To this end we use *exceptional sets* [BCPS18, DLSV20].

**Definition 3.1 (Exceptional set).** *An* exceptional set (modulo $N$) *is a set* $\mathbb{C} = \{c_0, \ldots, c_{k-1}\} \subseteq \mathbb{Z}_N$, *where the pairwise difference* $c_i - c_j$ *of all elements* $c_i \neq c_j$ *is invertible modulo* $N$.

Given $k$ and particular $N$ with smallest prime factor $q_1 \geq k$, there exists an efficient algorithm XSGen that outputs an exceptional set of size $k$ with integer elements, $\mathbb{C} = \{c_0 = 0, c_1 = 1, c_2, \cdots, c_{k-1}\}$.[1] In order for the exceptional set to have a specific target size $k \geq q_1$, we need to work in a subgroup $\mathbb{Z}_{N'}$, where $N' \mid N$ has smallest prime factor $q_1' \geq k$. To do this we factor out the smaller primes. The only restriction this puts on $N$ is that it is not $k$-smooth, which is a reasonable assumption for arbitrary composite numbers and $k \ll N$.

**The ID-Protocol.** We now describe the steps of our ID-protocol. Given a security parameter and the system parameters, the trusted authority samples a secret key $x \leftarrow \mathbb{Z}_N$, generates an exceptional set $\mathbb{C} = \{c_0 = 0, c_1 = 1, c_2, \cdots, c_{k-1}\}$ using XSGen and then generates the public key $(E_0, E_1, \ldots, E_{k-1})$, where $E_i = [c_i x] E_0$ for $i = 1 \ldots, k-1$. Note that we see $E_0$ as part of the public-key for simplicity and that $[0]$ denotes the neutral element of the group action. The trusted authority then sends the secret key to the prover, and the public key to both the prover and the verifier. Then, the prover can use the $\Sigma$-protocol in the figure below to convince the verifier about its *knowledge* of the secret key $x$.

---

**The Main ID Protocol Under a Trusted Setup with an Arbitrary $N$**

**Trusted Authority**

Use XSGen to obtain $\mathbb{C}$, where

$$\mathbb{C} = \{c_0 = 0, c_1 = 1, c_2, \cdots, c_{k-1}\}$$

$$x \leftarrow \mathbb{Z}_N, \text{ set } \{E_i = [c_i x] E_0\}_{i=1}^{k-1}$$

| $(x, (E_0, E_1, \cdots, E_{k-1}))$ | | $(E_0, E_1, \cdots, E_{k-1})$ |
|---|---|---|
| **Prover:** | | **Verifier:** |
| $b \leftarrow \mathbb{Z}_N, \; E_b \leftarrow [b] E_0$ | $\xrightarrow{\quad E_b \quad}$ | |
| | $\xleftarrow{\quad d \quad}$ | $d \leftarrow \{0, \ldots, k-1\}$ |
| $r \leftarrow b - c_d \cdot x \mod N$ | $\xrightarrow{\quad r \quad}$ | return $E_b \overset{?}{=} [r] E_d$ |

---

The following theorem proves the security of the proposed ID protocol.

**Theorem 3.1.** *Assuming the existence of an exceptional set* $\mathbb{C} = \{c_0 = 0, c_1 = 1, c_2, c_3, \cdots, c_{k-1}\}$, *the described ID-protocol is complete, HVZK, and special sound with soundness error rate* $\frac{1}{k}$.

---

[1] An easy approach is just to generate $k-2$ distinct elements from $\{2, \ldots, q_1\}$. In its simplest form, we have $\mathbb{C} = \{0, 1, 2, \cdots, k-1\}$.

*Proof.* For the completeness, the honest prover follows the protocol and additionally knows a secret $x$ such that $E_i = [c_i x] E_0$ for $i = 1, \ldots, k - 1$. The honest verifier checks whether $E_b = [r] E_d = [b - c_d x] E_d = [b - c_d x][c_d x] E_0 = [b] E_0$ which holds given the assumptions on the prover.

For the HVZK, we construct a simulator that given the honestly generated challenge $d$, samples $r$ randomly from $\mathbb{Z}_N$, then sets $E_b = [r] E_d$ and returns the transcript $(E_b, d, r)$. In both the real and the simulated transcripts, $r$ and $E_b$ are sampled uniformly at random, yielding indistinguishable distributions.

For special soundness, given two valid transcripts of the protocol, we build an efficient extraction algorithm that extracts the witness $x$. Let $(E_b, d, r)$ and $(E_b, d', r')$ be two acceptable transcripts of the protocol, where $d \neq d'$, consequently $r \neq r'$ (for non-zero $x$). From the verification equation, one can conclude that $[r] E_d = [r'] E_{d'}$, and from the (trusted) key generation we know that $E_i = [c_i x] E_0$ for $i = 1, \ldots, k - 1$. These imply that we have $[r][c_d x] E_0 = [r'][c_{d'} x] E_0$, which implies that $r - r' \equiv x(c_{d'} - c_d) \pmod{N}$. Considering the fact that both $c_d$ and $c_{d'}$ are sampled from the exceptional set $\mathbb{C}$, $c_{d'} - c_d$ is invertible modulo $N$, this allows the extraction of $x$ as $x = \frac{r - r'}{c_{d'} - c_d} \mod N$. $\qquad\square$

*Soundness Error Rate.* In its current form, our protocol has soundness error rate $1/k$. To achieve a target soundness error of $2^{-\lambda}$ for a given security parameter $\lambda$, we therefore have to repeat our protocol at least $\lceil \lambda \log_k 2 \rceil$ times.

**Making the Construction Non-interactive.** The described ID protocol is a public-coin $\Sigma$-protocol, therefore can be turned into a non-interactive ID protocol using the Fiat–Shamir transform [FS87]. To do so, let $t = t(k) = \lceil \lambda \log_k 2 \rceil$. The prover generates $t$ distinct elements $b_1, \ldots, b_t \leftarrow \mathbb{Z}_N$ and commits to $t$ elliptic curves $E_{b_i} = [b_i] E_0$ for $i = 1, \ldots, t$. Then the challenge is determined by hashing the commitments and the statements using a hash function $\mathsf{H} : \{0,1\}^* \to \{0,1\}^{t \lceil \log_2 k \rceil}$, modeled as a random oracle, and parsing it into $t$ challenges:

$$d = d_1 || \ldots || d_t = \mathsf{H}(E_0, \ldots, E_{k-1} || E_{b_1}, \ldots, E_{b_t}).$$

The response is given as $r = (r_1, \ldots, r_t) \equiv (b_1 - c_{d_1} x, \ldots, b_t - c_{d_t} x) \pmod{N}$. The prover publishes $(d, r)$ as its proof. The verifier then checks, whether

$$\mathsf{H}(E_0, \ldots, E_{k-1} || [r_1] E_{d_1}, \ldots, [r_t] E_{d_t}) \overset{?}{=} d.$$

**Lemma 3.1.** *The non-interactive version of our ID-protocol is a NIZK quantum proof of knowledge in the quantum random oracle model.*

*Proof.* The freeness of the group action implies that, if $[b] E_0 = [b'] E_0$, then $b = b'$. This immediately implies that our scheme has unique responses. Furthermore, the freeness of the group action also implies superlogarithmic collision-entropy of the commitments, since commitments will only collide if they are generated using the same $b$, which is a negligible function of the security parameter. Finally, the challenge space is of size $2^{t \lceil \log_2 k \rceil} \geq 2^\lambda$, thus superpolynomial in $\lambda$. Using our results for completeness, special soundness and HVZK from Theorem 3.1 this implies that our protocol is a quantum proof of knowledge using [DFMS19, Th. 25] and zero-knowledge against quantum adversaries [Unr17].    □

## 3.2   Optimizations and Efficiency

Similar to the proposal used in CSI-FiSh [BKV19], we can double our challenge space using twists. To this end, we assume that the underlying HHS is *symmetric* as by Definition 2.6. Defining $E_{-i} = [c_{-i}x]E_0 = [-c_ix]E_0$ allows challenges to be sampled from the set $d \leftarrow \{-(k-1), \ldots, k-1\}$ of size $2k-1$, while the response and verification steps proceed in exactly the same way as in the ID-protocol: In the case $d < 0$, the response is simply $r = b - c_{-d}x = b + c_dx$ and for the verification step, the verifier needs to compute $E_{-d} = [-c_dx]E_0$ via the efficient map from $E_d$, and check if $E_b = [r]E_{-d} = [b + c_dx][-c_dx]E_0$.

By this extension, our protocol achieves soundness error rate $\frac{1}{2k-1}$, and thus has to be repeated $t(2k-1) = \lceil \lambda \log_{2k-1} 2 \rceil$ times to achieve a target soundness error of at least $2^{-\lambda}$. Note that in the non-interactive case, the hash function needs to be redefined to have the output domain $\{0,1\}^{t(2k-1)\lceil \log_2(2k-1)\rceil}$.

However, there is another problem. To guarantee the special soundness proven in Theorem 3.1, we used exceptional sets (Definition 3.1), that guarantee that any pair of challenges allows the extraction of the secret $x$ by an extractor. Since we are implicitly extending our challenge space to also include negative values of the factors $c_i$, we have to guarantee that their pairwise sums are invertible too. We therefore define the notion of superexceptional sets.

**Definition 3.2 (Superexceptional set).** *A superexceptional set (modulo $N$) is a set $\mathbb{C} = \{c_0, \ldots, c_{k-1}\}$, where the pairwise difference $c_i - c_j$ of all distinct elements $c_i \neq c_j$ and the pairwise sum $c_i + c_j$ of all elements $c_i, c_j$ (including $c_i = c_j$) is invertible modulo $N$.*

Similarly to exceptional sets, we can define an efficient algorithm SXSGen for generating superexceptional sets modulo $N$ of size $k \leq \frac{1}{2}(q_1 + 1)$. By letting the trusted authority in our ID-protocol generate a superexceptional set instead of an exceptional one, and by assuming the underlying hard homogeneous space is symmetric around $E_0$, we have the following lemma.

**Lemma 3.2.** *Assuming the existence of a superexceptional set $\mathbb{C} = \{c_0 = 0, c_1 = 1, c_2, \ldots, c_{k-1}\}$, the described ID-protocol is complete, HVZK, and special sound with soundness error rate $\frac{1}{2k-1}$.*

*Proof.* We have already shown completeness. HVZK and special soundness closely follow the proof in Theorem 3.1. Note that because we also allow negative challenges, we can end up with three different scenarios for challenges $d, d'$: They can either be both positive, both negative or one positive and one negative. In the first two cases, the extractor will need to invert an element of the form $\pm(c_{|d'|} - c_{|d|})$ mod $N$, which is guaranteed to be possible in exceptional sets. In the third case, the extractor will end up with needing to invert an element of the form $\pm(c_{|d'|} + c_{|d|}) \mod N$, which is only guaranteed to be possible by using a superexceptional set $\mathbb{C}$. $\qquad\square$

**Computational Cost.** We establish the computational costs in terms of Group Actions (GAs) of our proposed protocol in the standard and in the symmetric case. We assume that we want to reach a target soundness error of $2^{-\lambda}$. Given a soundness error rate of $1/s$ per round, we need to repeat the underlying protocol $t(s) = \lceil \lambda \log_s 2 \rceil$ times. In both protocols, the prover and the verifier only need to compute a single GA per step thus, for both, the total cost in GAs is also expressed by $t(s)$. We find the following total costs:

- Standard ID-protocol: $t(k) = \lceil \lambda / \log_2 k \rceil$ GAs,
- Symmetric ID-protocol: $t(2k - 1) = \lceil \lambda / \log_2(2k - 1) \rceil$ GAs.

Assuming $k = 2^\kappa$, this implies $t(2) \approx \kappa t(k) \approx (\kappa + 1)t(2k - 1)$.

**Public Key Size.** Instead of a single set element, the public key now consists of $k - 1$ set elements, generated using the secret key $x$ and elements of the exceptional set $\mathbb{C}$.

**Proof Size.** We further establish the proof size of the non-interactive version of the ID-protocol in the standard and symmetric cases. To that end, we realize that the prover publishes the challenge-response pair $(d, r)$. The total challenge size is simply the size of the output domain of the hash function, which is $t(s)\lceil \log_2 s \rceil$ bits. The responses are $t(s)$ elements in $\mathbb{Z}_N$, thus have total size at most $t(s)\lceil \log_2 N \rceil$. This gives the total proof size of

- Standard ID-protocol: $\lceil \lambda / \log_2 k \rceil (\lceil \log_2 k \rceil + \lceil \log_2 N \rceil)$ bits,
- Symmetric ID-protocol: $\lceil \lambda / \log_2(2k - 1) \rceil (\lceil \log_2(2k - 1) \rceil + \lceil \log_2 N \rceil)$ bits.

# 4   Signatures from the Proposed ID Protocol

The ID protocol in Sect. 3 can be turned into a signature scheme using the Fiat–Shamir transform [FS87]. Let again $t = t(s) = \lceil \lambda \log_s 2 \rceil$, then the challenges are obtained by hashing the commitments $E_{b_1}, \ldots, E_{b_t}$ and the message $m$ to sign using a hash function $\mathsf{H} : \{0,1\}^* \to \{0,1\}^{t\lceil \log_2 s \rceil}$, modeled as a random oracle. The challenge is obtained as $d = d_1 \| \cdots \| d_t = \mathsf{H}(E_{b_1}, \ldots, E_{b_t} \| m)$.

The signature on $m$ consists of $(m; (r_1, d_1), \ldots, (r_t, d_t))$. The verifier recomputes the $E'_{b_i} = [r_i]E_i$ and checks that indeed $d = \mathsf{H}(E'_{b_1}, \ldots, E'_{b_t} \| m)$. The description of the trusted key generation, signing and verification of the signature scheme is presented in Fig. 1.

**Theorem 4.1.** *When the hash function* $\mathsf{H}$ *is modelled as a (quantum) random oracle, then the signature scheme in Fig. 1 is sEUF-CMA secure.*

*Proof.* In Lemma 3.1, we proved that the ID-protocol from Sect. 3 has special soundness and unique responses. Then by Theorem 25 of [DFMS19] the protocol enjoys the Quantum Proof of Knowledge property. This along with the fact that

---

The signature scheme based on our standard (resp. symmetric) ID protocol

$\mathsf{KGen}(1^\lambda)$:  To generate the keys, a *trusted authority* acts as follows,
  1. Sample $x \leftarrow \mathbb{Z}/N\mathbb{Z}$.
  2. Run algorithm $\mathsf{XSGen}$ (resp. $\mathsf{SXSGen}$) and obtain an exceptional (resp. superexceptional) set $\mathbb{C} = \{0, c_1 = 1, c_2, \cdots, c_{k-1}\}$
  3. For each $c_i \in \mathbb{C}$ set $E_i = [c_i x]E_0$.
  4. Return $\mathsf{sk} = x$, $\mathsf{pk} = (E_0, E_1, \ldots, E_{k-1})$.
$\mathsf{Sign}(\mathsf{sk}, m)$:  To sign a message $m$, the signer performs
  1. For $i = 1, 2, \ldots, t$:
    (a) $b_i \leftarrow \mathbb{Z}/N\mathbb{Z}$.
    (b) $E_{b_i} = [b_i]E_0$.
  2. Set $(d_1, \ldots, d_t) = \mathsf{H}(E_{b_1}, \ldots, E_{b_t} \parallel m)$.
  3. For $i = 1, 2, \ldots, t$:
    (a) set $r_i = b_i - c_{d_i} \cdot x \pmod{N}$.
  4. Return $\{(r_i, d_i)\}_{i=1}^t$.
$\mathsf{Vf}(\{(r_i, d_i)\}_{i=1}^t, m, \mathsf{pk})$:  To verify a signature $\{(r_i, d_i)\}_{i=1}^t$ on $m$, one performs:
  1. For $i = 1, 2, \ldots, t$: compute $E'_{b_i} = [r_i]E_i$.
  2. $(d'_1, d'_2, \ldots, d'_t) = \mathsf{H}(E'_{b_1}, \ldots, E'_{b_t} \parallel m)$.
  3. If $(d_1, d_2, \ldots, d_t) = (d'_1, d'_2, \cdots, d'_t)$ then return **valid**, else output **invalid**.

**Fig. 1.** The signature scheme based on our standard (resp. symmetric) ID protocol

the protocol has $\lambda$ bits of min entropy (Lemma 3.1) implies by Theorem 22 of [DFMS19] that the resulting signature scheme obtained via Fiat–Shamir is sEUF-CMA in the QROM. □

**Computational Cost and Signature Size.** We notice that the number of group actions to be performed in the signature and verification process are the same as in the proof and verification of the non-interactive ID protocol, respectively. Similarly, the size of the signature on $m$ is given by the size of the output domain of the hash function, which depends on inverse the soundness error rate $s$ and is therefore also equal to the proof size of the non-interactive ID protocol.

## 5   Eliminating the Trusted Setup

In the presented ID protocol (in Sect. 3), the need for a trusted authority mainly was for ensuring the *well-formedness* of the public key $\mathsf{pk}$. We call a public key $\mathsf{pk} := (E_0, E_1, \ldots, E_{k-1})$ *well-formed*, if for a secret key $x \in \mathbb{Z}_N$ and a set $\mathbb{C} = \{c_0, \ldots, c_{k-1}\}$ it holds that $E_i = [c_i x]E_0$ for $i = 1, \ldots, k-1$ and that $\mathbb{C}$ is a (super-)exceptional set for the case of a (symmetric) HHS.

The proof of special soundness in the main protocol relies on the fact that the elements of $\mathsf{pk}$ are well-formed and each one contains a particular multiple of $\mathsf{sk}$. In practice, this trust can be eliminated if the prover generates the keys and proves their *well-formedness*. This proof[2] needs to be generated only once, and a verifier can eliminate the need for a trusted party by verifying it and checking that $\mathbb{C}$ is a (super-)exceptional set (which can be done in polynomial time).

We present two $\Sigma$-protocols for a well-formedness proof. The first protocol is more general and proves that a given pk has the correct structure simply by showing that a single commitment-response pair applies to all elements of it. The second protocol, on the other hand, uses an incremental approach, where the correctness of an element $E_i$ of the pk is proven by using elements $E_0, \ldots, E_{i-1}$. By starting from $(E_0, E_1)$, which is well-formed by definition, we can then prove the well-formedness of the entire key incrementally. This approach will turn out to be much more efficient, but only works for exceptional sets of the form $\{0, 1, 2, \ldots, k-1\}$. This protocol also allows for a pk to be upgraded, i.e. to add a new element to a pk with a short proof, that the element is also well-formed.

Both protocols can be made non-interactive using the Fiat–Shamir transform.

## 5.1 First Approach: General Well-Formedness Proof

We present a $\Sigma$-protocol of the following *well-formedness* (WF) relation for a given $E_0$ and a particular $k$.

$$\mathbf{L}_{k-1}^{WF} := \{((E_0, E_1, \ldots, E_{k-1}), x, \mathbb{C} = \{c_1, \ldots, c_{k-1}\}) : \bigwedge_{i=1}^{k-1} F_i = [c_i x] E_0\}.$$

Namely, P needs to prove in zero-knowledge that all the elements of the pk are computed using the same secret key $x$ but with different public coefficients $c_1, \ldots, c_{k-1}$. This can be achieved in a straightforward fashion by sampling $b \leftarrow \mathbb{Z}_N$ and committing to $\hat{E}_i = [c_i b] E_0$ for $i = 1, \ldots, k-1$. The challenge $d$ is binary, or ternary if we assume a symmetric HHS, and the prover can respond with $r = b - dx \mod N$. Finally, the verifier checks if all $\hat{F}_i \stackrel{?}{=} [c_i r] E_{di}$.

**Theorem 5.1.** *The above $\Sigma$-protocol is correct, HVZK, and special sound with soundness error rate $\frac{1}{3}$.*

*Proof.* For completeness, we simply realize that $[c_i r] E_{di} = [c_i b - d c_i x][d c_i x] E_0 = [c_i b] E_0 = \hat{E}_i$, which shows that the honest verifier will return *accept*.

For special soundness, given two transcripts $((\hat{E}_1, \ldots, \hat{E}_{k-1}), d, r)$ and $((\hat{E}_1, \ldots, \hat{E}_{k-1}), d', r')$ where $d \neq d'$, and consequently $r \neq r'$ (for non-zero $x$), we have $[c_i r] E_{di} = [c_i r'] E_{d'i}$ for all $i = 1, \ldots, k-1$. Thus an extractor can extract the secret by computing $x = \frac{r-r'}{d'-d} \mod N$.

For the HVZK, given $d$, a simulator samples $r \leftarrow \mathbb{Z}_N$, then for $i = 1, \ldots, k-1$ sets $\hat{E}_i = [c_i r] E_{di}$. In both the real and the simulated transcripts, $r$ and $\hat{E}_i$ are sampled uniformly at random, leading to indistinguishable distributions. □

---

[2] Note that the proof does not need to be a proof of knowledge, rather a *sound* proof. Our presented protocol achieves special soundness, which is stronger than what we need. We consider constructing a sound proof system based on isogenies as an interesting future research direction.

## 5.2    Second Approach: Incremental Well-Formedness Proof

We present our second approach as an algorithm for upgrading a well-formed public key: To this end, assume a prover holds a well-formed public-key $PK_{k-1} = (E_0, E_1, \ldots, E_{k-1})$ of size $k$, where $E_c = [cx]E_0$ for $c = 1, \ldots, k-1$.[3] Now, assume the prover wants to add a new element $E_k = [kx]E_0$ to upgrade its public-key to $PK_k = (E_0, E_1, \ldots, E_{k-1}, E_k)$. Instead of repeating the full well-formedness proof of Sect. 5 for $PK_k$, the prover can create the following proof increment to show, that indeed $E_k = [kx]E_0$. Throughout this section, we denote $\mathbb{C}_k = \{0, \ldots, k\}$. We define the language of correct public-key increments

$$\mathbf{L}_k^{Incr.} = \{(PK_{k-1}, E_k) : \text{the new set } \{PK_{k-1} \cup E_k\} \text{ is well-formed}\}.$$

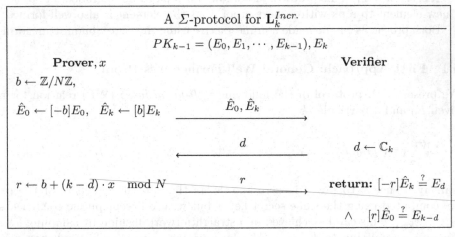

A $\Sigma$-protocol for $\mathbf{L}_k^{Incr.}$

$$PK_{k-1} = (E_0, E_1, \cdots, E_{k-1}), E_k$$

| **Prover**, $x$ | | **Verifier** |
|---|---|---|
| $b \leftarrow \mathbb{Z}/N\mathbb{Z}$, | | |
| $\hat{E}_0 \leftarrow [-b]E_0, \quad \hat{E}_k \leftarrow [b]E_k$ | $\xrightarrow{\hat{E}_0, \hat{E}_k}$ | |
| | $\xleftarrow{d}$ | $d \leftarrow \mathbb{C}_k$ |
| $r \leftarrow b + (k-d) \cdot x \mod N$ | $\xrightarrow{r}$ | **return:** $[-r]\hat{E}_k \stackrel{?}{=} E_d$ |
| | | $\wedge \quad [r]\hat{E}_0 \stackrel{?}{=} E_{k-d}$ |

**Theorem 5.2.** *The above $\Sigma$-protocol is correct, HVZK, and special sound with soundness error rate $\frac{1}{k}$.*

*Proof.* For completeness, we have that $[-r]\hat{E}_k = [-b - (k-d)x + b + kx]E_0 = [dx]E_0 = E_d$ and $[r]\hat{E}_0 = [b + (k-d)x - b] = [(k-d)x]E_0 = E_{k-d}$.

For special soundness, given two accepting transcripts $((\hat{E}_0, \hat{E}_k), d, r)$ and $((\hat{E}_0, \hat{E}_k), d', r')$ with $d \neq d'$, and consequently $r \neq r'$, we have $[r]E_d = [r']E_{d'}$ and $[-r]E_{k-d} = [-r']E_{k-d'}$, which implies that we can extract $x = \frac{r-r'}{d'-d} \mod N$ from either equation.

Finally, for the HVZK, given an honestly generated $d \leftarrow \mathbb{C}_k$, the simulator samples $r \leftarrow \mathbb{Z}_N$, then computes $\hat{E}_k = [r]E_d$ and $\hat{E}_0 = [-r]E_{k-d}$. Finally, it outputs $((\hat{E}_0, \hat{E}_k), d, r)$ as a simulated transcript.    □

## 5.3    Efficiency and Applications

In order to reach a soundness error of $\leq 2^{-\lambda}$, a protocol with soundness error $1/s$ needs to be repeated at least $t(s) = \lceil \lambda \log_s 2 \rceil$ times.

---

[3] Note that this protocol does not work for general exceptional sets, only for sets of the form $\{0, 1, \ldots, k\}$.

- The first protocol has soundness error $1/3$. For a public key $PK_k$, at each step, both the prover and verifier compute $k$ group actions, so that the full protocol results in $C_b(k,\lambda) = kt(3)$ group actions per party.
- The second protocol has soundness error $1/(k+1)$. At every step, the prover and verifier have to compute 2 group actions, yielding the total cost $c_I(k,\lambda) = 2t(k+1)$ for the proof of the increment $PK_{k-1} \to PK_k$. If we want to create the well-formedness proof using only incremented public keys, we find the total cost $C_I(k,\lambda) = \sum_{j=2}^{k} c_I(j,\lambda)$.

It is easy to see, that $c_I(2,\lambda) = C_b(2,\lambda)$ and that $c_I(k,\lambda) < C_b(k,\lambda)$ for $k > 2$. Numerically, we also find, that $C_I(k,\lambda) < C_b(k,\lambda)$ for $k > 16$, independent of $\lambda$. Finally, we can optimize well-formedness proofs by combining the two approaches and finding $l < k$, such that a combination of the full well-formedness proof and the incremental proof has minimal cost $C(k,l,\lambda) := C_b(l,\lambda) + \sum_{j=l+1}^{k} c_I(j,\lambda)$. Numerically, we find $l = 7,8$ to be optimal. Note that this is independent of $\lambda$. For $k < 7$, $l = k$ is optimal and equal to $C_b(k,\lambda)$. Asymptotically for $k \to \infty$, we have $C(k, l = 7, \lambda) \approx C_I(k,\lambda)$.

**Applications.** We realize that the cost of the well-formedness proofs established in the previous section are quite high for large public keys, which would allow a more efficient ID protocol as presented in Sect. 3.1. Note that the well-formedness proofs are not meant to be added to the ID-protocol at every invocation, since this would completely defeat the purpose of having a large public key to increase the efficiency in the first place.

Rather, the idea is to reduce the trust in comparison to our initial proposal in Sect. 3.1. There are many applications, where having a third party generating your private key is not an option. In such a case, a prover could simply generate its own key pair and send a proof of well-formedness to the trusted party. The trusted party verifies it and can then publish, that the well-formedness is accepted for that particular public key, by e.g. signing it. Thus, the expensive proof and verification have to be performed only once. An example of such an application could for instance be in TLS, where a certificate authority could verify the well-formedness of the public key, before issuing a certificate.

# 6 Instantiation with CSIDH-512

We instantiate our protocol using the known class-group and relation lattice of the CSIDH-512 parameter set, established in [BKV19]. In order to allow public-keys with more than 36 elements ($k \geq 37$), we work in the subgroup generated by $\mathfrak{g}^{111}$ and identify $N = \#\mathrm{Cl}(O)/111$, which has smallest prime divisor $q_1 = 1407181$ (cf. Sect. 2.3). We note that, $\log_2(q_1) \approx 2^{20.4}$, which allows our public key sizes to have that same size in case we work with exceptional sets, or up to $\approx 2^{19.4}$, if we work with superexceptional sets. Since the CSIDH-512 parameters set provides an instantiation of a symmetric HHS, we can choose the latter.

Table 1 summarizes different computational and communication costs related to our ID protocol. We use the complexity results established in Sect. 3.2. In our instantiation, we have the parameters $\lceil \log_2 N \rceil = 251$, $\lceil \log_2 p \rceil = 511$ and choose $\lambda = 128$. For simplicity, we bound the elements in $\mathbb{C}$ by $q_1$ and can express the public-key size as $(k - 1)\lceil \log_2 p \rceil + (k - 2)\lceil \log_2 q_1 \rceil = 532k - 553$. In order to give more descriptive examples for the runtime of our protocol, we further use the estimate of 35 ms per GA from [BDPV20], which uses the optimizations from [MR18].

**Table 1.** Public-key size, computational cost and estimated time of proof generation and verification, non-interactive proof size (or signature size), and computational cost of the optimal well-formedness proof established in Sect. 5 for various values of $k$ for standard HHS and symmetric HHS (SHHS). The row with $k = 2$, shows the efficiency of the basic ID protocol which has a binary challenge space. Runtimes are expressed in Group Actions (GA) and also using the estimate that each GA takes 35 ms for demonstration purposes.

| $k$ | Public-key size | Computational cost and run time of prover and verifier | | | | Proof size | | Well-formedness proof | |
| --- | --- | --- | --- | --- | --- | --- | --- | --- | --- |
| | | HHS | | SHHS | | HHS | SHHS | Cost (GA) | Time |
| $2^1$ | 64 B | 128 GA | 4480 ms | 81 GA | 2835 ms | 4032 B | 2552 B | – | – |
| $2^2$ | 197 B | 64 GA | 2240 ms | 46 GA | 1610 ms | 2024 B | 1455 B | 566 | 19.8 s |
| $2^5$ | 2.0 KB | 26 GA | 910 ms | 22 GA | 770 ms | 832 B | 704 B | 2082 | 72.8 s |
| $2^8$ | 16.6 KB | 16 GA | 560 ms | 15 GA | 525 ms | 518 B | 486 B | 10377 | 6.1 min |
| $2^{10}$ | 66.4 KB | 13 GA | 455 ms | 12 GA | 420 ms | 424 B | 392 B | 31761 | 18.5 min |
| $2^{12}$ | 265.9 KB | 11 GA | 385 ms | 10 GA | 350 ms | 362 B | 329 B | 101996 | 59.5 min |
| $2^{15}$ | 2.1 MB | 9 GA | 315 ms | 9 GA | 315 ms | 299 B | 299 B | 628528 | 6.1 h |
| $2^{18}$ | 16.6 MB | 8 GA | 280 ms | 7 GA | 245 ms | 269 B | 235 B | 4093141 | 1.7 days |

# 7  Conclusion

The ID protocol underlying CSI-FiSh [BKV19] allows one to prove knowledge of a secret isogeny, but suffers from a low constant soundness error rate. We were able to arbitrarily decrease the soundness error per round by sampling challenges from exceptional sets, namely sets having certain algebraic properties needed for the extraction. At the same time, this came at the cost of introducing new (structured) public keys that are indexed by the elements of the exceptional set. In the basic form of the protocol, we assumed that both the (structured) public key and the exceptional set were honestly generated by e.g. a trusted authority. We showed that with a 2.1 MB public key, this ID protocol generates proofs of size 299 bytes, and its prover and verifier can generate and verify a proof both in 315 milliseconds. Our ID protocol would allow to prove knowledge of the secret key sk of any CSIDH-based primitive with public-key pk $:= (E_0, E_1)$, where $E_1 := [\mathsf{sk}]E_0$.

We also showed how to get rid of the need for a trusted authority by presenting a protocol that allows the prover to convince the verifier that the keys have the required form. This proof takes a combined approach, by first proving the well-formedness of a small subset of the public key, and then iteratively using this to more efficiently prove the well-formedness of further elements.

We also presented the NIZK version of our ID protocol along with the resulting signature scheme obtained by the Fiat–Shamir transform [FS87]. We devote future work to improve the efficiency of the proof of well-formedness of the public keys, as this is the main bottleneck of the trustless version of our protocol. A possible improvement might come from designing *sound-only* proofs as this would not impose strong algebraic conditions on the challenge space for extraction.

**Acknowledgment.** We would like to thank the anonymous reviewers for their comments. This work has been supported in part by ERC Advanced Grant ERC-2015-AdG-IMPaCT, by the Defense Advanced Research Projects Agency (DARPA) under contract No. HR001120C0085, by the European Research Council (ERC) under the European Unions Horizon 2020 research and innovation programme (Grant agreement No. 101020788 - Adv-ERC-ISOCRYPT), by Research Council KU Leuven grant C14/18/067, and by CyberSecurity Research Flanders with reference number VR20192203. Any opinions, findings and conclusions or recommendations expressed in this material are those of the author(s) and do not necessarily reflect the views of the ERC, DARPA, the US Government, Cyber Security Research Flanders. The U.S. Government is authorized to reproduce and distribute reprints for governmental purposes notwithstanding any copyright annotation therein.

## A    Building Signatures from ID protocols

In order to build a signature scheme from a secure ID protocol, the Fiat–Shamir transformation [FS87] acts as follows. In nutshell, it makes an interactive ID protocol $\Pi = (\mathsf{KGen}, \mathsf{P}, \mathsf{V})$ with $c$-bit challenges for some integer $c \geq 1$, non-interactive using an RO to generate the challenges. Assume the ID protocol must be run in parallel $t$ times to achieve the soundness error rate $\frac{1}{2^{tc}}$. Let $H$ be an RO that outputs a bit string of length $c$. Then, the resulting signature can be expressed as follows,

- $(\mathsf{pk}, \mathsf{sk}) \leftarrow \mathsf{KGen}(1^\lambda)$: as in the setup phase of the ID protocol, given the security parameter, the key generation algorithm $\mathsf{KGen}$ returns the public key and secret key.
- $\sigma \leftarrow \mathsf{Sign}(\mathsf{sk}, m)$: given the secret key $\mathsf{sk}$ and a message $m$ to be signed, the signing algorithm $\mathsf{Sign}$ first computes the commitments $a_i \leftarrow \mathsf{P}(\mathsf{sk}, r_i)$ for $1 \leq i \leq t$. Then computes $h = H(m, a_1, \cdots, a_t)$. Parses $h$ as the $t$ values $c_i \in \{0,1\}^c$. Computes $z_i \leftarrow \mathsf{P}(\mathsf{sk}, r_i, a_i, c_i)$ for $1 \leq i \leq t$. Outputs the signature $\sigma = (a_1, \cdots, a_2, z_1, \cdots, z_t)$.
- $\{1,0\} \leftarrow \mathsf{Vf}(m, \sigma, \mathsf{pk})$: Given a signature, a message and the public key, it compute $h = H(m, a_1, \cdots, a_t)$. Parse $h$ as the $t$ values $c_i \in \{0,1\}^c$. Using the verifier of the ID protocol, checks that $\mathsf{V}(\mathsf{pk}, a_i, c_i, z_i) = 1$ for all $1 \leq i \leq t$. If $\mathsf{V}$ returns 1 for all $i$ then outputs 1, else outputs 0.

It is proven that, starting from a secure ID protocol, the above signature scheme derived by the Fiat–Shamir transform, is unforgeable against chosen-message attacks in the ROM [AABN02].

# References

[AABN02] Abdalla, M., An, J.H., Bellare, M., Namprempre, C.: From identification to signatures via the Fiat-Shamir transform: minimizing assumptions for security and forward-security. In: Knudsen, L.R. (ed.) EUROCRYPT 2002. LNCS, vol. 2332, pp. 418–433. Springer, Heidelberg (2002). https://doi.org/10.1007/3-540-46035-7_28

[BCPS18] Bishnoi, A., Clark, P.L., Potukuchi, A., Schmitt, J.R.: On zeros of a polynomial in a finite grid. Comb. Probab. Comput. **27**(3), 310–333 (2018)

[BDPV20] Beullens, W., Disson, L., Pedersen, R., Vercauteren, F.: CSI-RAShi: distributed key generation for CSIDH. In: Cheon, J.H., Tillich, J.-P. (eds.) PQCrypto 2021 2021. LNCS, vol. 12841, pp. 257–276. Springer, Cham (2021). https://doi.org/10.1007/978-3-030-81293-5_14

[BKV19] Beullens, W., Kleinjung, T., Vercauteren, F.: CSI-FiSh: efficient isogeny based signatures through class group computations. In: Galbraith, S.D., Moriai, S. (eds.) ASIACRYPT 2019. LNCS, vol. 11921, pp. 227–247. Springer, Cham (2019). https://doi.org/10.1007/978-3-030-34578-5_9

[CJS14] Childs, A., Jao, D., Soukharev, V.: Constructing elliptic curve isogenies in quantum subexponential time. J. Math. Cryptol. **8**(1), 1–29 (2014)

[CLM+18] Castryck, W., Lange, T., Martindale, C., Panny, L., Renes, J.: CSIDH: an efficient post-quantum commutative group action. In: Peyrin, T., Galbraith, S. (eds.) ASIACRYPT 2018. LNCS, vol. 11274, pp. 395–427. Springer, Cham (2018). https://doi.org/10.1007/978-3-030-03332-3_15

[Cou06] Jean Marc Couveignes: Hard homogeneous spaces. IACR Cryptol. ePrint Arch. **2006**, 291 (2006)

[DFG19] De Feo, L., Galbraith, S.D.: SeaSign: compact isogeny signatures from class group actions. In: Ishai, Y., Rijmen, V. (eds.) EUROCRYPT 2019. LNCS, vol. 11478, pp. 759–789. Springer, Cham (2019). https://doi.org/10.1007/978-3-030-17659-4_26

[DFKL+20] De Feo, L., Kohel, D., Leroux, A., Petit, C., Wesolowski, B.: SQISign: compact post-quantum signatures from quaternions and isogenies. In: Moriai, S., Wang, H. (eds.) ASIACRYPT 2020. LNCS, vol. 12491, pp. 64–93. Springer, Cham (2020). https://doi.org/10.1007/978-3-030-64837-4_3

[DFKS18] De Feo, L., Kieffer, J., Smith, B.: Towards practical key exchange from ordinary isogeny graphs. In: Peyrin, T., Galbraith, S. (eds.) ASIACRYPT 2018. LNCS, vol. 11274, pp. 365–394. Springer, Cham (2018). https://doi.org/10.1007/978-3-030-03332-3_14

[DFMS19] Don, J., Fehr, S., Majenz, C., Schaffner, C.: Security of the Fiat-Shamir transformation in the quantum random-oracle model. In: Boldyreva, A., Micciancio, D. (eds.) CRYPTO 2019. LNCS, vol. 11693, pp. 356–383. Springer, Cham (2019). https://doi.org/10.1007/978-3-030-26951-7_13

[DLSV20] Dalskov, A., Lee, E., Soria-Vazquez, E.: Circuit amortization friendly encodings and their application to statistically secure multiparty computation. In: Moriai, S., Wang, H. (eds.) ASIACRYPT 2020. LNCS, vol. 12493, pp. 213–243. Springer, Cham (2020). https://doi.org/10.1007/978-3-030-64840-4_8

[DPV19] Decru, T., Panny, L., Vercauteren, F.: Faster SeaSign signatures through improved rejection sampling. In: Ding, J., Steinwandt, R. (eds.) PQCrypto 2019. LNCS, vol. 11505, pp. 271–285. Springer, Cham (2019). https://doi.org/10.1007/978-3-030-25510-7_15

[FS87]  Fiat, A., Shamir, A.: How to prove yourself: practical solutions to identification and signature problems. In: Odlyzko, A.M. (ed.) CRYPTO 1986. LNCS, vol. 263, pp. 186–194. Springer, Heidelberg (1987). https://doi.org/10.1007/3-540-47721-7_12

[GPS17]  Galbraith, S.D., Petit, C., Silva, J.: Identification protocols and signature schemes based on supersingular isogeny problems. In: Takagi, T., Peyrin, T. (eds.) ASIACRYPT 2017. LNCS, vol. 10624, pp. 3–33. Springer, Cham (2017). https://doi.org/10.1007/978-3-319-70694-8_1

[HM89]  Hafner, J.L., McCurley, K.S.: A rigorous subexponential algorithm for computation of class groups. J. Am. Math. Soc. **2**(4), 837–850 (1989)

[JDF11]  Jao, D., De Feo, L.: Towards quantum-resistant cryptosystems from supersingular elliptic curve isogenies. In: Yang, B.-Y. (ed.) PQCrypto 2011. LNCS, vol. 7071, pp. 19–34. Springer, Heidelberg (2011). https://doi.org/10.1007/978-3-642-25405-5_2

[KLPT14]  Kohel, D., Lauter, K., Petit, C., Tignol, J.: On the quaternion-isogeny path problem. LMS J. Comput. Math. **17**(A), 418–432 (2014)

[MR18]  Meyer, M., Reith, S.: A faster way to the CSIDH. In: Chakraborty, D., Iwata, T. (eds.) INDOCRYPT 2018. LNCS, vol. 11356, pp. 137–152. Springer, Cham (2018). https://doi.org/10.1007/978-3-030-05378-9_8

[RS06]  Rostovtsev, A., Stolbunov, A.: Public-key cryptosystem based on isogenies. IACR Cryptol. ePrint Arch. **2006**, 145 (2006)

[Sch89]  Schnorr, C.P.: Efficient identification and signatures for smart cards. In: Brassard, G. (ed.) CRYPTO 1989. LNCS, vol. 435, pp. 239–252. Springer, New York (1990). https://doi.org/10.1007/0-387-34805-0_22

[Sho94]  Shor, P.W.: Algorithms for quantum computation: discrete logarithms and factoring. In: Proceedings of the 35th Annual Symposium on Foundations of Computer Science, pp. 124–134 (1994)

[Sto10]  Stolbunov, A.: Constructing public-key cryptographic schemes based on class group action on a set of isogenous elliptic curves. Adv. Math. Commun. **4**(2), 215 (2010)

[Sto12]  Stolbunov, A.: Cryptographic schemes based on isogenies (2012)

[Unr17]  Unruh, D.: Post-quantum security of Fiat-Shamir. In: Takagi, T., Peyrin, T. (eds.) ASIACRYPT 2017. LNCS, vol. 10624, pp. 65–95. Springer, Cham (2017). https://doi.org/10.1007/978-3-319-70694-8_3

[YAJ+17]  Yoo, Y., Azarderakhsh, R., Jalali, A., Jao, D., Soukharev, V.: A post-quantum digital signature scheme based on supersingular isogenies. In: Kiayias, A. (ed.) FC 2017. LNCS, vol. 10322, pp. 163–181. Springer, Cham (2017). https://doi.org/10.1007/978-3-319-70972-7_9

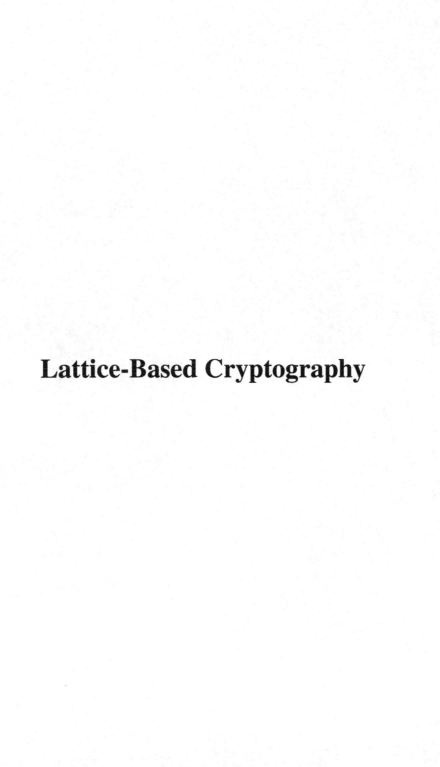

# Lattice-Based Cryptography

# An Extension of Kannan's Embedding for Solving Ring-Based LWE Problems

Satoshi Nakamura[1] and Masaya Yasuda[2]([✉])

[1] NTT Social Informatics Laboratories, Tokyo, Japan
satoshi.nakamura.xn@hco.ntt.co.jp
[2] Department of Mathematics, Rikkyo University, Tokyo, Japan
myasuda@rikkyo.ac.jp

**Abstract.** The hardness of the learning with errors (LWE) problem supports the security of modern lattice-based cryptography. Ring-based LWE is the analog of LWE over univariate polynomial rings that includes the polynomial-LWE and the ring-LWE, and it is useful to construct efficient and compact LWE-based cryptosystems. Any ring-based LWE instance can be transformed to an LWE instance, which can also be reduced to a particular case of the shortest vector problem (SVP) on a certain lattice by Kannan's embedding. In this paper, we extend Kannan's embedding for solving the search version of the ring-based LWE problem. Specifically, we propose a new extended lattice to include multiple short errors that are amplified by rotation operations for the coefficient vector of an error polynomial. Since multiple short errors have the same length and are embedded in our extended lattice, our extension could increase the success probability of solving the ring-based LWE problem by using the Block Korkine-Zorotarev (BKZ) algorithm that is widely used in cryptanalysis. We demonstrate the efficacy of our extension by experiments for solving various ring-based LWE instances.

**Keywords:** Ring-based LWE · Embeddings · Rotations · Lattices · BKZ

## 1 Introduction

The LWE problem is conjectured hard to be solved, and it is useful to construct various cryptosystems such as post-quantum cryptography and high-functional encryption. Informally, the (search) LWE problem asks us to find a solution $\mathbf{s} = (s_1, \ldots, s_n)$ over $\mathbb{Z}_q$ of an approximate linear system

$$
\begin{cases}
t_1 \equiv a_{11}s_1 + a_{21}s_2 + \cdots + a_{n1}s_n + e_1 \pmod{q} \\
t_2 \equiv a_{12}s_1 + a_{22}s_2 + \cdots + a_{n2}s_n + e_2 \pmod{q} \\
\vdots \qquad\qquad \vdots \\
t_d \equiv a_{1d}s_1 + a_{2d}s_2 + \cdots + a_{nd}s_n + e_d \pmod{q}
\end{cases}
$$

© Springer Nature Switzerland AG 2021
M. B. Paterson (Ed.): IMACC 2021, LNCS 13129, pp. 201–219, 2021.
https://doi.org/10.1007/978-3-030-92641-0_10

for an odd prime $q$, where the $a_{ij}$'s are chosen uniformly at random from $\mathbb{Z}_q$ and the $e_i$'s are small error terms in $\mathbb{Z}$. This system can be simply represented as a pair $(\mathbf{A}, \mathbf{t})$ satisfying $\mathbf{t} \equiv \mathbf{s}\mathbf{A} + \mathbf{e} \pmod{q}$, where $\mathbf{A} = (a_{ij}) \in \mathbb{Z}_q^{n \times d}$, $\mathbf{t} = (t_1, \ldots, t_d) \in \mathbb{Z}_q^d$, and $\mathbf{e} = (e_1, \ldots, e_d) \in \mathbb{Z}^d$. We call such a pair an LWE instance of size $n \times d$ with a secret $\mathbf{s}$ and an error $\mathbf{e}$. The condition $d > n$ is at least required to recover $\mathbf{s}$ uniquely, and the $e_i$'s are often sampled from the discrete Gaussian distribution. Any LWE instance $(\mathbf{A}, \mathbf{t})$ can be naturally regarded as an instance of the bounded distance decoding (BDD), a particular case of the closest vector problem (CVP), over a $q$-ary lattice $\Lambda_q(\mathbf{A})$ generated by $\mathbf{A}$ with a target $\mathbf{t}$ (see [19] for $q$-ary lattices). Furthermore, Kannan's embedding [15] can transform any BDD instance to an instance of the unique-SVP, a particular case of SVP. Specifically, the lattice of Kannan's embedding includes $\pm\mathbf{e}$ as unusually short lattice vectors, which can be recovered by using the BKZ algorithm [25]. Once the error is recovered, the secret can be also recovered by Gaussian elimination for the linear equation $\mathbf{t} - \mathbf{e} \equiv \mathbf{s}\mathbf{A} \pmod{q}$. This strategy for solving an LWE instance is referred to as the primal attack [4]. In addition, an improvement of Kannan's embedding was proposed by Bai and Galbraith [7] for a small secret.

Ring-based LWE is a generalization of LWE over univariate polynomial rings, and its setting includes the polynomial-LWE and the ring-LWE (see [10] for details). We focus on a ring $R = \mathbb{Z}[x]/(x^n + 1)$ for a 2-power integer $n$. (This ring is commonly used in structured lattice-based cryptography.) We let $R_q = R/qR$ for an odd prime $q$. Informally, the (search) ring-based LWE problem asks us to find a solution $s(x)$ over $R_q$ of a system

$$\begin{cases} t_1(x) = s(x)a_1(x) + e_1(x), \\ \quad \vdots \\ t_m(x) = s(x)a_m(x) + e_m(x), \end{cases} \tag{1}$$

where the $a_i(x)$'s are chosen uniformly at random from $R_q$ and the $e_i(x)$'s are 'small' elements of $R$. For every ring element $f(x) = f_0 + f_1 x + \cdots + f_{n-1}x^{n-1}$, we write its coefficient vector as $\mathbf{f} = (f_0, f_1, \ldots, f_{n-1})$. When we express every ring element as its coefficient vector, every ring-based LWE sample $(a_i(x), t_i(x))$ can be rewritten as an LWE instance $(\mathbf{A}_i, \mathbf{t}_i)$ of size $n \times n$ with a secret $\mathbf{s}$ and an error $\mathbf{e}_i$, where the matrix $\mathbf{A}_i$ is constructed from the coefficient vector $\mathbf{a}_i$ of $a_i(x)$ like Eq. (2) below. Furthermore, we concatenate $m$ LWE instances to obtain an LWE instance $(\widetilde{\mathbf{A}}, \widetilde{\mathbf{t}})$ of size $n \times d$ with a secret $\mathbf{s}$ and an error $\widetilde{\mathbf{e}} = (\mathbf{e}_1 \mid \cdots \mid \mathbf{e}_m)$, where $d = mn$, $\widetilde{\mathbf{A}} = (\mathbf{A}_1 \mid \cdots \mid \mathbf{A}_m)$ and $\widetilde{\mathbf{t}} = (\mathbf{t}_1 \mid \cdots \mid \mathbf{t}_m)$.

In this paper, we propose an extension of Kannan's embedding for solving an LWE instance $(\widetilde{\mathbf{A}}, \widetilde{\mathbf{t}})$, constructed from ring-based LWE samples. A key ingredient is the rotation operation that is defined as $\mathrm{rot}(\mathbf{f}) = (-f_{n-1}, f_0, f_1, \ldots, f_{n-2})$, which equals to the coefficient vector of $xf(x)$. We construct a new lattice including multiple short vectors $\mathrm{rot}^i(\widetilde{\mathbf{e}})$ that are amplified by rotation operations for $\widetilde{\mathbf{e}}$, where $\mathrm{rot}^i(\widetilde{\mathbf{e}})$ denotes the rotated vector for blocks as $(\mathrm{rot}^i(\mathbf{e}_1) \mid \cdots \mid \mathrm{rot}^i(\mathbf{e}_m))$. (We note that our extended lattice is similar to the NTRU lattice [14] that includes a short vector $(\mathbf{f}, \mathbf{g})$ and all of its rotated vectors $(\mathrm{rot}^i(\mathbf{f}), \mathrm{rot}^i(\mathbf{g}))$. We

also note that our extension is applicable to Bai-Galbraith's embedding [7].)
Specifically, since $\text{rot}^i(\widetilde{\mathbf{t}}) \equiv \text{rot}^i(\mathbf{s}) \cdot \widetilde{\mathbf{A}} + \text{rot}^i(\widetilde{\mathbf{e}}) \pmod{q}$, we append rotated vectors $\text{rot}^i(\widetilde{\mathbf{t}})$ to a basis of the lattice constructed in Kannan's embedding. Since multiple target vectors $\text{rot}^i(\widetilde{\mathbf{e}})$ have the same norm and they are embedded in our extended lattice, our extension could increase the success probability of solving the ring-based LWE problem by using BKZ. We show several experimental results to demonstrate the efficacy of our extended Kannan's embedding for solving various ring-based LWE instances. We also discuss trade-offs of our extension based on experimental results.

*Notation.* The symbols $\mathbb{Z}$ and $\mathbb{R}$ denote the ring of integers and the field of real numbers, respectively. For an odd prime $q$, let $\mathbb{Z}_q$ denote a set of representatives of integers modulo $q$ such as $\mathbb{Z}_q = \mathbb{Z} \cap \left[ -\frac{q}{2}, \frac{q}{2} \right)$. For two vectors $\mathbf{v} = (v_1, \ldots, v_d)$, $\mathbf{w} = (w_1, \ldots, w_d) \in \mathbb{R}^d$, let $\langle \mathbf{v}, \mathbf{w} \rangle$ denote the inner product $\sum_{i=1}^{d} v_i w_i$. We let $\|\mathbf{v}\|$ denote the Euclidean norm defined as $\|\mathbf{v}\| = \sqrt{\langle \mathbf{v}, \mathbf{v} \rangle}$. We write by $\mathbf{A}^\top$ (resp., $\mathbf{v}^\top$) the transpose of a matrix $\mathbf{A}$ (resp., a vector $\mathbf{v}$).

## 2  Preliminaries: Ring-Based LWE and Lattices

In this section, we recall a setting of ring-based LWE problem, and describe how to reduce it to lattice problems such as CVP and SVP (see [1,2,4] for details). We also recall lattice basis reduction such as the BKZ algorithm that is a strong tool to solve lattice problems (e.g., see [9,21] for lattice basis reduction).

### 2.1  Ring-Based LWE

Here we follow the ring-based LWE framework of [10] that contains the polynomial-LWE by Stehlé *et al.* [26] and the ring-LWE by Lyubashevsky *et al.* [18]. We focus on a ring $R = \mathbb{Z}[x]/(x^n + 1)$ for a 2-power integer $n$, which is commonly used in structured lattice-based cryptography (e.g., see [1]). We let $R_q = R/qR$ for a prime $q$, and $\chi$ an error distribution on $R$ outputting 'small' elements.

**Definition 1 (Search ring-based LWE).** *Fix an element $s(x)$ in $R_q$ that is called a "secret". The ring-based LWE distribution $A_{s,\chi}$ samples a pair*

$$(a(x), t(x)) \in R_q \times R_q, \quad t(x) = s(x)a(x) + e(x),$$

*where $a(x)$ is uniformly chosen at random from the quotient ring $R_q$ and $e(x)$ is sampled from the distribution $\chi$. Then the search ring-LWE problem asks us to find the secret $s(x)$ given any independent samples from $A_{s,\chi}$.*

**Rotation.** Any element of $R$ (resp., $R_q$) can be expressed as a polynomial of degree $n-1$ with coefficients in $\mathbb{Z}$ (resp., $\mathbb{Z}_q$). For any element $f(x) = f_0 + f_1 +$

$\cdots + f_{n-1}x^{n-1}$ of $R$ (resp., $R_q$), we write its coefficient vector in $\mathbb{Z}^n$ (resp., $\mathbb{Z}_q^n$) as $\mathbf{f} = (f_0, f_1, \ldots, f_{n-1})$. We define the rotation operation for $\mathbf{f}$ as

$$\mathrm{rot}(\mathbf{f}) = (-f_{n-1}, f_0, f_1, \ldots, f_{n-2}).$$

This is just the coefficient vector of the element $xf(x)$ in $R$. Similarly, for each $1 \le i \le n$, the $i$ times rotated vector $\mathrm{rot}^i(\mathbf{f})$ is the coefficient vector of $x^i f(x)$ in $R$. In particular, we have $\mathrm{rot}^n(\mathbf{f}) = -\mathbf{f}$ since $x^n = -1$ in $R$.

**Reduction to LWE.** We take a ring-based LWE sample $(a(x), t(x))$ from the ring-based LWE distribution $A_{s,\chi}$. For the coefficient vector $\mathbf{a} = (a_0, a_1, \ldots, a_{n-1})$ of $a(x)$, we set the $n \times n$ matrix

$$\mathbf{A} = \begin{pmatrix} \mathbf{a} \\ \mathrm{rot}(\mathbf{a}) \\ \vdots \\ \mathrm{rot}^{n-1}(\mathbf{a}) \end{pmatrix} = \begin{pmatrix} a_0 & a_1 & \cdots & a_{n-1} \\ -a_{n-1} & a_0 & \cdots & a_{n-2} \\ \vdots & \vdots & \ddots & \vdots \\ -a_1 & -a_2 & \cdots & a_0 \end{pmatrix}. \tag{2}$$

Then it holds $\mathbf{t} \equiv \mathbf{s}\mathbf{A} + \mathbf{e} \pmod{q}$, where $\mathbf{t}, \mathbf{s}, \mathbf{e}$ are coefficient vectors of three polynomials $t(x), s(x), e(x)$, respectively. Indeed, the ring-based LWE relation $t(x) = s(x)a(x) + e(x)$ can be rewritten as

$$\begin{aligned} \mathbf{t}\mathbf{x}^\top = t(x) &= s(x)a(x) + e(x) \\ &= \mathbf{s}\mathbf{x}^\top a(x) + \mathbf{e}\mathbf{x}^\top \\ &= \mathbf{s} \begin{pmatrix} a(x) \\ xa(x) \\ \vdots \\ x^{n-1}a(x) \end{pmatrix} + \mathbf{e}\mathbf{x}^\top = \mathbf{s} \begin{pmatrix} \mathbf{a} \\ \mathrm{rot}(\mathbf{a}) \\ \vdots \\ \mathrm{rot}^{n-1}(\mathbf{a}) \end{pmatrix} \mathbf{x}^\top + \mathbf{e}\mathbf{x}^\top \\ &= (\mathbf{s}\mathbf{A} + \mathbf{e})\mathbf{x}^\top, \end{aligned} \tag{3}$$

where $\mathbf{x} = (1, x, x^2, \ldots, x^{n-1})$ gives a basis of the ring $R$ (resp., $R_q$) as a $\mathbb{Z}$-module (resp., $\mathbb{Z}_q$-module). In other words, a ring-based LWE sample generates an LWE instance $(\mathbf{A}, \mathbf{t})$ of size $n \times n$ with a secret $\mathbf{s}$ and an error $\mathbf{e}$.

In Definition 1, we consider the number of given samples from $A_{s,\chi}$ as an additional parameter of ring-based LWE. For an integer $m \ge 1$, we take $m$ independent ring-based LWE samples $(a_1(x), t_1(x)), \ldots, (a_m(x), t_m(x))$ from $A_{s,\chi}$ (see the system (1) over $R_q$). Let $\mathbf{A}_i$ denote the $n \times n$ matrix corresponding to $a_i(x)$ like (2) for each $1 \le i \le m$. Then we have $m$ relations $\mathbf{t}_i \equiv \mathbf{s}\mathbf{A}_i + \mathbf{e}_i \pmod{q}$ for $1 \le i \le m$ from the previous paragraph. We can concatenate the $m$ relations to obtain an LWE instance of size $n \times d$ as

$$\left( \widetilde{\mathbf{A}}, \widetilde{\mathbf{t}} \right), \quad \widetilde{\mathbf{t}} \equiv \mathbf{s}\widetilde{\mathbf{A}} + \widetilde{\mathbf{e}} \pmod{q}, \tag{4}$$

where $d = mn$, $\widetilde{\mathbf{A}} = (\mathbf{A}_1 \mid \cdots \mid \mathbf{A}_m)$, $\widetilde{\mathbf{t}} = (\mathbf{t}_1 \mid \cdots \mid \mathbf{t}_m)$ and $\widetilde{\mathbf{e}} = (\mathbf{e}_1 \mid \cdots \mid \mathbf{e}_m)$. We note that the system (1) should be overdetermined, that is $m \ge 2$ (or $d > n$), to recover the secret $s(x)$ (or its coefficient vector $\mathbf{s}$) uniquely.

## 2.2 $q$-ary Lattices

**Basics on Lattices.** A *lattice* is a discrete additive subgroup of the Euclidean space $\mathbb{R}^d$. Any lattice $L$ is spanned over $\mathbb{Z}$ by some linearly independent vectors $\mathbf{b}_1, \ldots, \mathbf{b}_h$ in $\mathbb{R}^d$ as

$$L = \mathcal{L}(\mathbf{b}_1, \ldots, \mathbf{b}_h) = \left\{ \sum_{i=1}^{h} v_i \mathbf{b}_i : v_1, v_2, \ldots, v_h \in \mathbb{Z} \right\}.$$

The set of vectors $[\mathbf{b}_1, \ldots, \mathbf{b}_h]$ is called a *basis* of $L$, and the (maximal) number of linearly independent vectors spanning $L$ is called the *dimension* (or *rank*) of $L$, denoted by $\dim(L)$. In particular, a lattice $L$ in $\mathbb{R}^d$ is said to be *full-rank* when $\dim(L) = d$. There exist infinitely many bases of a lattice $L$ if $\dim(L) \geq 2$. The volume of $L$ is defined as $\mathrm{vol}(L) = \sqrt{\det(\mathbf{G})}$, where $\mathbf{G} = (\langle \mathbf{b}_i, \mathbf{b}_j \rangle)_{1 \leq i,j \leq h}$ denotes the Gram matrix of a basis $[\mathbf{b}_1, \ldots, \mathbf{b}_h]$ of $L$. The volume of a lattice is independent of the choice of bases of the lattice. Let $\lambda_1(L)$ denote the first successive minimum of a lattice $L$ that is equal to the norm of a shortest non-zero vector in $L$ (see [9,21] for the definition of other successive minima $\lambda_i(L)$).

**$q$-ary Lattices from LWE.** A full-rank lattice $L$ in $\mathbb{R}^d$ is said of *$q$-ary* for an odd prime $q$ if it satisfies $q\mathbb{Z}^d \subseteq L \subseteq \mathbb{Z}^d$. Given an LWE instance, the construction of several $q$-ary lattices is shown in [19] for reducing the instance to lattice problems such as SVP and CVP. We apply it to the LWE instance (4) to obtain a $q$-ary lattice

$$\Lambda_q(\widetilde{\mathbf{A}}) = \left\{ \widetilde{\mathbf{z}} \in \mathbb{Z}^d \mid \widetilde{\mathbf{z}} \equiv \mathbf{s}\widetilde{\mathbf{A}} \pmod{q}, \exists \mathbf{s} \in \mathbb{Z}^n \right\}. \tag{5}$$

We see that the rows of the $(d+n) \times d$ matrix $\begin{pmatrix} \widetilde{\mathbf{A}} \\ q\mathbf{I}_d \end{pmatrix}$ spans the $q$-ary lattice, where $\mathbf{I}_d$ denotes the identity matrix of size $d$. In addition, we can obtain a basis of the lattice by computing the Hermite normal form (or LLL which we shall present below) of such a generating matrix. It is known that it holds $\mathrm{vol}(\Lambda_q(\widetilde{\mathbf{A}})) = q^{d-n}$ for most matrices $\widetilde{\mathbf{A}}$.

**Reduction of LWE to CVP.** We can naturally regard the LWE instance (4) as a CVP instance over the $q$-ary lattice $\Lambda_q(\widetilde{\mathbf{A}})$ with a target vector $\widetilde{\mathbf{t}}$. In particular, the minimum distance between the target $\widetilde{\mathbf{t}}$ and the lattice vector $\mathbf{s}\widetilde{\mathbf{A}}$ in $\Lambda_q(\widetilde{\mathbf{A}})$ is equal to the length of the error $\widetilde{\mathbf{e}}$ by if the error is sufficiently short. (In a general setting of LWE, the error is considerably shorter than the modulus prime $q$.) Technically speaking, this is an instance of the *bounded distance decoding (BDD)* problem, a particular case of CVP with a promise about the minimum distance of a target from a lattice. (See [4] for other attacks against LWE.)

## 2.3 Lattice Basis Reduction

Given a basis of a lattice $L$, the goal of reduction is to seek a new basis $[\mathbf{b}_1, \ldots, \mathbf{b}_d]$ of $L$ with short and nearly orthogonal basis vectors $\mathbf{b}_i$'s in each other. Such algorithms give a strong tool for solving lattice problems such as CVP and SVP. To introduce reduction algorithms, we recall some basic definitions below.

The *Gram-Schmidt orthogonalization* of a basis $[\mathbf{b}_1, \ldots, \mathbf{b}_d]$ is the set of orthogonal vectors $\mathbf{b}_1^*, \ldots, \mathbf{b}_d^*$ defined recursively by

$$
\begin{cases}
\mathbf{b}_1^* := \mathbf{b}_1, \\
\mathbf{b}_i^* := \mathbf{b}_i - \sum_{j=1}^{i-1} \mu_{ij} \mathbf{b}_j^*, \quad \mu_{ij} := \dfrac{\langle \mathbf{b}_i, \mathbf{b}_j^* \rangle}{\|\mathbf{b}_j^*\|^2} \quad (i > j)
\end{cases}
\tag{6}
$$

for $2 \le i \le d$. Let $\mathbf{B}$ (resp., $\mathbf{B}^*$) denote the matrix whose rows are basis vectors $\mathbf{b}_i$'s (resp., Gram-Schmidt vectors $\mathbf{b}_i^*$'s). Let $\mathbf{U} = (\mu_{ij})$ denote the lower triangular matrix given by (6) with diagonal entries $\mu_{ii} = 1$. Then we have $\mathbf{B} = \mathbf{U}\mathbf{B}^*$, and hence $\mathrm{vol}(L) = \prod_{i=1}^{d} \|\mathbf{b}_i^*\|$ for the lattice $L = \mathcal{L}(\mathbf{B}) = \mathcal{L}(\mathbf{b}_1, \ldots, \mathbf{b}_d)$. For each $1 \le k \le d$, define an orthogonal projection map as

$$
\pi_k : \mathbb{R}^d \longrightarrow \langle \mathbf{b}_k^*, \ldots, \mathbf{b}_d^* \rangle_{\mathbb{R}}, \quad \pi_k(\mathbf{v}) = \sum_{i=k}^{d} \frac{\langle \mathbf{v}, \mathbf{b}_i^* \rangle}{\|\mathbf{b}_i^*\|^2} \mathbf{b}_i^* \quad (\mathbf{v} \in \mathbb{R}^d),
$$

where $\langle \mathbf{b}_k^*, \ldots, \mathbf{b}_d^* \rangle_{\mathbb{R}}$ is the sub-vector space spanned by Gram-Schmidt vectors $\mathbf{b}_k^*, \ldots, \mathbf{b}_d^*$. The lattice in $\mathbb{R}^d$ spanned by projected vectors $\pi_k(\mathbf{b}_k), \ldots, \pi_k(\mathbf{b}_d)$ is denoted by $\pi_k(L)$ and called a *projected lattice*. The projected lattice $\pi_k(L)$ is of dimension $n - k + 1$ and its volume is equal to $\prod_{i=k}^{d} \|\mathbf{b}_i^*\|$.

Below we recall two major algorithms of lattice basis reduction (e.g., see [28] for details of reduction algorithms).

**Lenstra-Lenstra-Lovász (LLL).** We say a basis $\mathbf{B} = [\mathbf{b}_1, \ldots, \mathbf{b}_d]$ to be $\delta$-*LLL-reduced* for a parameter $\frac{1}{4} < \delta < 1$ if (i) (Size-reduced) it holds $|\mu_{ij}| \le \frac{1}{2}$ for all $i > j$, and (ii) (Lovász' condition) $\delta \|\mathbf{b}_{k-1}^*\|^2 \le \|\pi_{k-1}(\mathbf{b}_k)\|^2$ for all $k$, where $\mu_{ij}$'s and $\mathbf{b}_k^*$'s are Gram-Schmidt coefficients and vectors of $\mathbf{B}$. For a $\delta$-LLL-reduced basis $\mathbf{B}$, it holds both $\|\mathbf{b}_1\| \le \alpha^{\frac{d-1}{2}} \lambda_1(L)$ and $\|\mathbf{b}_1\| \le \alpha^{\frac{d-1}{4}} \mathrm{vol}(L)^{\frac{1}{d}}$ for $L = \mathcal{L}(\mathbf{B})$ and $\alpha = \frac{4}{4\delta - 1}$. To find an LLL-reduced basis, the LLL algorithm [17] calls size-reduction as a subroutine, and it also swaps adjacent basis vectors that do not satisfy Lovász' condition. The LLL algorithm has complexity polynomial in $d$, and it is also useful to get rid of the linear dependency of vectors.

**Block Korkine-Zolotarev (BKZ).** For a basis $\mathbf{B} = [\mathbf{b}_1, \ldots, \mathbf{b}_d]$ of a lattice $L$, we set $\mathbf{B}_{[j:k]} = [\pi_j(\mathbf{b}_j), \pi_j(\mathbf{b}_{j+1}), \ldots, \pi_j(\mathbf{b}_k)]$ and $L_{[j:k]} = \mathcal{L}(\mathbf{B}_{[j:k]})$ for $j < k$. For a blocksize $\beta \ge 2$, a basis $\mathbf{B}$ is said to be $\beta$-*BKZ-reduced* if it is size-reduced and $\|\mathbf{b}_j^*\| = \lambda_1(L_{[j:k]})$ for every $1 \le j \le d - 1$ and $k = \min(j + \beta - 1, d)$. In the particular case $\beta = n$, it is called to be Hermite-Korkine-Zolotarev (HKZ) reduced. For a $\beta$-BKZ-reduced basis $\mathbf{B}$, it holds $\|\mathbf{b}_1\| \le \gamma_\beta^{\frac{d-1}{\beta-1}} \lambda_1(L)$ [23], where $\gamma_\beta$ denotes Hermite's constant of dimension $\beta$ (see [21] for Hermite's constants).

A $\beta$-BKZ-reduced basis can be found by the BKZ algorithm [25], in which LLL is called to reduce each block $\mathbf{B}_{[j:k]}$ before calling an exact-SVP algorithm (e.g., ENUM) over $L_{[j:k]}$. Since larger $\beta$ decreases $\gamma_\beta^{1/(\beta-1)}$, BKZ finds short lattice vectors, but its computational cost is much more expensive. The complexity of BKZ depends on that of an SVP algorithm over blocks $L_{[j:k]}$.

## 3   Extension of Kannan's Embedding for Ring-Based LWE

Kannan's embedding [15] is a method to transform CVP into SVP. In this section, we propose an extension of Kannan's embedding for solving the search ring-based LWE problem. We also give an application of our idea to Bai-Galbraith's embedding [7]. In addition, we describe how to solve the ring-based LWE problem in our extended Kannan's embedding by using the BKZ algorithm.

### 3.1   New Extended Lattices

We consider the LWE instance (4), constructed from ring-based LWE samples in Subsect. 2.1. We shall extend a basis $\mathbf{C}$ of the $q$-ary lattice (5) to define a new lattice. Specifically, we consider the $(d+k) \times (d+k)$ matrix

$$\mathbf{B} = \begin{pmatrix} \mathbf{C} & 0 & 0 & \cdots & 0 \\ \widetilde{\mathbf{t}} & \eta & 0 & \cdots & 0 \\ \mathrm{rot}(\widetilde{\mathbf{t}}) & 0 & \eta & \cdots & 0 \\ \vdots & \vdots & \vdots & \ddots & \vdots \\ \mathrm{rot}^{k-1}(\widetilde{\mathbf{t}}) & 0 & 0 & \cdots & \eta \end{pmatrix} \tag{7}$$

for an extension parameter $k$ and a small constant $\eta$, where $\mathrm{rot}^i(\widetilde{\mathbf{t}})$ denotes the rotated vector of $\widetilde{\mathbf{t}}$ for blocks as $\mathrm{rot}^i(\widetilde{\mathbf{t}}) = \left(\mathrm{rot}^i(\mathbf{t}_1) \mid \cdots \mid \mathrm{rot}^i(\mathbf{t}_m)\right)$. We let $\bar{\Lambda}_k$ denote the lattice of dimension $d+k$ generated by the rows of $\mathbf{B}$. Similarly to Eqs. (3), $m$ relations $x^i t_j(x) = x^i s(x) \cdot a_j(x) + x^i e_j(x)$ in $R_q$ for $1 \le j \le m$, ring-based LWE relations multiplied by $x^i$, can be rewritten as

$$\mathrm{rot}^i(\widetilde{\mathbf{t}}) \equiv \mathrm{rot}^i(\mathbf{s}) \cdot \widetilde{\mathbf{A}} + \mathrm{rot}^i(\widetilde{\mathbf{e}}) \pmod{q} \tag{8}$$

in $\mathbb{Z}_q^d$ for $1 \le i < k$, where $\mathrm{rot}^i(\widetilde{\mathbf{e}})$ denotes the rotated vector of $\widetilde{\mathbf{e}}$ for blocks like $\mathrm{rot}^i(\widetilde{\mathbf{t}})$. By Eq. (8) and the construction of $\mathbf{B}$ (note that $\mathcal{L}(\mathbf{C}) = \Lambda_q(\widetilde{\mathbf{A}})$), the extended lattice $\bar{\Lambda}_k$ includes $k$ short lattice vectors

$$\begin{cases} \bar{\mathbf{e}} = (\widetilde{\mathbf{e}} \mid \eta, 0, \ldots, 0), \\ \mathrm{rot}\,(\bar{\mathbf{e}}) = (\mathrm{rot}\,(\widetilde{\mathbf{e}}) \mid 0, \eta, \ldots, 0), \\ \quad \vdots \\ \mathrm{rot}^{k-1}\,(\bar{\mathbf{e}}) = \left(\mathrm{rot}^{k-1}\,(\widetilde{\mathbf{e}}) \mid 0, \ldots, 0, \eta\right). \end{cases} \tag{9}$$

These lattice vectors have the same length since the rotation operation does not change the length of a vector. In particular, the position of $\eta$ in the latter block in (4) indicates the number of rotation operations of the error vector $\bar{\mathbf{e}}$.

*Remark 1.* The case $k = 1$ is just the original Kannan's embedding [15]. In the original Kannan's embedding, the search ring-based LWE problem is reduced to the unique-SVP in which the unique unusual short lattice $\tilde{\mathbf{e}}$ is included. On the other hand, our extension is no longer a reduction of the unique-SVP for $k \geq 2$ like a reduction of the NTRU problem (e.g., see [1,2,4,14] for the NTRU lattice). In contrast, the extension parameter $k$ controls the number of rotated vectors $\mathrm{rot}^i(\tilde{\mathbf{e}})$ included in our extended lattice $\bar{\Lambda}_k$ for the search ring-based LWE problem. As another remark, in the particular case $k = n$, the lattice $\bar{\Lambda}_n$ admits the rotation operation like ideal lattices.

*Remark 2.* In a case of using large $k$ such as $k = n$, some combination of vectors in (9) with small integers can be a shortest non-zero vector in the lattice $\bar{\Lambda}_k$. If we find such a shortest non-zero vector, then the positions of scalers of $\eta$ help us to construct a system of linear equations to recover the non-rotated error $\tilde{\mathbf{e}}$. But in a case of using small $k$, any combination of vectors in (9) is rarely shorter than vectors in (9) in practice. (Indeed, the vectors in (9) seem to be the shortest in $\bar{\Lambda}_k \setminus \{\mathbf{0}\}$ in our experiments for $1 \leq k \leq 5$ below.)

*Remark 3.* Equation (8) can also be rewritten as

$$\mathrm{rot}^i(\tilde{\mathbf{t}}) \equiv \mathrm{rot}^{i-j}(\mathbf{s}) \cdot \mathrm{rot}^j(\tilde{\mathbf{A}}) + \mathrm{rot}^i(\tilde{\mathbf{e}}) \pmod{q}$$

for any integer $j$, where $\mathrm{rot}^j(\tilde{\mathbf{A}})$ the rotated matrix of $\tilde{\mathbf{A}}$ with respect to blocks as $\mathrm{rot}^j(\tilde{\mathbf{A}}) = \left(\mathrm{rot}^j(\mathbf{A}_1) \mid \cdots \mid \mathrm{rot}^j(\mathbf{A}_m)\right)$. Here $\mathrm{rot}^j(\mathbf{A}_h)$ denotes the $n \times n$ matrix whose rows are the $j$ times rotated rows of $\mathbf{A}_h$. Indeed, similarly to Eqs. (3), the relation $x^i t_h(x) = x^{i-j} s(x) \cdot x^j a_h(x) + x^i e_h(x)$ in $R_q$ can be rewritten as

$$\begin{aligned}
\mathrm{rot}^i(\mathbf{t}_h)\mathbf{x}^\top = x^i t_h(x) &= x^{i-j} s(x) \cdot x^j a_h(x) + x^i e_h(x) \\
&= \mathrm{rot}^{i-j}(\mathbf{s})\mathbf{x}^\top x^j a_h(x) + \mathrm{rot}^i(\mathbf{e}_h)\mathbf{x}^\top \\
&= \left(\mathrm{rot}^{i-j}(\mathbf{s}) \cdot \mathrm{rot}^j(\mathbf{A}_h) + \mathrm{rot}^i(\mathbf{e}_h)\right) \mathbf{x}^\top
\end{aligned}$$

for each $1 \leq h \leq m$. In addition, it follows from the construction of $\tilde{\mathbf{A}}$ that any rotation operation for $\tilde{\mathbf{A}}$ is just a permutation over the rows of $\tilde{\mathbf{A}}$. Hence the $q$-ary lattice $\Lambda_q(\mathrm{rot}^j(\tilde{\mathbf{A}}))$ is equal to the $q$-ary lattice (5) for any $j$.

*Remark 4.* The lower-right block of $\mathbf{B}$ is a diagonal matrix, and the volume of the lattice $\bar{\Lambda}_k$ is given by $\eta^k \cdot \mathrm{vol}(\Lambda_q(\tilde{\mathbf{A}}))$. We here modify the lower-right block of $\mathbf{B}$ to construct a lattice of the same dimension as $\bar{\Lambda}_k$ with a larger volume without increasing the length of embedded error vectors. (A large lattice volume is effective in solving LWE problems, see the next subsection.) For $k \geq 3$, we consider

$$
\mathbf{B}' = \begin{pmatrix}
\mathbf{C} & 0 & 0 & 0 & 0 & \cdots & 0 & 0 & 0 \\
\widetilde{\mathbf{t}} & \eta & \eta & 0 & 0 & \cdots & 0 & 0 & -\eta \\
\mathrm{rot}(\widetilde{\mathbf{t}}) & -\eta & \eta & \eta & 0 & \cdots & 0 & 0 & 0 \\
\mathrm{rot}^2(\widetilde{\mathbf{t}}) & 0 & -\eta & \eta & \eta & \cdots & 0 & 0 & 0 \\
\vdots & \vdots & \vdots & \vdots & \ddots & \ddots & \ddots & \vdots & \vdots \\
\vdots & \vdots & \vdots & \vdots & & \ddots & \ddots & \ddots & \vdots \\
\vdots & \vdots & \vdots & \vdots & \vdots & & \ddots & \ddots & \vdots \\
\mathrm{rot}^{k-2}(\widetilde{\mathbf{t}}) & 0 & 0 & 0 & 0 & \cdots & -\eta & \eta & \eta \\
\mathrm{rot}^{k-1}(\widetilde{\mathbf{t}}) & \eta & 0 & 0 & 0 & \cdots & 0 & -\eta & \eta
\end{pmatrix}.
$$

We let $\bar{\Lambda}'_k$ denote the lattice spanned by the rows of $\mathbf{B}'$. By determinant formulas of (ordinary) tridiagonal matrices (e.g., see [20]), the determinant of the lower-right block of $\mathbf{B}'$ is given by

$$
t_k = \eta^k \cdot \left\{ \mathrm{tr}(\mathbf{M}^k) + (-1)^{k+1} - 1 \right\}, \quad \mathbf{M} = \begin{pmatrix} 1 & 1 \\ 1 & 0 \end{pmatrix}.
$$

In particular, the trace values $f_k = \mathrm{tr}(\mathbf{M}^k)$ form a kind of the Fibonacci sequence $f_k = f_{k-1} + f_{k-2}$ starting with $f_1 = 1$ and $f_2 = 3$. Then the volume of the modified lattice $\bar{\Lambda}'_k$ is given by $t_k \cdot \mathrm{vol}(\Lambda_q(\widetilde{\mathbf{A}}))$, and it is considerably larger than the volume of the original lattice $\bar{\Lambda}_k$ for large $k$. In addition, from the same discussion as above, the modified lattice $\bar{\Lambda}'_k$ contains $k$ short vectors

$$
\begin{cases}
\bar{\mathbf{e}}' = (\widetilde{\mathbf{e}} \mid \eta, \eta, 0, \ldots, 0, -\eta), \\
\mathrm{rot}(\bar{\mathbf{e}}') = (\mathrm{rot}(\widetilde{\mathbf{e}}) \mid -\eta, \eta, \eta, 0 \ldots, 0), \\
\quad \vdots \\
\mathrm{rot}^{k-1}(\bar{\mathbf{e}}') = \left(\mathrm{rot}^{k-1}(\widetilde{\mathbf{e}}) \mid \eta, 0 \ldots, 0, -\eta, \eta\right).
\end{cases}
$$

These lattice vectors have the same length, whose size is slightly larger than the length of vectors (9). (The difference is that two more components with value $\pm\eta$ are added to the latter block.)

**Application to Bai-Galbraith's Embedding.** Bai-Galbraith's embedding [7] is an improvement of Kannan's embedding for solving LWE problems with a small secret. Similar to the case of Kannan's embedding, we shall extend Bai-Galbraith's embedding by using rotated vectors of $\widetilde{\mathbf{t}}$. For the LWE instance (4), we consider the $(d+n+k) \times (d+n+k)$ matrix

$$
\mathbf{B}'' = \begin{pmatrix}
q\mathbf{I}_d & 0 & 0 & 0 & \cdots & 0 \\
-\widetilde{\mathbf{A}} & \mathbf{I}_n & 0 & 0 & \cdots & 0 \\
\widetilde{\mathbf{t}} & 0 & \eta & 0 & \cdots & 0 \\
\mathrm{rot}(\widetilde{\mathbf{t}}) & 0 & 0 & \eta & \cdots & 0 \\
\vdots & \vdots & \vdots & \vdots & \ddots & \vdots \\
\mathrm{rot}^{k-1}(\widetilde{\mathbf{t}}) & 0 & 0 & 0 & \cdots & \eta
\end{pmatrix}
$$

with an extension parameter $k$ and a small constant $\eta$. We let $\bar{\Lambda}_k''$ be the lattice of dimension $d + n + k$ spanned by the rows of $\mathbf{B}''$. The case $k = 1$ is just the original Bai-Galbraith's embedding. By Eq. (8), the extended lattice $\bar{\Lambda}_k''$ includes $k$ short vectors

$$
\begin{cases}
\bar{\mathbf{e}}'' = (\tilde{\mathbf{e}} \mid \mathbf{s} \mid \eta, 0, \ldots, 0), \\
\mathrm{rot}(\bar{\mathbf{e}}'') = (\mathrm{rot}(\tilde{\mathbf{e}})) \mid \mathrm{rot}(\mathbf{s}) \mid 0, \eta, \ldots, 0), \\
\quad\quad\quad \vdots \\
\mathrm{rot}^{k-1}(\bar{\mathbf{e}}'') = (\mathrm{rot}^{k-1}(\tilde{\mathbf{e}})) \mid \mathrm{rot}^{k-1}(\mathbf{s}) \mid 0, 0, \ldots, \eta).
\end{cases}
$$

Like in Remark 4, we can modify this extended Bai-Galbraith's embedding to increase the lattice volume.

## 3.2    Recovering Short Lattice Vectors by BKZ

We recall the principle of finding any of short lattice vectors in (9) by using the BKZ reduction algorithm for a basis $\mathbf{B}$ of the lattice $\bar{\Lambda}_k$ of dimension $d + k$. Let $\mathbf{v} = \mathrm{rot}^h(\bar{\mathbf{e}}) \in \bar{\Lambda}_k$ be any of the vectors in (9) for some $0 \leq h \leq k - 1$. Note that if we find $\mathbf{v}$, then we can recover the error $\tilde{\mathbf{e}}$ and also the secret $\mathbf{s}$ by Gaussian elimination. (In particular, the position of $\eta$ in $\mathbf{v}$ helps to recover the non-rotated error $\tilde{\mathbf{e}}$.) We write the rows of $\mathbf{B}$ as $[\mathbf{b}_1, \ldots, \mathbf{b}_{d+k}]$, and let $[\mathbf{b}_1^*, \ldots, \mathbf{b}_{d+k}^*]$ denote its Gram-Schmidt vectors. Assume that $\mathbf{B}$ is almost $\beta$-BKZ-reduced for $\beta \geq 50$ before any of short vectors in (9) does not appear as a basis vector of $\mathbf{B}$. We also assume from [2,11,29] that the Gram-Schmidt lengths of $\mathbf{B}$ roughly hold

$$
\|\mathbf{b}_i^*\| \approx \delta_\beta^{d+k-1-2i} \mathrm{vol}(\bar{\Lambda}_k)^{\frac{1}{d+k}}, \quad \delta_\beta = \left( \frac{\beta}{2\pi e} (\pi\beta)^{\frac{1}{\beta}} \right)^{\frac{1}{2(\beta-1)}}
$$

for every $1 \leq i \leq d + k$, under the geometric series assumption (GSA) [24]. Precisely, the GSA does not hold for the last $\beta$ Gram-Schmidt lengths. Indeed, the last $\beta$ Gram-Schmidt lengths follow the HKZ shape. See also [2] for details. (We expect that the GSA approximations in [2,11,29] hold for our extended lattice $\bar{\Lambda}_k$ with small $k$.) It follows from the construction of $\mathbf{B}$ that the volume of the extended lattice is equal to $\mathrm{vol}(\bar{\Lambda}_k) = \eta^k q^{d-n}$ in most cases. As mentioned in [2,5], if the projected vector of $\mathbf{v}$ at index $d + k - \beta$ satisfies

$$
\|\pi_{d+k-\beta}(\mathbf{v})\| < \|\mathbf{b}_{d+k-\beta}^*\| \approx \delta_\beta^{2\beta-d-k-1} \mathrm{vol}(\bar{\Lambda}_k)^{\frac{1}{d+k}}, \tag{10}
$$

then the projected vector $\pi_{d+k-\beta}(\mathbf{v})$ is a shortest non-zero vector in the last $\beta$-dimensional block of $\mathbf{B}_{[d+k-\beta:d+k]}$. Therefore the projected vector can be found by (pruned) ENUM for the last block, and then it is inserted at index $d + k - \beta$. After that, our target vector $\mathbf{v}$ can be restored from the projected vector $\pi_{d+k-\beta}(\mathbf{v})$ by ENUM over the other block projected lattices (the vector $\mathbf{v}$ will appear as the first basis vector of $\mathbf{B}$, see Fig. 1 for an image of this principle). In particular, there are $k$ candidates of $\mathbf{v}$ in our extended lattice $\bar{\Lambda}_k$. Therefore

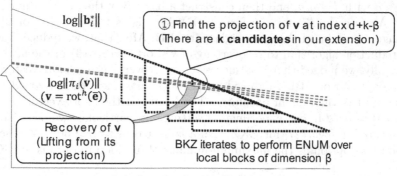

**Fig. 1.** An image of the GSA shape of a BKZ-reduced basis $\mathbf{B} = [\mathbf{b}_1, \ldots, \mathbf{b}_{d+k}]$ and the principle of recovering any of short vector $\mathbf{v} = \mathrm{rot}^h(\bar{\mathbf{e}}) \in \bar{\Lambda}_k$ in (9) for $0 \leq h \leq k-1$

as $k$ increases, it would increase the probability that the projected vector of $\mathbf{v}$ at index $d + k - \beta$ is found by ENUM for the last block $\mathbf{B}_{[d+k-\beta:d+k]}$.

The above discussion is referred to as "the 2016 estimate" by [5] in the literature, and it was experimentally confirmed in [3] that a target vector can be recovered with 'good' probability by BKZ with a blocksize $\beta$ satisfying the condition (10). However, the condition (10) on $\beta$ is sufficient to recover a target lattice vector, but not always necessary (e.g., see [22] for the success probability of the 2016 estimate). Hence we note that the condition (10) gives a just guide of choosing a blocksize $\beta$ of BKZ to recover a target vector.

## 4    Experiments

In this section, we show our experimental results for solving various ring-based LWE instances in our extended Kannan's embedding. We also discuss trade-offs of our extension based on experimental results.

### 4.1    Implementation

We implemented our extended Kannan's embedding for solving a ring-based LWE instance in SageMath [12], the Sage mathematics software (see Appendix A for a sample code). For our experiments, we used the ring-LWE oracle generator in SageMath to generate $m$ ring-LWE samples $\{(a_i(x), t_i(x)\}_{i=1}^m$ with a common secret $s(x)$ and $m$ errors $e_i(x)$ (that is, they satisfy $t_i(x) = s(x)a_i(x) + e_i(x)$ in $R_q$). In particular, we chose every coefficient of $s(x)$ uniformly from $\mathbb{Z}_q$, and used the discrete Gaussian sampler in SageMath for $\mathbb{Z}[x]$ to generate errors $e_i(x)$ whose coefficients are sampled independently from the discrete Gaussian distribution over $\mathbb{Z}$ with mean 0 and standard deviation $\sigma$ for a given constant $\sigma > 0$. In our implementation, we transform $m$ ring-LWE samples to an LWE instance (4) of size $n \times d$ with $d = mn$, and then construct a basis $\mathbf{B}$ of the $(d+k)$-dimensional lattice $\bar{\Lambda}_k$ (see Eq. (7) for the form of $\mathbf{B}$). We also set $\eta = 1$, $\lfloor \sigma \rceil$ or $2\lfloor \sigma \rceil$ as the diagonal entries of the lower right part of $\mathbf{B}$. After that, we reduce $\mathbf{B}$ by the BKZ reduction algorithm to recover any of $k$ short vectors (9) in the lattice $\bar{\Lambda}_k$. Specifically, we judged that it is successful to recovery such a short vector if the first basis vector of a BKZ-reduced basis has the norm less than $1.2\sigma\sqrt{d}$ and all the entries less than $4\sigma$ in absolute. (The length of the short vectors in (9) is estimated as $\sigma\sqrt{d}$ in our experimental setting.) In particular, we used BKZ 2.0 implemented in fpylll [27] for BKZ with a large blocksize $\beta \geq 50$. (We also used the loop_max option as the maximum number of full loop iterations of BKZ.)

## 4.2  Experimental Results

In Table 1, we show experimental results on the success probability of solving various ring-based LWE problems in our extended Kannan's embedding with an extension parameter $k$ with $1 \leq k \leq 5$. (Recall that the case $k = 1$ is the original

**Table 1.** Experimental results on the success probability of solving various ring-based LWE instances by our extended Kannan's embedding using BKZ with blocksizes $\beta \geq 50$ (Note that 'loop_max' denotes the maximum number of full loop iterations of BKZ)

| Experimental parameters of ring-based LWE and BKZ | | | Extension parameter $k$ in our extension | | | | |
|---|---|---|---|---|---|---|---|
| | | | $k = 1$ | $k = 2$ | $k = 3$ | $k = 4$ | $k = 5$ |
| $n = 32$ | $\sigma = 6.0$ | $\eta = 1$ | 36% | 20% | 23% | 19% | 10% |
| $q = 257$ | $\beta = 50$ | $\eta = \lfloor\sigma\rceil$ | 20% | **44%** | 38% | 32% | 34% |
| $d = 96$ | loop_max = 2 | $\eta = 2\lfloor\sigma\rceil$ | 6% | 13% | 20% | 34% | 28% |
| $(m = 3)$ | $\sigma = 8.0$ | $\eta = 1$ | 10% | 9% | 4% | 0% | 1% |
| | $\beta = 65$ | $\eta = \lfloor\sigma\rceil$ | 10% | **19%** | 14% | 12% | 10% |
| | loop_max = 2 | $\eta = 2\lfloor\sigma\rceil$ | 5% | 11% | 10% | 17% | 10% |
| $n = 32$ | $\sigma = 10.0$ | $\eta = 1$ | 35% | 27% | 22% | 13% | 3% |
| $q = 577$ | $\beta = 50$ | $\eta = \lfloor\sigma\rceil$ | 38% | **53%** | 46% | 46% | 37% |
| $d = 96$ | loop_max = 2 | $\eta = 2\lfloor\sigma\rceil$ | 15% | 20% | 29% | 37% | 39% |
| $(m = 3)$ | $\sigma = 11.0$ | $\eta = 1$ | 55% | 60% | 39% | 33% | 11% |
| | $\beta = 65$ | $\eta = \lfloor\sigma\rceil$ | 69% | 75% | 75% | 69% | 65% |
| | loop_max = 2 | $\eta = 2\lfloor\sigma\rceil$ | 62% | 67% | 78% | 76% | **79%** |
| $n = 64$ | $\sigma = 1.7$ | $\eta = 1$ | 19% | 20% | 18% | 19% | 11% |
| $q = 257$ | $\beta = 50$ | $\eta = \lfloor\sigma\rceil$ | 21% | 21% | **27%** | 18% | 21% |
| $d = 128$ | loop_max = 4 | $\eta = 2\lfloor\sigma\rceil$ | 0% | 0% | 0% | 0% | 1% |
| $(m = 2)$ | $\sigma = 2.0$ | $\eta = 1$ | 28% | 28% | 24% | 20% | 14% |
| | $\beta = 60$ | $\eta = \lfloor\sigma\rceil$ | 24% | 36% | **38%** | 20% | 17% |
| | loop_max = 4 | $\eta = 2\lfloor\sigma\rceil$ | 10% | 27% | 26% | 29% | 22% |
| $n = 64$ | $\sigma = 4.0$ | $\eta = 1$ | 19% | 20% | 14% | 9% | 4% |
| $q = 1153$ | $\beta = 55$ | $\eta = \lfloor\sigma\rceil$ | 18% | **22%** | 21% | 19% | 17% |
| $d = 128$ | loop_max = 4 | $\eta = 2\lfloor\sigma\rceil$ | 7% | 10% | 18% | 9% | 15% |
| $(m = 2)$ | $\sigma = 4.6$ | $\eta = 1$ | 24% | 26% | 14% | 6% | 4% |
| | $\beta = 65$ | $\eta = \lfloor\sigma\rceil$ | 24% | **32%** | 26% | 24% | 21% |
| | loop_max = 4 | $\eta = 2\lfloor\sigma\rceil$ | 13% | 23% | 26% | 27% | 24% |

Kannan's embedding.) Each success probability in Table 1 was obtained by performing 100 times experiments for each parameter setting. For each parameter setting, we selected $\beta \geq 50$ smaller than the minimum blocksize satisfying the condition (10) (the left-hand side of (10) is estimated as $\sigma\sqrt{\beta}$ from [3]). We see from Table 1 that the highest success probability is obtained in $k \geq 2$ for every parameter setting. In particular, cases $k = 2, 3$ with $\eta = \lfloor \sigma \rceil$ give higher success probability than the case $k = 1$. This is due to that as the extension parameter $k$ increases, the number of target errors in (9) increases, but the right-hand side of Eq. (10) decreases, and hence a large blocksize $\beta$ of BKZ is required for success. Similarly, larger $\eta$ increases the right-hand value of Eq. (10), but it also increases the length of embedded errors $\mathbf{v}$, and hence around $\eta \approx \sigma$ seems the best for our extended Kannan's embedding as in the original embedding.

In Fig. 2, we give an experimental comparison of success probabilities of our extended Kannan's embedding with extension parameters $1 \leq k \leq 5$ by using BKZ with blocksizes $\beta = 50$–$64$. Experimental parameters are from Table 1, and each success probability in Fig. 2 was obtained by performing 100 times experiments for each parameter as in Table 1. We see from Fig. 2 that success probabilities in cases $k = 2, 3, 4$ are higher than that of the case $k = 1$ (that is, the original Kannan's embedding) for each blocksize $\beta$. The condition (10) of the 2016 estimate indicates that around $\beta = 56$ is required for success with good probability for both parameters (a) and (b) in Fig. 2. Nevertheless, success probabilities in cases of $k = 2, 3, 4$ are still high even for smaller blocksizes such as $\beta = 52$ and 54.

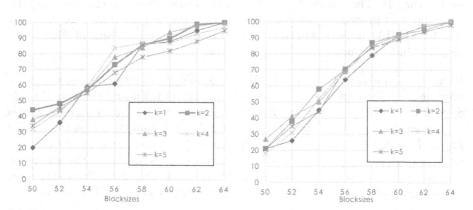

(a) Experimental parameters: $n = 32$, $q =$ 257, $d = 96$, $\sigma = 6.0$, $\eta = \lfloor \sigma \rceil$, loop_max $= 2$

(b) Experimental parameters: $n = 64$, $q =$ 257, $d = 128$, $\sigma = 1.7$, $\eta = \lfloor \sigma \rceil$, loop_max $= 4$

**Fig. 2.** Comparison of success probabilities of our extended Kannan's embedding with extension parameters $k = 1$–$5$ by using BKZ with blocksizes $\beta = 50$–$64$

### 4.3  Discussion on Trade-Offs of Our Extension

Our extended Kannan's embedding has a trade-off between a required blocksize $\beta$ of BKZ and the success probability for solving a ring-based LWE problem. Specifically, larger extension parameter $k$ increases the number of target short vectors (9) in the lattice $\bar{\Lambda}_k$, and it increases the success probability of finding any of target vector. On the other hand, Eq. (10) indicates that a larger extension parameter $k$ requires a larger blocksize $\beta$ for the success of recovering a target short vector. According to experimental results, extension parameters $k = 2, 3$ are suitable for blocksizes around $\beta = 50$–$60$ from the perspective of success probability. (In particular, Table 1 showed that $\eta \approx \sigma$ is suitable for our extension.) In contrast, we predict that larger $k$ would be suitable for larger $\beta$. Indeed, in using a large block (e.g., $\beta \geq 80$) for BKZ, the search tree of ENUM on $\beta$-dimensional blocks in BKZ should be pruned for good performance (see [13] for pruning of ENUM). As the number of target short vectors increases, it increases the probability of finding a target vector by pruned ENUM. For example, in the progressive BKZ of [6] with large blocksizes $\beta > 50$, the success probability of finding a short lattice vector by pruned ENUM is set as $p = \frac{2.0}{\alpha^\beta}$ for some constant $\alpha$ such as $\alpha = 1.05$. In the setting for our extension, a target projected lattice vector $\pi_{d+k-\beta}(\mathbf{v})$ can be recovered by pruned ENUM for the last block $\mathbf{B}_{[d+k-\beta:d+k]}$ with success probability $k \times p$.

From the construction of a basis $\mathbf{B}$ of the lattice $\bar{\Lambda}_k$ (see Eq. (7)), we can add the vector $(\mathrm{rot}^k(\widetilde{\mathbf{t}}) \mid 0, \cdots, 0, \eta)$ of length $d + k + 1$ to construct a basis of the $(d + k + 1)$-dimensional lattice $\bar{\Lambda}_{k+1}$ even during a processing of BKZ for reducing $\mathbf{B}$. The lattice $\bar{\Lambda}_{k+1}$ includes the $k$ times rotated error $\mathrm{rot}^k(\bar{\mathbf{e}})$. By repeating this procedure, we can increase the success probability for solving a ring-based LWE instance. On the other hand, the processing time of BKZ would increase since the lattice dimension increases.

*Remark 5 (Application to module-LWE).* Module-LWE is the analogue of LWE over modules, introduced in [8,16], which is between LWE and ring-based LWE. Specifically, module-LWE uses a free $R_q$-module of rank $m$ for a positive integer $m$. Like in the case of standard LWE, a module-LWE sample is a pair of $(\mathbf{a}, t) \in R_q^m \times R_q$ with $\mathbf{a} = (a_1, \ldots, a_m)$ satisfying $t = \sum_{i=1}^m a_i s_i + e$ over the ring $R_q$, where $\mathbf{s} = (s_1, \ldots, s_m) \in R_q^m$ is a secret and $e \in R_q$ is an error. The particular case $m = 1$ corresponds to ring-based LWE. From the same discussion as in Subsect. 2.1, a module-LWE sample can be rewritten as an LWE instance

$$\mathbf{t} \equiv (\mathbf{s}_1 \mid \cdots \mid \mathbf{s}_m) \begin{pmatrix} \mathbf{A}_1 \\ \vdots \\ \mathbf{A}_m \end{pmatrix} + \mathbf{e} \pmod{q},$$

where $\mathbf{t}$, $\mathbf{e}$ and the $\mathbf{s}_i$'s are coefficient vectors of ring elements $t$, $e$ and the $s_i$'s, respectively, and the $\mathbf{A}_i$'s are corresponding matrices of the $a_i$'s like Eq. (2). From this form, we can extend Kannan's embedding (or Bai-Galbraith's embedding) for any module-LWE instance as in Sect. 3.

# 5    Conclusion

We presented an extension of Kannan's embedding [15] specific to the ring-based LWE problem. We also applied our extension to Bai-Galbraith's embedding [7] for ring-based LWE with a small secret polynomial. Specifically, for an extension parameter $k$, we constructed a new extended lattice to embed $k$ short errors that are amplified by rotation operations for the coefficient vector of an error polynomial. We demonstrated by experiments that our extension can increase the success probability of Kannan's embedding by using BKZ for solving a ring-based LWE instance (see Table 1 and Fig. 1). Our experiments showed that parameters $k = 2, 3$ are suitable for blocksizes around $\beta = 50$–$60$ of BKZ from the perspective of success probability. (Our extension does not increase the running time of BKZ so much for small $k$.) As discussed in Subsect. 4.3, we predict that larger $k$ would be suitable for larger $\beta$.

# A    A Sample Code for Our Extended Kannan's Embedding

Here we give a sample Python code in SageMath [12] of our extended Kannan's embedding for solving a ring-based LWE instance. (We use the ring-LWE oracle generator in SageMath to generate ring-LWE samples, and also BKZ 2.0 in fpylll for BKZ. See also Subsect. 4.1 for details.)

```
1   from sage.crypto.lwe import RingLWE
2   from sage.crypto.lwe import
        DiscreteGaussianDistributionPolynomialSampler, RingLWE,
        RingLWEConverter
3   from sage.stats.distributions.discrete_gaussian_polynomial import
        DiscreteGaussianDistributionPolynomialSampler
4   from fpylll import *
5
6   # Rotation operation
7   def rot(v, l):
8           w = copy(v)
9           for i in range(1, l):
10                  w[i] = v[i-1]
11          w[0] = -v[l-1]
12          return w
13  #=================
14  # Setting of parameters
15  #=================
16  n = 64; N = 2*n  # security parameter
17  q = 1153    # modulus parameter
18  sigma = 4.0 # standard deviation of the discrete Gaussian
            distribution
19  m = 2   # number of ring-LWE samples
20  d = m*n # number of LWE samples
21  k = 5   # extension parameter for Kannan's embedding
```

```
22   # t = 1
23   # t = round(sigma)
24   t = 2*round(sigma)
25
26   #==============================
27   # Generation of ring-LWE samples
28   #==============================
29   D = DiscreteGaussianDistributionPolynomialSampler(ZZ['x'], euler_phi
         (N), sigma)
30   ringlwe = RingLWE(N, q, D, secret_dist='uniform')
31   a = Matrix(m, n)
32   b = Matrix(m, n)
33   for i in range(m):
34         Sample = ringlwe()
35         a[i] = copy(Sample[0])
36         b[i] = copy(Sample[1])
37
38   #==============================
39   # Contruction of a q-ary lattice
40   #==============================
41   A = Matrix(n, d)
42   for i in range(m):
43         v = copy(a[i])
44         for j in range(n):
45               for l in range(n):
46                     A[j, n*i + l] = v[l]
47               v = rot(v, n)
48   C = Matrix(n+d, d)
49   for i in range(n):
50         C[i] = copy(A[i])
51   for i in range(d):
52         C[i+n, i] = q
53   C = C.LLL()
54
55   #==============================
56   # Extended Kannan's embedding
57   #==============================
58   B = Matrix(ZZ, d+k, d+k)
59   for i in range(d):
60         for j in range(d):
61               B[i, j] = C[i+n, j]
62   for i in range(k):
63         B[d+i, d+i] = t
64         for j in range(m):
65               v = copy(b[j])
66               for l in range(n):
67                     B[d+i, n*j + l] = v[l]
68               b[j] = rot(b[j], n)
69
70   #==============================
```

```
71   # Lattice basis reduction (BKZ 2.0 in fpylll)
72   #=============================================
73   flags = BKZ.AUTO_ABORT|BKZ.MAX_LOOPS|BKZ.GH_BND
74   par = BKZ.Param(55, strategies=BKZ.DEFAULT_STRATEGY, max_loops=4,
         flags=flags)
75   A = IntegerMatrix(d+k, d+k)
76   for i in range(d+k):
77           for j in range(d+k):
78                   A[i, j] = B[i, j]
79   BB = BKZ.reduction(A, par)
80
81   tmp = 0
82   if BB[0].norm() >= 1.2*sigma*sqrt(d):
83           tmp = 1
84   else:
85           v = BB[0]
86           for i in range(d):
87                   if abs(v[i]) > 4*sigma:
88                           tmp = 1
89   if tmp == 0:
90           print("Success:_", BB[0])
91   else:
92           print("Failure")
```

# References

1. Albrecht, M.R., et al.: Estimate all the LWE, NTRU schemes! In: Catalano, D., De Prisco, R. (eds.) SCN 2018. LNCS, vol. 11035, pp. 351–367. Springer, Cham (2018). https://doi.org/10.1007/978-3-319-98113-0_19

2. Albrecht, M.R., Ducas, L.: Lattice attacks on NTRU and LWE: a history of refinements. IACR ePrint 2021/799 (2021)

3. Albrecht, M.R., Göpfert, F., Virdia, F., Wunderer, T.: Revisiting the expected cost of solving uSVP and applications to LWE. In: Takagi, T., Peyrin, T. (eds.) ASIACRYPT 2017. LNCS, vol. 10624, pp. 297–322. Springer, Cham (2017). https://doi.org/10.1007/978-3-319-70694-8_11

4. Albrecht, M.R., Player, R., Scott, S.: On the concrete hardness of learning with errors. J. Math. Cryptol. 9(3), 169–203 (2015)

5. Alkim, E., Ducas, L., Pöppelmann, T., Schwabe, P.: Post-quantum key exchange: a new hope. In: 25th USENIX Security Symposium, pp. 327–343 (2016)

6. Aono, Y., Wang, Y., Hayashi, T., Takagi, T.: Improved progressive BKZ algorithms and their precise cost estimation by sharp simulator. In: Fischlin, M., Coron, J.-S. (eds.) EUROCRYPT 2016. LNCS, vol. 9665, pp. 789–819. Springer, Heidelberg (2016). https://doi.org/10.1007/978-3-662-49890-3_30

7. Bai, S., Galbraith, S.D.: Lattice decoding attacks on binary LWE. In: Susilo, W., Mu, Y. (eds.) ACISP 2014. LNCS, vol. 8544, pp. 322–337. Springer, Cham (2014). https://doi.org/10.1007/978-3-319-08344-5_21

8. Brakerski, Z., Gentry, C., Vaikuntanathan, V.: (Leveled) fully homomorphic encryption without bootstrapping. ACM Trans. Comput. Theory (TOCT) **6**(3), 1–36 (2014)

9. Bremner, M.R.: Lattice Basis Reduction: An Introduction to the LLL Algorithm and Its Applications. CRC Press, Boca Raton (2011)

10. Castryck, W., Iliashenko, I., Vercauteren, F.: On error distributions in ring-based LWE. LMS J. Comput. Math. **19**(A), 130–145 (2016)

11. Chen, Y.: Réduction de réseau et sécurité concrete du chiffrement completement homomorphe. Ph.D. thesis, Paris 7 (2013)

12. Developers, T Sage: Sagemath (2016). https://www.sagemath.org/

13. Gama, N., Nguyen, P.Q., Regev, O.: Lattice enumeration using extreme pruning. In: Gilbert, H. (ed.) EUROCRYPT 2010. LNCS, vol. 6110, pp. 257–278. Springer, Heidelberg (2010). https://doi.org/10.1007/978-3-642-13190-5_13

14. Hoffstein, J., Pipher, J., Silverman, J.H.: NTRU: a ring-based public key cryptosystem. In: Buhler, J.P. (ed.) ANTS 1998. LNCS, vol. 1423, pp. 267–288. Springer, Heidelberg (1998). https://doi.org/10.1007/BFb0054868

15. Kannan, R.: Minkowski's convex body theorem and integer programming. Math. Oper. Res. **12**(3), 415–440 (1987)

16. Langlois, A., Stehlé, D.: Worst-case to average-case reductions for module lattices. Des. Codes Cryptogr. **75**(3), 565–599 (2015). https://doi.org/10.1007/s10623-014-9938-4

17. Lenstra, A.K., Lenstra, H.W., Lovász, L.: Factoring polynomials with rational coefficients. Mathematische Annalen **261**(4), 515–534 (1982)

18. Lyubashevsky, V., Peikert, C., Regev, O.: On ideal lattices and learning with errors over rings. In: Gilbert, H. (ed.) EUROCRYPT 2010. LNCS, vol. 6110, pp. 1–23. Springer, Heidelberg (2010). https://doi.org/10.1007/978-3-642-13190-5_1

19. Micciancio, D., Regev, O.: Lattice-based cryptography. In: Bernstein, D.J., Buchmann, J., Dahmen, E. (eds.) Post-Quantum Cryptography, pp. 147–191. Springer, Heidelberg (2009). https://doi.org/10.1007/978-3-540-88702-7_5

20. Molinari, L.G.: Determinants of block tridiagonal matrices. Linear Algebra Appl. **429**(8–9), 2221–2226 (2008)

21. Nguyen, P.Q.: Hermite's constant and lattice algorithms. In: Nguyen, P., Vallée, B. (eds.) The LLL Algorithm, pp. 19–69. Springer, Heidelberg (2009). https://doi.org/10.1007/978-3-642-02295-1_2

22. Postlethwaite, E.W., Virdia, F.: On the success probability of solving unique SVP via BKZ. In: Garay, J.A. (ed.) PKC 2021. LNCS, vol. 12710, pp. 68–98. Springer, Cham (2021). https://doi.org/10.1007/978-3-030-75245-3_4

23. Schnorr, C.P.: Block Korkin-Zolotarev bases and successive minima. International Computer Science Institute (1992)

24. Schnorr, C.P.: Lattice reduction by random sampling and birthday methods. In: Alt, H., Habib, M. (eds.) STACS 2003. LNCS, vol. 2607, pp. 145–156. Springer, Heidelberg (2003). https://doi.org/10.1007/3-540-36494-3_14

25. Schnorr, C.P., Euchner, M.: Lattice basis reduction: improved practical algorithms and solving subset sum problems. Math. Program. **66**, 181–199 (1994)

26. Stehlé, D., Steinfeld, R., Tanaka, K., Xagawa, K.: Efficient public key encryption based on ideal lattices. In: Matsui, M. (ed.) ASIACRYPT 2009. LNCS, vol. 5912, pp. 617–635. Springer, Heidelberg (2009). https://doi.org/10.1007/978-3-642-10366-7_36

27. The FPLLL development team: FPyLLL, a Python wrapper for the FPLLL lattice reduction library, Version: 0.5.6 (2021). https://github.com/fplll/fpylll

28. Yasuda, M.: A survey of solving SVP algorithms and recent strategies for solving the SVP challenge. In: Takagi, T., Wakayama, M., Tanaka, K., Kunihiro, N., Kimoto, K., Ikematsu, Y. (eds.) International Symposium on Mathematics, Quantum Theory, and Cryptography. MI, vol. 33, pp. 189–207. Springer, Singapore (2021). https://doi.org/10.1007/978-981-15-5191-8_15
29. Yu, Y., Ducas, L.: Second order statistical behavior of LLL and BKZ. In: Adams, C., Camenisch, J. (eds.) SAC 2017. LNCS, vol. 10719, pp. 3–22. Springer, Cham (2018). https://doi.org/10.1007/978-3-319-72565-9_1

# Black-Box Accumulation Based on Lattices

Sebastian H. Faller$^{(\boxtimes)}$, Pascal Baumer, Michael Klooß, Alexander Koch, Astrid Ottenhues, and Markus Raiber

Karlsruhe Institute of Technology (KIT), Karlsruhe, Germany
sebastian.faller@mailbox.org, ueeap@student.kit.edu,
{michael.klooss,alexander.koch,astrid.ottenhues,markus.raiber}@kit.edu

**Abstract.** Black-box accumulation (BBA) is a cryptographic protocol that allows users to accumulate and redeem points, e.g. in payment systems, and offers provable security and privacy guarantees. Loosely speaking, the transactions of users remain unlinkable, while adversaries cannot claim a false amount of points or use points from other users. Attempts to spend the same points multiple times (double spending) reveal the identity of the misbehaving user and an undeniable proof of guilt. Known instantiations of BBA rely on classical number-theoretic assumptions, which are not post-quantum secure. In this work, we propose the first lattice-based instantiation of BBA, which is plausibly post-quantum secure. It relies on the hardness of the Learning with Errors (LWE) and Short Integer Solution (SIS) assumptions and is secure in the Random Oracle Model (ROM).

Our work shows that a lattice-based instantiation of BBA can be realized with a communication cost per transaction of about 199MB if built on the zero-knowledge protocol by (CRYPTO 2019) and the CL-type signature of (ASIACRYPT 2017). Without any zero-knowledge overhead, our protocol requires 1.8 MB communication.

**Keywords:** Lattice-based cryptography · Black-box Accumulation (BBA) · Electronic funds transfer · Security and privacy · Learning with errors (LWE) · Short Integer Solution (SIS)

## 1 Introduction

Black-box accumulation (BBA), introduced in [24], allows the anonymous collection and redemption of points. BBA protocols feature two roles: users and operators. The users can accumulate and spend points on a cryptographic token issued by the operators, via the respective interactive protocols. In real-world scenarios like loyalty programs in shops or prepayment systems for public transport, users can collect incentives or bonus points. For the operators, the secure transfer of points is of paramount importance, whereas users want to protect their privacy. BBA offers a provably secure solution to both concerns. It allows users

© Springer Nature Switzerland AG 2021
M. B. Paterson (Ed.): IMACC 2021, LNCS 13129, pp. 220–246, 2021.
https://doi.org/10.1007/978-3-030-92641-0_11

to collect and redeem points in an unlinkable manner and it protects operators from malicious users trying to claim more points than collected.

Several works have extended the framework of BBA. BBA+ [22] added stronger notions of both security and privacy as well as offline-transactions (in the sense that no permanent connection to a central database is required). More recently, [6,7,23] improved several aspects of BBA+. However, all of the proposed instantiations are based on classical cryptographic building blocks whose security guarantees rely on number-theoretic assumptions which are broken by Shor's algorithms [33], rendering them insecure against quantum adversaries.

In contrast, lattice-based hardness assumptions have so-far withstood attempts to break them with quantum algorithms and allow to construct an extensive variety of cryptographic primitives, including commitments, public-key encryption [20,25,31,32] and fully homomorphic encryption (FHE) [19], and are hence considered an ideal candidate to achieve post-quantum (PQ) security. Moreover, lattice-based protocols usually feature good asymptotic efficiency, parallelism, and security under worst-case intractability assumptions. The downside is an increase in communication costs for certain important building blocks, such as zero-knowledge (ZK) proofs. As all known BBA constructions are heavily based on ZK proofs, it gives rise to the difficult question of how to instantiate BBA from lattice-based assumptions, while remaining relatively efficient.

**Contribution.** In this work, we propose the first lattice-based instantiation of BBA, called BABL (**B**lack-Box **A**ccumulation **B**ased on **L**attices). It relies on the LWE and SIS problems, and is proven secure in the ROM. We follow the security framework of [23], refered to as BBW in the following.

Moreover, we give a concrete instantiation, together with a suitable choice of lattice parameters, and evaluate the scheme's communication complexity. Without any zero-knowledge overhead, our protocol requires 1.8 MB communication, which shows that the efficiency baseline of our general approach/construction is low. When using the popular ZK proof system by Yang et al. [36], an optimized version requires 199 MB communication, too much to be practically usable. However, lattice-based ZK proofs are improving rapidly, see e.g. [35] for some performance comparisons. Thus, it is plausible that the added computation and communication cost shrinks to an actually practical level in the near future. Our construction is the most efficient lattice-based payment system (BBA or E-Cash, cf. Sect. 1) to date. The closest competitor, E-Cash, needs 262 MB per transaction, using the same ZK protocol. While this does not yet make our protocol fit for practice, it places lattice-based BBA schemes into the range of practicality, where a further round of optimizations could likely allow its real-world use.

**Our Construction in a Nutshell.** On a high level, our construction follows the approach of BBW [23], but it requires care to translate it to lattices, without reaching a giga-/terabyte range of communication cost per transaction. In BBW, the user holds a token which is basically a commitment whose contents are signed by the operator. This commitment contains a serial number for double-spending detection, a secret key uniquely identifying the user, and the amount of points. (For simplicity, we omit double-spending tags for now.) An update of the number of points (e.g. in a purchase) works as follows. The user sends a fresh (rerandomized) commitment to the operator, reveals the serial number, and proves in zero-knowledge that the commitment's contents are signed and that the new balance lies within admitted bounds. Using a property of the commitment scheme, the operator updates the balance while keeping the committed content intact. A serial number is chosen by a two-party coin-toss, to ensure it cannot be used to track users. Finally, the operator provides a signature for the new token.

To implement this strategy, [23] uses group-based commitments, ZK proofs, and so-called CL-type signatures [10,11], which have practically efficient ZK proofs for proving possession of a signature on a commitment or committed value. To replace Multi-Pedersen commitments, we use the lattice-based multi-block commitment scheme of [25], called KTX commitment in the following. We make use of a structural property of these commitments, which allows to "add blocks" to the committed message later, without knowing the messages in the other blocks, similar to Multi-Pedersen commitments. Finally, to replace the group-based CL-type signatures and ZK proofs, we rely on the ZK protocol of Yang et al.[36] combined with the CL-type signatures of Libert et al. [28].

**Related Work.** The previous BBA protocols by Blömer et al. [6], Bobolz et al. [7], Hartung et al. [22], Hoffmann et al. [23], and Jager and Rupp [24] are all based on number-theoretic hardness assumptions. While this allows them to be much more efficient, it also makes them insecure when quantum computers become available. We think that future privacy issues regarding payments made today, and the security of a users' collected points in the future are reason enough to switch to post-quantum payment systems in the long term. The closest relatives to BBA are Electronic Cash (E-Cash) cryptosystems [14]. The first *compact* E-Cash scheme was given in [9], where compact means that the complexity of withdrawal and spending is logarithmic in the size of an (electronic) wallet. In (compact) E-Cash, there exist three parties, namely a bank, a user, and a merchant. The bank allows withdrawing a wallet containing coins and depositing coins. The wallet is signed by the bank, to make it possible for a user to prove the legitimacy of their wallet. Further, the user can spend the coins from their withdrawn wallet in a privacy-preserving way at a merchant. This is achieved by proving in zero-knowledge the legitimacy of the origin of the coin. The merchant can then deposit the received coin at the bank. The bank can detect double-spenders and prove their guilt, if and only if they are guilty. There are two lattice-based versions of compact E-Cash in the literature: The work of Libert et al. [28] – which propose (implicit) CL-type signatures, and an abstraction of Stern-type ZK protocols [34] – and Yang et al. [36]'s system, which applies their ZK argument system and further optimizations to construct a more efficient system similar to [28]. [8] showed some major issues with the double-spending in compact E-Cash. [15] solved these problems with their lattice-based version of E-Cash.

We stress that E-Cash and BBA are quite different. Most importantly, BBA allows payments in both directions, i.e., points can be accumulated and spent. E-Cash does allow to deposit points but only at the bank, which means that a wallet cannot be "refilled". Instead, a new wallet with fresh coins has to be generated. Additionally, E-Cash and BBA have different assumptions on the involved parties. On the one hand, it is not possible in BBA to separate issuer and accumulator – such as when the issuer is an E-Cash bank, and the accumulator a merchant. Issuer and accumulator have the same secret key. On the other hand, a merchant and bank must not collude in E-Cash, as this can break privacy. A BBA issuer and an accumulator can collude without breaking privacy. This is necessary due to an impossibility result, cf. [12]. Further, E-Cash only allows the transferal of a single coin per transaction. The transaction value in BBA is an integer in a certain range (e.g. 32-bit integers). Hence, when payments for products with different prices are made, BBA requires just one transaction, whereas many E-Cash transactions would be necessary.

## 2    Preliminaries

**Notation.** We use $\lambda \in \mathbb{N}$ as security parameter. Vectors and matrices are in bold. For $n \in \mathbb{N}$ we write $\mathbf{I}_n$ for the identity matrix of dimension $n$. We denote by $\log$ the binary logarithm. $\|\cdot\|$ denotes the Euclidean norm and $\|\cdot\|_\infty$ the maximum norm. For $q \in \mathbb{N}$ we denote by $\mathbb{Z}_q = \{-\lfloor (q-1)/2 \rfloor, \ldots, \lceil (q-1)/2 \rceil\}$ the ring of congruence classes of integers modulo $q$. We denote by $x \leftarrow S$ that $x$ is drawn uniformly at random from set $S$ and by $y \leftarrow D$ that $y$ is drawn according to distribution $D$. We denote by $\cdot\|\cdot$ the concatenation of vectors, i.e., for $\mathbf{x}, \mathbf{y} \in \mathbb{Z}_q^n$ we have $(\mathbf{x}\|\mathbf{y}) \in \mathbb{Z}_q^{2n}$. For $\mathbf{x} \in \mathbb{Z}_q^m$, we denote by $\mathsf{bin}(\mathbf{x}) \in \mathbb{Z}_2^{m\lceil \log q \rceil}$ the binary decomposite of $\mathbf{x} \in \mathbb{Z}_q^m$, i.e. $\mathbf{x}_j = \sum_{i=0}^{\lceil \log q \rceil - 1} \mathsf{bin}(\mathbf{x})_{\lceil \log q \rceil \cdot j + i} \cdot 2^i$. Inversely, for a $\mathbf{y} \in \mathbb{Z}_2^{\lceil \log q \rceil}$, we denote by $\mathsf{toInt}(\mathbf{y}) := \sum_{i=0}^{\lceil \log q \rceil - 1} \mathbf{y}_i \cdot 2^i \in \mathbb{Z}_q$ the integer (modulo $q$) represented by $\mathbf{y}$. For a full-rank matrix $\mathbf{M} \in \mathbb{Z}_q^{n \times m}$, we denote by $\widetilde{\mathbf{M}}$ the Gram–Schmidt orthogonalization of $\mathbf{M}$'s columns.

### 2.1    Black-Box Accumulation

In this section, we give an overview of the BBW framework defined in [23], which we base this work on. It allows a user to anonymously collect (and redeem) points from the operators, which cover the following three roles: i) the *issuer* issues new tokens to the users of the system, ii) the *accumulator* adds points to a token, and iii) the *verifier* subtracts points from a token and verifies that a user's balance is large enough to perform that transaction. As these roles share the same key pair, we do not distinguish them within the paper and refer to them as the *operator*.

The protocols are *offline*, meaning transactions can be performed without a permanent connection of the operator to a database. Nonetheless, regular access to a shared database to store the double-spending tags is needed. We require a common reference string which is set-up by a Trusted Third Party (TTP).[1] Next, let us give the formal definition of a BBW scheme.

**Definition 2.1 (BBW Scheme).** *A* black-box wallet *scheme* BBW = (Setup, OGen, UGen, Issue, Update, UVer, IdentDS, VerifyGuilt) *consists of probabilistic polynomial time (PPT) algorithms* Setup, OGen *and* UGen, *interactive protocols* Issue *and* Update *and deterministic polynomial time algorithms* UVer, IdentDS *and* VerifyGuilt:

- CRS ← Setup($1^\lambda$): *On input* $1^\lambda$, *returns a common reference string* CRS. *All following algorithms always receive* CRS *(implicitly) as input.*
- ($pk_{\mathcal{O}}$, $sk_{\mathcal{O}}$) ← OGen(CRS): *Returns a public and secret key for operator* $\mathcal{O}$.
- ($pk_{\mathcal{U}}$, $sk_{\mathcal{U}}$) ← UGen(CRS): *Returns a public and secret key for user* $\mathcal{U}$.
- (($\mathcal{T}, b_{\mathcal{U}}$), $b_{\mathcal{O}}$) ← Issue⟨$\mathcal{U}$($pk_{\mathcal{O}}$, $pk_{\mathcal{U}}$, $sk_{\mathcal{U}}$), $\mathcal{O}$($pk_{\mathcal{O}}$, $sk_{\mathcal{O}}$, $pk_{\mathcal{U}}$)⟩: *User* $\mathcal{U}$ *communicates with operator* $\mathcal{O}$, *who produces a new token* $\mathcal{T}$ *for* $\mathcal{U}$ *with balance* 0. *The user's input is their key pair* ($pk_{\mathcal{U}}$, $sk_{\mathcal{U}}$), *and* $\mathcal{O}$'s *public key* $pk_{\mathcal{O}}$, *while* $\mathcal{O}$'s *input is its key pair* ($pk_{\mathcal{O}}$, $sk_{\mathcal{O}}$), *and the user's public key* $pk_{\mathcal{U}}$. *The bits* $b_{\mathcal{O}}$ *and* $b_{\mathcal{U}}$ *indicate whether* $\mathcal{O}$ *and* $\mathcal{U}$ *"accept" the protocol run, respectively.*
- (($\mathcal{T}^*, b_{\mathcal{U}}$), ($dstag, b_{\mathcal{O}}$)) ← Update⟨$\mathcal{U}$($pk_{\mathcal{O}}$, $pk_{\mathcal{U}}$, $sk_{\mathcal{U}}$, $\mathcal{T}$, $v$), $\mathcal{O}$($pk_{\mathcal{U}}$, $sk_{\mathcal{O}}$, $v$)⟩: *User* $\mathcal{U}$ *updates the token by interacting with the operator* $\mathcal{O}$. *Both get as inputs the public keys* $pk_{\mathcal{O}}$ *and* $pk_{\mathcal{U}}$ *and their respective secret key, and the (possibly negative) value* $v$ *to be added to the token's balance.* $\mathcal{U}$ *additionally gets their token* $\mathcal{T}$ *(with balance* $w$*) as input. In the end,* $\mathcal{U}$ *outputs an updated token* $\mathcal{T}^*$ *with balance* $w + v$, *and a bit* $b_{\mathcal{U}}$ *indicating acceptance of the execution. The operator outputs an acceptance bit* $b_{\mathcal{O}}$ *and a so-called double-spending tag* dstag *(which later allows detection of reuses of the same token).*[2]
- $b$ ← UVer($pk_{\mathcal{O}}$, $pk_{\mathcal{U}}$, $sk_{\mathcal{U}}$, $\mathcal{T}$, $w$): *User* $\mathcal{U}$ *verifies a token* $\mathcal{T}$, *given the operator's public key* $pk_{\mathcal{O}}$, *the user's key pair* ($pk_{\mathcal{U}}$, $sk_{\mathcal{U}}$), *and a value* $w$, *and outputs* 1 *if* $\mathcal{T}$ *is a valid token of* $\mathcal{U}$ *with balance* $w$, *or* 0 *otherwise.*
- ($pk_{\mathcal{U}}$, $\Pi$) ← IdentDS($pk_{\mathcal{O}}$, $dstag_1$, $dstag_2$): *Takes as input the operator's public key* $pk_{\mathcal{O}}$ *and two double-spending tags* $dstag_1$, $dstag_2$. *If* $dstag_1$, $dstag_2$ *come from a transaction with the same token, then* IdentDS *outputs the public key* $pk_{\mathcal{U}}$ *of the user* $\mathcal{U}$ *that "double-spent" their token and a proof of guilt* $\Pi$. ($\Pi$ *can later be verified by a third party, using the* VerifyGuilt *algorithm described next). Otherwise, it outputs an error symbol* $\bot$.
- $b$ ← VerifyGuilt($pk_{\mathcal{O}}$, $pk_{\mathcal{U}}$, $\Pi$): *Given a proof of guilt* $\Pi$, $\mathcal{O}$'s *and* $\mathcal{U}$'s *public keys* $pk_{\mathcal{O}}$, *and* $pk_{\mathcal{U}}$, *it outputs* 1 *if* $\mathcal{U}$ *is guilty of double-spending,* 0 *otherwise.*

---

[1] Our setup only requires a *uniform random string (URS)*, also called *transparent setup*. In practice, it can be heuristically chosen, e.g. as a hash image.

[2] Note, that [22–24] distinguish between an Add and a Sub transaction for updating the token, where the first one hides the user's balance and the latter one reveals it (or hides it via expensive range proofs). As we will discuss in Sect. 3 there is no need for us to distinguish those cases, as the balance is always hidden in our construction.

We say a BBW scheme is *correct* if the two interactive protocols Issue and Update and the algorithms UVer, IdentDS, and VerifyGuilt are correct. For Issue this means, if both parties follow the protocol, Issue outputs a valid token $\mathcal{T}$ (as verified by UVer) and both parties accept the execution. Similarly, Update is correct if both parties accept the execution and the output is a valid (as above) updated token (with new balance $w + v$) if the parties follow the protocol. Correctness of UVer, IdentDS, and VerifyGuilt are defined in the canonical way.

**Privacy and Security Properties.** We give an informal description of the security properties and refer to App. B for the full definitions.

On the system side we formalize security by three properties: i) a scheme is *owner-binding* if a token is bound to a unique user, and can only be used by it, ii) a scheme is *balance-binding* if no false balance can be claimed, i.e., one can only claim a certain (overall) balance for a token if this balance equals the exact amount of points that have been legitimately collected with this token up to this point in time, and iii) a scheme features *double-spending detection* if a user that presents an already used token in a transaction can be (provably) identified.

For the privacy of the user, we demand the following properties: i) the scheme is *privacy preserving*, i.e., an adversary is not able to link any transactions of the user, even with corrupt operators, ii) the scheme offers *false-accusation protection*, if no malicious operator can falsely produce a proof of guilt for an honest user, and iii) a scheme should feature *post-compromise security*, i.e., that after a temporary compromise of the user, the unlinkability (but not the false-accusation property) can be recovered (by introducing new randomness into the token).

A difference in the description of BBW and our framework is that BBW allows embedding attributes in the token, i.e., the token's expiration date or data for age verification. Including such attributes is direct, but omitted for simplicity.

## 2.2 Lattices

We recall the basics of lattice-based cryptography required for our construction.

**Definition 2.2.** *A lattice $\mathcal{L}$ is the group of all integer linear combinations of $k$ linearly independent vectors $\mathbf{B} = \{\mathbf{b}_1, \ldots, \mathbf{b}_k\} \subseteq \mathbb{R}^n$, for $k \in \mathbb{N}$: $\mathcal{L} = \mathcal{L}(\mathbf{B}) := \left\{ \sum_{i=1}^{k} z_i \cdot \mathbf{b}_i \mid z_i \in \mathbb{Z} \right\}$. Let $m \geq n \geq 1$, a prime number $q > 2$, $\mathbf{A} \in \mathbb{Z}_q^{n \times m}$ and $\mathbf{u} \in \mathbb{Z}_q^n$. We write:*

$$\Lambda_q^{\perp}(\mathbf{A}) := \{\mathbf{e} \in \mathbb{Z}^m \mid \mathbf{A}\mathbf{e} = \mathbf{0}^n \bmod q\}, \quad \Lambda_q^{\mathbf{u}}(\mathbf{A}) := \{\mathbf{e} \in \mathbb{Z}^m \mid \mathbf{A}\mathbf{e} = \mathbf{u} \bmod q\}.$$

**Definition 2.3 (Discrete Gaussian Distribution).** *For a lattice $\mathcal{L}$, a vector $\mathbf{c} \in \mathbb{R}^m$, and a real number $\sigma > 0$, define $\rho_{\sigma,\mathbf{c}}(\mathbf{x}) = \exp(--\pi\|\mathbf{x} --\mathbf{c}\|^2/\sigma^2)$. The discrete Gaussian distribution of support $\mathcal{L}$, center $\mathbf{c}$ and parameter $\sigma$ is defined as $D_{\mathcal{L},\sigma,\mathbf{c}}(\mathbf{y}) = \rho_{\sigma,\mathbf{c}}(\mathbf{y})/\rho_{\sigma,\mathbf{c}}(\mathcal{L})$ for any $\mathbf{y} \in \mathcal{L}$, where $\rho_{\sigma,\mathbf{c}}(\mathcal{L}) = \sum_{x \in \mathcal{L}} \rho_{\sigma,\mathbf{c}}(x)$. We denote by $D_{\mathcal{L},\sigma}(\mathbf{y})$ the distribution centered in $\mathbf{c} = \mathbf{0}^m$ and exploit the fact that samples from $D_{\mathcal{L},\sigma}$ have small maximum norm with high probability.*

**Lemma 1** ([5], **Lemma 1.5**)**.** For any lattice $\mathcal{L} \subset \mathbb{R}^n$ and positive real number $\sigma > 0$, we have $\mathrm{Pr}_{b \leftarrow D_{\mathcal{L},\sigma}}[\|\mathbf{b}\| \leq \sqrt{n}\sigma] \geq 1 - 2^{\Omega(n)}$.

The following lemmas specify how one can sample an (almost) random lattice basis of $\Lambda_q^{\perp}(\mathbf{A})$, together with a short trapdoor basis, and how to extend a basis:

**Lemma 2** ([4], **Theorem 3.2**)**.** There is a PPT algorithm TrapGen, that takes as input $1^n, 1^m$ and an integer $q > 2$ with $m \geq \Omega(n \log q)$, and outputs a matrix $\mathbf{A} \in \mathbb{Z}_q^{n \times m}$ and a basis $\mathbf{T}_{\mathbf{A}}$ of $\Lambda_q^{\perp}(\mathbf{A})$ such that $\mathbf{A}$ is within statistical distance $2^{-\Omega(n)}$ to the uniform distribution over $\mathbb{Z}_q^{n \times m}$ and $\|\widetilde{\mathbf{T}_{\mathbf{A}}}\| \leq \mathcal{O}(\sqrt{n \log q})$.

**Lemma 3** ([13], **Lemma 3.2**)**.** For $m' > m$, there exists a PPT algorithm ExtBasis that takes as inputs a matrix $\mathbf{B} \in \mathbb{Z}_q^{n \times m'}$ whose first $m$ columns span $\mathbb{Z}_q^n$, and a basis $\mathbf{T}_{\mathbf{A}}$ of $\Lambda_q^{\perp}(\mathbf{A})$ where $\mathbf{A}$ is the left $n \times m$ submatrix of $\mathbf{B}$, and outputs a basis $\mathbf{T}_{\mathbf{B}}$ of $\Lambda_q^{\perp}(\mathbf{B})$ with $\|\widetilde{\mathbf{T}_{\mathbf{B}}}\| \leq \|\widetilde{\mathbf{T}_{\mathbf{A}}}\|$.

### 2.3   Instantiation of Building Blocks

*KTX-Commitments.* In our construction, we use the commitment scheme of [25]. Let $n \in \mathcal{O}(\lambda)$, $q \in \mathcal{O}(n^4)$, $m_0, m_1 \in \Theta(n \log q)$, $0 < \sigma_{\mathsf{Com}} \in \mathbb{R}$, where $m_0$ is the size of the randomness vector $\mathbf{r}$, $m_1$ is the size of the message vector $\mathbf{m}$ and $\sigma_{\mathsf{Com}}$ is the parameter of the Gaussian distribution for the randomness. In the simplest case, one can commit to one message block $\mathbf{m} \in \mathbb{Z}_2^{m_1}$ by computing:

$$\mathsf{Gen}(1^{\lambda})\colon \mathbf{D}_0 \leftarrow \mathbb{Z}_q^{n \times m_0}, \mathbf{D}_1 \leftarrow \mathbb{Z}_q^{n \times m_1}, \text{ output } (\mathbf{D}_0, \mathbf{D}_1, \sigma_{\mathsf{Com}}).$$

$$\mathsf{Com}(\mathsf{params}, \mathbf{m}; \mathbf{r}) := \mathbf{D}_0 \cdot \mathbf{r} + \mathbf{D}_1 \cdot \mathbf{m} \in \mathbb{Z}_q^n,$$

where $\mathsf{params} = (\mathbf{D}_0, \mathbf{D}_1, \sigma_{\mathsf{Com}})$ are the public parameters.

The matrices $\mathbf{D}_0, \mathbf{D}_1$ are drawn uniformly at random. For each new commitment the randomness $\mathbf{r} \leftarrow D_{\mathbb{Z}_q^{m_0}, \sigma_{\mathsf{Com}}}$ is chosen according to the discrete Gaussian distribution $D_{\mathbb{Z}_q^{m_0}, \sigma_{\mathsf{Com}}}$. Usually, we set $m_0 = 2m_1$. A commitment $\mathbf{c}$ can be opened by showing $\mathbf{m}$ and $\mathbf{r}$. If it holds that $\mathbf{m} \in \mathbb{Z}_2^{m_1}$, $\|\mathbf{r}\| \leq \sigma_{\mathsf{Com}}\sqrt{m_0}$ and $\mathbf{c} = \mathbf{D}_0 \cdot \mathbf{r} + \mathbf{D}_1 \cdot \mathbf{m}$, the commitment is valid. This scheme is statistically hiding. It is computationally binding, which can be seen by a straightforward reduction on $SIS_{n,q,2\sigma_{\mathsf{Com}}\sqrt{m_0}, m_0+m_1}$. For $N \in \mathbb{N}$, the scheme can be extended to a commitment scheme on $N$ messages by using $N$ matrices. For the security proof of our construction, we require our commitment scheme to be equivocal. The scheme presented above can easily be turned into an equivocal commitment scheme, by using lattice trapdoor gadgets, as discussed in the full version [17] of this paper. It is necessary in the construction of the trapdoor to have $m_0 > n\lceil \log q \rceil$.

*Signature Scheme by Libert et al.* The scheme for obliviously signing committed messages by Libert et al. [27] consists of the two algorithms Gen, Vfy, and the interactive protocol OblSign (described in 1). It allows the signing of $N$-block messages $\mathbf{msg} = (\mathbf{m}_1, \ldots, \mathbf{m}_N)$, for $N = \mathsf{poly}(\lambda)$. In our construction we will

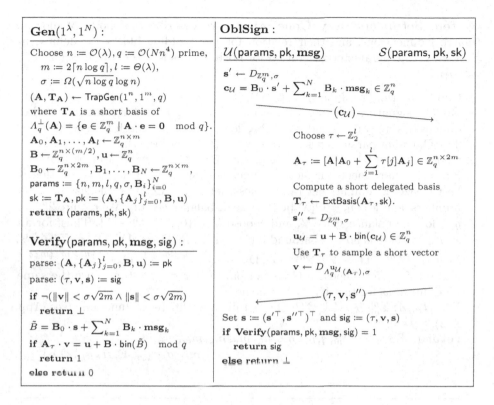

**Fig. 1.** Gen, Verify and OblSign algorithms of the signature scheme.

use the notation $\mathsf{OblSign}.\mathcal{S}(\mathsf{pk}, \mathsf{sk}, \mathbf{c}_\mathcal{U}) \to (\tau, \mathbf{v}, \mathbf{s}'')$ to denote the part of the protocol, which is executed by the signer, where params is derived from the relevant parts of the implicitly given CRS. The algorithm takes a key pair $(\mathsf{pk}, \mathsf{sk})$ and a commitment $\mathbf{c}_\mathcal{U}$ and outputs the signer's part of the signature $(\tau, \mathbf{v}, \mathbf{s}'')$ on the content of the commitment $\mathbf{c}_\mathcal{U}$. See the full version [17] of this paper for a proof sketch or [28, Theorem 2] for a full proof of Lemma 4. In the full-version, we additionally give a formal definition of the security, which was only implicit in [27,28].

**Lemma 4 ([28], Theorem 2).** Let $\beta' := \sigma^2 m\sqrt{2m}(l+2) + \sigma m\sqrt{m}$ and $\beta'' = \sigma^2 m\sqrt{2m} + \sqrt{2m} + 4\sigma m\sqrt{2m\log q}$. Then the above scheme is secure if the $SIS_{n,q,\beta',m}$ and $SIS_{n,q,\beta'',m}$ assumptions hold.

## 3 Our Construction of **BABL**

We denote by S the signature scheme of [28] (cf. Section 2.3) and by C the commitment scheme of [25] used in Issue and Update (cf. Sect. 2.3). The two zero-knowledge proof systems P1 and P2 are instantiations of the ZK scheme from [36] and are used in Issue and Update, respectively. (For a general description of the building blocks and their security notions, see Appendix A.2).

**System Setup and Key Generation.** We describe the choice of moduli, (matrix) dimensions, and their relation for the building blocks (as defined in Sect. 2.3). The parameter generation for both parties is described in Fig. 2.
**Setup($1^\lambda$):**

- Choose a prime modulus $q_0 = \mathcal{O}(\lambda^4)$.
- For the signature scheme, set the modulus to $q = q_0^e$ for some $e > 0$. Let dimensions $n_S = \mathcal{O}(\lambda)$ and $m_S = 2n_S\lceil\log q\rceil$, and tag length $l_\tau = \Theta(\lambda)$.
- The Gaussian parameter is set to $\sigma = \Omega(\sqrt{n_S\log q}\log n_S)$.
- Choose $n_{sk} = \mathcal{O}(\lambda)$, $m_{sk} = n_{sk}\log q_0$ and draw $\mathbf{F} \leftarrow \mathbb{Z}_{q_0}^{n_{sk}\times m_{sk}}$ (for $pk_\mathcal{U}$ later).
- For the commitment scheme, let dimension $n_C = n_S$. Let $m_r = 2n_C\lceil\log q\rceil$ be the size of commitment randomness, let $m_{nr} = \mathcal{O}(\lambda)$ be the size of serial numbers, and let $m_b = \mathcal{O}(\lambda)$ be the size of balance vectors. We require $2^{m_b} < q/4$ for the balance space $\mathbb{V}$, and choose $\mathbb{V} = \{0,\ldots,2^{m_b}-1\}$. Thus, for all $x, y \in \mathbb{V}$, there is no wrap-around for $x + y$. Draw $\mathbf{D}_0 = (\mathbf{D}_0^0, \mathbf{D}_0^1) \leftarrow \mathbb{Z}_q^{n_C\times 2m_r}$, $\mathbf{D}_1 \leftarrow \mathbb{Z}_q^{n_C\times m_{sk}}$, $\mathbf{D}_2 \leftarrow \mathbb{Z}_q^{n_C\times m_b}$, $\mathbf{D}_3, \mathbf{D}_4 \leftarrow \mathbb{Z}_q^{n_C\times m_{nr}\lceil\log q_0\rceil}$, $\mathbf{D}_5 \leftarrow \mathbb{Z}_q^{n_C\times m_{sk}\lceil\log q_0\rceil}$ and set $N = 5$.[3] Choose a Gaussian parameter $\sigma_{Com} > 0$ and use the same modulus $q$, as for the signature scheme.
- Let $H_{FRD}\colon \mathbb{Z}_{q_0}^{m_{sk}} \to \mathbb{Z}_{q_0}^{m_{sk}\times m_{sk}}$ be a full-rank difference function, (see App. A.2).
- **return** CRS $:= (1^\lambda, q_0, q, n_S, m_S, n_C, m_r, n_{sk}, m_{sk}, m_b,$
$$m_{nr}, \sigma, \sigma_{Com}, \mathbf{F}, H_{FRD}, \{\mathbf{D}_i\}_{i=0}^5).$$

| **OGen(CRS)** | **UGen(CRS)** |
|---|---|
| Generate $(params', pk_S, sk_S) \leftarrow S.Gen(1^\lambda, 1^5)$ | Draw $sk_\mathcal{U} \leftarrow \mathbb{Z}_2^{m_{sk}}$ |
| **return** $(sk_\mathcal{O} := sk_S, pk_\mathcal{O} := pk_S)$ | **return** $(pk_\mathcal{U} := \mathbf{F}\cdot sk_\mathcal{U}, sk_\mathcal{U})$ |

**Fig. 2.** Generation algorithms **OGen**, **UGen** for operators and user, respectively

**Issuing a New Token.** In this protocol, the user $\mathcal{U}$ interacts with the operator $\mathcal{O}$ (in the issuer role) to get a fresh token with balance $\mathbf{b} = \mathbf{0}$. The token is a tuple of the form $\mathcal{T} = (\mathbf{c}, \mathbf{r}, sk_\mathcal{U}, \mathbf{b}, \mathbf{s}_\mathcal{U}, \mathbf{s}_\mathcal{O}, \mathbf{u}_\mathcal{U}, sig)$, where $\mathbf{c}$ is a multi-block commitment to the values $sk_\mathcal{U}, \mathbf{b}, \mathbf{s}_\mathcal{U}, \mathbf{s}_\mathcal{O}$, and $\mathbf{u}_\mathcal{U}$ with randomness $\mathbf{r}$. Here, $sk_\mathcal{U}$ is the user's secret key, and the vectors $\mathbf{s}_\mathcal{U}$ and $\mathbf{s}_\mathcal{O}$ are the two shares of the token's serial number, chosen by $\mathcal{U}$ and $\mathcal{O}$, respectively. The vector $\mathbf{u}_\mathcal{U}$ is randomly drawn by the user and is used in the generation of the $\mathbf{t}$-part of the double-spending tag (to be explained below). Finally, $sig$ is a signature on the commitment $\mathbf{c}$.

The Issue protocol is the only protocol in which the operator sees $pk_\mathcal{U}$, the public key of the user. In subsequent transactions of Update, possession of $sk_\mathcal{U}$ (and thus, of $pk_\mathcal{U}$) is proven via ZK proof.

---

[3] We will use these matrices for the signature, too. We ignore $params'$, output by S.Gen.

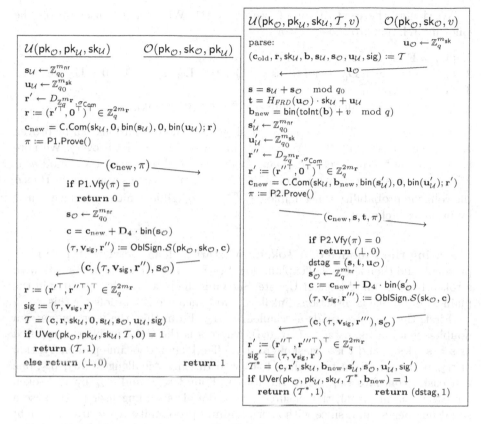

**Fig. 3.** Protocols for issuing (left) and updating (right) a token $\mathcal{T}$.

Figure 3 (left) shows the Issue protocol in detail. First, the user $\mathcal{U}$ draws their part of the serial number $\mathbf{s}_{\mathcal{U}} \leftarrow \mathbb{Z}_{q0}^{m_{nr}}$, the vector $\mathbf{u}_{\mathcal{U}} \leftarrow \mathbb{Z}_{q0}^{m_{sk}}$ for the computation of the double-spending tag, and a random vector for the commitment $\mathbf{r}' \leftarrow D_{\mathbb{Z}_q^{m_r},\sigma_{\text{Com}}}$. The other half of the randomness vector $\mathbf{r} \in \mathbb{Z}_q^{2m_r}$ is set to 0, so the randomness chosen by $\mathcal{O}$ can later be added (after $\mathcal{U}$ received $\mathbf{r}''$ from $\mathcal{O}$). $\mathcal{U}$ then commits (using randomness $\mathbf{r}'$) on a five-block message, containing the secret key $\text{sk}_{\mathcal{U}}$, $\mathbf{s}_{\mathcal{U}}$ and $\mathbf{u}_{\mathcal{U}}$, with the second and fourth message block of the commitment being initialized to $\mathbf{0}$. This is because the second block represents the balance of the token, and is supposed to be $\mathbf{0}$ after issuance of the token, and the fourth block is zero for the operator to later add their share $\mathbf{s}_{\mathcal{O}}$ of the serial number to the block. Afterwards, the user sends the commitment to $\mathcal{O}$, together with a ZK proof $\pi$ that ensures that the commitment contains the secret key which belongs to the user's public key.

After verification of $\pi$, $\mathcal{O}$ proceeds by adding their share $\mathbf{s}_{\mathcal{O}}$ of the serial number $(\mathbf{s}_{\mathcal{U}}, \mathbf{s}_{\mathcal{O}})$ to the commitment. Then, the operator signs the committed message obliviously and sends the final commitment and the signature back to the user. The user verifies if the token is correct and accepts if this is the case.

We denote the used ZK proof system by P1. With P1, the user proves the following relations to the operator:

1. $\mathsf{pk}_\mathcal{U} = \mathbf{F} \cdot \mathsf{sk}_\mathcal{U} \mod q_0$
2. $\mathbf{c}_{\mathrm{new}} = \mathbf{D}_0^0 \cdot \mathbf{r}' + \mathbf{D}_0^1 \cdot \mathbf{0} + \mathbf{D}_1 \cdot \mathsf{sk}_\mathcal{U} + \mathbf{D}_2 \cdot \mathbf{0} + \mathbf{D}_3 \cdot \bar{\mathbf{s}}_\mathcal{U} + \mathbf{D}_4 \cdot \mathbf{0} + \mathbf{D}_5 \cdot \bar{\mathbf{u}}_\mathcal{U}$
3. $\|\mathbf{r}'\| \le \sigma_{\mathsf{Com}} \sqrt{m_\mathbf{r}}$
4. $\mathsf{sk}_\mathcal{U}, \bar{\mathbf{s}}_\mathcal{U}, \bar{\mathbf{u}}_\mathcal{U}$ are binary and $\mathsf{bin}(\mathbf{s}_\mathcal{U}) = \bar{\mathbf{s}}_\mathcal{U}$, $\mathsf{bin}(\mathbf{u}_\mathcal{U}) = \bar{\mathbf{u}}_\mathcal{U}$

In the full-version [17] of this paper, we show how these equations can be proven via the ZK protocol of [36]. We denote this proof by $\pi := \mathsf{P1.Prove}()$. We note here, that the "actual" serial number of the token will be $\mathbf{s} = \mathbf{s}_\mathcal{U} + \mathbf{s}_\mathcal{O} \mod q_0 \in \mathbb{Z}_{q_0}^{m_{\mathrm{nr}}}$. Thus, $\mathbf{s}$ is uniformly random in $\mathbb{Z}_{q_0}^{m_{\mathrm{nr}}}$ if one of the parties was honest. Hence, the collision probability is negligible if $q_0^{-m_{\mathrm{nr}}}$ is negligible, which must be ensured by parameter choices.

**Updating the Balance of a Token.** We start with an overview of the update protocol, and then a detailed explanation. See Fig. 3 (right). The user starts with a token from a run of Issue or Update. Showing the token to the operator in the plain would make transactions linkable – we hence use ZK proofs for this.

First, the operator sends a "challenge" $\mathbf{u}_\mathcal{O}$. From this, the user generates a double-spending tag $\mathsf{dstag} = (\mathbf{s}, \mathbf{t}, \mathbf{u}_\mathcal{O})$, where $\mathbf{s}$ is the serial number, computed as $\mathbf{s} = \mathbf{s}_\mathcal{U} + \mathbf{s}_\mathcal{O}$, and $\mathbf{t}$ is a masking of $\mathsf{sk}_\mathcal{U}$, effectively a one-time pad encryption of $\mathsf{sk}_\mathcal{U}$ with $\mathbf{u}_\mathcal{U}$. Given two values $\mathbf{t}, \mathbf{t}'$ with distinct "challenges" $\mathbf{u}_\mathcal{O}$, $\mathbf{u}'_\mathcal{O}$, one can easily compute $\mathsf{sk}_\mathcal{U}$. Since the user is bound to $\mathbf{s}$ and $\mathsf{sk}_\mathcal{U}$ by the token (and the commitment), this ensures that a double-spending user must reuse a serial number $\mathbf{s}$, and, since with overwhelming probability $\mathbf{u}_\mathcal{O} \ne \mathbf{u}'_\mathcal{O}$, is caught and deanonymized when doing so. This implements double spending detection. (Note, that a benign user can not be deanonymized).

The user also sets up a new (partial) token $\mathbf{c}_{\mathrm{new}}$, analogous to the Issue protocol, but with balance set $\mathsf{toInt}(\mathbf{b}) + v$, according to the transaction. Then it proves that $\mathbf{c}_{\mathrm{new}}$ is a valid token (analogous to Issue) with correct balance, its connection and the validity of the "old" token (and its balance), and also, that the double spending tag $\mathsf{dstag} = (\mathbf{s}, \mathbf{t}, \mathbf{u}_\mathcal{O})$ was correctly computed.

As in Issue, the operator first verifies the proof. It then chooses its part $\mathbf{s}'_\mathcal{O}$ of the new serial number and obliviously signs the adapted commitment $\mathbf{c}$. Also as in Issue, the user verifies the commitment and signature. After the transaction, the user has a freshly updated token, and the operator a double-spending tag.

Now, we describe the relevant parts in more detail. Update is defined as an interactive protocol between user $\mathcal{U}$ and operator $\mathcal{O}$. Both parties take as inputs their key pairs, and the transaction value $v \in \mathbb{V}$. Additionally, the user gets as input the operator's public key and the old token $\mathcal{T}$ containing their current balance $\mathsf{toInt}(\mathbf{b}) \in \mathbb{V}$. The protocol outputs for $\mathcal{U}$ and $\mathcal{O}$ consist of a new token $\mathcal{T}^*$ and a double-spending tag $\mathsf{dstag}$, respectively, as well as the output bits $b_\mathcal{U}, b_\mathcal{O}$, respectively, indicating a party accepts the execution of the protocol.

The user's token is $\mathcal{T} = (\mathbf{c}_{\mathrm{old}}, \mathbf{r}, \mathsf{sk}_\mathcal{U}, \mathbf{b}, \mathbf{s}_\mathcal{U}, \mathbf{s}_\mathcal{O}, \mathbf{u}_\mathcal{U}, \mathsf{sig})$. As explained above, the protocol generates a new token, but with a different balance and additional consistency proofs and double-spending detection. This is reflected by the variables with an additional prime, corresponding to those of Issue. The updated balance is $\mathbf{b}_{new} := \mathsf{bin}(\mathsf{toInt}(\mathbf{b}) + v \mod q)$. The partial commitment is of the form

$$\mathbf{c}_{new} = \mathbf{D}_0^0 \cdot \mathbf{r}' + \mathbf{D}_1 \cdot \mathsf{sk}_{\mathcal{U}} + \mathbf{D}_2 \cdot \mathbf{b}_{new} + \mathbf{D}_3 \cdot \mathsf{bin}(\mathsf{s}_{\mathcal{U}}') + \mathbf{D}_5 \cdot \mathsf{bin}(\mathsf{u}_{\mathcal{U}}'), \quad (1)$$

which differs from Issue in the term $\mathbf{D}_2 \cdot \mathbf{b}_{new}$, where $\mathbf{b}_{new} = \mathbf{0}$. As in Issue, the new serial number is calculated from $(\mathsf{s}_{\mathcal{U}}', \mathsf{s}_{\mathcal{O}}')$ chosen by user and operator, respectively. Also note the user only adds by $\mathbf{D}_0^0 \cdot \mathbf{r}'$ the first half of the randomness to the commitment. The second half will be chosen by the operator. For double-spending detection, $\mathcal{O}$ sends $\mathbf{u}_{\mathcal{O}} \leftarrow \mathbb{Z}_{q_0}^{m_{sk}}$. The user calculates the vector $\mathbf{s} := \mathbf{s}_{\mathcal{U}} + \mathbf{s}_{\mathcal{O}} \mod q_0$, and $\mathbf{t} := H_{FRD}(\mathbf{u}_{\mathcal{O}}) \cdot \mathsf{sk}_{\mathcal{U}} + \mathbf{u}_{\mathcal{U}}$. Recall that $H_{FRD}$ denotes the full-rank difference function from Appendix A.2. Also note, that $\mathbf{u}_{\mathcal{U}}$ perfectly masks $H_{FRD}(\mathbf{u}_{\mathcal{O}}) \cdot \mathsf{sk}_{\mathcal{U}}$, as it is a uniformly random value (chosen when $\mathbf{c}_{old}$ was issued). Hence, $\mathbf{t}$ reveals nothing about $\mathsf{sk}_{\mathcal{U}}$. However, if the user double-spends by reusing an old token, given $\mathbf{u}_{\mathcal{O}} \neq \mathbf{u}_{\mathcal{O}}'$ in these two executions (which happens with overwhelming probability), then $(H_{FRD}(\mathbf{u}_{\mathcal{O}}) - H_{FRD}(\mathbf{u}_{\mathcal{O}}'))^{-1}(\mathbf{t}' - \mathbf{t}'') = \mathsf{sk}_{\mathcal{U}}$. Thus, the identity of the misbehaving user is revealed. We denote by P2 a non-interactive ZK proof system, and by $\pi := \mathsf{P2.Prove}()$ its output. P2 proves following equations:

1. $\mathsf{Vfy}(\mathsf{pk}_{\mathcal{O}}, \mathsf{sig}, (\mathsf{sk}_{\mathcal{U}}, \mathbf{b}, \bar{\mathsf{s}}_{\mathcal{U}}, \bar{\mathsf{s}}_{\mathcal{O}}, \bar{\mathsf{u}}_{\mathcal{U}})) = 1$
2. $\mathbf{s} = \mathbf{s}_{\mathcal{U}} + \mathbf{s}_{\mathcal{O}} \mod q_0$
3. $\mathbf{t} = H_{FRD}(\mathbf{u}_{\mathcal{O}}) \cdot \mathsf{sk}_{\mathcal{U}} + \mathbf{u}_{\mathcal{U}} \mod q_0$
4. $\mathbf{c}_{new} = \mathbf{D}_0^0 \cdot \mathbf{r}'' + \mathbf{D}_0^1 \cdot \mathbf{0} + \mathbf{D}_1 \cdot \mathsf{sk}_{\mathcal{U}} + \mathbf{D}_2 \cdot \mathbf{b}_{new} + \mathbf{D}_3 \cdot \bar{\mathsf{s}}_{\mathcal{U}}' + \mathbf{D}_5 \cdot \bar{\mathsf{u}}_{\mathcal{U}}'$
5. $\mathbf{b}_{new} = \mathsf{bin}(\mathsf{toInt}(\mathbf{b}) + v \mod q))$
6. $\|\mathbf{r}'\| \leq \sigma_{Com}\sqrt{m_r}$
7. $\mathsf{sk}_{\mathcal{U}}, \bar{\mathsf{s}}_{\mathcal{U}}, \bar{\mathsf{s}}_{\mathcal{O}}, \bar{\mathsf{u}}_{\mathcal{U}}, \bar{\mathsf{u}}_{\mathcal{U}}', \mathbf{b}_{new}, \bar{\mathsf{s}}_{\mathcal{U}}'$ are binary, $\mathsf{bin}(\mathsf{s}_{\mathcal{U}}) = \bar{\mathsf{s}}_{\mathcal{U}}, \mathsf{bin}(\mathsf{s}_{\mathcal{O}}) = \bar{\mathsf{s}}_{\mathcal{O}},$ $\mathsf{bin}(\mathsf{u}_{\mathcal{U}}) = \bar{\mathsf{u}}_{\mathcal{U}}, \mathsf{bin}(\mathsf{u}_{\mathcal{U}}') = \bar{\mathsf{u}}_{\mathcal{U}}',$ and $\mathsf{bin}(\mathsf{s}_{\mathcal{U}}') = \bar{\mathsf{s}}_{\mathcal{U}}'$

The equations prove that the old token was valid, and its contents were used to compute $\mathbf{b}_{new}$, dstag and $\mathbf{c}_{new}$. Items 2 and 3 are for showing that the serial number $\mathbf{s}$ and tag $\mathbf{t}$ were computed correctly (from these values). The remaining equations prove the well-formedness of the new token, similar to Issue. In the full-version [17] of this paper, we show how the equations can be transformed into the generic form $\mathbf{A} \cdot \mathbf{x} = \mathbf{y} \mod q$, where $\mathbf{A}$ is a public matrix, $\mathbf{y}$ is a public vector and $\mathbf{x}$ is the secret witness. Once the equations are in this form, the ZK protocol from [36] can be leveraged.

The user sends $(\mathbf{c}_{new}, \mathbf{s}, \mathbf{t}, \pi)$ to $\mathcal{O}$, who checks the validity of the proof. The remainder of the protocol is essentially as in Issue, i.e. $\mathcal{O}$ picks their share $\mathbf{s}_{\mathcal{O}}$ of the serial number, obliviously signs the extended commitment $\mathbf{c}$, and sends the respective values to $\mathcal{U}$. The double-spending tag dstag $= (\mathbf{s}, \mathbf{t}, \mathbf{u}_{\mathcal{O}})$ is stored in a database of the operator, after the transaction ended successfully. If an entry $(\mathbf{s}, \mathbf{t}')$ is already recorded, IdentDS can be used to identify the offending user.

*Security of the Construction.* We give an intuition on why the protocol is secure (see App. B.3 for the formal version of the argument): the commitment binds the user to the values in a token. The ZK property of the proof system protects the user's actions from being linked between executions. Its soundness ensures that the user cannot cheat. Thus, at the end of the protocol, the user has a new token with an updated balance. The operator only learns that the old and new token are valid, the value $v$ of the transaction, and the double-spending tag.

*Discussion.* We point out a difference between our construction of BBA and previous ones [22–24]. There, range proofs were expensive and therefore optional. However, going without range proofs was only possible if the user revealed the balance when spending points, leaking a lot of information. Due to the lattice-based setting, our ZK proofs implicitly ensure that the balance is within the allowed range $\mathbb{V}$. This is because our proofs rely on bit decomposition. That is, we prove $\mathsf{toInt}(\mathbf{x}) = \sum_{i=0}^{m_b-1} \mathbf{x}_i \cdot 2^i \in \{0, \ldots, 2^{m_b} - 1\} = \mathbb{V}$ and $\mathbf{x} \in \{0,1\}^{m_b}$. Consequently, $\mathsf{toInt}(\mathbf{x})$ is a positive integer. (Recall that $2^{m_b} < q/4$, so the unique representative of the congruence class in $\mathbb{Z}_q$ is positive.) More precisely, we prove that $\mathbf{b_{new}}$ is of the form $\mathbf{b_{new}} = \mathsf{bin}(\mathsf{toInt}(\mathbf{b}) + v \mod q)$. Now, if $\mathsf{toInt}(\mathbf{b}) + v \mod q$ would be negative or bigger than $2^{m_b} - 1$, the user could not generate a ZK proof which would be accepted by the operator.

**Detecting Double-Spending.** To identify a double-spender, in other words, a user who tries to spend the same token twice, the operator runs the IdentDS algorithm (see Fig. 4). For double-spending detection, the operator requires access to the database of double-spending tags. When the user did double-spend, the operator can calculate the user's secret-key $\mathsf{sk}_\mathcal{U}$ from the double-spending tags.

| $\mathsf{UVer}(\mathsf{pk}_\mathcal{O}, \mathsf{pk}_\mathcal{U}, \mathsf{sk}_\mathcal{U}, \mathcal{T}, \mathbf{b})$ | $\mathsf{IdentDS}(\mathsf{pk}_\mathcal{O}, (\mathbf{s}, z_1), (\mathbf{s}', z_2))$ |
|---|---|
| parse: $(\mathbf{c}, \mathbf{r}, \mathsf{sk}_\mathcal{U}, \mathbf{b}, \mathbf{s}_\mathcal{U}, \mathbf{s}_\mathcal{O}, \mathbf{u}_\mathcal{U}, \mathsf{sig}) := \mathcal{T}$ | parse: $(\mathbf{t}, \mathbf{u}_\mathcal{O}) := z_1, (\mathbf{t}', \mathbf{u}'_\mathcal{O}) := z_2$ |
| parse: $(\tau_\mathsf{sig}, \mathbf{v}_\mathsf{sig}, \mathbf{r}) := \mathsf{sig}$ | if $\mathbf{s} \neq \mathbf{s}' \vee \mathbf{u}_\mathcal{O} = \mathbf{u}'_\mathcal{O}$   return $\perp$ |
| $\mathsf{msg} := \mathsf{sk}_\mathcal{U}, \mathbf{b}, \mathsf{bin}(\mathbf{s}_\mathcal{U}), \mathsf{bin}(\mathbf{s}_\mathcal{O}), \mathsf{bin}(\mathbf{u}_\mathcal{U})$ | else |
| if $\mathbf{c} = \mathsf{C.Com}(\mathsf{msg}; \mathbf{r})$ | $\quad \mathsf{sk}_\mathcal{U} := (\mathbf{t} - \mathbf{t}')$ |
| $\quad \wedge \mathsf{S.Verify}(\mathsf{pk}_\mathcal{O}, \mathsf{sig}, \mathsf{msg}) = 1$ | $\quad \cdot (H_{FRD}(\mathbf{u}_\mathcal{O}) - H_{FRD}(\mathbf{u}'_\mathcal{O}))^{-1} \mod q_0$ |
| $\quad$ return 1 | $\quad \mathsf{pk}_\mathcal{U} := \mathbf{F} \cdot \mathsf{sk}_\mathcal{U}$ |
| else return 0 | $\quad$ return $(\mathsf{pk}_\mathcal{U}, \Pi = \mathsf{sk}_\mathcal{U})$ |

**Fig. 4.** UVer for token verification, and IdentDS to handle double-spending.

The VerifyGuilt algorithm takes the users public key $\mathsf{pk}_\mathcal{U}$ and a proof $\Pi$ of double-spending. The algorithm outputs 1 if $\mathbf{F} \cdot \Pi = \mathsf{pk}_\mathcal{U} \mod q_0 \wedge \|\Pi\|_\infty \leq 1$. Note, that it is not possible to generate a proof of guilt for benign user, as our construction offers *false-accusation protection*.

**User-Verify Algorithm.** The UVer algorithm (see Fig. 4) checks if the commitment $\mathbf{c}$ contained in the token is truly a commitment on the messages $sk_{\mathcal{U}}, \mathbf{b}, bin(s_{\mathcal{U}}), bin(s_{\mathcal{O}})$ and $bin(\mathbf{u}_{\mathcal{U}})$ with randomness $\mathbf{r}$. Further the algorithm checks if sig is a valid signature on the commitment $\mathbf{c}$ under the operator's secret key. The algorithm outputs 1 if both conditions are fulfilled, otherwise 0.

# 4    Efficiency Evaluation

In this section, we evaluate the efficiency of our construction. We concentrate on the communication cost, as this is the main bottleneck for mobile payments. Therefore, we first analyze the communication cost of an Update transaction. Next, we briefly explain our choice of parameters and calculate the concrete communication cost of Update and Issue given those parameters. We also compare the efficiency of our instantiation to similar protocols.

**Communication Cost.** From Fig. 3 (right) we can derive the cost of Update. We denote the communication cost by $\mathcal{C}_{\text{Update}}$ and we write $|\mathbf{vec}|$ for the number of bits needed to represent a vector $\mathbf{vec}$.

$$\mathcal{C}_{\text{Update}} = |\mathbf{u}_{\mathcal{O}}| + |\mathbf{c}_{\text{new}}| + |\mathbf{s}| + |\mathbf{t}| + |\pi| + |\mathbf{c}| + |(\tau, \mathbf{v}_{\text{sig}}, \mathbf{r}'')| + |\mathbf{s}'_{\mathcal{O}}|$$

The biggest part of this sum is $|\pi|$. Therefore, we will further analyze the size of the proof. According to Yang et al. [36] the size of this proof is

$$|\pi| = (\log(2p+1) + \kappa + (3l_1 + 2l_2 + 2m_{\text{Update}}$$
$$+ 2l_{\text{Update}}) \cdot \log q) \cdot N + (l_1 + m_{\text{Update}}) \cdot \log q, \quad (2)$$

where $p, \kappa, l_1, l_2, N$ are parameters of the zero-knowledge protocol, $m_{\text{Update}}$ is the length of the witness and $l_{\text{Update}}$ is the size of the set $\mathcal{M}$.

Using the fast mode [36] to prove the norm bounds on $\mathbf{r}$ and $\mathbf{v}$ we arrive at the size $m_{\text{Update}} := |\tau| + 2n_S|\tau| + 2m_S + n_C \log q + 2m_\mathbf{r} + m_{\text{sk}} + 2m_\mathbf{b} + 3m_{\text{nr}} \log q_0 + 2m_{\text{sk}} \log q_0 + m_\mathbf{r} + b\lambda(\log(10m_S\beta/b)+1)$ for the witness and $l_{\text{Update}} := |\tau| + n_S|\tau| + n_C \log q + 2m_\mathbf{b} \log q_0 + 3m_{\text{nr}} \log q_0 + 2m_{\text{sk}} + b\lambda(\log(10m_S\beta/b)+1)$ for $\mathcal{M}$, where $b$ allows for a trade-off between proof size and tightness of the proven bound.

Next, we look at the signature $|\text{sig}|$. By definition, we have $\text{sig} = (\tau, \mathbf{v}, \mathbf{s})$, where $\tau \in \mathbb{Z}_2^l, \mathbf{v} \in \mathbb{Z}_q^{2m_S}$ and $\mathbf{s} \in \mathbb{Z}_q^{2m_S}$. Hence, we get $|\text{sig}| = l + 4m_S \cdot \log(\beta)$ bits.

**Choice of Parameters.** To provide practical parameters for our scheme, we follow the heuristic approach of setting parameters high enough to withstand best-known attacks instead of deriving them from a reduction to a hard lattice problem such as SVP. For the sake of comparison we choose parameters for 80-bit security. In real-world scenarios, a higher level of security is desirable. To do so, we examine the root Hermite factor (RHF) [18] of our SIS/LWE problems. According to [36], to achieve 80-bit security a RHF of at most 1.0048 is required. We follow [36] and estimate the required RHF as

$$\text{RHF}(SIS_{n,q,\beta}) \approx 2^{\frac{\log^2 \beta}{4n \log q}} \quad \text{resp.} \quad \text{RHF}(LWE_{n,q,\alpha}) \approx 2^{\frac{\log^2 \frac{\alpha}{5.31}}{4n \log q}}$$

see [26], resp. [3]. BABL relies on the the following assumptions:

- $SIS_{n_{sk},q,\sqrt{m_{sk}}}$ so it is infeasible to derive the secret key from the public key.
- $SIS_{n_C,q,2\sigma_{Com}\sqrt{2m_r}\frac{m_r}{b}}$ for the commitment scheme to be binding.
- $SIS_{n_S,q,\beta'\frac{m_S}{b}}$, $SIS_{n_S,q,\beta''\frac{m_S}{b}}$ for the signature to be secure.
- $SIS_{l_1,q,\beta_1}$, $SIS_{l_2,q,\beta_2}$ and $LWE_{l_2,q,\alpha}$ for the zero-knowledge protocol [36].

where factors $\frac{m_r}{b}$, $\frac{m_s}{b}$ are due to the soundness loss from the fast mode of [36]. From the ZK argument we have the constraints that $q_0 > p$ and $q > \max(\beta_1, \beta_2)$, where we repeat the proof $\lceil 2^{80}/p \rceil$ times to achieve a soundness error of $2^{-80}$.

**Table 1.** Concrete choices of parameters and resulting values for the underlying assumptions of the zero-knowledge proof (left), the signature scheme (middle), the commitment scheme (right) and for the secret keys (bottom right).

| Param. | Value | Param. | Value | Param. | Value |
|---|---|---|---|---|---|
| $p$ | $2^{80}$ | $\log q_0$ | 100 | $\log q$ | 200 |
| $l_1$ | 7050 | $n_S$ | 880 | $n_C$ | 880 |
| $l_2$ | 7000 | $m_S$ | 352 000 | $m_r$ | 352 000 |
| $\sigma_3$ | 67 | $l_\tau$ | 80 | $\sigma_{Com}$ | 4195.0 |
| $\sigma_4$ | $5.96 \times 10^{30}$ | $\sigma$ | 671.0 | $m_{nr}$ | 1 |
| $\beta_1$ | $1.75 \times 10^{59}$ | $\beta$ | 8055.0 | $m_b$ | 32 |
| $\beta_2$ | $8 \times 10^{58}$ | $\beta'$ | $9.6 \times 10^{20}$ | | |
| $\alpha$ | $1.05 \times 10^{-58}$ | $\beta''$ | $1.29 \times 10^{19}$ | | |
| $b$ | 16 | | | $n_{sk}$ | 9 |
| $\kappa$ | 128 | | | $m_{sk}$ | 900 |
| | RHF | | RHF | | RHF |
| $SIS_{l_1,q,\beta_1}$ | 1.0048 | $SIS_{n_S,q,\beta'}$ | 1.0048 | $SIS_{n_C,q,2\sqrt{2m_r}\sigma_{Com}\frac{m_r}{b}}$ | 1.0014 |
| $SIS_{l_2,q,\beta_2}$ | 1.0048 | $SIS_{n_S,q,\beta''}$ | 1.004 | $SIS_{n_{sk},q,\sqrt{m_{sk}}}$ | 1.0046 |
| $LWE_{l_2,q,\alpha}$ | 1.0047 | | | | |

We tested for values of $p = 2^{10}$ up to $p = 2^{80}$ and arrived at the smallest proof size for $p = 2^{80}$. Then we set $q_0$ such that $q = q_0^2$ is just big enough. Finally we set all dimensions $n$ just high enough to achieve the desired RHF of 1.0048. This resulted in the parameters shown in Table 1. The size of the proof $\pi$ is 197 MB. Overall, the communication cost for Update is 199MB and for Issue 70 MB.

**Comparison with Similar Protocols.** In Table 2, we compare the result for our instantiation with other protocols. The given values for our construction, and E-Cash of [36] and of [28] are theoretical estimations, while the values for BBA+ [24] and BBW [22] are results of empirical experiments on a software implementation (the benchmarks are described in [22]). Therefore, the comparison should be taken with a grain of salt. However, it suffices to illustrate the efficiency gap between the lattice-based constructions and the elliptic curve-based ones. Note, that our construction is slightly more efficient than the construction of [36]. Even though we used the same zero-knowledge proof, we do not need to prove statements about the correct evaluation of weak pseudorandom functions.

**Table 2.** Comparison of the efficiency of similar protocols with our work

| Protocol | Issuance | Transaction | Token/Wallet | Based on |
|----------|----------|-------------|--------------|----------|
| Our work | 70 MB | 199MB | 11 MB | Lattices |
| E-Cash [28] | 33 TB | 720 TB | 4 MB | Lattices |
| E-Cash [36] | 53 MB | 262 MB | 4 MB | Lattices |
| BBA+ [24] | 1 kB | 14 kB | <1 kB | Elliptic curves |
| BBW [22] | 1 kB | 5 kB | <1 kB | Elliptic curves |

## 5 Future Work

*Post-Quantum Security.* Despite recent progress in proving Fiat–Shamir transformations of $\Sigma$-protocols secure in the quantum random oracle model [16,30] none of the results seems to apply to our setting. That is, even if we assume that the results apply to [36], the resulting notion of security is not sufficient for our proofs. We essentially require witness-extended emulation (WEE) [21,29], i.e., except with negligible probability an accepting proof can be extracted. This is a stronger notion than the knowledge soundness, which [16,30] use. In the classical setting, the difference is small since amplification (via rewinding) can be used to obtain WEE from knowledge soundness [29]. In the quantum setting, this is unclear. A possible remedy would be a transformation which allows online extraction of the witness, e.g. by (additionally) committing to the witness with an extractable commitment scheme or a dual-mode commitment scheme. Knowledge of the extraction trapdoor allows to prove "operator soundness", while the hiding property still ensures the "privacy notions". However, this would further increase proof sizes and introduce a global system trapdoor (which is undesirable).

*Efficiency.* As seen in Sect. 4, our construction requires a high amount of network traffic. For real-world scenarios this cost is still unacceptably high. Basing a construction on the stronger assumptions of Ring-LWE and Ring-SIS should allow more efficient schemes. However, while more efficient zero-knowledge proofs are known in the ring setting, we are not aware of more efficient CL-type signatures. Thus, this remains the most important open question.

**Acknowledgement.** We thank the anonymous reviewers for their feedback. The work presented in this paper has been funded by the German Federal Ministry of Education and Research (BMBF) under the project "PQC4MED" (ID 16KIS1044) and the topic Engineering Secure Systems of the Helmholtz Association (HGF) and by KASTEL Security Research Labs.

# A   Hardness Assumptions and Cryptographic Building Blocks

## A.1   Lattice-based Hardness Assumptions

**Definition A.1 (Short Integer Solution).** *Given a modulus $q \in \mathbb{N}$, $m \in \mathbb{N}$ uniformly random vectors $\mathbf{a}_i \in \mathbb{Z}_q^n$ (written as a matrix $\mathbf{A} \in \mathbb{Z}_q^{n \times m}$), and a uniformly random vector $\mathbf{u} \in \mathbb{Z}_q^n$, the* Inhomogeneous Short Integer Solution *(ISIS) problem is to find a non-zero integer vector $\mathbf{z} \in \mathbb{Z}^m$ of norm $\|\mathbf{z}\| \leq \beta$ such that*

$$\mathbf{A}\mathbf{z} = \sum_{i=1}^{m} \mathbf{a}_i \cdot z_i = \mathbf{u} \in \mathbb{Z}_q^n,$$

*where $\beta \in \mathbb{R}$ is a parameter with $\beta < q$.*

*In the case where $\mathbf{u}$ is not uniform but fixed to $\mathbf{0}$, the problem is called* Short Integer Solution *(SIS). We write $SIS_{n,q,\beta,m}$, if we want to emphasize the respective parameters.*

For typical parameter choices, SIS and ISIS are equivalent. Ajtai showed in his seminal work [2] that the average-case SIS problem can be reduced in polynomial time to the short integer vector problem (SIVP), a worst-case problem on lattices.

Regev [32] introduced the LWE problem and gave a quantum reduction to SIVP. We define the decisional variant of the respective hardness assumption.

**Definition A.2 (Learning with Errors).** *$LWE_{n,q,\chi,m}$: For a secret vector $\mathbf{s} \in \mathbb{Z}_q^n$ and a probability distribution $\chi$ over $\mathbb{Z}_q^m$, sample a matrix $\mathbf{A} \in \mathbb{Z}_q^{n \times m}$ uniformly at random and a vector $\mathbf{e} \leftarrow \chi$. Given $(\mathbf{A}, \mathbf{b}^*)$ where $\mathbf{b}^*$ is either $\mathbf{b}_0$ or $\mathbf{b}_1$, where $\mathbf{b}_0^\top = \mathbf{s}^\top \mathbf{A} + \mathbf{e} \mod q$ and $\mathbf{b}_1$ is chosen uniformly at random. Decide whether $\mathbf{b}^* = \mathbf{b}_0$ or $\mathbf{b}^* = \mathbf{b}_1$.*

## A.2   Building Blocks

We give a brief overview of the used building blocks. In Sect. 2.3, we give instantiations of these building blocks based on the hardness of SIS and LWE.

*Commitments.* A *commitment scheme* allows one to *commit* to (i.e., fix) a value, without revealing it immediately. At a later point, the commitment can be *opened* and the committed value is revealed. A commitment scheme consists of two PPT algorithms: The parameter generation $Gen(1^\lambda)$ outputs public parameters params, and the commitment algorithm $Com(params, m; r) \to c$ outputs, for a given message $m$, some explicit randomness $r$ and the public parameters params, a commitment $c$ on that value $m$. We often omit the input of the public parameters.

To open the commitment $c$, one can reveal the randomness $r$, to check, if $Com(params, m; r) = c$ holds. Informally, we want a commitment scheme to be *hiding*, i.e. no (efficient) adversary can learn anything about the message $m$ in a commitment, prior to opening. Furthermore, a commitment should be *binding* which means it should be (computationally) infeasible to open a commitment on $m$ to any other value than $m$. A commitment scheme is *equivocal*, if there exist an additional trapdoor generation algorithm $EqGen(1^\lambda)$ that outputs the public parameters params, together with a trapdoor td. With the trapdoor td, it is possible to open a commitment $c$ on the value $m$ to another value $m'$ with $m' \neq m$, by running a second algorithm, called $Equiv(td, c, m')$ that outputs a randomness value $r'$ for opening $c$ to $m'$. We require the two setups via Gen and EqGen to be computationally indistinguishable.

*Oblivious Signing of Committed Messages.* In our construction, we use the signature scheme of Libert et al. [28]; in particular, their protocol for obliviously signing a committed message (see Sect. 2.3). A *signature scheme for oblivious signing of committed messages* consists of the following algorithms/protocols:

- A key-generation algorithm $Gen(1^\lambda)$ that outputs (params, pk, sk), namely public parameters params, and a pair consisting of a public and a secret key.
- $OblSign\langle \mathcal{U}(params, pk, m), \mathcal{S}(params, pk, sk)\rangle$, an interactive protocol, where a user $\mathcal{U}$ interacts with a signer $\mathcal{S}$ to obtain a signature on a message $m$ inside of a commitment. In this protocol, $\mathcal{U}$ sends a commitment $c \leftarrow Com(m; r)$ on $m$ to the signer $\mathcal{S}$ and eventually $\mathcal{U}$ outputs a valid signature on $m$.
- a verification algorithm $Vfy(params, pk, m, sig) \to b$ that allows to check, whether sig is a valid signature on message $m$ public key pk.

The signer does not learn anything about $m$, as the commitment scheme is hiding. This protocol offers a security notion that is almost identical to common EUF-CMA security but takes into account that the user sends commitments and not plain messages. Libert et al. forgo an abstract definition of the signature's security as they directly apply the signature scheme to their E-Cash. We give a formal definition in the full-version [17] of this paper.

*Zero-Knowledge Proofs.* A proof system allows a party, called *prover*, to prove to another party, called *verifier*, that some statement is true. It is a *zero-knowledge (ZK)* protocol, if (informally) the verifier gains no additional knowledge, except for the truth of the statement. More precisely, the prover can convince the verifier that a word $x$ belongs to a certain $\mathcal{NP}$-language $L$, while even a malicious verifier learns nothing about $x$ except for the truth of $x \in L$. The protocol is a *proof of knowledge (PoK)*, or *extractable*, if a convincing prover must know an $\mathcal{NP}$-witness $w$. For example, if $x = m$, $w = \sigma$, and the language is "I know a signature $\sigma$ on message $m$", then a ZK-PoK guarantees that a convincing prover knows a signature $\sigma$, yet, the verifier learns nothing about $\sigma$. A ZK-PoK is correct, if an honest execution with correct statement always accepts. It has *soundness error* $p \in [0,1]$, if the probability that the verifier accepts a false statement is at most $p$.

*Full-Rank Difference Function.* We define full-rank differences as introduced by Agrawal, Boneh, and Boyen [1], and refer to them for a concrete instantiation. We use this in the calculation of the double-spending tag. Let $q \in \mathbb{N}$ be a prime and $n \in \mathbb{N}$. A *full-rank difference function* is an efficiently computable function $H_{FRD} \colon \mathbb{Z}_q^n \to \mathbb{Z}_q^{n \times n}$ satisfying that for all distinct $u, v \in \mathbb{Z}_q^n$, the matrix $H_{FRD}(u) - H_{FRD}(v) \in \mathbb{Z}_q^{n \times n}$ is full rank.

# B     Security and Privacy Notions

In this section we render the precise definitions of the security and privacy notions as defined by [23].

**Definition B.1 (Correctness of BABL).** *Similar to [22] the BABL scheme is called correct if the following holds: If the system is set up by the Setup algorithm, the keys are generated by UGen and OGen, all parties follow the protocol honestly, then, the following properties hold: (1) Correctness of the Issue protocol: Both parties return as acceptance bit 1. (2) Correctness of the Update protocol: For all valid tokens and balances, after adding a value the user always returns as acceptance bit 1.*

**Definition B.2 (Oracles, from [23] Def. 3.2).** MalIssue lets the adversary initiate the Issue protocol with an honest issuer $\mathcal{O}$ provided that there is no pending MalIssue call for $\mathsf{pk}_\mathcal{U}$ and $\mathsf{pk}_\mathcal{U}$ has also not been used in a successful call to MalIssue before. MalUpdate lets the adversary initiate the Update protocol with an honest operator $\mathcal{O}$ for an input value $v$. We say that a call to an oracle is successful if the honest party represented by the oracle accepts the run.

## B.1     System Security

We denote by $\mathcal{T}_{\lambda,\mathsf{CRS}}^{\mathsf{Update}}$ the set of all transcripts of Update transactions, meaning all exchanged messages from the beginning, until both parties terminate.

**Definition B.3.** *A scheme is called* simulation-linkable *if it satisfies the following conditions:*

**Completeness:** *Let $n \in \mathbb{N}, \mathsf{CRS} \leftarrow \mathsf{Setup}(1^\lambda)$ and $tr \in \mathcal{T}_{\lambda,\mathsf{CRS}}^{\mathsf{Update}}$ be a transcript. Then there exist inputs $\mathsf{pk}_\mathcal{U}, \mathsf{sk}_\mathcal{U}, \mathcal{T}, \mathbf{b}$ and random choices for an honest user $\mathcal{U}$ and honest operator $\mathcal{O}$ such that a run of the Update protocol between $\mathcal{U}$ and $\mathcal{O}$ with those inputs leads to the same transcript $tr$.*

**Extractability:** *There exists a PPT algorithm* ExtractUID *that, given two related transcripts* $tr_1, tr_2 \in \mathcal{T}_{\lambda,\mathsf{CRS}}^{\mathsf{Update}}$ *produced by the interaction of a honest user* $\mathcal{U}$ *with public key* $\mathsf{pk}_\mathcal{U}$ *with a honest operator* $\mathcal{O}$ *outputs the public key* $\mathsf{pk}_\mathcal{U}$. *Two transcripts* $tr_1, tr_2$ *are called related if they are identical except for the zero-knowledge challenges, output by the Random Oracle.*

*Additionally, there exists an expected PPT algorithm* **GenerateTranscripts** *that, given access to a transcript oracle* $\mathcal{O} = \langle \mathcal{U}, \mathcal{O} \rangle$ *which outputs transcripts between a user and an operator, outputs two related transcripts* $tr_1, tr_2 \in \mathcal{T}_{\lambda,\mathsf{CRS}}^{\mathsf{Update}}$ *with overwhelming probability.* **GenerateTranscripts** *is allowed to rewind* $\mathcal{O}$ *and reprogram the Random Oracle.*

**Definition B.4.** *A simulation-linkable scheme is called* owner-binding *if for any PPT adversary* $\mathcal{A}$ *in the experiments* $\mathsf{Exp}_{\mathsf{BABL},\mathcal{A}}^{\mathsf{ob\text{-}issue}}(\lambda)$ *and* $\mathsf{Exp}_{\mathsf{BABL},\mathcal{A}}^{\mathsf{ob\text{-}update}}(\lambda)$ *from Fig. 5 the advantages of* $\mathcal{A}$ *defined by*

$$\mathsf{Adv}_{\mathsf{BABL},\mathcal{A}}^{\mathsf{ob\text{-}issue}}(\lambda) = \Pr\left[\mathsf{Exp}_{\mathsf{BABL},\mathcal{A}}^{\mathsf{ob\text{-}issue}}(\lambda) = 1\right]$$

$$\mathsf{Adv}_{\mathsf{BABL},\mathcal{A}}^{\mathsf{ob\text{-}update}}(\lambda) = \Pr\left[\mathsf{Exp}_{\mathsf{BABL},\mathcal{A}}^{\mathsf{ob\text{-}update}}(\lambda) = 1\right]$$

*are negligible in* $\lambda$.

---

**Experiment** $\mathsf{Exp}_{\mathsf{BABL},\mathcal{A}}^{\mathsf{ob\text{-}issue}}(\lambda)$
$\mathsf{CRS} \leftarrow \mathsf{Setup}(1^\lambda)$
$(\mathsf{pk}_\mathcal{O}, \mathsf{sk}_\mathcal{O}) \leftarrow \mathsf{OGen}(\mathsf{CRS})$
$(\mathsf{pk}_\mathcal{U}, \mathsf{sk}_\mathcal{U}) \leftarrow \mathsf{UGen}(\mathsf{CRS})$
$b \leftarrow \mathcal{A}^{\mathsf{MalIssue},\mathsf{MalUpdate}}(\mathsf{CRS}, \mathsf{pk}_\mathcal{O}, \mathsf{pk}_\mathcal{U})$
The experiment outputs 1 iff $\mathcal{A}$ made a successful call to $\mathsf{MalIssue}(\mathsf{pk}_\mathcal{U})$.


**Experiment** $\mathsf{Exp}_{\mathsf{BABL},\mathcal{A}}^{\mathsf{ob\text{-}update}}(\lambda)$
$\mathsf{CRS} \leftarrow \mathsf{Setup}(1^\lambda)$
$(\mathsf{pk}_\mathcal{O}, \mathsf{sk}_\mathcal{O}) \leftarrow \mathsf{OGen}(\mathsf{CRS})$
$b \leftarrow \mathcal{A}^{\mathsf{MalIssue},\mathsf{MalUpdate}}(\mathsf{pk}_\mathcal{O})$
The experiment outputs 1 iff $\mathcal{A}$ made a successful call to $\mathsf{MalUpdate}$ such that $\mathsf{ExtractUID}$ applied to that call outputs a public key $\mathsf{pk}_\mathcal{U}$, for which $\mathsf{MalIssue}$ has never been called before.

---

**Fig. 5.** Owner-binding experiment

**Definition B.5.** *A simulation-linkable scheme ensures* doubles-spending detection *if for any PPT adversary* $\mathcal{A}$ *in the experiments* $\mathsf{Exp}_{\mathsf{BABL},\mathcal{A}}^{\mathsf{dsd}}(\lambda)$ *from Fig. 6 the advantage of* $\mathcal{A}$ *defined by*

$$\mathsf{Adv}_{\mathsf{BABL},\mathcal{A}}^{\mathsf{dsd}}(\lambda) = \Pr\left[\mathsf{Exp}_{\mathsf{BABL},\mathcal{A}}^{\mathsf{dsd}}(\lambda) = 1\right]$$

*is negligible in* $\lambda$.

---

**Experiment** $\mathsf{Exp}^{\mathsf{dsd}}_{\mathsf{BABL},\mathcal{A}}(\lambda)$

$\mathsf{CRS} \leftarrow \mathsf{Setup}(1^\lambda)$
$(\mathsf{pk}_\mathcal{O}, \mathsf{sk}_\mathcal{O}) \leftarrow \mathsf{OGen}(\mathsf{CRS})$
$b \leftarrow \mathcal{A}^{\mathsf{MalIssue},\mathsf{MalUpdate}}(\mathsf{pk}_\mathcal{O})$

The experiment outputs 1 iff $\mathcal{A}$ did two successful MalUpdate calls resulting in two double-spending tags $dstag_1 = (\mathbf{s}, z_1)$ and $dstag_2 = (\mathbf{s}, z_2)$ with extracted public keys $\mathsf{pk}^{(1)}_\mathcal{U}$ and $\mathsf{pk}^{(2)}_\mathcal{U}$ such that at least one of the following conditions is satisfied:

- $\mathsf{pk}^{(1)}_\mathcal{U} \neq \mathsf{pk}^{(2)}_\mathcal{U}$ or
- $\mathsf{IdentDS}(\mathsf{pk}_\mathcal{O}, dstag_1, dstag_2) \neq (\mathsf{pk}^{(1)}_\mathcal{U}, \pi)$ or
- $\mathsf{IdentDS}(\mathsf{pk}_\mathcal{O}, dstag_1, dstag_2) = (\mathsf{pk}^{(1)}_\mathcal{U}, \pi)$ but
  $\mathsf{VerifyGuilt}(\mathsf{pk}_\mathcal{O}, \mathsf{pk}^{(1)}_\mathcal{U}, \pi) \neq 0$.

---

**Fig. 6.** Double-spending experiment

**Definition B.6.** *A simulation-linkable scheme is called* balance-binding *if for any PPT adversary $\mathcal{A}$ in the experiments* $\mathsf{Exp}^{\mathsf{bb}}_{\mathsf{BABL},\mathcal{A}}(\lambda)$ *from Fig. 7 the advantage of $\mathcal{A}$ defined by*

$$\mathsf{Adv}^{\mathsf{bb}}_{\mathsf{BABL},\mathcal{A}}(\lambda) = \Pr\left[\mathsf{Exp}^{\mathsf{bb}}_{\mathsf{BABL},\mathcal{A}}(\lambda) = 1\right]$$

*is negligible in $\lambda$.*

---

**Experiment** $\mathsf{Exp}^{\mathsf{bb}}_{\mathsf{BABL},\mathcal{A}}(\lambda)$

$\mathsf{CRS} \leftarrow \mathsf{Setup}(1^\lambda)$
$(\mathsf{pk}_\mathcal{O}, \mathsf{sk}_\mathcal{O}) \leftarrow \mathsf{OGen}(\mathsf{CRS})$
$b \leftarrow \mathcal{A}^{\mathsf{MalIssue},\mathsf{MalUpdate}}(\mathsf{pk}_\mathcal{O})$

The experiment outputs 1 iff $\mathcal{A}$ made a successful call to MalUpdate with extracted user public-key $\mathsf{pk}_\mathcal{U}$, s.t.

- all successful MalIssue / MalUpdate calls produce unique token version numbers,
- the claimed balance $w \in \mathbb{V}$ does not equal the sum of previously collected accumulation values $v$ for $\mathsf{pk}_\mathcal{U}$, i.e. $w \neq \sum_{v \in V_{\mathsf{pk}_\mathcal{U}}} v$ where $V_{\mathsf{pk}_\mathcal{U}}$ is the list of all accumulation values $v \in \mathbb{V}$ that appeared in previous successful calls to MalUpdate for which $\mathsf{pk}_\mathcal{U}$ could be extracted using ExtractUID.

---

**Fig. 7.** Balance-binding experiment

## B.2   User Security and Privacy

User security is defined using the real/ideal world paradigm. The adversary can query the HonUser oracle to spawn new users. In the real world, the adversary interacts with oracles RHonIssue and RHonUpdate implementing the real user protocols. In the ideal world, the adversary interacts with a simulator. The simulator has to play the role of the oracles, but without receiving any private user information. We denote this by SHonIssue, SHonUpdate. In both worlds, the adversary can query RCorrupt or SCorrupt, respectively, to corrupt a user. By this, they learn all private information of the respective user.

**Definition B.7.** *A scheme is called* privacy-preserving *if there exist PPT algorithms* SimSetup *and* SCorrupt *as well as PPT protocols* SHonIssue, SHonUpdate *that receive no private user information, such that for all PPT adversaries* $\mathcal{A} = (\mathcal{A}_1, \mathcal{A}_2)$ *in the experiment depicted in Fig. 8, the advantage* $\mathsf{Adv}^{\mathsf{priv}}_{\mathsf{BABL},\mathcal{A}}(\lambda)$ *of* $\mathcal{A}$ *defined by*

$$\left| \Pr\left[ \mathsf{Exp}^{\mathsf{priv\text{-}real}}_{\mathsf{BABL},\mathcal{A}}(\lambda) = 1 \right] - \Pr\left[ \mathsf{Exp}^{\mathsf{priv\text{-}ideal}}_{\mathsf{BABL},\mathcal{A}}(\lambda) = 1 \right] \right|$$

*is negligible in* $\lambda$.

---

**Experiment** $\mathsf{Exp}^{\mathsf{priv\text{-}real}}_{\mathsf{BABL},\mathcal{A}}(\lambda)$
CRS $\leftarrow$ Setup($1^\lambda$)
$(\mathsf{pk}_\mathcal{O}, state) \leftarrow \mathcal{A}_1(\mathsf{CRS})$
$b \leftarrow \mathcal{A}_2^{\mathsf{HonUser},\mathsf{RHonIssue},\mathsf{RHonUpdate},\mathsf{RCorrupt}}(\mathsf{pk}_\mathcal{O}, state)$
**return** $b$

---

**Experiment** $\mathsf{Exp}^{\mathsf{priv\text{-}ideal}}_{\mathsf{BABL},\mathcal{A}}(\lambda)$
$(\mathsf{CRS}, td_{sim}) \leftarrow \mathsf{SimSetup}(1^\lambda)$
$(\mathsf{pk}_\mathcal{O}, state) \leftarrow \mathcal{A}_1(\mathsf{CRS})$
$b \leftarrow \mathcal{A}_2^{\mathsf{HonUser},\mathsf{SHonIssue},\mathsf{SHonUpdate},\mathsf{SCorrupt}}(\mathsf{pk}_\mathcal{O}, state)$
**return** $b$

---

**Fig. 8.** Real/Ideal world privacy experiment

**Definition B.8.** *A* simulation-linkable *scheme ensures* false-accusation protection *if for any PPT adversary* $\mathcal{A} = (\mathcal{A}_1, \mathcal{A}_2)$ *in the experiments* $\mathsf{Exp}^{\mathsf{facp}}_{\mathsf{BABL},\mathcal{A}}(\lambda)$ *from Fig. 9 the advantage of* $\mathcal{A}$ *defined by*

$$\mathsf{Adv}^{\mathsf{facp}}_{\mathsf{BABL},\mathcal{A}}(\lambda) = \Pr\left[ \mathsf{Exp}^{\mathsf{facp}}_{\mathsf{BABL},\mathcal{A}}(\lambda) = 1 \right]$$

*is negligible in* $\lambda$. *(Note, that this does not guarantee anything, once the user was compromised.)*

## B.3  Security and Privacy

Our construction fulfills the desired security and privacy properties mentioned in Sect. 2.1. We formulate the theorems and give proof sketches. Note, that the proofs follow closely the proofs from [23]. Only small changes were necessary to adopt the proofs to the lattice-setting:

---

Experiment $\mathrm{Exp}^{\mathsf{facp}}_{\mathsf{BABL},\mathcal{A}}(\lambda)$

$\mathsf{CRS} \leftarrow \mathsf{Setup}(1^\lambda)$

$(\mathsf{pk}_\mathcal{O}, \mathsf{sk}_\mathcal{O}) \leftarrow \mathcal{A}_1(\mathsf{CRS})$

$(\mathsf{pk}_\mathcal{U}, \mathsf{sk}_\mathcal{U}) \leftarrow \mathsf{UGen}(\mathsf{CRS})$

$\pi \leftarrow \mathcal{A}_2^{\mathsf{RHonIssue},\mathsf{RHonUpdate}}(\mathsf{pk}_\mathcal{O}, \mathsf{pk}_\mathcal{U})$

Return 1 iff $\mathsf{VerifyGuilt}(\mathsf{pk}_\mathcal{O}, \mathsf{pk}_\mathcal{U}, \pi) = 1$.

---

**Fig. 9.** False-accusation experiment

**Theorem B.1 (Simulation-Linkability).** *Suppose* BABL *is correct,* S *is secure and* P1, P2 *are sound. Then* BABL *is simulation-linkable.*

*Proof Sketch (Simulation-Linkability (Theorem B.1)).* As by definition, a scheme is called simulation-linkable when it is complete and extractable, we have to show that BABL fulfills these properties.

Completeness requires, that for every accepted transcript, there is a choice of parameters, such that the transcript is the result of an honest protocol run. This is given in our case, as the sum of the serial number and the t-part of the double-spending tag are indistinguishable from random values. Further, as the transcript is accepted, the soundness property of the zero-knowledge protocol from [36] guarantees that a commitment is well-formed. It remains to show that the signature is honestly generated, but as the token is accepted by the user and the signature is secure, this is given.

To prove the extractability property we can rely on the fact that the protocol from [36] is extractable, because it is a proof of knowledge.

**Theorem B.2 (Owner-Binding w.r.t. Issue).** *Suppose the* $SIS_{n_{\mathsf{sk}},q,\sqrt{m_{\mathsf{sk}}}}$ *assumption holds and* P1 *is extractable. Then* BABL *is owner-binding w.r.t.* Issue.

*Proof Sketch (Owner-Binding wrt. Issue (Theorem B.2)).* Proving this property is a straightforward reduction on $SIS_{n_{\mathsf{sk}},q,\sqrt{m_{\mathsf{sk}}}}$.

**Theorem B.3 (Owner-Binding w.r.t. Update).** *Suppose* BABL *is simulation-linkable,* P2 *is extractable and* S *is secure. Then* BABL *is owner-binding w.r.t.* Update.

*Proof Sketch (Owner-Binding wrt. Update (Theorem B.3)).* To prove the owner-binding property for the Update protocol we define a series of games for a hybrid argument. In these games, we test the required properties for the owner-binding property step by step. Finally, we show that the advantage of the adversary to win in the original game differs only negligibly from the other games.

First, we show that it is indeed possible to extract the user's secret key by reducing this problem on the already proven simulation-linkability property of our scheme. Then it is possible to extract witnesses for all occurred zero-knowledge proofs as the zero-knowledge argument from [36] is extractable. Finally, as there are extracted witnesses, the only way left for the adversary to win the owner-binding game is to forge a signature. This is prevented by the security of our signature. Note here, that the security of the signature is not exactly the usual EUF-CMA security, as the user sends commitments and the signer signs the committed messages (and not the commitment itself). However, the notion of security given in the full-version [17] of this paper suffices for our proofs.

**Theorem B.4 (Double-Spending Detection).** *Suppose* BABL *is simulation-linkable, the* $SIS_{n_{sk}, q, \sqrt{m_{sk}}}$ *assumption holds,* P2 *is extractable and* S *is secure. Then* BABL *ensures double-spending detection.*

*Proof Sketch (Double-Spending Detection (Theorem B.4)).* Similar to the last theorem, we prove this property with a hybrid argument. In particular, we consider all ways in which IdentDS (Fig. 4) could be tricked into not recognizing an actual act of double-spending. We show that an adversary would therefore either be able to find a collision on the serial number, or they were was able to manipulate the double-spending tag in a specific way. The former happens only with negligible probability, as the serial number is chosen in a coin-toss-like manner. The latter happens only with negligible probability, as the double-spending certainly includes values that the operators drew at random, and as the zero-knowledge proof is sound.

**Theorem B.5 (Balance-Binding).** *Suppose* P1 *and* P2 *are extractable and sound and* C *is statistically hiding, and* S *is secure Then* BABL *is balance-binding.*

*Proof Sketch (Balance-Binding (Theorem B.5)).* Similar to the proofs for the previous properties, we prove the balance-binding property by defining several games, where we show step by step, that the probability for an adversary to break the balance-binding property of BABL is negligible. More precisely, we interpret every transaction as a node in a graph. Two nodes are connected if the output serial number of the first transaction is the input serial number of the last. We ensure through the game hops, that all nodes have an indegree of exactly one (except for the issuance of the token) and outdegrees of at most one. If this was not the case, there would be collisions on the serial number, double-spendings, or forged signatures. Additionally, every such chain of transactions must be started by the issuance of a token and the balance must only change according to the transaction values of the nodes.

**Theorem B.6 (Privacy-Preserving).** *Suppose* P1 *and* P2 *are zero-knowledge and* C *is equivocal. Then* BABL *is privacy-preserving.*

*Proof Sketch (Privacy-Preserving (Theorem B.6)).* We prove this property by defining several games, where the oracles of the real experiment are step-by-step replaced by oracles that hold no personal information of the user, called the ideal world. By showing that an adversary is only with negligible probability able to tell apart the real from the ideal world, we prove that BABL is indeed privacy-preserving. In more detail, we make use of the fact that the zero-knowledge proof from [36] is indeed zero-knowledge and the commitment scheme is equivocal. We use the equivocality property to replace the real values in the token with random ones, which makes it impossible to extract personal information from the user in the ideal world.

**Theorem B.7 (False-Accusation Protection).** *Suppose the $SIS_{n_{sk},q,\sqrt{m_{sk}}}$ assumption holds and the scheme ensures double-spending detection. Then* BABL *ensures false-accusation protection.*

*Proof Sketch (False-Accusation Protection (Theorem B.7)).* Just like in the privacy-preserving proof we use the real/ideal world paradigm. Now, if the adversary is able to output a false proof of guilt for an honest user, one can directly construct an adversary breaking the $SIS_{n_{sk},q,\sqrt{m_{sk}}}$ assumption. If the adversary is not able to output a proof of guilt for a guilty user, this can be leveraged to distinguish the real world from the ideal world.

# References

1. Agrawal, S., Boneh, D., Boyen, X.: Efficient lattice (H)IBE in the standard model. In: Gilbert, H. (ed.) EUROCRYPT 2010. LNCS, vol. 6110, pp. 553–572. Springer, Heidelberg (2010). https://doi.org/10.1007/978-3-642-13190-5_28

2. Ajtai, M.: Generating hard instances of lattice problems (extended abstract). In: 28th ACM STOC, pp. 99–108. ACM Press (1996). https://doi.org/10.1145/237814.237838

3. Albrecht, M.R., Player, R., Scott, S.: On the concrete hardness of learning with errors. Cryptology ePrint Archive, Report 2015/046. https://eprint.iacr.org/2015/046

4. Alwen, J., Peikert, C.: Generating shorter bases for hard random lattices. Cryptology ePrint Archive, Report 2008/521. https://eprint.iacr.org/2008/521

5. Banaszczyk, W.: New bounds in some transference theorems in the geometry of numbers. Mathe. Annalen **296**(1), 625–635 (1993). https://doi.org/10.1007/BF01445125

6. Blömer, J., Bobolz, J., Diemert, D., Eidens, F.: Updatable anonymous credentials and applications to incentive systems. In: Cavallaro, L., Kinder, J., Wang, X., Katz, J. (eds.) ACM CCS 2019, pp. 1671–1685. ACM Press (2019). https://doi.org/10.1145/3319535.3354223

7. Bobolz, J., Eidens, F., Krenn, S., Slamanig, D., Striecks, C.: Privacy-preserving incentive systems with highly efficient point-collection. In: Sun, H.M., Shieh, S.P., Gu, G., Ateniese, G. (eds.)ASIACCS 2020, pp. 319–333. ACM Press (2020). https://doi.org/10.1145/3320269.3384769

8. Bourse, F., Pointcheval, D., Sanders, O.: Divisible e-cash from constrained pseudorandom functions. In: Galbraith, S.D., Moriai, S. (eds.) ASIACRYPT 2019. LNCS, vol. 11921, pp. 679–708. Springer, Cham (2019). https://doi.org/10.1007/978-3-030-34578-5_24

9. Camenisch, J., Hohenberger, S., Lysyanskaya, A.: Compact e-cash. In: Cramer, R. (ed.) EUROCRYPT 2005. LNCS, vol. 3494, pp. 302–321. Springer, Heidelberg (2005). https://doi.org/10.1007/11426639_18

10. Camenisch, J., Lysyanskaya, A.: A signature scheme with efficient protocols. In: Cimato, S., Persiano, G., Galdi, C. (eds.) SCN 2002. LNCS, vol. 2576, pp. 268–289. Springer, Heidelberg (2003). https://doi.org/10.1007/3-540-36413-7_20

11. Camenisch, J., Lysyanskaya, Anna: Signature schemes and anonymous credentials from bilinear maps. In: Franklin, M. (ed.) CRYPTO 2004. LNCS, vol. 3152, pp. 56–72. Springer, Heidelberg (2004). https://doi.org/10.1007/978-3-540-28628-8_4

12. Canard, S., Gouget, A.: Anonymity in transferable e-cash. In: Bellovin, S.M., Gennaro, R., Keromytis, A., Yung, M. (eds.) ACNS 2008. LNCS, vol. 5037, pp. 207–223. Springer, Heidelberg (2008). https://doi.org/10.1007/978-3-540-68914-0_13

13. Cash, D., Hofheinz, D., Kiltz, E., Peikert, C.: Bonsai trees, or how to delegate a lattice basis. J. Cryptol. **25**(4), 601–639 (2011). https://doi.org/10.1007/s00145-011-9105-2

14. Chaum, D.: Blind signatures for untraceable payments. In: Chaum, D., Rivest, R.L., Sherman, A.T. (eds.) Adv. Cryptol., pp. 199–203. Springer, Boston (1983). https://doi.org/10.1007/978-1-4757-0602-4_18

15. Deo, A., Libert, B., Nguyen, K., Sanders, O.: Lattice-based e-cash, revisited. In: Moriai, S., Wang, H. (eds.) ASIACRYPT 2020. LNCS, vol. 12492, pp. 318–348. Springer, Cham (2020). https://doi.org/10.1007/978-3-030-64834-3_11

16. Don, J., Fehr, S., Majenz, C., Schaffner, C.: Security of the fiat-shamir transformation in the quantum random-oracle model. In: Boldyreva, A., Micciancio, D. (eds.) CRYPTO 2019. LNCS, vol. 11693, pp. 356–383. Springer, Cham (2019). https://doi.org/10.1007/978-3-030-26951-7_13

17. Faller, S.H., Baumer, P., Klooß, M., Koch, A., Ottenhues, A., Raiber. M.: Black-box accumulation based on lattices. Cryptology ePrint Archive, Report 2021/1303. https://eprint.iacr.org/2021/1303

18. Gama, N., Nguyen, P.Q.: Predicting lattice reduction. In: Smart, N. (ed.) EUROCRYPT 2008. LNCS, vol. 4965, pp. 31–51. Springer, Heidelberg (2008). https://doi.org/10.1007/978-3-540-78967-3_3

19. Gentry, C.: Fully homomorphic encryption using ideal lattices. In: Mitzenmacher, M. (ed.) 41st ACM STOC, pp. 169–178. ACM Press (2009). https://doi.org/10.1145/1536414.1536440

20. Gentry, C., Peikert, C., Vaikuntanathan, V.: Trapdoors for hard lattices and new cryptographic constructions. In: Ladner, R.E., Dwork, C. (eds.) 40th ACM STOC, pp. 197–206. ACM Press (2008). https://doi.org/10.1145/1374376.1374407

21. Groth, J., Ishai, Y.: Sub-linear zero-knowledge argument for correctness of a shuffle. In: Smart, N. (ed.) EUROCRYPT 2008. LNCS, vol. 4965, pp. 379–396. Springer, Heidelberg (2008). https://doi.org/10.1007/978-3-540-78967-3_22

22. Hartung, G., Hoffmann, M., Nagel, M., Rupp, A.: BBA+: improving the security and applicability of privacy-preserving point collection. In: Thuraisingham, B.M., Evans, D., Malkin, T., Xu, D. (eds.) ACM CCS 2017, pp. 1925–1942. ACM Press (2017). https://doi.org/10.1145/3133956.3134071

23. Hoffmann, M., Klooß, M., Raiber, M., Rupp, A.: Black-box wallets: Fast anonymous two-way payments for constrained devices. PoPETs **2020**(1), 165–194 (2020). https://doi.org/10.2478/popets-2020-0010

24. Jager, T., Rupp, A.: Black-box accumulation: collecting incentives in a privacy-preserving way. PoPETs **2016**(3), 62–82 (2013). https://doi.org/10.1515/popets-2016-0016

25. Kawachi, Ai., Tanaka, K., Xagawa, K.: Concurrently secure identification schemes based on the worst-case hardness of lattice problems. In: Pieprzyk, J. (ed.) ASIACRYPT 2008. LNCS, vol. 5350, pp. 372–389. Springer, Heidelberg (2008). https://doi.org/10.1007/978-3-540-89255-7_23

26. Kosba, A., et al.: C0c0: a framework for building composable zero-knowledge proofs. Cryptology ePrint Archive, Report 2015/1093. https://eprint.iacr.org/2015/1093

27. Libert, B., Ling, S., Mouhartem, F., Nguyen, K., Wang, H.: Signature schemes with efficient protocols and dynamic group signatures from lattice assumptions. In: Cheon, J.H., Takagi, T. (eds.) ASIACRYPT 2016. LNCS, vol. 10032, pp. 373–403. Springer, Heidelberg (2016). https://doi.org/10.1007/978-3-662-53890-6_13
28. Libert, B., Ling, S., Nguyen, K., Wang, H.: Zero-knowledge arguments for lattice-based PRFs and applications to e-cash. In: Takagi, T., Peyrin, T. (eds.) ASI-ACRYPT 2017. LNCS, vol. 10626, pp. 304–335. Springer, Cham (2017). https://doi.org/10.1007/978-3-319-70700-6_11
29. Lindell, Y.: Parallel coin-tossing and constant-round secure two-party computation. In: Kilian, J. (ed.) CRYPTO 2001. LNCS, vol. 2139, pp. 171–189. Springer, Heidelberg (2001). https://doi.org/10.1007/3-540-44647-8_10
30. Liu, Q., Zhandry, M.: Revisiting post-quantum fiat-shamir. In: Boldyreva, A., Micciancio, D. (eds.) CRYPTO 2019. LNCS, vol. 11693, pp. 326–355. Springer, Cham (2019). https://doi.org/10.1007/978-3-030-26951-7_12
31. Peikert, C., Waters, B.: Lossy trapdoor functions and their applications. In: Ladner, R.E., Dwork, C. (eds.) 40th ACM STOC, pp. 187–196. ACM Press (2008). https://doi.org/10.1145/1374376.1374406
32. Regev, O.: On lattices, learning with errors, random linear codes, and cryptography. In: Gabow, H.N., Fagin, R. (eds.) 37th ACM STOC, pp. 84–93. ACM Press (2005). https://doi.org/10.1145/1060590.1060603
33. Shor, P.W.: Algorithms for quantum computation: Discrete logarithms and factoring. In: 35th FOCS, pp. 124–134. IEEE Computer Society Press (1994). https://doi.org/10.1109/SFCS.1994.365700
34. Stern, J.: A new paradigm for public key identification. IEEE Trans. Inf. Theory 42(6), 1757–1768 (1996). https://doi.org/10.1109/18.556672
35. Weng, C., Yang, K., Katz, J., Wang, X.: Wolverine: fast, scalable, and communication-efficient zero-knowledge proofs for boolean and arithmetic circuits. Cryptology ePrint Archive, Report 2020/925. https://eprint.iacr.org/2020/925
36. Yang, R., Au, M.H., Zhang, Z., Xu, Q., Yu, Z., Whyte, W.: Efficient lattice-based zero-knowledge arguments with standard soundness: construction and applications. In: Boldyreva, A., Micciancio, D. (eds.) CRYPTO 2019. LNCS, vol. 11692, pp. 147–175. Springer, Cham (2019). https://doi.org/10.1007/978-3-030-26948-7_6

# How to Find Ternary LWE Keys Using Locality Sensitive Hashing

Elena Kirshanova[1,2] and Alexander May[1(✉)]

[1] Horst Görtz Institute for IT-Security, Ruhr University Bochum, Bochum, Germany
{elena.kirshanova,alex.may}@rub.de
[2] Immanuel Kant Baltic Federal University, Kaliningrad, Russia

**Abstract.** Let $As = b+e \bmod q$ be an LWE-instance with ternary keys $s, e \in \{0, \pm 1\}^n$. Let $s$ be taken from a search space of size $\mathcal{S}$. A standard Meet-in-the-Middle attack recovers $s$ in time $\mathcal{S}^{0.5}$. Using the representation technique, a recent improvement of May shows that this can be lowered to approximately $\mathcal{S}^{0.25}$ by guessing a sub-linear number of $\Theta(\frac{n}{\log n})$ coordinates from $e$. While guessing such an amount of $e$ can asymptotically be neglected, for concrete instantiations of e.g. NTRU, BLISS or GLP the additional cost of guessing leads to complexities around $\mathcal{S}^{0.3}$.

We introduce a locality sensitive hashing (LSH) technique based on Odlyzko's work that avoids any guessing of $e$'s coordinates. This LSH technique involves a comparably small cost such that we can significantly improve on previous results, pushing complexities towards the asymptotic bound $\mathcal{S}^{0.25}$. Concretely, using LSH we lower the MitM complexity estimates for the currently suggested NTRU and NTRU Prime instantiations by a factor in the range $2^{20} - 2^{49}$, and for BLISS and GLP parameters by a factor in the range $2^{18} - 2^{41}$.

**Keywords:** Ternary LWE · Combinatorial attack · Representations · LSH

## 1 Introduction

The LWE problem is currently without a doubt the richest source for constructing efficient quantum-resistant cryptography. Let $(A, b) \in \mathbb{F}_q^{n \times n} \times \mathbb{F}_q^n$ be an LWE public key with secret key $s \in \mathbb{F}_q^n$ satisfying $As = b + e \bmod q$ for some error $e \in \mathbb{F}_q^n$. The unknown vectors $s, e$ have entries significantly smaller than $q$. For efficiency reasons, many modern LWE variants even use ternary secrets $s, e \in \{0, \pm 1\}^n$. Thus, it is of uttermost interest to understand the complexity of ternary key LWE – also called NTRU-type – schemes.

Elena and Kirshanova: Supported by the Ministry of Science and Higher Education of the Russian Federation (agreement no. 075-02-2021-1748) and the "Young Russian Mathematics" grant.

© Springer Nature Switzerland AG 2021
M. B. Paterson (Ed.): IMACC 2021, LNCS 13129, pp. 247–264, 2021.
https://doi.org/10.1007/978-3-030-92641-0_12

A standard Meet-in-the-Middle algorithm (MitM) splits $s = s_1 + s_2$ with $s_1 \in \{0, \pm 1\}^{n/2} \times 0^{n/2}$ and $s_2 \in 0^{n/2} \times \{0, \pm 1\}^{n/2}$. Therefore, we obtain the identity

$$As_1 = -As_2 + b + e \bmod q. \tag{1}$$

One then computes for all potential $s_1, s_2$ the values $As_1$ and $-As_2 + b$. With high probability only for the correct pair $s_1, s_2$ these values are apart by a ternary error $e \in \{0, \pm 1\}^n$. The correct pair is efficiently identified by a locality sensitive hash function proposed by Odlyzko, mentioned in the original NTRU paper [HPS98].

Recently, the above MitM attack has been improved by May [May21], based on the representation techniques that was developed in [HJ10, BCJ11, BJMM12]. The key idea in [May21] is to search over all $s_1, s_2 \in \{0, \pm 1\}^n$ that satisfy Eq. (1) on $k = \Theta(\frac{n}{\log n})$ coordinates exactly, and on the remaining $n-k$ coordinates up to the entries of $e$ (using Odylzko's hashing). This in turn implies that we have to initially guess $k$ coordinates of $e$ to realize the exact matching.

*Our Contribution.* We show that a suitable modification of Odylzko's locality sensitive hash function (LSH) allows to avoid any error guessing in [May21]. Since the cost of our LSH function is comparatively small, in turn we significantly improve over the MitM complexities given in [May21], see Table 1.[1]

**Table 1.** Results of our LSH meet-in-the-middle attack.

|  | $(n, q, w)$ | $\mathcal{S}$ [bit] | [May21] [bit] | Our [bit] | [DDGR20] Core-SVP |
|---|---|---|---|---|---|
| NTRU IEEE [IEE08] | $(659, 2048, 76)$ | 408 | 146 | **135** | 151 |
|  | $(761, 2048, 84)$ | 457 | 166 | **162** | 176 |
|  | $(1087, 2048, 126)$ | 680 | 243 | **221** | 260 |
|  | $(1499, 2048, 158)$ | 877 | 315 | **283** | 358 |
| NTRU [CDH+20] | $(509, 2048, 254)$ | 754 | 227 | **191** | 124 |
|  | $(677, 2048, 254)$ | 891 | 273 | **226** | 167 |
|  | $(821, 4096, 510)$ | 1286 | 378 | **358** | 197 |
|  | $(701, 8192, 468)$ | 1101 | 327 | **295** | 155 |
| NTRU Prime [BBC+20] | $(653, 4621, 288)$ | 925 | 272 | **228** | 148 |
|  | $(761, 4591, 286)$ | 1003 | 301 | **268** | 174 |
|  | $(857, 5167, 322)$ | 1131 | 338 | **315** | 196 |
| BLISS I+II [DDLL13] | $(512, 12289, 154)$ | 597 | 187 | **159** | 102 |
| GLP I [GLP12] | $(512, 8383489, 342)$ | 802 | 225 | **184** | 60 |

In comparison to the results in [May21], for the encryption schemes NTRU and NTRU Prime we gain a run time factor between $2^{20}$ for NTRU-821 and $2^{49}$

---

[1] The scripts to reproduce the tables are available at https://github.com/Elena Kirshanova/ntru_with_lsh.

for NTRU-677. For the signatures schemes we gain a $2^{18}$ factor for BLISS I+II, and a $2^{41}$-factor for GLP I.

In terms of the search space size $\mathcal{S}$ for the secret key, we obtain attacks in the range $\mathcal{S}^{0.23}$ for GLP-I and $\mathcal{S}^{0.28}$ for NTRU-821. These exponents in the range $[0.23, 0.28]$ are close to the asymptotic exponents achieved in [May21], and thus indicate the optimality of our LSH approach.

Another direction of improvement is the use of the representation technique not only for the enumeration of $s$ as in [May21], but also for the error vector $e$. This approach yields comparable improvements to our LSH technique: we provide more details in Appendix A of the full version [KM21]. Since LSH and representations of $e$ are somewhat orthogonal techniques to exploit the structure of $e$, we currently do not see a way to combine both approaches.

In comparison to the (highly optimized) lattice attacks in the Core-SVP metric from [DDGR20], our estimates are still a tad bit away. However, we beat current lattice estimates for a selection of the NTRU IEEE 1363-2008 standard [IEE08], see Table 1. For instance, for the ees1499ep1 parameter set we further improve the attack of [May21] by another 32 bits, now beating current lattice estimates by 75 bits.

This demonstrates that our purely combinatorial attack shows its strength in the small weight regime, e.g. for ees1499ep1 with only $w = 158$ non-zero secret key coefficients. We would like to point out that current cold-boot attack scenarios such as [ADP18] live in the (really) small weight regime. We provide cold-boot applications of our attack in Sect. 6.

On the technical level, we have to construct an LSH approach that realizes an approximate hashing over many levels of a search tree. This is not straightforward, since Odlyzko's original LSH function does not provide linearity. We realize an LSH hashing over search trees via suitable combinations of projections. Given the importance of search tree constructions optimizations with LSH [MO15], we hope that our projection technique will find more applications.

*Notations.* We denote by $\mathbb{Z}_q$ the ring of integers modulo $q \geq 2$. Vectors are denoted by lowercase letters, matrices by uppercase letters. The $n \times n$ identity matrix is denoted by $I_n$. The $\ell_\infty$-norm of vector $x$, denoted by $\|x\|_\infty$, is $\max_i |x_i|$. For a set $S$, we denote by $|S|$ its size.

We shall also make use of multinomial coefficients: for positive integers $n$, $\{n_i\}_{i \leq k}$ such that $n = n_1 + \ldots + n_k$, the multinomial coefficient, denoted by $\binom{n}{n_1, \ldots, n_{k-1}, \cdot}$, is the product $\binom{n}{n_1} \cdot \binom{n-n_1}{n_2} \cdot \ldots \cdot \binom{n-\sum_{i<k} n_i}{n_k}$.

## 2  Generalizing Odlyzko's LSH

In order to generalize Odlyzko's LSH to search trees, we consider the following problem abstraction that we face for every node of our search tree constructions.

**Definition 1 (Close pairs problem in $\ell_\infty$-norm).** *Given two equal-sized lists $L_1, L_2$ of iid. uniform random vectors from $\mathbb{Z}_q^n$, find an $(1 - o(1))$-fraction of all* *pairs* $(x_1, x_2) \in L_1 \times L_2$ *that satisfy* $\|(x_1 - x_2) \bmod q\|_\infty = 1$. *Any such pair is called* 1-*close.*

This is an average-case version of the close pairs problem and we shall make use of the distribution in our analysis. In particular, we assume that elements from the lists $L_1, L_2$ do not cluster, i.e., there is no subset of vectors with small diameter. For the worst-case version of the problem, an algorithm is given by Indyk in [Ind01]. Note also that we are in the special case of the $\ell_\infty$ norm on the torus $\mathbb{Z}_q = \{0, \ldots, q - 1\}$, i.e., it holds that $\|0 - (q - 1)\|_\infty = 1$. Furthermore, the lists $L_1, L_2$ are assumed to be of $\exp(n)$-size.

The close pairs problem is solved using the so-called *locality-sensitive hash functions* (LSH) [IM98, AI06]. Informally, such a hash function has higher collision probability for elements that are close than for those that are far apart.

For the $\ell_\infty$-norm over $\mathbb{Z}_q$, Odlyzko proposed a construction of a locality-sensitive hash (LSH) function [HPS98]. Odlyzko's LSH splits $\mathbb{Z}_q$ into two halves: $[0, \lfloor q/2 \rfloor - 1]$ and $[\lfloor q/2 \rfloor, q - 1]$, and assigns the 0-label to the first half and the 1-label to the second half. It is extended to vectors coordinate-wise thus mapping $\mathbb{Z}_q^n$ to $\{0, 1\}^n$. It is likely that close vectors have the same label under this mapping. In order to avoid losing close pairs, Odlyzko suggests to assign both 0- and 1-labels to the "border" values $\lfloor q/2 \rfloor - 1$ and $\lfloor q/2 \rfloor$. We do not perform such a double assignment, but instead we re-randomize the function as we explain below.

The choice to split $\mathbb{Z}_q$ into two halves works particularly well when there is a unique close pair in the sense that the other pairs have a different label under Odlyzko's mapping. In our average case setting non-close pairs differ by label with probability $1 - 2^{-n}$, since the probability that two uniform random elements from $\mathbb{Z}_q$ are in the same half wrt. to $\lfloor q/2 \rfloor$ is $1/2$.

In our applications we will be in the setting where a solution may not be unique and thus we require in Definition 1 to output (almost) all close pairs. Odlyzko's LSH generalises to this setting by

1. dividing the $\mathbb{Z}_q$ torus into more than 2 parts, and
2. re-randomizing the hash function (see also [Ngu21]) so that we can handle border values in a more elegant way than assigning multiple labels[2].

More precisely, consider the following straightforward generalisation of Odlyzko's LSH. For a fixed bound $B \in \{1, \ldots, q\}$ and a uniformly chosen shift-vector $u \in \mathbb{Z}_q^n$ define

$$h_{u,B} : \mathbb{Z}_q^n \to \left[0, \ldots, \left\lceil \frac{q}{B} \right\rceil - 1\right]^n$$

$$(x_1, \ldots, x_n) \mapsto \left(\left\lfloor \frac{x_1 + u_1}{B} \right\rfloor, \ldots, \left\lfloor \frac{x_n + u_n}{B} \right\rfloor\right).$$

---

[2] In fact, the 'multiple' labels assignment is what is done in [Ind01] to handle worst-case inputs. We could also use this algorithm but it turns out to be less memory-efficient than what we propose for the average-case setting.

In the original Odlyzko's LSH, $B$ is set to $q/2$. We choose a uniform random function from the family $H_B = \{h_{u,B} \mid u \in \mathbb{Z}_q^n\}$. For a list $L_1 \subset \mathbb{Z}_q^n$, the shift $L_1 + u$ is just a rotation of all the elements on the $\mathbb{Z}_q$ torus. Any function $h_{u,B}$ can be evaluated in $\mathcal{O}(n)$ operations over $\mathbb{Z}_q$.

---

**Algorithm 1.** Our LSH-ODLYZKO algorithm for finding 1-close pairs

---

**Input:** $L_1, L_2$ – list of iid. uniform vectors from $\mathbb{Z}_q^n$, each of size $|L|$.
**Output:** $(1 - o(1))$-fraction of all pairs $(x_1, x_2) \in L_1 \times L_2$ such that $\|(x_1 - x_2) \bmod q\|_\infty = 1$

1: Choose $B \geq \frac{q}{|L|^{1/n}} \in \{1, \ldots, q\}$ suitably. Choose $u \xleftarrow{\$} \mathbb{Z}_q^n$.
2: Apply $h_{u,B}$ to $L_1, L_2$. Sort $L_1, L_2$ according to the hash values.
3: Merge the sorted lists according to their hash labels. Output only those pairs $(x_1, x_2) \in L_1 \times L_2$ that satisfy $\|(x_1 - x_2) \bmod q\|_\infty = 1$
4: Repeat Steps 1–3 $N$ times, where

$$N = \left(\frac{B}{B-1}\right)^n \cdot n \log n \qquad (2)$$

---

Let us now provide our algorithm LSH-ODYLZKO (Algorithm 1) that solves the close pairs problem from Definition 1. For our NTRU-type applications, we later solve close pairs problems on suitably chosen projections of all $n$ coordinates. Notice that $h_{u,B}$ can easily applied on projections, since it works coordinate-wise.

**Theorem 1 (Adapted from [IM98]).** *Given two lists $L_1, L_2$ of equal size $|L|$ with iid. Elements taken from the uniform distribution on $\mathbb{Z}_q^n$, LSH-ODLYZKO (Algorithm 1) solves the close pairs problem from Definition 1 in space and time complexities*

$$S = \max\left\{|L|, |L|^2 \cdot \left(\frac{3}{q}\right)^n\right\} \cdot \text{poly}(n),$$

$$T_{\mathsf{LSH}}(|L|, n, B) = \max\left\{S, |L|^2 \left(\frac{B^2}{(B-1)q}\right)^n \cdot \text{poly}(n)\right\}.$$

*Proof.* The proof is an adaptation of [IM98, Theorem 5] to the average-case $\ell_\infty$-norm setting.

We start with the analysis of Steps 1–3 of Algorithm 1.

In Step 2, hashing and sorting can be performed within time and memory complexity $\tilde{\mathcal{O}}(|L|) = |L| \cdot \text{poly}(n)$.

Notice that our choice of $B$ in Step 1 implies $|L|\left(\frac{B}{q}\right)^n \geq 1$, which is the expected number of elements from $L_1$ (or $L_2$) that receive the same hash label. Thus the number of elements in $L_1 \times L_2$ that match by hash label is $|L|^2 \left(\frac{B}{q}\right)^n$, and these pairs can be found in Step 3 in time $|L|^2 \left(\frac{B}{q}\right)^n \cdot \text{poly}(n)$ time. Among the pairs $(x_1, x_2) \in L_1 \times L_2$ we filter out all those that are not 1-close in $\ell_\infty$ norm.

Notice that in total we expect $|L|^2 \cdot \left(\frac{3}{q}\right)^n$ 1-close pairs. However, since we consider only those pairs with matching LSH-label, in each iteration we only obtain a certain fraction of all 1-close pairs. It remains to show that by our choice of $N$ repetitions in Step 4 we eventually find almost all 1-close pairs.

Let $(x_1, x_2) \in L_1 \times L_2$ be a solution to the close pairs problem, and consider the event $E$ that $h_{u,B}(x_1) = h_{u,B}(x_2)$, i.e., $x_1, x_2$ receive the same hash label for a random hash function. Then

$$\Pr[E] = \prod_{i=1}^n \left(1 - \Pr_{h_{u,B}}\left[\left\lfloor \frac{x_i + u_i}{B} \right\rfloor \neq \left\lfloor \frac{x_i' + u_i}{B} \right\rfloor\right]\right) = \left(1 - \frac{q/B}{q}\right)^n = (1 - 1/B)^n.$$

Thus, $E$ happens after $N = (\Pr[E])^{-1} n \log n$ repetitions with probability

$$1 - (1 - \Pr[E])^N \leq 1 - e^{-n \log n}.$$

Taking the union bound over all $\exp(n)$-many potentially 1-close pairs $(x_1, x_2) \in L_1 \times L_2$ ensures that we find with high probability an $(1 - o(1))$-fraction of all 1-close pairs.                                                                    □

Notice that Algorithm 1 requires some optimization of $B$. The larger $B$, the larger is the number of 1-close pairs that we find per iteration, and the smaller the required number $N$ of iterations. In our applications, we found the optimal value $B$ that minimizes $T_{\text{LSH}}(|L|, n)$ in Theorem 1 by an exhaustive search.

*Combining Approximate with Exact Matching.* Algorithm 1 can be easily adapted to exact matching by setting $B = q$, $N = 0$, and the whole process will correspond to simple merge sort. Now, assume we need to combine approximate matching on some $k_1$ coordinates and exact matching on some other $k_2$ coordinates. A hash label is then a concatenation of an approximate label of dimension $k_1$ and an exact label of dimension $k_2$. Then the number of elements in $L_1 \times L_2$ that have the same label is $|L|^2 \left(\frac{B}{q}\right)^{k_1} \left(\frac{1}{q}\right)^{k_2}$. The space and time complexity of this combined LSH+Exact algorithm are up to $\text{poly}(n)$ terms

$$S = \max\left\{|L|, |L|^2 \cdot \left(\frac{3}{q}\right)^{k_1} \left(\frac{1}{q}\right)^{k_2}\right\},$$

$$T_{\text{LSH+Exact}}(|L|, k_1, k_2, B) = \max\left\{S, |L|^2 \left(\frac{B}{q}\right)^{k_1} \left(\frac{1}{q}\right)^{k_2} \cdot N\right\}. \tag{3}$$

## 3 Our LSH-Based MitM with Rep-0 Representations

Since our algorithm builds on top of the representation technique-based MEET-LWE algorithm of [May21], let us briefly sketch the idea of representations, how they are used inside MEET-LWE, and how our LSH-technique for 1-close pairs from Sect. 2 leads to an improved LSH-MEET-LWE algorithm. As a warm-up, for didactical reasons we describe in this section the idea how to use our LSH technique with depth-2 search trees, where our technique is only used once to construct the level-1 lists $L_1^{(1)}$ and $L_2^{(1)}$ (the upper index denotes the level of the lists in Fig. 1). In the subsequent sections, we show how to generalize the technique to larger depth.

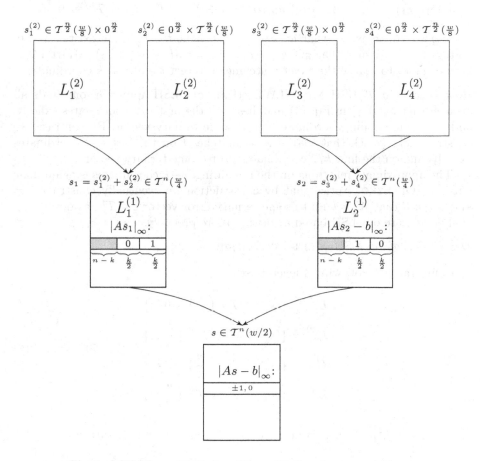

**Fig. 1.** LSH-MEET-LWE algorithm with Rep-0 representations

*Reprentations and* MEET-LWE. Let $\mathcal{T}^n = \{0, \pm 1\}^n \cap \mathbb{F}_q^n$ denote the set of ternary vectors. Moreover we denote by $\mathcal{T}^n(w/2)$ the set of ternary vectors having weight $w$ with exactly $w/2$ 1-entries and $w/2$ $(-1)$-entries.

Let $As = b + e \bmod q$ be the LWE key equation with $e \in \mathcal{T}^n$ and $s \in \mathcal{T}^n(w/2)$. We represent $s = s_1 + s_2$ where $s_1, s_2 \in \mathcal{T}^n(w/4)$, i.e. $s_1, s_2$ have exactly $w/4$ 1- and $(-1)$-entries each. Notice that there are $\mathcal{R} = \binom{w/2}{w/4}^2$ ways to represent $s$ as a sum of two weight $w/2$-vectors $s_1, s_2$. We call each such a tuple $(s_1, s_2)$ a REP-0-*representation* of $s$.

Choose $k$ maximal such that $q^k < \mathcal{R}$. Assume that on level 1 of the search tree, we first match on $k$ coordinates, and on level 0 we match on the remaining $n - k$ coordinates. Further let $\pi_k : \mathbb{F}_2^n \to \mathbb{F}_2^k$ denote the projection on the first $k$ coordinates.

We rewrite the LWE MitM identity from Eq. (1) as

$$\pi_k(As_1 + e_1) = \pi_k(b - As_2 + e_2) \text{ for some } e_1 \in 0^{k/2} \times \mathcal{T}^{k/2}, e_2 \in \mathcal{T}^{k/2} \times 0^{k/2}. \quad (4)$$

Since $q^k < R$, we expect that for each target value $t \in \mathbb{F}_q^k$ there exists a representation $(s_1, s_2)$ such that $\pi_k(As_1 + e_1) = t = \pi_k(b - As_2 + e_2)$. MEET-LWE guesses $e_1, e_2$ to realize the exact matching to target $t$ on these $k$ coordinates.

*High-Level Idea of* LSH-MEET-LWE. Using our LSH approach, one finds all $s_1$ such that $\pi_k(As_1)$ in Eq. (4) matches $t$ on the first $k/2$ coordinates exactly, and on the remaining coordinates up to some ternary vector. By contrast, we construct all $s_2$ such that $\pi_k(b - As_2)$ matches $t$ on the last $k/2$ coordinates exactly, and on the first $k/2$ coordinates up to some ternary vector.

The approximate matching on the remaining $n - k$ coordinates is again done via LSH-ODLYZKO. Notice that by construction we eventually construct $s = s_1 + s_2$ such that $As = b$ up to some ternary error vector $e \in \mathcal{T}^n$, as desired.

Let us state our LSH-based algorithm more precisely.

*Description of our* LSH-MEET-LWE *Algorithm*.

1. Enumerate the following 4 level-2 lists:

$$L_1^{(2)} = \{(s_1^{(2)} \in \mathcal{T}^{\frac{n}{2}}\left(\frac{w}{8}\right) \times 0^{\frac{n}{2}})\},$$

$$L_2^{(2)} = \{(s_2^{(2)} \in 0^{\frac{n}{2}} \times \mathcal{T}^{\frac{n}{2}}\left(\frac{w}{8}\right))\},$$

$$L_3^{(2)} = \{(s_3^{(2)} \in \mathcal{T}^{\frac{n}{2}}\left(\frac{w}{8}\right) \times 0^{\frac{n}{2}})\}, \quad (5)$$

$$L_4^{(2)} = \{(s_4^{(2)} \in 0^{\frac{n}{2}} \times \mathcal{T}^{\frac{n}{2}}\left(\frac{w}{8}\right))\}.$$

2. Let $\mathcal{R} = \binom{w/2}{w/4}^2$. Choose a positive even integer $k < n$ that satisfies

$$k = \left\lfloor \frac{\log_2(\mathcal{R})}{\log_2 q - 0.5 \log_2 3} \right\rfloor.$$

This choice of $k$ allows to expect one solution to survive during the merge of $L_1^{(2)}$ with $L_2^{(2)}$ and $L_3^{(2)}$ with $L_4^{(2)}$ as we find exact matches on $k/2$ coordinates and all 1-close pairs on another $k/2$ coordinates, hence we expect $\mathcal{R} \approx q^{\frac{k}{2}} \left(\frac{q}{3}\right)^{\frac{k}{2}}$.

3. Find all $(As_1^{(2)}, As_2^{(2)})$ that
   (a) match (sum to 0) on the coordinates $[k/2 + 1, k]$, and are

(b) 1-close on the coordinates $[1, k/2]$.

Analogously, find all $(As_3^{(2)}, As_4^{(2)})$ that

(a) match (sum to 0) on the coordinates $[1, k/2]$, and are

(b) 1-close on the coordinates $[k/2 + 1, k]$.

Use our LSH-ODLYZKO (Algorithm 1) with optimal $B$ to find 1-close pairs. This gives us two lists

$$L_1^{(1)} = \{(s_1 \in T^n \left(\frac{w}{4}\right) \ : \ As_1 \in \mathbb{Z}_q^{n-k} \times 0^{k/2} \times \{\pm 1, 0\}^{k/2})\}$$

$$L_2^{(1)} = \{(s_2 \in T^n \left(\frac{w}{4}\right) \ : \ As_2 \in \mathbb{Z}_q^{n-k} \times \{\pm 1, 0\}^{k/2} \times 0^{k/2})\}.$$

4. Use LSH-ODLYZKO again to find pairs from $L_1^{(1)}, L_2^{(1)}$ that are 1-close on the remaining $n - k$ coordinates.

Let $|L^{(j)}|$ denote the common length of all level-$j$ lists. Notice that on level 1 we obtain expected list length

$$\left|L_1^{(1)}\right| = \left|L_1^{(2)}\right|^2 \cdot \left(\frac{3}{q}\right)^{k/2} \cdot \left(\frac{1}{q}\right)^{k/2}.$$

Using Theorem 1 and ignoring polynomial factors, the running time of LSH-MEET-LWE with REP-0 representations is (here $N$ is given in Eq (2))

$$T_{\text{REP-0}} = \max\left\{|L^{(2)}|, \ T_{\text{LSH+Exact}}\left(|L^{(2)}|, \frac{k}{2}, \frac{k}{2}, B\right), \ T_{\text{LSH}}(|L^{(1)}|, n - k, q/2)\right\}$$

$$= \max\left\{|L^{(2)}|, \left|L^{(2)}\right|^2 \cdot \left(\frac{B}{q} \cdot \frac{1}{q}\right)^{k/2} \cdot N, \left|L^{(2)}\right|^4 \cdot \left(\frac{3}{q^2}\right)^k \cdot N \cdot 2^{-(n-k)}\right\}.$$

Table 1 gives concrete values of $T_{\text{REP-0}}$. For all of them the optimal value of the LSH-ODLYZKO parameter is $B = 3$. For concrete parameters, $B$ can be found using a brute-force search.

## 4  Generalizing Our LSH-Based MitM to Rep-1 Representations

The algorithm from the previous section can be generalised and improved by

1. representing weight-$w$ secrets $s = s_1 + s_2$ with $s_1, s_2$ having weight larger than $w/2$. As opposed to Sect. 3 this allows to represent 0-coordinates of $s$ not only by $0 + 0$, but also as $-1 + 1$ or as $1 + (-1)$. These are called REP-1 representations in [May21]. Notice that REP-1 in comparison to REP-0 increases the search space.

2. by constructing a deeper search tree to amortize the increased search space over many levels.

**Table 2.** Comparison bit complexities for REP-0 using our LSH-MEET-LWE and MEET-LWE.

| | $(n, q, w)$ | LSH-MEET-LWE | | MEET-LWE |
|---|---|---|---|---|
| | | REP-0 | $\log_2(N), k$ | [May21] |
| NTRU-Enc | $(509, 2048, 254)$ | 299 | 16, 24 | 305 |
| | $(677, 2048, 254)$ | 360 | 18, 24 | 364 |
| | $(821, 4096, 510)$ | 509 | 27, 44 | 520 |
| | $(701, 8192, 468)$ | 449 | 22, 36 | 461 |
| NTRU-Prime | $(653, 4621, 288)$ | 370 | 17, 24 | 370 |
| | $(761, 4591, 286)$ | 407 | 18, 24 | 408 |
| | $(857, 5167, 322)$ | 473 | 20, 26 | 459 |
| BLISS I+II | $(512, 12289, 154)$ | 267 | 7, 10 | 247 |
| GLP I | $(512, 8383489, 342)$ | 326 | 9, 14 | 325 |

Let us describe the depth-3 version of our LSH-MEET-LWE with REP-1. The reader is advised to follow Fig. 2. We implicitly assume that all fractions that appear are integers by appropriate rounding. We count the levels from bottom to top starting with 0, e.g., on level 3 we have 8 lists. The upper index of the elements refers to the level. In Fig. 2, we also visualize how we define suitable projections such that our LSH-ODLYZKO eventually finds 1-close pairs.

LSH-MEET-LWE *for* REP-1 *with Depth* 3. The eight top-most lists are of the form

$$L_i^{(3)} = \left\{ s_i^{(3)} \in \mathcal{T}^{\frac{n}{2}} \left( \frac{w}{16} + \frac{\varepsilon[1]}{4} + \frac{\varepsilon[2]}{2} \right) \times 0^{\frac{n}{2}} \right\} \quad \text{for odd } i,$$

$$L_i^{(3)} = \left\{ s_i^{(3)} \in 0^{\frac{n}{2}} \times \mathcal{T}^{\frac{n}{2}} \left( \frac{w}{16} + \frac{\varepsilon[1]}{4} + \frac{\varepsilon[2]}{2} \right) \right\} \quad \text{for even } i,$$

where $\varepsilon[i]$ describes the number of additional 1's we add in the representation of the secret $s$ on level $i$. More precisely, on the bottom level, we target the solution $s$ of weight $w$, i.e., $s \in \mathcal{T}^n(w/2)$. We split $s$ into $s = s_1^{(1)} + s_2^{(1)}$, where each $s_1^{(1)}, s_2^{(1)} \in \mathcal{T}^n(w/4 + \varepsilon[1])$ for some $\varepsilon[1] \geq 0$. This gives us, as in the previous section, $\binom{w/2}{w/4}^2$ ways to represent 1's and $-1$'s in $s$, and in addition $\binom{n-w}{\varepsilon[1], \varepsilon[1], \cdot}$ ways to represent 0's in $s$. The total number of representations for $s$ on level 1 is therefore

$$\mathcal{R}^{(1)} = \binom{w/2}{w/4}^2 \cdot \binom{n-w}{\varepsilon[1], \varepsilon[1], \cdot}.$$

Next, we go one level up by splitting $s_1^{(1)}$ (analogously for $s_2^{(1)}$) into two vectors $s_1^{(2)}, s_2^{(2)}$, each from $\mathcal{T}^n(\frac{w}{8} + \frac{\varepsilon[1]}{2} + \varepsilon[2])$. Therefore, the 1's and $-1$'s

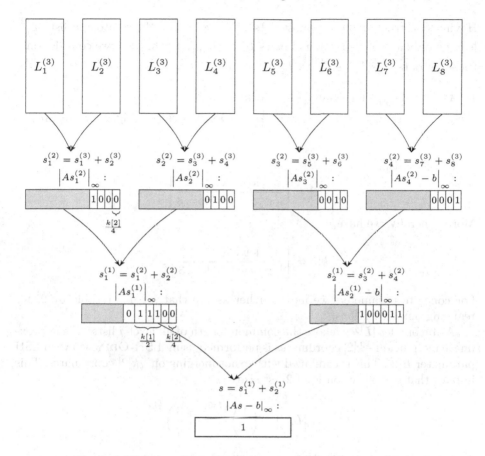

**Fig. 2.** LSH-MEET-LWE algorithm using REP-1 with depth 3

in $s_1^{(1)}$ can be represented in $\binom{w/4+\varepsilon[1]}{w/8+\varepsilon[1]/2}^2$ ways, while for 0's of $s_1^{(1)}$ we have $\binom{n-w/2-2\varepsilon[1]}{\varepsilon[2],\varepsilon[2],\cdot}$ representations. In total, the number of level-2 representations is

$$\mathcal{R}^{(2)} = \binom{w/4+\varepsilon[1]}{w/8+\varepsilon[1]/2}^2 \cdot \binom{n-w/2-2\varepsilon[1]}{\varepsilon[2],\varepsilon[2],\cdot}.$$

If we wanted to construct a tree of depth larger than 3, we would continue with representations for $s_1^{(2)}, s_2^{(2)}$. Instead, our depth-3 algorithm enumerates $s_1^{(2)}, s_2^{(2)}$ a standard Meet-in-Middle way by considering $s_1^{(2)} = s_1^{(3)} + s_2^{(3)}$, where $s_i^{(3)} \in \mathcal{T}^{n/2}(\frac{w}{16} + \frac{\varepsilon[1]}{4} + \frac{\varepsilon[2]}{2})$.

The cost of building the top-level lists is determined by their sizes, i.e.,

$$T[3] = \left| L_i^{(3)} \right|.$$

Having constructed the top-most lists $L_i^{(3)}$, we merge them into the lists $L_i^{(2)}$ leaving only a $1/\mathcal{R}^{(2)}$-fraction of pairs $L_i^{(3)} \times L_{i+1}^{(3)}$. To this end, we consider only those pairs $(s_i^{(3)}, s_{i+1}^{(3)}) \in L_i^{(3)} \times L_{i+1}^{(3)}$ for which

1. $As_i^{(3)} = As_{i+1}^{(3)}$ on certain $\frac{3}{4}k[2]$-coordinates, and
2. $\left| As_i^{(3)} - As_{i+1}^{(3)} \right|_\infty \leq 1$ on certain $\frac{1}{4}k[2]$-coordinates (see Fig. 2 for our projections).

Here, $k[2]$ satisfies

$$k[2] = \left\lfloor \frac{\log_2(\mathcal{R}^{(2)})}{\log_2 q - 0.5^2 \log_2 3} \right\rfloor .$$

More generally, we have

$$k[i] = \left\lfloor \frac{\log_2(\mathcal{R}^{(i)})}{\log_2 q - 0.5^i \log_2 3} \right\rfloor .$$

For concrete parameters we must further assure that $k[i]$ is divisible by $2^i$ for realizing our projections.

As before, let $|L^{(j)}|$ denote the common length of all level-$j$ lists. The approximate merging on $\frac{1}{4}k[2]$ coordinates is performed using LSH-ODLYZKO with LSH parameter $B[2]$. This is combined with exact merging on $\frac{3}{4}k[2]$ coordinates. This implies that we expect on level 2 list size

$$\left| L_i^{(2)} \right| = \left| L_i^{(3)} \right|^2 \cdot \left( \frac{1}{q} \right)^{\frac{3}{4}k[2]} \cdot \left( \frac{3}{q} \right)^{\frac{1}{4}k[2]} .$$

The complexity of constructing level-2 lists is

$$T[2] = \max \left\{ T_{\text{LSH+Exact}} \left( |L^{(3)}|, \frac{1}{4}k[2], \frac{3}{4}k[2], B[2] \right), |L_i^{(2)}| \right\}$$

$$= N[2] \cdot (q^{\frac{3}{4}k[2]} \cdot \lceil (q/B[2]) \rceil^{\frac{1}{4}k[2]}) \cdot \left( \left| L_i^{(3)} \right| \cdot \left( \frac{1}{q} \right)^{\frac{3}{4}k[2]} \left( \frac{B[2]}{q} \right)^{\frac{1}{4}k[2]} \right)^2 .$$

Level-1 lists are constructed in a similar way to level-2 lists. Concretely, $L_1^{(1)}, L_2^{(1)}$ are constructed via approximate matching on $\frac{1}{2}k[1]$ coordinates and exact matching on $\frac{1}{2}k[1]$ coordinates. Note that by our construction the elements from $L_1^{(1)}, L_2^{(1)}$ are already 1-close on $k[2]/2$ coordinates. The expected level-1 list size is therefore

$$\left| L_i^{(1)} \right| = \left| L_i^{(2)} \right|^2 \cdot \left( \frac{1}{q} \right)^{\frac{1}{2}k[1]-\frac{1}{2}k[2]} \left( \frac{3}{q} \right)^{\frac{1}{2}k[1]-\frac{1}{2}k[2]} .$$

The complexity of constructing level-1 lists is

$$T[1] = \max\left\{T_{\mathsf{LSH+Exact}}\left(L^{(2)}, \frac{1}{2}(k[1]-k[2]), B[1]\right), |L^{(1)}|\right\}$$

$$= N[1]\left(q^{\frac{k[1]}{2}-\frac{k[2]}{2}} \cdot \left\lceil \frac{q}{B[1]} \right\rceil^{\frac{k[1]}{2}-\frac{k[2]}{2}}\right)\left(|L_i^{(2)}| \cdot \left(\frac{1}{q}\right)^{\frac{k[1]}{2}-\frac{k[2]}{2}}\left(\frac{B[1]}{q}\right)^{\frac{k[1]}{2}-\frac{k[2]}{2}}\right)^2.$$

In order to construct the final list and determine the solution $s$, we use LSH-ODYLZKO once again on the remaining $n - k[1]$ coordinates with parameter $B[0] = q/2$ in time

$$T[0] = |L_i^{(1)}| \cdot 2^{n-k[1]}.$$

Overall, the asymptotic time and memory complexities of LSH-MEET-LWE on REP-1 with depth 3 are respectively

$$T = \max_{0 \le i \le 3}\{T[i]\} \quad \text{and} \quad S = \max_{0 \le i \le 3}\{L[i]\}.$$

## 5   Results: LSH-Meet-LWE (Rep-1) Compared to Lattices

Let us compare the performance of LSH-MEET-LWE to lattice attacks on NTRU-type cryptosystems. Concrete bit securities of proposed NTRU parameter sets are shown in Table 3.

The estimates for lattice attacks are computed with the help of the "leaky-LWE-Estimator" available at https://github.com/lducas/leaky-LWE-Estimator[3]. We used this estimator in the so-called Probabilistic-simulation regime, which gives slightly more accurate figures than, e.g., predictions from [ACD+18].

The estimator, based on the results from [DDGR20], produces bit securities for the so-called primal lattice attack. This attack runs a BKZ-reduction algorithm on the $2n$-dimensional lattice $\Lambda = \{(x,y) \in \mathbb{Z}^{2n} : [A|I_n]\begin{bmatrix} x \\ y \end{bmatrix} = 0 \bmod q\}$, where $[A|I_n]$ is the column-wise concatenation of matrices $A$ and $I_n$.

The estimator, given the NTRU parameters, produces a block-size parameter $\beta$, which determines the hardness of the BKZ reduction. In particular, we conservatively assume that the lattice attack will run in time $2^{0.292\beta+16.4}$ [BDGL16] (the constant 16.4 replaces $o(\beta)$ in the asymptotic SVP complexity $2^{0.292\beta+o(\beta)}$, see [APS15]). The values for $\beta$ as well as the bit complexities of the primal attack are given in the last column of Table 3.

*Parameter Sets.* In Table 3 we consider three different NTRU encryption schemes: the IEEE-2008 NTRU standard from [IEE08] with 12 different parameter sets, 4 parameter sets from the NIST standardisation candidate

---

[3] We used commit 4027151 of the branch NTRU_keygen, https://github.com/lducas/leaky-LWE-Estimator/tree/NTRU_keygen.

**Table 3.** Bit complexities for our LSH-MEET-LWE using Rep-0, Rep-1 from Sects. 3 and 4 with depths-$\{2-4\}$ search trees. We give the optimized values of $\varepsilon$ in square brackets. The last column provides the complexity of lattice-based attacks relying on the results of [DDGR20].

| $(n, q, w)$ | REP-0 [bit] | REP-1 depth 2 [bit], $\varepsilon$ | REP-1 depth 3 [bit], $\varepsilon$ | REP-1 depth 4 [bit], $\varepsilon$ | Lattices [DDGR20] $\beta$, $0.292\beta + 16.4$ |
|---|---|---|---|---|---|
| NTRU IEEE-2008 [IEE08] | | | | | |
| $(401, 2048, 226)$ | 260 | 237, [2] | **179**, [11,2] | 180, [39,18,3] | 273, **96** |
| $(449, 2048, 268)$ | 290 | 271, [2] | 208, [13,4] | **180**, [31,13,3] | 318, **109** |
| $(677, 2048, 314)$ | 414 | 362, [4] | 287, [25,6] | **242**, [31,13,2] | 522, **169** |
| $(1087, 2048, 240)$ | 445 | 375, [10] | **289**, [28,8] | 306, [38,13,3] | 835, **260** |
| $(541, 2048, 98)$ | 213 | 177, [8] | **144**, [13, 3] | 160, [27,8,1] | 372, **126** |
| $(613, 2048, 110)$ | 221 | 192, [6] | **160**, [10,3] | 174, [26,11,1] | 435, **143** |
| $(887, 2048, 162)$ | 342 | 287, [12] | 231, [19,6] | **230**, [26,13,4] | 677, **214** |
| $(1171, 2048, 212)$ | 427 | 365, [12] | 300, [23,6] | **283**, [35,14,3] | 945, **292** |
| $(659, 2048, 76)$ | 191 | 156, [6] | **135**, [13,4] | 167, [27,11,1] | 460, **151** |
| $(761, 2048, 84)$ | 221 | 179, [6] | **162**, [12,1] | 181, [37,17,5] | 545, **176** |
| $(1087, 2048, 126)$ | 311 | 251, [8] | **221**, [16,4] | 230, [38,17,4] | 835, **260** |
| $(1499, 2048, 158)$ | 389 | 324, [12] | 286, [26,7] | **283**, [28,10,0] | 1170, **358** |
| NTRU [CDH+20] | | | | | |
| $(509, 2048, 254)$ | 299 | 282, [6] | 203, [12, 4] | **191**, [27, 16, 3] | 369, **124** |
| $(677, 2048, 254)$ | 360 | 322, [6] | 244, [20, 6] | **226**, [27, 16, 3] | 517, **167** |
| $(821, 4096, 510)$ | 509 | 501, [2] | 374, [18, 5] | **358**, [27, 8, 1] | 619, **197** |
| $(701, 8192, 468)$ | 449 | 441, [0] | 336, [27, 4] | **295**, [23, 14, 2] | 474, **155** |
| NTRU Prime [BBC+20] | | | | | |
| $(653, 4621, 288)$ | 370 | 333, [4] | 265, [22, 3] | **228**, [26, 15, 4] | 449, **148** |
| $(761, 4591, 286)$ | 407 | 359, [6] | 276, [24, 6] | **268**, [24, 6, 5] | 539, **174** |
| $(857, 5167, 322)$ | 473 | 413, [8] | 317, [27, 8] | **315**, [27, 10, 4] | 615, **196** |
| BLISS I+II [DDLL13] | | | | | |
| $(512, 12289, 154)$ | 267 | 216, [6] | 166, [15, 3] | **159**, [23, 11, 1] | 292, **102** |
| GLP I [GLP12] | | | | | |
| $(512, 8383489, 342)$ | 326 | 326, [0] | 262, [10, 0] | **184**, [27, 11, 2] | 148, **60** |

NTRU [CDH+20], and 3 parameter sets from the alternative NIST standardisation candidate NTRU Prime [BBC+20]. We also consider two signature schemes based on ternary LWE: BLISS with parameter sets I and II from [DDLL13] and GLP [GLP12]. Except BLISS, all these schemes the weight of $e$ is chosen to be $2 \cdot \lfloor n/3 \rfloor$. Note that the exact value of the error weight is relevant only for the lattice attack, while our LSH-MEET-LWE's complexity algorithm is independent of $e$'s weight, but highly sensitive to the weight of the secret $s$. Both LSH-MEET-LWE and lattice reduction require memory exponential in $n$.

*Conclusions.* From Table 3 we observe that our combinatorial LSH-MEET-LWE attack highly profits from small weight. For example, the third package of NTRU IEEE-2008 parameters (speed optimized according to the specification [IEE08]) has smallest weight relative to $n$. For all four instances of this package, our estimates outperform the lattice estimates.

The decision to choose larger weights in recent standardization proposals such as NTRU [CDH+20] and NTRU Prime [BBC+20] appears to be a wise decision in light of our new combinatorial attack results. For these instances, we cannot compete with current lattice estimates.

We note that the figures in Table 3 both for lattices and LSH-MEET-LWE are likely to underestimate actual costs. For lattices, the $2^{0.292\beta+16.4}$ Core-SVP model does not include several SVP calls within the BKZ reduction, and also hides the complexity of decoding random spherical codes of length $\mathcal{O}(\sqrt{\beta})$. For LSH-MEET-LWE, we omit polynomial factors for LSH-ODLYZKO and sorting.

# 6   Cold Boot Attack

Our combinatorial Rep-1 attack performs best when the secret is sparse. In some cases, see Table 3, it even outperforms lattice-based attacks. Sparse secrets also naturally appear in the so called cold boot attack scenario [HSH+09]. Belonging to the class of side-channel attacks, in an cold-boot attack one has read-access to RAM where the secret key is stored, but some small fraction of bits in this RAM is flipped (after power shut-down).

Thus an attacker obtains a noisy version $s'$ of the secret key $s$. Concretely, let $s' = s + \Delta$, where $\Delta$ is of small Hamming weight $w_\Delta$. With this noisy secret $s'$, the attacker produces from the original ternary LWE instance $(A, b)$ a new instance $(A, b')$, where

$$b' = b - As' = A \cdot \Delta + e,$$

i.e., we replace the secret $s$ by $\Delta$.

Following [HSH+09, ADP18], let us assume a typical average bit flip rate of 0.55%. In order to estimate $w_\Delta$, we notice that a ternary NTRU secret key requires $2n$ bits of storage, since each coefficient occupies 2 bits. Therefore, we expect $w_\Delta = \lceil 2n \cdot \frac{0.55}{100} \rceil$. For the concrete cryptographic parameters in Table 4 this translates to $w_\Delta$ in a range between 6 and 10.

**Table 4.** Bit complexities for the cold boot attack on NTRU-type encryption schemes and signatures. Lattice-based attacks are estimated using the results from [ACD+18].

| $(n, q, w, w_\Delta)$ | REP-1 [bit], $\varepsilon$ | Lattices [ACD+18] $0.292\beta + 16.4$ |
|---|---|---|
| NTRU [CDH+20] | | |
| $(509, 2048, 254, 6)$ | **40**, [0] | 41 |
| $(677, 2048, 254, 8)$ | **42**, [0] | 48 |
| $(821, 4096, 510, 10)$ | 60, [2] | 56 |
| $(701, 8192, 468, 8)$ | **43**, [0] | 47 |
| NTRU Prime [BBC+20] | | |
| $(653, 4621, 288, 8)$ | **42**, [0] | 47 |
| $(761, 4591, 286, 9)$ | 57, [2] | 48 |
| $(857, 5167, 322, 10)$ | 60, [2] | 55 |
| BLISS I+II [DDLL13] | | |
| $(512, 12289, 154, 6)$ | 41, [0] | 38 |
| GLP I [GLP12] | | |
| $(512, 8383489, 342, 6)$ | 40, [0] | 33 |

We note that some implementations may choose to store the secret keys differently than just two bits per coefficient, and this will impact the efficiency of our cold boot attack. For example, [CDH+20] describes a compression mechanism of ternary keys to bit-strings. Thus, flipping one bit of the bit-string may impact many entries in the ternary key. For simplicity of exposition, we ignore such implementation subtleties here.

Let us now apply our Rep-1 attack to this new extremely sparse secret LWE setup. Concrete figures are given in Table 4. Since the secret is very sparse, we do not have to construct deep search trees to outperform lattice attacks. It is suffices to the consider depth-2 Rep-1 (or even sometimes Rep-0) algorithm. To estimate lattice-based attacks for sparse secret we use the estimator from [ACD+18] since it incorporates the so-called 'drop-and-solve' guessing technique for sparse secret, see [ACW19].

This 'drop-and-solve' technique can be applied as well to our algorithm: we guess that a certain $c$ coordinates of $s'$ are 0 and remove these columns from the matrix $A$. The probability of guessing the 0's correctly is $p_0 = \binom{w_\Delta}{n-c}/\binom{w_\Delta}{n}$. The LWE problem becomes easier as the dimension is now $n - c$, but the overall runtime has to take the guessing into account. We find the optimal choice for $c$ by exhaustive search. For our attack, the total saving is around a factor of 2 (i.e., one bit in the security level). For the parameter sets from Table 4 our Rep-1 attack performs similar to or even better than lattice-based attacks.

# References

[ACD+18] Albrecht, M.R., et al.: Estimate all the LWE, NTRU schemes! In: Catalano, D., De Prisco, R. (eds.) SCN 2018. LNCS, vol. 11035, pp. 351–367. Springer, Cham (2018). https://doi.org/10.1007/978-3-319-98113-0_19

[ACW19] Albrecht, M.R., Curtis, B.R., Wunderer, T.: Exploring trade-offs in batch bounded distance decoding. In: Paterson, K.G., Stebila, D. (eds.) SAC 2019. LNCS, vol. 11959, pp. 467–491. Springer, Cham (2020). https://doi.org/10.1007/978-3-030-38471-5_19

[ADP18] Albrecht, M.R., Amit, D., Paterson, K.G.: Cold boot attacks on ring and module LWE keys under the NTT. IACR TCHES **2018**(3), 173–213 (2018). https://tches.iacr.org/index.php/TCHES/article/view/7273

[AI06] Andoni, A., Indyk, P.: Near-optimal hashing algorithms for approximate nearest neighbor in high dimensions. In: 47th FOCS, pp. 459–468. IEEE Computer Society Press, October 2006

[APS15] Albrecht, M.R., Player, R., Scott, S.: On the concrete hardness of learning with errors. J. Math. Cryptol. **9**(3), 169–203 (2015)

[BBC+20] Bernstein, D.J., et al.: NTRU Prime: round 3 (2020). https://ntruprime.cr.yp.to/nist/ntruprime-20201007.pdf

[BCJ11] Becker, A., Coron, J.-S., Joux, A.: Improved generic algorithms for hard knapsacks. In: Paterson, K.G. (ed.) EUROCRYPT 2011. LNCS, vol. 6632, pp. 364–385. Springer, Heidelberg (2011). https://doi.org/10.1007/978-3-642-20465-4_21

[BDGL16] Becker, A., Ducas, L., Gama, N., Laarhoven, T.: New directions in nearest neighbor searching with applications to lattice sieving. In: Krauthgamer, R. (ed.) 27th SODA, pp. 10–24. ACM-SIAM, January 2016

[BJMM12] Becker, A., Joux, A., May, A., Meurer, A.: Decoding random binary linear codes in $2^{n/20}$: How $1 + 1 = 0$ improves information set decoding. In: Pointcheval, D., Johansson, T. (eds.) EUROCRYPT 2012. LNCS, vol. 7237, pp. 520–536. Springer, Heidelberg (2012). https://doi.org/10.1007/978-3-642-29011-4_31

[CDH+20] Chen, C., et al.: PQC round-3 candidate: NTRU. Technical report (2020). https://ntru.org/f/ntru-20190330.pdf

[DDGR20] Dachman-Soled, D., Ducas, L., Gong, H., Rossi, M.: LWE with side information: attacks and concrete security estimation. In: Micciancio, D., Ristenpart, T. (eds.) CRYPTO 2020. LNCS, vol. 12171, pp. 329–358. Springer, Cham (2020). https://doi.org/10.1007/978-3-030-56880-1_12

[DDLL13] Ducas, L., Durmus, A., Lepoint, T., Lyubashevsky, V.: Lattice signatures and bimodal gaussians. In: Canetti, R., Garay, J.A. (eds.) CRYPTO 2013. LNCS, vol. 8042, pp. 40–56. Springer, Heidelberg (2013). https://doi.org/10.1007/978-3-642-40041-4_3

[GLP12] Güneysu, T., Lyubashevsky, V., Pöppelmann, T.: Practical lattice-based cryptography: a signature scheme for embedded systems. In: Prouff, E., Schaumont, P. (eds.) CHES 2012. LNCS, vol. 7428, pp. 530–547. Springer, Heidelberg (2012). https://doi.org/10.1007/978-3-642-33027-8_31

[HJ10] Howgrave-Graham, N., Joux, A.: New generic algorithms for hard knapsacks. In: Gilbert, H. (ed.) EUROCRYPT 2010. LNCS, vol. 6110, pp. 235–256. Springer, Heidelberg (2010). https://doi.org/10.1007/978-3-642-13190-5_12

[HPS98]   Hoffstein, J., Pipher, J., Silverman, J.H.: NTRU: a ring-based public key cryptosystem. In: Buhler, J.P. (ed.) ANTS 1998. LNCS, vol. 1423, pp. 267–288. Springer, Heidelberg (1998). https://doi.org/10.1007/BFb0054868

[HSH+09]  Halderman, J.A., et al.: Lest we remember: cold-boot attacks on encryption keys. Commun. ACM **52**(5), 91–98 (2009)

[IEE08]   IEEE standard specification for public key cryptographic techniques based on hard problems over lattices. IEEE Std 1363.1-2008, pp. 1–81 (2008)

[IM98]    Indyk, P., Motwani, R.: Approximate nearest neighbors: towards removing the curse of dimensionality. In: Proceedings of the Thirtieth Annual ACM Symposium on Theory of Computing, STOC 1998, pp. 604–613 (1998)

[Ind01]   Indyk, P.: On approximate nearest neighbors under $\ell_\infty$-norm. J. Comput. Syst. Sci. **63**(4), 627–638 (2001)

[KM21]    Kirshaniva, E., May, A.: How to find ternary LWE keys using locality sensitive hashings. Cryptology ePrint Archive, Report 2021/1255 (2021). https://eprint.iacr.org/2021/1255

[May21]   May, A.: How to meet ternary LWE keys. In: Malkin, T., Peikert, C. (eds.) CRYPTO 2021. LNCS, vol. 12826, pp. 701–731. Springer, Cham (2021). https://doi.org/10.1007/978-3-030-84245-1_24

[MO15]    May, A., Ozerov, I.: On computing nearest neighbors with applications to decoding of binary linear codes. In: Oswald, E., Fischlin, M. (eds.) EURO-CRYPT 2015. LNCS, vol. 9056, pp. 203–228. Springer, Heidelberg (2015). https://doi.org/10.1007/978-3-662-46800-5_9

[Ngu21]   Nguyen, P.: Boosting the hybrid attack on NTRU: Torus LSH, permuted HNF and boxed sphere (2021). https://csrc.nist.gov/Presentations/2021/boosting-the-hybrid-attack-on-ntru

# When HEAAN Meets FV: A New Somewhat Homomorphic Encryption with Reduced Memory Overhead

Hao Chen[1], Ilia Iliashenko[2(✉)], and Kim Laine[3]

[1] Facebook, Cambridge, USA
[2] imec-COSIC, Department of Electrical Engineering, KU Leuven, Leuven, Belgium
ilia@esat.kuleuven.be
[3] Microsoft Research, Redmond, USA
kim.laine@microsoft.com

**Abstract.** We demonstrate how to reduce the memory overhead of somewhat homomorphic encryption (SHE) while computing on numerical data. We design a hybrid SHE scheme that exploits the packing algorithm of the HEAAN scheme and the variant of the FV scheme by Bootland et al. The ciphertext size of the resulting scheme is 3–18 times smaller than in HEAAN to compute polynomial functions of depth 4 while packing a small number of data values. Furthermore, our scheme has smaller ciphertexts even with larger packing capacities (256–2048 values).

## 1 Introduction

Homomorphic encryption (HE) [21] is a family of encryption schemes that allow computation on encrypted messages without decryption. Several types of such schemes have been proposed in the last 40 years, including *partially* homomorphic encryption (e.g. [11,15,19,22]), which can perform either addition or multiplication, *somewhat* homomorphic encryption (SHE), which supports functions of a limited multiplicative depth, and *fully* homomorphic encryption (FHE) [14] capable to compute any function on encrypted data.

Despite their universality, SHE/FHE schemes have a significant disadvantage in practice. In particular, they introduce a huge memory overhead per encrypted bit value, which makes even simple arithmetic operations on numerical data impractically slow. To mitigate this overhead various encoding algorithms have been proposed that exploit the structure of typical plaintext spaces used in SHE/FHE [2–4,6,7,10]. They deviate from bit-wise encryption to so-called 'word-wise' encryption where one (or even several) data values can be encrypted per ciphertext. Unfortunately, these algorithms perform correctly only if the ciphertext modulus grows exponentially with the depth of the circuit.

A more efficient approach was proposed by Cheon et al. [5], who introduced a new type of HE schemes, called *approximate* HE (AHE). The crucial idea is to allow an additional error while performing homomorphic operations. For

© Springer Nature Switzerland AG 2021
M. B. Paterson (Ed.): IMACC 2021, LNCS 13129, pp. 265–285, 2021.
https://doi.org/10.1007/978-3-030-92641-0_13

example, multiplication of two encrypted plaintexts $ct_1 = \mathtt{Encrypt}(pt_1)$ and $ct_2 = \mathtt{Encrypt}(pt_2)$ results in another ciphertext $ct_3$, which is decrypted to $\mathtt{Decrypt}(ct_3) = pt_1 \cdot pt_2 + e$ where $e$ is a so-called 'noise'. The size of $e$ defines the approximation 'closeness' between decrypted and expected results.

AHE is suitable for handling non-integer data types such as real, rational or complex numbers. Computation on such numerical types in computer systems is inherently prone to numerical errors. Thus, the results of such computation are only correct up to a certain precision. Approximation errors introduced by AHE can be treated as a part of these numerical errors.

The drawback of the first AHE scheme from [5], called HEAAN, is that its ciphertext size should be set quite large to be able to compute even simple polynomial functions with a decent precision. This problem is mitigated by packing, which is an encoding technique that allows to encrypt several data values into one ciphertext. In addition, computations on these packed values can be performed in the Single-Instruction Multiple-Data (SIMD) manner.

The packing method of HEAAN permits thousands of data values to be encrypted into a single ciphertext, thus significantly reducing the amortized ciphertext expansion per data value. However, various applications do not require such a large packing capacity and assume modest computational resources, especially in the use cases where embedded devices are used [12,16,18].

For example, such a device can collect data about vital organs (e.g. heart, blood pressure) and constantly sends it to a special service that runs a private prediction model of a heart attack in a privacy-preserving manner. Each message from the device contains a smaller amount of values (dozens, maybe a hundred of measurements) in comparison to the dimension of plaintexts in FHE schemes (thousands). In addition, each message should be as small as possible to fit constraints of the device, but at the same time it should be large enough to let the service perform homomorphic computations of certain depth.

To reduce ciphertext size, one can resort to so-called 'high-precision' SHE schemes [3,4] that trade packing capacity for additional homomorphic operations. Thus, relatively deep computations can be performed with modest encryption parameters of these schemes. The known high-precision SHE schemes are variants the FV scheme [13]. FV is not AHE, but its encryption function is very similar to the one of HEAAN. Furthermore, the variant of FV by Bootland et al. [3] supports complex-number arithmetic as HEAAN.

*Our Contribution.* In this work, we design a new SHE scheme that can perform computations on numerical data with smaller ciphertexts than in HEAAN.

The core idea is to exploit the recent variant of the FV scheme [13] due to Bootland et al. [3], where the integer plaintext modulus is replaced by a polynomial $X^m + b$ for some $m$ and $b$. The plaintext space of this scheme is $\mathbb{Z}[X]/(X^n + 1, X^m + b)$, which is isomorphic to the ring of cyclotomic integers $\mathbb{Z}[\zeta_{2m}]/(b^{n/m} + 1)$ if $n$ and $m$ are powers of 2 and $b$ is an $m$th power modulo $b^{n/m} + 1$. This FV variant natively supports homomorphic computation on large cyclotomic integers $\mathbb{Z}[\zeta_{2m}]$ with small encryption parameters.

We combine this scheme with the HEAAN packing algorithm, which maps complex-valued vectors into cyclotomic integers. More precisely, it encodes elements of $\mathbb{C}^{m/2}$ into the aforementioned ring $\mathbb{Z}[\zeta_{2m}]$, which can be easily embedded into $\mathbb{Z}[\zeta_{2m}]/(b^{n/m} + 1)$, the plaintext space of Bootland's variant of FV.

As a result we obtain a hybrid SHE scheme which follows the following diagram

$$\mathbb{C}^{m/2} \xrightarrow{\text{HEAAN packing}} \mathbb{Z}[\zeta_{2m}]/(b^{n/m} + 1) \xrightarrow{\text{FV encryption}} R_q^2 = (\mathbb{Z}[X]/(X^n + 1))^2 ,$$

where $R_q^2$ is the ciphertext space. This hybrid leverages the advantages of both schemes: the small memory overhead of Bootland's FV variant and the large packing capacity of HEAAN. Furthermore, since our technique only changes the way how the plaintext space of Bootland's scheme is used, the security analysis of our hybrid scheme is exactly the same as for the FV scheme.

We describe a family of arithmetic circuits where our scheme have a smaller memory and running time overhead than HEAAN. In addition, we illustrate the difference between these schemes by computing several important analytic functions.

## 2    Preliminaries

For any $a \in \mathbb{N}$, we denote the set of integers $\{1, \ldots, a\}$ by $[a]$. Vectors and matrices are denoted by boldface lower- and upper-case letters, respectively. Vectors are written in column form.

Let $n$ be a positive power of 2. Let $K$ be a cyclotomic number field constructed by adjoining a primitive complex $2n$-th root of unity to the field of rational numbers. We denote this root of unity by $\zeta_{2n}$, so $K = \mathbb{Q}(\zeta_{2n})$. The ring of integers of $K$, denoted by $R$, is isomorphic to $\mathbb{Z}[X]/(X^n + 1)$.

For any $a \in K$ its coefficient vector $(a_0, \ldots, a_{n-1})$ in the power basis is denoted by $\mathbf{a}$. The infinity norm of $a$ is equal to $|a|_\infty = |\mathbf{a}|_\infty = \max_{i=0}^{n-1} |a_i|$. The product of any $a, b \in K$ satisfies the following bound $|ab|_\infty \leq n \cdot |a|_\infty \cdot |b|_\infty$, see [9] for more details.

Let $R_a$ be the quotient of $R$ modulo an ideal $(a)$. If $a$ is a natural number, we take representatives of $\mathbb{Z}/a\mathbb{Z}$ from the half-open interval $[-a/2, a/2)$.

The semantic security of encryption schemes presented in this paper is based on the RLWE problem introduced in [17].

**Definition 1 (RLWE problem).** *Let $q > 2$ be an integer. Let $s \in R_q$ be a random secret element, $a, a', b' \in R_q$ be uniformly random elements and $e \in R_q$ be a random element sampled from some known distribution over $R_q$. The RLWE problem is to distinguish between $(a, b = as + e)$ and $(a', b')$.*

The hardness of the RLWE problem implies that the above pair $(a, b)$ is pseudorandom. Thus, it can be exploited as a random mask in encryption and key generation (see more details in [17]).

## 3   HEAAN Packing Method

In this section, we describe the HEAAN method for packing complex-valued vectors as presented in [5]. This packing method exploits the canonical embedding of cyclotomic fields.

Let $K' = \mathbb{Q}\left(\zeta_{2m}\right)$, where $m$ is a power of two and $m$ divides $n$. Clearly, $K'$ is a subfield of $K$. We denote the ring of integers of $K'$ by $R'$. Since $[K' : \mathbb{Q}] = m$, there exist $m$ field homomorphisms $\sigma'_i : K' \to \mathbb{C}$ with $i \in [m]$ that fix every element of $\mathbb{Q}$. In particular, each $\sigma'_i$ is a complex embedding that maps $\zeta_{2m}$ to $\zeta_{2m}^{2i-1}$. These are the only field homomorphisms from $K'$ to $\mathbb{C}$.

Let $H'$ be a vector subspace of $\mathbb{C}^m$ such that $H' = \{(x_1, \ldots, x_m)^{\mathsf{T}} : x_{m-j+1} = \hat{x}_j, \forall j \in [m/2]\}$. This space is equipped with a projection map $\pi : H' \to \mathbb{C}^{m/2}$ that discards either of complex conjugate components. Conversely, the inverse map $\pi^{-1}$ appends a vector from $\mathbb{C}^{m/2}$ with the conjugates of its coordinates in the order compliant with $H'$.

The *canonical embedding* of $K'$ is the map $\sigma' : K' \to H'$ defined as $\sigma'(a) = (\sigma'_1(a), \ldots, \sigma'_m(a))$. By analogy, we can define the canonical embedding of $K$ denoted by $\sigma$, which endows $K$ with the canonical norm via $\|a\|^{\mathrm{can}} = |\sigma(a)|_{\infty}$ for any $a \in K$. Since $n$ is a power of two, $|a|_{\infty} \leq \|a\|^{\mathrm{can}}$ as shown in [9]. In addition, $\|ab\|^{\mathrm{can}} \leq \|a\|^{\mathrm{can}} \|b\|^{\mathrm{can}}$ for any $a, b \in K$.

Let $\mathbf{a} = (a_0, a_1, \ldots, a_{m-1})$ be the coefficient vector of $a \in K'$ in the power basis of $K'$. Then, the canonical embedding $\sigma'$ transforms $\mathbf{a}$ into

$$\mathbf{\Sigma} \cdot \begin{pmatrix} a_0 \\ \vdots \\ a_{m-1} \end{pmatrix} = \begin{pmatrix} \sigma'_1(a) \\ \vdots \\ \sigma'_m(a) \end{pmatrix}$$

where $\mathbf{\Sigma} = (\zeta_{2m}^{j(2i+1)})_{i,j}$ is a Vandermonde matrix. Since $\mathbf{\Sigma}$ is nonsingular, the inverse of the canonical embedding is correctly defined by $\mathbf{\Sigma}^{-1} = \left(\frac{1}{m}\zeta_{2m}^{-i(2j+1)}\right)_{i,j}$. Thus, the composition map $\sigma'^{-1} \circ \pi^{-1}$ encodes vectors from $\mathbb{C}^{m/2}$ into $K'$.

To finish packing, elements of $K'$ should end up in the ring of cyclotomic integers $R'$. This can be done using discretization to the lattice $\sigma'(R')$, which boils down to coefficient-wise rounding with relation to the power basis of $R'$ over $\mathbb{Z}$. However, this rounding introduces an error that might damage significant bits of input values. To eliminate this error, an input vector is scaled up by some value $\Delta$. To summarize, the complete packing pipeline consists of the following map chain

- $\mathtt{Pack}(\Delta) : \mathbb{C}^{m/2} \xrightarrow{\cdot\Delta} \mathbb{C}^{m/2} \xrightarrow{\pi^{-1}} H' \xrightarrow{\sigma'^{-1}} K' \xrightarrow{\lfloor \cdot \rceil} R'$.

The unpacking algorithm is the inverse map of Pack without the rounding step, namely

- $\mathtt{Unpack}(\Delta') : R' \xrightarrow{\sigma'} H' \xrightarrow{\pi} \mathbb{C}^{m/2} \xrightarrow{\cdot\Delta'^{-1}} \mathbb{C}^{m/2}$.

The size of $\Delta$ is defined by the input precision $p$ and the input dimension $m$ according to the following lemma.

**Lemma 1.** *Given an input vector $\mathbf{z} \in \mathbb{C}^{m/2}$ and a positive integer $p$, the vector $\mathbf{z}' = \mathtt{Unpack}(\Delta, \mathtt{Pack}(\Delta, \mathbf{z}))$ satisfies $|\mathbf{z} - \mathbf{z}'|_\infty < \frac{1}{p}$, if $\Delta > \frac{pm}{2}$.*

*Proof.* Let $\mathbf{u} \in H'$ be the output of the first two steps of the $\mathtt{Pack}$ algorithm, namely $\mathbf{u} = \pi^{-1}(\Delta \cdot \mathbf{z})$. Then, the final output $a \in R'$ can be represented in matrix notation as

$$\mathbf{a} = \lfloor \mathbf{\Sigma}^{-1} \cdot \mathbf{u} \rceil = \mathbf{\Sigma}^{-1} \cdot \mathbf{u} + \mathbf{e}$$

with $|\mathbf{e}|_\infty \leq 1/2$. Computing $\mathtt{Unpack}(\Delta, a)$, we obtain

$$\mathbf{z}' = \frac{1}{\Delta}\pi\,(\mathbf{\Sigma}\mathbf{a}) = \frac{1}{\Delta}\pi(\mathbf{u} + \mathbf{\Sigma}\mathbf{e}) = \mathbf{z} + \frac{1}{\Delta}\pi(\mathbf{\Sigma}\mathbf{e})\,.$$

Hence, the difference between the input $\mathbf{z}$ and its packed approximation $\mathbf{z}'$ satisfies the following bound

$$|\mathbf{z} - \mathbf{z}'|_\infty = \max_{i \in [m/2]} \left| \frac{1}{\Delta} \sum_{j=0}^{m-1} e_j \cdot \zeta_{2m}^{j(2i-1)} \right| \leq \frac{m}{2\Delta}\,,$$

which immediately leads to the desired lower bound on $\Delta$. $\qquad\square$

## 4    FV Scheme with a Polynomial Plaintext Modulus

In this section we describe the variant of the FV scheme given by Bootland et al. in [3], which is based on the work of Chen et al. [4]. The main difference of this variant from the original FV scheme [13] consists in switching from an integer plaintext modulus $t$ to a polynomial $X^m + b$.

Let $q$ be an integer. The ciphertext space is defined as $R_q = R/(q)$. Take an integer $b$ such that $2 \leq |b| \ll q$. Let $m$ be a positive integer dividing $n$. The quotient ring $R_{X^m+b} = R/(X^m + b)$ serves as the plaintext space. We define the encryption scaling factor $\Delta_b$ as follows

$$\Delta_b = \left\lfloor \frac{q}{X^m + b} \bmod (X^n + 1) \right\rceil = \left\lfloor -\frac{q}{b^{n/m} + 1} \sum_{i=1}^{n/m}(-b)^{i-1} \cdot X^{n-im} \right\rceil .$$

Let $\chi_e$ be the error distribution on $R$, which is a coefficient-wise discrete Gaussian distribution with respect to the power basis. The standard deviation of $\chi_e$ is $\sigma$. The key distribution $\chi_k$ generates uniformly random elements of $R$ with ternary coefficients (again, with respect to the power basis). We also set an integer $w > 1$ and call it the decomposition base. Let $\ell = \lfloor \log_w q \rfloor$.

Given this set-up, the basic FV scheme with polynomial plaintext modulus is defined as follows.

- KeyGen($1^n$): Let $s \leftarrow \chi_k$ and $e, e_0, \ldots e_\ell \leftarrow \chi_e$. Generate uniformly random $a, a_0, \ldots, a_\ell \in R_q$ and compute $b_i = \left[-(a_i \cdot s + e_i) + w^i \cdot s^2\right]_q$. Output
  - the secret key $\text{sk} = s$,
  - the public key $\text{pk} = \left([-(a \cdot s + e)]_q, a\right)$,
  - the evaluation key $\text{rlk} = \{(b_i, a_i)\}_{i=0}^{\ell}$.
- Encrypt ($\text{pk}, \text{msg} \in R_{X^m+b}$): Sample $u \leftarrow \chi_k$ and $e_0, e_1 \leftarrow \chi_e$. Set $p_0 = \text{pk}[0]$ and $p_1 = \text{pk}[1]$. Output $\text{ct} = (c_0, c_1)$, where

$$c_0 = [\Delta_b \cdot \text{msg} + p_0 \cdot u + e_0]_q, \qquad c_1 = [p_1 \cdot u + e_1]_q$$

- Decrypt ($\text{sk}, \text{ct}$): Return

$$\text{msg}' = \left\lfloor \frac{X^m + b}{q} [c_0 + c_1 \cdot s]_q \right\rceil \mod (X^m + b).$$

As shown in [17], this encryption scheme is semantically secure assuming the hardness of the RLWE problem.

### 4.1    Homomorphic Operations

It is easy to adapt the homomorphic operations of FV to the new plaintext modulus as shown below.

- Add($\text{ct}_0, \text{ct}_1$): Return $\text{ct}_{\text{Add}} = \left([\text{ct}_0[0] + \text{ct}_1[0]]_q, [\text{ct}_0[1] + \text{ct}_1[1]]_q\right)$.
- BasicMul($\text{ct}_0, \text{ct}_1$): Return $\text{ct}_{\text{BasicMul}} = (c_0, c_1, c_2)$, where

$$c_0 = \left[\left\lfloor \frac{X^m + b}{q} \cdot \text{ct}_0[0] \cdot \text{ct}_1[0] \right\rceil\right]_q, \quad c_2 = \left[\left\lfloor \frac{X^m + b}{q} \cdot \text{ct}_0[1] \cdot \text{ct}_1[1] \right\rceil\right]_q,$$

$$c_1 = \left[\left\lfloor \frac{X^m + b}{q} \cdot (\text{ct}_0[0] \cdot \text{ct}_1[1] + \text{ct}_0[1] \cdot \text{ct}_1[0]) \right\rceil\right]_q.$$

- Relin($\text{ct}_{\text{BasicMul}}, \text{rlk}$): Writing $\text{ct}_{\text{BasicMul}} = (c_0, c_1, c_2)$, expand $c_2$ in base $w$ such that $c_2 = \sum_{i=0}^{\ell} c_{2,i} \cdot w^i$ with $|c_{2,i}|_\infty \leq w/2$. Compute

$$c_0' = c_0 + \sum_{i=0}^{\ell} \text{rlk}[i][0] \cdot c_{2,i}, \qquad c_1' = c_1 + \sum_{i=0}^{\ell} \text{rlk}[i][1] \cdot c_{2,i}$$

and output $c_{\text{Relin}} = (c_0', c_1')$.
- Mul($\text{ct}_0, \text{ct}_1, \text{rlk}$): Return $c_{\text{Mul}} = (c_0', c_1') = \text{Relin}(\text{BasicMul}(\text{ct}_0, \text{ct}_1), \text{rlk})$.

### 4.2    Ciphertext Size

In this section we describe the memory overhead of FV with a polynomial plaintext modulus.

The memory overhead is defined by two encryption parameters: the ciphertext modulus $q$ and the ring dimension $n$. Furthermore, the same parameters and the standard deviation $\sigma$ determine the security level of an HE scheme. In practice, $n$ and $\sigma$ are usually fixed whereas $q$ is chosen according to the desired security level and homomorphic operations to be performed. If no appropriate $q$ is found, then this search is repeated for a larger $n$.

The security level of the parameter triple $(q, n, \sigma)$ can be computed via the LWE-estimator of Albrecht et al. [1]. To find $q$ that guarantees decryption correctness for the output of a given homomorphic circuit, one can use the following heuristic analysis with fixed $n$ and $\sigma$.

The decryption correctness is closely related to the size of the ciphertext invariant noise. The *invariant noise* of a ciphertext $\mathtt{ct} = (c_0, c_1)$ encrypting a plaintext $\mathtt{msg} \in R_{X^m + b}$ is an element $v \in K$ with the smallest canonical norm such that

$$\frac{X^m + b}{q} \cdot [c_0 + c_1 \cdot s]_q = \mathtt{msg} + v + g \cdot (X^m + b)$$

for some $g \in R$. It is easy to see that $\mathtt{Decrypt}$ returns $\mathtt{msg}$ if $|v|_\infty < 1/2$, i.e. the rounding step removes $v$. Since $|v|_\infty \leq \|v\|^{\mathrm{can}}$, one can switch to the heuristic analysis of the canonical norm to show that $\|v\|^{\mathrm{can}} < 1/2$.

*Fresh Noise Heuristic* [3]. Let $\mathtt{ct}$ be a fresh ciphertext $\mathtt{ct} = \mathtt{Encrypt}(\mathtt{pk}, \mathtt{msg})$, then the invariant noise $v$ of $\mathtt{ct}$ is bounded with very high probability by

$$\|v\|^{\mathrm{can}} \leq \frac{b+1}{q} \left( \|\mathtt{msg}\|^{\mathrm{can}} \cdot n\sqrt{3n} + 2\sigma\sqrt{12n^2 + 9n} \right). \tag{1}$$

Since the right-hand side should be smaller than $1/2$, the minimal ciphertext modulus supporting the decryption correctness should satisfy $q \in \Omega\left(b^2 n\sqrt{n}\right)$.

Homomorphic arithmetic operations increase the invariant noise. It can be easily seen that homomorphic addition results in an additive noise growth, whereas homomorphic multiplication induces a linear growth as shown below.

*Multiplication Noise Heuristic* [3]. Let $\mathtt{ct}(\mathtt{msg}, v)$ be a ciphertext encrypting message $\mathtt{msg} \in R_{X^m + b}$ with invariant noise $v$. Given two ciphertexts $\mathtt{ct}_1 = \mathtt{ct}(\mathtt{msg}_1, v_1)$ and $\mathtt{ct}_1 = \mathtt{ct}(\mathtt{msg}_2, v_2)$, the function $\mathtt{Mul}(\mathtt{ct}_1, \mathtt{ct}_2, \mathtt{rlk})$ outputs a ciphertext $\mathtt{ct}_{\mathtt{Mul}} = \mathtt{ct}(\mathtt{msg}_1 \cdot \mathtt{msg}_2, v_{\mathtt{Mul}})$ with

$$\|v_{\mathtt{Mul}}\|^{\mathrm{can}} \leq (b+1)\sqrt{3n + 2n^2} \left(\|v_1\|^{\mathrm{can}} + \|v_2\|^{\mathrm{can}}\right) + 3\|v_1\|^{\mathrm{can}}\|v_2\|^{\mathrm{can}}$$
$$\frac{b+1}{q}\sqrt{3n + 2n^2 + 4n^3/3} + \frac{b+1}{q}\sigma n w \sqrt{3(\ell+1)} \tag{2}$$

with very high probability. Let $v_{\mathtt{Mul}}^L$ be an invariant noise after $L$ multiplicative levels. If $L = 0$, then it follows from (1) and the additive noise growth after homomorphic addition that $\left\|v_{\mathtt{Mul}}^0\right\|^{\mathrm{can}} \in O\left(b^2 n\sqrt{n}/q\right)$. Computing $\left\|v_{\mathtt{Mul}}^1\right\|^{\mathrm{can}}$, one can notice that the first term of the right-hand side in (2) is dominant and thus $\left\|v_{\text{Mul}}^1\right\|^{\text{can}} \in O\left(bnv_{\text{Mul}}^0\right)$, or $\left\|v_{\text{Mul}}^1\right\|^{\text{can}} \in O\left(b^3n^2\sqrt{n}/q\right)$. By induction, we obtain

$$\left\|v_{\text{Mul}}^L\right\|^{\text{can}} \in O\left(\frac{b^{L+2}n^{L+1}\sqrt{n}}{q}\right).$$

Given that $\left\|v_{\text{Mul}}^L\right\|^{\text{can}}$ should be less than $1/2$ to guarantee the decryption correctness, the ciphertext modulus should satisfy

$$q \in \Omega\left(b^{L+2}n^{L+1}\sqrt{n}\right). \tag{3}$$

## 5  Encoding of Packed Values into FV

To employ the HEAAN packing method in the FV scheme, we need to map elements of $R'$ to the plaintext ring $R_{X^m+b}$. For this purpose, we resort to the encoding algorithm of Bootland et al. [3], which maps cyclotomic integers from $R' = \mathbb{Z}[\zeta_{2m}]$ to the plaintext space $R_{X^m+b}$ isomorphic to $\mathbb{Z}[X]/(X^n + 1, X^m + b)$. A similar technique was given by Chen et al. [4] for the plaintext modulus $X + b$.

Let $\hat{a} \in \mathbb{Z}/(b^{n/m}+1)\mathbb{Z}$ be the representative of an integer $a$ modulo $b^{n/m}+1$ in the symmetric interval $\left[-(b^{n/m}+1)/2, (b^{n/m}+1)/2\right)$. Assume that $\hat{b} = \hat{a}^m$ for some $\alpha$. This assumption might seem too strong for the reader but there exist special forms of $b$ such that $\hat{a}$ is efficiently computable; we discuss them later in this section. Since $b$ is co-prime to $b^{n/m}+1$, there exist the multiplicative inverse of $\hat{a}$, denoted $\hat{\beta}$. This implies that $\beta X$ is a primitive $2m$-th root of unity in $R_{X^m+b}$, namely $(\hat{\beta}X)^m = \hat{a}^{-m}X^m = \hat{b}^{-1}X^m = -1$. Therefore, the map $\zeta_{2m} \mapsto \hat{\beta}X$ induces the following ring homomorphism

$$\mathbb{Z}[\zeta_{2m}] \to R_{X^m+b} : \quad \sum_{i=0}^{m-1} a_i\zeta_{2m}^i \mapsto \sum_{i=0}^{m-1} \hat{a}_i\hat{\beta}^iX^i. \tag{4}$$

This map outputs polynomials of degree less than $m$ with coefficients exponential in $b$. Such large coefficients drastically increase the invariant noise as you can see in (1). Therefore, the next step is to switch to another representative modulo $X^m + b$ by spreading this polynomial across the power range $1, X, \ldots, X^{n-1}$ while making the plaintext coefficients smaller. It can be done by computing the balanced $b$-ary expansion of each coefficient and then mapping powers of $b$ to corresponding powers of $-X^m$. The result is then lifted to $R = \mathbb{Z}[X]/(X^n + 1)$ and fed to the FV scheme.

The homomorphism (4) is surjective with kernel $\left(b^{n/m}+1\right)$. Therefore, it induces an isomorphism between cyclotomic integers from $\mathbb{Z}[\zeta_{2m}]/\left(b^{n/m}+1\right)$ and $R_{X^m+b}$; thus, the encoding and the decoding maps are well defined. To decode an element $c \in R_{X^m+b}$, we first compute $c' = c \bmod (X^m + b)$ and then map $X$ to $\hat{\alpha} \cdot \zeta_{2m}$, which results in

$$c' = \sum_{i=0}^{m-1} \hat{c}_iX^i \mapsto \sum_{i=0}^{m-1} \hat{c}_i\hat{\alpha}^i\zeta_{2m}^i.$$

As a result, the homomorphism defined by (4) serves as an encoding map from cyclotomic integers to the plaintext space $R_{X^m+b}$. Using this map together with the `Pack` function from Sect. 3, we can encrypt $m/2$ complex numbers into FV without using previously known packing techniques based on the Chinese Remainder Theorem [24].

The advantage of this encoding technique is that the unused part of the plaintext space coming from the large dimension $n$ is transformed into a larger integral modulus, reflected in the exponent $n/m$. However, the encoding algorithm of HEAAN, where $\zeta_{2m}$ is mapped to $X^{n/m}$, is not surjective as plaintexts belong to an $m$-dimensional subspace of the plaintext space. Thus, a large part of the plaintext space remains unused.

## 5.1 Choice of $b$

As mentioned earlier, the encoding algorithm assumes that $b$ is an $m$-th power residue modulo $b^{n/m} + 1$. Moreover, its $m$-th root $\alpha$ is efficiently computable. When $m$ is a positive power of 2, finding $\alpha$ is at least as hard as finding a square root of $b$. Since factoring $b^{n/m} + 1$ and extracting square roots modulo $b^{n/m} + 1$ are computationally equivalent [20], an efficient algorithm for computing $\alpha$ implies the existence of an efficient factoring algorithm for generalized Fermat numbers of the form $b^{2^k} + 1$. Unfortunately, no efficient prime factorization algorithm for these numbers is found.

There exists a specific $b$ whose $m$-th roots are efficiently computable. In particular, if $b = 2^{m/2}$ then $\alpha$ must be congruent to the square root of 2 modulo $b^{n/m} + 1 = 2^{n/2} + 1$. In this case, it is easy to verify that $\alpha = 2^{n/8} \left(2^{n/4} - 1\right)$. Unfortunately, such $b$ is exponential in $m$, so invariant noise grows exponentially faster as the number of packing slots increases. Therefore, fewer homomorphic operations are affordable when the packing capacity increases.

Another interesting choice of $b$ is when $b < 2^{m/2}$ and $b^{n/m} + 1$ becomes a generalized Fermat prime. Thus, $\alpha$ can be efficiently computed by the Tonelli-Shanks algorithm [23]. Note that in this case $b$ must be even, or $b = 2^k c$ for some $k > 0$ and odd $c$. It follows from [3, Lemma 1] that if $b$ is an $m$-th power residue, then $2n$ divides $b^{n/m} = 2^{kn/m} c^{n/m}$. As a result, $n$ should divide $2^{kn/m-1}$. Since $n$ is a power of two, we obtain that $\log_2 n \leq kn/m - 1$. Given this constraint and the fact that $n/m$ is at most $2^{16}$ in practice, we can find numerous suitable bases $b$ of generalized Fermat primes, see Table 6 in Appendix A.

To be decoded correctly, a cyclotomic integer $a$ from $\mathbb{Z}[\zeta_{2m}]$ should have an infinity norm bounded as follows

$$|a|_\infty < \frac{b^{n/m} + 1}{2}. \tag{5}$$

Let $a_i \in \mathbb{Z}[\zeta_{2m}]$ be output values of `Pack`$(\mathbf{z}_i)$ for complex vectors $\mathbf{z}_i \in \mathbb{C}^{m/2}$ with $|\mathbf{z}_i|_\infty \leq B$ for some $B$. According to Sect. 3, the infinity norm of $a_i$ represented in the power basis of $\mathbb{Z}[\zeta_{2m}]$ is bounded by

$$|a_i|_\infty = \left\| \left[ \frac{\Delta}{m} \cdot \Sigma^{-1} \mathbf{z}_i \right] \right\|_\infty \leq \Delta B + \frac{1}{2}. \tag{6}$$

It follows from Lemma 1 that the packing scale $\Delta$ must be at least $\frac{pm}{2} + \varepsilon$ for small $\varepsilon > 0$ to pack $\mathbf{z}_i$ with precision $p$. Hence, the infinity norm of $a_i$ has the following upper bound $|a_i|_\infty \leq V = \left( \frac{pm}{2} + \varepsilon \right) \cdot B + \frac{1}{2}$. For any $a_i, a_j$ it holds $|a_i a_j|_\infty \leq mV^2$. It follows by induction that after $L$ multiplicative levels the infinity norm increases up to $m^{2^L-1}V^{2^L}$. From the decoding requirement (5) we obtain that $m^{2^L-1}V^{2^L}$ must be smaller than $\frac{b^{n/m}+1}{2}$, which leads to $b \in \Omega\left( m^{\frac{m}{n}(2^{L+1}-1)} \cdot (pB)^{\frac{m}{n} \cdot 2^L} \right)$. Substituting this estimation into (3), we can see how the ciphertext modulus depends on the ring dimension $n$, the packing capacity $m$, the input precision $p$, the input bound $B$ and the circuit depth $L$, namely

$$q \in \Omega\left( m^{\frac{m}{n}(2^{L+1}-1)(L+2)} \cdot (pB)^{\frac{m}{n}2^L(L+2)} \cdot n^{L+1}\sqrt{n} \right). \tag{7}$$

## 6     Asymptotic Comparison with HEAAN

We start the comparison of our scheme with HEAAN by estimating how large should be the ciphertext modulus in this scheme to support correct evaluation of given circuits. Let us first describe the HEAAN scheme as defined in [5].

Let $q_L > \cdots > q_\ell > \cdots > q_0$ be a ladder of ciphertext moduli. Take a large integer $P \simeq q_L$. Let $h$ be a positive integer. The key distribution $\chi_k$ draws random elements from $R$ with ternary coefficients and Hamming weight $h$.

The basic encryption functions of HEAAN are the following:

- KeyGen($1^n$): Let $s \leftarrow \chi_k$ and $e, e' \leftarrow \chi_e$. Sample uniformly random $a \in R_{q_L}$ and $a' \in R_{P \cdot q_L}$. Output
  - the secret key $\mathsf{sk} = s$,
  - the public key $\mathsf{pk} = \left( [-a \cdot s + e]_{q_L}, a \right)$,
  - the evaluation key $\mathsf{rlk} = \left( [-a' \cdot s + e' + P \cdot s^2]_{P \cdot q_L}, a' \right)$.
- Encrypt ($\mathsf{pk}, \mathsf{msg} \in R_{q_L}$): Sample $u \leftarrow \chi_k$ and $e_0, e_1 \leftarrow \chi_e$. Set $p_0 = \mathsf{pk}[0]$, $p_1 = \mathsf{pk}[1]$ and output $\mathsf{ct} = (c_0, c_1)$ where

$$c_0 = [\mathsf{msg} + p_0 \cdot u + e_0]_{q_L}, \qquad c_1 = [p_1 \cdot u + e_1]_{q_L}.$$

- Decrypt ($\mathsf{sk}, \mathsf{ct}$): Return $\mathsf{msg}' = [c_0 + c_1 \cdot s]_{q_L}$.

To encode a cyclotomic integer $a \in \mathbb{Z}[\zeta_{2m}]$ with $|a|_\infty < q_L/2$, we embed $a$ to $R_{q_L}$ using the map $\zeta_{2m} \mapsto X^{n/m}$ and the reduction modulo $q_L$. Notice that the decryption algorithm outputs $\mathsf{msg}' = \mathsf{msg} + e'$ with a noisy component $e' = e_0 + e_1 s + ue$. Therefore, to encrypt a complex vector $\mathbf{z} \in \mathbb{C}^{m/2}$ with the input precision $p$ in HEAAN, the packing scale $\Delta$ must be larger than in Lemma 1 to compensate a precision loss induced by this noise. Let $\mathbf{z}' = \texttt{Unpack}(\texttt{Decrypt}(\texttt{Encrypt}(\texttt{Pack}(\mathbf{z}))))$, then, following the reasoning of Lemma 1, we obtain

$$|\mathbf{z} - \mathbf{z}'|_\infty = \max_i \left| \frac{1}{\Delta} \sum_{k=0}^{m-1} (e_k + e'_k) \cdot \zeta_{2m}^{ik} \right| \leq \frac{m}{2\Delta} + \frac{mr}{\Delta}$$

where $|e'|_\infty \leq r \in O(n)$. To have $|\mathbf{z} - \mathbf{z}'|_\infty < 1/p$, the packing scale $\Delta$ must then satisfy the following bound

$$\Delta > mp\left(\frac{1}{2} + r\right), \tag{8}$$

which results in $\Delta \in \Omega(mpn)$.

## 6.1 Homomorphic Operations

In HEAAN, homomorphic operations can output ciphertexts with a smaller ciphertext modulus in comparison to their input. Therefore, ciphertext moduli of input ciphertexts lie between $q_0$ and $q_L$. Below we assume that ciphertexts $\texttt{ct}_1$ and $\texttt{ct}_2$ are given modulo $q_\ell$. The basic homomorphic operations such as addition and multiplication are defined as follows.

- $\texttt{Add}(\texttt{ct}_0, \texttt{ct}_1)$: Return $\texttt{ct}_{\texttt{Add}} = \left( [\texttt{ct}_0[0] + \texttt{ct}_1[0]]_{q_\ell}, [\texttt{ct}_0[1] + \texttt{ct}_1[1]]_{q_\ell} \right)$.
- $\texttt{BasicMul}(\texttt{ct}_0, \texttt{ct}_1)$: Return $\texttt{ct}_{\texttt{BasicMul}} = (c_0, c_1, c_2)$ where

$$c_0 = [\texttt{ct}_0[0] \cdot \texttt{ct}_1[0]]_{q_\ell}, \quad c_1 = [\texttt{ct}_0[0] \cdot \texttt{ct}_1[1] + \texttt{ct}_0[1] \cdot \texttt{ct}_1[0]]_{q_\ell},$$
$$c_2 = [\texttt{ct}_0[1] \cdot \texttt{ct}_1[1]]_{q_\ell}.$$

- $\texttt{Relin}(\texttt{ct}_{\texttt{BasicMul}}, \texttt{rlk})$: Output $c_{\texttt{Relin}} = (c'_0, c'_1)$ where

$$c'_0 = \left[ c_0 + \lfloor P^{-1} \cdot c_2 \cdot \texttt{rlk}[0] \rceil \right]_{q_\ell}, \quad c'_1 = \left[ c_1 + \lfloor P^{-1} \cdot c_2 \cdot \texttt{rlk}[1] \rceil \right]_{q_\ell}$$

- $\texttt{Mul}(\texttt{ct}_0, \texttt{ct}_1, \texttt{rlk})$: Return $\texttt{ct}_{\texttt{Mul}} = (c'_0, c'_1) = \texttt{Relin}(\texttt{BasicMul}(\texttt{ct}_0, \texttt{ct}_1), \texttt{rlk})$.

In addition, HEAAN has a special function called rescaling, which imitates rounding. Rescaling discards least significant bits of a given ciphertext and reduces the ciphertext modulus.

- $\texttt{Rescale}(\texttt{ct}, \ell, \ell')$: Output $\texttt{ct}_{\texttt{Rescale}} = \left( \lfloor \frac{q_{\ell'}}{q_\ell} c_0 \rceil, \lfloor \frac{q_{\ell'}}{q_\ell} c_1 \rceil \right) \in R_{q_{\ell'}}^2$.

Note that if the input ciphertext $\texttt{ct}$ encrypts a plaintext $\texttt{msg}$, then $\texttt{ct}_{\texttt{Rescale}}$ is a valid encryption of $(q_{\ell'}/q_\ell) \cdot \texttt{msg}$. Hence, rescaling can help to control the coefficient size of plaintexts, especially after multiplication. Let $\texttt{ct}_0$ and $\texttt{ct}_1$ be ciphertexts of two complex vectors $\mathbf{z}_1$ and $\mathbf{z}_2$ packed with scale $\Delta$. The product of these ciphertexts is an encryption of the Hadamard product $\mathbf{z} = \mathbf{z}_1 \odot \mathbf{z}_2$ with scale $\Delta^2$. If $q_{\ell'}/q_\ell \simeq \Delta$, then $\texttt{Rescale}(\texttt{ct})$ outputs a ciphertext, which again encrypts $\mathbf{z}$ but with packing scale $\Delta$. As a result, the unpacking scale $\Delta'$ in HEAAN can be equal to $\Delta$ for any circuit, whereas in our scheme the depth of a circuit should be known to set $\Delta'$ to a correct power of $\Delta$.

## 6.2  Ciphertext Size

Let $\mathsf{msg}_i$ be plaintext messages encoding complex vectors $\mathbf{z}_i \in \mathbb{C}^{m/2}$ with $|\mathbf{z}_i|_\infty \leq B$ for some $B$. To be decrypted and then decoded correctly, a plaintext should have an infinity norm smaller than $q_0/2$. As in Sect. 4, we switch to the canonical norm in order to analyze how plaintexts approach this bound. The canonical norm of each $\mathsf{msg}_i$ is bounded by $|\Delta\mathbf{z}_i|_\infty + \|e\|^{\mathrm{can}} = \Delta B + m/2$ where $e$ is the rounding error. Let $V = \Delta B + m/2$.

Assume that $q_\ell/q_{\ell-1} \simeq \Delta$ for any $\ell \in [L]$. After multiplication and rescaling we obtain a ciphertext encrypting a plaintext $\mathsf{msg}$ such that $\|\mathsf{msg}\|^{\mathrm{can}} \leq \frac{(V+\|E_e\|^{\mathrm{can}})^2}{\Delta} + \|E_r\|^{\mathrm{can}}$ where $E_e$ is the encryption noise and $E_r$ is the noise introduced by $\mathtt{Relin}$ and $\mathtt{Rescale}$. Since $\|E_e\|^{\mathrm{can}}, \|E_r\|^{\mathrm{can}} \in O(n)$ according to [5, Lemmas 1–3], it follows from (8) that $\|\mathsf{msg}\|^{\mathrm{can}} \in O(\Delta B^2)$. Hence, after $L$ multiplicative levels the canonical norm of a resulting plaintext satisfies $\|\mathsf{msg}\|^{\mathrm{can}} \in O\left(\Delta B^{2^L}\right)$. As $\|\mathsf{msg}\|^{\mathrm{can}}$ should be smaller than $q_0/2$, we obtain that $q_0 \in \Omega\left(\Delta B^{2^L}\right)$. Since rescaling decreases the ciphertext modulus $L$ times to reach $q_0$, the initial ciphertext modulus should be set to $q_L \simeq q_0 \cdot \Delta^L$. Thus, $q_L \in \Omega\left(\Delta^{L+1} B^{2^L}\right)$ and (8) yields $q_L \in \Omega\left(m^{L+1} \cdot p^{L+1} \cdot B^{2^L} \cdot n^{L+1}\right)$. Comparing the above estimation with its analog for our scheme, we can see that if $\frac{m}{n} = \frac{1}{2^{L+1}}$, then (7) turns into $q \in \Omega\left(m^{(L+2)\left(1-\frac{1}{2^{L+1}}\right)} \cdot (pB)^{\frac{L+2}{2}} \cdot n^{L+1}\sqrt{n}\right)$. It implies that when $B > (m\sqrt{n})^{1/2^{L-1}}$, our scheme requires a smaller ciphertext modulus. More specifically, our approach results in a smaller memory overhead in comparison to $\mathtt{HEAAN}$ in the following cases:

- in shallow circuits with large ratios between the packing capacity and the dimension of $R$, namely $m/n \leq 1/4$;
- in deep circuits with a small packing capacity, i.e. $m = n/2^{L+1}$.

## 7  Practical Comparison with $\mathtt{HEAAN}$

In this section we demonstrate the efficiency of our scheme in comparison to the $\mathtt{HEAAN}$ scheme. In particular, we homomorphically computed the functions presented in [5, Section 5] including power functions, the exponential function and the logistic regression function. In addition, we performed experiments with the sine function.

We implemented our scheme and two versions of $\mathtt{HEAAN}$ in SageMath [25]. The implementation script can be found at https://github.com/iliailia/heaan-vs-fv-sage. One version of $\mathtt{HEAAN}$ corresponds to the original scheme given in [5] with sparse secret keys and the relinearization method described in Sect. 6.1. While these features can speed up computations, they introduce a larger memory overhead than in our scheme as larger encryption parameters are needed to support the same security level. To perform a fair comparison with our scheme, we implemented a second variant of $\mathtt{HEAAN}$, denoted $\mathtt{HEAAN}^*$, without sparse secret keys and with the same relinearization method (see Sect. 4.1) as in our scheme.

For all the implemented schemes we found minimal encryption parameters that support both correct computation of the above functions and a security level of at least 128 bits. To achieve this security level we set the parameters of the original HEAAN scheme according to the recent recommendations for sparse-secret RLWE [8]. Namely, we set the sparsity parameter $h = 128$. The standard deviation $\sigma$ of the error distribution $\chi_e$ is set to 3.19.

## 7.1 Non-polynomial Functions: Logistic Regression, Sine and Exponential Function

**Table 1.** The ciphertext size and the running time to compute the logistic function in the interval $[-2.1, 2.1]$.

| #slots | 1 | 2 | $2^2$ | $2^3$ | $2^4$ | $2^5$ | $2^6$ | $2^7$ | $2^8$ | $2^9$ |
|---|---|---|---|---|---|---|---|---|---|---|
| Our scheme | | | | | | | | | | |
| Size, KB | 94 | 97 | 104 | 228 | 238 | 238 | 238 | 244 | 334 | 704 |
| Time, sec | 6.04 | 6.75 | 6.21 | 13.52 | 12.92 | 12.76 | 12.80 | 12.99 | 18.16 | 38.81 |
| HEAAN | | | | | | | | | | |
| Size, KB | 448 | 464 | 476 | 492 | 512 | 528 | 548 | 568 | 584 | 604 |
| Time, sec | 18.22 | 18.18 | 17.61 | 17.97 | 18.76 | 18.97 | 18.24 | 18.09 | 18.28 | 18.89 |
| HEAAN* | | | | | | | | | | |
| Size, KB | 274 | 284 | 292 | 302 | 312 | 322 | 332 | 342 | 352 | 362 |
| Time, sec | 14.48 | 14.45 | 14.28 | 14.46 | 14.52 | 16.98 | 18.07 | 18.14 | 18.00 | 18.24 |

**Table 2.** The ciphertext size and the running time to compute the sine in the interval $[-\pi, \pi]$.

| #slots | 1 | 2 | $2^2$ | $2^3$ | $2^4$ | $2^5$ | $2^6$ | $2^7$ | $2^8$ | $2^9$ | $2^{10}$ | $2^{11}$ |
|---|---|---|---|---|---|---|---|---|---|---|---|---|
| Our scheme | | | | | | | | | | | | |
| Size, KB | 94 | 97 | 104 | 228 | 238 | 238 | 238 | 264 | 380 | 796 | 1292 | 2680 |
| Time, sec | 5.85 | 6.52 | 6.25 | 12.34 | 13.22 | 12.83 | 12.70 | 14.63 | 18.75 | 43.48 | 73.84 | 155.66 |
| HEAAN | | | | | | | | | | | | |
| Size, KB | 564 | 580 | 600 | 620 | 640 | 660 | 680 | 1400 | 1440 | 1480 | 1520 | 1560 |
| Time, sec | 18.14 | 18.13 | 18.25 | 18.55 | 19.67 | 19.58 | 19.56 | 40.21 | 40.40 | 44.57 | 47.20 | 50.27 |
| HEAAN* | | | | | | | | | | | | |
| Size, KB | 310 | 320 | 330 | 340 | 350 | 360 | 370 | 380 | 390 | 400 | 410 | 420 |
| Time, sec | 14.52 | 16.79 | 16.93 | 17.07 | 17.62 | 17.58 | 16.80 | 17.23 | 17.49 | 19.20 | 19.89 | 21.74 |

**Table 3.** The ciphertext size and the running time to compute $e^x$ in the interval $[-2.3, 2.3]$.

| #slots | 1 | 2 | $2^2$ | $2^3$ | $2^4$ | $2^5$ | $2^6$ | $2^7$ | $2^8$ | $2^9$ | $2^{10}$ |
|---|---|---|---|---|---|---|---|---|---|---|---|
| Our scheme | | | | | | | | | | | |
| Size, KB | 87 | 89 | 95 | 105 | 105 | 105 | 107 | 224 | 310 | 652 | 1044 |
| Time, sec | 6.42 | 6.00 | 5.83 | 6.92 | 6.85 | 6.68 | 7.07 | 14.73 | 18.23 | 43.88 | 68.05 |
| HEAAN | | | | | | | | | | | |
| Size, KB | 480 | 500 | 520 | 540 | 560 | 580 | 600 | 620 | 640 | 660 | 680 |
| Time, sec | 19.63 | 20.02 | 20.20 | 20.30 | 20.25 | 20.41 | 20.53 | 20.76 | 21.50 | 21.87 | 23.74 |
| HEAAN* | | | | | | | | | | | |
| Size, KB | 290 | 300 | 310 | 320 | 330 | 340 | 350 | 360 | 370 | 380 | 390 |
| Time, sec | 15.57 | 15.43 | 15.66 | 18.22 | 18.64 | 18.67 | 18.74 | 18.78 | 18.65 | 19.71 | 20.76 |

As in [5], we approximate the logistic function $1/(1 + e^{-x})$ and the sine with Maclaurin series of degree 9. The exponential function $e^x$ is evaluated via its Maclaurin series of degree 8. These approximations are accurate up to 7 bits of binary precision in $[-2.1, 2.1]$ for the logistic regression, $[-\pi, \pi]$ for the sine function and $[-2.3, 2.3]$ for the exponential function.

We conducted experiments with encryption and packing parameters that support homomorphic evaluation of the above series within 7 bits of binary precision. More detailed description of these parameters is given in Appendix B. The results of our experiments are presented in Tables 1–2. In particular, our scheme needs 4–6 times and around 3 times less memory than HEAAN and HEAAN*, respectively, to perform computations on a small number of data slots. This advantage is declining with an increasing number of slots as predicted by the theoretical estimations of Sect. 6. Starting from only 512–2048 packing slots both versions of HEAAN need less memory than our scheme.

## 7.2 Power Functions

We also computed two simple polynomial functions $x^{16}$ and $x^2$ with input values taken from $[-2.1, 2.1]$ and $(-2^{15}, 2^{15})$, respectively. As for non-linear functions we aim to achieve 7 bits of binary precision for output values.

As seen in Tables 5 and 4, our scheme with a small number of slots requires around 18 and 4 times less memory than HEAAN and HEAAN*, respectively. However, the memory overhead of our method grows exponentially with the number of slots. The maximal number of slots where our scheme still outperforms HEAAN is 512 for $x^{16}$ and 2048 for $x^2$. Comparing with HEAAN*, these numbers are 256 for $x^{16}$ and 1024 for $x^2$.

**Table 4.** The ciphertext size and the running time to compute $x^2$ in the interval $(-2^{15}, 2^{15})$.

| #slots | 1 | 2 | $2^2$ | $2^3$ | $2^4$ | $2^5$ | $2^6$ | $2^7$ | $2^8$ | $2^9$ | $2^{10}$ | $2^{11}$ | $2^{12}$ |
|---|---|---|---|---|---|---|---|---|---|---|---|---|---|
| Our scheme | | | | | | | | | | | | | |
| Size, KB | 24 | 24.5 | 25.5 | 25.5 | 25.5 | 25.5 | 26 | 54 | 66 | 102 | 212 | 360 | 740 |
| Time, sec | 0.22 | 0.20 | 0.19 | 0.19 | 0.19 | 0.19 | 0.20 | 0.44 | 0.62 | 0.80 | 1.71 | 2.57 | 4.93 |
| HEAAN | | | | | | | | | | | | | |
| Size, KB | 388 | 396 | 404 | 412 | 420 | 428 | 436 | 444 | 452 | 460 | 468 | 476 | 484 |
| Time, sec | 1.47 | 1.41 | 1.39 | 1.47 | 1.47 | 1.48 | 1.42 | 1.49 | 1.47 | 1.50 | 1.58 | 1.68 | 1.98 |
| HEAAN* | | | | | | | | | | | | | |
| Size, KB | 97 | 99 | 101 | 103 | 105 | 107 | 109 | 222 | 226 | 230 | 234 | 238 | 242 |
| Time, sec | 0.60 | 0.61 | 0.61 | 0.61 | 0.61 | 0.60 | 0.61 | 1.33 | 1.32 | 1.35 | 1.43 | 1.60 | 1.79 |

**Table 5.** The ciphertext size and the running time to compute $x^{16}$ in the interval $[-2.1, 2.1]$.

| #slots | 1 | 2 | $2^2$ | $2^3$ | $2^4$ | $2^5$ | $2^6$ | $2^7$ | $2^8$ | $2^9$ | $2^{10}$ |
|---|---|---|---|---|---|---|---|---|---|---|---|
| Our scheme | | | | | | | | | | | |
| Size, KB | 95 | 98 | 105 | 230 | 242 | 242 | 260 | 360 | 756 | 1176 | 2496 |
| Time, sec | 2.88 | 3.08 | 3.13 | 6.53 | 6.37 | 6.56 | 7.70 | 8.88 | 19.15 | 33.42 | 70.72 |
| HEAAN | | | | | | | | | | | |
| Size, KB | 1672 | 1712 | 1752 | 1792 | 1832 | 1872 | 1912 | 1952 | 1992 | 2032 | 2072 |
| Time, sec | 20.76 | 20.38 | 20.57 | 20.70 | 20.45 | 20.96 | 21.02 | 21.91 | 22.06 | 23.56 | 23.70 |
| HEAAN* | | | | | | | | | | | |
| Size, KB | 408 | 418 | 428 | 876 | 896 | 916 | 936 | 956 | 976 | 996 | 1016 |
| Time, sec | 8.42 | 8.43 | 8.66 | 18.45 | 18.98 | 19.73 | 19.53 | 20.29 | 20.95 | 20.33 | 22.46 |

## 8 Conclusion

While the HEAAN scheme has achieved significant success in recent years, especially in privacy-preserving machine learning applications, in many cases computations are not as highly parallelizable as would be optimal for the HEAAN scheme. In this work we have demonstrated how in these cases an approach generalizing that of Bootland et al. and Chen et al. can yield significant performance improvements in terms of encryption parameter sizes and subsequently in ciphertext sizes. This can be particularly important when using homomorphic encryption in low-latency applications, where communication complexity quickly becomes a bottleneck.

**Acknowledgements.** The second author started this work while being an intern at Microsoft Research. He is also supported by a Junior Postdoctoral Fellowship from the Research Foundation – Flanders (FWO) and by CyberSecurity Research Flanders with reference number VR20192203.

# A    Examples of $b$

As shown in Sect. 5, the plaintext space parameter $b$ must be an $m$th power residue modulo $b^{n/m} + 1$ and its $m$ root must be efficiently computable to allow the HEAAN encoding of complex numbers. Here we present a collection of these parameters for given practical choices of the ring dimension $n$ and the packing capacity $m$.

**Table 6.** Examples of $b$ such that $b$ is an $m$-th power residue modulo $b^{n/m} + 1$ for practical choices of $m$ and $n$. Numbers in parentheses are equal to $\left\lfloor \log_2(b^{n/m} + 1) \right\rfloor$, which is the maximal coefficient size of HEAAN encodings. For each $b$ we precomputed its $m$-th root using several calls of the Tonelli-Shanks algorithm (square_root_mod_prime) in SageMath.

| $m$ | $n$ | | | | | |
|---|---|---|---|---|---|---|
| | $2^{11}$ | $2^{12}$ | $2^{13}$ | $2^{14}$ | $2^{15}$ | $2^{16}$ |
| 2 | 2 | 2 | 2 | 2 | 2 | 2 |
| | (1024) | (2048) | (4096) | (8192) | (16384) | (32768) |
| $2^2$ | 4 | 4 | 4 | 4 | 4 | 4 |
| | (1024) | (2048) | (4096) | (8192) | (16384) | (32768) |
| $2^3$ | 16 | 16 | 16 | 16 | 16 | 16 |
| | (1024) | (2048) | (4096) | (8192) | (16384) | (32768) |
| $2^4$ | 120 | 256 | 46 | 256 | 150 | 256 |
| | (884) | (2048) | (2828) | (8192) | (14804) | (32768) |
| $2^5$ | 274 | 120 | 278 | 46 | 824 | 150 |
| | (518) | (884) | (2078) | (2828) | (9918) | (14804) |
| $2^6$ | 884 | 274 | 120 | 278 | 46 | 824 |
| | (313) | (518) | (884) | (2078) | (2828) | (9918) |
| $2^7$ | 984 | 884 | 274 | 120 | 278 | 46 |
| | (159) | (313) | (518) | (884) | (2078) | (2828) |
| $2^8$ | 1028 | 984 | 884 | 274 | 120 | 278 |
| | (80) | (159) | (313) | (518) | (884) | (2078) |
| $2^9$ | 9872 | 1028 | 984 | 884 | 274 | 120 |
| | (53) | (80) | (159) | (313) | (518) | (884) |
| $2^{10}$ | 9600 | 9872 | 1028 | 984 | 884 | 274 |
| | (26) | (53) | (80) | (159) | (313) | (518) |
| $2^{11}$ | $2^{15}$ | 9600 | 9872 | 1028 | 984 | 884 |
| | (16) | (26) | (53) | (80) | (159) | (313) |
| $2^{12}$ | x | $2^{15}$ | 9600 | 9872 | 1028 | 984 |
| | | (16) | (26) | (53) | (80) | (159) |

# B    Results of experiments

The following tables present the detailed encoding and encryption parameters used in the experiments conducted in Sect. 7. This data is the full version of Tables 1, 2, 3, 4 and 5 from Sect. 7. In all the tables, $\Delta$ denotes the packing scale, $n$ is the dimension of the cyclotomic ring $R$ and $b$ is the constant term of the plaintext modulus. The total running time is averaged over 10 runs (Tables 7, 8, 9, 10 and 11).

**Table 7.** Encryption parameters to compute the logistic function in the interval $[-2.1, 2.1]$. The (*) symbol indicates that the maximal number of slots supported by the plaintext space is $2^6$ for our scheme.

| #slots | 1 | 2 | $2^2$ | $2^3$ | $2^4(*)$ | $2^5(*)$ | $2^6$ | $2^7$ | $2^8$ | $2^9$ |
|---|---|---|---|---|---|---|---|---|---|---|
| **Our scheme** | | | | | | | | | | |
| $\Delta$ | $2^{16}$ | $2^{17}$ | $2^{18}$ | $2^{19}$ | $2^{20}$ | $2^{21}$ | $2^{22}$ | $2^{23}$ | $2^{24}$ | $2^{25}$ |
| $n$ | $2^{12}$ | $2^{12}$ | $2^{12}$ | $2^{13}$ | $2^{13}$ | $2^{13}$ | $2^{13}$ | $2^{13}$ | $2^{13}$ | $2^{14}$ |
| $\log q$ | 94 | 97 | 104 | 114 | 119 | 119 | 119 | 122 | 167 | 176 |
| b | 2 | 4 | 16 | 46 | 102 | 102 | 102 | 156 | 3.3e4 | 5.1e4 |
| Size, KB | 94 | 97 | 104 | 228 | 238 | 238 | 238 | 244 | 334 | 704 |
| Time, sec | 6.04 | 6.75 | 6.21 | 13.52 | 12.92 | 12.76 | 12.80 | 12.99 | 18.16 | 38.81 |
| **HEAAN** | | | | | | | | | | |
| $\Delta$ | $2^{21}$ | $2^{22}$ | $2^{23}$ | $2^{24}$ | $2^{25}$ | $2^{26}$ | $2^{27}$ | $2^{28}$ | $2^{29}$ | $2^{30}$ |
| $n$ | $2^{14}$ | $2^{14}$ | $2^{14}$ | $2^{14}$ | $2^{14}$ | $2^{14}$ | $2^{14}$ | $2^{14}$ | $2^{14}$ | $2^{14}$ |
| $\log q_L$ | 112 | 116 | 119 | 123 | 128 | 132 | 137 | 142 | 146 | 151 |
| Size, KB | 448 | 464 | 476 | 492 | 512 | 528 | 548 | 568 | 584 | 604 |
| Time, sec | 18.22 | 18.18 | 17.61 | 17.97 | 18.76 | 18.97 | 18.24 | 18.09 | 18.28 | 18.89 |
| **HEAAN\*** | | | | | | | | | | |
| $\Delta$ | $2^{27}$ | $2^{28}$ | $2^{29}$ | $2^{30}$ | $2^{31}$ | $2^{32}$ | $2^{33}$ | $2^{34}$ | $2^{35}$ | $2^{36}$ |
| $n$ | $2^{13}$ | $2^{13}$ | $2^{13}$ | $2^{13}$ | $2^{13}$ | $2^{13}$ | $2^{13}$ | $2^{13}$ | $2^{13}$ | $2^{13}$ |
| $\log q_L$ | 137 | 142 | 146 | 151 | 156 | 161 | 166 | 171 | 176 | 181 |
| Size, KB | 274 | 284 | 292 | 302 | 312 | 322 | 332 | 342 | 352 | 362 |
| Time, sec | 14.48 | 14.45 | 14.28 | 14.46 | 14.52 | 16.98 | 18.07 | 18.14 | 18.00 | 18.24 |

**Table 8.** Encryption parameters to compute the sine in the interval $[-\pi, \pi]$. The (*) symbol indicates that the maximal number of slots supported by the plaintext space is $2^6$ for our scheme.

| #slots | 1 | 2 | $2^2$ | $2^3$ | $2^4(*)$ | $2^5(*)$ | $2^6$ | $2^7$ | $2^8$ | $2^9$ | $2^{10}$ | $2^{11}$ |
|---|---|---|---|---|---|---|---|---|---|---|---|---|
| **Our scheme** | | | | | | | | | | | | |
| $\Delta$ | $2^{23}$ | $2^{24}$ | $2^{25}$ | $2^{26}$ | $2^{27}$ | $2^{28}$ | $2^{29}$ | $2^{30}$ | $2^{31}$ | $2^{32}$ | $2^{33}$ | $2^{34}$ |
| $n$ | $2^{12}$ | $2^{12}$ | $2^{12}$ | $2^{13}$ | $2^{13}$ | $2^{13}$ | $2^{13}$ | $2^{13}$ | $2^{13}$ | $2^{14}$ | $2^{14}$ | $2^{15}$ |
| $b$ | 2 | 4 | 16 | 46 | 102 | 102 | 102 | 562 | 4.6e5 | 7.1e5 | 1.1e12 | 2.6e12 |
| $\log q$ | 94 | 97 | 104 | 114 | 119 | 119 | 119 | 132 | 190 | 199 | 323 | 335 |
| Size, KB | 94 | 97 | 104 | 228 | 238 | 238 | 238 | 264 | 380 | 796 | 1292 | 2680 |
| Time, sec | 5.85 | 6.52 | 6.25 | 12.34 | 13.22 | 12.83 | 12.70 | 14.63 | 18.75 | 43.48 | 73.84 | 155.66 |
| **HEAAN** | | | | | | | | | | | | |
| $\Delta$ | $2^{27}$ | $2^{28}$ | $2^{29}$ | $2^{30}$ | $2^{31}$ | $2^{32}$ | $2^{33}$ | $2^{34}$ | $2^{35}$ | $2^{36}$ | $2^{37}$ | $2^{38}$ |
| $n$ | $2^{14}$ | $2^{14}$ | $2^{14}$ | $2^{14}$ | $2^{14}$ | $2^{14}$ | $2^{14}$ | $2^{15}$ | $2^{15}$ | $2^{15}$ | $2^{15}$ | $2^{15}$ |
| $\log q_L$ | 141 | 145 | 150 | 155 | 160 | 165 | 170 | 175 | 180 | 185 | 190 | 195 |
| Size, KB | 564 | 580 | 600 | 620 | 640 | 660 | 680 | 1400 | 1440 | 1480 | 1520 | 1560 |
| Time, sec | 18.14 | 18.13 | 18.25 | 18.55 | 19.67 | 19.58 | 19.56 | 40.21 | 40.40 | 44.57 | 47.20 | 50.27 |
| **HEAAN\*** | | | | | | | | | | | | |
| $\Delta$ | $2^{30}$ | $2^{31}$ | $2^{32}$ | $2^{33}$ | $2^{34}$ | $2^{35}$ | $2^{36}$ | $2^{37}$ | $2^{38}$ | $2^{39}$ | $2^{40}$ | $2^{41}$ |
| $n$ | $2^{13}$ | $2^{13}$ | $2^{13}$ | $2^{13}$ | $2^{13}$ | $2^{13}$ | $2^{13}$ | $2^{13}$ | $2^{13}$ | $2^{13}$ | $2^{13}$ | $2^{13}$ |
| $\log q_L$ | 155 | 160 | 165 | 170 | 175 | 180 | 185 | 190 | 195 | 200 | 205 | 210 |
| Size, KB | 310 | 320 | 330 | 340 | 350 | 360 | 370 | 380 | 390 | 400 | 410 | 420 |
| Time, sec | 14.52 | 16.79 | 16.93 | 17.07 | 17.62 | 17.58 | 16.80 | 17.23 | 17.49 | 19.20 | 19.89 | 21.74 |

**Table 9.** Encryption parameters to compute $e^x$ in the interval $[-2.3, 2.3]$. The (*) symbol indicates that the maximal number of slots supported by the plaintext space is $2^5$ for our scheme.

| #slots | 1 | 2 | $2^2$ | $2^3(*)$ | $2^4(*)$ | $2^5$ | $2^6$ | $2^7$ | $2^8$ | $2^9$ | $2^{10}$ |
|---|---|---|---|---|---|---|---|---|---|---|---|
| **Our scheme** | | | | | | | | | | | |
| $\Delta$ | $2^{18}$ | $2^{19}$ | $2^{20}$ | $2^{21}$ | $2^{22}$ | $2^{23}$ | $2^{24}$ | $2^{25}$ | $2^{26}$ | $2^{27}$ | $2^{28}$ |
| $n$ | $2^{12}$ | $2^{12}$ | $2^{12}$ | $2^{12}$ | $2^{12}$ | $2^{12}$ | $2^{12}$ | $2^{13}$ | $2^{13}$ | $2^{14}$ | $2^{14}$ |
| $b$ | 2 | 4 | 16 | 102 | 102 | 102 | 132 | 156 | 2.9e4 | 4.3e4 | 4.1e9 |
| $\log q$ | 87 | 89 | 95 | 105 | 105 | 105 | 107 | 112 | 155 | 163 | 261 |
| Size, KB | 87 | 89 | 95 | 105 | 105 | 105 | 107 | 224 | 310 | 652 | 1044 |
| Time, sec | 6.42 | 6.00 | 5.83 | 6.92 | 6.85 | 6.68 | 7.07 | 14.73 | 18.23 | 43.88 | 68.05 |
| **HEAAN** | | | | | | | | | | | |
| $\Delta$ | $2^{23}$ | $2^{24}$ | $2^{25}$ | $2^{26}$ | $2^{27}$ | $2^{28}$ | $2^{29}$ | $2^{30}$ | $2^{31}$ | $2^{32}$ | $2^{33}$ |
| $n$ | $2^{14}$ | $2^{14}$ | $2^{14}$ | $2^{14}$ | $2^{14}$ | $2^{14}$ | $2^{14}$ | $2^{14}$ | $2^{14}$ | $2^{14}$ | $2^{14}$ |
| $\log q_L$ | 120 | 125 | 130 | 135 | 140 | 145 | 150 | 155 | 160 | 165 | 170 |
| Size, KB | 480 | 500 | 520 | 540 | 560 | 580 | 600 | 620 | 640 | 660 | 680 |
| Time, sec | 19.63 | 20.02 | 20.20 | 20.30 | 20.25 | 20.41 | 20.53 | 20.76 | 21.50 | 21.87 | 23.74 |
| **HEAAN\*** | | | | | | | | | | | |
| $\Delta$ | $2^{28}$ | $2^{29}$ | $2^{30}$ | $2^{31}$ | $2^{32}$ | $2^{33}$ | $2^{34}$ | $2^{35}$ | $2^{36}$ | $2^{37}$ | $2^{38}$ |
| $n$ | $2^{13}$ | $2^{13}$ | $2^{13}$ | $2^{13}$ | $2^{13}$ | $2^{13}$ | $2^{13}$ | $2^{13}$ | $2^{13}$ | $2^{13}$ | $2^{13}$ |
| $\log q_L$ | 145 | 150 | 155 | 160 | 165 | 170 | 175 | 180 | 185 | 190 | 195 |
| Size, KB | 290 | 300 | 310 | 320 | 330 | 340 | 350 | 360 | 370 | 380 | 390 |
| Time, sec | 15.57 | 15.43 | 15.66 | 18.22 | 18.64 | 18.67 | 18.74 | 18.78 | 18.65 | 19.71 | 20.76 |

**Table 10.** Encryption parameters to compute $x^{16}$ in the interval $[-2.1, 2.1]$. The (*) symbol indicates that the maximal number of slots supported by the plaintext space is $2^5$ for our scheme.

| #slots | 1 | 2 | $2^2$ | $2^3$ (*) | $2^4$ (*) | $2^5$ | $2^6$ | $2^7$ | $2^8$ | $2^9$ | $2^{10}$ |
|---|---|---|---|---|---|---|---|---|---|---|---|
| **Our scheme** | | | | | | | | | | | |
| $\Delta$ | $2^{25}$ | $2^{26}$ | $2^{28}$ | $2^{29}$ | $2^{30}$ | $2^{31}$ | $2^{32}$ | $2^{33}$ | $2^{34}$ | $2^{35}$ | $2^{36}$ |
| $n$ | $2^{12}$ | $2^{12}$ | $2^{12}$ | $2^{13}$ | $2^{13}$ | $2^{13}$ | $2^{13}$ | $2^{13}$ | $2^{14}$ | $2^{14}$ | $2^{15}$ |
| b | 2 | 4 | 16 | 46 | 120 | 120 | 412 | 1.4e5 | 1.9e5 | 3.8e10 | 1.5e11 |
| $\log q$ | 95 | 98 | 105 | 115 | 121 | 121 | 130 | 180 | 189 | 294 | 312 |
| Size, KB | 95 | 98 | 105 | 230 | 242 | 242 | 260 | 360 | 756 | 1176 | 2496 |
| Time, sec | 2.88 | 3.08 | 3.13 | 6.53 | 6.37 | 6.56 | 7.70 | 8.88 | 19.15 | 33.42 | 70.72 |
| **HEAAN** | | | | | | | | | | | |
| $\Delta$ | $2^{38}$ | $2^{39}$ | $2^{40}$ | $2^{41}$ | $2^{42}$ | $2^{43}$ | $2^{44}$ | $2^{45}$ | $2^{46}$ | $2^{47}$ | $2^{48}$ |
| $n$ | $2^{15}$ | $2^{15}$ | $2^{15}$ | $2^{15}$ | $2^{15}$ | $2^{15}$ | $2^{15}$ | $2^{15}$ | $2^{15}$ | $2^{15}$ | $2^{15}$ |
| $\log q_L$ | 209 | 214 | 219 | 224 | 229 | 234 | 239 | 244 | 249 | 254 | 259 |
| Size, KB | 1672 | 1712 | 1752 | 1792 | 1832 | 1872 | 1912 | 1952 | 1992 | 2032 | 2072 |
| Time, sec | 20.76 | 20.38 | 20.57 | 20.70 | 20.45 | 20.96 | 21.02 | 21.91 | 22.06 | 23.56 | 23.70 |
| **HEAAN*** | | | | | | | | | | | |
| $\Delta$ | $2^{37}$ | $2^{38}$ | $2^{39}$ | $2^{40}$ | $2^{41}$ | $2^{42}$ | $2^{43}$ | $2^{44}$ | $2^{45}$ | $2^{46}$ | $2^{47}$ |
| $n$ | $2^{13}$ | $2^{13}$ | $2^{13}$ | $2^{14}$ | $2^{14}$ | $2^{14}$ | $2^{14}$ | $2^{14}$ | $2^{14}$ | $2^{14}$ | $2^{14}$ |
| $\log q_L$ | 204 | 209 | 214 | 219 | 224 | 229 | 234 | 239 | 244 | 249 | 254 |
| Size, KB | 408 | 418 | 428 | 876 | 896 | 916 | 936 | 956 | 976 | 996 | 1016 |
| Time, sec | 8.42 | 8.43 | 8.66 | 18.45 | 18.98 | 19.73 | 19.53 | 20.29 | 20.95 | 20.33 | 22.46 |

**Table 11.** Encryption parameters to compute $x^2$ in the interval $(-2^{15}, 2^{15})$. The (*) symbol indicates that the maximal number of slots supported by the plaintext space is $2^5$ for our scheme.

| #slots | 1 | 2 | $2^2$ | $2^3$ (*) | $2^4$ (*) | $2^5$ | $2^6$ | $2^7$ | $2^8$ | $2^9$ | $2^{10}$ | $2^{11}$ | $2^{12}$ |
|---|---|---|---|---|---|---|---|---|---|---|---|---|---|
| **Our scheme** | | | | | | | | | | | | | |
| $\Delta$ | $2^{21}$ | $2^{23}$ | $2^{24}$ | $2^{25}$ | $2^{26}$ | $2^{27}$ | $2^{28}$ | $2^{29}$ | $2^{30}$ | $2^{31}$ | $2^{32}$ | $2^{33}$ | $2^{34}$ |
| $n$ | $2^{11}$ | $2^{11}$ | $2^{11}$ | $2^{11}$ | $2^{11}$ | $2^{11}$ | $2^{11}$ | $2^{12}$ | $2^{12}$ | $2^{12}$ | $2^{13}$ | $2^{13}$ | $2^{14}$ |
| b | 2 | 4 | 16 | 30 | 30 | 30 | 44 | 74 | 2.9e3 | 1.0e7 | 1.4e7 | 4.0e14 | 8.0e14 |
| $\log q$ | 48 | 49 | 51 | 51 | 51 | 51 | 52 | 54 | 66 | 102 | 106 | 180 | 185 |
| Size, KB | 24 | 24.5 | 25.5 | 25.5 | 25.5 | 25.5 | 26 | 54 | 66 | 102 | 212 | 360 | 740 |
| Time, sec | 0.22 | 0.20 | 0.19 | 0.19 | 0.19 | 0.19 | 0.20 | 0.44 | 0.62 | 0.80 | 1.71 | 2.57 | 4.93 |
| **HEAAN** | | | | | | | | | | | | | |
| $\Delta$ | $2^{33}$ | $2^{34}$ | $2^{35}$ | $2^{36}$ | $2^{37}$ | $2^{38}$ | $2^{39}$ | $2^{40}$ | $2^{41}$ | $2^{42}$ | $2^{43}$ | $2^{44}$ | $2^{45}$ |
| $n$ | $2^{14}$ | $2^{14}$ | $2^{14}$ | $2^{14}$ | $2^{14}$ | $2^{14}$ | $2^{14}$ | $2^{14}$ | $2^{14}$ | $2^{14}$ | $2^{14}$ | $2^{14}$ | $2^{14}$ |
| $\log q_L$ | 97 | 99 | 101 | 103 | 105 | 107 | 109 | 111 | 113 | 115 | 117 | 119 | 121 |
| Size, KB | 388 | 396 | 404 | 412 | 420 | 428 | 436 | 444 | 452 | 460 | 468 | 476 | 484 |
| Time, sec | 1.47 | 1.41 | 1.39 | 1.47 | 1.47 | 1.48 | 1.42 | 1.49 | 1.47 | 1.50 | 1.58 | 1.68 | 1.98 |
| **HEAAN*** | | | | | | | | | | | | | |
| $\Delta$ | $2^{33}$ | $2^{34}$ | $2^{35}$ | $2^{36}$ | $2^{37}$ | $2^{38}$ | $2^{39}$ | $2^{40}$ | $2^{41}$ | $2^{42}$ | $2^{43}$ | $2^{44}$ | $2^{45}$ |
| $n$ | $2^{12}$ | $2^{12}$ | $2^{12}$ | $2^{12}$ | $2^{12}$ | $2^{12}$ | $2^{12}$ | $2^{13}$ | $2^{13}$ | $2^{13}$ | $2^{13}$ | $2^{13}$ | $2^{13}$ |
| $\log q_L$ | 97 | 99 | 101 | 103 | 105 | 107 | 109 | 111 | 113 | 115 | 117 | 119 | 121 |
| Size, KB | 97 | 99 | 101 | 103 | 105 | 107 | 109 | 222 | 226 | 230 | 234 | 238 | 242 |
| Time, sec | 0.60 | 0.61 | 0.61 | 0.61 | 0.61 | 0.60 | 0.61 | 1.33 | 1.32 | 1.35 | 1.43 | 1.60 | 1.79 |

# References

1. Albrecht, M.R., Player, R., Scott, S.: On the concrete hardness of learning with errors. J. Math. Cryptol. **9**(3), 169–203 (2015)
2. Bonte, C., Bootland, C., Bos, J.W., Castryck, W., Iliashenko, I., Vercauteren, F.: Faster homomorphic function evaluation using non-integral base encoding. In: Fischer, W., Homma, N. (eds.) CHES 2017. LNCS, vol. 10529, pp. 579–600. Springer, Cham (2017). https://doi.org/10.1007/978-3-319-66787-4_28
3. Bootland, C., Castryck, W., Iliashenko, I., Vercauteren, F.: Efficiently processing complex-valued data in homomorphic encryption. Spec. Issue J. Math. Cryptol.: Mathcrypt **14**, 55–65 (2018)
4. Chen, H., Laine, K., Player, R., Xia, Y.: High-precision arithmetic in homomorphic encryption. In: Smart, N.P. (ed.) CT-RSA 2018. LNCS, vol. 10808, pp. 116–136. Springer, Cham (2018). https://doi.org/10.1007/978-3-319-76953-0_7
5. Cheon, J.H., Kim, A., Kim, M., Song, Y.: Homomorphic encryption for arithmetic of approximate numbers. In: Takagi, T., Peyrin, T. (eds.) ASIACRYPT 2017, Part I. LNCS, vol. 10624, pp. 409–437. Springer, Cham (2017). https://doi.org/10.1007/978-3-319-70694-8_15
6. Costache, A., Smart, N.P., Vivek, S.: Faster homomorphic evaluation of discrete Fourier transforms. In: Kiayias, A. (ed.) FC 2017. LNCS, vol. 10322, pp. 517–529. Springer, Cham (2017). https://doi.org/10.1007/978-3-319-70972-7_29
7. Costache, A., Smart, N.P., Vivek, S., Waller, A.: Fixed-point arithmetic in SHE schemes. In: Avanzi, R., Heys, H. (eds.) SAC 2016. LNCS, vol. 10532, pp. 401–422. Springer, Cham (2017). https://doi.org/10.1007/978-3-319-69453-5_22
8. Curtis, B.R., Player, R.: On the feasibility and impact of standardising sparse-secret LWE parameter sets for homomorphic encryption. In: WAHC 2019. ACM Press (2019)
9. Damgård, I., Pastro, V., Smart, N., Zakarias, S.: Multiparty computation from somewhat homomorphic encryption. In: Safavi-Naini, R., Canetti, R. (eds.) CRYPTO 2012. LNCS, vol. 7417, pp. 643–662. Springer, Heidelberg (2012). https://doi.org/10.1007/978-3-642-32009-5_38
10. Dowlin, N., Gilad-Bachrach, R., Laine, K., Lauter, K.E., Naehrig, M., Wernsing, J.: Manual for using homomorphic encryption for bioinformatics. Proc. IEEE **105**(3), 552–567 (2017)
11. ElGamal, T.: A public key cryptosystem and a signature scheme based on discrete logarithms. IEEE Trans. Inf. Theory **31**, 469–472 (1985)
12. Erkin, Z., Troncoso-Pastoriza, J.R., Lagendijk, R.L., Pérez-González, F.: Privacy-preserving data aggregation in smart metering systems: an overview. IEEE Signal Process. Mag. **30**(2), 75–86 (2013)
13. Fan, J., Vercauteren, F.: Somewhat practical fully homomorphic encryption. Cryptology ePrint Archive, Report 2012/144 (2012). http://eprint.iacr.org/2012/144
14. Gentry, C.: Fully homomorphic encryption using ideal lattices. In: Mitzenmacher, M. (ed.) 41st ACM STOC, pp. 169–178. ACM Press (May/June 2009)
15. Goldwasser, S., Micali, S.: Probabilistic encryption and how to play mental poker keeping secret all partial information. In: 14th ACM STOC, pp. 365–377. ACM Press (May 1982)
16. Kocabas, O., Soyata, T., Couderc, J.P., Aktas, M., Xia, J., Huang, M.: Assessment of cloud-based health monitoring using homomorphic encryption. In: 2013 IEEE 31st International Conference on Computer Design (ICCD), pp. 443–446. IEEE (2013)

17. Lyubashevsky, V., Peikert, C., Regev, O.: On ideal lattices and learning with errors over rings. In: Gilbert, H. (ed.) EUROCRYPT 2010. LNCS, vol. 6110, pp. 1–23. Springer, Heidelberg (2010). https://doi.org/10.1007/978-3-642-13190-5_1
18. Malina, L., Hajny, J., Fujdiak, R., Hosek, J.: On perspective of security and privacy-preserving solutions in the Internet of Things. Comput. Netw. **102**, 83–95 (2016)
19. Paillier, P.: Public-key cryptosystems based on composite degree residuosity classes. In: Stern, J. (ed.) EUROCRYPT 1999. LNCS, vol. 1592, pp. 223–238. Springer, Heidelberg (1999). https://doi.org/10.1007/3-540-48910-X_16
20. Rabin, M.O.: Digitalized signatures and public-key functions as intractable as factorization. Tech. rep., Massachusetts Inst of Tech Cambridge Lab for Computer Science (1979)
21. Rivest, R.L., Adleman, L., Dertouzos, M.L.: On data banks and privacy homomorphisms. Found. Secur. Comput. **4**(11), 169–180 (1978)
22. Rivest, R.L., Shamir, A., Adleman, L.M.: A method for obtaining digital signatures and public-key cryptosystems. Commun. Assoc. Comput. Mach. **21**(2), 120–126 (1978)
23. Shanks, D.: Five number-theoretic algorithms. In: Proceedings of the Second Manitoba Conference on Numerical Mathematics (1973)
24. Smart, N.P., Vercauteren, F.: Fully homomorphic SIMD operations. Des. Codes Cryptogr. **71**(1), 57–81 (2012). https://doi.org/10.1007/s10623-012-9720-4
25. The Sage Developers: SageMath, the Sage Mathematics Software System (Version 8.9) (2019). https://www.sagemath.org

# Multiparty Computation

# Secure Multiparty Computation
# in the Bounded Storage Model

Jiahui Liu[(✉)] and Satyanarayana Vusirikala

The University of Texas at Austin, Austin, USA
jiahui@cs.utexas.edu

**Abstract.** Most cryptography is based on assumptions such as factoring and discrete log, which assume an adversary has bounded computational power. With the recent development in quantum computing as well as concern with everlasting security, there is an interest in coming up with information-theoretic constructions in the bounded storage model.

In this model, an adversary is computationally unbounded but has limited space. Past works have constructed schemes such as key exchange and bit commitment in this model. In this work, we expand the functionalities further by building a semi-honest MPC protocol in the bounded storage model. We use the hardness of the parity learning problem (recently shown by Ran Raz (FOCS '16) without any cryptographic assumptions) to prove the security of our construction, following the work by Guan and Zhandry (EUROCRYPT '19).

## 1 Introduction

Many schemes in cryptography rely on various computational assumptions such as factoring, discrete log and Learning with Errors. Even though these assumptions are well-believed to be true, recent advances in quantum computing show that factoring and discrete log problems could be solved efficiently by quantum computers [10,23]. It, therefore, could be dangerous to base the security of global user information on these assumptions. An adversary can store ciphertext and attempt to decrypt it later when his computational power increases or quantum computers come into existence. The current systems, therefore, do not provide everlasting security. Alternately, one could construct schemes in the information-theoretic model, where no computational power of the adversary is assumed. However, many of these information-theoretic systems such as one-time pad are impractical to use.

In the face of the above issues, Maurer proposed bounded storage model [17] in which we do not assume any computational restrictions on the adversary. Rather, we assume that the adversary has bounded storage and is unable to store a long conversation. In this model, [17] constructed a key exchange protocol assuming a publicly accessible long random stream of bits. In his protocol, Alice and Bob respectively record a private random subset of $n$ bits from a stream of $n^2$ random bits. They later send their recorded positions to each other, and the

© Springer Nature Switzerland AG 2021
M. B. Paterson (Ed.): IMACC 2021, LNCS 13129, pp. 289–325, 2021.
https://doi.org/10.1007/978-3-030-92641-0_14

secret key is set as the bit at their commonly recorded position in the stream. Note that they will record at least one-bit position in common with a constant probability according to the birthday paradox. An eavesdropping adversary with $Cn^2$ (for some constant $C < 1$) storage can only obtain the secret key with $1/C$ probability.

Many sequence of works [1–7,12,16–18,21,22] have given increasingly secure and efficient protocols for key exchange, oblivious transfer, commitments and timestamping in this model. Most of these works rely on the birthday paradox. Unfortunately, this has several disadvantages. For example, in the above protocol, (1) The honest parties can succeed with only constant probability. To achieve high success probability, the protocol has to be repeated several times. (2) The adversary can succeed with constant probability. To achieve statistical security, a randomness extractor has to be applied to the obtained secret key. (3) The birthday paradox does not have a rich structure that can be exploited to construct advanced protocols.

Recently, Ran Raz et al. [15,19,20] proposed a new class of techniques that can be used to construct cryptographic schemes in the bounded storage model. Specifically, they studied the hardness of solving *parity learning* problem in bounded space. In this problem, a secret string $k$ is sampled uniformly at random from $\{0,1\}^n$. A learner has to compute the secret $k$ when given a stream of samples $(a_1, b_1), (a_2, b_2), \cdots$, where each $a_i$ is sampled uniformly at random from $\{0,1\}^n$, and $b_i$ is the inner product of $a_i$ and $k$ mod 2. Roughly speaking, [19] proved that any (computationally unbounded) learner that uses less than $n^2/20$ space requires either an exponential number of samples or has an exponentially small probability of outputting the correct answer. [19] used the hardness of solving the parity learning problem to construct a simple secret key encryption protocol – The secret key $k$ is randomly sampled from $\{0,1\}^n$. To encrypt a bit $b$, sample $x \leftarrow \{0,1\}^n$ and output $(x, x \cdot k + b \bmod 2)$. In this protocol, the honest users require only $O(n)$ space, whereas a dishonest user requires more than $n^2/20$ space to break security.

Guan and Zhandry [11] used the hardness of solving parity learning problem to construct key exchange, oblivious transfer, and bit commitment protocols in the bounded storage model.

Even after 28 years after the introduction of the bounded storage model, constructing a general multi-party computation protocol in this model using any techniques is still an open problem. To the best of our knowledge MPC in the bounded storage model has not yet been defined in any past work. In this work, we define semi-honest secure MPC in the bounded storage model and construct it based on the hardness of solving parity learning in bounded space.

## 1.1    Our Results and Technical Overview

In a multi-party computation scenario, there are $k$ parties $\mathcal{P}_i$ ($i \in [k]$) each holding a private input $x_i$. The parties would like to know the output of a joint function $y = f(x_1, \cdots x_k)$ without leaking any information about its private input to the other parties. We would like to develop a protocol, where the parties can send messages to each other in rounds and finally compute $y$ based on the transcript. To enable the communication between parties, we model the parties as interactive Turing machines that have additional read and write communication tapes. Many MPC protocols have been proposed in the computational model [9,13,14,24] predominantly based on oblivious transfer (OT). As [11] showed how to build oblivious transfer in the bounded storage model based on the hardness of parity learning [19], one simple idea could be to directly substitute Guan Zhandry's OT construction in any of the existing MPC constructions.

However, there are few subtleties here. First, as we base our MPC protocol on the hardness of parity learning, we would like to show that if an adversary can break the security of our MPC protocol in bounded space, then he can solve the parity learning problem in bounded space. To model the adversarial behaviors in MPC properly, we model the adversaries as interactive Turing machines. However, the notion of bounded storage for interactive Turing machines is not well-defined in this context. We therefore need to first give a formal characterization of bounded-storage interactive Turing machines and show the parity learning hardness in the setting.

*Review of Parity Learning for Branching Programs* [19]. We first give a brief overview on the branching program adversary model used in [19] and why we need to properly remodel the problem when it comes to Turing machines.

When proving the hardness of parity learning, [19] modeled the learning algorithm as a deterministic branching program and not as a probabilistic interactive Turing machine.

At a high level, a branching program is a graph, with vertices arranged in layers, and edges between the vertices in adjacent layers marked by parity learning samples $(a, b) \in \{0,1\}^n \times \{0,1\}$. Intuitively, each layer of the graph represents a time step and the vertices in each layer represent the possible states of the learning algorithm at that time step. The learner initializes his state with the vertex in the first layer. When the learner receives a stream of parity learning samples $(a_1, b_1), (a_2, b_2), \cdots$, the learner follows the edges corresponding to the samples. When it reaches a vertex in the last layer, it outputs a key $k \in \{0,1\}^n$ depending on the vertex. [19] showed that either the width of the branching program (number of vertices in a layer) has to be $2^{cn^2}$ or the length of the branching program (total number of layers which also represents the number of samples) has to be exponential in $n$ in order to solve the parity learning problem with non-negligible advantage. This implies any learner with access to an only polynomial number of samples should have space at least $cn^2$ (for some constant $c$) to store the state. Intuitively, [19] defined the notion of the learner's space as the amount of storage required to store the state of the learner and did not include the amount of space required to store the transition function.

## Parity Learning Hardness for Bounded-Storage Turing Machines. In the Turing machine model, we let the learner receive a stream of parity learning

samples via its read communication tape[1] and has to write its output key on the output tape. The learner can additionally sample randomness via its random tape, interact with other Turing machines using its other communication tapes, and additionally take an advice string on its input tape.[2] What should be an analogous definition of space in case of (probabilistic interactive) Turing machines?[3] Should we include the space required to store the transition function? What about the space required to store the advice string on input tape, or the space required to store the output?

To address these questions, we first define a notion called "space characteristic" for Turing machines. We then prove that any Turing machine with bounded *space characteristic* has an exponentially small probability of solving the parity learning problem with a polynomial number of samples.

In order to prove the hardness result, we show that for every Turing machine that solves the parity learning problem, there exists a corresponding branching program that solves the problem with the same advantage. For simplicity, let us first consider the case of deterministic Turing machines which do not interact with other parties. Roughly speaking, we define a configuration of the Turing machine to be a tuple containing (state of the TM, input tape pointer, work tape contents, work tape pointer, output tape contents, output tape pointer). In this case, the vertices of the constructed branching program correspond to all possible configurations of the Turing machine, and the edges between the vertices correspond to how the Turing machine configuration changes when given a parity learning sample on its read comm. tape. We define the space characteristic of the TM to be the space required to store a configuration. Note that this does not include the storage required for input tape contents or state transition function. We give a more general definition of "space characteristic" for non-uniform probabilistic interactive TMs in Definition 1, and extend the hardness result to these general Turing machine learners in Sect. 3.

**MPC in Bounded Storage Model.** In this work, we construct a semi-honest secure $k$-party MPC protocol secure against $k - 1$ corruptions in the bounded storage model. In this model, the corrupted parties try to learn more information from the union of their protocol transcripts but do not deviate from the protocol. As we base our security on the hardness of parity learning problem, the honest

---

[1] The Turing machine has only read once access to this tape and thereby cannot move its tape head to the left.

[2] Looking forward, given an adversary that breaks the security of our MPC protocol, we build a reduction algorithm that solves the parity learning problem. In this case, the reduction algorithm interacts with the adversary. The reduction algorithm uses the circuit $C$ and input tuple $(x_1, \cdots x_k)$ for which the adversary has a high advantage as an advice string written on its input tape.

[3] We note that [11] built various protocols where the parties are modeled as Turing machines. Unfortunately, they ignored the gap between Raz's theorem [19] and Turing machines, and used the traditional space complexity definition to define the space of a Turing machine.

parties can run the protocol in $O(n)$ space, whereas the dishonest parties need at least $\Omega(n^2)$ space to break the protocol.

At a high level, we follow the GMW semi-honest MPC protocol approach [9]. The functionality is first represented as a circuit $C$ containing only XOR and AND gates. When the circuit $C$ is evaluated on input $(x_1, \cdots, x_k)$, let the bit value obtained at each wire $w$ be $v_w$. The goal is to enable all the parties $\mathcal{P}_i$ to hold a secret share $r_{i,w}$ of $v_w$ (i.e., $\sum_i r_{i,w} = v_w \bmod 2$) for each wire $w$. In order to do this, each party $\mathcal{P}_i$ first secret shares its private input $x_i$ with all the other parties. Now, each party holds a secret share of $v_w$ for all the input wires $w$.

The parties now proceed to process gate by gate in a logical order. If a gate is an XOR gate, the parties simply XOR the shares of their input wires locally to obtain a share of the output wire i.e., perform $r_{i,c} = r_{i,a} + r_{i,b} \bmod 2$, where $a, b$ are input wires and $c$ is the output wire of the gate. If the gate is an AND gate, then the parties would like to obtain secret shares of the bit $v_a * v_b = (\sum_i r_{i,a}) * (\sum_i r_{i,b}) = (\sum_i r_{i,a} * r_{i,b}) + \sum_{i<j}(r_{i,a} * r_{j,b} + r_{i,b} * r_{j,a})$. Each party $\mathcal{P}_i$ could locally compute $r_{i,a} * r_{i,b}$ term. To secret share the $(r_{i,a} * r_{j,b} + r_{i,b} * r_{j,a})$ term, the party $\mathcal{P}_i$ first samples a bit $\alpha \leftarrow \{0,1\}$, and sets $m_{(p,q)} = \alpha + p * r_{i,b} + q * r_{i,a}$ for each $p, q \in \{0,1\}$. The parties $\mathcal{P}_i$ and $\mathcal{P}_j$ now run an 1-out-of-4 oblivious transfer protocol[4], where $\mathcal{P}_i$ acts as the sender with input messages $(m_{(0,0)}, m_{(0,1)}, m_{(1,0)}, m_{(1,1)})$, and $\mathcal{P}_j$ acts as the receiver with $(r_{j,a}, r_{j,b})$ as its choice. The party $\mathcal{P}_j$ adds the OT output $\alpha + (r_{i,a} * r_{j,b} + r_{i,b} * r_{j,a})$ to its share of output wire $r_{j,c}$. The party $\mathcal{P}_i$ adds $\alpha$ to its share of the output wire $r_{i,c}$. After processing all the gates, each party sends their secret share corresponding to all the output wires to the other parties. Each party can compute the desired output by summing up the received secret shares.

**1-Out-of-4 Oblivious Transfer Protocol.** In order for the above construction to work, we need a semi-honest secure 1-out-of-4 bit oblivious transfer protocol in the bounded storage model. However, [11] built only a 1-out-of-2 bit oblivious transfer based on the hardness of parity learning. In this work, we provide a generic way to transform any 1-out-of-2 OT to 1-out-of-4 OT in the bounded storage model. Let the sender's input messages be $(m_0, m_1, m_2, m_3)$ and the receiver's choice be $d$. At a high level, the sender samples 3 uniformly random mask bits $r_{i,1}, r_{i,2}, r_{i,3}$ for each message $m_i$. For each pair $(i, j) \in [3] \times [3]$, the receiver chooses to obtain either a mask bit of $m_i$ or a mask bit of $m_j$ by performing a 1-out-of-2 OT with the sender. At the end, the sender masks each message $m_i$ with the corresponding mask bits and sends $y_i = m_i + r_{i,1} + r_{i,2} + r_{i,3}$ (for each $i \in [3]$) to the receiver. Clearly, during the 1-out-of-2 OT invocations, if the receiver always chooses to obtain the mask bit corresponding to $m_d$, then the receiver can decrypt $y_d$ and obtain $m_d$.

The above transformation is secure because the receiver cannot obtain information about other messages as for each $i \neq d$, the receiver does not know a

---

[4] In 1-out-of-$t$ oblivious transfer protocol, the sender takes $t$ messages $(m_1, \cdots m_t)$ as input. The receiver chooses an index $c$ and obtains the message $m_c$, without letting the sender know about the choice $c$ and without gaining any information about the other messages.

mask bit corresponding to $m_i$. The sender cannot obtain any information about the choice $d$ because the only messages he receives are part of the underlying 1-out-of-2 OT protocol. As the underlying 1-out-of-2 OT is secure, the sender cannot obtain any more information throughout the protocol. The above transformation can be extended to a general 1-out-of-$k$ case by running 1-out-of-2 OT protocol $\binom{k}{2}$ times.

## 1.2  Related Works

A recent concurrent work [?] achieves simulation-based security for MPC based on the method from [7], but in the slightly different streaming BSM, compared to the traditional BSM used in [7]: the honest parties are less restricted and meanwhile the adversary is given less power. The protocols built in [11](and thus ours) can be viewed as similar to the streaming BSM, but the honest parties only use a single or very limited number of "long" rounds where they stream long messages to each other and therefore achieve better in terms of communication complexity.

## 2  Preliminaries

In this section, we first recall the definition of interactive turing machines and define a new parameter of ITMs called "space characteristic". We then define the notions of multiparty computation and oblivious transfer in the bounded storage model.

### 2.1  Interactive Turing Machines

An interactive turing machine (ITM) is a multi-tape turing machine. The functionality and access restrictions of each tape are described below.

- Space Parameter tape (read-only): This tape stores a value of the form $1^n$. Here $n$ is called the "space parameter" which determines the upper bound on the space that could be used by the turing machine. This is analogous to the security parameter typically used in the computational model.
- Input tape (read-only): The ITM receives its input on this tape.
- Output tape (write only): The ITM places its final output on this tape.
- Work tape (read & write): The ITM uses this for its internal storage during the computation.
- Random tape (read once): The ITM receives random bits on this tape.
- $r$ read communication tapes (read once): These tapes are used to receive messages from other turing machines in an interactive protocol. Each tape is given a unique identifier in the set $[r]$.
- $w$ write communication tapes (write-once): These tapes are used to send messages to other turing machines in an interactive protocol. Each tape is given a unique identifier in the set $[w]$.

For the tapes with read once (or write-once) access, the state machine can access each bit on the tape only once i.e., the head pointer of the turing machine is only allowed to move in the forward direction. In this paper, we assume that a uniformly random bit is sampled and placed on a cell of the random tape only at the time step at which the cell is accessed by the turing machine. In an interactive protocol, we can connect write tape $i$ of an ITM $\mathcal{A}$ to a read tape $j$ of a different ITM $\mathcal{B}$. In such a case, every bit written by $\mathcal{A}$ on it's $i^{th}$ write tape is copied immediately to the first blank cell of ITM $\mathcal{B}$'s $j^{th}$ read tape. At every time step, if an ITM has a non-blank cell at any of its read tape heads, then the ITM has to definitely read the cell and move its head to right.[5] For any turing machine $\mathcal{A}$, we denote $\mathcal{A}(1^n)$ to be the turing machine obtained by fixing the space parameter tape to $1^n$.

We now define a new parameter for an ITM called "space characteristic". Looking ahead, we construct a multi-party computation protocol and show that no (computationally unbounded) adversary with small *space characteristic* can break the security of the protocol.

**Definition 1 (Space Characteristic).** *Consider any interactive turing machine $M$ with $r$ read comm. tapes, $w$ write comm. tapes, alphabet size $a$, and $Q$ states in its state machine. Suppose for every random string on the random tape, the execution of $M$ on an input $x$ (of length ip) and space parameter $n$ uses at most $T$ work tape cells, rnd random tape cells[6] and outputs a string of length at most op on its output tape. Then the space characteristic of $M$ on the input $x$ is given by*

$$(T + \mathsf{op} + 2(r + w)) \cdot \log_2 a + \log_2(n \cdot Q \cdot T \cdot \mathsf{ip} \cdot \mathsf{op} \cdot \mathsf{rnd}).$$

Intuitively, the first term $(T + \mathsf{op} + 2(r+w)) \cdot \log_2 a$ is the total amount of storage (in bits) required to store work tape, output tape and few symbols of each of the communication tapes. The second term intuitively represents the space required to store the current state, work tape pointer, input tape pointer, output tape pointer, space tape pointer and random tape pointer locations. The necessity for the second term would be more clear in Sect. 3. Note that the definition of space characteristic is different from that of space complexity. Space complexity typically does not include the space required to store the output, whereas the definition of space characteristic includes op term. Moreover, the definition of space characteristic includes $\log Q$ term, which is typically not included in the space complexity.

**Definition 2 (s-space bounded ITM).** *For any function $s : \mathbb{N} \to \mathbb{N}$, we say that an interactive turing machine $M$ is s-space bounded for an input class*

---

[5] Note that a turing machine could have multiple read tapes and all the tapes could receive messages from other turing machines at the same time. The turing machine has to read all the read tape cells at once, but can only copy one symbol to its work tape at a timestep. We solve this by problem by allowing our work tape to use large alphabet size.

[6] In case the turing machine does not use randomness, we fix $\mathsf{rnd} = 1$.

$\{\mathcal{X}_n\}_{n \in \mathbb{N}}$, if for all space parameters $n \in \mathbb{N}$, and inputs $x \in \mathcal{X}_n$, the turing machine $M$ has a space characteristic $s(n)$.

When the input class is clear from the context, we simply call an ITM to be $s$-space bounded.

## 2.2 Secure Multiparty Computation

In this section, we define Multiparty Computation protocols in the Bounded Storage Model. In this scenario, we have $k$ parties $\mathcal{P}_i$ $(i \in [k])$ each holding a private input $x_i$. Each party $\mathcal{P}_i$ would like to know the output of a joint function $y_i = f_i(x_1, \cdots x_k)$ without leaking any information about its private input to the other parties. This is represented using a $k$-party functionality $\mathbf{f} = (f_1, f_2, \cdots f_k)$. To compute $(y_1, \cdots y_k)$, we would like to develop a protocol, where the parties can send messages to each other in rounds. In each round, the message sent by $\mathcal{P}_i$ to $\mathcal{P}_j$ (for any $i, j \in [k]$) depends on $\mathcal{P}_i$'s input, its random coins and all the messages it received in the previous rounds. At the end of the protocol, each party $\mathcal{P}_i$ computes $y_i = f_i(x_1, x_2, \cdots, x_k)$. As we are working in the bounded storage model, we are only interested in protocols where the algorithm used by each party $\mathcal{P}_i$ has small space characteristic. More formally,

**Definition 3 (MPC protocol).** *A $k$-party MPC protocol $\Pi$ is described by ITMs $(\Pi_i)_{i \in [k]}$ and a simulator $\mathsf{Sim}$[7]. The $i^{th}$ ITM is used by party $\mathcal{P}_i$. Each ITM has $k$ read communication tapes and $k$ write communication tapes. The simulator has $k$ write tapes. For every $j \neq i \in [k]$, the $j^{th}$ write communication tape of $\Pi_i$ is connected to the $i^{th}$ read communication tape of $\Pi_j$ i.e., this tape is used by the party $\mathcal{P}_i$ to send messages to the party $\mathcal{P}_j$. To initiate the protocol for a functionality $\mathbf{f}$, each party $\mathcal{P}_i$ first places $(\mathbf{f}, x_i)$ on the input tape of its ITM $\Pi_i$ and then runs the turing machine.*

**Definition 4 ($s$-Correctness).** *For any function $s : \mathbb{N} \to \mathbb{N}$, we say that a $k$-party MPC protocol $\Pi = (\Pi_i)_{i \in [k]}$ $s$-correctly computes a class of $k$-party functionalities $\{\mathcal{F}_n\}_{n \in \mathbb{N}}$ if for every space parameter $n \in \mathbb{N}$, every functionality $\mathbf{f} = (f_1, \cdots, f_k) \in \mathcal{F}_n$, for every input vector $(x_1, \cdots, x_k)$ of the functionality, every set of random coins used by $\Pi$, when each party $\Pi_i$ is run on input $(\mathbf{f}, x_i)$ and space parameter $1^n$, the output tape of each $\Pi_i$ at the end of the protocol is equal to $f_i(x_1, \cdots, x_k)$, and each ITM $\Pi_i$ has a space characteristic at most $s(n)$.*

**Semi-honest Security.** We now provide a security definition for MPC protocols against semi-honest adversaries in the bounded storage model. Intuitively, a semi-honest adversary can corrupt any subset of parties $\mathcal{I}$ before starting the protocol and then obtain their inputs $\{x_i\}_{i \in \mathcal{I}}$, random coins and transcript of the messages received by the parties. However, the adversary cannot force the corrupted parties to deviate from the protocol. Let the view of the adversary be all the information

---

[7] The simulator is used only in the security definition but not in the real protocol.

obtained by the adversary. The folklore definition says that an MPC protocol $\Pi$ for some functionality $\mathbf{f}$ is semi-honest secure if there exists a simulator such that no semi-honest adversary can distinguish between the following two distributions: (1) view obtained by running the protocol $\Pi$ on input $\{x_i\}_{i \in [k]}$, and (2) the output of the simulator on input $\mathbf{f}, \mathcal{I}, \{x_i\}_{i \in \mathcal{I}}, \{f_i(x_1, x_2, \cdots, x_k)\}_{i \in \mathcal{I}}$. Intuitively, if an MPC protocol satisfies such a security definition, it guarantees that the adversary cannot learn any more information by looking at the random coins and transcript of the messages other than what he can learn based on the inputs and outputs of the corrupted parties.

However, such a security definition would not work in bounded storage model. This is because the adversary and the simulator can only have bounded space $s$, and the view generated by the protocol execution could be much larger than $s$. As a result, the simulator may not be able to generate the complete view on its output tape and send it to the adversary. Therefore, we model the adversary and the simulator as bounded space interactive turing machines that exchange stream of bits via their read and write communication tapes. Formally,

**Definition 5 (Semi-honest Security).** *For any functions $s_1 : \mathbb{N} \to \mathbb{N}$, $s_2 : \mathbb{N} \to \mathbb{N}$ and $\epsilon : \mathbb{N} \to [0, 1]$, we say that a $k$-party protocol $\Pi = \{\Pi_i\}_{i \in [k]}$ $(s_1, s_2, \epsilon)$-securely computes a class of $k$-party functionalities $\{\mathcal{F}_n\}_{n \in \mathbb{N}}$ if*

*(1) The simulator* Sim *is $s_1$-space bounded, and*

*(2) For every $s_2$-space bounded adversary $\mathcal{A}$ with $k$ read tapes there exists an integer $N_0$ s.t. for every space parameter $n > N_0$, for any functionality $\mathbf{f} = (f_1, f_2, \cdots f_k) \in \mathcal{F}_n$, all input tuples $\mathbf{x} = (x_1, \cdots, x_k)$ belonging to the domain of $\mathbf{f}$, and for every subset $\mathcal{I} \subset [k]$, we have*

$$| \Pr[\mathsf{GameSH}^{\mathcal{A}}_{1^n, \mathbf{f}, \mathcal{I}, \mathbf{x}}(0) = 1] - \Pr[\mathsf{GameSH}^{\mathcal{A}}_{1^n, \mathbf{f}, \mathcal{I}, \mathbf{x}}(1) = 1]| \leq \epsilon(n),$$

*where* GameSH *is described in Fig. 1 and the probability is taken over the random coins used by the simulator, the adversary and the challenger.*

### 2.3 Oblivious Transfer

In this section, we define 1-out-of-$k$ oblivious transfer in bounded storage model. In our scenario, we have 2 parties – a sender and a receiver. The sender takes as input $k$ message bits $\{m_i\}_{i \in [k]}$ and the receiver takes as input a selector $c \in [k]$. The goal is to enable the receiver to obtain the message $m_c$. At the same time, we do not want the receiver to learn anything about the other messages, and we do not want the sender to learn anything about the selector $c$. To that end, we model the sender and the receiver as interactive turing machines $(\Pi_{\mathsf{sender}}, \Pi_{\mathsf{receiver}})$ each with 1 read and 1 write tape. The parties receive their input on input tape, send messages to each other using their read and write communication tapes, and finally write their output to the output tape. In the bounded storage model, we assume both the sender and the receiver have bounded space characteristic. We require that an honest sender and receiver can run the protocol using at most

---

**GameSH$_{1^n, \mathbf{f}, \mathcal{I}, \mathbf{x}}^{\mathcal{A}}(b)$**

- If $b = 0$: For each $i \in I$, the challenger connects the $i^{th}$ write tape of the simulator Sim to the $i^{th}$ read tape of the adversary $\mathcal{A}$. The challenger then runs the simulator Sim$(1^n, (\mathbf{f}, \mathcal{I}, (x_j)_{j \in \mathcal{I}}, (f_j(\mathbf{x}))_{j \in \mathcal{I}}))$ and the adversary $\mathcal{A}(1^n, (\mathbf{f}, \mathcal{I}, \mathbf{x}))$.
- Else if $b = 1$: The challenger runs the adversary $\mathcal{A}(1^n, (\mathbf{f}, \mathcal{I}, \mathbf{x}))$. It then places (Input, $(\mathbf{f}, x_i)$) on the $i^{th}$ read tape of $\mathcal{A}$ for each $i \in \mathcal{I}$. The challenger runs the real protocol $\Pi$ on input $(\mathbf{f}, \mathbf{x})$ and space parameter $n$. At each step of the protocol $\Pi$, if any party $i \in I$,
    - reads a bit $c$ on its random tape, then the challenger places (sample, $c$) on the $i^{th}$ read tape of the adversary $\mathcal{A}$.
    - receives a bit $c$ from $j^{th}$ read tape $(j \neq i)$, then the challenger places (receive, $j, c$) on the $i^{th}$ read tape of the adversary $\mathcal{A}$.
- At the end of the protocol, the adversary $\mathcal{A}$ writes a guess bit $b'$ on its output tape, which is considered as the output of the game.

---

**Fig. 1.** Security game for MPC against semi-honest adversary $\mathcal{A}$

space $s_1$, and any dishonest (computationally unbounded) sender and receiver with space less than $s_2$ cannot break the protocol. For the sake of security definition, we add two additional ITMs SenderSim and ReceiverSim, each having 1 write tape, to the protocol description. We first define the correctness of an OT protocol.

**Definition 6 (s-Correctness).** *We say that a protocol $\Pi = (\Pi_{\text{sender}}, \Pi_{\text{receiver}})$ s-correctly performs a 1-out-of-k OT if for every input vector $(m_1, \cdots, m_k) \in \{0, 1\}^k$, every set of random coins used by the ITMs, the output tape of $\Pi_{\text{sender}}$ is empty and the output tape of $\Pi_r$ is $m_c$ at the end of the protocol, and both $\Pi_{\text{sender}}$ and $\Pi_{\text{receiver}}$ uses at most s space through out the protocol.*

**Semi-honest Security.** In this section, we define the notion of semi-honest security of oblivious transfer in the bounded storage model. In the semi-honest model, the parties run the protocol honestly but try to deduce more information than what is described by the functionality from the view of the protocol. The security definition is analogous to the general semi-honest security of MPC protocols for the functionality $f(\{m_i\}_{i \in [k]}, c) = (\phi, m_c)$, where $\phi$ denotes the empty string. To be more concrete, the semi-honest OT protocol has to 2 security requirements – security against a semi-honest sender, and security against a semi-honest receiver. When the sender is semi-honest, we require that the view of the sender (which constitutes its input, sampled randomness and set of all messages received) can be simulated by a space bounded ITM which takes as input $\{m_i\}_{i \in [k]}$. We require that any space-bounded sender (adversary) cannot distinguish between the real view and the simulated view. As we allow the size of the protocol's view to be more than the bound on the space of the turing machines, the simulator does not send the entire view at once. Rather, the simulator sends the view to the adversary as a stream of bits via a communication tape. The adversary has only read once access to this stream of bits. If the adversary needs to access any of the bits multiple times, it can copy onto its (bounded space) work tape. Similarly, when the receiver is semi-honest, we require that the view of the receiver can be simulated by a space bounded ITM which takes as input $(c, m_c)$. Formally,

**Definition 7 (Security against Semi-honest Sender).** *For any functions $s_1 : \mathbb{N} \to \mathbb{N}$, $s_2 : \mathbb{N} \to \mathbb{N}$ and $\epsilon : \mathbb{N} \to [0,1]$, we say that a 1-out-of-k oblivious transfer (OT) protocol $\Pi = (\Pi_{\text{sender}}, \Pi_{\text{receiver}}, \text{SenderSim}, \text{ReceiverSim})$ is $(s_1, s_2, \epsilon)$-secure against a semi-honest sender if*
*(1) The simulator SenderSim has space characteristic at most $s_1$, and*
*(2) For every $s_2$-space bounded adversary $\mathcal{A}$ with 1 read tape, there exists an integer $N_0$ s.t. for all space parameters $n > N_0$, for all message bit tuples $\{m_i\}_{i \in [k]}$ and for every selector bit $d \in [k]$, we have*

$$| \Pr[\text{GameSHSender}^{\mathcal{A}}_{1^n, \{m_i\}_{i \in [k]}, d}(0) = 1] - \Pr[\text{GameSHSender}^{\mathcal{A}}_{1^n, \{m_i\}_{i \subset [k]}, d}(1) = 1]| \leq \epsilon(n),$$

*where the game GameSHSender is described in Fig. 2 and the probability is taken over the random coins used by the simulator, adversary and challenger.*

---

$$\text{GameSH}^{\mathcal{A}}_{1^n, \{m_i\}_{i \in [k]}, d}(\beta)$$

- If $\beta = 0$: The challenger connects the write communication tape of the simulator SenderSim to the read communication tape of the adversary $\mathcal{A}$. The challenger then runs the simulator SenderSim$(1^n, \{m_i\}_{i \in [k]})$ and the adversary $\mathcal{A}(1^n, (\{m_i\}_{i \in [k]}, d))$.
- Else if $\beta = 1$: The challenger runs the adversary $\mathcal{A}(1^n, (\{m_i\}_{i \in [k]}, d))$. It then runs the protocol $\Pi$ with sender's input $\{m_i\}_{i \in [k]}$ and receiver's input $d$. The challenger then places (input, $d$) on the read tape of the adversary. Whenever $\Pi_{\text{sender}}$ reads a bit $b$ on its random tape, the challenger places (sample, $b$) on the read tape of the adversary $\mathcal{A}$. Similarly, whenever $\Pi_{\text{sender}}$ receives a bit $b$ from $\Pi_{\text{receiver}}$, then the challenger places (receive, $b$) on the read tape of the adversary $\mathcal{A}$.
- At the end of the protocol, the adversary $\mathcal{A}$ writes $\beta'$ on its output tape, which is considered as the output of the game.

---

**Fig. 2.** Security game for OT against Semi-honest Sender $\mathcal{A}$

**Definition 8 (Security against Semi-honest Receiver).** *For any functions $s_1 : \mathbb{N} \to \mathbb{N}$, $s_2 : \mathbb{N} \to \mathbb{N}$ and $\epsilon : \mathbb{N} \to [0,1]$, we say that a 1-out-of-k oblivious transfer (OT) protocol $\Pi = (\Pi_{\text{sender}}, \Pi_{\text{receiver}}, \text{SenderSim}, \text{ReceiverSim})$ is $(s_1, s_2, \epsilon)$-secure against a semi-honest receiver if*
*(1) The simulator ReceiverSim has space characteristic at most $s_1$, and*
*(2) For every $s_2$-space bounded adversary $\mathcal{A}$ with 1 read tape, there exists an integer $N_0$ s.t. for all space parameters $n > N_0$, for all message bit tuples $\{m_i\}_{i \in [k]}$ and for every selector bit $d \in [k]$, we have*

$$| \Pr[\text{GameSHReceiver}^{\mathcal{A}}_{1^n, \{m_i\}_{i \in [k]}, d}(0) = 1] - \Pr[\text{GameSHReceiver}^{\mathcal{A}}_{1^n, \{m_i\}_{i \in [k]}, d}(1) = 1]| \leq \epsilon(n),$$

*where GameSHReceiver is described in Fig. 3 and the probability is taken over the random coins used by the simulator, adversary and challenger.*

---

$$\mathsf{GameSHReceiver}^{\mathcal{A}}_{1^n, \{m_i\}_{i \in [k]}, d}(\beta)$$

- If $\beta = 0$: The challenger connects the write communication tape of the simulator ReceiverSim to the read communication tape of the adversary $\mathcal{A}$. The challenger then runs the simulator ReceiverSim$(1^n, (d, m_d))$ and the adversary $\mathcal{A}(1^n, (\{m_i\}_{i \in [k]}, d))$.
- Else if $\beta = 1$: The challenger runs the adversary $\mathcal{A}(1^n, (\{m_i\}_{i \in [k]}, d))$. It then runs the protocol $\Pi$ with sender's input $\{m_i\}_{i \in [k]}$ and receiver's input $d$. The challenger then places (input, $d$) on the read tape of the adversary. Whenever $\Pi_{\mathsf{receiver}}$ reads a bit $b$ on its random tape, the challenger places (sample, $b$) on the read tape of the adversary $\mathcal{A}$. Similarly, whenever $\Pi_{\mathsf{receiver}}$ receives a bit $b$ from $\Pi_{\mathsf{sender}}$, then the challenger places (receive, $b$) on the read tape of the adversary $\mathcal{A}$.
- At the end of the protocol, the adversary $\mathcal{A}$ writes $\beta'$ on its output tape, which is considered as the output of the game.

---

**Fig. 3.** Security game for OT against Semi-honest Receiver $\mathcal{A}$

## 3  Time-Space Lower Bound for Parity Learning for Turing Machines

In this section, we recall the time-space lower bounds for the parity learning problem proved in [19] and adapt the theorems in the context of turing machines. In the parity learning problem, a secret string $k$ is sampled uniformly at random from $\{0,1\}^n$. A learner has to compute the secret $k$ when given a stream of samples $(a_1, b_1), (a_2, b_2), \cdots$, where each $a_i$ is sampled uniformly at random from $\{0,1\}^n$, and $b_i$ is the inner product of $a_i$ and $k$ mod 2. Roughly speaking, Raz [19] proved that any (computationally unbounded) learner that uses less than $n^2/20$ space requires either an exponential number of samples or has an exponentially small probably of outputting the correct answer.

To prove the theorem, Raz modeled the learning algorithm as a branching program. A branching program of length $\ell$ and width $d$ is a directed acyclic graph with vertices arranged as $\ell + 1$ layers, each layer containing at most $d$ vertices. Roughly speaking, each layer represents a time step and a vertex in each layer represents the state of the learning algorithm. Vertices with out-degree 0 are called leaf vertices. The first layer has only one vertex, representing the initial state of the learner. Every non-leaf vertex in the first $\ell$ layers has $2^{n+1}$ outgoing edges connected to the vertices in the next layer. Each of the outgoing edges is labelled with an $n + 1$-bit string $(a, b)$, where $a \in \{0,1\}^n, b \in \{0,1\}$. Intuitively, an edge labelled by $(a, b)$ represents how the learner modifies its state after processing the sample $(a, b)$. Every leaf vertex is associated with a subspace $S \subseteq \{0,1\}^n$. Given a stream of samples $(a_1, b_1), (a_2, b_2), \cdots$, the learner follows the computation path defined by the branching program and outputs the subspace $S$ associated with the final vertex. We interpret the output as the learner guessing that the secret $k \in S$. Formally, [19] proves the following theorem.

**Theorem 1** ([19]). *For any $c < 1/20$, there exists $\alpha > 0$, such that for any $m \leq 2^{\alpha n}$, and a branching program $\mathcal{A}$ of width at most $2^{cn^2}$ and length $m$, that takes a stream of samples $(a_1, b_1)$, $(a_2, b_2)$, $\cdots (a_m, b_m)$, where $k, a_i$ are sampled uniformly from $\{0, 1\}^n$ and $b_i = a_i \cdot k \mod 2$ for every $i$, outputs $\tilde{k} \in \{0, 1\}^n$, then $\Pr[\tilde{k} = k] \leq O(2^{-\alpha n})$.*

The [20] theorem states the lower bound only for deterministic branching programs, whereas we need to model our adversary as a probabilistic interactive turing machine. Therefore, we now prove an analogous time-space lower bound for the parity learning problem modeling the learner as a probabilistic ITM.

*Time-Space Lower Bound for Deterministic Turing Machines.* For the sake of simplicity, we first prove lower bounds for deterministic ITMs without the random tape. We later reduce the lower bounds for probabilistic ITMs to the lower bounds for deterministic ITMs.

In this model, the learner has a space parameter tape storing $1^n$, an input tape, an output tape, and one read comm. tape on which he receives a stream of samples $(a_1, b_1), (a_2, b_2), \cdots$. At the end of the stream, a special symbol $\#$ is given as input to denote the end. The learner has to halt by outputting an $n$-bit string $k$ on its output tape and moving its read comm. tape pointer to the cell next to $\#$. Note that we do not input the stream of samples via the input tape because the ITM has read-only access to the input tape, and the input tape pointer is allowed to move in both directions. As we consider non-uniform learners, the ITM is allowed to have any advice string written on its input tape.

We will present the theorem statement and the proof as below.

**Theorem 2.** *For any $c < 1/20$, there exists $\alpha > 0$, such that for every non-uniform deterministic turing machine $\mathcal{A}$ with 1 read comm. tape and space characteristic $s_c$, where $s_c(n) = cn^2$, for every space parameter $n \in \mathbb{N}$, if $\mathcal{A}(1^n)$ is run with any advice string $x$ of length at most $2^{cn^2/4}$ on its input tape, and a stream of samples $(a_1, b_1), (a_2, b_2), \cdots (a_m, b_m)$ on its read comm. tape, where $m \leq 2^{\alpha n}$, $k, a_i$ are sampled uniformly from $\{0, 1\}^n$ and $b_i = a_i \cdot k \mod 2$ for every $i$, then if $\mathcal{A}$ outputs $\tilde{k} \in \{0, 1\}^n$, the success probability $\Pr[\tilde{k} = k] \leq O(2^{-\alpha n})$.*

*Proof.* For the sake of contradiction, suppose there exists a constant $c < 1/20$ s.t. for any $\alpha > 0$, there exists a non-uniform deterministic $s_c$-space bounded ITM $\mathcal{A}_\alpha$, a space parameter $n$ and an advice string $x$ s.t. $\mathcal{A}_\alpha(1^n, x)$ solves parity learning problem with $m \leq 2^{\alpha n}$ samples and success probability $\epsilon > O(2^{-\alpha n})$. Using this, we show a contradiction to Raz's lower bound. Specifically, for any such $\mathcal{A}_\alpha$, space parameter $n$ and advice string $x$, we construct a corresponding branching program $\mathcal{B}$ that solves the parity learning problem with success probability more than $O(2^{-\alpha n})$.

At any time step during the execution of a turing machine, let us define its configuration to be a tuple containing (state, work tape content, work tape pointer, output tape content, output tape pointer, input tape pointer, space tape pointer). Note that we do not include input tape content as part of the configuration as it does not change during the execution. In the constructed branching program $\mathcal{B}$ vertices in every layer correspond to the possible configurations in the turing machine. As per our definition of space characteristic (Definition 1), the number of possible configurations of $\mathcal{A}$ is $2^{s_c(n)}$ and therefore the width of the branching program $\mathcal{B}$ is $2^{s_c(n)}$. We now describe how the edges are connected between adjacent layers. Consider any vertex $v$ of the branching program and let its corresponding configuration be con. Consider any $n+1$-bit string $(a, b)$, where $a \in \{0, 1\}^n, b \in \{0, 1\}$. We run the turing machine $\mathcal{A}(1^n)$ starting from this configuration con by placing $x$ on its input tape, $(a, b)$ on read comm. tape and placing pointer for read comm. tape at the starting cell of $(a, b)$. When the read comm. tape pointer first reaches the cell next to $b$, let its configuration be con'. Note that there exists only one possible configuration con' as $\mathcal{A}$ is deterministic.[8] In $\mathcal{B}$, we place a directed edge from vertex $v$ to the vertex $w$ in the next layer which corresponds to the configuration con'. We now describe how to associate any vertex $v$ in the final layer with an $n$-bit string $k$. Let the configuration corresponding to $v$ be con. Run the turing machine $\mathcal{A}(1^n)$ from this configuration con by placing $x$ on its input tape, $\#$ on read comm. tape and placing the pointer for read comm. tape at $\#$. When $\mathcal{A}$ runs and places its read comm. tape pointer to the cell next to $\#$, let the output written on its output tape be $y$. We associate the vertex $v$ with the string $y$. Note that the branching program $\mathcal{B}$ has length $m$, width $2^{cn^2}$ and solves parity learning with success probability $\epsilon$ which is more than $O(2^{-\alpha n})$, thereby violating Raz's time-space lower bound.

*Time-Space Lower Bound for Probabilistic Turing Machines.* We now give an analogous time-space lower bound theorem for probabilistic ITMs.

**Theorem 3.** *For any $c < 1/20$, there exists $\alpha > 0$, such that for every non-uniform probabilistic turing machine $\mathcal{A}$ with 1 read comm. tape and space characteristic $s_c$, where $s_c(n) = cn^2$, for every space parameter $n \in \mathbb{N}$, if $\mathcal{A}(1^n)$ is run with any advice string $x$ on its input tape, and a stream of samples $(a_1, b_1)$, $(a_2, b_2), \cdots (a_m, b_m)$ on its read comm. tape, where $m \leq 2^{\alpha n}$, $k, a_i$ are sampled uniformly from $\{0, 1\}^n$ and $b_i = a_i \cdot k \mod 2$ for every $i$, then if outputs $\tilde{k} \in \{0, 1\}^n$, the success probability $\Pr[\tilde{k} = k] \leq O(2^{-\alpha n})$.*

*Proof.* For the sake of contradiction, suppose there exists a constant $c < 1/20$ s.t. for any $\alpha > 0$, there exists a non-uniform probabilistic $s_c$-space bounded ITM $\mathcal{A}_\alpha$, a space parameter $n_\alpha$ and an advice string $x_\alpha$ s.t. $\mathcal{A}_\alpha(1^{n_\alpha}, x_\alpha)$ solves parity learning problem with success probability $\epsilon > O(2^{-\alpha n_\alpha})$ using at most $m \leq 2^{\alpha n_\alpha}$ samples. Using this, we show a contradiction to Raz's lower bound. Specifically, for any $\alpha > 0$, we construct a non-uniform deterministic $s_{c'}$-space bounded ITM $\mathcal{B}_\alpha$ and an advice string $x'_\alpha$ that solves parity learning problem with success probability more than $O(2^{-\alpha n_\alpha})$.

---

[8] Observe that the transition function in the resulting branching program is deterministic even if the output tape contents are not included in the configuration definition. We include the output tape contents in the configuration so that every vertex in the final layer corresponds to an output key as defined by the turing machine.

For any $\alpha > 0$, let the success probability of $\mathcal{A}_\alpha(1^{n_\alpha}, x_\alpha)$ in solving the parity learning problem be $\epsilon$, where the probability is taken over the random coins used to create samples $(a_i, b_i)$ and the random coins used by $\mathcal{A}_\alpha$. Let rnd be the upper bound on the random coins used by $\mathcal{A}_\alpha$[9]. We know that there exists a bit $r_1 \in \{0,1\}$ s.t. $\mathcal{A}_\alpha(1^{n_\alpha}, x_\alpha)$ solves the parity learning problem with success probability at least $\epsilon$, when the first cell of $\mathcal{A}_\alpha$'s random tape is fixed to be $r_1$. Extending this argument, we know that there exists a rnd-bit string $r_\alpha$ s.t. $\mathcal{A}_\alpha(1^{n_\alpha}, x_\alpha)$ solves the parity learning problem with success probability at least $\epsilon$, when the entire random tape is fixed to $r_\alpha$. For any $\alpha > 0$, let us now construct the ITM $\mathcal{B}_\alpha$ along with an advice string $x'_\alpha$. At a high level, we let $x'_\alpha$ be equal to $x_\alpha$ concatenated with $r_\alpha$ i.e., the random coins on which $\mathcal{A}_\alpha$ has high success probability are given as part of advice string to $\mathcal{B}_\alpha$. $\mathcal{B}_\alpha(1^{n_\alpha}, x'_\alpha)$ emulates $\mathcal{A}_\alpha(1^{n_\alpha}, x_\alpha)$ with random coins hardcoded to $r_\alpha$. Whenever $\mathcal{A}_\alpha$ reads a bit from its random tape, $\mathcal{B}_\alpha$ reads the corresponding bit from its advice string.

We now analyze the space characteristic of $\mathcal{B}_\alpha$. Clearly, $\mathcal{B}_\alpha$ uses the same number of work tape and output tape cells as $\mathcal{A}_\alpha$. The space characteristic of $\mathcal{A}_\alpha$ has $\log(|x_\alpha| \cdot \text{rnd})$ term in it, whereas the space characteristic of $\mathcal{B}_\alpha$ has only $\log(|x'_\alpha|) = \log(|x_\alpha| + \text{rnd})$ term in it. The number of states of $\mathcal{B}$ is only a small constant times the number of states in $\mathcal{A}$. Therefore, $\mathcal{B}_\alpha$ is $s_c$-space bounded ITM. Moreover, the success probability of $\mathcal{B}_\alpha$ is at least $\epsilon$, and thereby breaks the time-space lower bound for deterministic ITMs.

*Time-Space Lower Bound for Interactive Turing Machines.* In the above theorems, we restricted the learner to receive only the stream of parity learning samples and not interact with any other ITMs. Looking forward, we construct an OT protocol based on parity learning and prove that if there exists an adversary $\mathcal{A}$ that breaks OT security, then there exists a reduction algorithm $\mathcal{B}$ that solves parity learning problem within low space characteristic. In the proof, $\mathcal{B}$ has to interact with $\mathcal{A}$ to solve the parity learning problem. In the standard model where the adversary is computationally bounded, this is not an issue because $\mathcal{B}$ can internally interact with $\mathcal{A}$ in poly time. However, in the bounded storage model, we need to be careful as we need to ensure $\mathcal{B}$ can internally run the conversation with $\mathcal{A}$ in bounded space. As similar scenario occurs in every proof where we need to construct a reduction algorithm, we present a general theorem which roughly states that if $\mathcal{B}$ solves a problem by interacting with $\mathcal{A}$, then there exists another TM $\mathcal{C}$ which can solve the problem without interacting with any other ITMs. At a high level, $\mathcal{C}$ runs both $\mathcal{A}$ and $\mathcal{B}$ internally, emulates their interaction using its work tape, and finally outputs whatever $\mathcal{B}$ outputs.

Formally, in this model, we have two ITMs – $\mathcal{A}$ and $\mathcal{B}$. $\mathcal{B}$ has $t_1 + 1$ read comm. tapes and $t_2$ write comm. tapes for some integers $t_1, t_2$. Similarly, $\mathcal{A}$ has $t_2$ read comm. tapes and $t_1$ write comm. tapes. $\mathcal{B}$ receives a stream of bits sampled from some distribution $\mathcal{D}$ from a challenger on its first read comm. tape, and uses the rest of its tapes to send and receive messages from $\mathcal{A}$. Both $\mathcal{A}, \mathcal{B}$ are allowed to be randomized and have any advice string on their input tapes. At the end of

---

[9] Note that $\mathcal{A}_\alpha$ can use only at most $2^{s_c(n)}$ bits of randomness as it is $s_c$-space bounded.

the execution, the string written by $\mathcal{B}$ on its output tape is considered to be the output of $(\mathcal{A}, \mathcal{B})$ pair. We now show that there exists an ITM $\mathcal{C}$ with only 1 read tape using which $\mathcal{C}$ receives a stream of bits sampled from the challenger, s.t. for any distribution of $\mathcal{D}$ used by the challenger, the output distribution of $\mathcal{C}$ is same as that of $(\mathcal{A}, \mathcal{B})$.

**Theorem 4.** *For any pair of ITMs $(\mathcal{A}, \mathcal{B})$ described above with space characteristic $s_A$ and $s_B$ respectively, there exists another ITM $\mathcal{C}$ with 1 read comm. tape and space characteristic $2(s_A + s_B) + \Delta$, where $\Delta$ is a constant that depends only number of tapes in $(\mathcal{A}, \mathcal{B})$, s.t. for any pair of advice strings $x_A, x_B$ given to $\mathcal{A}, \mathcal{B}$ respectively, there exists an advice string $x_C$, s.t. for any space parameter $n$ and any distribution $\mathcal{D}$ used by the challenger, the output distribution of $(\mathcal{A}, \mathcal{B})$ is same as the output distribution of $\mathcal{C}$.*

*Proof.* Let us first construct the ITM $\mathcal{C}$ along with its advice string $x_C$. For each symbol $\beta$ present in the alphabet of $\mathcal{A}, \mathcal{B}$, we include the symbol $\beta$ along with a fresh symbol $\underline{\beta}$ in the alphabet of $\mathcal{C}$. We also include a fresh symbol \$ which we call 'tape separator'. Intuitively, $\mathcal{C}$ internally runs both $\mathcal{A}, \mathcal{B}$ by maintaining many of the $\mathcal{A}, \mathcal{B}$'s tapes on its work tape. Specifically, the work tape of $\mathcal{C}$ is divided into many sections separated by the symbol \$. Each of the sections is used to simulate one of the following – work tape of $\mathcal{A}$, work tape of $\mathcal{B}$, output tape of $\mathcal{A}$, communication tapes between $\mathcal{A}$ and $\mathcal{B}$. Let the total number of communication tapes between $\mathcal{A}$ and $\mathcal{B}$ be $t$.[10] The work tape of $\mathcal{C}$ looks as follows.

$\mathcal{A}$'s work tape \$ $\mathcal{B}$'s work tape \$ $\mathcal{A}$'s output tape \$ comm. tape 1 \$ $\cdots$ \$ comm. tape t \$

The sections reserved for internal communication tapes store only last cell that is not yet read by the other turing machine. The input tape of $\mathcal{C}$ is also divided into 2 sections to simulate the input tapes of $\mathcal{A}$ and $\mathcal{B}$. So, the advice string $x_C$ is given by $x_A||\$||x_B$, where $||$ denotes concatenation. The output tape of $\mathcal{C}$ is used to store the output tape of $\mathcal{B}$. The random tape of $\mathcal{C}$ is used to provide randomness required to run both $\mathcal{A}$ and $\mathcal{B}$ internally. At any time step, the fresh symbols with an underscore are used to mark the tape heads for each of these internal tapes.

At a high level, $\mathcal{C}$ first runs the transition function of $\mathcal{A}$ internally for one step and then runs the transition function of $\mathcal{B}$ internally for another step and repeats. $\mathcal{C}$ internally runs the transition function of $\mathcal{A}$ (similarly for $\mathcal{B}$) in multiple steps – (1) $\mathcal{C}$ first scans the entire work tape and input tape. For each section of the tapes, $\mathcal{C}$ stores the symbol at the internal tape head (the symbols with an underscore) in its state. (2) $\mathcal{C}$ then runs the transition function of $\mathcal{A}$ and stores the set of actions to be performed (such as moving internal tapes heads to left or right) in its state. (3) Finally, $\mathcal{C}$ scans the entire work tape, input tape, and output tapes and performs the required actions. (4) $\mathcal{C}$ finally switches its

---

[10] Note that $\mathcal{B}$ has 1 additional read communication tape to receive a stream of bits from the challenger.

state to perform the next transition for $\mathcal{B}$. In order to enable $\mathcal{C}$ to perform these actions, we design the state space of $\mathcal{C}$ in the following way. A state of $\mathcal{C}$ is a tuple consisting of

($\mathcal{A}'$s state, $\mathcal{B}'$s state, mode, tape head contents/actions to be performed, current section)

Here, the *mode* indicates, whether $\mathcal{C}$ is currently reading contents of internal tape heads, or performing a transition for $\mathcal{A}$ or $\mathcal{B}$. *Current section* indicates the internal section at which the tape head of $\mathcal{C}$ is currently located at.

Let us now analyze the space characteristic of ITM $\mathcal{C}$. Let the number of states, number of work tape cells, number of input tape cells, number of output tape cells, alphabet size and total number of communication tapes $\mathcal{A}$ be $Q_A, W_A, \mathsf{ip}_A, \mathsf{op}_A, \alpha_A, t$ Let the corresponding values for ITM $\mathcal{B}$ be $Q_B, W_B, \mathsf{ip}_B, \mathsf{op}_B, \alpha_B, t+1$ respectively. The number of work tape cells of $\mathcal{C}$ including the tape separators is given by $W_C = (W_A + W_B + \mathsf{op}_A + 2t + 3)$. For the sake of simplicity, let us assume both $\mathcal{A}, \mathcal{B}$ use alphabet of same size $\alpha$.[11] The number of input tape, output tape cells, and alphabet size of $\mathcal{C}$ is given by $\mathsf{ip}_C = \mathsf{ip}_A + \mathsf{ip}_B + 1$, $\mathsf{op}_C = \mathsf{op}_B$, $\alpha_C = 2 * \alpha$ respectively[12]. The number of states in $\mathcal{C}$ is given by $Q_C = Q_A \cdot Q_B \cdot (2\alpha_C)^t \cdot (\log t) \cdot K$, for some constant $K$. $\mathcal{C}$ has only one read communication tape to receive inputs from the challenger. The amount of randomness uses by $\mathcal{C}$ is $\mathsf{rnd}_C = \mathsf{rnd}_A + \mathsf{rnd}_B$. Therefore, the space characteristic of $\mathcal{C}$ is given by

$$(W_C + \mathsf{op}_C + 3)\log_2 \alpha_C + \log_2(n \cdot Q_C \cdot W_C \cdot \mathsf{ip}_C \cdot \mathsf{op}_C \cdot \mathsf{rnd}_C)$$
$$\leq 2[(W_A + \mathsf{op}_A + 2t)\log_2(\alpha) + \log_2(n \cdot Q_A \cdot W_A \cdot \mathsf{ip}_A \cdot \mathsf{op}_A \cdot \mathsf{rnd}_A)]$$
$$+ 2[(W_B + \mathsf{op}_B + 2t + 2)\log_2(\alpha) + \log(n \cdot Q_B \cdot W_B \cdot \mathsf{ip}_B \cdot \mathsf{op}_B \cdot \mathsf{rnd}_B)] + \Delta$$
$$= 2(s_A + s_B) + \Delta$$

for some constant $\Delta$ that depends only on $t$.     ∎

## 3.1 Indistinguishability Parity Learning

The Guan-Zhandry 1-out-of-2 OT construction [11] is based on indistinguishability version of the Raz's parity learning space lower bound so that they can give indistinguishability security proofs for the construction. To extend the hardness result for the computational problem to the hardness result for the indistinguishability problem, they use the Goldreich-Levin algorithm, denoted as GL for the rest of the paper.

---

[11] If $\mathcal{A}$ uses an alphabet of size $\alpha_A$ and $\mathcal{B}$ uses an alphabet of size $\alpha_B$, then we can first convert them into turing machines $\mathcal{A}', \mathcal{B}'$ both using an alphabet of size two, and then apply the Theorem 4. Each symbol of $\mathcal{A}$ is represented using $\log \alpha_A$ symbols in $\mathcal{A}'$. $\mathcal{A}'$ internally runs the transition function of $\mathcal{A}$ in multiple stages. It reads a sequence of $\log \alpha_A$ bits from each tape and stores as part of the state, and then apply the transition function of $\mathcal{A}$ by writing $\log \alpha_A$ symbols to each tape.

[12] We could eliminate the need of introducing a new symbol for the tape separator by reusing the other fresh symbols introduced in $\mathcal{C}$.

**Theorem 5 (Goldreich-Levin Algorithm [8]).** *Assume that there exists a function* $f : \{0,1\}^n \to \{0,1\}$ *s.t. for some unknown* $x \in \{0,1\}^n$, *we have*

$$\Pr_{r \in \{0,1\}^n}[f(r) = \langle \boldsymbol{x}, \boldsymbol{r} \rangle] \geq \frac{1}{2} + \epsilon$$

*Then there exists an algorithm that runs in time* $O(n^2 \epsilon^{-4} \log n)$, *makes* $O(n^2 \epsilon^{-4} \log n)$ *oracle queries to the function* $f$, *and outputs* $x$ *with probability* $\Omega(\epsilon^2)$.

Importantly, the GL algorithm also has $O(n)$ space characteristic so that we can use it during reduction.

We review the definition for the indistinguishability security game of parity learning, denoted as $\mathsf{PL}_{\mathcal{A},\delta}(n,\ell)$.

**Definition 9. (Indistinguishability Parity Learning** $PL_{\mathcal{A},\delta}(n,\ell)$**).** *The challenger's input is* $(1^n, 1^\ell)$

1. *The challenger chooses a random* $k \in \{0,1\}^n$.
2. *For* $i = 1, \cdots, \ell$:
   - *The challenger writes* $(\boldsymbol{a}_i, b_i)$ *on the communication tape, where* $\boldsymbol{a}_i \leftarrow \{0,1\}^n$ *is uniformly random and* $b_i = \boldsymbol{a}_i \cdot \boldsymbol{k}$.
3. *The challenger writes* $(\boldsymbol{a}_\ell, b_\ell)$ *on the communication tape, where* $\boldsymbol{a}_\ell \leftarrow \{0,1\}^n$ *is uniformly random and chooses a random bit* $\delta \in \{0,1\}$:
   - *If* $\delta = 0$, $b_\ell = \boldsymbol{a}_\ell \cdot \boldsymbol{k}$.
   - *If* $\delta = 1$, $b_\ell$ *is a random bit.*
4. *Finally,* $\mathcal{A}$ *outputs a guess* $\delta'$ *for* $\delta$. $\mathcal{A}$*'s advantage is defined as* $(\Pr[\delta' = \delta] - 1/2)$.

Next, we give a security proof in the ITM setting so that we can use the indistinguishability parity learning lower bound in later sections.

**Theorem 6.** *For any* $c < 1/20$, *there exists* $\alpha > 0$ *such that for all ITM adversary* $\mathcal{A}$ *with* $cn^2$*-space characteristic and that receives at most* $2^{\alpha n}$ *parity learning tuples,* $\mathcal{A}$ *has advantage* $O(2^{-\alpha n/2})$ *in* $PL_{\mathcal{A},\delta}(n, 2^{\alpha n})$, *for all* $n \in \mathbb{N}$.

*Proof.* For the sake of contradiction, suppose there is some $c < 1/40$ such that for all $\alpha > 0$, there exists an ITM adversary $\mathcal{A}$ with $cn^2$-space characteristic and using at most $2^{\alpha n}$ parity learning tuples solves the above PL problem with advantage $\beta = \Omega(2^{-\alpha n/2})$ in $\mathsf{PL}_{\mathcal{A},\delta}(n, 2^{\alpha n})$. We show that there exists an ITM adversary $\mathcal{A}'$ with $(2cn^2 + O(n))$-space characteristic, which uses at most $2^{\alpha n}$ parity learning tuples and solves the parity learning problem with advantage $\beta' = \Omega(2^{-\alpha n})$, which would contradict Theorem 3. There exists some $N_0$, such that for all $n > N_0$, there exists some $c' < 1/20$ such that $c'n^2 \geq 2cn^2 + O(n)$.

As a first step, we show that if an adversary can distinguish between $(\mathbf{a}_\ell, b_\ell \leftarrow \{0,1\})$ and $(\mathbf{a}_\ell, b_\ell = \mathbf{a}_\ell \cdot \mathbf{k})$ with large probability, then we can have an algorithm that outputs $f(\mathbf{a}_\ell) = \mathbf{a}_\ell \cdot \mathbf{k}$ on input $\mathbf{a}_\ell$ with large probability.

*Claim.* If there exists some $c_1 < 1/20$, we have an ITM $\mathcal{A}$ with space characteristic $c_1 n^2$ that can distinguish between $(\mathbf{a}_\ell, b_\ell \leftarrow \{0,1\})$ and $(\mathbf{a}_\ell, b_\ell = \mathbf{a}_\ell \cdot \mathbf{k})$ with probability $p$, given $\{(\mathbf{a}_i, b_i = \mathbf{a}_1 \cdot \mathbf{k})\}_{i=1,\cdots,\ell-1}$ in a stream; then we can have an ITM $\mathcal{B}$ with space characteristic $c_2 n^2$ for some $c_2 < 1/20$, $\mathcal{B}$ outputs $\mathbf{a}_\ell \cdot \mathbf{k}$, with probability $p$.

*Proof.* Let $\mathcal{A}$ output $(d, b_\ell)$ where $d$ is a bit indicating $\mathcal{A}$'s guess. If $\mathcal{A}$ thinks $b_\ell = \mathbf{a}_\ell \cdot \mathbf{k}$, then $d = 0$; if it thinks $b_\ell \leftarrow \{0,1\}$, then $d = 1$. $\mathcal{B}$ outputs $(b_\ell + d)$ as its guess for the value $\mathbf{a}_\ell \cdot \mathbf{k}$. Since $\mathcal{A}$ is correct with probability $p$, then $\mathcal{B}$ outputs the correct value $\mathbf{a}_\ell \cdot \mathbf{k}$ with probability $p$.

Let the challenger in $\mathsf{PL}_{\mathcal{A},\delta}(n, \ell)$ be an adversary $\mathcal{A}'$ in a modified parity learning game. a tuple in which $b_\ell$ can be a real inner product or uniformly random described as below.

**Definition 10 (Modified Parity Learning $\mathsf{MPL}_{\mathcal{A},\delta}(n, m, \ell)$).** *The challenger's input is* $(1^n, 1^m, 1^\ell)$.

1. *The challenger chooses a random* $k \in \{0,1\}^n$.
2. *For* $i = 1, \cdots, m$:

   *If* $i < \ell$:
   - *The challenger writes* $(\mathbf{a}_i, b_i)$ *on the communication tape, where* $\mathbf{a}_i \leftarrow \{0,1\}^n$ *is uniformly random and* $b_i = \mathbf{a}_i \cdot \mathbf{k}$.
   *Else if* $i \geq \ell$:
   - *The challenger writes* $(\mathbf{a}_i, b_i)$ *on the communication tape, where* $\mathbf{a}_i \leftarrow \{0,1\}^n$ *is uniformly random and chooses a random bit* $\lambda \leftarrow \{0,1\}$:
     - *If* $\lambda = 0$, $b_i = \mathbf{a}_i \cdot \mathbf{k}$.
     - *If* $\lambda = 1$, $b_i$ *is a random bit.*
3. *Finally,* $\mathcal{A}$ *outputs a guess* $k'$ *for* $k$ *and wins if* $k' = k$.

$\mathcal{A}'$ receives parity learning tuples $(\mathbf{a}_i, b_i)_{i=1,\cdots,\ell}$ from the $\mathsf{MPL}_{\mathcal{A},\delta}(n, m, \ell)$ challenger and writes it on the communication tape to $\mathcal{A}$. The first $(\ell - 1)$ tuples are used as the stream of parity learning tuples in $\mathsf{PL}_{\mathcal{A},\delta}(n, \ell)$ and the rest $(m - \ell)$ tuples each is used as a challenge tuple in $\mathsf{PL}_{\mathcal{A},\delta}(n, \ell)$.

The advantage of $\mathcal{A}$ is $\beta = |\Pr[\mathsf{PL}_{\mathcal{A},0}(n, \ell) = 0] - \Pr[\mathsf{PL}_{\mathcal{A},1}(n, \ell) = 1]|$. In other words, we have an ITM $\mathcal{A}$ that given $(\mathbf{a}_1, b_1), \cdots, (\mathbf{a}_{\ell-1}, b_{\ell-1})$ on the read tape, can distinguish between $(\mathbf{a}_\ell, b_\ell \leftarrow \{0,1\})$ and $(\mathbf{a}_\ell, b_\ell = \mathbf{a}_\ell \cdot \mathbf{k})$ with probability $(1 + \beta)/2$. According to Sect. 3.1, given unknown $\mathbf{k} \in \{0,1\}^n$ and $\mathbf{a}_\ell \in \{0,1\}^n$ the function $f(\mathbf{a}_\ell) = \langle \mathbf{a}_\ell, \mathbf{k} \rangle$ can be computed with probability $(1 + \beta)/2$.

After receiving every $\ell$ tuples from the $\mathsf{MPL}_{\mathcal{A},\delta}(n, m, \ell)$ challenger, $\mathcal{A}'$ can obtain $f(\mathbf{a}_i) = \langle \mathbf{a}_i, \mathbf{k} \rangle$ for each $\mathbf{a}_i$ with probability $(1 + \beta)/2$, where $i \geq l$, ; $\mathcal{A}'$ runs the GL algorithm from Theorem 5 along with obtaining $O(n^2 \beta^4 \log n)$ number of inner products of $\mathbf{k}$ with $\mathbf{a}_i$ by invoking $\mathcal{A}$. By Theorem 5 $\mathcal{A}'$ can output correct $\mathbf{k}$ with probability $\Omega(\beta^2)$ in the end. $\mathcal{A}'$ simulates $\mathcal{A}$ using $cn^2$ space and running GL algorithm takes $O(n)$ space; $\mathcal{A}$'s space characteristic is $(2cn^2 + O(n))$ ; according to Theorem 3, $\mathcal{A}'$'s advantage is $O(2^{-\alpha n})$ and we must have $\Omega(\beta^2) \leq O(2^{-\alpha n})$. Hence, using $cn^2$ space and at most $2^{\alpha n}$ tuples, adversary $\mathcal{A}$'s advantage is at most $\beta = O(2^{-\alpha n/2})$.

## 4   1-Out-of-4 Semi-honest OT Construction

In this section, we describe our 1-out-of-4 oblivious transfer based on 1-out-of-2 oblivious transfer in the bounded storage model. In summary, we perform six 1-out-of-2 oblivious transfer with random input bits.

1. Let the sender's input be $(m_0, m_1, m_2, m_3)$, and the receiver's input be $t \in \{0, 1, 2, 3\}$.
2. For each pair $(a, b) \in \{0, 1, 2, 3\}^2$ s.t $a < b$,

   Sender samples uniformly random bits denoted by $r_{a,b}^a, r_{a,b}^b \leftarrow \{0, 1\}$. If $t = a$, receiver sets $c = 0$, else if $t = b$ receiver sets $c = 1$, else receiver samples $c \leftarrow \{0, 1\}$. The sender and the receiver performs 1-out-of-2 OT with sender's input $(r_{a,b}^a, r_{a,b}^b)$ and receiver's input $c$.
3. The Sender sends the following 4 bits $(y_0, y_1, y_2, y_3)$ to the receiver.

$$y_0 = m_0 + r_{0,1}^0 + r_{0,2}^0 + r_{0,3}^0$$

$$y_1 = m_1 + r_{0,1}^1 + r_{1,2}^1 + r_{1,3}^1$$

$$y_2 = m_2 + r_{0,2}^2 + r_{1,2}^2 + r_{2,3}^2$$

$$y_3 = m_3 + r_{0,3}^3 + r_{1,3}^3 + r_{2,3}^3$$

4. The receiver computes $m_t$ from $y_t$ as he has all the 3 mask bits from the 1-out-of-2 oblivious transfers.

We will leave the proofs for correctness and security to Appendix A. We also review the 1-of-2 OT construction from [11] in Sect. B.

## 5   MPC Protocol in Bounded Storage

In this section, we describe our $k$-party semi-honest secure MPC protocol (for any integer $k$) in the bounded storage model from semi-honest secure 1-out-4 OT protocol in the bounded storage model.

Consider any functionality $\mathbf{f} = (f_1, f_2, \cdots f_k)$. Let the private input of each party $\mathcal{P}_i$ be $x_i$. The party $\mathcal{P}_i$ intends to compute $f_i(x_1, x_2, \cdots x_k)$. We first represent the functionality as a circuit $C$ containing only XOR and AND gates, which takes the inputs of all the parties and computes the output of all the parties. Let us denote the space parameter used by the protocol to be $n$, and let $\mathcal{C}_n$ be the set of all $n$-gate circuits. We describe our MPC protocol for the class of functionalities $\{\mathcal{C}_n\}_{n \in \mathbb{N}}$. We show that an honest party can run the protocol within $O(n)$ space characteristic, whereas any dishonest set of parties require at least $O(n^2)$ space characteristic to break the security.

**Notations.** Let us first introduce some notations. We order the gates of the circuit in such a way that $g_1, g_2 < g_3$ if the output wires of gates $g_1, g_2$ are used as input wires for gate $g_3$. We call such an order as a logical order. We denote the set of input wires and output wires of the circuit that belong to the party $\mathcal{P}_i$ be Input($i$) and Output($i$) respectively. Also for any input wire $w$, let the party that holds the private input corresponding to the wire be Party($w$). Similarly, for any output wire $w$, let the party that is entitled to receive output from the wire be Party($w$). Let the input of the circuit $C$ on input $\mathbf{x} = (x_1, \cdots, x_k)$ be $\mathbf{y} = (y_1, \cdots, y_k)$. For any input wire $w$ that belongs to the party $\mathcal{P}_i$, let $\mathcal{P}_i$'s input bit corresponding to the wire $w$ be $x_i[w]$. Similarly, for any output wire $w$ that belongs to the party $\mathcal{P}_i$, let $\mathcal{P}_i$'s output bit corresponding to the $w$ be $y_i[w]$. When the circuit $C$ is run on the input $(x_1, \cdots, x_k)$, let the value at any wire $w$ be $v_w$.

At a high level, the algorithm is similar to the GMW protocol [9]. Each party $\mathcal{P}_i$ first secret shares its input $x_i$ with all the parties. Each of the parties now holds a secret share of $v_w$ for each input wire $w$. The parties now run a 1-out-of-4 OT protocol to compute secret shares of $v_w$ for each of the internal and output wires. Finally, for each output wire $w$, each party sends its secret share of $v_w$ to the party that is entitled to receive the value of wire $w$ (i.e., Party($w$)). Each party $\mathcal{P}_i$ now computes its output from the received shares.

Let $\mathsf{OT}_4 = (\Pi_{\mathsf{sender}}, \Pi_{\mathsf{receiver}}, \mathsf{SenderSim}, \mathsf{ReceiverSim})$ be a 1-out-of-4 oblivious transfer protocol secure in the bounded storage model. For the sake of simplicity, we assume that the receiver's choice in the $\mathsf{OT}_4$ protocol is chosen from $\{(0,0), (0,1), (1,0), (1,1)\}$ intead of $\{0,1,2,3\}$. The algorithm used by each party $\mathcal{P}_i$ is formally described in Fig. 4. Note that all the computations over bits are done over $\mathsf{GF}(2)$.

## 5.1   Security Proof for MPC Protocol

We present the proof of security and correctness for the MPC protocol in Sect. 5 here.

*Correctness.* Throughout the protocol, we maintain an invariant that the values $\{r_{i,w}\}_i$ for any wire $w$ form a secret sharing of the bit $v_w$ i.e., $\sum_{i \in [k]} r_{i,w} = v_w$. We can prove this via induction. Clearly, the invariant is satisfied if $w$ is an input wire. Suppose the invariant is satisfied for the input wires $a, b$ of any gate $g$. If $g$ is an XOR gate, then $\sum_i r_{i,c} = \sum_i r_{i,a} + \sum_i r_{i,b} = v_a + v_b = v_c$ and the invariant is satisfied for the output wire. Suppose $g$ is an AND gate, each pair of parties $(i, j)$ perform 1-out-4 OT and obtain a secret sharing of $r_{i,a} * r_{j,b} + r_{i,b} * r_{j,a}$. Therefore, $\sum_i r_{i,c} = \sum_i r_{i,a} * r_{i,b} + \sum_{i \neq j}(r_{i,a} * r_{j,b} + r_{i,b} * r_{j,a}) = (\sum_i r_{i,a}) * (\sum_i r_{i,b}) = v_a * v_b = v_c$.

We now argue that if $\mathsf{OT}_4$ is $s$-correct for some function $s : \mathbb{N} \to \mathbb{N}$, then all the parties in the above protocol have space characteristic at most $O(s + n)$ for the class of $n$-gate functionalities. Observe that work tape of each party needs to store at most 1 bit per each wire, along with work tape contents needed for oblivious transfer. Both the input and output tapes need to store at most $n$ bits, as we are dealing with $n$-gate functionalities. Moreover, the number of states required by the protocol is only constant times that of the number of states in $\mathsf{OT}_4$. Therefore, the above MPC protocol has space characteristic $O(s + n)$.

$$\Pi_i(1^n, C, x_i)$$

**Input Phase:**

For each input wire $w \in \mathsf{Input}(i)$:
    For $j = 1$ to $k$ s.t. $j \neq i$:
        Sample random bit $r_{j,w}$ and send it to party $\mathcal{P}_j$.
    Set $r_{i,w} = x_i[w] + \sum_{j \neq i} r_{j,w}$.
For each input wire $w \notin \mathsf{Input}(i)$:
    Receive bit $r_{i,w}$ from other parties. This corresponds to the party $\mathcal{P}_i$'s share of the
    input at wire $w$.

**Eval Phase:**
For each gate $g$ in logical order:

- Let $a, b$ be the input wires and $c$ be the output wire of gate $g$.
- If $g$ is XOR gate, set $r_{i,c} = r_{i,a} + r_{i,b}$.
- If $g$ is AND gate:
  - For $j = 1$ to $i - 1$:
    Run $\mathsf{OT}_4.\Pi_{\mathsf{receiver}}$ algorithm with $(r_{i,a}, r_{i,b})$ as input and party $\mathcal{P}_j$ as the OT sender.
    Let the received message bit be $\beta_j$.
  - For $j = i + 1$ to $k$:
    Sample bit $\alpha_j \leftarrow \{0, 1\}$.
    For each $(x, y) \in \{0, 1\}^2$, compute message $m_{(x,y)} = \alpha_j + x * r_{i,b} + y * r_{i,a}$.
    Run $\mathsf{OT}_4.\Pi_{\mathsf{sender}}$ algorithm with input messages $(m_{(0,0)}, m_{(0,1)}, m_{(1,0)}, m_{(1,1)})$ and $\mathcal{P}_j$ as the OT receiver.
  - Set the party $\mathcal{P}_i$'s share for wire $c$ as $r_{i,c} = r_{i,a} * r_{i,b} + \sum_{j=1}^{i-1} \beta_j + \sum_{j=i+1}^{k} \alpha_j$.

**Output Phase:**
For each output wire $w$:

- If $w \notin \mathsf{Output}(i)$, send the party $\mathcal{P}_i$'s share $r_{i,w}$ to the party $\mathsf{Party}(w)$.
- If $w \in \mathsf{Output}(i)$, receive secret shares of the wire $w$ from the other parties i.e.,
  For $j = 1$ to $k$ s.t. $j \neq i$:
      Receive bit $r_{j,w}$ from party $\mathcal{P}_j$.
  Compute the output bit $y[w] = \sum_{j=1}^{k} r_{j,w}$ and write it to the output tape.

**Fig. 4.** The algorithm used by the party $\mathcal{P}_i$ in the MPC protocol.

If $\mathsf{OT}_4$ scheme presented in the Sect. 4 is used, the space characteristic of the protocol is $O(n)$.

## 5.2   Proof of Security

We now prove that the above scheme is semi-honest secure against adversaries that have space characteristic less than $n^2/80$. Formally, we prove the following theorem.

**Theorem 7.** *For any functions $s_1, s_2, s_3 : \mathbb{N} \to \mathbb{N}$, and $\epsilon : \mathbb{N} \to [0, 1]$, assuming $\mathsf{OT}_4$ is $s_1$-correct (as per Definition 6), $(s_2, s_3, \epsilon)$-secure against semi-honest sender and $(s_2, s_3, \epsilon)$-secure against semi-honest receiver (as per Definitions 7 and 8),[13] the above $k$-party MPC protocol is $(O(s_1 + s_2 + kn), s_2/2 - (s_1 + s_3 + O(n)), \epsilon \cdot n \cdot k^2)$ semi-honest secure for the class of the $n$-gate functionalities $\{\mathcal{C}_n\}_{n \in \mathbb{N}}$.*

*Proof.* To prove security, we first build a simulator Sim which given a circuit $\mathcal{C}$, a set of parties $\mathcal{I}$ along with their input-output pairs, outputs a view of the parties in the set $\mathcal{I}$. We then argue that the simulator has $O(s_1 + s_2 + kn)$ space characteristic, and prove that any adversary with space characteristic at most $1/2 \cdot s_3 - (s_1 + s_2 + O(n))$ cannot distinguish between the views generated by the simulator, and the views generated during the real execution of the protocol with advantage more than $\epsilon \cdot n \cdot k^2$ probability.

At a high level, the simulator works as follows. The simulator has $k$ write communication tapes, each indexed by an integer in $[k]$. The simulator writes the view of the $i^{th}$ party to its $i^{th}$ communication tape, which we hereby denote WriteTape$_i$. We present a formal description of the algorithm used by the simulator in Fig. 5. Observe that the simulator has to internally run an $\mathsf{OT}_4$ protocol, run ReceiverSim and SenderSim algorithms and store at most $k$ bits per each gate. Therefore, the Sim can be run within space characteristic $O(s_1 + s_2 + kn)$.

We now prove that the distribution of the views generated by the real protocol and the simulator are indistinguishable for any space bounded adversary via a hybrid argument. The hybrids are indexed by a tuple $(t, \ell, m)$, where $t$ is an integer in $[1, n]$, and $\ell, m$ are integers in $[k]$ s.t. $\ell < m$. In any hybrid $H_{t,\ell,m}$, the hybrid simulator HSim$_{t,\ell,m}$ (described in Fig. 6) is used to generate a view of the parties in the set $\mathcal{I}$. Unlike the simulator Sim, this hybrid simulator is given access to inputs $x_j$ of all the $k$ parties.

At a high level, the hybrid simulator HSim$_{t,\ell,m}$ algorithm first secret shares the input during the *input phase* just like the simulator Sim. The hybrid simulator, therefore, knows the secret shares $r_{i,w}$ for all the parties $\mathcal{P}_i$ in the set $\mathcal{I}$ and all the input wires $w$. Then during the *eval phase*, the hybrid simulator HSim$_{t,\ell,m}$ processes all the gates $g < t$ just like the simulator Sim, and processes gates $g > t$ by internally running the real protocol. For the gate $g = t$, for all party pairs $(i, j)$ s.t. $(i, j) \succeq (\ell, m)$,[14] the hybrid simulator internally run a real oblivious transfer protocol, whereas for the party pairs $(i, j) \prec (\ell, m)$,[15] the hybrid simulator simulates the view of the oblivious transfer. We formally describe the sequence of hybrids described in Fig. 6. The differences from the Sim algorithm are marked in red color.

---

[13] For the sake of simplicity, we assume $\mathsf{OT}_4$ is $(s_2, s_3, \epsilon)$-secure against semi-honest receiver. A similar proof works even if we assume $\mathsf{OT}_4$ is $(s_4, s_5, \epsilon')$ for some other functions $s_4, s_5, \epsilon'$.

[14] We say that $(i, j) \succeq (\ell, m)$ iff $(i > \ell) \vee (i = \ell \wedge j >= m)$.

[15] We say that $(i, j) \prec (\ell, m)$ if $(i < \ell) \vee (i = \ell \wedge j < m)$.

---

$$\mathsf{Sim}(1^n, C, \mathcal{I}, (x_j)_{j \in \mathcal{I}}, (y_j)_{j \in \mathcal{I}})$$

**Input Phase:**

For each party $i \in \mathcal{I}$:
  Include the input in the party $P_i$'s view i.e., Write $(\mathsf{input}, (C, x_i))$ to $\mathsf{WriteTape}_i$.
For each party $i \in \mathcal{I}$ and each input wire $w \in \mathsf{Input}(i)$:
  For $j = 1$ to $k$ s.t. $j \neq i$:
    Sample party $\mathcal{P}_j$'s share of the input at wire $w$ as $r_{j,w} \leftarrow \{0,1\}$. Write $(\mathsf{sample}, r_{j,w})$ to $\mathsf{WriteTape}_i$. Set the party $\mathcal{P}_i$'s share of wire $w$ to be $r_{i,w} = x_i[w] + \sum_{j \neq i} r_{j,w}$.
For each $i \in \mathcal{I}$ and each input wire $w \notin \mathsf{Input}(i)$:
  If $\mathsf{Party}(w) \notin \mathcal{I}$, sample bit $r_{i,w} \leftarrow \{0,1\}$.
  Write $(\mathsf{receive}, \mathsf{Party}(w), r_{i,w})$ to $\mathsf{WriteTape}_i$.

**Eval Phase:**
For each gate $g$ in the logical order:

- Let $a, b$ be the input wires and $c$ be the output wire of gate $g$.
- If $g$ is XOR gate, for each $i \in \mathcal{I}$, set $r_{i,c} = r_{i,a} + r_{i,b}$.
- If $g$ is AND gate:
  - For each $i \in \mathcal{I}$, set $r_{i,c} = r_{i,a} * r_{i,b}$.
  - For each $i = 1$ to $k-1$ & $j = i+1$ to $k$:
    * If both $\mathcal{P}_i$ and $\mathcal{P}_j$ are in the set $\mathcal{I}$ ($i \in \mathcal{I}$ & $j \in \mathcal{I}$),
      · Sample bit $\alpha \leftarrow \{0,1\}$.
      · For each $(x,y) \in \{0,1\}^2$, compute the message bit $m_{(x,y)} = \alpha + x * r_{i,b} + y * r_{i,a}$.
      · Perform 1-out-of-4 OT internally with $(m_{(0,0)}, m_{(0,1)}, m_{(1,0)}, m_{(1,1)})$ as sender's input and $(r_{j,a}, r_{j,b})$ as receiver's input.
      · During the OT protocol, write the sender's transcript on tape $\mathsf{WriteTape}_i$ and receiver's transcript on $\mathsf{WriteTape}_j$.
      · Set $r_{i,c} = r_{i,c} + \alpha$ and $r_{j,c} = r_{j,c} + \alpha + r_{i,a} * r_{j,b} + r_{i,b} * r_{j,a}$.
    * Else if only $\mathcal{P}_i$ is in the set $\mathcal{I}$ ($i \in \mathcal{I}$ & $j \notin \mathcal{I}$),
      · Sample bit $\alpha \leftarrow \{0,1\}$ and set $r_{i,c} = r_{i,c} + \alpha$.
      · For each $(x,y) \in \{0,1\}^2$, compute the message bit $m_{(x,y)} = \alpha + x * r_{i,b} + y * r_{i,a}$.
      · Internally, run $\mathsf{SenderSim}(1^n)$ on input $(m_{(0,0)}, m_{(0,1)}, m_{(1,0)}, m_{(1,1)})$ using $\mathsf{WriteTape}_i$ as its write comm. tape.
    * Else if only $\mathcal{P}_j$ is in the set $\mathcal{I}$ ($i \notin \mathcal{I}$ & $j \in \mathcal{I}$),
      · Sample bit $\beta \leftarrow \{0,1\}$ and set $r_{j,c} = r_{j,c} + \beta$.
      · Internally, run $\mathsf{ReceiverSim}(1^n)$ on input $(\beta, (r_{j,a}, r_{j,b}))$ using $\mathsf{WriteTape}_i$ as its write comm. tape.

**Output Phase:**
For each output wire $w$ s.t. $\mathsf{Party}(w) \in \mathcal{I}$,
  For each $i \notin \mathcal{I}$, sample $r_{i,w} \leftarrow \{0,1\}$ under the constraint $\sum_{i=1}^{k} r_{i,w} = y[w]$.
  For each $j \neq i$, write $(\mathsf{receive}, j, r_{j,w})$ on tape $\mathsf{WriteTape}_i$.

---

**Fig. 5.** Algorithm used by simulator to generate the view of parties in set $\mathcal{I}$. The simulator writes the view of party $\mathcal{P}_i$ on $\mathsf{WriteTape}_i$.

Throughout the execution, the hybrid simulator maintains an invariant that it knows secret share $r_{i,w}$ for any party $i \in \mathcal{I}$ and wire $w$. For any gate $g < t$ and its output wire $c$, the hybrid simulator $\mathsf{HSim}_{t,\ell,m}$ has no information about

---

**The algorithm used by** $\mathsf{HSim}_{t,\ell,m}(\mathcal{I}, C, (x_j)_{j \in [k]})$:

Input Phase: The input phase runs similar to the $\mathsf{Sim}$ algorithm. Additionally, for each input wire $w$, set $v_w = \mathbf{x}[w]$.
Eval Phase:
For each gate $g$ in the logical order:

- Let $a, b$ be the input wires and $c$ be the output wire of gate $g$.
- If $g$ is XOR gate, set $v_c = v_a + v_b$. For each $i \in \mathcal{I}$, $r_{i,c} = r_{i,a} + r_{i,b}$.
- If $g$ is AND gate, set $v_c = v_a * v_b$.
  - For each $i \in \mathcal{I}$, set $r_{i,c} = r_{i,a} * r_{i,b}$.
  - For each $i = 1$ to $k - 1$ & $j = i + 1$ to $k$:
    * If $(g, i, j) \succeq (t, \ell, m)$ and one of the parties $i, j$ is in $\mathcal{I}$:
      · For any party $p \in \{i, j\}$ and wire $w \in \{a, b\}$, if bit $r_{p,w}$ is not set, then sample $r_{p,w}$ uniformly at random subject to constraint $\sum_{q=1}^{k} r_{q,w} - v_w$, and set $r_{p,c} = r_{p,a} * r_{p,b}$.
      · Sample bit $\alpha \leftarrow \{0, 1\}$.
      · For each $(x, y) \in \{0, 1\}^2$, compute the message bit $m_{(x,y)} = \alpha + x * r_{i,b} + y * r_{i,a}$.
      · Perform 1-out-of-4 OT internally with $(m_{(0,0)}, m_{(0,1)}, m_{(1,0)}, m_{(1,1)})$ as sender's input and $(r_{j,a}, r_{j,b})$ as receiver's input.
      · During the OT protocol, write the sender's transcript on tape $\mathsf{WriteTape}_i$ and receiver's transcript on $\mathsf{WriteTape}_j$.
      · Set $r_{i,c} = r_{i,c} + \alpha$ and $r_{j,c} = r_{j,c} + \alpha + r_{i,a} * r_{j,b} + r_{i,b} * r_{j,a}$.
    * Else if both $\mathcal{P}_i$ and $\mathcal{P}_j$ are in the set $\mathcal{I}$ ($i \in \mathcal{I}$ & $j \in \mathcal{I}$), run similar to the $\mathsf{Sim}$ algorithm
    * Else if only $\mathcal{P}_i$ is in set $\mathcal{I}$ ($i \in \mathcal{I}$ & $j \notin \mathcal{I}$), run similar to the $\mathsf{Sim}$ algorithm
    * Else if only $\mathcal{P}_j$ is in set $\mathcal{I}$ ($i \notin \mathcal{I}$ & $j \in \mathcal{I}$), run similar to the $\mathsf{Sim}$ algorithm.
  - If there exists a party $\mathcal{P}_i$ not in the set $\mathcal{I}$, and some other party $\mathcal{P}_j$ s.t. either $(i, j) \prec (\ell, m)$ or $(j, i) \prec (\ell, m)$, then delete the bit $r_{i,c}$.

Output Phase:
For each output wire $w$ s.t. $\mathsf{Party}(w) \in \mathcal{I}$,
    For each $i \notin \mathcal{I}$ s.t. $r_{i,w}$ is not set, sample $r_{i,w} \leftarrow \{0, 1\}$ under the constraint $\sum_{i=1}^{k} r_{i,w} = v_w$.
    For each $j \neq i$, write $(\mathsf{receive}, j, r_{j,w})$ on tape $\mathsf{WriteTape}_i$.

---

**Fig. 6.** Algorithm used by the hybrid simulator $\mathsf{HSim}_{t,\ell,m}$ ($t \in [n], \ell \in [k], m > \ell$) to generate the view of set of parties $\mathcal{I}$. The simulator writes the view of party $\mathcal{P}_i$ on $\mathsf{WriteTape}_i$ (Color figure online).

shares $r_{i,c}$ for parties $\mathcal{P}_i \notin \mathcal{I}$ after processing the gate $g$. In case the wire $c$ is the output wire of the circuit or if $c$ is used as input wire to another gate $g'$ for which the real OT protocol is used to process the gate, then $r_{i,c}$ is sampled at that point. When processing the gate $g = t$, suppose the oblivious transfer for party pair $(i, j)$ is simulated and the party $\mathcal{P}_i$ is not in the set $\mathcal{I}$. Then the party $\mathcal{P}_i$'s share $r_{i,c}$ of the output wire $c$ that is computed by $\mathsf{HSim}_{t,\ell,m}$ is not complete, as the party $\mathcal{P}_i$'s output of the OT between $(i, j)$ parties is not included in the share $r_{i,c}$. Therefore, $\mathsf{HSim}_{t,\ell,m}$ deletes the share $r_{i,c}$ in such a case. The hybrid simulator acts similarly if the oblivious transfer for party pair $(i, j)$ is simulated and $\mathcal{P}_j$ is not the set $\mathcal{I}$.

Let us introduce some notations. For any set of integers $(g_1, i_1, j_1, g_2, i_2, j_2)$, we say that $(g_1, i_1, j_1) \prec (g_2, i_2, j_2)$ if $g_1 < g_2$ or $(g_1 = g_2 \land i_1 < i_2)$ or $(g_1 = g_2 \land i_1 = i_2 \land j_1 < j_2)$. We say that $(g_1, i_1, j_1) \succeq (g_2, i_2, j_2)$ if $(g_2, i_2, j_2) \prec (g_1, i_1, j_1) \lor (g_2, i_2, j_2) = (g_1, i_1, j_1)$. For any tuple of integers $(g, i, j) \in [n] \times [k] \times [k]$ s.t. $j > i$, we define the function $\mathsf{Next}(g, i, j) =$

$$\begin{cases} (g+1, 1, 2) & \text{if } i = k-1 \land j = k \\ (g, i+1, i+2) & \text{if } i < k-1 \land j = k. \\ (g, i, j+1) & \text{if } j < k \end{cases}$$

Consider any adversary $\mathcal{A}$ which has $k$ read tapes. Let $\Pr[H^{\mathcal{A}}_{t.\ell.m}(1^n, C, \mathcal{I}, (x_i)_{i \in [k]}) = 1]$ be the probability that $\mathcal{A}$ outputs 1 when its read tapes are connected to the write tapes of $\mathsf{HSim}(1^n, (C, \mathcal{I}, (x_i)_{i \in [k]}))$. We now prove that each adjacent pair of hybrids are indistinguishable to a space bounded adversary.

**Lemma 1.** *For any space parameter $n \in \mathbb{N}$, any circuit $C \in \mathcal{C}_n$, any input tuple $(x_1, \cdots, x_k)$ belonging to the domain of $C$ and any set $\mathcal{I} \subset [k]$, the distribution of views of parties in the set $\mathcal{I}$ generated by the real protocol is identical to the views generated by $\mathsf{HSim}_{1,1,2}$.*

*Proof.* This follows from the definition of the hybrids.

**Lemma 2.** *For any functions $s_1, s_2, s_3 : \mathbb{N} \to \mathbb{N}$ and $\epsilon : \mathbb{N} \to [0, 1]$, assuming $\mathsf{OT}_4$ is $s_1$-correct (as per Definition 6), $(s_2, s_3, \epsilon)$-secure against semi-honest sender and $(s_2, s_3, \epsilon)$-secure against semi-honest receiver (as per Definitions 7 and 8), then for every $s_3/2 - (s_1 + s_2 + kn)$-space bounded adversary $\mathcal{A}$, there exists an integer $N_0$ s.t. for every space parameter $n > N_0$, for every circuit $C \in \mathcal{C}_n$, every set of parties $\mathcal{I} \subset [k]$, every input tuple $(x_1, \cdots, x_k)$ belonging to the circuit's domain, any indices $(t, \ell, m) \in [n] \times [k] \times [k]$ s.t. $\ell < m$, the advantage $|\Pr[H^{\mathcal{A}}_{t.\ell.m}(1^n, C, \mathcal{I}, (x_i)_{i \in [k]}) = 1] - \Pr[H^{\mathcal{A}}_{t'.\ell'.m'}(1^n, C, \mathcal{I}, (x_i)_{i \in [k]}) = 1]| \leq \epsilon(n)$, where $(t', \ell', m') = \mathsf{Next}(t, \ell, m)$.*

*Proof.* For the sake of contradiction, let us assume there exists an $s_2/2 - (s_1 + s_3 + kn)$-space bounded adversary $\mathcal{A}$ s.t. for every integer $N_0$, there exists an $n > N_0$, circuit $C \in \mathcal{C}_n$, set of parties $\mathcal{I} \subset [k]$, input tuple $(x_1, \cdots, x_k)$, indices $(t, \ell, m) \in [n] \times [k] \times [k]$ s.t. $\ell < m$, the advantage $|\Pr[H^{\mathcal{A}}_{t.\ell.m}(1^n, C, \mathcal{I}, (x_i)_{i \in [k]}) = 1] - \Pr[H^{\mathcal{A}}_{t'.\ell'.m'}(1^n, C, \mathcal{I}, (x_i)_{i \in [k]}) = 1]| > \epsilon(n)$, where $(t', \ell', m') = \mathsf{Next}(t, \ell, m)$. We now show how to break the semi-honest security of the underlying $\mathsf{OT}_4$ scheme.

We know that the Hybrids $H_{t.\ell.m}$ and $H_{t'.\ell'.m'}$ are identical if (1) the gate $t$ is an XOR gate or (2) $t$ is an AND gate and both the parties $\mathcal{P}_\ell, \mathcal{P}_m$ are in the set $\mathcal{I}$ or (3) $t$ is an AND gate and both $\mathcal{P}_\ell, \mathcal{P}_m$ are not in the set $\mathcal{I}$. As the adversary $\mathcal{A}$ can distinguish between these hybrids, we know that $t$ is an AND gate and exactly one of the parties $\mathcal{P}_\ell, \mathcal{P}_m$ is not in the set $\mathcal{I}$. Suppose $\mathcal{P}_\ell \notin \mathcal{I}$ and $\mathcal{P}_m \in \mathcal{I}$, we break the security of $\mathsf{OT}_4$ scheme against semi-honest receiver[16]. Specifically, we show that there exists an $s_3$-space bound adversary $\mathcal{A}'$ s.t. for every $N'_0$, there

---

[16] In case, $\mathcal{P}_\ell \in \mathcal{I}$ and $\mathcal{P}_m \notin \mathcal{I}$, we can break the security of $\mathsf{OT}_4$ scheme against semi-honest sender. This case can be handled analogously.

exists a space parameter $n' > N_0'$, message bits $(m_{(0,0)}, m_{(0,1)}, m_{(1,0)}, m_{(1,1)})$ and receiver's choice $(d_1, d_2)$ s.t. the advantage in GameSHReceiver is atleast $\epsilon(n')$.

We prove the argument in two steps – We first show that there exists a pair of ITMs $(\mathcal{A}_1, \mathcal{A}_2)$ s.t. $\mathcal{A}_1$ is $1/2 \cdot s_3 - (s_1 + s_2 + kn)$-space bounded, $\mathcal{A}_2$ is $(kn + s_1 + s_2)$-space bounded, $\mathcal{A}_2$ receives oblivious transfer challenge view on one of its read tapes, interacts with $\mathcal{A}_1$ using its other tapes and finally solves the oblivious transfer game GameSHReceiver with $\epsilon$ advantage. We then invoke Theorem 4 to construct an $s_3$-space bounded adversary $\mathcal{A}'$ that solves game GameSHReceiver with $\epsilon$ advantage. At a high level, we simply set $\mathcal{A}_1$ to be equal to the adversary $\mathcal{A}$ which can distinguish between the hybrids $(t, \ell, m)$ and $(t', \ell', m')$ with advantage more than $\epsilon$. The algorithm $\mathcal{A}_2$ takes $(C, \mathcal{I}, (x_1, \cdots, x_k), t, \ell, m)$ on its input tape as an advice string. The algorithm $\mathcal{A}_2$ has $k$ write tapes that are connected to the $k$ read tapes of $\mathcal{A}_1$. $\mathcal{A}_2$ runs similar to the $\mathsf{HSim}_{t.\ell.m}$ algorithm to generate the views for each oblivious transfer corresponding to the pairs $(g, i, j) \neq (t, \ell, m)$. When processing the gate $t$ and oblivious transfer for party pair $(\ell, m)$, $\mathcal{A}_2$ samples a random bit $\alpha \leftarrow \{0, 1\}$ and invokes OT challenger with the sender's input sampled similar to $\mathsf{HSim}_{t.\ell.m}$, and the receiver's input as $(\alpha, r_{j,a}, r_{j,b})$. The OT challenger samples a bit $b \leftarrow \{0, 1\}$. If $\beta = 0$, the OT challenger sends the real view of party $\mathcal{P}_j$ in the oblivious transfer to $\mathcal{A}_2$. If $\beta = 1$, the OT challenger sends the simulated view of party $\mathcal{P}_j$ in the oblivious transfer to $\mathcal{A}_2$. $\mathcal{A}_2$ copies this message onto its $j^{th}$ write tape i.e., includes party $\mathcal{P}_j$'s view. At the end of the game, $\mathcal{A}_1$ sends a guess bit to $\mathcal{A}_2$, which $\mathcal{A}_2$ outputs as its guess in the OT game.

We now analyze the advantage of $(\mathcal{A}_1, \mathcal{A}_2)$ pair in the OT game. If $\beta = 0$, the messages received by $\mathcal{A}_1$ is identical to hybrid $H_{t.\ell.m}$. Otherwise, it is identical to hybrid $H_{t'.\ell'.m'}$. Therefore, the pair $(\mathcal{A}_1, \mathcal{A}_2)$ has advantage $\epsilon(n)$ in distinguishing between the two cases. ∎

**Corollary 1.** *For any $c < 1/80$, there exists an $\alpha$ s.t. the above $k$-party MPC protocol is $(O(kn), cn^2 - O(n), O(2^{-\alpha n}))$ semi-honest secure for the class of $n$-gate functionalities $\{\mathcal{C}_n\}_{n \in \mathbb{N}}$.*

## Supplementary Material

## A    Security Proof for 1-Out-of-4 OT in Bounded-Storage Model

In this section we present proof for correctness and security for the OT protocol in Sect. 4.

*Correctness.* We now prove the correctness property of the scheme in Sect. 4.

**Claim 1.** *If the underlying 1-out-of-2 OT scheme is $O(n)$-correct, then the 1-out-of-4 OT scheme described above is $O(n)$-correct.*

*Proof.* By the correctness property of the 1-out-of-2 scheme, after step 2, the receiver will correctly compute $r_{t,b}^t$ for all $b > t$ and $r_{a,t}^t$ for all $a < t$, which are the 3 masking bits it needs to decrypt the message $y_t$. The receiver can then correctly decrypt $y_t$ to get $m_t$. The sender and reciever runs six 1-out-of-2 OT protocols. If the underlying 1-out-of-2 OT scheme run within $O(n)$ space characteristic, then both the receiver and sender can run within $O(n)$ space.

## A.1    Proof of Security

Now we prove that the construction is semi-honest secure in the bounded storage model as per Definitions 7 and 8, assuming the underlying 1-out-of-2 OT protocol is semi-honest secure in the bounded storage model. For simplicity, we denote the underlying 1-out-of-2 OT scheme by $\mathsf{OT}_2$ and the 1-out-of-4 OT scheme constructed above by $\mathsf{OT}_4$.

At a high level, the $\mathsf{OT}_4$ scheme is secure against a semi-honest sender with bounded space, because all the message that the sender receives are part of one of the underlying $\mathsf{OT}_2$ invocations. As any bounded space semi-honest sender cannot extract more information from the 1-out-of-2 protocol transcript, he cannot extract more information from the 1-out-of-4 OT protocol transcript as well.

In order to argue that the $\mathsf{OT}_4$ scheme is secure against a semi-honest receiver with bounded space, let us consider an example when the receiver's choice $t$ is 1. By the security of the $\mathsf{OT}_2$ scheme, the receiver does not have any information about the bits $r_{(0,1)}^0, r_{(1,2)}^2, r_{(1,3)}^3$. As these bits are used to mask the messages $m_0, m_2, m_3$. The receiver cannot distinguish $y_0, y_2, y_3$ from uniformly random bits.

*Security Against Semi-honest Sender*

**Theorem 8.** *For any constants $c, \alpha$, if $\mathsf{OT}_2$ scheme is $O(n)$-correct and $(O(n), cn^2, O(2^{-\alpha n}))$-secure against semi-honest sender, then there exists corresponding constants $c', \alpha'$ s.t. the above $\mathsf{OT}_4$ scheme is $(O(n), c'n^2, O(2^{-\alpha' n}))$-secure against semi-honest sender.*

*Proof.* We first construct a simulator $\mathsf{OT}_4.\mathsf{SenderSim}_4$ which outputs a simulated view of the sender in $\mathsf{OT}_4$ protocol, given input $\{m_j\}_{j \in [3]}$. The simulator outputs the view via its write communication tape.

$\mathsf{SenderSim}_4(1^n, (m_0, m_1, m_2, m_3))$ :
Write $(\mathsf{Input}, (m_0, m_1, m_2, m_3))$ on the write communication tape.
For each pair $(a, b) \in \{0, 1, 2, 3\}^2$ s.t. $a < b$:
   – Sample uniformly random $(r_{a,b}^a, r_{a,b}^b) \leftarrow \{0,1\}^2$, and write $(\mathsf{sample}, r_{a,b}^a), (\mathsf{sample}, r_{a,b}^b)$ to the write tape.
   – Run $\mathsf{OT}_2.\mathsf{SenderSim}_2(1^n, (r_{a,b}^a, r_{a,b}^b))$, and write the generated view on the write tape.

The $OT_4$ simulator internally invokes $OT_2$ simulator 6 times sequentially. As the $OT_2$ simulator has space characteristic $O(n)$, the $OT_4$ simulator also has space characteristic $O(n)$. We now prove that a space bounded adversary cannot distinguish between the views generated by the real protocol and the simulator via a hybrid argument. First let us order the six tuples $(a, b) \in \{0, 1, 2, 3\}^2$ s.t. $a < b$ in any order from 1 to 6. Let the order of any tuple $(a, b)$ be $\mathsf{Order}(a, b)$.

At a high level, in the hybrid $H_i$, for the tuples with order less than or equal to $i$, a real $OT_2$ protocol is run internally to generate the corresponding view, whereas for the tuples with order more than $i$, $OT_2.\mathsf{SenderSim}_2$ is used to generate the view of the corresponding 1-out-of-2 OT. The description of the algorithm used in $H_i$ is formally described below. Note that unlike the $\mathsf{SenderSim}_4$, these intermediate hybrids additionally take the receiver's choice $t$ as input.

$H_i(1^n, (m_0, m_1, m_2, m_3), t) \ (0 \le i \le 6)$ :
  Write $(\mathsf{Input}, (m_0, m_1, m_2, m_3))$ on the write communication tape.
  For each $(a, b) \in \{0, 1, 2, 3\}^2$ s.t. $a < b$,
    - Sample uniformly random $(r_{a,b}^a, r_{a,b}^b) \leftarrow \{0, 1\}^2$, and write $(\mathsf{sample}, r_{a,b}^a), (\mathsf{sample}, r_{a,b}^b)$ to the write tape.
    - If $\mathsf{Order}(a, b) \le i$, If $t = a$, set $c = 0$. If $t = b$, set $c = 1$. Otherwise, sample $c \leftarrow \{0, 1\}$. Internally run the $OT_2$ protocol with sender's input $(r_{a,b}^a, r_{a,b}^b)$, and the receiver's input $c$. Throughout the protocol, write the sender's transcript on the write tape.
    - If $\mathsf{Order}(a, b) > i$, run $OT_2$ simulator $\mathsf{SenderSim}_2(1^n, (r_{a,b}^a, r_{a,b}^b))$, and write the generated view on the write tape.

Clearly, the distribution of the view generated by Hybrid $H_0$ is identical to the view generated in the real protocol. Similarly, the distribution of the view generated by final hybrid $H_6$ is identical to the view generated by the simulator $OT_4.\mathsf{SenderSim}_4$. We now show that if a space-bounded adversary can distinguish between the hybrids $H_i$ and $H_{i+1}$ with an $\epsilon$ advantage, then there exists a space-bounded reduction algorithm that can break the 1-out-of-2 OT security with $\epsilon$ advantage. Formally we state the lemma below. Consider any adversary $\mathcal{A}$ with 1 read-tape. For any hybrid $H_i$, we let $\Pr[H_i^{\mathcal{A}}(1^n, (m_0, m_1, m_2, m_3), t) = 1]$ to be the probability that the adversary outputs 1 when the write tape of $H_i(1^n, (m_0, m_1, m_2, m_3), t)$ algorithm is connected to the read tape of the adversary.

**Lemma 3.** *For any constants $c, \alpha$, if the underlying $OT_2$ scheme is $O(n)$-correct and $(O(n), cn^2, O(2^{-\alpha n}))$-secure against semi-honest sender, then there exists corresponding constants $c', \alpha'$ s.t. for every $c'n^2$-space bounded adversary $\mathcal{A}$, there exists an integer $N_0$ s.t. for any space parameter $n > N_0$, any sender's input tuple $(m_0, m_1, m_2, m_3)$, receiver's choice $t$, any index $0 \le i < 6$, $|\Pr[H_i^{\mathcal{A}}(1^n, (m_0, m_1, m_2, m_3), t) = 1] - \Pr[H_{i+1}^{\mathcal{A}}(1^n, (m_0, m_1, m_2, m_3), t) = 1]| \le O(2^{-\alpha' n})$.*

*Proof.* We show that if for all $c', \alpha'$ s.t. there is a $c'n^2$-space bounded adversary $\mathcal{A}$, for all integer $N_0$ s.t. there exists space parameter $n > N_0$, some sender's input tuple $(m_0, m_1, m_2, m_3)$, some receiver's choice $t$, some index $0 \le i < 6$,

$|\Pr[H_i^{\mathcal{A}}(1^n, (m_0, m_1, m_2, m_3), t) = 1] - \Pr[H_{i+1}^{\mathcal{A}}(1^n, (m_0, m_1, m_2, m_3), t) = 1]| \geq \Omega(2^{-\alpha'n})$; then there exists constants $c, \alpha$, such that there is a $cn^2$-space characteristic semi-honest sender adversary $\mathcal{A}'$ that breaks the underlying $\mathsf{OT}_2$ scheme with $\Omega(2^{-\alpha n})$ advantage.

Let the challenger in hybrid $H_i$ be an adversary $\mathcal{A}'$ in an $\mathsf{OT}_2$ security game against the semi-honest sender. In the reduction during $H_i$, for all ordered tuples $(a, b)$ where $\mathsf{Order}(a, b) < i$, $\mathcal{A}'$ runs a real $\mathsf{OT}_2$ protocol as described above and writes the sender's view on the read tape of adversary $\mathcal{A}$; for $k = i+1$, $\mathcal{A}'$ receives the sender adversary's view from the challenger in $\mathsf{GameSHSender}_{(r_{a,b}^a, r_{a,b}^b),c}^{\mathcal{A}}$ against semi-honest sender, where $\mathsf{Order}(a, b) = i + 1$; $\mathcal{A}'$ writes this view on the read tape of $\mathcal{A}$; for $k > i+1$, $\mathcal{A}'$ runs $\mathsf{SenderSim}_2$ as described above for $H_i$.

At the end of the game, $\mathcal{A}$ outputs a bit $b' \in \{0, 1\}$ and $\mathcal{A}'$ passes it as its own output to the challenger in $\mathsf{GameSHSender}_{(r_{a,b}^a, r_{a,b}^b),c}^{\mathcal{A}}$, where $\mathsf{Order}(a, b) = i + 1$. $\mathcal{A}'$ has advantage $|\Pr[H_i^{\mathcal{A}}(1^n, (m_0, m_1, m_2, m_3), t) = 1] - \Pr[H_{i+1}^{\mathcal{A}}(1^n, (m_0, m_1, m_2, m_3), t) = 1]|$. Hence if there exists $\mathcal{A}$ that has $\Omega(2^{-\alpha'n})$ advantage difference between two hybrids, $\mathcal{A}'$ has $\Omega(2^{-\alpha'n})$ advantage in winning $\mathsf{GameSHSender}_{(r_{a,b}^a, r_{a,b}^b),c}^{\mathcal{A}}$ against semi-honest sender.

By triangle inequality, the advantage of adversary $\mathcal{A}$ in the $\mathsf{OT}_4$ game $\mathsf{GameSH}_{\{m_j\}_{j \in [3]}, t}^{\mathcal{A}}$ is

$$|\Pr[H_0^{\mathcal{A}}(1^n, (m_0, m_1, m_2, m_3), t) = 1] - \Pr[H_6^{\mathcal{A}}(1^n, (m_0, m_1, m_2, m_3), t) = 1]|$$

$$\leq \sum_{i=0}^{5} |\Pr[H_i^{\mathcal{A}}(1^n, (m_0, m_1, m_2, m_3), t) = 1] - \Pr[H_{i+1}^{\mathcal{A}}(1^n, (m_0, m_1, m_2, m_3), t) = 1]|$$

If there exists $\mathcal{A}$ that has $\Omega(2^{-\alpha n})$ advantage in $\mathsf{GameSHSender}_{\{m_j\}_{j \in [3]}, t}^{\mathcal{A}}$, then there must exist some $\alpha'$ such that some adversary $\mathcal{A}'$ has advantage $\Omega(2^{-\alpha'n}) = \Omega(2^{-\alpha n}/6)$ in $\mathsf{OT}_2$ semi-honest sender security game on some input $((r_{a,b}^a, r_{a,b}^b), c)$, which contradicts the proved security of $\mathsf{OT}_2$.

**Corollary 2.** *For any $c < 1/40$, there exists $\alpha > 0$ such that the above 1-out-of-4 OT construction is $(O(n), c \cdot n^2, O(2^{-\alpha n}))$-secure against semi-honest sender.*

The corollary follows when the above $\mathsf{OT}_4$ scheme is used with the $\mathsf{OT}_2$ construction described in Sect. B.

*Security Against Semi-honest Receiver*

**Theorem 9.** *If the underlying $\mathsf{OT}_2$ scheme is $O(n)$-correct and $(O(n), \infty, O(2^{-n}))$-secure against semi-honest receiver, then the above 1-out-of-4 OT construction is $(O(n), \infty, O(2^{-n}))$-secure against semi-honest receiver.*

*Proof.* We first construct a receiver simulator for $\mathsf{OT}_4$, $\mathsf{ReceiverSim}_4$ which outputs a simulated view of the receiver in the $\mathsf{OT}_4$ protocol, given the receiver's choice $t \in \{0, 1, 2, 3\}$ and the receiver's output bit $m_t$. The simulator outputs the view via its write communication tape.

ReceiverSim$_4$($1^n$, $(t, m_t)$) :
  - Write (Input, $(t, m_t)$) to the write communication tape.
  - For each pair $(a, b) \in \{0, 1, 2, 3\}^2$ s.t. $a < b$:
    If $t = a$, sample $r_{a,b}^a \leftarrow \{0, 1\}$, run OT$_2$.ReceiverSim$_2$($1^n$, $(0, r_{a,b}^a)$).
    If $t = b$, sample $r_{a,b}^b \leftarrow \{0, 1\}$, run OT$_2$.ReceiverSim$_2$($1^n$, $(1, r_{a,b}^b)$).
    Else, sample $c \leftarrow \{0, 1\}$ and write (sample, $c$) to the write tape.
        If $c = 0$, sample $r_{a,b}^a \leftarrow \{0, 1\}$ and run OT$_2$.ReceiverSim$_2$($1^n$, $(0, r_{a,b}^a)$).
        If $c = 1$, sample $r_{a,b}^b \leftarrow \{0, 1\}$ and run OT$_2$.ReceiverSim$_2$($1^n$, $(1, r_{a,b}^b)$).
    In all the cases, copy the view generated by OT$_2$ simulator to the write tape.
  - Sample $y_j \leftarrow \{0, 1\}$ for $j \neq t$. Compute $y_t$ by encrypting $m_t$ as in the real game. Write (receive, $(y_0, y_1, y_2, y_3)$) on the write tape.

The OT$_4$ simulator internally invokes OT$_2$ simulator 6 times sequentially. As the OT$_2$ simulator has space characteristic $O(n)$, the OT$_4$ simulator also has space characteristic $O(n)$, the OT$_4$ simulator also has space characteristic $O(n)$. We now prove that a space bounded adversary cannot distinguish between the views generated by the real protocol and the simulator via a hybrid argument. Recall that we order all possible tuples in $\{0, 1, 2, 3\}^2$ by numerical order and denote that the $k$-th tuple has Order($a, b$) = $k$.

At a high level, in the hybrid $H_i$, for the tuples with order less than or equal to $i$, a real OT$_2$ protocol is run internally to generate the corresponding view; whereas for the tuples with order more than $i$, OT$_2$.ReceiverSim$_2$ is used to generate the view of the corresponding 1-out-of-2 OT.

The distribution of the view generated by Hybrid $H_0$ is identical to the view generated in the real protocol. Similarly, the distribution of the view generated by the final hybrid $H_6$ is identical to the view generated by the simulator OT$_4$.ReceiverSim$_4$. We now show that if an adversary can distinguish between the hybrids $H_i$ and $H_{i+1}$ with an $\epsilon$ advantage, then there exists a space-bounded reduction algorithm that can break the 1-out-of-2 OT security against semi-honest receiver with $\epsilon$ advantage. Formally we state the lemma below. Consider any adversary $\mathcal{A}$ with 1 read-tape. For any hybrid $H_i$, we let $\Pr[H_i^{\mathcal{A}}(1^n, (m_0, m_1, m_2, m_3), t) = 1]$ to be the probability that the adversary outputs 1 when the write tape of $H_i(1^n, (m_0, m_1, m_2, m_3), t)$ algorithm is connected to the read tape of the adversary.

**Lemma 4.** *If the underlying* OT$_2$ *scheme is* $O(n)$-*correct and* $(O(n), \infty,$ $O(2^{-n}))$-*secure against semi-honest receiver, then for every adversary* $\mathcal{A}$*, there exists an integer* $N_0$ *s.t. for any space parameter* $n > N_0$*, any sender's input tuple* $(m_0, m_1, m_2, m_3)$*, receiver's choice* $t$*, for any index* $0 \leq i < 6$*,* $|\Pr[H_i^{\mathcal{A}}(1^n,$ $(m_0, m_1, m_2, m_3), t) = 1] - \Pr[H_{i+1}^{\mathcal{A}}(1^n, (m_0, m_1, m_2, m_3), t) = 1]| \leq O(2^{-n})$*.*

*Proof.* We show that if there is some adversary $\mathcal{A}$, for all integer $N_0$ s.t. there exists space parameter $n > N_0$, some sender's input tuple $(m_0, m_1, m_2, m_3)$, some receiver's choice $t$, some index $0 \le i < 6$, $|\Pr[H_i^{\mathcal{A}}(1^n, (m_0, m_1, m_2, m_3), t) = 1] - \Pr[H_{i+1}^{\mathcal{A}}(1^n, (m_0, m_1, m_2, m_3), t) = 1]| \ge \Omega(2^{-\alpha' n})$; then there exists some semi-honest receiver adversary $\mathcal{A}'$ that breaks the underlying $\mathsf{OT}_2$ scheme with $\Omega(2^{-n})$ advantage.

Let the challenger in hybrid $H_i$ be an adversary $\mathcal{A}'$ in an $\mathsf{OT}_2$ security game against the semi-honest receiver. In the reduction during $H_i$, for all ordered tuples $(a, b)$ where $\mathsf{Order}(a, b) \le i$, $\mathcal{A}'$ runs a real $\mathsf{OT}_2$ protocol as described above; for $\mathsf{Order}(a, b) = i + 1$, $\mathcal{A}'$ gets the adversary's view from the challenger in $\mathsf{GameSHReceiver}^{\mathcal{A}}_{(r^a_{a,b}, r^b_{a,b}), c}$ against semi-honest receiver, and then $\mathcal{A}'$ writes this view on the read tape of $\mathcal{A}$; for $\mathsf{Order}(a, b) > i + 1$, $\mathcal{A}'$ runs $\mathsf{ReceiverSim}_2$ as described above for $H_i$.

At the end of the game, $\mathcal{A}$ outputs a bit $b' \in \{0, 1\}$ and $\mathcal{A}'$ passes it as its own output to the challenger in $\mathsf{GameSHReceiver}^{\mathcal{A}}_{(r^a_{a,b}, r^b_{a,b}), c}$, $\mathsf{Order}(a, b) = i + 1$. $\mathcal{A}'$ has advantage $|\Pr[H_i^{\mathcal{A}}(1^n, (m_0, m_1, m_2, m_3), t) = 1] - \Pr[H_{i+1}^{\mathcal{A}}(1^n, (m_0, m_1, m_2, m_3), t) = 1]|$. Hence if there exists $\mathcal{A}$ that can distinguish between two hybrids with probability $\Omega(2^{-n})$, $\mathcal{A}'$ has $\Omega(2^{-n})$ advantage in winning $\mathsf{GameSHReceiver}^{\mathcal{A}}_{(r^a_{a,b}, r^b_{a,b}), c}$ against semi-honest receiver.

**Conclusion.** By triangle inequality, the advantage of adversary $\mathcal{A}$ in the $\mathsf{OT}_4$ game $\mathsf{GameSH}^{\mathcal{A}}_{\{m_j\}_{j \in [3]}, t}$ is given by

$$|\Pr[H_0^{\mathcal{A}}(1^n, (m_0, m_1, m_2, m_3), t) = 1] - \Pr[H_6^{\mathcal{A}}(1^n, (m_0, m_1, m_2, m_3), t) = 1]|$$

$$\le \sum_{i=0}^{5} |\Pr[H_i^{\mathcal{A}}(1^n, (m_0, m_1, m_2, m_3), t) = 1] - \Pr[H_{i+1}^{\mathcal{A}}(1^n, (m_0, m_1, m_2, m_3), t) = 1]|$$

If there exists $\mathcal{A}$ that has $\Omega(2^{-n})$ advantage in $\mathsf{GameSHReceiver}^{\mathcal{A}}_{\{m_j\}_{j \in [3]}, t}$, then there must exist some adversary $\mathcal{A}'$ has advantage $\Omega(2^{-n}) = \Omega(2^{-n}/6)$ in $\mathsf{OT}_2$ semi-honest receiver security game on some input $((r^a_{a,b}, r^b_{a,b}), c)$, which contradicts the proved security of $\mathsf{OT}_2$.

# B     Review of 1-Out-of-2 Semi-honest OT Protocol

In this section, we recall the 1-out-of-2 OT construction by Guan and Zhandry [11] and prove its security. [11] proposed an indistinguishability based security definition for 1-out-of-2 OT, whereas we need simulation-based secure OT in our construction of MPC protocol. We thereby prove the security of their construction as per Definitions 7 and 8.

At a high level, the OT construction proceeds as follows. Let $(x_0, x_1)$ be the sender's input message bits, and let $d$ be the receiver's choice bit. The receiver sends a randomly sampled stream of parity learning tuples $(a_1, b_1), \cdots (a_\ell, b_\ell)$ to the sender. The sender stores two random linear combinations $(L_0, q_0)$ and

$(L_1, q_1)$ of these samples. For a sufficiently large $m$, these samples stored by the sender statistically resemble a fresh parity learning samples. The receiver then encrypts its choice bit $d$ i.e., creates a fresh parity learning sample $(a, b)$ and sends $(a, b + d)$ to the sender. The sender then computes encryptions of $(1 - d) \cdot x_0$ and $d \cdot x_1$, rerandomizes these by adding $(L_0, q_0)$ and $(L_1, q_1)$ and sends them to the receiver. The receiver can decrypt $(1 - d) \cdot x_0$ and $d \cdot x_1$ using its secret key and obtain $x_d$.

We now describe the protocol formally. The construction is parameterized by a space parameter $n$. Intuitively, the honest parties can run the protocol within space characteristic $O(n)$, whereas the dishonest parties with space characteristic $O(n^2)$ cannot break the security of the protocol.

1. The receiver samples a random key $\mathbf{k} \leftarrow \{0, 1\}^n$. The sender sets $\mathbf{L} = \{0\}^{2 \times n}$ and $\mathbf{q} \leftarrow [0, 0]^\top$. Let $\ell = 2n$.
2. For $i = 1$ to $\ell$,
   The receiver samples $\mathbf{a}_i \leftarrow \{0, 1\}^n$ and sends $(\mathbf{a}_i, \mathbf{a}_i \cdot \mathbf{k} \bmod 2)$ to the sender. Upon receiving $(\mathbf{a}_i, b_i)$, the sender first samples $\mathbf{M}_i \leftarrow \{0, 1\}^2$ and updates
   $$\mathbf{L} \leftarrow \mathbf{L} + \mathbf{M}_i \cdot \mathbf{a}_i \text{ and } \mathbf{q} \leftarrow \mathbf{q} + \mathbf{M}_i \cdot b_i,$$
   where $\mathbf{a}_i$ is interpreted as a row vector and $\mathbf{M}_i$ is interpreted as a column vector.
3. The receiver then samples a random $\mathbf{y} \leftarrow \{0, 1\}^n$ and sends a tuple $(\mathbf{y}, \mathbf{y} \cdot \mathbf{k} + d)$ to the sender.
4. Let us denote $\mathbf{L}_0, \mathbf{L}_1$ as the first and second rows of $\mathbf{L}$, and denote $q_0, q_1$ to be the first and second element in $\mathbf{q}$. The sender sends the following encryptions of $(1 - d)x_0, dx_1$ to the receiver:

$$(\mathbf{L}_0, q_0) + x_0 \cdot (\mathbf{y}, \mathbf{y} \cdot \mathbf{k} + 1 - d) = (\mathbf{L} + x_0 \cdot \mathbf{y}, (\mathbf{L} + x_0 \cdot \mathbf{y}) \cdot \mathbf{k} + x_0(1 - d))$$

and

$$(\mathbf{L}_1, q_1) + x_1 \cdot (\mathbf{y}, \mathbf{y} \cdot \mathbf{k} + d) = (\mathbf{L} + x_1 \cdot \mathbf{y}, (\mathbf{L} + x_1 \cdot \mathbf{y}) \cdot \mathbf{k} + x_1 d).$$

5. Let the values received by the receiver be $(c_0, c'_0) \in \{0, 1\}^n \times \{0, 1\}$ and $(c_1, c'_1) \in \{0, 1\}^n \times \{0, 1\}$. The receiver computes $c'_0 - c_0 \cdot k \bmod 2$ and $c'_1 - c_1 \cdot k \bmod 2$. If both values are 0, the receiver outputs 0. Otherwise, the receiver outputs 1.

*Correctness.* Note that in the last step, $c'_0 - c_0 \cdot k \bmod 2$ evaluates to $x_0 \cdot (1 - d)$, and $c'_1 - c_1 \cdot k \bmod 2$ evaluates to $x_1 \cdot d$. In case the chosen message $x_d = 0$, then both the values are 0 and the receiver outputs 0. Whereas if $x_d = 1$, then one of these values is 1, and the receiver outputs 1.

The above protocol can be run within $O(n)$ space characteristic. This is because, at each step of the protocol, the receiver has to store the key $k$ and at most two other $n$-bit messages. The sender only maintains $\mathbf{L}, q$ which also requires only $O(n)$ space.

## B.1    Proof of Security

**Theorem 10.** *For any $c < 1/40$, there exists $\alpha > 0$ such that the above 1-out-of-2 OT construction is $(O(n), c \cdot n^2, O(2^{-\alpha n}))$-secure against semi-honest sender.*

*Proof.* We first build a simulator SenderSim which outputs the simulated view of the sender given its input messages $(x_0, x_1)$. The simulator outputs the view via its write communication tape.

SenderSim($1^n, (x_0, x_1)$):
  – Place (Input, $(x_0, x_1)$) on the write comm. tape.
  – Sample $\mathbf{k} \leftarrow \{0,1\}^n$.
  – For $i = 1$ to $2n$,
     Sample $\mathbf{a}_i \leftarrow \{0,1\}^n$, compute $b_i = \mathbf{a}_i \cdot \mathbf{k} \bmod 2$, and write
     (receive, $(\mathbf{a}_i, b_i)$) on the write tape.
     Sample $\mathbf{M}_i \leftarrow \{0,1\}^2$, and write (sample, $\mathbf{M}_i$) on the write tape.
  – Sample $\mathbf{y} \leftarrow \{0,1\}^n$ and a bit $r \leftarrow \{0,1\}$, and write (receive, $(\mathbf{y}, r)$) on the write tape.

To prove Theorem 10, we prove that if there exists a space bounded semi-honest sender that can break the security defined above, then we can construct a space bounded adversary that breaks the indistinguishability version of parity learning, defined in 9 in this paper.

For the sake of contradiction, suppose there exists some $c < 1/40$, for all $\alpha > 0$, there exists a $cn^2$-space bounded adversary such that for all $N_0 \in \mathbb{N}$, there is some $n > N_0, \{x_i\}_{i \in [k]} \subseteq \mathcal{M}, d \in \{0,1\}$ where $\mathcal{A}$ has advantage $\Omega(2^{-\alpha n})$ in the GameSHSender$^{\mathcal{A}}_{\{x_i\}_{i \in [1]}, c}$ security game; then for all $\alpha' > 0$, there is a $(2cn^2 + O(n))$-space bounded adversary $\mathcal{A}'$ where $\mathcal{A}'$ has advantage $\Omega(2^{-\alpha' n})$ in the indistinguishability parity learning security game. There exists some $N_0$, such that for all $n > N_0$, there exists some $c' < 1/20$ such that $c'n^2 \geq 2cn^2 + O(n)$.

The challenger in the semi-honest sender security game GameSHSender$^{\mathcal{A}}_{\{x_j\}_{j \in [1]}, c}$ is an adversary $\mathcal{A}'$ in the indistinguishability parity learning security game denoted as PL$_{\mathcal{A}', \delta}(n, 2n+1)$, where the secret key of parity learning has length $n$ and the adversary will receive $2n$ parity learning tuples plus one challenge tuple.

If $\mathcal{A}'$'s coin flip is $b = 1$, $\mathcal{A}'$ runs the real-world OT$_2$ protocol, regardless of the PL$_{\mathcal{A}', \delta}(n, 2n+1)$ challenger. If $\mathcal{A}'$'s coin it flips $b = 0$, then $\mathcal{A}'$ writes the parity learning tuples from PL$_{\mathcal{A}', \delta}(n, 2n+1)$ on communication tape of the simulator. In the reduction, the simulator in GameSHSender$^{\mathcal{A}}_{\{x_j\}_{j \in [1]}, d}$ does not sample $\mathbf{k}, \mathbf{r}_i, \mathbf{y}$ by itself but instead gets $(\mathbf{r}_i, a_i), i \in [2n+1]$ from the PL$_{\mathcal{A}, \delta}(n, 2n+1)$ game. For the first $2n$ tuples $(\mathbf{a}_i, b_i), i \in [2n]$, the simulator uses them as the tuples in protocol step 2; when $i = 2n+1$, the sender simulator sets $\mathbf{y} = \mathbf{a}_{2n+1}$ and sets $r = b_{2n+1}$.

Recall that when $i = 2n + 1$, the PL$_{\mathcal{A}', b}(n, 2n + 1)$ challenger flips a coin $\delta \leftarrow \{0, 1\}$; it sends $b_{2n+1} = \mathbf{a}_{2n+1} \cdot \mathbf{k}$ to $\mathcal{A}'$ if $\delta = 0$ and sends uniformly random

$b_{2n+1} \leftarrow \{0, 1\}$ to the $\mathcal{A}'$ if $\delta = 1$. At the end of the game, $\mathcal{A}$ outputs a bit $b'$; $\mathcal{A}'$ passes $\mathcal{A}$'s output $b'$ to the the $\mathsf{PL}_{\mathcal{A}',b}(n, 2n+1)$ challenger as its own output $\delta'$. $\mathcal{A}'$ has space characteristic $(cn^2 + O(n))$ where $cn^2$ space is used to simulate the $\mathcal{A}$ and $O(n)$ for interaction with challenger. Suppose $\mathcal{A}$ has advantage $\epsilon = \Omega(2^{-\alpha n})$, then $\mathcal{A}'$ has advantage $\epsilon/2 = \Omega(2^{-\alpha' n})$ in $\mathsf{PL}_{\mathcal{A}',b}(n, 2n+1)$, which forms a contradiction with 6.

**Theorem 11.** *The above 1-out-of-2 OT construction is $(O(n), \infty, O(2^{-n}))$-secure against semi-honest receiver.*

*Proof.* We first build a simulator ReceiverSim which outputs the simulated view of the receiver given the choice bit $d$ and the receiver's output $x_d$. The simulator outputs the view via its write communication tape.

ReceiverSim$(1^n, (d, x_d))$ :
- Write (Input, $(d, x_d)$) to the write comm. tape.
- Sample key $\mathbf{k} \leftarrow \{0, 1\}^n$, and place (sample, $\mathbf{k}$) on the write tape.
- For $i = 1$ to $2n$, sample key $\mathbf{a}_i \leftarrow \{0, 1\}^n$, and write (sample, $\mathbf{a}_i$) on the write tape.
- Sample $\mathbf{y} \leftarrow \{0, 1\}^n$, and place (sample, $\mathbf{k}$) on the write tape.
- Sample uniformly random $\mathbf{U} \leftarrow \{0, 1\}^{2*n}$. Let $\mathbf{U}_0, \mathbf{U}_1$ be the first and second row vectors.
- If $d = 0$:
  Write (receive, $(\mathbf{U}_0, \mathbf{U}_0 \cdot \mathbf{k} + x_0)$) and (receive, $(\mathbf{U}_1, \mathbf{U}_1 \cdot \mathbf{k})$) on the write tape.
  else if $d = 1$:
  Write (receive, $(\mathbf{U}_0, \mathbf{U}_0 \cdot \mathbf{k})$) and (receive, $(\mathbf{U}_1, \mathbf{U}_1 \cdot \mathbf{k} + x_1)$) on the write tape.

Notice that other than the final step, rest of the view generated by the simulator is identical to the view of the receiver in the real protocol. Suppose $d = 0$. In the final step, the receiver in the real protocol receives $(\mathbf{L}_0 + x_0 \cdot \mathbf{y}, (\mathbf{L}_0 + x_0 \cdot \mathbf{y}) \cdot \mathbf{k} + x_0)$, $(\mathbf{L}_1 + x_1 \cdot \mathbf{y}, (\mathbf{L}_1 + x_1 \cdot \mathbf{y}) \cdot \mathbf{k} + 0)$, where $\mathbf{L}_0, \mathbf{L}_1$ are random linear combinations of $\mathbf{a}_i$ vectors. Note that the stream of randomness $\{\mathbf{a}_i\}_{i \in [2n]}$ can be viewed as a $2n \times n$ matrix, and with all but exponentially small probability, the matrix has rank $n$. Therefore, a random linear combination of these rows $(\mathbf{L}_0, \mathbf{L}_1)$ are statistically indistinguishable from uniform sampled vectors in $\{0, 1\}^n$. Consequently, $(\mathbf{L}_0 + x_0 \cdot \mathbf{y}, (\mathbf{L}_0 + x_0 \cdot \mathbf{y}) \cdot \mathbf{k} + x_0)$, $(\mathbf{L}_1 + x_1 \cdot \mathbf{y}, (\mathbf{L}_1 + x_1 \cdot \mathbf{y}) \cdot \mathbf{k} + 0)$ are statistically indistinguishable from $(\mathbf{U}_0, \mathbf{U}_0 \cdot \mathbf{k} + x_0)$ and $(\mathbf{U}_1, \mathbf{U}_1 \cdot \mathbf{k})$. Similar analysis works even when $d = 1$.

# References

1. Aumann, Y., Ding, Y.Z., Rabin, M.O.: Everlasting security in the bounded storage model. IEEE Trans, Inf. Theory **48**, 668–1680 (2002)
2. Aumann, Y., Rabin, M.O.: Information theoretically secure communication in the limited storage space model. In: Wiener, M. (ed.) CRYPTO 1999. LNCS, vol. 1666, pp. 65–79. Springer, Heidelberg (1999). https://doi.org/10.1007/3-540-48405-1_5

3. Cachin, C., Maurer, U.: Unconditional security against memory-bounded adversaries. In: Kaliski, B.S. (ed.) CRYPTO 1997. LNCS, vol. 1294, pp. 292–306. Springer, Heidelberg (1997). https://doi.org/10.1007/BFb0052243

4. Ding, Y.Z., Rabin, M.O.: Hyper-encryption and everlasting security. In: Alt, H., Ferreira, A. (eds.) STACS 2002. LNCS, vol. 2285, pp. 1–26. Springer, Heidelberg (2002). https://doi.org/10.1007/3-540-45841-7_1

5. Dowsley, R., Lacerda, F., Nascimento, A.C.A.: Oblivious transfer in the bounded storage model with errors. In: IEEE International Symposium on Information Theory (2014)

6. Dziembowski, S., Maurer, U.: Tight security proofs for the bounded-storage model. In: STOC, pp. 341–350 (2002)

7. Dziembowski, S., Maurer, U.: On generating the initial key in the bounded-storage model. In: Cachin, C., Camenisch, J.L. (eds.) EUROCRYPT 2004. LNCS, vol. 3027, pp. 126–137. Springer, Heidelberg (2004). https://doi.org/10.1007/978-3-540-24676-3_8

8. Goldreich, O., Levin, L.A.: A hard-core predicate for all one-way functions. In: Proceedings of the Twenty-First Annual ACM Symposium on Theory of Computing, STOC 1989, pp. 25–32. Association for Computing Machinery, New York (1989). https://doi.org/10.1145/73007.73010

9. Goldreich, O., Micali, S., Wigderson, A.: How to play any mental game or a completeness theorem for protocols with honest majority. In: STOC 1987 (1987)

10. Grover, L.K.: A fast quantum mechanical algorithm for database search. In: STOC (1996)

11. Guan, J., Zhandary, M.: Simple schemes in the bounded storage model. In: Ishai, Y., Rijmen, V. (eds.) EUROCRYPT 2019, Part III. LNCS, vol. 11478, pp. 500–524. Springer, Cham (2019). https://doi.org/10.1007/978-3-030-17659-4_17

12. Harnik, D., Naor, M.: On everlasting security in the *Hybrid* bounded storage model. In: Bugliesi, M., Preneel, B., Sassone, V., Wegener, I. (eds.) ICALP 2006, Part II. LNCS, vol. 4052, pp. 192–203. Springer, Heidelberg (2006). https://doi.org/10.1007/11787006_17

13. Ishai, Y., Prabhakaran, M., Sahai, A.: Founding cryptography on oblivious transfer – efficiently. In: Wagner, D. (ed.) CRYPTO 2008. LNCS, vol. 5157, pp. 572–591. Springer, Heidelberg (2008). https://doi.org/10.1007/978-3-540-85174-5_32

14. Kilian, J.: Founding cryptography on oblivious transfer. In: STOC (1988)

15. Kol, G., Raz, R., Tal, A.: Time-space hardness of learning sparse parities. In: STOC (2017)

16. Lu, C.-J.: Hyper-encryption against space-bounded adversaries from on-line strong extractors. In: Yung, M. (ed.) CRYPTO 2002. LNCS, vol. 2442, pp. 257–271. Springer, Heidelberg (2002). https://doi.org/10.1007/3-540-45708-9_17

17. Maurer, U.M.: Conditionally-perfect secrecy and a provably-secure randomized cipher. J. Cryptol. **5**(1), 53–66 (1992). https://doi.org/10.1007/BF00191321

18. Moran, T., Shaltiel, R., Ta-Shma, A.: Non-interactive timestamping in the bounded-storage model. J. Cryptol. **22**, 189–226 (2009)

19. Raz, R.: Fast learning requires good memory: a time-space lower bound for parity learning. In: FOCS (2016)

20. Raz, R.: A time-space lower bound for a large class of learning problems. In: FOCS (2017)

21. Savaş, E., Sunar, B.: A practical and secure communication protocol in the bounded storage model. In: Lorenz, P., Dini, P. (eds.) ICN 2005, Part II. LNCS, vol. 3421, pp. 707–717. Springer, Heidelberg (2005). https://doi.org/10.1007/978-3-540-31957-3_80

22. Shikata, J., Yamanaka, D.: Bit commitment in the bounded storage model: tight bound and simple optimal construction. In: Chen, L. (ed.) IMACC 2011. LNCS, vol. 7089, pp. 112–131. Springer, Heidelberg (2011). https://doi.org/10.1007/978-3-642-25516-8_8
23. Shor, P.W.: Algorithms for quantum computation: discrete logarithms and factoring. In: FOCS (1994)
24. Yao, A.: How to generate and exchange secrets. In: FOCS (1986)

# Author Index

Printed in the United States
by Baker & Taylor Publisher Services